Popular Protest in Late Medieval English Towns

D1423737

Contrary to received opinion, revolts and popular protests in medieval English towns were as frequent and as sophisticated, if not more so, as those in the countryside. This groundbreaking study refocuses attention on the varied nature of popular movements in towns from Carlisle to Dover and from the London tax revolt of Longbeard in 1196 to Jack Cade's Rebellion in 1450, exploring the leadership, social composition, organization, and motives of popular rebels. The book charts patterns of urban revolt in times of strong and weak kingship, contrasting them with the broad sweep of ecological and economic change that inspired revolts on the Continent. Samuel K. Cohn, Jr demonstrates that the timing and character of popular revolt in England differed radically from revolts in Italy, France, and Flanders. In addition, he analyses the repression of, and waves of hate against, Jews, foreigners, and heretics, opening new vistas in the comparative history of late medieval Europe.

SAMUEL K. COHN, JR is Professor of Medieval History at the University of Glasgow. His work over the past decade has concentrated on plague and the history of popular insurrection, and his previous publications include *Cultures of Plague: Medical Thinking at the End of the Renaissance* (2010) and *Lust for Liberty: The Politics of Social Revolt in Medieval Europe, 1200–1425* (2006).

Popular Protest in Late Medieval English Towns

Samuel K. Cohn, Jr

With assistance from Douglas Aiton

CAMBRIDGE
UNIVERSITY PRESS

CAMBRIDGE
UNIVERSITY PRESS

University Printing House, Cambridge CB2 8BS, United Kingdom

Cambridge University Press is part of the University of Cambridge.

It furthers the University's mission by disseminating knowledge in the pursuit of education, learning and research at the highest international levels of excellence.

www.cambridge.org
Information on this title: www.cambridge.org/9781107529359

© Samuel K. Cohn, Jr, 2013

First published 2013
First paperback edition 2015

A catalogue record for this publication is available from the British Library

Library of Congress Cataloguing in Publication data

Cohn, Samuel Kline.
  Popular protest in late medieval English towns / Samuel K. Cohn, Jr.;
with assistance from Douglas Aiton.
      p.   cm.
  ISBN 978-1-107-02780-0 (Hardback)
  1. Protest movements–England–History–To 1500.   2. England–Social
conditions–1066–1485.   3. Great Britain–History–1066–1687.   I. Aiton,
Douglas.   II. Title.
  HN398.E5C64 2012
  303.60941–dc23

                                                2012017173

ISBN 978-1-107-02780-0 Hardback
ISBN 978-1-107-52935-9 Paperback

Dedicated to
Rudolph Binion (1927–2011)
friend, colleague, and master craftsman
of comparative history

Contents

vii

Maps

Acknowledgements

An ESRC three-year small research grant awarded in October 2007 (000–22–2339) made this project possible. Having just defended a Ph.D. thesis on the Jacquerie, Douglas Aiton served as the research assistant, Matthew Strickland was the adviser, and I was the principal investigator. In his ten-month stint, Aiton read and selected between two-thirds and three-quarters of the chronicles and documents from the Calendar of Patent Rolls analysed for this book. He also made several trips to TNA to check a sample of original documents with those edited at the end of the nineteenth and early twentieth century in the CPR. Over the next three years I checked and coded the records and searched for further examples of popular protest, reading additional chronicles and volumes from the CPR and a large array of published documents and secondary sources. I compiled the databases and wrote versions of the present book that were first commented upon and criticized by Strickland and Aiton and afterwards circulated for a one-day workshop at the University of Glasgow, attended by seven senior scholars and four post-graduates (in addition to the three grant holders). They included William Hepburn, Colette Bowie, Laura Crombie, Fergus Oakes, Neil Murphy, Hamish Scott, Graeme Small, Patrick Lantschner, Andrew Prescott, Christian Liddy, and Chris Dyer. I thank all these scholars for their time and intellectual generosity, but especially the three principal interlocutors – Prescott, Liddy, and Dyer – who submitted detailed reports and criticisms and were extraordinarily generous afterwards in offering materials from their own published, as well as unpublished, research. With their comments and criticisms, I returned to the drawing board for an intense period of reading, rethinking, and redrafting. Finally, Andrew Roach, an authority on European heresy, commented on Chapter 13.

In addition, Kathryn Dutton and especially Laura Crombie assisted for shorter periods, researching place names for the maps and compiling bibliographies. Early on in the writing, I benefited from discussions with, and the fine personal library of, Maryanne Kowaleski. Finally, I am indebted to both Elizabeth Friend-Smith and the anonymous readers at Cambridge University Press for their detailed, critical, and informed reports that went beyond the call of duty.

Abbreviations

BIHR	*Bulletin of the Institute of Historical Research*
BJRL	*Bulletin of the John Rylands Library*
CCR	*Calendar of the Close Rolls Preserved in the Public Record Office, 1227–1509*, 63 vols. (London, 1900–63)
CEMCR	*Calendar of Early Mayor's Court Rolls, a.d. 1298–1307*, ed. A. H. Thomas (Cambridge, 1924)
CFR	*Calendar of the Fine Rolls Preserved in the Public Records Office, 1272–1509*, 22 vols. (London, 1911–62)
CPMR	*Calendar of Plea and Memoranda Rolls Preserved among the Archives of the Corporation of the City of London at the Guildhall, 1323–1482*, ed. A. H. Thomas, 6 vols. (Cambridge, 1926–61)
CPR	*Calendar of Patent Rolls Preserved in the Public Record Office, 1216–1452*, 49 vols. (London, 1901–9)
CS	Camden Society
CUHB	*The Cambridge Urban History of Britain*, vol. I, ed. D. M. Palliser (Cambridge, 2000)
EcHR	*Economic History Review*, 2nd series
EHR	*English Historical Review*
JBS	*Journal of British Studies*
JIDH	*Journal of Interdisciplinary History*
JMH	*Journal of Medieval History*
JUST	*Justices in Eyre, of Assize, of Oyer and Terminer* in TNA
KB	King's Bench in TNA
King's Bench	*Select Cases in the Court of King's Bench*, ed. G. O. Sayles, 7 vols., Selden Society, LV, LVII, LVIII, LXXIV, LXXVI, LXXXII, LXXXVIII (London, 1936–71)
LB	*Calendar of Letter Books Preserved among the Archives of the Corporation of the City of London at the Guildhall: Letter-Book A-K*, 9 vols., ed. Reginald R. Sharpe (London, 1899–1912)

ML   *Memorials of London and London Life in the XIIIth, XIVth,*
                and XVth Centuries Being a Series of Extracts, Local, Social,
                and Political from the Early Archives of the City of London
                A.D. 1276–1419, ed. Henry T. Riley (London, 1868)
ODNB   *Oxford Dictionary of National Biography,* online edn
                (Oxford, September 2004–10)
P&P   *Past and Present*
PROME   *The Parliament Rolls of Medieval England, 1275–1504*
                [Electronic resource], ed. Chris Given-Wilson, The
                National Archives, The History of Parliament Trust
                (Leicester, 2005)
RS   Rolls Series: *Rerum Britannicarum medii aevi scriptores,*
                119 vols. (London, 1858–96)
SCBKC   *Select Cases Before the King's Council 1243–1482,* ed.
                I. S. Leadam and J. F. Baldwin, Selden Society, XXXV
                (Cambridge, MA, 1918)
SHF   Société de l'histoire de France
TNA   The National Archives, formerly the Public Record Office
UH   *Urban History*
VCH   *Victorian County History*

Part I

The setting

1 Introduction: questions and sources

More research has been devoted to the English Peasants' Revolt of 1381[1] than to any uprising of the Middle Ages; more than to the Tumult of the Ciompi, the Jacquerie, and the widespread rebellions in Flanders of 1297–1305 and 1323–8 combined.[2] Research on the English Peasants' Revolt has been interdisciplinary, principally the work of historians and literary scholars,[3]

[1] There are serious objections to calling the wide arc of revolts in 1381 the 'Peasants' Revolt'. Not only did townsmen revolt in great numbers in cities and towns within Kent and Essex, but the rebels who converged on London in June or rebelled in their own communities came predominantly from market towns in these counties, places such as Ware and Thaxted, along with small towns surrounding the capital, and many practised crafts or came higher up in the social hierarchy; see Andrew Prescott, 'London in the Peasants' Revolt: A Picture Gallery', *London Journal*, 7 (1981): 128–30; Herbert Eiden, 'Joint Action Against "Bad" Lordship: The Peasants' Revolt in Essex and Norfolk', *History* 83 (1998): 5–30, p. 10; Paul Strohm, '"A Revelle!": Chronicle Evidence and the Rebel Voice', pp. 33–56, in *Hochon's Arrow: The Social Imagination of Fourteenth-Century Texts* (Princeton, 1992), p. 36. Nonetheless, throughout this book, the common label for these revolts – 'the Peasants' Revolt of 1381' will be employed. Others such as Christopher Dyer, 'The Social and Economic Background to the Rural Revolt of 1381', pp. 9–42, in *The English Rising of 1381*, ed. Rodney Hilton and T. H. Aston (Cambridge, 1984), find nothing here to contradict the traditional label, at least within Kent, Essex, Hertfordshire, and the region around London. On the origins of the name and its replacement of rival tags in the 1880s, see R. B. Dobson, 'Remembering the Peasants' Revolt 1381–1981', in *Essex and the Great Revolt of 1381: Lectures Celebrating the Six Hundredth Anniversary*, ed. W. H. Liddell and R. G. E. Wood, Essex Record Office Publication no. 84 (Essex, 1982), p. 16. For its renaming as a 'rising', see Paul Strohm, 'A Peasants' Revolt?' in *Misconceptions about the Middle Ages*, ed. Stephen J. Harris and Bryon L. Grigsby (New York, 2007), pp. 197–203.
[2] For a guide to these numbers in articles published since 1964, see the *Brepols Online International Medieval Bibliography*.
[3] For notable literary analyses of the English Peasants' Revolt, see Strohm, '"A Revelle!"'; Steven Justice, *Writing and Rebellion: England in 1381* (Berkeley, 1994); Richard F. Green, 'John Ball's Letters: Literary History and Historical Literature', in *Chaucer's England: Literature in Historical Context*, ed. Barbara Hanawalt (Minneapolis, 1992), pp. 176–200; Susan Crane, 'The Writing Lesson of 1381', in ibid., pp. 201–21; or more recently, Christopher Baswell, 'Aeneas in 1381', pp. 7–58, in *New Medieval Literatures*, 5, ed. Rita Copeland, David Lawton, and Wendy Scase (Oxford, 2003); Conrad Van Dijk, 'Simon Sudbury and Helenus in John Gower's *Vox Clamantis*', *Medium Aevum*, 77 (2008): 313–18; and Alexander L. Kaufman, *The Historical Literature of the Jack Cade Rebellion* (Farnham, 2009).

and international.[4] Paradoxically, beyond this revolt and, secondarily, Cade's Rebellion in 1450,[5] scholars have paid much less attention to a wide range of medieval uprisings in England than to ones on the Continent,[6] and especially in comparison with the outpouring of publications on popular revolt in early modern England.[7] Furthermore, the work on medieval English revolts has concentrated on the countryside, making excellent use of England's exceptionally rich manorial rolls and court records. By contrast, little attention has been directed towards popular protest in English towns and cities, and with few exceptions this work has been restricted to individual uprisings or experiences within individual towns, most prominently, London.[8] Moreover, much of the work on late medieval insurrection in towns outside the capital and not during the Peasants' Revolt has appeared in local historical and

---

[4] See André Réville and Charles Petit-Dutaillis, *Le soulèvement des travailleurs d'Angleterre en 1381* (Paris, 1898); Stefano Simonetta, 'Wyclif e la rivolta di 1381', in *John Wyclif: logica, politica, teologia. Atti del Convegno Internazionale, Milano, 12–13 febbraio 1999*, ed. M. Fumugalli Beonio Brocchierri and Stefano Simonetta (Florence, 2003), pp. 143–79; Theo Stemmler, 'Der Bauernaufstand von 1381 in der zeitgenössichen Literatur Englands', in *Historisches und fiktioales Erzählen in Mittelalter*, ed. Fritz Peter Knapp and Manuela Niesner (Berlin, 2002), pp. 45–62; Herbert Eiden, 'Norfolk, 1382: A Sequel to the Peasants' Revolt', *EHR* 114 (1999): 370–7; Herbert Eiden, 'Der Richter, der seinen Kopfverlor: Leben und Sterben des Sir John Cavendish (*1381*), Chief Justice of the King's Bench', in *Landesgeschichte als multidisziplinäre Wissenschaft. Festgabe für Franz Irsigler zum 60. Geburtstag*, ed. Dietrich Ebeling and Franz Irsigler (Trier, 2001), pp. 197–222; and Herbert Eiden, '*In der Knechtschaft werdet ihr verharren*': Ursachen in Verlauf des englischen Bauernaufstandes von 1381 (Trier, 1995).

[5] Before Ralph A. Griffiths, *The Reign of King Henry VI: The Exercise of Royal Authority, 1422–1461* (London, 1981), with its extensive research on Cade's revolt (pp. 610–65), only one major study of this revolt had appeared, and that by a German, a century earlier: George Kriehn, *The English Rising in 1450* (Strasbourg, 1892).

[6] See Michel Mollat and Philippe Wolff, *The Popular Revolutions of the Late Middle Ages*, trans. A. L. Lytton-Sells (London, 1973); Guy Fourquin, *Anatomy of Popular Rebellion in the Middle Ages*, trans. A. Chesters (Amsterdam, 1978); Marc Boone and Maarten Prak, 'Rulers, Patricians and Burghers: The Great and the Little Traditions of Urban Revolt in the Low Countries', in *A Miracle Mirrored: The Dutch Republic in European Perspective*, ed. Karel Davids and Jan Lucassen (Cambridge, 1995), pp. 99–134; Rinaldo Comba, 'Rivolte e ribellioni fra tre e quattrocento', in *La storia: I grandi problemi*, ed. Nicola Tranfaglia and Massimo Firpo (Turin, 1988) II, Part 2, pp. 673–91; Samuel K. Cohn, Jr, *Lust for Liberty: The Politics of Social Revolt in Medieval Europe, 1200–1425* (Cambridge, MA, 2006).

[7] See, for instance, Roger B. Manning, *Village Revolts: Social Protest and Popular Disturbances in England, 1509–1640* (Oxford, 1988); John Walter, *Crowds and Popular Politics in Early Modern England* (Manchester, 2006); Andy Wood, *Riot, Rebellion and Popular Politics in Early Modern England* (Houndmills, 2002); and Andy Wood, *The 1549 Rebellions and the Making of Early Modern England* (Cambridge, 2008).

[8] Most importantly, see Gwyn A. Williams, *Medieval London: From Commune to Capital* (London, 1963). Also, the attention given to insurrection in Bury St Edmunds stands out, especially M. D. Lobel, *The Borough of Bury St Edmund's: A Study in the Government and Development of a Monastic Town* (Oxford, 1935), pp. 118–70.

archaeological journals and, as with Bristol's remarkable and long resistance to the Crown during Edward II's reign, was written over a century ago.[9] Excellent descriptions and effective use of archival sources can be found in these early works, but they mostly studied individual uprisings within the contexts of single towns, or only at specific moments in their town's histories.[10] Few have attempted to find patterns in urban protest over time or space, or between types of towns that tended to revolt, such as royal boroughs or monastic ones,[11] or to compare English revolts with ones on the Continent. Comparisons and overviews, few in number, have been confined to brief sections in books and at best have reflected a dozen or fewer cases of factional or class conflict over the long-term of the Middle Ages.[12] As a result, untested assumptions have passed from one publication to the next, such as the notion that insurrections in towns were less frequent and less significant than in the countryside, and that the aims and ideology of urban rebels were less developed and less radical than those of late medieval English peasants.[13] According to

[9] Rodney Hilton, *English and French Towns in Feudal Society: A Comparative Study* (Cambridge, 1992), p. 136, gives this revolt scant notice and reduces it to a class struggle between elite merchants and commoners (which it was not), with the Crown supporting the elites. An exception is Michael Prestwich's brief summary of it in *Plantagenet England 1225–1360: The New Oxford History of England* (Oxford, 2005), p. 480.

[10] See for instance E. A. Fuller, 'The Tallage of 6 Edward II (Dec. 16, 1312) and the Bristol Rebellion', *Transactions of the Bristol and Gloucestershire Archaeological Society*, 19 (1894–5): 171–278.

[11] The major exception being Norman Maclaren Trenholme, *The English Monastic Boroughs: A Study in Medieval History* in The University of Missouri Studies 3 (1927).

[12] The only overviews we know are comments in Trenholme, *The English Monastic Boroughs*, especially Chapter 2; Susan Reynolds, *An Introduction to the History of English Medieval Towns* (Oxford, 1977), parts of chapters 6–8; S. H. Rigby and Elizabeth Ewan, 'Government, Power, and Authority 1300–1540', *CUHB*, pp. 291–312; and very briefly, W. M. Ormrod, *The Reign of Edward III: Crown and Political Society in England 1327–1377* (New Haven, 1990), Chapter 9; Prestwich, *Plantagenet England*, Chapter 18; and Hilton, *English and French Towns*, Chapter 6. Moreover, occasionally Williams, *Medieval London*, draws comparisons; for baronial revolts against the Crown from Magna Carta to the mid-fifteenth century, in which peasants and townsmen participated, see Claire Valente, *The Theory and Practice of Revolt in Medieval England* (Aldershot, 2003).

[13] See, for instance, Christopher Dyer, 'Small-town Conflict in the Later Middle Ages: Events at Shipston-on-Stour, *UH*, 19 (1992), p. 208; Rodney Hilton, 'Popular Movements in England at the End of the Fourteenth Century', in *Il Tumulto dei Ciompi: Un momento di storia fiorentina ed europea* (Florence, 1981), p. 227; and Rodney Hilton, 'Towns in English Society', in *The English Medieval Town: A Reader in English Urban History 1200–1540*, ed. R. C. Holt and G. Rosser (London, 1990), pp. 19–28: 'In practice, the most serious conflict in feudal society was that between peasants and landowners, but the tensions in urban society . . . also had to be faced' (p. 28). A similar view was held in older, standard political and constitutional histories of England; see May McKisack, *The Fourteenth Century 1307–1399* (Oxford, 1959), pp. 50–1: English towns experienced few uprisings because they lacked 'the political vitality or civic independence of the great cities of the Continent'. Also, May McKisack, 'London and the Succession to the Crown during the Middle Ages', in

Rodney Hilton, '[I]n so far as there was a potentially anti-feudal class in medieval society it was the peasantry.'[14]

This book will raise questions about popular protest in English towns from the London revolt led by William fitzOsbert, called Longbeard, of 1196 to Jack Cade's in 1450. It will describe the varieties of popular protest and consider to what extent they differed from those on the Continent, principally in Italy, France, and Flanders. Through concentrating largely on two types of sources – chronicles and Patent Rolls – the book analyses the variety of revolt and popular violence, the leadership, social composition, organization, and as best the sources allow, ideologies and motives of urban movements. In outlining patterns of revolt over time, it charts the ebb and flow of revolt against times of strong and weak kingship (including the absences of kings and their retinues from England), and against ecological disasters and economic depression, such as the Great Famine of 1315–17, the economic depression of the 1340s, the Black Death and the period of economic dislocation to c. 1375, and the general improvements that then followed in the material conditions of most commoners during the last quarter of the fourteenth century and into the fifteenth.[15]

Studies in Medieval History Presented to Fredrick Maurice Powicke, ed. R. W. Hunt, W. A. Pantin, and R. W. Southern (Oxford, 1948), pp. 76–89. Reynolds, An Introduction, is more cautious and probably correct: 'On present knowledge one can only conclude tentatively that so far as there was an English urban proletariat, it was less revolutionary than were the peasants.' But what about other groups in urban society, such as enfranchised artisans, craftsmen, or the lower echelons of urban elites and the ruling councils themselves? Even more problematic, others have assumed that peasant revolt was the dominant form of popular protest across Continental Europe; see for instance, Mollat and Wolff, The Popular Revolutions of the Late Middle Ages; William H. TeBrake, A Plague of Insurrection: Popular Politics and Peasant Revolt in Flanders, 1323–1328 (Philadelphia, 1993), p. 7; and implicitly, Marc Bloch, in his famous comparison: 'peasant revolts were as natural to traditional Europe as strikes are today': French Rural History: An Essay on its Basic Characteristics, trans. Janet Sondheimer (London, 1966 [Antwerp, 1931]), p. 170. Later Rodney Hilton, 'Révoltes rurales et révoltes urbaines au Moyen Age', in Révolte et société: Actes du IVe colloque d'histoire au present, Paris, mai 1988, ed. Fabienne Gambrelle and Michel Trebitsch, 2 vols. (Paris, 1989), I, p. 25, commented that historians generally saw peasant revolts as being the dominant ones of the Middle Ages, a position with which he did not disagree, but added that they often have overlooked the class antagonism within towns. In English and French Towns, p. 150, Hilton maintained that 'the most important class division' in medieval society was between 'landed aristocracy and peasants', but concluded that the tax revolt in towns was the equivalent of revolts over feudal rent in the countryside.

[14] Hilton, 'Popular Movements in England', p. 227.

[15] For the contours of these changes and their effects on the well-being of various classes and social groups across the Middle Ages, see Christopher Dyer, Standards of Living in the Later Middle Ages: Social Change in England c. 1200–1520 (Cambridge, 1989); Christopher Dyer, Everyday Life in Medieval England (London, 2001); and Christopher Dyer, Making a Living in the Middle Ages: The People of Britain 850–1520 (New Haven, 2002).

The book will make several overarching hypotheses: firstly, that urban revolt in England was more frequent and important than historians have assumed. With the exception of the English Peasants' Revolt of 1381 (which in fact combined revolts in towns and the countryside), urban protest generally had a more pronounced impact on national and royal politics than corresponding disturbances in the countryside. On the other hand, revolts in English towns were less frequent than on the Continent, especially as regards movements of disenfranchised artisans, or artisans in guilds against mercantile elites or their employers in textiles or other handicraft industries. Secondly, in contrast to the Continent, urban artisans rarely led challenges against municipal governments or the Crown. Thirdly, revolts in English towns fit more neatly with models of so-called 'pre-industrial revolt' that may later have become more or less common in early modern states of Western Europe. Certainly, they fit these models better than late medieval ones on the Continent. In contrast to those in Italy, France, and Flanders, (a) leaders of English revolts came less often from the rank-and-file of artisans and workers and instead relied heavily on those outside their social ranks – on barons, wealthy mayors, aldermen, and the clergy, from itinerant priests such as John Ball to the Archbishop of York; (b) far more often than on the Continent, urban movements in late medieval England were stimulated by, attached to, and organized to a considerable degree by larger baronial movements against the monarchy that originated outside towns; (c) more often than on the Continent, English insurgents idealized, or at least praised, the monarchy in rallying their supporters and relied on it to resolve their conflicts with other authorities such as monasteries, cathedral priories, employers, or entrenched oligarchs within towns. In contrast to the Continent, English rebels often expressed awe and respect for the monarch and blamed his corrupt advisers for their oppression, most famously seen with peasants' and townsmen's insignia and pleas to Richard II at London in mid-June 1381. Rarely did insurgents declare open war against their monarchs (even when they actually rebelled against the king, as with their participation in baronial wars or when Bristol's rebels refused to allow agents of the Crown to enter the town's gates or collect royal tallages). The Lollard revolts of the last decades of the fourteenth and early fifteenth century and immediately after Cade's in 1450 may have begun to break this mould; however, Cade's revolt firmly upheld the traditional lines. These rebels refused to attack the king directly and instead blamed his 'evil' advisers. Finally, women appear more often in official lists of English insurgents and in chronicle descriptions of revolts than on the Continent. Occasionally, they even emerge as leaders.

In addition to describing and arguing for these differences, the book attempts to explain why late medieval English urban revolts differed from contemporaneous Continental ones. In brief, we argue that the differences stem from the precocious nature of the English monarchy, its ability to intervene rapidly and effectively in local affairs of towns (at least compared with the Continent), and its oversight of and attention to resolving social conflict and suppressing urban threats to government both at municipal and national levels. As a result, more than on the Continent, the chronology of urban social movements in England clusters in periods of transitional and weak kingship, as with the troubled periods of baronial warfare and civil war, or when the king was overextended, waging wars, or absent from England. Not only could ruling elites in English towns, whether secular or religious, turn to the more effective and stronger repressive powers of a centralized monarchy, but other avenues of conflict resolution – appeals to the king and use of his commissions and courts – were more readily available than on the Continent. Even though the royal commissions, and courts such as King's Bench, almost invariably ruled in favour of elites, lower classes continued to rely on these legal channels through the two-and-half centuries studied in this book.[16] The same, moreover, can be said of the London courts, as seen in their Letter-books and in the mayor's memoranda, explored in Chapter 2.[17] By contrast, while peasants and artisans might petition their urban rulers on the Continent,[18] few cases appear there of artisans, workers, or other groups, c. 1200 to 1425, pooling resources to resolve grievances against local rulers or employers in legal tribunals. According to historians, increased access to legal alternatives became a vital escape valve in early

[16] See numerous cases scattered through this book; and for rural villeins' collection of fees to pay lawyers to bring cases against their lords, see Christopher Dyer, *An Age of Transition? Economy and Society in England in the Later Middle Ages: The Ford Lectures Delivered in the University of Oxford in Hilary Term 2001* (Oxford, 2005), p. 35.

[17] Penelope Tucker, *Law Courts and Lawyers in the City of London 1300–1550* (Cambridge, 2007), pp. 327–37, maintains that the mayor's and sheriff's courts, if not the Husting Court, were accessible to a wide social range of plaintiffs, and informal assistance occasionally was granted to the poor. However, 'the type of dispute resolution offered to the poor ... differed from and was limited compared to that available to wealthier individuals'. She points to factors such as the physical environments of courts, and language barriers, but does not chart the success or failure of litigants based on class differences.

[18] See, for instance, the peasant petitions beseeching tax breaks and other matters in fourteenth- and fifteenth-century Florence; Samuel K. Cohn, Jr, *Creating the Florentine State: Peasants and Rebellion, 1348–1434* (Cambridge, 1999). Peasants and townsmen also presented petitions to the king in late medieval England, and these sources (which have not been tapped in this study) deserve systematic attention for the history of popular protest.

modern England that lessened the pressure and frequency of open revolt.[19] By our evidence, that alternative was already alive in the later Middle Ages.

Before embarking on the sources and analysis of English urban revolt, the four terms of the book's title – English, town, popular, and protest – must be defined. To be sure, the English sources concern much more than what constitutes England today, partly because issues outside the island impinged on it, such as the decisions of popes or the territorial ambitions of kings and members of the royal family, as with the involvement of Henry III's brother, Richard of Cornwall, in the Holy Roman Empire, John of Gaunt's forays into Castile and, later, Portugal, or the marriage of Lionel of Antwerp (Edward III's third son and Duke of Clarence) to Violante, daughter of Galeazzo Visconti, and possible ambitions by the throne to have him become Lord of Milan, or even the Holy Roman Emperor.[20] More significantly, England ruled vast territories in present-day France – the Pas de Calais, Ponthieu and Aquitaine, which at different moments covered territories in Saintonge, the Agenais and the dioceses of Limoges, Cahors, and Périgueux, and extended into the Massif Central.[21] Following the English conquest of Rouen in 1419, England controlled Normandy and parts of northern France, including the Île de France and Paris, under the Dual Lancastrian Monarchy until the mid-fifteenth century resurgence of French power under Charles VII.[22] In addition, England attempted to exercise overlordship to all or parts of Wales, Ireland, and Scotland during periods covered by this study. While attentive to revolts outside

[19] Wood, *Riot, Rebellion and Popular Politics*, pp. 46, 78–80; Manning, *Village Revolts*, pp. 54, 75, and 80; Steve Hindle, *State and Social Change in Early Modern England, c. 1550–1640* (London, 2000), pp. 87–93, 114–15, 235–8. Historians of early modern Europe outside England have described a similar transformation of political protest; Winfried Schulze, 'Peasant Resistance in Sixteenth- and Seventeenth-Century Germany in a European Context', in *Religion, Politics and Social Protest: Three Studies on Early Modern Germany*, ed. Kapsar van Greyerz (London, 1984), p. 82; and William Beik, *Urban Protest in Seventeenth-Century France* (Cambridge, 1997), p. 171.

[20] For these ambitions, cut short by Lionel's early death soon after his marriage, see W. M. Ormrod, *Edward III*, Yale English Monarchs Series (New Haven, 2012), p. 443.

[21] For the shifting of the boundaries of English sovereignty and control in France during the reign of Edward III, see ibid., especially chapters 15 and 18.

[22] See Jean-Philippe Genet, *La genèse de l'état moderne: Culture et société politique en Angleterre* (Paris, 2003), p. 2; Griffiths, *The Reign of King Henry VI*, chapters 17 and 18; Michael K. Jones, 'War on the Frontier: The Lancastrian Land Settlement in Eastern Normandy, 1435–50', *Nottingham Medieval Studies*, 33 (1989): 104–21; and C. T. Allmand, *Lancastrian Normandy, 1415–1450: The History of Medieval Occupation* (Oxford, 1993).

present-day England, we have not concentrated on them. For instance, the Welsh rose against the English on numerous occasions from 1200 to 1450, in 1212, 1244–5, 1256, 1275–6, 1281–3, 1285–6, 1287, 1288–90, 1294–5, 1314–15, 1316, and 1400–9.[23] We have not investigated these to ask to what extent they may have been acts of war between two competing kingdoms or possible examples of popular insurrection against foreign occupation. The one Welsh revolt to find some analysis in this book, that of Owain Glyn Dŵr, 1400 to 1409, has been viewed not for its causes and inner dynamics (which have been the subject of numerous studies) as for its impact and spread across the marches into towns of present-day England.[24] We have spotted only two incidents possibly of popular insurrection from Scotland – an insurrection of 1222 against the former bishop and abbot in Caithness (probably not a town even by late medieval Scottish standards) and in Berwick-upon-Tweed, a town fiercely contested between the two kingdoms during most of the period of this study.[25] The protests and revolts we have discovered in chronicles and Patent Rolls cluster overwhelmingly in southern and eastern England, from Canterbury to Bristol to York with a few from Cornwall in the far west, Carlisle in the northwest, and Newcastle in the northeast. (See maps 1 and 2.) Further-flung regions of the English Crown may have been as rebellious or even more so than the centre, as has been argued for other frontier places during the central Middle Ages[26] and can be seen at times in the later Middle

[23] These are noted in the chronicles of Matthew Paris; *Chronicle of Pierre de Langtoft, in French Verse from the Earliest Period to the Death of Edward I*, ed. T. Wright. 2 vols., RS, 47 (1866–8), II; *The Chronicle of Adam Usk 1377–1421*, ed. and trans. Chris Given-Wilson (Oxford, 1997); *Continuatio Chronici Florentii Wigorniensis*, in *Florentii Wigorniensis monachi chronicon ex chronicis*, ed. Benjamin Thorpe, 2 vols. (London, 1848–9), II, pp. 238, 275; and others.

[24] Welsh historians have analysed these revolts in great detail; see Rees Davies, *The Age of Conquest: Wales 1063–1415* (Oxford, 1987), pp. 443–59, and Rees Davies, *The Revolt of Owain Glyn Dŵr* (Oxford, 1995). Also, Seymour Phillips, *Edward II*, Yale English Monarchs Series (New Haven, 2010), pp. 270–1. On the complexities of considering Owain Glyn Dŵr's revolt as 'popular', especially after 1403 when he sought to dissociate the revolution from one of class to a nationalist movement, see Andrew Prescott, '"Meynteyn him als his brother": Rebellion, Power and Knowledge in Late Medieval Britain' (forthcoming). For a short description and analysis of Welsh revolts from 1282 to 1410, see Robin Frame, *The Political Development of the British Isles 1100–1400* (Oxford, 1990), pp. 207–12.

[25] As Frame, *The Political Development*, has commented: 'in Wales, Scotland and Ireland the silence of the popular voice is deafening' (p. 199). To what extent this reflects the historiography, the sources, or realities is not clear. On the pivotal political and economic importance of Berwick during the fourteenth century, see Ormrod, *Edward III*, pp. 158–9, 178.

[26] James Given, *Society and Homicide in Thirteenth-Century England* (Stanford, 1977). For the fifteenth century, see the characterization of violence and disorder in the marches of

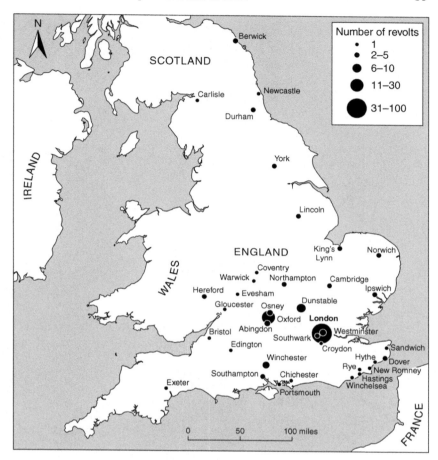

Map 1: Distribution of incidents according to the chronicles, 1196–1450.

Ages for border towns such as Carlisle, Berwick, and Newcastle, where urban rebels could take advantage of the political instability created by threats from Scotland. Our sources, however, show only occasional evidence for it.

Scotland in J. R. Lander, *Conflict and Stability in Fifteenth-Century England*, 3rd edn (London, 1977), pp. 178–80; and for Devon and Cornwall, Hannes Kleineke, 'Why the West was Wild: Law and Disorder in Fifteenth-Century Cornwall and Devon', in *The Fifteenth Century*, III: *Authority and Subversion*, ed. Linda Clark (Woodbridge, 2003), pp. 75–93.

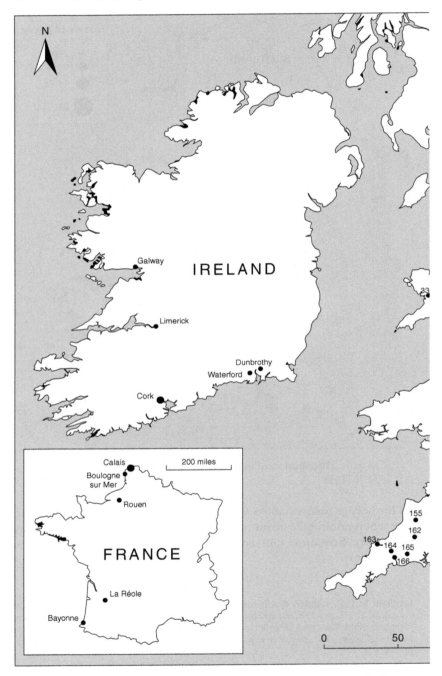

Map 2: Distribution of incidents according to the Patent Rolls, 1196–1450.

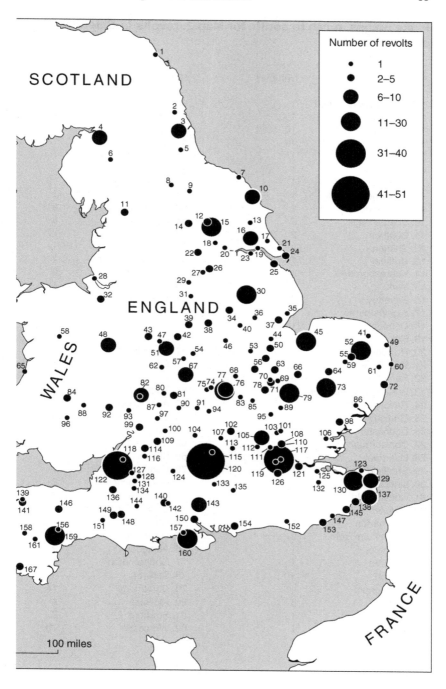

Place names, north to south, for Map 2: revolts in Calendar of Patent Rolls

Name	Numbers	Name	Numbers
1. Berwick-upon-Tweed	1	42. Burton on Trent	3
2. Morpeth	1	43. Stafford	2
3. Newcastle	10	44. Spalding	1
4. Carlisle	10	45. Lynn	12
5. Durham	1	46. Melton Mowbray	1
6. Penrith	1	47. Rugeley	1
7. Whitby	1	48. Shrewsbury	10
8. Richmond	1	49. Caister	1
9. Northallerton	1	50. Crowland	2
10. Scarborough	9	51. Lichfield	8
11. Bentham	2	52. Norwich	27
12. Shipton	2	53. Stamford	1
13. Driffield	1	54. Market Bosworth	1
14. Knaresborough	2	55. Wymondham	3
15. York	28	56. Peterborough	2
16. Beverley	7	57. Atherstone	1
17. Sigglesthorne	1	58. Montgomery	1
18. Osgodby	1	59. Attleborough	1
19. Hull	6	60. Lowestoft	1
20. Howden	1	61. Beccles	1
21. Withernsea	1	62. Birmingham	1
22. Pontefract	3	63. Ramsey	3
23. Barton upon Humber	1	64. Thetford	2
24. Ravenserodd	3	65. Aberystwyth	1
25. Grimsby	2	66. Ely	3
26. Doncaster	2	67. Coventry	10
27. Conisbrough	1	68. Kettering	1
28. Liverpool	1	69. St Ives	1
29. Sheffield	1	70. Huntingdon	1
30. Lincoln	16	71. Godmanchester	2
31. Chesterfield	1	72. Dunwich	2
32. Chester	3	73. Bury St Edmunds	11
33. Caernarfon	1	74. Norton	1
34. Newark on Trent	2	75. Daventry	1
35. Wrangle	1	76. Abingdon	9
36. Sleaford	1	77. Northampton	12
37. Boston	4	78. St Neots	2
38. Nottingham	4	79. Cambridge	14
39. Derby	5	80. Alcester	1
40. Grantham	1	81. Stratford	2
41. Worstead	1	82. Worcester	10

Map 2: (cont.)

Name	Numbers	Name	Numbers
83. Lavendon	1	126. Croydon	2
84. Builth	2	127. Bath	1
85. Bedford	1	128. Bradford	1
86. Ipswich	1	129. Sandwich	6
87. Evesham	1	130. Canterbury	12
88. Hay	1	131. Norton St Philip	1
89. Royston	1	132. Maidstone	1
90. Shipston	3	133. Basingstoke	1
91. Banbury	1	134. Frome	1
92. Hereford	2	135. Farnham	1
93. Ledbury	1	136. Wells	3
94. Brackley	1	137. Dover	6
95. Baldock	1	138. Hythe	4
96. Brecon	1	139. Barnstaple	1
97. Winchcombe	1	140. Wilton	2
98. Colchester	3	141. Bishop's Taunton	3
99. Gloucester	4	142. Salisbury	1
100. Northleach	1	143. Winchester	9
101. Ware	1	144. Gillingham	1
102. Aylesbury	3	145. New Romney	4
103. Hertford	1	146. Bampton	2
104. Eynsham	1	147. Winchelsea	1
105. St Albans	9	148. Sherbourne	3
106. Maldon	1	149. Yeovil	2
107. Thame	1	150. Southampton	5
108. Cheshunt	3	151. Crewkerne	1
109. Cirencester	5	152. Lewes	1
110. Waltham Cross	5	153. Hastings	4
111. Chipping Barnet	1	154. Chichester	4
112. Watford	1	155. Holsworthy	1
113. High Wycombe	1	156. Coleridge	1
114. Tetbury	2	157. Lymington	1
115. Crowmarsh Gifford	1	158. Okehampton	1
116. Norton	1	159. Exeter	11
117. London	39	160. Yarmouth	16
118. Winterbourne	1	161. Chagford	1
119. Westminster	1	162. Launceston	1
120. Oxford	51	163. Padstow	1
121. Dartford	3	164. Bodmin	1
122. Bristol	36	165. Liskeard	1
123. Reculver	1	166. Lostwithiel	1
124. Marlborough	1	167. Plympton	2
125. Rochester	1		

Map 2: (cont.)

As is well-rehearsed in the literature, towns differed in England from the Continent, especially in comparison with northern Italian city-states. Firstly, few English towns[27] possessed jurisdiction over their surrounding hinterland or county, and the majority of those that did gained these privileges only after the period of our analysis, in what Martin Weinbaum labelled 'The Classic Age of Incorporation', during the reign of Henry VI in the second half of the fifteenth century or later:[28] the earlier exceptions were London from the late twelfth century, despite repeated suspensions of its liberties from the reign of Henry III through Richard II,[29] Bristol (1373),[30] York (1396),[31] Newcastle upon Tyne in 1400, Norwich (1404),[32] Lincoln (1409),[33] Hull (1440),[34] Southampton (1445),[35] and Coventry (1451).[36] However, as Jenny Kermode has commented: 'By 1500, only a few towns had reached the apex of constitutional autonomy, that of a county . . .'[37] Even after reaching this peak, no town or city possessed the virtual independence from larger, centralized authorities that numerous Italian towns and several Swiss ones such as Berne,[38] and to a lesser extent ones in southern France, such as Toulouse, in Germany, such as Erfurt, and in Flanders had at certain times during the late Middle Ages. Secondly, except for the capital, towns in England were considerably smaller than Continental ones such as pre-plague Paris, where the population was estimated at between

---

[27] See for instance D. M. Palliser, 'Towns and the English State: 1066–1500', in *The Medieval State: Essay Presented to James Campbell*, ed. J. R. Maddicott and D. M. Palliser (London, 2000), p. 134, even regarding London's limited control in Middlesex.

[28] Martin Weinbaum, *The Incorporation of Boroughs* (Manchester, 1937), pp. 63–96.

[29] Reynolds, *An Introduction*, pp. 104 and 109.

[30] Ibid., p. 113; Peter Fleming and Kieran Costello, *Discovering Cabot's Bristol: Life in the Medieval and Tudor Town* (Bristol, 1998), p. 21; and Christian D. Liddy, *War, Politics and Finance in Late Medieval English Towns: Bristol, York and the Crown, 1350–1400* (Woodbridge, 2005), pp. 11, 13, and Chapter 5. For the transcription and translation of Bristol's charter of incorporation, see *Bristol Charters 1155–1373*, ed. M. Dermont Harding (Bristol, 1930), I, pp. 119–45.

[31] Liddy, *War, Politics and Finance*, p. 11 and Chapter 5. The charters of 1373, 1393, and 1396 freed Bristol and York, and later other towns and cities, from the interference of royal officials located in their hinterlands.

[32] *The Records of the City of Norwich*, ed. William Hudson and John Cottingham Tingey, 2 vols. (Norwich, 1906), I, p. lxiii, puts it in 1426.

[33] Weinbaum, *The Incorporation of Boroughs*, p. 59.   [34] Ibid., pp. 65–6.

[35] Colin Platt, *Medieval Southampton: The Port and Trading Community, AD 1000–1600* (London, 1973), p. 166.

[36] P. R. Coss, 'Coventry before Incorporation: A Re-interpretation', *Midland History* 2 (1974): 135–51, p. 151. Weinbaum, *The Incorporation of Boroughs*, p. 132, dates its charter of incorporation to 1345, but it did not then have powers over its county.

[37] Jenny Kermode, *Medieval Merchants: York, Beverley and Hull in the Later Middle Ages* (Cambridge, 1998), p. 28.

[38] Tom Scott, *The City-State in Europe, 1000–1600: Hinterland, Territory, Region* (Oxford 2012).

50,000 and 280,000,[39] Ghent with 60,000 to 80,000,[40] Florence at 120,000,[41] and others in Italy which are more difficult to estimate but that were larger than Florence, such as Milan, Naples, and Venice.[42] Even after the Black Death, cities such as Florence ranged from 40,000 to at least 60,000 in the second half of the fourteenth century,[43] while Milan, Venice, and Naples grew larger, perhaps attaining 150,000 by the end of the fifteenth century. Meanwhile, populations of previously smaller cities such as Verona would surpass the Arno city by the end of the Middle Ages.[44] By contrast, only sixteen towns in England at most possessed populations over 10,000 at their peak, circa 1300, and London had between 60,000 and 80,000,[45] or 100,000 if its suburbs are included.[46] From the subsidies of 1377, Rodney Hilton estimated London's post-plague numbers to have been between 45,000 and 50,000, but only four towns held between 8,000 and 15,000, eight between 5,000 and 8,000, and twenty-seven between 2,000 and 5,000.

[39] See, for instance, David Herlihy, *Opera Muliebria: Women and Work in Medieval Europe* (New York, 1990), pp. 127–30. Scholars now think the population was about 210,000 in 1328; see Sharon Farmer, *Surviving Poverty in Medieval Paris: Gender, Ideology and the Daily Lives of the Poor* (Ithaca, 2002), p. 17.

[40] Most recently, Marc Boone, *A la recherché d'une modernité civique: La société urbaine des anciens Pays-Bas au bas Moyen Age* (Brussels, 2010), p. 62, following Walter Prevenier, puts it at 64,000 before the Black Death.

[41] David Herlihy and Christiane Klapisch-Zuber, *Les Toscans et leurs familles: Une étude du catasto florentin de 1427* (Paris, 1978), pp. 175–6; and Samuel K. Cohn, Jr, 'Epidemiology of the Black Death and Successive Waves of Plague', in *Pestilential Complexities: Understanding Medieval Plague*, ed. Vivian Nutton, *Medical History*, Supplement no. 27 (London, 2008), p. 83.

[42] Herlihy and Klapisch-Zuber, *Les Toscans*, p. 187. Precise population statistics for Milan and Venice do not survive until the sixteenth century; see Karl Julius Beloch, *Bevölkerungsgeschichte italiens*, 3 vols. (Berlin, 1937–61), III, pp. 1–8 and 168–71. By the mid-sixteenth century, both cities numbered over 150,000.

[43] Samuel K. Cohn Jr, *Women in the Streets: Essays on Sex and Power in Renaissance Italy* (Baltimore, 1996), p. 22.

[44] See Beloch, *Bevölkerungsgeschichte italiens*, II, pp. 169–73; III, pp. 1–8 and pp. 168–71.

[45] See Christopher Dyer, 'The Hidden Trade of the Middle Ages: Evidence from the West Midlands of England', *Journal of Historical Geography* 18 (1992), p. 141. It has been estimated as low as 25–35,000 in 1300; see David Nicholas, *The Later Medieval City, 1300–1500* (Harlow, 1997), p. 50; and Tucker, *Law Courts and Lawyers*, p. 20, although she relies on the higher figure of 80,000 (p. 155).

[46] Richard Britnell, 'Town Life', in *A Social History of England 1200–1500*, ed. Rosemary Horrox and W. M. Ormrod (Cambridge, 2006), p. 145; J. L. Bolton, 'Introduction', in *The Alien Communities of London in the Fifteenth Century: The Subsidy Rolls of 1400 & 1483–4* (Stamford, 1998), p. 8, has downsized the estimate for London including its suburbs, *c.* 1300, to 75,000. After the Black Death, historians have estimated from tax records that London's population was around 40,000 and that the next two largest towns, York and Bristol, had populations of 15,000 and 12,000 respectively; see Liddy, *War, Politics and Finance*, p. 11. For a contrast between English and Italian urbanization, see R. H. Britnell, 'The Towns of England and Northern Italy in the Early Fourteenth Century', *EcHR*, 44 (1991): 21–35.

Five hundred market towns of between 500 and 2,000 inhabitants may have contained half of England's urban population.[47]

Our operating definition of towns and cities (seats of bishoprics) follows closely that of recent English historians: population is not the crucial variable; nor should the possession of a charter or constitution as a free borough determine it.[48] By this standard, medieval St Albans – 'comfortably the largest and most important town in Hertfordshire' according to the subsidy of 1334 and which Jean Froissart from the densely populated urban Low Countries (Valenciennes) described as 'a large town (une grosse ville)' in 1400[49] – must be considered part of England's countryside.[50] Contemporary documents, moreover, show that these inhabitants considered themselves burgesses even if the abbey persisted in calling them villeins, refusing them status as free burghers.[51]

Instead of a threshold population or the survival of a charter, urban functions and the inhabitants' occupations are now seen as critical for distinguishing an English town from a village. Thus Palliser (relying on Reynolds) has defined a town as 'a permanent and concentrated human settlement in which a significant proportion of the population is engaged in non-agricultural occupations ... lives, at least in part, off food

[47] Rodney Hilton, 'Towns in Societies – Medieval England', *Urban History Yearbook* (1982): 8–9. According to the subsidies of 1520, an average country town in southern and central England had a population of between 500 and 600; Colin Platt, *The English Medieval Town* (London, 1976), p. 15. According to Britnell, 'Towns of England and Northern Italy', p. 24, at least 444 places in England *c.* 1300 were known as boroughs. Also see Liddy, *War, Politics and Finance*, p. 11, for the populations of Bristol and York.

[48] See most prominently James Tait, *The Medieval English Borough: Studies on its Origins and Constitutional History* (Manchester, 1936). On this historiography and its change in the 1970s to a broader social definition of towns, see R. C. Holt and G. Rosser, 'Introduction: The English Town in the Middle Ages', in *The English Medieval Town: A Reader in English Urban History 1200–1540*, ed. R. C. Holt and G. Rosser (London, 1990), pp. 3–4. In contrast to the historians above, Prestwich also finds difficulties with the economic-functional criteria for defining communities as towns.

[49] Jean Froissart, *Œuvres de Froissart: chroniques*, ed. M. le baron Kervyn de Lettenhove, 25 vols. (Brussels, 1867–77), XVI, p. 227.

[50] In 1265, *Opus Chronicorum*, ed. Henry T. Riley, RS, 28 (1866), III, p. 20, called St Albans, 'Little London' because of its impressive fortifications and security.

[51] Mark Freeman, *St Albans: A History* (Lancaster, 2008), pp. 89 and 93. See Pamela Nightingale's critique of earlier juridical definitions of towns by the great legal historians of the late nineteenth century, Charles Gross and F. W. Maitland, who stressed administrative independence (*A Medieval Mercantile Community: The Grocers' Company and the Politics and Trade of London, 1000–1485* [New Haven, 1995], p. 227) and D. M. Palliser, 'Introduction', 3–15 in *CUHB*, p. 4. For other examples, where the juridical criteria do not match the economic and demographic characteristics of an urban place, see Prestwich, *Plantagenet England*, pp. 468–73: Boston, for instance, was listed and taxed as a village, but by the subsidy of 1334 was the fifth wealthiest community in England.

produced by people who live outside it ... regard themselves and are regarded by the inhabitants of predominantly rural settlements, as a different sort of people'.[52] No more precise but perhaps a better key, given the limited demographic sources for late medieval English towns, Holt and Rosser have emphasized 'heterogeneity', particularly diversity in occupations, as the defining characteristic.[53] As Hilton argued, '[e]ven small towns of less than a thousand inhabitants were character- ized by occupational heterogeneity, and contained a minority only of full time cultivators'.[54]

The problem, of course, and one largely unexamined by these historians, is that these criteria are quantitative, and the English sources for urban places, particularly at the lower end of the spectrum of towns, rarely allow such quantitative scrutiny. The two national records of late medieval England that historians have most often called upon to estimate population and draw social demarcations – the pre-1334 lay subsidy and the poll tax of 1377 – listed few by occupation, and I know of no work to utilize these sources to distin- guish urban from rural places by calculating ratios of full-time cultivators to those who were not. One work to establish that a moderately small community was urban by quantifying professions is E. M. Carus-Wilson's of Stratford-upon-Avon. Here, the survival of a remarkable town survey of 1251–2 lists the borough's 234 burgesses. Yet, even this unusual record, providing one demographic snapshot over the entirety of the Middle Ages, identifies only 27 per cent by a profession. Carus-Wilson, however, also emphasized a second meas- ure for distinguishing urban from rural – a high percentage of recent immigrants.[55] But few documents allow us to separate communities along these lines as well.

---

[52] D. M. Palliser, 'Introduction', 3–15 in *CUHB*, p. 5.

[53] Holt and Rosser, 'Introduction', p. 4. Also, Hilton, *English and French Towns*, pp. 6–10, where he stresses heterogeneity of occupations, a permanent market, and basic liberties – 'to be as free as possible from seigneurial jurisdiction, to be justiciable in their own town court' (p. 10). By this later definition, late medieval St Albans would not qualify as a town. For a similar definition stressing occupations and the economic functions of communities as urban, but where recognition of non-servile status is not essential, see Dyer, 'Small-town Conflict'; Dyer, 'The Hidden Trade', p. 145; and Christopher Dyer, 'Bromsgrove: A Small Town in Worcestershire in the Middle Ages', *Worcestershire Historical Society, Occasional Publications*, no. 9 (2000), pp. 2–3.

[54] Hilton, 'Towns in English Society', in *The English Medieval Town*, p. 27.

[55] E. M. Carus-Wilson, 'The First Half-century of the Borough of Stratford-upon-Avon', *EcHR* 18 (1965): 49–70. York's civic ordinances in 1301 provide data to access the occupational character of a community, but here there is no question that York was a town; see *York Civic Ordinances, 1301*, ed. Michael Prestwich, Borthwick Papers, no. 49 (York, 1976), pp. 7, 10–18.

In addition, it is often difficult to know, particularly in the Patent Rolls, whether an insurrection had taken place in the countryside, towns, or both; whether the commoners were rural tenants or townsmen. Such was a commission in 1394 to the king's cousin, Henry, Earl of Derby, 'to arrest and imprison until further order all persons causing insurrections, insolences, commotions, congregations or unlawful assemblies or exciting the people thereof, in the counties of York, Derby, Stafford, Lancaster or Chester, with power to suppress them by force if necessary'.[56] An entry from Walsingham's *Annales* gives further details. Purportedly, 20,000 men had risen against the king, angered by his peace negotiation at Calais that year (which threatened the livelihoods of these men, who in the main were soldiers). Moreover, commoners ('populum'), joined the archers and men-at-arms ('multitudo armatorum et arcitenentium'), 'who in various places held assemblies'. Further, they communicated their demands and recruited followers across four counties – Chester, Lancaster, Gloucester, and Derby – 'not just by individual messengers' ('Haec non solum inter se privatim nunciabant') but even by fixing written handbills on parish doors (something that clearly astonished the chronicler). They also resented Richard II's threats to their county liberties, which he wished to sweep away ('avitasque eorum libertates auferre voluisse'). But even with these added details, it remains difficult to know whether any, many, or most, of the armed rebels of military background or the commoners who joined them came from rural villages or towns.[57]

In this book we may have erred on the side of excluding as urban places some small market towns that might with detailed investigation fit the functional criteria above. For instance, without Christopher Dyer's study of Shipston-on-Stour, Warwickshire, a manor of Worcester Cathedral priory, which shows from a wide variety of sources that it was 'truly urban' – its inhabitants 'engaged in a multiplicity of activities, a substantial proportion of which are non-agrarian'[58] – this town would easily have slipped through our net. Without Zvi Razi's and Hilton's

[56] *CPR 1391–6*, p. 433, 1394.iii.21.

[57] Thomas Walsingham, *Annales Ricardi Secundi et Henrici Quarti*, ed. Henry T. Riley, RS, 28 (1866), III, pp. 153–420 (1392–1406), p. 159. According to the editors of the new edition and translation of Walsingham, *The St Albans Chronicle: The Chronica maiora of Thomas Walsingham*, ed. John Taylor and Wendy R. Childs, trans. Leslie Watkiss, 2 vols. (Oxford, 2003–11), II, pp. xlii–xlvi, Walsingham was the author of this chronicle until 1405; it is believed, based on stylistic grounds, that afterwards the chronicle had several authors, of which one was Walsingham, until his death in 1422. On the incident above, also see McKisack, *The Fourteenth Century*, p. 469; and Nigel Saul, *Richard II*, Yale English Monarchs Series (New Haven, 1997), pp. 219–21.

[58] Dyer, 'Small-town Conflict', p. 189.

studies, the same would have been true of Halesowen, part of a manor then in Shropshire, whose inhabitants were legally 'villeins'.[59]

Thirdly, we have followed the broad definitions of 'popular' outlined earlier in *Lust for Liberty*. First, 'popular' takes on a relative meaning that could relate to any class beneath the aristocracy,[60] depending on the nature of the struggle, as with conflicts of burgesses against their monastic, Episcopal, or secular lords, or against royal power.[61] This book, however, looks at baronial revolts only when they clearly galvanized support from peasants and townsmen, especially those beneath the patriciate, as with the waves of rebellion in London, Oxford, and other towns from 1263 to 1265. At the upper end, organized by mayors, aldermen, and bailiffs, towns and cities revolted against royal taxation and perceived infringements against communal liberties of exercising justice and other previously granted privileges, as with the struggles of Bristol between 1312 and 1316 or those against monastic lords in towns such as St Albans or Bury St Edmunds to acquire self-rule, economic rights over markets, or the use of their own mills.[62]

---

[59] Zvi Razi, *Life, Marriage, and Death in a Medieval Parish: Economy and Demography in Halesowen 1270–1400* (Cambridge, 1980); and Rodney Hilton, 'Small Town Society in England before the Black Death', in *The English Medieval Town: A Reader in English Urban History 1200–1540*, ed. R. C. Holt and G. Rosser (London, 1990) p. 96, who argues convincingly that it was 'genuinely a borough', even if it was at the lower end of urbanized places. Also, see Hilton, *English and French Towns*, pp. 55–7. In addition, see the example of Bromsgrove, which was not a borough, held no courts, and possessed no elected officials. However, from its economic functions and occupations of its tenants, Dyer ('Bromsgrove') assesses that it was a small town. We have relied on Dyer's unpublished lists of market towns.

[60] In the English context, it would include the gentry, nobility, and upper echelons of the clergy, secular and regular.

[61] According to Michael Bush, 'The Risings of the Commons in England, 1381–1549', in *Orders and Hierarchies in Late Medieval and Renaissance Europe*, ed. Jeffrey Denton (Manchester, 1999), p. 109, 'commons' in England designated those beneath the nobility and clergy. For Benjamin R. McRee, 'Peacemaking and Its Limits in Late Medieval Norwich', *EHR*, 109 (1994), p. 836, commoners constituted 'the larger but less powerful group' of citizens, 'all those below the rank of bailiff', as opposed to the smaller governing group of *probi homines*. Nonetheless, *commune(s)*/common(s) have complex and numerous permutations and have long been subject to debate by political historians; see W. M. Ormrod, 'Murmur, Clamour and Noise: Voicing Complaint and Remedy in Petitions to the English Crown, c. 1300–c.1460', in *Medieval Petitions: Grace and Grievance*, ed. W. M. Ormrod, Gwilym Dodd, and Anthony Musson (York, 2009), p. 152. John Watts, 'Public or Plebs: The Changing Meaning of "The Commons", 1381–1549', in *Power and Identity in the Middle Ages: Essays in Memory of Rees Davies*, ed. Huw Pryce and John Watts (Oxford, 2007), pp. 242–60, argues convincingly that commons 'did not mean "lower class"' (pp. 244–5) until the sixteenth century, although subtle changes in the terminology can be seen at least by the time of Cade's Rebellion, when it was becoming 'a more routine term for the lower orders', even if it did not yet connote 'simply lower-class people'.

[62] On these struggles, see Trenholme, *The English Monastic Boroughs*.

At the lower end of the social spectrum – artisans and workers – the English sources reveal much less conflict than was seen in numerous urban places on the Continent. Although also somewhat infrequent on the Continent, no cases of riots by the *miserabile* against high bread or grain prices during periods of severe scarcity (like those which erupted in Siena, Rome, and Florence during the 1320s and 1340s) appear in the English sources we have examined.[63] On the other hand, there is no reason to doubt that wide swathes of the English population suffered any less than those on the Continent from famine, pressures of war, and excessive taxation,[64] especially before the Black Death, as with 'inclement air', plague ('peste'), and famine around Easter in 1196,[65] famine in 1234,[66] again in Wales in 1245,[67] pestilence, drought, famine, and a murrain of sheep in 1252 and 1253.[68] Famine and pestilence in 1258 caused high mortalities in London and elsewhere.[69] Triggered by heavy rains and flooding, followed by high corn prices, the scarcity that year caused the poor 'to eat horsemeat, bark off trees and more unpleasant things. Many died of famine.'[70] Late harvests, hail storms, and pestilence struck England again the following year and again in 1260;[71] in October 1271, thunder, lightning, rain, and flooding to an extent 'never seen or heard before' brought 'extreme famine' through the region of Canterbury.[72] 'Drought, heat, and death' in 1285,[73] dearth of corn in 1289,[74] and 'Dearth throughout England'

---

[63] For these, see Cohn, *Lust for Liberty*, pp. 70–5.

[64] A. R. Bridbury, 'English Provincial Towns', *EcHR*, 34 (1981): 15 and 17, suggests that taxation in England, even the poll taxes that led to the Peasants' Revolt, was not so burdensome. He does not support his assertion, however, with any analysis of the data, qualitatively or quantitatively. For another view, see J. R. Maddicott, *The English Peasantry and the Demands of the Crown 1294–1341*, *Past & Present* Supplement, 1 (Oxford, 1975).

[65] *The Chronicle of Walter of Guisborough*, ed. H. Rothwell (CS, 3rd series, 89, 1957), p. 137. Furthermore, price series suggest bad harvests at the end of the twelfth and the beginning of the next century; see Christopher Dyer, 'Did the Peasants Really Starve in Medieval England?', in *Food and Eating in Medieval Europe*, ed. Martha Carlin and Joel T. Rosenthal (London, 1998), pp. 54–5.

[66] Matthew Paris, *Chronica majora*, ed. Henry Richards Luard, 7 vols., RS, 57 (1874), III, p. 299. This followed bad harvests in 1293–5; Dyer, 'Did Peasants Really Starve', p. 61.

[67] Paris, *Chronica majora*, IV, p. 486.

[68] Ibid., V, pp. 316, 321, and 370. Also in 1252, 'an exceptionally hot simmer killed many people'; *The Chronicle of Bury St Edmunds*, p. 18.

[69] Paris, *Chronica majora*, V, pp. 690–3; and *Continuatio chronici Florentii Wigorniensis*, II, p. 187.

[70] *The Chronicle of Bury St Edmunds*, pp. 22–3.

[71] *Willelmi Rishanger, monachi S. Albani, chronica*, ed. Henry T. Riley, RS 28.2 (1865), II, 1–230, pp. 3 and 7.

[72] *The Chronicle of Walter of Guisborough*, p. 212.   [73] Ibid., p. 112.

[74] Ibid., p. 119.

in 1294 led to further 'poverty and death',[75] coupled with continuous rain, so that few crops were harvested. Warfare and probably the highest period of royal taxation in late medieval England[76] further fuelled ecological disaster, with famine spreading through England from 1294 to the end of the century.[77] The Great Famine of 1315–17 was England's worst pre-plague disaster. London's *Great Chronicle* reported that 'the pouere people ete for hunger Cattes and hors and houndes ... And the pouere peple stolen children and eten hem And than after fille a grete pestilence'.[78] Scarcity and hardship returned with war and high taxation in the 1330s, especially in 1336; heavy rain caused wheat prices to soar, and the year witnessed 'a grete moreyn of beestes and of men'.[79]

Bad times did not cease with the Black Death or after the general recovery for labourers in the 1370s and 1380s, though chroniclers reported them less often: exceptions included 1371,[80] the end of 1390 into 1391,[81] and the 1430s, with bad wheat harvests in 1430, pestilence in 1431 and again in 1437, followed by three years of scarcity at the beginning of the next decade.[82] The word 'fames', however, had vanished from these post-plague descriptions. With the scarcity of 1438, an anonymous chronicler of London was shocked that men and women were reduced to eating bread made of beans, peas, and

---

[75] Ibid., p. 143; also see *The Chronicle of Bury St Edmunds*, p. 123; and *Continuatio chronici Florentii Wigorniensis*, II, p. 273.

[76] See Maddicott, *The English Peasantry*, pp. 6–7; Barbara A. Hanawalt, 'Peasant Resistance to Royal and Seignorial Impositions', in *Social Unrest in the Late Middle Ages: Papers of the Fifteenth Annual Conference of the Center for Medieval and Early Renaissance Studies*, ed. Francis X. Newman (Binghamton, New York, 1986), p. 27; and for these taxes and that of 1334, see Sir Maurice Powicke, *The Thirteenth Century 1216–1307* (Oxford, 1953), pp. 534–5 and 618.

[77] *The Chronicle of Bury St Edmunds 1212–1301*, ed. Antonia Gransden (London, 1964), p. 123.

[78] *The Great Chronicle of London*, ed. A. H. Thomas and I. D. Thornley (London, 1938), p. 27. Also see the 'Poem on the Evil Times of Edward II', in *The Political Songs of England from the Reign of John to that of Edward II*, ed. Thomas Wright, CS, 6 (London, 1839), pp. 323 and 342, which laments the price of corn, death of animals, hunger, dearth, and starvation at the beginning of Edward's reign, even before the onset of the Great Famine. ('Whii hunger and derthe on eorthe the pore hath undernome,/Whii bestes ben thus storve, whii corn hath ben so dere').

[79] *A Chronicle of London, from 1089 to 1483, Written in the Fifteenth Century*, ed. N. H. Nicolas and E. Tyrell (London, 1827), p. 55.

[80] Ibid., p. 68.

[81] *The Westminster Chronicle 1381–1394*, ed. L. C. Hector and Barbara F. Harvey (Oxford, 1982), p. 475.

[82] *Chronicon rerum gestarum in monasterio S. Albani (1422–1431) a quodam auctore ignoto compilatum*, ed. Henry T. Riley, 2 vols. RS, 28/5 (1870–1), I, pp. 55 and 62; and *Annales monasterii S. Albani, a Johanne Amundesham (AD 1421–1440)*, in ibid., II, pp. 127 and 223.

vetches,[83] a far cry from the pre-plague horrors of the poor driven to eat cats, hounds, even children.[84] Both the Crown and municipal governments also appear to have become better adept at managing subsistence crises, as noted in a memorandum from London's Guildhall in 1391:

> Since in these days the scarcity of wheat and especially of corn has been greatly increased and since the Most High of His abundant grace has permitted a great part of the wheat, coming from distant foreign parts for the sustenance and aid of His common people, to be brought to the city of London so that scarcity has in great part been diminished there.[85]

And with the scarcity of 1438, the mayor of London purchased wheat supplies from Danzig.[86] The growing effectiveness of parish charities and almshouses, moreover, matched for the provinces and countryside that achieved in towns.[87] According to Dyer, a turning-point in English history occurred around 1375, ushering 'in a new era of cheap and plentiful food' that marked an end to 'hunger-driven mortality'.[88]

In addition to the absence of riots spawned by hunger, English sources detail extremely few protests in which clearly identified disenfranchised workers struggled for rights, fought in the streets against their employers, or protested by initially peaceful means such as strikes and other forms of collective action. In contrast to the Continent, terms such as *menu peuple*, or *popolo minuto*, or expressions such as 'those without underwear' (meaning without means and privileges of citizenship) surface rarely in the English sources. Even when terms such as *plebes*, the poor, *mediocres*, *minores*, or *minor pars et infirmior* appear, it is difficult to know

---

[83] *A Chronicle of London*, p. 124. According to John Hatcher, 'The Great Slump of the Mid-Fifteenth Century', in *Progress and Problems in Medieval England: Essays in Honour of Edward Miller*, ed. R. H. Britnell and John Hatcher (Cambridge, 1996), p. 246, the 1430s were the coldest decade in England between 1100 and 1970, and closed with three extremely poor harvests; wheat prices soared with average yields for barley on a par with 'the very worst harvest on record, that of 1316'. For this scarcity in Cheshire, see Jane Laughton, *Life in a Late Medieval City: Chester 1275–1520* (Oxford, 2008), p. 34.

[84] *A Chronicle of London*, p. 45.

[85] *CPMR*, III: 1381–1412, p. 174, 1391.ii.8. According to *A Chronicle of London*, p. 79, it was the mayor of London, not the king, who 'sente his men over the see with gold into divers contres and broughte home corn, so that the prys was well amendyd'.

[86] Bolton, 'Introduction', p. 33. Also, in 1437 the mayor of London was commissioned to block exports of wheat from the port of London, 'to cause such wheat to be taken back to London to feed the people'; *CPR 1436–41*, p. 144, 1437.ix.17; similar commissions were appointed to prosecute forestallers of wheat in the hundred of Alton, Hampshire; ibid., p. 145, 1437.x.7; and in Kent in 1438 and 1439, ibid., p. 266, 1438.xii.12 and p. 369, 1439.x.14.

[87] Dyer, 'Did the Peasants Really Starve', p. 70; and Majorie K. McIntosh, 'Local Responses to the Poor in Late Medieval and Tudor England', *Continuity and Change*, 3 (1988): 214–17.

[88] Dyer, 'Did the Peasants Really Starve', p. 70.

what social, occupational, or juridical groups are being discussed: were they citizens or not, guildsmen or disenfranchised workers?[89] Instead, English chroniclers usually employed the still vaguer terms 'commoners', or 'populares', to describe those who struggled for rights in urban places: these terms could include citizens, even mayors and aldermen, as well as peasants.[90] In places such as London and the Cinque Ports, mayors, aldermen, bailiffs, and sheriffs, along with patrician merchants and seamen had acquired baronial status since the end of the twelfth century. Chronicles and official documents often distinguished them from other burgesses in these towns, as on 18 July 1392, when King Richard II summoned to Windsor the twenty-four aldermen 'and 400 others, described as commoners, of the city of London' for a collective pardon to the city on payment of a colossal fine. However, these 'others' were hardly the disenfranchised: 'each craft came out in its own livery ... handed the king a sword and keys to the city ...'[91]

Only rarely, such as with a London insurrection against excessive taxes organized by William fitzOsbert in 1196, did chroniclers divide commoners into rich and poor ('divites et paupers'), at one another's throats in the days leading up to the revolt,[92] or by other divisions within the 'commoners'. According to Matthew Paris in 1257, a squire in the service of the king's half-brother wounded several citizens of London and afterwards 'gave utterance to insults and threats, trusting to the usual protection of his lord. The lower orders of citizens ("plebei"),

---

[89] For these and other divisions, such as between *probi homines* and those who were not worthy (usually without a specific term for the latter) taken from imaginative literature, see Hilton, *English and French Towns*, pp. 114–15. He does not draw differences with the Continent; instead he concludes that France and England were similar in their nomenclatures. For the vagueness of the term 'small people' used by the scribe Thomas Usk in cataloguing John of Northampton's crimes after his failed bid for mayor in 1383 and the absence of terminology to distinguish the lower echelons of citizens from non-citizens and the marginalized, see C. M. Barron, 'Searching for the "Small People" of Medieval London', *The Local Historian*, 38 (2008): 83–6.

[90] E. F. Jacob, *Studies in the Period of Baronial Reform and Rebellion, 1258–1267* (Oxford, 1925), pp. 135–6, asserts that at towns such as Lincoln 'distinct classes of *magni*, *secundarii*, and *minores*' can be discerned, but he points to no documents that separate these groups economically, politically, or juridically. Further, he asserts that the bachelors during the baronial revolts of the 1260s were the equivalent of *gens de métier*, even wool workers who went on strike contemporaneously on the Continent, though again without evidence of such among English bachelors (pp. 134–5).

[91] *The Westminster Chronicle 1381–1394*, pp. 503 and 505.

[92] Ralph de Diceto, *Radulphi de Diceto decani Lundoniensis opera historica: The Historical Work of Master Ralph de Diceto, Dean of London*, ed. William Stubbs, 2 vols., RS, 68 (1876), I, pp. 143–4. The same division of London's population into rich and poor is found in another description of fitzOsbert's revolt (perhaps borrowed from the other) in Walter of Coventry, *Memoriale fratris Walteri de Coventria: The Historical Collections of Walter Coventry*, ed. William Stubbs, 2 vols., RS, 58 (1872–3), II, pp. 97–8.

however, rushed on him in crowds, being neither able nor willing to put up with his arrogance', and killed him with stones and staves. Henry III summoned the mayor to account for the murder and, according to Paris, replied 'My lord king, I cannot check the violence of the lower orders of the citizens'.[93] A similar division, even a tripartite one, is found in another struggle the following year:

> the citizens of London, of the middle and lower orders, made a serious complaint to the king, that those appointed to collect the money for rebuilding the walls of the city, as the king had ordered for their honour, had fraudulently kept the greatest part of this money in their own purses, to the injury of the lower order of citizens.[94]

In 1364, John of Reading reported a conflict between the 'majores et populares Londoniarum', in which many were wrongfully imprisoned.[95] Unfortunately, neither Paris nor Reading specified who belonged to these two urban groups, as chroniclers often did on the Continent, or whether the distinctions were juridically defined as being between barons and commoners, or *popolani* versus magnates in late medieval Italian city-states.[96] Nor do London's detailed Letter-books or the Crown's voluminous Patent Rolls draw with any precision such social distinctions.

Finally, our title's fourth term, 'protest', poses problems. Firstly, this book will only touch on the legal means by which peasants, artisans, and the lower echelons of burgesses redressed social, economic, and political grievances through peaceful collective petition in municipal or royal courts. In addition, as Lorraine Attreed and Ben McRee have shown, processes of informal negotiations and formal appeals to appointed arbitrators could resolve even bitter disputes over contested city elections without resort to costly legal battles or appeals to the king. As important as these avenues were for dispute settlement and even class struggle in late medieval England, they will not be this book's focus.[97] Instead, while these forms of protest are not ignored, the book will concentrate on collective action that took place only after such legal

---

[93] Paris, *Chronica majora*, V, pp. 643–4 'De morte cujusdam armigeri Willelmi de Walentia'.

[94] Ibid., V, p. 663.

[95] *Chronica Johannis de Reading, et Anonymi Cantuariensis, 1346–1367*, ed. James Tait, Publications of the University of Manchester, Historical Series, 20 (Manchester, 1914), p. 161.

[96] See for instance, Cohn, *Lust for Liberty*, pp. 55–6.

[97] Lorraine C. Attreed, 'Arbitration and the Growth of Urban Liberties in Late Medieval England', *JBS*, 31 (1992): 205–35; Lorraine C. Attreed, 'Urban Identity in Medieval English Towns', *JIDH*, 32 (2002): 571–92; and McRee, 'Peacemaking'.

means had faltered and the aggrieved had formed illegal assemblies, had planned tactics rulers called conspiracy, or had engaged in collective violence against rulers and their symbols of power.

Another distinction implicit in this book is between riot and revolt: the former connotes collective street violence without a clear sense from the documents of expressed demands beyond anger, possibly personal gain, or criminality, while the latter were struggles for rights or to redress specified abuses by employers, lords, or rulers.[98] These actions challenged the status quo of social and political realities, the imbalances between rulers and the ruled, or between corporate entities such as the Church and burgesses, even if the protesters' objectives were not always to oust a current regime or overturn the political and economic structure of a town or rural community. The authors of our medieval sources – royal clerks or ecclesiastical chroniclers – certainly made no such distinctions. At best, their interest was to judge what was legal or moral by their terms, predicated on the maintenance of hierarchical stability, embedded within feudal and religious notions of the

---

[98] Historians such as Mollat, Wolff, and Fourquin have used slightly different words and have made other distinctions. For Mollat and Wolff, 'A revolution is something planned and prepared; it has a programme. A revolt is a spontaneous reaction, a reflex of anger or self-defence, sometimes of both' (*The Popular Revolutions of the Late Middle Ages*, p. 91). The authors judged most of what they found to be revolts, not revolutions. Similarly, Fourquin, *Anatomy of Popular Rebellion in the Middle Ages*, pp. 20–1, 24–5, 83, 101–2, and 109, distinguished between 'revolt' and 'rebellion'. His definition was more restrictive than Mollat's and Wolff's; 'rebellion' was 'the complete overthrow of a society's foundations', which he deemed impossible for the Middle Ages; it had to await the French Revolution (p. 20). Instead, medieval 'insurgents' were 'imbued with a messianic spirit', yearning 'to get back to the good old days' (p. 21). Following the political philosopher, Jacques Ellul (1912–94), Fourquin maintained that 'revolt is never for; by its very essence it is against' (p. 22). According to Fourquin, victory was something the 'insurgent' never tasted: 'revolt led only to repression and not to revolution' (p. 25). As shown in *Lust for Liberty* and as will be illustrated here, such a stark, negative, and one-dimensional analysis of medieval revolt does little justice to the sources or the realities they describe. More recently, Patrick Lantschner, 'The Logic of Political Conflict in the Late Middle Ages: A Comparative Study of Urban Political Conflicts in Italy and the Southern Low Countries, c. 1370–1440', D.Phil. thesis, University of Oxford, 2012, p. 15, has distinguished 'revolt' from all other forms of political protest, whether legal or illegal, violent or non-violent, factional or class-bound. His notion of revolt approaches Fourquin's of rebellion, in turning over agencies of government. Unlike Fourquin, however, Lantschner sees such turnovers as characteristic of late medieval urban politics, even if the agents of this change were often members of the ruling class. An important collaborative work on community and revolt in the early modern period, *Resistance, Representation, and Community*, ed. Peter Blickle (Oxford, 1997), uses resistance for all forms and levels of conflicts, individual as well as collective, with subsidiary terms such as rebellion, riots, risings, uprisings, conflicts, conspiracies, disturbances, and popular movements employed interchangeably.

three orders of society.[99] Nonetheless, we have not used 'riot' and 'revolt' interchangeably as the sources often do. Tavern brawls that spiralled into pitched battles between scholars and townsmen, for instance, are called riots, no matter how large and devastating to communities, when the documents suggest no struggle for rights or other specific objectives. Yet at the same time we fully recognize that incidents that appear as 'riots' from the sources may well have been 'revolts', provoked by abuses of power or resentment against unfair and injurious prerogatives, and that aimed to gain or restore rights; they may even have had explicit or written demands, which the chronicler or clerk of a Patent Roll felt no need to divulge, or purposefully covered up. To obtain a sense of such resentments and demands from the margins of documents is in fact more difficult with English sources than with Continental ones. While the latter often reported rebels' chants or described newly invented flags and other insignia that expressed their solidarity, corporate identity, and occasionally aspects of their allegiances and ideology, the English ones rarely reveal such direct expressions of their zeal and objectives.

With terms such as 'popular', 'protest', 'revolt' or 'riot', grey areas emerge, as they do on the Continent. However, late medieval England does not pose exactly the same problems in definition. In Italy, Flanders, and France, for instance, it was occasionally difficult to decide whether a town's struggle against the incursions of a larger territorial state, the liberation from such a state, or resistance to domination by the pope or Holy Roman Emperor should be considered popular rebellion or war between two different states of unequal size and importance. The revolt of the subject town of Gallicano in 1372 against Lucchese rule[100] was counted as an act of popular insurrection, as was the defence staged by Ypres' satellite town, Poperinge, against economic domination by its

---

[99] As Wood, *Riot, Rebellion and Popular Politics*, shows for early modern England, legal definitions did not distinguish between riot, sedition, and rebellion; instead, they defined the gamut of 'popular politics as tumultuous, and thereby sought to deny it a public voice' (p. 17). The same can be said of the Middle Ages. Until the Riot Act of 1715, common-law definitions of riot and their penalties were open, vague, and flexible; such collective acts could involve as few as three persons and their 'violence' could be limited to intimidating words. On the other hand, riot also encompassed widespread enclosure movements across regions, even those events well-recorded and part of the historical canon, such as Cade's and Kett's rebellions; see ibid. pp. 38–42. Similarly, in late medieval law and political theory (Emperor Henry VII's declaration of 12 April 1313 and Bartolus da Sassaferrato's tract on rebellion), any disobedience amounted to rebellion; see Lantschner, 'The Logic of Political Conflict', pp. 44–5.

[100] Samuel K. Cohn, Jr, *Popular Protest in Late Medieval Europe: Italy, France, and Flanders*, Medieval Sources Series (Manchester, 2004), document no. 85.

larger neighbour in 1340.[101] On the other hand, Florence's struggle to maintain independence against domination by its larger political rival Milan, or wars by independent city-states against papal incursions into city liberties, such as the War of Eight Saints in the 1370s, were seen principally as warfare between unequal rivals, not popular protest, even though guild militias and artisans may have patriotically repulsed these outside threats by princes. Because of the strength and unity of the English Crown, hostilities between cities that reached open warfare, or between cities and their surrounding countryside,[102] rarely erupted in the later Middle Ages. When Southampton threatened London's domination of the Italian wool trade, the violence that arose between the two was limited to the assassination of a single Italian trader.[103] On the other hand, more violent trade wars, piracy, and squabbles arose between the 'barons' of the Cinque Ports and other English coastal towns, especially with Great Yarmouth in Norfolk, as in 1265,[104] 1297,[105] 1316,[106] 1318,[107] or between Great Yarmouth and Winchelsea in 1254,[108] and Little Yarmouth and Gorleston in 1334.[109] Edward II's difficulties opened further opportunities for inter-city conflict between these towns, with consequences that reached the city of London: its mayor and aldermen complained that their merchants were caught in the cross-fire, and that the internecine quarrels had damaged their curing-sheds in Little Yarmouth.[110] Although these feuds and acts of piracy continued to the reign of Henry VIII,[111] we have not included them in our tallies of popular protest.

Other struggles straddle the grey areas of popular violence and war and are difficult to define as 'popular movements', even though they relied on popular elements, as with various followings of urban forces behind the barons and their wars with the king. In addition, chroniclers recorded numerous outbreaks of town–gown violence, but often it is

---

[101] Cohn, *Lust for Liberty*, p. 56; and Boone, *A la recherché d'une modernité civique*, p. 69.
[102] Hilton, 'Towns in Societies', p. 13.   [103] See below, Chapter 13, n. 68.
[104] *CPR 1258–66*, pp. 491–2, 1265.x.4.
[105] Margaret Brentnall, *The Cinque Ports and Romney Marsh* (London, 1972), p. 9.
[106] *CPR 1313–17*, p. 583, 1316.vii.18   [107] *CPR 1317–21*, p. 290, 1318.xi.12.
[108] Matthew Paris, *Historia Anglorum, sive, ut vulgo dicitur, historia minor*, ed. Frederic Madden, 3 vols., RS, 44 (1866–9), III, p. 335.
[109] *CPR 1330–4*, pp. 577–8, 1334.iv.20. Also, more generally, see N. A. M. Rodger, *The Safeguard of the Sea: A Naval History of Britain, I 660–1649*, 2 vols. (London, 1997), p. 126, on the century-long 'private war' between Yarmouth and the Cinque Ports.
[110] *CPMR*, I, pp. 34–5.
[111] Brentnall, *The Cinque Ports*, p. 9; also see F. W. Brooks, 'The Cinque Ports', *The Mariner's Mirror*, 15 (1929): 176–86, for descriptions of these feuds, which he claims were 'the most desperate that existed in medieval England' (p. 177). They were principally between the Cinque Ports and Yarmouth over fishing rights.

difficult to understand who was oppressing whom or whether these were protests over city liberties, internecine conflict, personal adventure, or youthful violence exploding from bar-room brawls to urban war, ending in mass bloodshed and destruction. Violence against Jews and against foreigners fills another grey area. Often the violence was without clearly described signs of protest, beyond irrational hatred or personal opportunism. Yet these acts and movements of urban violence, where they involved groups of burgesses or artisans and when not limited to individual acts of criminality, have been tallied as popular movements.

Not all forms of popular protest need have resulted in violent action. On the Continent, peace demonstrations such as those of children opposed to Queen Joanna's war with Sicily in 1347[112] or the movement of children and adolescents in Parma in 1331 that led to dancing in streets, chants against war and taxes, and resulted in the deposition of their hated ruler Riccardo, King Robert II's agent, did not spill over into mass violence.[113] Similar peace movements (whether peaceful or not) do not appear in the English sources we have examined. On the other hand, the English populace organized other forms of protest, particularly against ecclesiastical lords, which did not depend on violence (at least as recorded by chroniclers or the Patent Rolls). On a number of occasions, villagers and townsmen took their protests for rights or against abuses to outside authorities, most often the king. Such cases depended on extensive mobilization and organization of popular groups, peasants, and small townsmen, involving the collection of funds for legal assistance, travel to the king's courts, and payment of fines, as well as the organization of assemblies and actions that were regarded by their lords, chroniclers, and clerks as illegal.[114] For instance, from 1395 to 1403, the townsmen of Shipston-on-Stour struggled against impositions of seigneurial rights such as heriot and the priory's monopoly over mills. The tenants formed 'conventicles', raised funds, and presented their case at King's Bench in 1398; they withheld their rents and other dues, avoided tolls and a tax on ale, and built horse mills to grind their own malt against the priory's customs and privileges. But the only suggestion of violence occurred in 1402, when the priory's servants, who were sent to collect tolls, were threatened (but seemingly only threatened) with physical injury.[115]

---

[112] Cohn, *Lust for Liberty*, p. 93.   [113] Ibid., pp. 93–4.   [114] See Chapter 3.

[115] Dyer, 'Small-town Conflict', pp. 200–3. Also see Razi, 'The Struggles', for other cases of manors and market villages resisting seigneurial exactions and impositions through secret meetings, and pooling resources to pursue suits in royal courts against lords such as the Abbot of Halesowen. Often they appealed to the Domesday Book, to prove they

In addition, the long history of London's resistance to the Crown, especially as regards the king's requests for loans and increased taxation, which were fought within Parliament and the courts, forms an important chapter in the constitutional history of medieval and early modern England but is rarely presented here as a form of 'popular' protest, even though the contours of this constitutional history may have rested more on pressure from below, violent or non-violent, than either chroniclers or modern historians have admitted or explored. Occasionally, chroniclers described the populace as the ones resisting a king's attempt to change their constitutional rights. And in these cases, the events were tallied as popular insurgence. Such resistance could lead to bloodshed but it need not, as in London in 1250. Before proposing to set off on a crusade to the Holy Land, Henry III tried to force Londoners to grant many of their franchises to the Abbot of Westminster. At the abbey, he planned a ceremonial handover of the privileges with the mayor, aldermen, and other citizens in attendance, but 'the whole of the commons . . . exclaiming with one voice' opposed the king, the abbey, and the London patriciate, 'that in no point would they recede from their wonted franchises'.[116] In the long struggle between London and Richard II during the 1380s and 1390s, popular resistance could influence events and blunt the king's efforts in imposing emergency loans or new taxes. Such popular pressure could be achieved without recourse to arms. In 1387, London's mayor promised to raise the £50,000 demanded by the king for war, but Londoners rebuffed their mayor:

the greater part of them answered, with one voice and mind, that they could not and would not go to fight those who were friends of the king and the kingdom, and defenders of the truth, and in the present business like to be, with God's help, powerful champions of the poor, but they were now and would always be ready to turn out against enemies of the king and the kingdom.[117]

---

were tenants of the Crown's ancient demesne, as did Halesowen's tenants, albeit unsuccessfully, in 1278 (p. 161). Despite numerous attempts by peasants, almost inevitably these suits failed. See Hanawalt, 'Peasant Resistance', pp. 39–40; and John H. Tillotson, 'Peasant Unrest in England of Richard II', *Historical Studies*, 16 (1974): 3–6.

[116] *'Liber de Antiquis Legibus'*, attributed to Arnald Fitz-Thedmar, in *Chronicles of the Mayors and Sheriffs of London, 1188–1274*, ed. H. T. Riley (London, 1863), p. 17. Paris, *Chronica majora*, V, pp. 127–8, speculated that the king 'shamelessly violated' the charters of Londoners, 'perhaps because of the pope's example', I imagine, reflecting on Innocent III's struggles against the prerogatives of Frederick II. He also added that Londoners sought the support of Richard, Earl of Cornwall, and other nobles against the king's demands.

[117] *Knighton's Chronicle 1337–1396*, ed. and trans. G. H. Martin (Oxford, 1995), p. 407; *The Westminster Chronicle*, pp. 497 and 503, put the loan at 5,000 marks and the price of Richard's pardon at £40,000; John Capgrave, *Chronicle of England*, ed. F. C. Hingeston, RS, 1 (1858), p. 293, writing more than a generation after the event, dated it to 1390.

Finally, in English history, as on the Continent, factional conflict between contending parties of elites, aided by artisans or even by ones further down the social hierarchy, is often difficult to distinguish from popular revolt. Such factional conflict could also express class interests, as seen in disputes over municipal elections, especially of mayors. Most notable of these were the mayoral struggles in London between John of Northampton and Nicholas Brembre during the 1380s and 1390s. While little may have separated the two as regards their social and economic status, Northampton appealed to the populace, and craftsmen organized in his support, showing that class interests played a part in these disputed elections.[118]

The mix of factional and class interests continued into the fifteenth century, when the wealthy merchant Ralph Holland led struggles of tailors against drapers, supported by members of the grocers' guild and other merchants from traditional London elites in the early 1440s. The elites rejected the lower guildsmen's candidates for chamberlain in 1442 and mayor the following year. Holland drew support from tailors, skinners, and other London artisans outside the ruling class, who at the same time allied with elites, such as their own candidate for mayor in 1443, the grocer William Cottesbroke, who they supported against the incumbent grocer of nine years, John Chichele. As Caroline Barron has persuasively argued, these artisans had their own voice and agenda, to preserve the rights and representation of the city's entire commonalty in municipal government as guaranteed in charters of the early fourteenth century.[119] We question Pamela Nightingale's conclusions that these movements led (but only in part) by Northampton or Holland arose solely from conflicts of interests within the ruling class, that these leaders merely 'exploited popular grievances to obtain political power and to disguise their factional and personal aims'.[120] In summary, popular protest will be delimited in this study

---

[118] Also, the factional disputes in London that supported or opposed Richard in the late 1380s and 1390s; *The Westminster Chronicle*, pp. 217–33.

[119] See C. M. Barron, 'Ralph Holland and the London Radicals, 1438–1444', in *The English Medieval Town: A Reader in English Urban History 1200–1540*, ed. R. C. Holt and G. Rosser (London, 1990), pp. 160–83; C. M. Barron, 'The Political Culture of Medieval London', in *The Fifteenth Century, IV: Political Culture in Late Medieval Britain*, ed. Linda Clark and Christine Carpenter (Woodbridge, 2004), pp. 111–33. S. H. Rigby, 'Urban "Oligarchy" in Late Medieval England', in *Towns and Townspeople in the Fifteenth Century*, ed. John A. F. Thomson (Gloucester, 1988), p. 69; *The Great Chronicle of London*, pp. 175–6; and 'Eighth Book of the *Polychronicon* from Caxton', in *Ranulphi Higden monachi Cestrensis*, ed. J. R. Lumby, 9 vols., RS, 41 (1865–6), VIII, appendix 4, p. 567.

[120] Nightingale, *A Medieval Mercantile Community*, esp. pp. 564–6. For different and more balanced views of Northampton's and Brembre's class interests, see the *Westminster*

to include struggles where conflict can be detected between different social strata, which may have used legal avenues such as arbitration or the royal courts but ultimately resorted to illegal assembly and collective street action for threats of physical intimidation to class war.

Sources

Certainly, a book attempting to trace broad patterns over centuries and comparisons with the Continent must select sources and create samples. This book relies principally on chronicles and the royal miscellanea of records called Patent Rolls. Unlike in city-states of central and northern Italy and to a large extent in northern France and in Germany, a tradition of local, municipal chronicles is largely missing for medieval England, with the limited exception of London, and that primarily for the fifteenth century on. In addition, overwhelmingly, the chroniclers of medieval England were ecclesiastical, secular and monastic, although several served as royal clerks.[121] As a consequence, their focus was either on the narrow affairs of a monastic house or the principal national and international events concerning the Crown or the Church. Municipal matters, especially in places far removed from Westminster and London, even by chroniclers who lived in monasteries in the north of England, are often left unnoticed unless they concerned wars with Scotland, Wales, or Ireland, or had an immediate impact on the Crown or Church with national or international repercussions. As can be seen in some of the best known of the English chroniclers, as with Matthew Paris and Thomas Walsingham, both monks at the Benedictine

---

Chronicler; Ruth Bird, *The Turbulent London of Richard II* (London, 1949); Wendy Scase, *Literature and Complaint in England, 1272–1553* (Oxford, 2007), pp. 68–9; Prescott, 'London in the Peasants' Revolt', p. 133; C. M. Barron, 'Richard II and London', in *Richard II: The Art of Kingship*, ed. Anthony Goodman and James L. Gillespie (Oxford, 1999), pp. 145–9; and comments in the next chapter. Moreover, Brembre's constitutional directives returned to the elites of the wards the rights to elect the common council, revoked the ban on aldermen serving for two consecutive years, and restricted the common council's role in electing the mayor, and the wards' role in electing aldermen, and deciding who was eligible to be a candidate for mayor. These measures led in 1394 to aldermen being elected for life; Rigby, 'Urban "Oligarchy"', p. 72. For the historiography of the Northampton–Brembre conflict, from George Unwin's study of London guilds (1908) to Nightingale, see Frank Rexroth, *Deviance and Power in Late Medieval London*, trans. Pamela Selwyn (Cambridge, 2007; 1999), pp. 130–7, which mostly supports Nightingale's conclusions. For Ralph Holland, see Barron, 'Ralph Holland'.

[121] Chris Given-Wilson, *Chronicles: The Writing of History in Medieval England* (London, 2004), p. 156.

Abbey of St Albans,[122] events in Paris or Rome were more likely to enter their accounts than serious class conflict at Carlisle, Newcastle, or within larger and more centrally located English cities such as Norwich, Bristol, and York, even when municipal strife was crucial to royal authority.[123]

The Patent Rolls, by contrast, present a much broader geographical coverage within England. (See maps.) These records, originating as early as the beginning of John's reign – a separate roll for letters patent opening in 1201–2[124] – were royal letters, issued unsealed and not closed, hence their name and contrast with a set of letters and mandates known as the 'Close Rolls'.[125] Entries within the Patent Rolls do not, however, begin to mount in number until the reign of Henry III (1216), and only at this point did a government commission of 1901 decide to begin its publication of the calendar of these royal documents. Until the second half of the thirteenth century, however, these documents give little hint of popular protest in towns or the countryside.[126] Even then, the most important documents for our purposes had yet to appear – commissions to examine disturbances of the peace, known as 'oyer et terminer' (to hear and determine, in other words, pass judgement on bills and complaints) and commissions for general inquiries into breaches of the king's peace. These concerned serious cases of 'trespasses, oppressions, extortions, conspiracies and rebellion', and by Edward II's reign were opened to complaints even by lesser burgesses and peasants of official abuses and corruption. As Richard Kaeuper has shown, cases covered by these commissions varied widely in scope and purpose.[127]

---

[122] For the chronicle tradition of St Albans, see Antonia Gransden, *Historical Writing in England*, 2 vols. (London, 1974–82), II, Chapter 5.

[123] On the varied and complex history of chronicle and annalist writing in England from the early Middle Ages to the early modern period, see ibid.

[124] David Carpenter, '"In Testimonium Factorum Brevium": The Beginnings of the English Chancery Rolls', pp. 1–28, in *Records, Administration and Aristocratic Society in the Anglo-Norman Realm: Papers Commemorating the 800th Anniversary of King John's Loss of Normandy*, ed. Nicholas Vincent (Woodbridge, 2009), especially pp. 24 and 28. He speculates that chancery rolls may have had an earlier origin.

[125] Certain years of these records, such as from 1346 to 1349, have also been sampled: they report far fewer examples of collective popular protest and conflict.

[126] Alan Harding, 'Plaints and Bills in the History of English Law, Mainly the Period 1250–1330', in *Legal History Studies 1972: Papers Presented to the Legal History Conference, Aberystwyth, 18–21 July 1972*, ed. Dafydd Jenkins (Cardiff, 1975), p. 74.

[127] Richard W. Kaeuper, 'Law and Order in Fourteenth-Century England: The Evidence of Special Commissions of Oyer and Terminer', *Speculum*, 54 (1979): 734–84, especially 739–40. For the variety and procedures of these commissions to gather information, arrest, and prosecute rebels of 1381, see Andrew Prescott, 'Judicial Records of the Rising of 1381', Ph.D. thesis, Bedford College, University of London (1984), Chapter 1.

Political parties and individuals could abuse them, using them as legal weapons to injure enemies.[128] During the first twenty years of Henry III's reign, documents in the Patent Rolls were mostly 'mandates' – protection granted to monasteries and individuals, grants of safe conduct and passage, communiqués with knights, charitable gifts to monasteries, guarantees to boroughs such as Devizes in 1218, that the king would not jeopardize their ancient liberties and customs,[129] grants of the assizes of bread and market privileges in towns to feudal lords.[130] Only rarely can noises of urban crowds or evidence of violence be heard in these documents (and here only at the margins), as with disturbances in the annual markets at Great Yarmouth in a royal mandate granted to that town in 1222.[131]

In the latter years of Henry's reign and more so during Edward I's (1272–1307), these rolls developed into a vast miscellanea of royal acts – writs, grants, protections, mandates, appointments, presentations, legal examinations and investigations, pardons, letters of enquiry, and most importantly for studying popular protest, the appointment of special and general commissions of inquiry, especially those of 'oyer et terminer', which examined cases of collective violence, trespass, and revolt in towns and the countryside.[132] The first of these commissions appears in 1248 but did not adjudicate any acts of violence (popular or otherwise).[133] Commissions containing specific descriptions of collective violence rise

<hr>

[128] In addition to Kaeuper on these special commissions, see A. L. Brown, *The Governance of Late Medieval England 1272–1461* (London, 1989), pp. 116–17; Scase, *Literature and Complaint*, pp. 44–5; Harding, 'Plaints and Bills', pp. 78–80; and Harding, 'The Revolt against the Justices', in *The English Rising*. Checking the Patent Roll originals with those published in the Calendars, Kaeuper, 'Law and Order', p. 740, finds that the Calendars present an accurate and full list of the commissions. In addition, Douglas Aiton compared a sample of the original membranes of Patent Rolls in TNA with edited ones in *CPR*, concluding that the editors fulfilled the aims of the early editor, Maxwell Lyte: 'I have caused the abstracts in the Calendar to be made so full that in ordinary cases no further information can be obtained from the Rolls themselves' (*CPR 1327–30*, p. vii). In checking names and occupations in long lists of rebels, for instance, Aiton has found that the editors did not abridge this information. The Chancery, however, issued commissions that were never recorded in the Patent Rolls; from other evidence, however, only a few are known not to have been enrolled.

[129] *CPR 1216–25*, p. 142, 1218. [130] See for instance, ibid. p. 153.

[131] *CPR 1216–25*, pp. 340–1.

[132] According to Brown, *The Governance*, p. 116, only with Edward I's reign in 1272 do they increase significantly in number. After the Black Death, the numbers of special commissions of oyer et terminer began to decline, to be replaced by more specialized forms of oyer et terminer proceedings held by justices of the peace; see Anthony Musson and W. M. Ormrod, *The Evolution of English Justice: Law, Politics and Society in the Fourteenth Century* (Basingstoke, 1999), p. 50; also Edward Powell, *Kingship, Law, and Society: Criminal Justice in the Reign of Henry V* (Oxford, 1989), pp. 12–18.

[133] *CPR 1247–58*, p. 30, 1248.vi.15.

significantly only at the end of the thirteenth century. Thus, for the first century of our analysis, understanding of popular protest must rely on chronicles almost alone. Even afterwards, during the fourteenth and fifteenth centuries, these royal administrative records had shortcomings. Rarely do they document motives behind collective violence, making it often difficult to know whether attacks on feudal, monastic, or royal manors were opportunistic raids for profit or motivated by social, economic, or political grievances.[134]

Other sources remain to be tapped for evidence of popular insurrection in towns. These include, most importantly, the records of King's Bench[135] and municipal archives of town governments and guilds held in TNA and in individual towns across England. Some have been published and are utilized in our analysis, especially Chapter 2. These court records, however, were not mutually exclusive: commissions of inquiry initiated by the Crown or private parties could enter municipal records along with being adjudicated at King's Bench. Nonetheless, investigation of these tribunals' holdings would certainly increase our sample of incidents and enrich our findings.[136]

Only future work will show to what extent the broad interpretative patterns suggested by this study should be seriously altered, such as our finding of a great decline in most forms of popular revolt as early as the first decades of the fourteenth century, well before the Black Death and 'the meteoric rise of Justices of the Peace after 1350', the Ricardian Statutes of Livery and Forcible Entry, and the Statute of 1411, which gave Justices of the Peace summary powers for dealing with riots. As Edward Powell has argued, the rise of the JPs and new peace commissions did not supplant the functions of the two older officials concerned with criminal justice in the shires: the coroner and the sheriff.[137] Commissions of oyer et terminer, of general inquiries, pardons, and mandates found in the Patent

---

[134] According to Kaeuper, 'Law and Order', pp. 750, 752, 781, and 784, a sizeable majority of the commissions of oyer et terminer were 'in large measure' disputes among feuding gentry in the countryside, in which the courts themselves were used to gain land and power, contributing to further disorder rather than resolving it. Also, see cases from these commission inquiries of 'noble lawlessness' in Griffiths, *The Reign of King Henry VI*, pp. 569–92.

[135] On the jurisdiction and prosecution of cases in King's Bench, especially regarding rebels, see Prescott, 'Judicial Records', Chapter 4, pp. 194–252.

[136] Still other sources, such as the records of the Sheriffs' Court of London, the busiest and 'by far the most important of the city courts', might provide further cases of civil unrest in London; however, their survival is extremely fragmentary. Further, this court heard minor criminal and civil cases, not ones of serious collective action. The Mayor's Court (whose published records are considered in Chapter 2), dealt with major city disturbances; see Tucker, *Law Courts and Lawyers*, pp. 7, 12–15, 19, 98–9, 155.

[137] Powell, *Kingship, Law, and Society*, p. 60.

Rolls, along with the chronicles, record all the major revolts presently discussed in the secondary literature of the first half of the fifteenth century – the Lollard conspiracies and revolts of Sir John Oldcastle, John Grace and Jack Sharp, the Londoners' protests and bill casting against Bishop Beaufort in 1425, electoral riots at Norwich in 1437, as well as numerous descriptions of Cade's Revolt of 1450. In addition, our records reflect on less studied incidents of riot and revolt, including ones yet to be analysed by historians, such as a revolt over a mayoral election at Lincoln in 1393, which split the city along class lines,[138] or a revolt on 5 June 1402 of shipmen and skinners, who 'rose in insurrection' at Hull (a place supposedly where violence between the town's rulers and its ruled failed to flare in the Middle Ages).[139] In Hull, the rebels broke into the king's prison, liberated their comrades in stocks, and attempted to kill the mayor and his servants. This revolt was one of the very few to record the chants of English rebels, 'fire, fire, fire' and 'doune with the maire, doune with hym'.[140] Further unnoticed revolts include the many 'congregations and conventicles in taverns and other suspected places of the city with the intention of making rancour, dissension, and discord in it' at Bath in 1422,[141] a royal commission granted to the mayor of London in 1437 to investigate and prosecute 'riots, congregations and unlawful assemblies, which have recently occurred in such large numbers' in the city and suburbs of London,[142] or the 'invasions, slaughters, burnings, plunderings' organized by those of the hinterland of Waterford, Ireland, in 1448 against the town's mayor and the English Crown,[143] to name only a few.

One purpose of this study is to encourage historians to study the records comparatively across Britain and not just to increase our repertoire of popular protests in single towns. The next chapter investigates an aspect of urban popular struggle that rarely appears in either chronicles or Patent Rolls: economic and social struggles between workers or artisans and their employers. Further exploration of municipal archives will no doubt shed more light on these conflicts. For this chapter, we turn to published records for towns such as Lincoln, Norwich, and Lynn but mostly to London. The book will then explore forms of protest that by comparison with the Continent were rare in late medieval England; then to those that filled the vacuum, firstly against the Crown, its ministers, and other secular authorities; then, against the Church, and finally movements of hate that targeted Jews, foreigners, and heretics.

---

[138] See p. 189 below. [139] See Chapter 5, note 53.
[140] *CPR 1401–5*, p. 115, 1402.vii.5. [141] *CPR 1416–22*, p. 447, 1422.vii.11.
[142] *CPR 1436–41*, p. 145, 1437.ix.3.
[143] *CPR 1446–52*, p. 132, 1448.iv.8; and p. 67 below.

2   Class struggle in English towns: workers and bosses

English chronicles and Patent Rolls reveal few examples of conflict between apprentices, wage earners, or journeymen on the one hand; their bosses on the other, or struggles between rivalling guilds of comparable class status. These appear far less frequently than is seen on the Continent from chroniclers alone. Nonetheless, much of what we know of Continental popular protest at the bottom rungs of urban society of disenfranchised workers, apprentices, and journeymen against the demands and abuses of their employers comes from administrative and juridical sources. In northern Europe, these are primarily town statutes and petitions; in France, royal pardons or remissions of justice; and in Italy, criminal inquisitions and sentences.[1] For instance, relying on chroniclers, the early strikes in thirteenth- or fourteenth-century Douai,[2] the first recorded association of disenfranchised wool workers in Florence with a community chest and strike fund in 1345, or the strikes of dyers between 1369 and 1371 in that city would not be known.[3]

On the Continent, however, chroniclers were neither blind nor indifferent to conflicts of *menu peuple* or *popolo minuto* against city officials or clashes in which workers confronted their masters in armed combat, as with the disputes over wages by the wool carders of Siena, known as the Bruco, in 1370 and 1371. Initially, these targeted the wool carders' employers, but escalated later that year in a march on city hall, in which wool carders assaulted town magistrates and threatened to kill their bosses. Surviving administrative records for this, Siena's most remarkable urban rising of workers, do not figure; rather the descriptions come from a city chronicler, Neri di Donato.[4] Other chronicles, such as the *Chronicon Parmense* for Parma, the *Corpus chronicorum Boniensium*

---

[1] On these sources and examples of popular protest, see *Popular Protest in Late Medieval Europe: Italy, France, and Flanders*, ed. and trans. Samuel K. Cohn, Jr, Medieval Sources Series (Manchester, 2004).

[2] Among other places, see Cohn, *Lust for Liberty*, p. 54.

[3] Ibid., p. 63.   [4] Ibid., pp. 58–9.

for Bologna, those of Giovanni and Matteo Villani, three anonymous chroniclers of the Tumult of the Ciompi, Marchionne di Coppo Stefani, and Andrea Minerbetti for Florence, Agnolo di Tura del Grasso for Siena, and many others, reported numerous risings of disenfranchised workers in the wool industry, as well as of artisans in other trades, challenging their employers, or fiscal or juridical abuses imposed on them by elites. Many of these chroniclers were merchants, residents of towns and often directly involved in these battles. By contrast, before the mid-fifteenth century, few chronicles written by merchants survive for England.[5]

At the same time, however, precious few merchant chroniclers survive for late medieval northern France and the Low Countries, in cloth-manufacturing cities such as Bruges, Ghent, and Ypres, as well as in cities that were not cloth producers, such as Liège before the fifteenth century. Yet chroniclers who belonged to religious institutions – the continuators of the *Chronique latine de Guillaume de Naugis*, *Chronicon Girardi de Fracheto*, *Les grandes chroniques de France*, *Chronicon Cornelii Zanteliet*, *Chronicon comitum Flandrensium*, *Chronica Aegidii Li Muisis*, *Chronique des Pays-Bas*, *Annales Gandenses*, *Chronique du religieux de Saint-Denys*, and others – reported strikes, guild strife, and revolts organized and staffed by disenfranchised wool workers and artisans in their towns and in neighbouring places.[6]

Although revolts of cloth workers and other disenfranchised workers over wages and injustices at the point of production never predominated among Continental revolts, they were conspicuous in Flanders and northern France from the mid-thirteenth century and in Italy just before the Black Death and more so thereafter.[7] By contrast, these

---

[5] Several mid-fifteenth-century London chroniclers may have been merchants; see Kaufman, *The Historical Literature*, as with an earlier collection of chroniclers, which included sheriffs or mayors, most prominently, Arnold Fitzthedmar [Thedmar] (1201–74/5). Before becoming an alderman, he had prospered in the Baltic trade; see Catto, 'Fitzthedmar'. Another important chronicle, probably by a merchant, was the *Annales Londonienses*, which Andrew Horn, fishmonger and chamberlain of London from about 1320, may have authored; see Gransden, *Historical Writing*, I, p. 3; II, pp. 508–9. In her exhaustive works on English chroniclers, she does not mention a merchant chronicler outside London before 1450. Merchant chroniclers increase in number in London during the first half of the fifteenth century; all but one – the skinner, William Gregory – however, were anonymous, and only one more is known from the second half of the century – the draper Robert Fabyan; ibid., II, p. 230. The first merchant chronicler mentioned in the secondary literature from any other town was Robert Ricart, town clerk of Bristol in 1479; Rigby, 'Urban "Oligarchy"', p. 62.

[6] For these, see Cohn, *Lust for Liberty*, especially Chapter 3.

[7] Among other places, see ibid., Chapter 3; Mollat and Wolff, *The Popular Revolutions of the Late Middle Ages*; Marc Boone, 'Urban Space and Political Conflict in Late Medieval Flanders', *JIDH*, 32 (2002): 621–40; Boone, *A la recherché d'une modernité civique*,

revolts are wholly missing from the ninety-three English chronicles surveyed in this study, as well as from thousands of pardons, special and general commissions, royal writs, and other documents contained in the voluminous Patent Rolls from the late thirteenth to the mid-fifteenth centuries. Only one case of a wage dispute emerges from the chroniclers, but it was not a revolt or a dispute of disenfranchised workers or of other artisans. Instead, it comes at the end of our analysis and involved the king's sailors and soldiers. On 11 January 1449, the king sent Master Adam Moleyns, Bishop of Chichester and keeper of the king's seal, to Portsmouth to pay royal soldiers and sailors their wages ('certeyn soudiers and shippemen'). Altercations arose when the bishop tried to cut their pay ('wolde haue abrigged their wages'). As a result, they 'fell on hym and ther killed hym'.[8] Another case involving sailors may have also concerned wages or working conditions. The chronicler's pithy entry of 23 June 1324, however, makes it difficult to know whether it was a conflict between sailors and their masters taking place simultaneously in two ports on opposite sides of the Channel – Dover and Wissant [Witsand] in the Pas-de-Calais – or (more likely) a rivalry among sailors (*fuit discordia inter nautas de Doveria et Witsand*) 'that caused ships not to sail for a long time'.[9]

Other incidences of class altercation between masters and servants found in chronicles suggest underlying tensions, but few of these point explicitly to troubles at the workplace. For instance, a chronicler records a fight at Smithfield between an armourer of Fleet Street and his servant on the eve of Cade's Rebellion that had broken out over slurs the servant allegedly made against the king, and in which the servant slew his master.[10] This may well have been a conflict over ideologies or

---

pp. 65–76; Boone and Prak, 'Rulers, Patricians and Burghers'; Jan Dumolyn and Jelle Haemers, 'Patterns of Urban Rebellion in Medieval Flanders', *JMH* 31 (2005): 369–93; and Jelle Haemers, 'A Moody Community? Emotion and Ritual in Late Medieval Urban Revolts', in *Emotions in the Heart of the City (14th–16th Century)*, Studies in European Urban History, 5, ed. Elodie Lecuppre-Desjardin and Anne-Laure Van Bruaene (Tournhout, 2005), pp. 63–81.

[8] *An English Chronicle, 1377–1461: Edited from Aberystwyth, National Library of Wales MS 21068 and Oxford, Bodleian Library MS Lyell 34*, ed. William Marx (Woodbridge, Suffolk, 2003), p. 67.

[9] *Annales Paulini*, in *Chronicles of the Reigns of Edward I and Edward II*, ed. William Stubbs, 2 vols. RS, 76 (1882–3), I, p. 307. The Parliament Rolls list other complaints of unpaid wages to soldiers, as in 1376 with the troops of Lord Neville. His men-at-arms and archers, however, did not take their frustrations out on Lord Neville, who 'would take no notice of their complaint'; instead they pillaged the town of Winchester. See A. Audrey Locke, 'Political History', in *VCH: A History of Hampshire and the Isle of Wight*, vol. XII, ed. William Page (London, 1912), p. 314.

[10] *Chronicle of the Grey Friars of London*, CS, old series, 53, ed. J. G. Nichols (London, 1852), p. 18.

national loyalties, but it did not concern working conditions or wages and was individual, not collective action. Strife involving 'men practising various handicrafts ... some of them workingmen, who conspired to rise against the clergy and their lay neighbours' at Croydon on 13 January 1390 may have involved economic demands or the overthrow of local governors. The chronicler of Westminster does not, however, supply any details of their organization, motives, or actions, except that the authorities took the workers' intentions seriously: sixteen were arrested, and three were drawn and hanged.[11] Finally, class tensions may have been mounting in London during Henry VI's minority in 1425, at the height of factional strife between Bishop Beaufort, chancellor of England, and the king's uncle, Humphrey, Duke of Gloucester.[12] The spark came with a new ordinance of the mayor and aldermen of London against masons, carpenters, tilers, daubers, and other labourers accepting excessive wages. The labourers' resentment and anger, however, was not directed against their employers and never reached the boiling point of revolt, even though the chronicler (or at least Bishop Beaufort) suspected that Duke Humphrey did little to contain it and may have encouraged their 'dysobeyssaunce'. Only the casting of 'mony hevynesses and cedicious billes under the names of suche labourers Thretyng Rysing' ensued.[13]

Incidents of strife between guilds or among apprentices also leave few traces in medieval English chronicles. The few to arise, moreover, come exclusively from London or its suburbs. Two revolved around contested or allegedly corrupt elections of mayors. The first, well covered by the *Westminster Chronicle*, involved the famous contest between Northampton and Brembre in the 1380s, the former, a draper, representing mostly the non-victualling trades, especially in cloth production; the latter, a prominent member of the grocers' guild, representing merchant purveyors of food and traders in wool (grocers, fishmongers, and mercers).[14] The near-three-decade struggle, however, also had a class

---

[11] *The Westminster Chronicle*, p. 411.

[12] On this tension within Henry VI's protectorate, see Griffiths, *The Reign of King Henry VI*, Chapter 4; and G. L. Harriss, 'Humphrey [Humfrey or Humphrey of Lancaster], Duke of Gloucester', *ODNB* (2004).

[13] *The Great Chronicle of London*, p. 143. Also, *A Chronicle of London* reported that the mayor and 'peple' of London came out well armed in support of the Duke of Gloucester against the chancellor, 'but thankyd God there was non harme don on neythir partye' (p. 114). On Duke Humphrey, see H. S. Bennett, *Six Medieval Men and Women* (Cambridge, 1955), pp. 1–29; and Harriss, 'Humphrey'.

[14] For the most recent and detailed investigation of this two-decade controversy, see Nightingale, *A Medieval Mercantile Community*, chapters 10–12, who sees it simply as a power-play between elites. By her view, Northampton was the corrupt opportunist demagogue, fanning the rage of commoners, and Brembre the scapegoat, who paid with

dimension, seen not only in court records but also in chronicle accounts. On 11 February 1384, a cordwainer, John Constantyn, 'excited as some will have it, by a spirit sent from the Devil, careered through the streets of London urging the populace to rise against the mayor [Brembre], whom he declared to be bent on smashing all those who supported John of Northampton'. Clearly, the Westminster chronicler had no sympathy for the cordwainer's cause (which may well have been broader than simply supporting Northampton, as later decrees of Brembre against the cordwainers' and other craft guilds suggest): 'A righteous and merciful God, however, unwilling that the emergence of serious sedition in the densely populated city should lead, because of a single individual, to people's destroying one another, ordained a better course.'[15] Constantyn was arrested, condemned to death, his head severed and placed above Newgate. The mayor then 'set industriously to appease those of the city crafts which were in conflict with each other'.[16] The second case of a craft guild taking collective action again concerned a contested London election, this one in 1440, when the tailors rebelled in the Guildhall ('a stryffe in the yelde halle for chesynge of the mayer, by the crafte of the taylors').[17]

Three further cases arise during troubled times of national civil strife between magnates and kings, one following the revolt of Simon de Montfort against Henry III, and two at the end of Edward II's reign. On 25 November 1267, armed conflict between guildsmen spread through London with 'great assemblages' over three days and nights, which (according to the chronicler) engaged five hundred craftsmen and resulted in bodies thrown into the Thames. Thirty were seized and imprisoned at Newgate, and several were hanged. On one side were the guilds of goldsmiths and tailors; on the other tradesmen of parmenters (embroiderers) and tawyers (preparers of white leather).

his life because of the economic recession of the 1380s and the failures of Richard II's government. She ignores evidence such as that cited above from the royal courts (*SCBKC*), in which various lower guilds – the saddlers, tailors, cordwainers, spinners, blacksmiths, and embroiderers – lost their guild privileges as a result of Brembre's rule, and protested against him. She also fails to consider evidence from *The Westminster Chronicle*, pp. 60–5, 95–7, 101–3, 137, 149, 207, 215, 309, 315, on Brembre's brutality, abuses of power, and electoral corruption. In addition, see below for his use of the mayoral court to silence his enemies, largely artisans; see *CPMR*, IV, pp. 50–64; and Chapter 13, pp. 306–7 below.

[15] *The Westminster Chronicle*, p. 65.
[16] Ibid., p. 65. *The Chronica maiora of Thomas Walsingham, 1376–1422*, ed. James Clark and trans. David Preest (Woodbridge, Suffolk, 2005), p. 214, translates 'ex arte sutoria' incorrectly as tailor; see Thomas Walsingham Chronica monasterii S. Albani, historia anglicana, ed. Henry T. Riley, 2 vols., RS, 28 (1863–4), II, pp. 110–11; also *LB, H*, pp. 229 and 231.
[17] *Chronicle of the Grey Friars of London*, p. 17.

The chronicle, however, fails to reveal whether the dispute concerned working conditions, inter-guild trade, or other demands.[18]

In 1324 another 'major dispute' erupted among London guildsmen; this one between goldsmiths and weavers ('telarios') with battles of rocks, bows, arrows, and crossbows through the entire city, with deaths on both sides. The anonymous chronicler, however, fails to mention if it hinged on economic or political objectives or grievances.[19] Two years later, a third case appears in the same chronicle: 'a major dispute' at Westminster between two groups of the king's apprentices – 'the northerners' and 'the southerners' – who worked on his accounts ('inter apprenticios de Banco domini regis'). It led to 'many killings through the city of London', but the chronicler again fails to specify the reasons for violence.[20]

Similarly, the Patent Rolls give only occasional glimpses of struggles between crafts or between employers and their workers, whether in London or other towns. At Bristol in 1363 the commonalty and those in its suburbs complained to the king concerning business practices and prices set by tanners and their mistery. The townsmen accused the tanners of price gouging since the time of Roger Turtle's mayoralty (c. 1340s). While they purchased their hides for 2s or 3s, they sold tanned ones on to cobblers for 5s or 6s. Forced to buy their raw materials at 'such an excessive price', the cobblers were then compelled to sell their shoes and other items of their mistery at much higher prices with 'great clamour and strife among the people'. It is not evident, however, that this 'great clamour' escalated into violence or popular rebellion.[21] Instead, these cases appear limited to formal litigation and without popular leaders or organized forms of protest beyond the law courts. Compare these experiences of infra-guild struggle with Flanders', especially after the Peace of Athis in 1305, when fullers and weavers were allowed to establish their own separate guilds. Conflict between them over their share of power and economic rights in Ghent, Bruges, Ypres, and smaller towns became almost incessant. For Ghent alone at least thirteen major and violent armed struggles between fullers and weavers ripped the city apart between 1311 and 1375.[22] Unlike the evidence of inter and infra-guild conflict in London (which appears limited to struggles within the courts), the Flemish challenges for power were

---

[18] *Chronicles of the Mayors and Sheriffs*, p. 104.   [19] *Annales Paulini*, p. 307.
[20] Ibid., p. 313. The murder of a mercer at Blackheath in 1372 set off another case of inter-craft strife in London (*Chronicles of London*, ed. C. L. Kingsford [Oxford, 1905], p. 14). The chronicle report, however, is so brief that not even the crafts of those involved are mentioned, only that of the victim.
[21] *CPR 1361–4*, pp. 297–8, 1363.ii.1.
[22] Boone, *A la recherché d'une modernité civique*, p. 69.

violent, contested by mass collective action in the streets, and were repressed with executions, wholesale exile, and heavy financial punishment in 1326, 1328, 1337, 1349, 1353, and 1356–9, and so on. These conflicts, moreover, were a major force shaping the political contours of the Low Countries, at least until Philip van Artevelde's defeat in 1382.[23]

Class struggle in municipal records: London

Numerous municipal documents published over the past century and a half fail to reveal many further conflicts between workers (journeymen or apprentices) and their bosses, or between minor and major guildsmen even in London, the largest and perhaps the most politically and socially contentious city in medieval England.[24] The detailed London Letter-books of the deliberations, decisions, and ordinances of London's mayors and aldermen, a near two-century series from Edward I to Henry VI, expose only five such conflicts between artisans and their bosses, and none before the Black Death.[25] The earliest, 17 August 1387, was initiated in the Court of the Mayor and Aldermen by the mistery of cordwainers, which charged its journeymen and apprentices ('serving-men') of illegal assembly at the Friar Preachers. The cordwainers accused the servants of

---

[23] In addition to references above, see among other places, David Nicholas, *Medieval Flanders* (London, 1992); David Nicholas, *The Metamorphosis of a Medieval City: Ghent in the Age of the Arteveldes, 1302–1390* (Leiden, 1987); David Nicholas, *The van Arteveldes of Ghent: The Varieties of Vendetta and the Hero in History* (Ithaca, 1988); and Haemers, 'A Moody Community?', pp. 76–7. On the mass and brutal repression of these revolts, see Boone, *A la recherché d'une modernité civique*, pp. 70–1.

[24] Williams, *Medieval London*; and Bird, *The Turbulent London*. While Nightingale, *A Medieval Mercantile Community*, contests interpretations, especially of Williams, who showed sympathy with London rebels, she nonetheless unearths further examples of urban conflict in the capital during the Middle Ages. Monographs of other towns that have probed municipal archives support the impression of relatively little open conflict between artisans and their employers; see Gervase Rosser, *Medieval Westminster 1200–1540* (Oxford, 1989), who finds no significant class struggles or factional conflict in Westminster and attributes it to the town's 'multifarious, cross-cutting loyalties' (p. 247). His broader 'Crafts, Guilds and the Negotiation of Work in the Medieval Town', *P&P* 154 (1997), despite an absence of comparative analysis, shows artisan strikes and armed protests on the Continent, but little of them in late medieval England. Similarly, R. H. Britnell, *Growth and Decline in Colchester, 1300–1525* (Cambridge, 1986), finds few traces of social strife in medieval Colchester, not even in 1381, even though it was the major town of one of the two epicentres of the insurrection, p. 124; for Bristol and York, see Liddy, *War, Politics, and Finance*. Finally, Henry Summerson, *Medieval Carlisle: The City and the Borders from the Late Eleventh to the mid-Sixteenth Century*, 2 vols. (Stroud, 1993), I, pp. 329–30, has gone through Carlisle's fourteenth- and fifteenth-century mayoral court records, as well as King's Bench, but reports not a single incident of collective protest by servants, workers, or artisans against their masters or city authorities. Work in progress by Christian Liddy in provincial archives will certainly unearth more incidents.

[25] *LB, A-K*; and *CEMCR*.

assaulting a guild member and paying the friar William Bartone to bring their suit to the Court of Rome, to persuade the pope to approve the legitimacy of their fraternity. The serving-men lost the case and were imprisoned.[26] Despite their defeat and repression, their efforts to form their own society did not disappear. On 9 September 1396, the cordwainers petitioned the mayor and aldermen, alleging that their serving-men had violated guild ordinances again by forming their own fraternity. Again, the servants lost and now faced a mammoth fine of £10 a head, clearly beyond the means of apprentices or journeymen. But even in these rare cases the records reveal little violence, little that can be conjectured as riot, much less revolt; instead, their actions appear confined to the courts.[27]

In the same year, employers in another craft accused their apprentices and journeymen of similarly forming illicit societies. Master saddlers alleged that their journeymen ('servientes'), calling themselves 'yomen', donned livery at an annual festival and held meetings at Stratford and elsewhere, within and outside the city without their masters' consent, 'to the great prejudice of the mistery'. The masters further alleged that these wage-earners ('servientes stipendiarios') sought to boost their pay and neglected work.[28] Their fraternity and festive practices were not, however, new; instead, as the masters confessed, these men 'had been accustomed to have a fraternity and livery time out mind'.[29] What was new appears to have been the masters' zeal to repress any organization or assemblies of their subordinate craftsmen.

In the second decade of the fifteenth century, the Letter-books reveal similar movements within cloth manufacture. On two occasions, master tailors brought law suits against their apprentices and journeymen. Firstly, on 19 April 1415 they challenged their servants' right to live in their own dwellings, assemble freely, and continue to belong to their own fraternity; then on 5 August 1417 they forbade them holding their annual church gathering near Smithfield on the feast of the Decollation, making offerings 'for the brethren and sisters of the fraternity of yoman taillours', or performing other religious rites.[30] The masters complained: the servants in these unsupervised dwellings had behaved 'in an unruly manner'; their fraternity 'would lead to disturbances, as similar assemblies of the same mistery had done before'. As appears to have been the rule, the masters won, with an end put to the former rights and movements of the journeymen. In the future, the 'yoman taillours' were permitted to

---

[26] *LB, H*, pp. 311–12. On craftsmen's religious fraternities in late medieval England and France, see Hilton, *English and French Towns*, pp. 72–5.
[27] *LB, H*, pp. 432–3.   [28] Ibid., pp. 431–2. Also, *ML*, pp. 542–4.
[29] *LB, H*, p. 432.   [30] Ibid., pp. 136–7; and *ML*, pp. 609–12.

hold 'conventicles' only within the church of St John in the presence of their masters.[31] In October 1441, the wardens of the bakers' guild and 'householders in the City' appeared before the mayor and aldermen, charging that their servants revelled and drank on holy days and so did 'no good werk a daye after'.[32] Yet this case went beyond rights of forming a religious society and performance of religious rites. The bakers further complained that their journeymen and apprentices possessed their own 'brotherhode & clithyng' and that they had refused to work unless paid higher wages or work from Saturday afternoon to Sunday in the evening to eight or nine o'clock – a rare instance of strike activity.[33] On 22 November, the mayor and aldermen summoned all these guild servants to appear before them to defend their actions. Despite claims that their company and 'Revelyng Hall' were not new but had existed 'time out of mind', the mayor sided with the masters and prohibited the workers from any 'maner of confederacie', from possessing any livery, and their wages were to remain 'the same as of old'.[34]

Finally, at the end of our period, the struggle between tailors and drapers flared under the guidance in part of the wealthy tailor and draper Ralph Holland over rights to examine ('search') work, prosecute those guilty of defective work, and over the right of tailors to elect their own representatives to the ranks of city aldermen and thereby potentially as mayors of London.[35] This infra-guild struggle of the 1440s widened into a conflict between these different levels of independent craftsmen and merchants over the right of the larger guild community of poorer freemen to elect chamberlains, sheriffs, and the mayor. Again, the actions of the lesser ranks ended in repression: in 1441 eleven artisan ringleaders were imprisoned, and in 1442 a clergyman, who preached 'a seditious sermon' at St Paul's Cross, claiming that 'the first and best Mayor had been a Cordwainer named Walsh', was prosecuted. More significantly, in October 1443, a major conspiracy with secret meetings involving two thousand artisans, armed with swords, poleaxes, and other weapons, was organized to protest against mayoral elections. A month earlier, their efforts to elect their candidate for chamberlain had failed,

---

[31] *LB, I*, pp. 187–8; and *ML*, pp. 651–3.

[32] On drinking feasts and drinking fraternities called 'scotalla' or 'scotals' in Herefordshire and bishops' attempts to ban them, see *Registrum Ade de Orleton, episcopi Herefordensis, 1317–27*, ed. A. T. Bannister, Canterbury and York Series, 5 (London, 1908), pp. 316–18 (1325); and *Regestrum Johannis de Trillek, episcopi Herefordensis, AD 1344–1361*, ed. Joseph H. Parry, Canterbury and York Society, 8 (London, 1914), p. 224 (1354).

[33] *LB, K*, p. 263.   [34] Ibid., pp. 264–6.

[35] On the importance of 'searchers' in craft legislation, see Heather Swanson, 'The Illusion of Economic Structure: Craft Guilds in Late Medieval English Towns', *P&P*, 121 (1988): 43.

and the king had issued a new oligarchic charter to the aldermen that stripped away earlier privileges possessed by the poorer freemen of the city. But no such revolt materialized; evidently the Crown or city oligarchs nipped it in the bud. The upshot of these years of artisan protest, led in large part by sympathetic members of the London elites, was failure. The London oligarchy eradicated the liberties and privileges of free artisans, those of London's lower guilds such as the tailors, who earlier had won charters such as the 1319 'Magna Carta of the London commonalty', 'the highest peak of achievement that a popular movement ever attained in medieval London'.[36] After the abortive struggles of the 1440s, earlier possibilities held by the fourteenth-century charters were swept aside. The tailors now were firmly defined as a second-tier guild and not one of merchants; for the future they came under the drapers' jurisdiction, especially as regards enforcing standards of work, or 'searching'.[37]

A possible sixth dispute, the only one before the Black Death, was not, however, a controversy between employers and employees but between a more privileged guild – the saddlers – and three independent guilds – the joiners, painters, and lorimers in copper and iron – that sold their wares and services to the saddlers. This dispute was violent. On 20 May 1327, the three minor guilds brought their trade disputes into the streets of Cheapside, Cripplegate, and elsewhere, ending with some killed, and others 'mortally wounded', and requiring mayoral intervention.[38] According to the testimony of joiners, painters, and lorimers delivered at the Guildhall, the saddlers had violated the franchises of the others by forcing them to sell their goods only to saddlers. The saddlers rejected the charges and countered 'by force of arms ... beating and maltreating the tradesmen in their own houses and in the high streets'; several were left dead. As a result of the intimidation and violence, the tradesmen claimed they were afraid to ask the saddlers for debts owed to them for their goods. The saddlers denied the charges and presented counter-charges, accusing the men of the three guilds of taking an oath: if any suffered attacks from saddlers or from any other trades they would cease work and close their stands ('selds'). Against the grain of

---

[36] Williams, *Medieval London*, pp. 282–3. For the ineffectiveness of this charter, at least as regards the annual single-terms of aldermen, see Bird, *The Turbulent London*, p. 30.

[37] See Barron, 'Ralph Holland'. Further examples come to light principally through archival records, in this case, the Journals of the City Government of London.

[38] *ML*, pp. 156–62. Because Riley had previously transcribed this agreement, Sharpe (*LB, E*, pp. 219–20) abbreviated it. However, even its brief five-line description shows discrepancies with Riley's: by Sharpe's the agreement is between the 'mistery of the Saddlers' on the one part, and the 'mistery of Fusters [makers of the woodwork of saddles] and Lorimers of copper and iron' on the other, and is dated 21 May, instead of 20 May.

other cases, the mayor and aldermen appear to have sided mainly with the lesser guildsmen, but did not punish the saddlers for their violence and intimidation; instead they only threatened that if their violence continued, they would have to provide the lower guildsmen with ten tuns of good wine and the mayor and commonalty with another ten.[39] The date, no doubt, influenced the decision: the incident was brewing at the time of Edward's deposition, when lesser commoners were supporting the barons and momentarily gained an upper hand in city politics.[40] These were clearly different times for workers and artisans in the capital than those that would ensue for them after the Peasants' Revolt.

Like the Letter-books, London's *Plea and Memoranda Rolls* reveal numerous quarrels between individual masters and apprentices, including breaches of contract, misbehaviour, and masters' failures to provide proper living conditions and education.[41] These were not, however, matters of collective action, either in the streets or courts. Nonetheless, these rolls add a few further examples of collective protest from London's lower guildsmen and journeymen. They clustered immediately after the Black Death and pertained to the new bargaining positions of wage earners in the wake of plague, in violation not only of the Ordinances and Statutes of Labourers but also against city proclamations to limit prices and wages. On 18 July 1349, five named servants of bakers in Holborn and unidentified others were indicted 'for forming a conspiracy' not to work for their masters except at double or treble the wages formerly given, violating the Ordinances passed a month before.[42] In October, the mayor's court charged ten 'wyndrawers' with demanding double the rates set in a post-plague city proclamation 'to take no more than he was wont ... during the last five or six years'.[43] The same day, five named cordwainers and others were charged with making 'a conspiracy' to sell shoes at 8d or 9d instead of the former 6d 'in contempt of the recent proclamation'.[44] The next month, the most serious charge of workingmen's collusion to set wages and prices surfaced. A group of master cordwainers (nine named) brought a case against their servants, numbering sixty, accused of joining a 'confederacy', having 'conspired' not to serve their masters 'except by the day and on their own terms ... in contravention of the masters' right to rule the

---

[39] Also see Mrs J. R. Green [Alice Stopford], *Town Life in the Fifteenth Century*, 2 vols. (London, 1894), II, pp. 163–5.

[40] Williams, *Medieval London*, p. 296.

[41] *CPMR*, I, p. 41. These were adjudicated in the Mayor's Court. On this and other London courts, their procedures, accessibility, use of legal advice, and independence from central royal courts, see Tucker, *Law Courts and Lawyers*.

[42] *CPMR*, I, p. 225.   [43] Ibid., I, pp. 228–9.   [44] Ibid., I, p. 229.

trade'. They were found guilty and sent to Newgate prison, to be released only if they promised to work for their former wages.[45]

The next violation of post-plague wage and price laws does not emerge until 1355, when eight Flemish weavers were arrested for forming a confederacy, refusing to work for less than 7d a day. Their resolution appears to have gone beyond those of other workers and artisans in 1349. The Flemings[46] swore if any of them were imprisoned, the rest would strike until that member was freed. Further, they allegedly threatened their Flemish bailiffs, charged with governing 'their nation' resident in London. The weavers were found guilty and sent to Newgate.[47] One further case of collective action demanding new wages or prices of goods surfaces in these volumes. On the eve of the Peasants' Revolt, an inquest before the mayor indicted thirteen, and later another eleven, journeymen spurriers of forming a 'covin and confederacy' that had convened nine years earlier in a London garden called 'Hyginesgardyn'. There they 'ordained' that none should make a quartern of spurs for less than 20d nor accept less than 2s for polishing them. Afterwards, they formed a religious confraternity restricted to journeymen spurriers who met monthly in St Bartolomew's, Smithfield. In these meetings, they passed ordinances and collected dues and pledges deposited in a common box 'for the maintenance of their ordinances'. They fined members for failing to attend meetings and agreed that all would cease work and leave their masters, if any master employed a foreigner. The court declared the fraternity illegal and threatened its members with penalties of £100 and the pillory for any renewed collusion.[48] As interesting as these cases may be, they comprised small groups of journeymen, confined to single trades and single neighbourhoods, such as Holborn. They fail to compare with the general strikes and armed combat against town councils, regional princes, and even kings, when hundreds, in some cases, thousands, of workers and artisans mobilized on the Continent: for example, the Brugse Metten of 1302, revolts of the *menu peuple* in Paris, the Sienese Bruco, Florence's Ciompi, and more. On occasion, these united townsmen with peasants and could endure for years, as with the late thirteenth- and fourteenth-century revolts in the Low Countries.

Mayors' memoranda rolls reveal further actions and protests of London artisans, but again they are few in number, comprise small groups, and are confined to single misteries and neighbourhoods. For

---

[45] Ibid., I, pp. 231–2.
[46] On the vagueness of the word 'Flemings', see Bolton, 'Introduction', p. 1: it could mean anyone from the Low Countries or northwestern Europe.
[47] *CPMR*, I, p. 248, 1355.iii.24.   [48] Ibid., II (1364–81), pp. 291–4, 1381.iv.9.

the most part they cluster in the 1360s, as in 1365, when three cordwainers were arrested, charged with rebelling against their masters, and found guilty of threatening to redress the wrongs suffered from their masters 'as soon as the present Mayor was out of office'. They were imprisoned and forced to swear never to join covins or confederacies in the future.[49] In the same month, the mayor and aldermen summoned eight tawyers (those who worked with the fur of squirrel, not the white-tawyers), read them the guild ordinances, and asked whether they would abide by them. Twice they refused and were sent to Newgate.[50] The next day, fourteen servants of several of the masters condemned the day before were called to court in an inquest to uncover other 'evildoers' who had disturbed the king's peace. Here, in a curious shift in alliances, workers had gone on strike to support their masters. 'By common assent' they closed the doors and windows of their masters' shops throughout the city, refused to work, and then as 'a body' went to Horrsedone [Bermondsey, south London], where they rioted.[51] The following Sunday, fourteen master fullers and three journeymen of the craft 'assembled a great general congregation of the mistery of Fullers' in St Paul's Cathedral. The 'great assembly', however, did not press for new economic or political rights, but gathered to assault a fellow fuller for undisclosed reasons.[52] In the same year, the mayor's court summoned the bailiffs of the Flemish weavers, because they had refused to inform the mayor and aldermen about Flemish weavers making 'covins and assemblies' and for levying unlawful tolls in their neighbour-hoods. Allegedly, their bailiffs had told the weavers that they need not work, 'thus allowing them to wander about the city'.[53] Finally, in 1368, the mayor's court sentenced three from the mistery of skinners for unspecified crimes, but it must have involved unlawful assembly amongst their trade: they were made to promise not to form 'congregations, unions and covins in taverns'.[54]

Except for the 1381 'covin' of spurriers above, no further cases appear in the mayors' pleas and memoranda of specific artisan groups contesting their masters or demanding political and economic rights. The closest possible exception might have been disturbances on the eve of the Peasants' Revolt, which appear not to have aroused comment from chronicles (even from Thomas Walsingham, who was then following

[49] Ibid., II, pp. 22–3, 1365.iii.5
[50] Ibid., II, pp. 28–9, 1365.iii.31. The editor surmises that the conflict concerned these artisans' relations with skinners, for whom they worked and who set the price of tawyers' finished goods. The new ordinances read to the tawyers do not survive; ibid., note on p. 28.
[51] Ibid., II, p. 29, 1365.iv.1.   [52] Ibid., III, pp. 54–6.
[53] Ibid., III, p. 65, 1366.x.30.   [54] Ibid., III, pp. 88–9; 1368.vi.20.

closely events in the capital, especially reactions against John of Gaunt after the Good Parliament of 1376). It was a letter from the king, requesting information on 'certain disturbances and disputes in the City, which were reported as having been raised by the commons'. The mayor answered in a contradictory fashion: 'there had been no such great commotions ... and such disturbances as had occurred had been punished'.[55] The identity of those committing 'such disturbances' is left opaque.

To be sure, a number of charges against illegal assemblies and covins appear in the mayors' and aldermen's memoranda after the Peasants' Revolt and after Brembre's election of May 1384 in his reign of intimidation against competitors for city offices. These accusations, however, did not relate to workers' or journeymen's unions or confraternities but were 'covins' of factions, those who allegedly had supported Northampton for mayor.[56] Nonetheless, Brembre's charges show that these 'covins' had trade, even class dimensions: numerous artisans were arrested, charged with speaking 'indecent words' against Brembre and his government.[57]

As Richard Britnell has commented, conflicts between masters and their men may have been 'seriously under-recorded'; they 'find mention only at the moment when they were outlawed by the borough authorities'.[58] A proclamation issued by London's mayor and aldermen after Walter Stapeldon was beheaded in November 1326 perhaps suggests that such discontent of the disenfranchised was rumbling beneath the surface of towns and cities more often than chronicles and the surviving court records indicate:

That the good men of the City, who have their apprentices, hired men or servants, working with their hands or trading, shall cause them to work or trade as they were wont to do, and inform the Mayor, officers and other good men of the City of any that be rebellious, who shall duly be punished as a warning to others.[59]

A year later, with Edward II deposed, tensions from below continued to simmer. The mayor of London delivered a proclamation that 'Aggrieved persons must not form covins, but complain to the Wardens of their misteries, or sue at law .... The wardens of the misteries must keep their men at work and report any rebellious behaviour to the Mayor and good men of the City.'[60] Yet when records of tribunals adjudicating

[55] Ibid., III, p. 275, 1380.xi.12.   [56] Ibid., IV, pp. 54, and 62.
[57] See pp. 306–7 below.   [58] Britnell, 'Town Life', p. 174.   [59] CPMR, I, pp. 15–16.
[60] Ibid., I, p. 34. This undergrowth of more or less constant rumbling and discontent of labourers in late medieval Europe supports the thesis of Jan Dumolyn and Jelle Haemers, '"A Bad Chicken was Brooding": Subversive Speech in Late Medieval

tensions between masters and journeymen or apprentices survive, as with London's mayoral court rolls from 1298 to 1307, conflict was confined almost exclusively to grievances between individuals.[61] Unlike the kind of labourers' organized violence seen in inquisitions issued by Italian communes, the London ones describe only litigation in courts without resort to collective violence in streets. On several occasions, individuals slandered the mayor, aldermen, or tax collectors of the wards when collecting 'courtesy gifts' for the king, queen, or other magnates,[62] or for undisclosed reasons, as in the summer of 1307, when a rag-and-bones man mocked the mayor, aldermen, and guardians of the peace as they came riding down his street. He neighed at them like a horse and hurled 'abusive words of contempt'.[63] Few cases even cast shadows of collective action by artisans, journeymen, or apprentices that concerned economic grievances. On 23 October 1303, eight named journeymen cordwainers 'and others' summoned their masters before a jury appointed by the mayor, charging that their piece-work wages for shoes and ankle boots had been unfairly lowered. As seen with similar litigation in the Letter-books, the masters won the case: the journeymen 'were told to work well and faithfully, and serve their masters and the people'. They were prohibited from demanding any more than what their masters set, and adding salt to the wound, were fined, and held 'in mercy for their false claim'. As with so much of the conflict at this level, inevitably the masters won, and in this case, no evidence of collective actions in the streets preceded, accompanied, or followed the journeymen's failed courtroom challenge.[64]

Several years later (1306), efforts by the London masons may have been an exception to the rule, but their success, this time, depended on action beyond the courts. The mayor's tribunal charged a London mason with intimidating the king's labourers, who had been brought to London to work on a project for the queen: they had been told that if they accepted lower wages than those of the city's masons, they would be beaten. The outcome of the case is unclear, but the queen's work was left unfinished.[65]

Flanders', *P&P*, 214 (2012): 45–86; and Jan Dumolyn, '"Criers and Shouters": The Discourse on Radical Urban Rebels in Late Medieval Flanders', *Journal of Social History*, 42 (2008): 111–35.

[61] Ibid., pp. 46, 47–8, 82, 158–9, 166, 170, 171, 222, present numerous cases in which individual apprentices or their fathers accused masters of maltreatment, unfair dismissal, or failing to feed, clothe, or instruct apprentices. These plaintiffs almost inevitably lost their court battles against masters' counter-claims.

[62] Ibid., pp. 216–17, 219, and 222.

[63] Ibid., p. 261.   [64] Ibid., pp. 148–9.   [65] Ibid., p. 251.

Events of the early fifteenth century support trends noticed by S. H. Rigby, Elizabeth Ewan, Caroline Barron, Jenny Kermode, and others: English towns were becoming less 'democratic' and more oligarchic.[66] These forces affected elections even within minor guilds. On 10 January 1434, 'the valets or servants of "Weavers", called "jorneymen"' came before the mayor and aldermen, protesting that for the past six years they had not been allowed to elect their guild wardens, which formerly had been their prerogative: now the masters claimed it as belonging to them alone 'and not to the serving men'. Having heard both parties, the mayor and aldermen sided with the masters, entitling them to elect the mistery's wardens.[67] Two further guilds, the mistery of goldbeaters and writers of text-letters, called 'Illuminators', may have experienced conflict within their ranks at the beginning of the fifteenth century. These guildsmen (the goldbeaters on 20 September 1400;[68] the illuminators on 12 July 1403)[69] petitioned the court to be allowed to elect two wardens to punish any 'who rebel' against the ordinances of their guild. Presumably, the motion was to control more stringently their journeymen and apprentices.

[66] Rigby, 'Urban "Oligarchy"', pp. 76–80; Rigby and Ewan, 'Government, Power, and Authority', pp. 310–11; Barron, 'London 1300–1540', in *CUHB*, p. 406; Kermode, *Medieval Merchants*, p. 53; and Green, *Town Life*, I, pp. 221–2 and 240–65, following Charles Gross (*The Gild Merchant: A Contribution to British Municipal History*, 2 vols. [Oxford, 1890]), argued that the trend originated from the early fourteenth century across England. For Charles W. Colby, 'The Growth of Oligarchy in English Towns', *EHR* 5 (1890): 633–53, the trend for most towns began in Edward I's reign and was complete by the War of the Roses. On the other hand, Nightingale, *A Medieval Mercantile Community*, disputes such a trend in late medieval London. As with the decline of towns debate at the end of the Middle Ages (see for instance R. B. Dobson, 'Urban Decline in Late Medieval England' [1977], in *The English Medieval Town: A Reader in English Urban History 1200–1540*, ed. R. C. Holt and G. Rosser [London, 1990], pp. 265–86), not all towns may have had the same experiences during the fifteenth century. For instance, Richard C. Holt, 'Gloucester in the Century after the Black Death', *Transactions of the Bristol and Gloucestershire Archaeological Society*, 103 (1985): 156, argues that Gloucester burgesses became more effective at resisting the domination over the town by ecclesiastical lords, Lanthony priory, and secondarily, the Abbey of St Peter, around 1400. On the other hand, the secular government could have become more oligarchic at the same time, a question Holt does not address. In other towns such as Exeter, oligarchic rule by merchant elites appears well entrenched early in the fourteenth century without any appreciable change in the fifteenth, although artisans and craftsmen were allowed some participation in the lower tiers of government; see Maryanne Kowaleski, 'The Commercial Dominance of a Medieval Provincial Oligarchy: Exeter in the Late Fourteenth Century', in *The English Medieval Town: A Reader in English Urban History 1200–1540*, ed. R. C. Holt and G. Rosser (London, 1990), pp. 184–215. On the emergence of oligarchies in the fourteenth century, see also Peter R. Coss, 'Coventry before Incorporation: A Reinterpretation', *Midland History*, 2 (1974), especially p. 140, who argues that Coventry was ruled by a merchant oligarchy from 1345 on.

[67] *LB, K*, p. 290.   [68] *LB, I*, p. 9.   [69] Ibid., pp. 25–6.

The sharp rise in nominal, then real, wages after the Black Death and the vigilance of London's mayors and aldermen with Crown backing to control them may have been the stimulus for masters' new aggression against their servants and labourers. According to Robert Braid, Edward III's legislation was in part based on regulations to control artisans' movement, wages, and prices already promulgated by London's mayor and aldermen.[70] Immediately after the Black Death, mayors also created new posts within artisan guilds, such as those of the fullers and dyers in 1353, to assure 'that no one took more for his labour than he was accustomed to take before the Pestilence'.[71] In 1355 and 1359, mayors, aldermen, sheriffs, and commissioners were issued writs to enforce the Ordinances and Statutes of Labourers against workmen who demanded excessive wages, as well as to punish abuses of weights and measures.[72] In 1363, the mayor and aldermen forced masons, carpenters, plasterers, tilers, 'and all kind of labourers' to redress the damages incurred by artisans 'taking exceedingly more than they ought'.[73] In 1426 an ordinance was decreed against 'the excessife taking of Masons Carpenters, Tylers, dawbers [plasterers] and other labourers'.[74] For the most part, these writs and proclamations do not necessarily point to strife between different tiers within guild hierarchies – between masters and journeymen – but instead between labourers and artisans, on the one hand, and the municipal government and consumers on the other. In 1362, however, the mayor and aldermen enforced the master saddlers' decision to punish their 'vadlets and servants', who formed 'secret' covins to obtain higher wages.[75] And the new ordinances of the fullers of 1364 imposed severe penalties on valets or servants, 'combining to obtain more than their proper wage', to be imprisoned for a year and fined at the discretion of the mayor and aldermen.[76]

---

[70] Robert Braid, 'Peste, prolétaires et politiques: la législation du travail et les politiques économiques en Angleterre aux XIIIeme et XIVeme siècles. Concepts, réalités et contexte européen'. Ph.D. thesis, Université Paris, 7 (Paris, 2008).

[71] *LB, G*, p. 14.   [72] Ibid., pp. 37 and 115–18.   [73] Ibid., p. 148.

[74] *The Great Chronicle of London*, p. 143. In the previous year, Commons passed national legislation against masons congregating and making confederacies 'in their general Chapters', stating that such assemblies violated the Statutes of Labourers and that the convicted would be judged as felons. The statute did not, however, specify the masons' objectives or where they had been congregating; *Statutes of the Realm*, 11 vols. (London, 1810–28), II, p. 227.

[75] *LB, G*, pp. 141–3.

[76] Ibid., p. 160. Other court records, such as those brought before the king's councils, show at least one case of artisan guilds petitioning against the actions of their mayor. In 1386, Cordwainers, Founders, Saddlers, Painters, Armourers, Pinners, Embroiderers, Spinners, and the Blacksmiths petitioned Parliament against Brembre's use of armed force to assault and intimidate his opponents and secure his election, as in 1383. In addition, tailors complained to the king in 1386 that Brembre had removed their guild charter, and cancelled their rights to hold annual meetings and promulgate their own

In addition, cases of unspecified disturbances of the peace, which appear not to have arisen from questions at the workplace, but in which journeymen or apprentices were predominant were also rare. On a Friday in November 1304, the mayor and aldermen arrested five tailors, a servant of one of these tailors, a cordwainer, and a parish clerk for assault and disturbing the peace 'with swords and other arms'.[77] The incident may have had political motives, but may well have been no more than a Friday-night bar-room brawl.

Finally, conflicts between opposing artisan guilds, more or less on the same economic plane, were equally rare. Only three cases appear over the 187-year history covered by the published London Letter-books. From late July to mid-September 1336, the weavers made a writ to the mayor and sheriffs of London, complaining that the burellers were exercising the weavers' craft without belonging to the weavers' guild. Eventually, the mayor and sheriffs ruled in the burellers' favour – the higher status of the two[78] – declaring that as freemen they were entitled 'to set up looms in their hostels and elsewhere to weave cloth and sell the same at will'.[79] Similar conflicts appear between 'Cordewaners and Cobelers', and on 10 December 1410, the two agreed on the manufacturing boundaries of their respective crafts.[80] On 24 July 1425, a three-way controversy came before the mayor and aldermen of London from the misteries of pinners, iron-wire-drawers, and card-makers concerning their craft boundaries, all three claiming that previous infringements had caused them to lose work over the past six or seven years.[81] Other municipal records, such as the London coroners' rolls, which reported accidental deaths, murders, and other forms of criminality that led to death, also fail to highlight internecine artisan struggle or class conflict between employers and workers.[82]

Class struggle in municipal records: other English towns

Even less is seen of popular protest and insurrection in the published municipal records of other towns. Philippa Maddern's investigation of

ordinances, calling his actions 'a horrible trespass done against the crown' (p. 75); *SCBKC*, pp. xcvii–xcviii, 74–6.

[77] *LB, C*, pp. 139–40.

[78] Burellers could be cloth entrepreneurs, as in their quarrels with weavers in London at the beginning of the fourteenth century; see Williams, *Medieval London*, p. 174.

[79] *LB, E*, pp. 296–8.   [80] *LB, I*, p. 96.   [81] *LB, K*, pp. 42–3.

[82] *Calendar of Coroners Rolls of the City of London, AD 1300–1378* (London, 1913); and *Select Cases from the Coroners' Rolls 1265–1413*, ed. Charles Gross, Selden Society (London, 1896). On these records see Barbara Hanawalt, *Medieval Crime and Social Control* (Minneapolis, 1999).

coroners' rolls from medieval Norwich – the only records to document 'a significant proportion of cases of violent crime in the medieval city' – fails to uncover examples of popular insurrection.[83] Norwich was among the largest of England's cities before the Black Death; according to the subsidies of 1377, it was one of only four towns ranked behind the capital, with populations between 8,000 and 15,000.[84] As commented on by chroniclers, its violent assault on the priory and cathedral of Norwich in 1272 and the repression that followed was one of the most notable examples of popular insurrection before the English Peasants' Revolt. In addition, on at least four occasions the city experienced 'mass public outbreaks' – 1235, 1272, 1381, and 1443 – that have gained attention from historians. Yet Maddern has claimed that these four insurrections 'hardly constitute continuous social disorder over the space of 265 years from 1235 to 1500 ... an average rate of one major outbreak every sixty-six years'.[85] Instead, she stresses the city's political stability and low levels of murder and criminal violence. As will be discussed, the Patent Rolls tell another story, revealing twenty-two riots and revolts between 1267 and 1437, constituting an insurrection every eight years in the city. These included artisan armed violence, unlawful assemblies, leagues, and conspiracies, assaults on high-ranking citizens, coroners, bailiffs, and other officials, disruptions to municipal elections, attempts to overthrow city government, and confederacies against the king, marking it as one of England's most insurrectionary towns behind Oxford, London, Bristol, and York in the number of incidents.[86]

Nonetheless, at least as regards conflict among artisans and workers against guild masters and employers, the published municipal records of Norwich lend some support to Maddern's claims. Selections of records from TNA [then the Public Record Office] and the municipal archives of the city published at the beginning of the twentieth century give evidence of crises and conflicts that confronted various classes within Norwich and its surrounding countryside from the thirteenth to the fifteenth centuries. For the most part, however, these are the sorts of incidents that can be gleaned from contemporary chronicles and the Patent Rolls, and like them, they do not show class struggle emerging from the lower

---

[83] Philippa Maddern, 'Order and Disorder', in *Medieval Norwich*, ed. Carole Rawcliffe and Richard Wilson (London, 2004), pp. 188–212.
[84] Hilton, 'Towns in Societies', pp. 8–9.   [85] Maddern, 'Order and Disorder', p. 198.
[86] In contrast to Maddern, Wood, *The 1549 Rebellions*, especially p. 1 and Chapter 6, has stressed the late medieval insurrectionary tradition in southeast England, particularly at Norwich, from the Peasants' Revolt to Kett's Rebellion in 1549. Earlier, Charles Oman, *The Great Revolt of 1381*, new edition with introduction by E. B. Fryde (Oxford, 1969 [1906]), p. 114, suggested the same.

rungs of Norwich society. For instance, 'Ancient Petitions' reveal that in 1253 country people close to Norwich opposed the enclosure of the city,[87] and in 1326 'the middle people of Norwich' protested against tallages of 200 marks levied on them by the 'Baillifs and the Rich', contrary to previous promises and without their consent. They claimed the rich 'threaten to make a higher tallage from one day to another at their will'.[88] Complaints lodged by the city's 'Major Part of the Commonalty' against the prerogatives of the city's sheriffs and its twenty-four ruling 'Prudhommes' ('Venerabiliores ciues') formed a special commission headed by Sir Thomas Erpingham in 1414, and from it litigation ensued that split Norwich's citizens into two rival factions with a class dimension. These concerned constitutional issues of consent and elections of bailiffs, sheriffs, the treasurer, and mayor along with protectionism for Norwich cloth manufacturers and dealers to sell at a specific place, a building called the Worsted Seld. The controlled monopolistic trade in cloth against foreigners favoured the larger part of burgesses and not the more elite bachelors of the city, 'la bachelery' and the 'Prudhommes'.[89] It was not, however, a struggle that penetrated to issues involving lower artisans, journeymen, or apprentices.

As Ben McRee has shown, formal and informal negotiation without any recorded resort to violence ultimately resolved this long-festering dispute.[90] As early as 1377, representatives of Norwich's governing elites had negotiated secretly with the king to strip the broad body of commoners from electing the city's highest officials. These agreements became widely known to commoners only with the city's grant of a new charter of incorporation in 1404, and became contentious still later, during an election of 1414. This conflict was not, however, one between elites and those without citizenship, employers and labourers, or haves and have-nots, as surface often on the Continent. Instead, the published Norwich municipal records fail to uncover a single incident of strife between the disenfranchised and city rule or ones when apprentices or journeymen opposed their guild masters, either in the law courts (as seen with similar records for London) or in the streets. For one of medieval England's largest cities, not even the dozen or so examples gleaned from London's municipal records of small groups of journeymen confronting employers over wages, petitioning to wear livery on festive days, or forming their own trade fraternities, appear in Norwich's published records.[91]

---

[87] *The Records of the City of Norwich*, I, pp. 59–60.   [88] Ibid., pp. 61–2.
[89] Ibid., pp. 66–77, 81–2.   [90] McRee, 'Peacemaking', pp. 847–52.
[91] *The Records of the City of Norwich*, I, however, transcribed only a small portion of the city's late medieval registers.

Published documents from Lynn's municipal archives and TNA reveal much the same. They illustrate numerous conflicts between burgesses, their bishop, and other ecclesiastical bodies over rights and privileges and against royal authorities and others who controlled their port and tolls, but conflicts at the point of production fail to appear.[92] Occasionally, traces of struggles between masters and journeymen in provincial towns emerge, as in Chester in 1399, when a group of master craftsmen in clothmaking attacked their own journeymen in front of St Peter's 'with pole-axes, daggers and iron-pointed staves'.[93] This, however, was the rare exception, at least as revealed by our survey of published sources and the secondary literature. The surviving minutes from Oxford's town council do not reveal a single case, collective or individual, of labour strife within its guilds, between them, or between employers and their journeymen or apprentices.[94] The same holds for the borough records of Leicester: from the beginning of the twelfth century to the end of our study in 1450, only one dispute between a master and his apprentice appears and that is a court case over the alleged early departure of the apprentice.[95] The closest hint of any possible popular collective protest seen in these records concerns a woman, Christiana le Mustarder, convicted in the mayor's court for verbally abusing a tax collector in the midst of a crowd on the city's high street ('in alta strata coram populo') 'to the damage and shame of the entire community'.[96] Could she have been the leader of that crowd and

---

[92] Dorothy M. Owen, *The Making of King's Lynn: A Documentary Study*, Records of Social and Economic History, new series IX (London, 1984); see below for these conflicts beyond the workplace.

[93] Jane Laughton, 'Economy and Society, 1350–1500', pp. 34–90, in *VCH: Chester*, ed. C. P. Lewis and A. T. Thacker (London, 2003), V, Part 1, pp. 74–6; and Laughton, *Life in a Late Medieval City*, p. 129. From municipal registers, Laughton also finds one case of internecine artisan violence: in 1360, Chester's tanners squabbled with shoemakers over the right to produce leather; ibid., p. 114. In addition, armed attacks between bakers and millers, she maintains, were common (Laughton, 'Economy and Society, 1350–1500', p. 72).

[94] *Munimenta Civitatis Oxonie*, ed. H. E. Salter, Oxford Historical Society, 71 (Oxford, 1920), p. 178. There is one quarrel between two saddlers, *c.* 1400, but they appear to be on the same social footing and the case involves wrongful prosecution, which did not concern their trade.

[95] *Records of the Borough of Leicester*, ed. Mary Bateson, 2 vols. (London, 1899–1901), II, pp. 179–80 (from Portmanmoot Rolls 1378–9).

[96] Ibid., I, p. 309 (8 September 1318, from the Merchant Guild Rolls). Over our period at least another ten cases of individuals abusing tax collectors 'with contumelious words', occur in these records. None of these, however, appears to have gone beyond words or suggests any collective action; ibid., I, 230, 251, 275, 294, 307; II, 92, 107, 130. In addition, neither Audrey M. Erskine, 'Political and Administrative History, 1066–1509', in *VCH: Leicester, Vol. IV: The City of Leicester*, ed. R. A. McKinley, (London, 1958), pp. 1–30, nor Marian K. Dale, 'Social and Economic History,

her cries the consequence of collective protest? More likely, or at least from the court's clipped and no doubt biased presentation of the event, that 'coram populo' was simply an assemblage of innocent bystanders.[97]

In conclusion, chronicles, Patent Rolls, and published municipal records across England reveal extremely few incidents of labourers or disenfranchised craftsmen challenging their guild masters, especially compared with the Continent. The few to arise come predominantly from London and most of these were pursued within mayoral courts or through other legitimate channels that eschewed collective violence. From this rarity of conflict at the point of production and from the lower tiers of artisans and labourers, should we then conclude that English towns were free of popular protest with clear economic or political objectives? As the following chapters will show, the chronicles and Patent Rolls, despite their many pitfalls, rule out any such conclusion.

1066–1509', in ibid., pp. 31–54, points to any incidents of popular protest at Leicester during the Middle Ages, whether or not at the workplace. The first two volumes of the *Records of the Borough of Nottingham*, ed. W. H. Stevenson et al., 9 vols. (London, 1882–1956), from 1155 to 1452, show less – no cases even of commoners verbally abusing tax collectors.

[97] Her entry is the longest and is the most elaborate of the eleven charges found in these records against individuals verbally abusing tax officials. Such attention might suggest that more was at stake here than simply one woman 'cursing and villifying' an official.

3   Varieties of revolt

Putting forms of popular protest into discrete categories is fraught with difficulties. A tax revolt was simultaneously an economic revolt and a protest against the political body imposing the tax – the king, a town's oligarchy, or a monastic corporation. Simon de Montfort's baronial revolt against Henry III galvanized support from peasants, who also revolted for their own purposes,[1] as did towns and cities such as Oxford and London. At the same time, these revolts were tinged with anti-Semitic movements of violence.[2] The categorization of popular protest also depends on what aspect of a riot, revolt, or movement is being examined – on whether the focus falls on the participants, as with peasant versus urban revolts, or with revolts of labourers, burgesses, or those vaguely defined as commoners. On the other hand, the causes and objectives can be key, as with tax revolts, or collective violence arising from bad harvests and high grain prices, or uprisings against abuses of power, fiscal corruption, or rigged mayoral elections. Thirdly, popular revolt can be defined according to the targets of the protesters' animosity – for example, the king, municipal government, or monastic rule. And on top of this grid, revolts can have more than a single set of participants, causes, or objectives. Nonetheless, in the following chapters, we have used the criteria of who participated and what were

[1] David Carpenter, 'Simon de Montfort: The First Leader of a Political Movement in English History', *History* 76 (1991): 3–23; and David Carpenter, 'English Peasants in Politics 1258–1267', *P&P*, 136 (1992): 3–42, show the importance of peasants in English politics during the thirteenth century; these movements, however, essentially involved the barons' struggle: they were the leaders. Through a wide range of court records, Valente, *The Theory and Practice of Revolt*, p. 95, estimates that 'rural dwellers below the level of knights, i.e. freeholders and villeins' made up half of the rebels overall.
[2] In analysing revolts in the Low Countries from the thirteenth to sixteenth century, Jan Dumolyn and Kristof Papin, 'Y avait-il "révoltes fiscales" dans les villes médiévales des Pays-Bas méridionaux? L'exemple de Saint-Omer en 1467', *Revue du Nord* (forthcoming), show a rich history of fiscal revolt, but argue that taxes rarely were the central issue. They propose getting rid of the category 'tax revolt' altogether. This book upholds their first proposition, but not their second.

the causes and the objectives, to interpret patterns of revolts in English towns portrayed in chronicles and the Patent Rolls and to compare these with Continental ones. We begin with what was mostly missing from the English protests.

Riots against the papal legate

No matter how protests are defined in late medieval England, their overall character differs starkly from those on the Continent, as seen in Italy, France, and Flanders.[3] Certain categories prominent on the Continent, especially in Italy, are altogether missing or extremely rare with the English cases; some of these might hardly seem surprising, such as revolts against the Holy Roman Emperor or the papacy. Yet the pope was not so distant from English affairs as geography might at first suggest. As is well known, the pope on several occasions played a direct and crucial role in English politics. At the beginning of our period, a clash between king and pope was dramatic and may have been more important than the Thomas Becket–Henry II controversy in shaping subsequent political developments. The stand-off between Innocent III and King John over ecclesiastical liberties – John's refusal to accept Innocent's choice, Stephen Langton, as Archbishop of Canterbury – led to Innocent's interdict of England and excommunication of the king. John retaliated by confiscating Church property. The battle between king and pope shifted the balance of power between France and England, with the pope calling a crusade armed by the French king, Philip II, against England. These international events in turn destabilized internal relations between John and his barons. With the reversal of John's position towards Innocent on 15 May 1213, foreign and domestic relations transformed almost overnight. The crusade against England abruptly ended, and Innocent, now the king's overlord, became his staunchest supporter against his rebellious barons, quashing Magna Carta soon after its signing. As C. R. Cheney observed: 'The king and the country had recognized as never before that Rome could play a part in secular politics.'[4]

Future popes continued to be intimately involved with English internal and foreign politics, as with the pope's disastrous grant of the

---

[3] For the patterns of these revolts, see Cohn, *Lust for Liberty*, Chapter 3.
[4] C. R. Cheney, *Pope Innocent III and England*, Päpste und Papsttum, 9 (Stuttgart, 1976), p. 400. Also see Alan Harding, *England in the Thirteenth Century* (Cambridge, 1993): 'For both medieval chroniclers and sixteenth-century protestants, the struggle of king and pope, not that of king and barons, was the significant event of [John's] reign' (p. 266).

Sicilian throne to Henry's second son, Edmund, in 1254. Less has been written, however, on the papacy's role in municipal disputes. Through letters, bulls, other mandates, and the periodic presence of legates, the pope played a role in conflicts such as in 1239, when the canons and congregation of the diocese of Lincoln opposed their bishop. Against 'the custom of the church from time immemorial', the bishop had deposed the dean of the cathedral. The canons retaliated, 'stirring up angry feelings'. They barred the bishop from entering the cathedral chapter and making his accustomed visitations: 'A great dispute arose, and after no small useless expense on both sides', the chapter appealed to the pope, sending an advocate to Rome to argue their case.[5] In addition, with papal letters and edicts, the pope intervened in other English affairs and conflicts, as in 1328 when a controversy led to fisticuffs, bloody faces, and clerics flung from London's cathedral. It concerned filling the position of a prebend at St Paul's, which the bishop had left in abeyance for some time (no doubt collecting its living in the meantime). Order was restored only with intervention from the Bishop of Corbie (near Amiens), who came armed with papal privileges.[6] More significantly, and as far as the urban laity was concerned, the pope was a key supporter of the Benedictine monks of Norwich in their negotiations with the king and in further crushing the burgesses following their armed revolt in 1272. The monks sent letters to the pope against the commune and presented their case at his court in Rome.[7] Similarly, after a burgess revolt of 1264 at Bury St Edmunds, the monastery appealed to Rome, and England's papal legate Ottoboni excommunicated the rebels, creating such a hostile environment that many townsmen fled.[8]

Moreover, English clerics and townsmen could challenge papal authority by attacking his legate sent to inspect English monastic or other ecclesiastical institutions. One struggle between clerics and commoners led to an attack on a papal legate himself, and his officers, that began on the night of 23 April 1238: it was one of the most commented-upon incidents of riot and strife found in our sample of chronicles. At least twelve chroniclers and one entry in the Patent Rolls – a mandate pardoning Osmund the Clerk of the diocese of Salisbury[9] (not mentioned in any of the chronicles) – described the 'discordia' that erupted 'between Oxford' and the cardinal and apostolic

---

[5] Paris, *Chronica majora*, III, pp. 528–9.   [6] *Annales Paulini*, p. 340.
[7] Bartholomew de Cotton, *Historia Anglicana (AD 449–1298)*, ed. Henry Richards Luard, RS, 16 (1859), pp. 150–1.
[8] Lobel, *The Borough of Bury St Edmunds*, p. 130.   [9] *CPR 1232–47*, p. 297.

legate Lord Otto.[10] By some accounts, the violence appeared when Otto first entered the city to conduct a synod between scholars and members of the legate's retinue.[11] He then retreated to the canons' residence at Osney just outside Oxford, where he was held in the canons' tower until eventually the king and his troops, stationed nearby at Abingdon, freed him.[12] By other accounts, it was a battle between the legate and the clerics of Oxford, who after being insulted at Osney, returned to Oxford, rang their town bells and brought armed force against the abbey, suggesting some collusion and support from the town.[13] By still others, especially Matthew Paris, the longest and most elaborate account, the legate was at first 'received with the highest honour, as was due to him'. While Otto was at Osney, the scholar-clerks of the university wished to pay their respect, presenting him with gifts. However, the 'transalpine porter', 'after the manner of the Romans', haughtily rebuffed the request. During the melee that followed, a poor Irish chaplain arrived seeking food at the kitchen's door; the master of the legate's cooks (charged with ensuring that poison was not added to the broth, 'which the legate greatly feared') threw boiling fat into the poor man's face. The poor clerk then drew a bow (which he just happened to be carrying) and shot the chef. According to Paris, the legate then took fright, locked himself in the tower 'clad in his canonical hood', and secured the doors behind him.

According to the *Annals of Thomas Wykes*, the legate's servants were instead the aggressors; they threw the boiling broth on the clerics' clothes and into their faces. By Paris' account alone, the legate was portrayed heroically, able to escape the abbey on his own, with help only

[10] *Annales de Tewksbury (1066–1263)* in *Annales monastici*, ed. Henry Richards Luard, 5 vols., RS, 36 (1864–9), I, p. 106; *Chronicles of the Reigns of Edward I and Edward II*, I, p. 35; *Annals of Dunstable* in *Annales monastici*, ed. Henry Richards Luard, 5 vols., RS 35 (London, 1864–9), III, p. 147; *Annals of Osney* in *Annales monastici*, vol 5, pp. 84–6; *Annals of Osney/Thomas Wykes* in *Annales monastici*, IV, pp. 429–31; *Continuatio chronici Florentii Wigorniensis*, II, p. 176; Paris, *Chronica majora*, III, pp. 482–4; *Chronica majora: Matthew Paris's English History: From the Year 1235 to 1273*, trans. J. A. Giles, 3 vols. (London, 1852–4), III, pp. 126–9; *The Chronicle of Walter of Guisborough*, p. 177; *Chronicon Angliae Petriburgense*, ed. J. A. Giles (London, 1845), p. 135; and *Cronica Buriensis, AD 1020–1346*, ed. T. Arnold, RS, 96 (1896), III, p. 28. *The Chronicle of Bury St Edmunds*, pp. 9–11, reports Otto's visitation at Bury St Edmunds and conflicts with Dominican and Franciscan orders over his rights of inspection.

[11] See, for instance, *The Chronicle of Bury St Edmunds*, p. 9; *Continuatio chronici Florentii Wigorniensis*, II, p. 176; and Janet Cooper and Alan Crossley, 'Medieval Oxford', 3–74, in *VCH: Oxford, Vol. IV: The City of Oxford*, ed. Alan Crossley (Oxford, 1979), p. 13.

[12] *Annals of Osney*, pp. 84–6; *Annals of Osney/Thomas Wykes*, pp. 430–1; and especially *The Chronicle of Walter of Guisborough*, saw the conflict first in Oxford with the papal legate, then seeking refuge at Osney.

[13] *Annales de Tewksbury*, p. 106. According to *Annals of Dunstable*, p. 147, the student siege also resulted in the death of one of the cook's kinsmen.

from a local guide and without the king's entry into Osney: Otto mounted his best stead, crossed the river 'with much danger', and arrived before the king 'breathless'. Again, by Paris' account alone, the clerks,

carried away by rage, continued to seek for the legate in the most secret hiding-places, crying out 'Where is that simoniacal usurer, that plunderer of revenues, and thirster for money, who perverts the king, subverts the kingdom, and enriches foreigners with spoils taken from us?'

If true, their cries suggest that more was at stake than simply the taunts and arrogance of the legate's concierge. Paris, again unlike other chroniclers, praised the legate, saying that he 'patiently endured' the clerics' taunts, though without the power to refute them. The king, 'astonished at his pitiable story', sent the Earl of Warene to Oxford to rescue the Romans and arrest the scholars. By all accounts, Oxford was put under interdict, and those found guilty excommunicated by the legate. Studies at the university were suspended for the summer term; prisoners were carted to London and deprived of their incomes.[14]

According to Paris, the legate returned hurriedly to London from his planned visitations in northern England, and the king had to place him under armed guard of the mayor and citizens of London. On 17 May, the legate summoned the Archbishop of York and all the bishops of England to meet at London. A dispute arose between the English clergy and the legate's men, and according to the *Annals of Burton*, the English 'got the worst of it', with a large portion of them sent to prison. The rest were forced to show submission before the legate at a place three days' ride from Oxford. Along with the bishops, the students processed by foot to St Paul's, London, where they humbly beseeched the legate for a pardon. After their humiliation, the legate restored the university's privileges and withdrew his interdict and sentences of excommunication.[15] According to the *Annales Londonienses*, the humiliation and pardon were more elaborate: the canons of Osney and secular magistrates of Oxford also processed 'barefoot, their heads uncovered, and stripped of the outer garments and signs of distinction' to London.[16] The legate

---

[14] Paris, *Chronica majora*, III, 484. By the Malmesbury monks' account, the students were the ones excommunicated, the university suspended, and scholars moved temporarily to Salisbury; *Eulogium (historiarum sive temporis): chronicon ab orbe condito usque ad annum Domini M.CCC.LXVI*, ed. Frank Scott Haydon, 3 vols., RS, 9 (1863), III, p. 118.

[15] For the London convocation, also see *Annales of Burton (AD 1004–1263)* in *Annales monastici*, ed. Henry Richards Luard, 5 vols., RS, 36 (1864–9), I, pp. 253–4.

[16] *Annales Londonienses*, in *Chronicles of the Reigns of Edward I and Edward II: Edited from Manuscripts*, ed. William Stubbs, 2 vols., RS, 76 (1882–3), I, p. 35. Also, *Annals of Osney/Thomas Wykes*, pp. 430–1. The pardon found in *CPR* does nothing to resolve any of the chronicles' discrepancies.

had offended more than students at Oxford, and burgesses from both Oxford and London had been involved.

In summary, the papacy, via its letters, courts, and legates, could successfully intervene in English affairs and exert power, leading to social conflict involving clerics, students, and the laity, as well as protests from the Commons against the pope's installation of alien favourites on prized English abbeys and priories.[17] Yet the case of Osney, despite all its attention and its consequences for Oxford, London, and the north of England, cannot compare to the long and embittered armed struggles of the populace against papal power seen on the Continent, and not only in Italy. No other papal legate of the later Middle Ages sparked such outrage in England again.

Struggles between towns

On the Continent, revolts by smaller towns against political or economic domination by larger ones were common, as with Montalcino's struggle for independence against Siena in 1359,[18] Poperinge's against Ypres's economic domination, battles over tolls between the Franc of Bruges and Sluis in 1398, or over the sale of cloth between Bruges and Sluis in 1400.[19] In England, the closest approximations to such economic or political struggles were those of the Cinque Ports against their competitors, especially those concerning the port of Great Yarmouth, battles over fishing rights, and the cloth trade led by merchants on land and the open seas.[20] The conflicts also involved squabbles over local markets, as seen in early records of the Patent Rolls.[21] These struggles, however, appear to have been more internecine conflict among equals, than struggles for independence or liberties, even if the rulers of the Cinque Ports had entitlements as barons.

---

[17] F. M. Powicke, *King Henry III and the Lord Edward: The Community of the Realm in the Thirteenth Century*, 2 vols. (Oxford, 1947), I, pp. 351–3, spends ample space on Henry's dependence on Otto and the legate's politics in England but mentions only in passing the riot at Osney (p. 352). For protests against Rome's interference with 'free elections' of the English Church, see p. 209, note 51.

[18] Cohn, *Popular Protest*, pp. 122–3.

[19] See for instance Jan Dumolyn, 'Privileges and Novelties: the Political Discourse of the Flemish Cities and Rural Districts in their Negotiations with the Dukes of Burgundy (1384–1506)', *UH*, 35 (2008): 20.

[20] See for instance *CPR 1313–17*, p. 583. On 18 July 1316, Edward II appointed a committee to prevent further acts of piracy by those of Yarmouth who attacked merchants and stole their cargoes in Cinque Ports, Portsmouth, near the Isle of Wight, Southampton, Shoreham in Sussex, and along the coast of Norfolk. They had made similar raids during Edward I's reign.

[21] *CPR 1216–25*, p. 340, 1222.ix.22.

To be sure, disputes arose between larger and smaller towns within regions, such as with Lincoln, Boston, and Grimsby, or smaller places in Lincolnshire, such as Louth and Sleaford, on the one hand, and Lincoln on the other, over tolls, rights to fairs, and monopolies over foreign trade. But in citing many examples of these from the thirteenth to the fifteenth century, the historian of Lincoln describes none that percolated beyond the courts to rioting, much less to organized armed assaults by one town against another.[22] Occasionally, local city identity and pride could lead to inter-city violence significant enough to draw a chronicler's attention, as in 1260, when Londoners attending a fair at Northampton came to blows with residents, leaving a few from Northampton wounded and one killed. 'Envious of the Londoners', the Northampton bailiffs seized four Londoners, took their goods, imprisoned them, charged them with death penalties, and afterwards seized other goods from Londoners. Matters escalated, and the king had to intervene.[23] As we will see, the Patent Rolls are filled with controversies that arose in local urban settings, especially on market days and at annual fairs between indigenous populations and outsiders, both from abroad, as with Flemish and Italian traders, and those from other towns in England. But the imperialism of larger cities subjugating politically or economically smaller towns, or efforts by subordinate towns to claw back liberties from larger ones, are missing from the annals of late medieval England. Without doubt, the Crown's centrality and strength kept such urban aggrandizement in check.

Colonial wars

Another form of political and popular movements active on the Continent was colonial struggle for independence, as against Genoa's and Venice's occupations of towns and territories along the Dalmatian coast, in Crete, Turkey, and Corsica. Late medieval England also experienced difficulties in its dominance over territories and cities in Ireland, Wales, Scotland, Gascony, Normandy, and other regions in France. To what extent these struggles were popular or urban conflict is often difficult to tell: were matters such as William Wallace's rising against the English warfare between opposing states, or popular struggles for collective liberties and the eradication of abuses? Certainly, in Ireland

---

[22] J. W. F. Hill, *Medieval Lincoln* (Cambridge, 1948), pp. 318–22. Moreover, I find none in the documentary collection assembled by Owen, *The Making of King's Lynn*, even though a great many of these documents focus on the urban economy.

[23] '*Liber de Antiquis Legibus*', p. 49.

and Scotland, the conflicts could touch towns, as in Waterford in 1358, when men in the counties of Kerry, Cork, and Limerick captured the king's castles and manors, and lands of the Earl of Desmond, who held them in chief from the king.[24] A month later, a second commission, headed by the justiciary of Ireland, focused more clearly on Waterford's citizens, addressing a petition by some who had been charged with 'contempts, rebellions and disobediences', and had been captured and placed in the king's prisons.[25] Unfortunately, the documents fail to specify the citizens' motives or grievances, other than 'rebellion'.

Such struggles against royal domination did not always present a united front between citizens of towns and those of the countryside. In 1448, rebels in the counties of Kilkenny, Tipperary, Wexford, and Waterford united with other of the king's 'Irish enemies and divers other nations' to 'perpetrate invasions, slaughters, burnings, plunderings, robberies, captures, fines, ransoms, hangings, and other intolerable misdeeds'. Unlike in 1358, however, the butt of revolt was not only the English but the mayor, bailiffs, and citizens of Waterford, who now served as a bulwark against Irish rebellion from smaller towns and villages. The king granted the citizens rights to assemble an army under their standards to attack the rebels.[26]

Internal struggles against English possessions in Gascony and later in the north of France, such as during the siege of Calais in 1346–7 and the resistance of Rouen against the English in 1418 and 1419, must certainly have been in part popular resistance against foreign domination. For the latter, the *Mémoires de Pierre de Fenin* recounts the urban population's terrible suffering: the wealthy forced to eat their horses, while the poor ate dogs, cats, rats, and mice.[27] News of urban resistance to English rule in France occasionally filters through the Patent Rolls, as in a revolt of La Réole[28] against Henry III in 1254. The Crown appealed to the local bishop of Bazas, calling the town's rebellion 'insolent war'. The centre of resistance came from the town's eighth-century monastery, fortified by townsmen and monks, transformed into 'a tower of Babylon', to assault

---

[24] *CPR 1358–61*, p. 75, 1358.v.28.   [25] Ibid., p. 79, 1358.vi.22.

[26] *CPR 1446–52*, p. 132, 1448.iv.8; also, Griffiths, *The Reign of King Henry VI*, p. 420.

[27] *Mémoires de Pierre de Fenin, comprenant le récit des événements qui se sont passés en France et en Bourgogne sous les règnes de Charles VI et Charles VII (1407–1427)*, ed. Mlle DuPont, SHF (Paris, 1837), p. 104.

[28] After Bordeaux, it was the second town of Guyenne, significant in the English wine trade, as is reflected in a street name of medieval London; see Williams, *Medieval London*, p. 12. Its population was around 2,500, *c*. 1400; Malcolm Vale, *The Angevin Legacy and the Hundred Years War 1250–1340* (Oxford, 1990), p. 144.

the adjacent royal castle. The rebels succeeded in taking the castle from the king, which resulted in 'so many evils and unspeakable slaughters that they could scarcely be allayed by the king's utmost endeavours'. Eventually, Henry's troops prevailed, and he demolished the monastery.[29]

Another conflict on French soil gives further overtones of popular revolt that go beyond the horrors of warfare between rival monarchs. In 1370, Limoges and other towns and surrounding incastellated villages rebelled against the Black Prince. The initial motive is clear: taxes ('propter graves exactiones et impositiones'). The Black Prince responded by recapturing Limoges, and even according to English chronicles, his punishment of the rebel inhabitants was 'vindictive'.[30] Similarly, English taxation in Normandy, combined with a sudden shift of English fortunes in northern France following the death of John, Duke of Bedford, in 1435, and the alliance between France and Burgundy the same year, triggered a revolt of Caux's peasantry against the English the following year. Led by Norman lords and French military captains, they captured English towns and castles between Dieppe and Harfleur but lost their attempt to take the English capital, Rouen. As earlier with the inhabitants of Limoges, the rebels were brutally repressed.[31]

---

[29] *CPR 1247–58*, pp. 339–40, 1254.ix.29. Powicke, *King Henry III and the Lord Edward*, I, p. 228, mentions the incident only in passing, but gives no hint that the conflict involved the local population or resistance against English occupation. Margaret Wade Labarge, *Gascony, England's First Colony 1204–1453* (London, 1980), p. 41, mentions the role of the 15-year-old Edward in the town's pacification, but nothing about the popular protest. On the repression of the rebels, also see J. R. Maddicott, *Simon de Montfort* (Cambridge, 1994), p. 124.

[30] Walsingham, *Historia Anglicana*, I, pp. 311–12; Walsingham, *Ypodigma Neustriae*, ed. Henry T. Riley, RS, 28, 7 (London, 1876), pp. 316–17; and 'Continuation of the English translation … MS Harl 2,261', in *Ranulphi Higden monachi Cestrensis*, ed. J. R. Lumby, 9 vols., RS, 41 (1865–6), VIII, Appendix 3, p. 440, which claims that the Black Prince 'allemoste destroyede that cite to the grownde'. Drawing on Froissart's account, Labarge, *Gascony*, pp. 164–5, comments on the Black Prince's ruthless suppression of the town, but gives no hint that Limoges had risen against English taxes. In 1390, Walsingham, *Historia Anglicana*, II, p. 196, mentions that Calais rose up 'again' against English rule, its leaders dragged and hanged. There is no mention of the previous insurrection, of who the rebels were, or of their demands. Another rebuff against English rule in France comes from Bordeaux in 1393, when the 'Burdegalenses' refused to allow Henry Percy the Younger to enter town and assume his post as warden. The *Annales Ricardi Secundi*, p. 158, does not describe who these people were, or their actions in refusing their new local ruler entry; eventually, Percy was allowed to exercise his duties. For factional conflicts that fed on urban insurrections at Bordeaux in 1249, when Simon de Montfort was Henry III's representative in Gascony and sided with one local faction against another, see Vale, *The Angevin Legacy*, p. 162.

[31] See Guy Bois, *Crise du féodalisme: économie rurale et démographie en Normandie orientale du début du 14e siècle au milieu du 16e siècle* (Paris, 1976), pp. 300–4; Jones, 'War on the Frontier', pp. 114–15; Allmand, *Lancastrian Normandy*, pp. 40 and 234; and Graeme Small, *Later Medieval France* (Basingstoke, 2009), pp. 72–3.

By contrast, the wars for independence in Scotland,[32] and the English conquest of Wales, which comprise long and venerable historiographies in the British Isles, are difficult to define as popular revolt, especially as ones in towns. This is even true of Owain Glyn Dŵr's proto-nationalist revolt from 1400–9, and the fortification of towns by the English, to control and discriminate against the Welsh. Berwick's resistance to Edward I in 1296 might be seen as an exception: a ship carrying supplies for his troops, who were camped outside Berwick, ran aground, prompting the town's commoners to attack the ship. They put it to flames and cut down its men. In retaliation, the king's army attacked the ditches where townsmen had made their defences. By nightfall, Edward had captured the town and its castle.[33] Yet because he had not occupied it by the day's start (30 March), the townsmen's attack on the supply ship was not an indigenous urban population resisting 'colonial' occupation but an act of war, even if the defenders were commoners. Despite England's possessions and wars of aggression in Ireland, Scotland, Wales, and France, further examples of popular conflict against colonial rule are difficult to spot and disentangle from near incessant warfare between monarchs, certainly more so than with the myriad uprisings against Italian city-state colonial rule by Pisa, Genoa, and Venice during the later Middle Ages.

Riots of children and youth movements

Still other forms of revolt prevalent on the Continent leave few traces in the English sources. Small children sometimes comprised the rank and file of peace movements, as at Naples in 1347. Moreover, Continental children and adolescents led pro-war riots, as in Florence in 1323 when they hurled rocks at the windows of the Palazzo Signoria, then cajoled adults from the labouring classes (*popolo minuto*) to pressure the government into forcing their noble commanders stationed outside Prato, reluctant to fight for a popular regime, to attack Lucca's forces under Castruccio Castracce's command.[34] In the last stages of a tax revolt organized by craftsmen in Tournai in 1365, children joined the insurgents, disguising themselves by blackening their faces and wearing strange clothes.[35] In another incident, this one in Paris in 1404,

---

[32] See G. W. S. Barrow, *Robert Bruce and the Community of the Realm of Scotland* (Edinburgh, 1976).

[33] Sir Thomas Gray, *Scalacronica 1272–1363*, ed. Andy King (Woodbridge, 2005), p. 37.

[34] Cohn, *Lust for Liberty*, p. 94.   [35] Ibid., p. 95.

school-aged children threw stones and mud at the Duke of Savoy's valets, who retaliated against the schoolchildren. The encounter ended with the banishment of members of the royal family and the demolition of a grand Parisian palace.[36] More significant for the history of late medieval popular protest was the 1383 revolt of Perugia, in which the city's youth led a major artisan revolt to overthrow the government.[37]

Nothing so formidable appears in the English sources. The chroniclers present less than a handful of incidents of collective violence instigated largely or entirely by children or adolescents and these hardly could be called revolts. Three occurred in London, all involved games, none of which, however, can easily be interpreted as collective protest with political or economic aims. The first, described by two chronicles, began as a wrestling match between London youth ('cives juniores de Londoniis') and servants of the Abbot of Westminster in 1223. With several wounded on both sides, the abbey won the match, and the Londoners were poor losers. A major conflict then ensued. The next morning, Londoners chose a new mayor, 'assembled armed mercenaries under the city standard', set out against the abbey, and attacked houses belonging to the abbot's seneschal in the city and suburbs. After the abbot's complaints to the king, strife between London and Westminster widened: citizens threw rocks from the banks of the Thames at monks, and the mayor and chief men of the city organized a full-scale assault against the abbot and his property. The king intervened, taking sixty citizens hostage and imposing a fine of 'many thousand marks'. This rare example of internecine conflict between two towns was not, however, a political or economic conflict of the sort seen in Flanders or central Italy; nor was it a youth movement or protest with any purpose other than restoration of pride, and that pride from the morning after the match was the adults'. As far as the chronicle accounts go, the youth had vanished from the scene.[38]

---

[36] Ibid., p. 93.   [37] Ibid., pp. 94–5.

[38] *Annales monasterii de Waverleia (AD 1–1291)* in *Annales monastici*, II, p. 297; *Annals of Dunstable*, pp. 78–9, partially translated in William Robieson, *The Growth of Parliament and the War with Scotland, 1216–1307* (London, 1914), pp. 9–10. Paris, *Historia Anglorum*, II, p. 251 and III, pp. 71–3, also reports the incident and dates it to 25 July 1222. For a comparison of this event to games out of control in Italy, see Samuel K. Cohn, Jr, 'Revolts of the Late Middle Ages and the Peculiarities of the English', in *Survival and Discord in Medieval Society: Essays in Honour of Christopher Dyer*, ed. Richard Goddard, John Langdon, and Miriam Müller (Turnhout, 2010), pp. 269–85, pp. 284–5. Powicke, *King Henry III and the Lord Edward*, p. 56, mentions the riot in passing and dismisses it as devoid of historical interest.

The second example also related by two chroniclers – one a terse entry from John of Oxenedes,[39] the other by the elaborate storyteller Paris[40] – involved youth play gone wrong a generation later. This time, the poor losers were noble youth at the king's court; yet Londoners again incurred royal wrath and were forced to pay another large fine. In 1252 (according to Oxenedes), 1253 (according to Paris), forty youth of London were playing a match on horseback, called Quintina, with a peacock as the prize. The king's youth taunted the boys, calling them 'rustics, scurvy and soapy wretches' (according to Paris), and then entered the field with lances and other weapons ('contis et lanceis'). But with broken pike handles, the Londoners prevailed over their better-armed opponents, throwing them from their horses and forcing them to flee. 'With clasped hands and gushing tears' (according to Paris), 'lacerated and dripping with blood' (according to John) the losers beseeched the king not to allow their defeat to pass unpunished: London's price of victory was a thousand-mark fine.[41]

Another game gone wrong, again in London, erupted during a critical year for English kingship, 1400. On 7 December, 'a great multitude' of boys gathered in St Paul's cemetery to enact a pretend battle between the different monarchies of Britain. Starting as child's play, it soon became serious, especially between those who chose to be Scots and those supporting England. The pretend battles ended with blood, even death, grave enough to attract the notice of the chronicler closest to being England's official royal chronicler. The author, however, made no hints that the disorder was tied to the current troubled royal politics of 1399 to 1400, or that it possessed any other political overtones.[42]

---

[39] *Chronica Johannis de Oxenedes*, ed. H. Ellis (London, 1859), pp. 195–6.

[40] *Matthew Paris's English History*, III, p. 18. Wrestling matches in London continued to spark collective violence throughout our period. They were not, however, necessarily of youth, of popular culture, or expressions of social, political, or economic aims. In 1453, 'jentilmen' of St John's priory disturbed the peace at 'a grete game of wrestlynge' in Clerkenwell. The mayor (apparently in attendance) called the sheriff to make arrests. Under the influence of alcohol, others from St John's resisted arrest, leaving a yeoman dead and others injured. Afterwards the mayor banned wrestling in London (*Chronicles of London*, p. 164).

[41] Another wrestling match sparked a quarrel at Northampton in 1309: a son of a carpenter, shot by an arrow, recovered but died soon afterwards of a disease called 'le flux' [dysentery?]; *Select Cases from the Coroners' Rolls*, p. 61.

[42] Walsingham, *The St Albans Chronicle*, II, pp. 300–3; perhaps this was the same battle reported by Usk, *The Chronicle*, pp. 94–7: during Lent 1400, thousands of apprentices in London banded together to choose their kings and fight amongst themselves, from which 'many died'. By some sources (but none of the chronicles we have sampled), young men from Durham aided the priory and monks of the city to attack the Archbishop of York during his visitation in 1283; Margaret E. Cornford, 'Religious Houses of Durham', in *VCH: Durham*, ed. William Page (London, 1907), II,

No cases of collective violence involving children or adolescents surface from our examination of Patent Rolls.

If not disturbed by children or adolescents, English towns could, nonetheless, be split between younger citizens and older established elites. As we will see, Thomas Wykes claimed that during the barons' war against Henry III, towns were divided between city magnates and 'bachelors' but gives little evidence of it.[43] Furthermore, exactly who the 'bachelors' were, especially in towns, has been debated. E. F. Jacob argues that in the countryside they were knights with limited holdings, who did not carry their own banner into the field of battle but were not young landless nobles 'of little experience'. Similarly, for towns, he interpreted the chronicle evidence to mean that 'bachelors' had nothing to do with age but instead with class, seeing them as the equivalent of *gens de métier*, or craftsmen, of Flemish towns in the late thirteenth and fourteenth centuries.[44] On the evidence of the Letter-books of London and cases from Norwich's town minutes, such a parallel seems doubtful, at least by the fourteenth and fifteenth centuries. As we have seen with political and economic strife at Norwich in 1414, the city's bachelors were elites united with the 'Prudhommes' against a commonalty, which in fact included merchants. The ages of these and other English bachelors are difficult to know. Certainly, they were not property-less youth without any stake in urban society and politics (as with Perugia's youth in 1383). In at least one case, however, during the Henrician civil war, an English bachelor society connoted a division by age. At Bury St Edmunds, a guild of youth ('gilda iuventum') played a leading role in the burgesses' revolt of 1264 that briefly won rights to elect their mayor and aldermen,[45] and rose a second time against the established burgesses of Bury and the abbey in 1266.[46] Beyond their title as bachelors and their formation of a youth guild, we know nothing of their social and economic backgrounds; no lists of rebels survive as they do for Bury's next big revolt in 1327, when these bachelors no longer played a role as rebels.

According to Mary Lobel, young men of Cirencester made a similar effort to overthrow abbey rule in 1210. We know, however, even less about them. As far as the surviving sources go, they did not form a 'gilda iuventum'.[47] If Wykes were correct and these bachelors and youth guilds

pp. 86–103. In addition, a sporting event was at the origins of the Norwich revolt of 1272, but no evidence ties it to children or youth.

[43] See pp. 84–5 below and Powicke, *King Henry III and the Lord Edward*, p. 448.
[44] Jacob, *Studies in the Period of Baronial Reform*, pp. 126–43.
[45] See p. 216 below.   [46] Lobel, *The Borough of Bury St Edmunds*, pp. 127–32.
[47] Ibid., p. 126.

had formed through towns and cities, at least during crisis moments, such as with de Monfort's rebellion in the 1260s, then such an undercurrent of youth protest may have been as prevalent as on the Continent. Only one revolt in our sample, however, resembles those revolts on the Continent. In 1282, 'the older and more lawful men' of Scarborough protested against 'strangers' in town and young men, who had resisted the rule of the old, made themselves governors, and appropriated £16 from mills and other properties belonging to the town. They refused to appear in municipal courts and 'subverted other customs, rights and liberties of the town and the church'. As with revolts possibly of youth in Cirencester and Bury, no lists of occupations or other indications of social status survive. At Scarborough these younger men (their ages indeterminate) had in effect created a system of dual power. The king's commission ordered them severely punished to serve as 'a warning to others'.[48] But were these rebels 'youth' or adolescents, or even necessarily all younger than those they opposed? As with the dual meaning of 'vassal', meaning 'puer' or 'young boy', and later taking on the meaning of subservience and dependence between grown men, or 'boy' for black men in menial jobs in the American south until very recent times, notions of status overlapped and coloured terms for age in the later Middle Ages.[49]

The paucity of evidence from these sources on youth movements and insurrection does not, however, mean that town youth were not an active part of the criminal underworld. A case from the capital in 1326 suggests that a youth culture of violence not only existed but could terrorize burgesses, even noble elites. 'The cruelty and iniquity of youths' in London was so widespread, according to the *Annales Paulini*, that 'the mayor, aldermen, and elder burgesses of the city were insecure and dared not to resist them'. From this fear, Robert de Baldock removed his wealth kept at St Paul's, and the Earl of Arundel took his from the priory of the Holy Trinity. At night, gangs, called 'Rifflinge' ('chisellers'), after their mode of robbery, and their booty

---

[48] *CPR 1281–92*, p. 50, 1282.x.20. In addition, Helmut Hinck, 'The Rising of 1381 in Winchester', *EHR* 125 (2010): 124, argues that in 1381, 'the ambitions of some young aspiring men' against an older generation of city oligarchs fuelled the revolt at Winchester. This was not, however, a youth movement, or one like Scarborough's, comprised of resident non-citizens allied with aliens.

[49] See Marc Bloch, *Feudal Society*, trans. L. A. Manyon, 2 vols. (Chicago, 1961 [Paris, 1939–49]), I, pp. 155–6. Similarly, the double meaning of 'valet' would endure through the Middle Ages. For notions of youth and service and the 'delicate interplay between age, precedence, "place" and authority' (pp. 100–1) in early modern London, see Paul Griffiths, *Youth and Authority: Formative Experiences in England 1560–1640* (Oxford, 1996), pp. 76–78, and 96–110. I thank Christian Liddy for this last reference.

('Riffleres'), stole the treasury of Hugh Despenser, the younger, kept in the city with the Florentine Bardi bank.[50] On the other hand, while both the Patent Rolls and chronicles report virtually no cases of youth protest with clear political or economic objectives, except possibly for Bury in 1264 and Scarborough in 1282, they point to an abundance of cases of town–gown conflict to be examined later, especially at Oxford. These involved students, young clerics, and their masters, but rarely give signs of being struggles over liberties or political power.

Revolts against military occupation

Protests of burgesses against soldiers billeted within their walls, enraged by soldiers' thieving, consumption of resources, arrogance, and abuses, especially sexual ones, are another form of urban revolt that prevailed on the Continent but finds scant traces in late medieval England. On the Continent, these revolts engendered greater and longer-term conse-quences for towns than the peace movements of children; among the former can be counted several of the most explosive of Continental popular revolts. Sexual abuses committed against indigenous popula-tions by occupying French troops led to the Sicilian Vespers of 1282, which resulted in the massacre of thousands, and ultimately the collapse of French power in the island kingdom. Less famous, though even more disastrous for an urban population, were the consequences of billeted soldiers and their abuses at Cesena in 1377. First, indigenous butchers revolted against the billeted Breton mercenaries, murdering a hundred of them. In retaliation, Cardinal Robert of Geneva (soon to become anti-pope) hired John Hawkwood to lead Bretons and other mercenaries back to Cesena, where they pillaged, raped, and slaughtered civilians, leaving this major commercial centre of Romagna uninhabited for two years.[51] Abuses by billeted troops provoked similar protests and disasters in French towns, as in 1414, when those of Noyon violently confronted the king and burnt part of their town to prevent his troops billeting there, or in 1417 when Rouen's *menu peuple* answered royal orders to billet troops by 'madly' charging through the streets and squares, stealing the keys to their gates, chasing out royal guards, and killing the king's chief officer and other royal officials in the city.[52]

By contrast, the English sources give only a few hints of commoners' actions against soldiers in their towns and in some it may have been more a conflict between commoners and magnates or internecine

[50] *Annales Paulini*, p. 321.   [51] Cohn, *Lust for Liberty*, pp. 103–4.
[52] Ibid., p. 84.

struggles between rival towns than ones directed against soldiers *per se*, or ones with long-term consequences. The earliest possible example appears on 30 September 1321, when thirty ships from Southampton sailed into the port of Winchelsea to aid the town against a threatened naval attack from foreigners ('contra venientes alienigenas'). The rulers of Southampton ('majores') consigned two of these ships and their equipment over to Winchelsea, but those of Winchelsea ('Illi vero de Wynchelse') – exactly who they were is not specified – were incensed and 'foolishly' burnt fifteen ships while anchored in their harbour and a further two the following day.[53] Was this a reaction against a billeted navy or a rivalry between towns?

On 29 July 1322, the movement of the king's army 'with an armed foot-man from every town in England' appears to have set off a mutiny of the king's common soldiers against their officers, who allied with townsmen, possibly against the principle of troops occupying one's own country. At the same time in Newcastle upon Tyne, foot soldiers allied with commoners and killed the knight John of Penrith, along with squires, on the town's bridge. According to the chronicler, they met their death because 'they wanted to have the malefactors arrested so as to put an end to the riot, so impudent were the commoners in their doings'.[54] The chronicler, however, does not explain what the riot that led to the massacre of the knight and his squires concerned. Had it arisen from abuses of a large army moving through a provincial town, and if so, what exactly had the knight and his squires done to have aroused their own foot soldiers to unite with Newcastle's commoners?

A later case also points to the tensions between a resident urban population and billeted soldiers, in this case, sailors in London in 1377 during the troubled last year of Edward III's reign, with tensions on the rise between Gaunt and the capital's inhabitants. For reasons which the chronicler claimed only the duke knew, John had gathered the whole of the English fleet in London. After having been stationed there 'for a considerable length of time', a certain squire, with the approval of the king's mistress (Alice Perrers), again for undisclosed reasons, murdered one of the sailors. His comrades first pursued their case in the king's court, the Marshalsea,[55] but on hearing that Alice would see that the man was given immunity, the sailors took the law into their own hands,[56]

---

[53] *Annales Paulini*, p. 298.   [54] Gray, *Scalacronica*, p. 89.

[55] Marshalsea was the King's Bench prison, located in Southwark; see Harding, 'The Revolt against the Justices', p. 177.

[56] On Alice's power and influence over Edward III, especially in 1377, and the animosity she aroused from knights, clergy, and possibly commoners, see George Holmes, *The Good Parliament* (Oxford, 1975), pp. 103–4, 136–9, 164.

broke into the prison, and after begrudgingly allowing him confession and the last sacraments, dragged him to the gallows and killed him 'without mercy'. They then had a flute player accompany them to their fleets, 'where they passed the rest of the day in great rejoicing'. Londoners did not take this abrogation of justice lightly and warned that such actions would not go unpunished, but it seems that they did, in this year of heightened conflict in London and across the countryside, of dynastic strife and royal weakness.[57]

An enigmatic chronicle entry from the *St Albans Chronicle* refers perhaps to another case of local resentment towards the abuses of billeted troops, in this case those of Henry IV in 1401, but exactly where in England is unspecified: 'At that time rumbling ['murmur'] from the populace erupted against the king, especially given that foodstuff was taken but not paid for.'[58] Another case two years earlier, however, shows the tell-tale signs of false promises, soldiers' arrogance, and their destruction of towns and villages which are so often heard in chronicles on the Continent. The *Dieulacres Chronicle* and Adam Usk tell similar stories of the encampment of Duke Henry's troops on the outskirts of Chester in 1399, when he challenged the kingship of his cousin. The duke assured the townsmen that his men would not kill anyone, seize any goods, or destroy anything. However, that night, perhaps in revenge against the Cheshire men, long loyal to Richard, Henry's troops:

seized enormous riches, devastating the countryside and secretly carrying things off with them, smashing open wine-casks and emptying them, making off everywhere with treasure and all sorts of other things which had been buried in the ground. They even destroyed the corn and slaughtered the cattle – young and old alike – in the fields and meadows, leaving the carcasses to lie there; ladders, chests, harrows, and all the implements so essential to rural life, they burned everywhere.[59]

The duke, however, was not yet king and these were not the king's troops; instead, at this moment, the soldiers were those of an invading army. Besides, no popular revolt followed on from this invasion and abuse of a local population, although it may well have conditioned burgess resentment that flared against Henry a year later.[60]

---

[57] On 1377, see pp. 99–104 below.

[58] Walsingham, *St Albans Chronicle*, II, pp. 314–15.

[59] *Dieulacres Chronicle* in *Chronicles of the Revolution 1397–1400: The Reign of Richard II*, trans. and ed. Chris Given-Wilson (Manchester, 1993), pp. 152–3. Also see *Chronicle of Dieulacres Abbey, 1381–1403*, ed. M. V. Clarke and V. H. Galbraith, in 'The Deposition of Richard II', *BJRL*, 7 (1930): 125–81.

[60] Peter McNiven, 'The Cheshire Rising of 1400', *BJRL*, 52 (1969–70): 375–96.

Finally, the chronicle of an anonymous monk of Malmesbury describes what appears to have had the beginnings of an English Sicilian Vespers. With the young Edward III poised to invade Scotland with a mix of English and Hainault troops, a dispute ('contumeliam') erupted between the billeted Hainaulters and burgesses of York in its suburb of St Nicholas in Ousegate in 1328. As with so many similar incidents on the Continent, the revolt's trigger was (according to this chronicler) soldiers' abuse of local women: 'the foreigners' had raped ('ceperunt ... per vim') burgesses' wives, daughters, and female servants. A pitched battle ('modo bellico') ensued, bringing 500 into the streets and leaving twenty-seven mortally wounded. On the third day, the entire town assembled before dawn. One hundred and twenty-six of the Hainaulters and 241 of the English were slain, their bodies thrown into the river Ouse. The Hainaulter soldiers retaliated, burning the entire parish of St Nicholas to the ground.[61]

No other English chronicle describes these events; nor do the Patent, Close, or Fine Rolls mention them, at least for 1328. However, Geoffrey le Baker describes a conflict arising between York's citizens and soldiers from Hampshire that resulted in soldiers setting fire to part of the town in 1327.[62] This event receives greater attention from an eye-witness of the events – the Flemish chronicler, courtier, and canon, Jean le Bel, then in the entourage of Edward's and John of Hainault's troops. His story differs from that of the Malmesbury monk, and not only with a different month (June) and year (1327) for the incident. The first difference is that in his account, the quarrel's spark was a game of dice, not sex. More fundamentally, the struggle was not between a billeted army and an indigenous urban population, but a conflict, even a war, between two military forces, supposedly on the same side, encamped outside York to make raids on Scotland (even if the town's professional archers eventually joined the English archers against the Hainaulters). In addition, the figures of those involved and the casualties differ widely between le Bel and the anonymous monk. By Jean le Bel's count, 2,000 English archers alone were involved, and 316 of the Bishop of Lincoln's archers were slain.[63] The king ordered a royal commission to investigate this quarrel a week after Jean le Bel's date of its outbreak. Its brief

---

[61] *Eulogium*, pp. 199–200.
[62] *Chronicon Galfridi le Baker de Swynebroke*, ed. E. M. Thompson (Oxford, 1889), p. 35.
[63] *Chronique de Jean le Bel*, ed. Jules Viard and Eugène Déprez, SHF, 317, 2 vols. (Paris, 1904), pp. 42–3; and Matthew Strickland and Robert Hardy, *The Great Warbow: From Hastings to the Mary Rose* (Stroud, 2005), pp. 180–1.

description corroborates le Bel's characterization of it as a battle between the two nations of soldiers,

resulting in murders, robberies and other crimes, between the men of Hainault who lately came at the king's request to assist him in his expedition against Scotland, and the king's footsoldiers who lately came to York for the same purpose from the counties of Lincoln and Northampton.[64]

In conclusion, struggles of dependent artisans and disenfranchised workers against their masters, riots against popes and their legates, subjugation of smaller towns by larger ones, colonial struggles against dominant regimes, protests of children and youth movements, and especially revolts against billeted troops and their abuses of local populations, were characteristic forms of urban protest on the Continent that could have disastrous and long-term consequences. By contrast, these forms of protest and revolt find only weak appearances in the English sources. What then were the predominant forms of revolt in late medieval English towns?

[64] *CPR 1327–30*, p. 152.

Part II

Crown and town: strife with secular authority

4   Revolts against the Crown: crises of kingship from John Lackland to Henry VI

Revolts against the Crown – attacks on the king, his decrees or taxes, against his justiciars and other officers, or against the queen – comprise a large proportion of the urban revolts reported by contemporary chroniclers: they make up forty-seven of 231 incidents, which we have evaluated as cases of popular movements or collective protest in English towns, or 20 per cent of them.[1] This percentage more than doubles that of our earlier database for the Continent, taken primarily from chroniclers in Italy, France, and Flanders, which showed that 87 of 1,112 (or 7.8 per cent) of revolts were directed at the Crown.[2] However, absolutely and relative to other forms of popular protest, these attacks against and resistance to the Crown may not have been so extraordinarily high (at least from these sources) as first appears. City-states of central and northern Italy were rarely subjected to royal power. There were exceptions, as with Parma in the 1320s and 1330s: under the suzerainty of

---

[1] We have collected over 400 examples from chronicles, but there is considerable repetition, especially with chronicles copying from one another. As Gransden, *Historical Writing*, I, describes: 'the fashion developed of lending the chronicle of one house to another, where they would be copied' (p. 318). For instance, nine chroniclers in our sample reported in various ways the revolt of Londoners allied with barons against Edward II that led to the beheading of Edward's principal advisers and his loss of the throne. Still more chronicles (15) reported the Norwich burgesses' revolt against their city's priory and its privileges in 1272. The Patent Rolls record many more attacks against the Crown, or royal ministers, or situations where the Crown intervened to restore order (263 of 651 cases that we have tallied as municipal disturbances). However, these royal rolls were in fact established principally to investigate and adjudicate attacks against the king and disturbances to his peace. In addition, these show the extent to which the Crown regularly intervened into the affairs of towns, even beneath the level of municipal government, to the duties of guildsmen, as in 1327, when a royal commission judged that 'bakers, taverners, millers, cooks, poulterers, fishmongers, butchers, brewers, corn-chandlers and others in the city of London' had become lax in their duties as officers of their misteries, and as a result 'evildoers by night and day with swords, clubs, bucklers and other arms march through the city . . . beat and illtreat individuals'. The commission commanded the mayor and sheriffs 'to redress these matters by corporal punishment or otherwise'; *CPR 1327–30*, p. 185, 1327.xi.18.

[2] Cohn, *Lust for Liberty*, pp. 79–84.

Robert of Naples and his representative at Parma, the much-hated notary, Riccardo, the populace of Parma in 1331 revolted against royal taxation and its war policy. Florence's contestations against their regal sovereign, Walter of Brienne, in the early 1340s also can be interpreted as a revolt against royal power, Walter being a member of the French royal dynasty. Over half the cases of revolt in that database (604 of 1,112) occurred within these Italian city-states. As might be expected, incidents of popular protest against kings and queens and their officials came mostly from the kingdoms of Sicily and Naples and France, as well as from Flanders, where French royal intervention often incited revolt. Here, attacks against royal power constituted 17 per cent of the cases, only slightly below that found in the English chronicle accounts. Yet, as we have seen, with artisan struggles in towns such as London (and unlike revolts in the city-states of Italy and Flanders, or even in France) the king often intervened and his courts were the ultimate arbiter of these conflicts within and between guilds and between artisans and town governments. As we will see with a plethora of revolts of burgesses against a wide array of ecclesiastical bodies, such revolts in England also reached the king's ear and involved royal judicial and military intervention. The king and his advisers interpreted these revolts as attacks against the king himself; yet these have not been included as 'royal' revolts.

Furthermore, in contrast to the Continental cases, English urban disturbances were often allied with, or followed on from, the great uprisings of magnates against the Crown during periods of national dynastic crises and civil war. Because Westminster was the principal residence of the king and centre of royal administration throughout most of this period, London was the arena of these struggles and its mayor, aldermen, citizens, and the faceless crowds (at least in the chronicle reports), were overwhelmingly those of urban rebels. Many of these struggles are well known from standard surveys and constitutional histories of the British Isles by authors such as William Stubbs, F. M. Powicke, E. F. Jacob, and more recently David Carpenter and Claire Valente; they need little rehearsing here, except to emphasize and trace their urban and popular elements. Often they may also push the boundaries of what reasonably might be claimed as a 'popular' rebellion. The earliest of these in our study is a case in point, the great rising of magnates against King John, from 1215 to 1216: of known townsmen, only the wealthiest and most elite of London's citizenry ('civium, ut dicitur, parte majore et sanorie') seem to have taken part.[3] On a last

---

[3] Walter of Coventry, *Memoriale fratris Walteri de Coventria*, II, p. 220.

attempt to win over the city, John negotiated a charter granting rights to
elect yearly their mayor and abolish all tallages not granted by common
consent of the kingdom and city.[4] Artisans or others beneath magnate
citizens, who may have fought, and then negotiated, for urban liberties
are not mentioned, and unlike other English cities and towns (with the
exception of the Cinque Ports), the burgesses of the ruling elites in
London – its mayors, aldermen, sheriffs, and wealthy merchants – were,
in fact, barons.[5]

Rebellion also erupted against John in Northampton with the
massacre of many of the king's men stationed there. A few days later,
the king retaliated by burning most of the town.[6] From chronicle
descriptions, it is difficult to know if any were townsmen. Roger of
Wendover relates the pillaging and damages John's troops inflicted on
other towns – Lynn, Colchester, and especially Lincoln – but fails to
describe any resistance by townspeople, or to say whether they participated alongside the barons.[7] Nonetheless, despite the paucity of
evidence, this baronial unrest (as with later baronial wars) appears to
have created opportunities for burgesses to revolt against other authorities in towns. During John's rule, for example, citizens of Norwich
revolted against their priory for the first time, and their struggle concerned rights to common lands and other liberties.[8]

The baronial revolt against Henry III

For the next significant baronial revolt, Simon de Montfort's against
Henry III, more chroniclers describe events in London and other towns:
Oxford, Northampton, Lynn, Hereford, and Norwich. It was another
period of royal weakness. Not only did de Montfort, the barons, and civil
war cut across vast expanses of England, and challenge royal authority,
but rebellion in Wales, the king's loss of support in the Welsh marches,
and long-term disaffection among the London populace, as well as from
other towns, the friars and other clergy, and the country gentry, further

---

[4] Williams, *Medieval London*, pp. 5–6.
[5] See for instance the description of *Matthew Paris's English History*, III, p. 18: 'the citizens
of London (whom we usually call barons, owing to the dignity of their city, and to the
ancient liberty of its citizens)'; and Nightingale, *A Medieval Mercantile Community*, p. 49.
[6] *Memoriale fratris Walteri de Coventria*, pp. 220–1.
[7] Cited in Paris, *Historia Anglorum*, II, pp. 182 and 184; for Lincoln, Matthew Paris,
Chronica majora, III, p. 23. He also describes the atrocities of John's armies in the
counties of Essex, Hertford, Middlesex, Cambridge, and Huntingdon; ibid., II, p. 637.
[8] W. Rye, 'The Riot between the Monks and Citizens of Norfolk in 1272', *Norfolk
Antiquarian Miscellany*, first series, 2 (1880): 17–18, does not indicate exactly when this
riot took place, except that it was during John's reign.

weakened Henry's hand.[9] In addition, in September 1262, a strange disease afflicted Henry and large numbers of his court while at Paris, causing him to remain absent from England, first because of illness, then convalescence, and finally to go on pilgrimage to pay spiritually for his recovery. These concomitant struggles and problems opened opportunities to the baronial opposition.[10] In Oxford, the revolt fed into the recurrent battles between burgesses and the university. From the town's resentment over the king's granting of special privileges to the university, violence erupted between the two on 21 September 1263.[11] Later, students and Jews, who had escaped de Monfort's anti-Semitic pogroms in London, battled on the king's behalf at Oxford.[12] In Hereford, rebels ('ruffians' employed by the barons, according to the chronicler) dragged the bishop from his church and threw him into prison, and at Norwich, its bishop had to flee to Bury St Edmunds.[13] Lynn lost its royal privileges (as had other towns, according to the continuator of Matthew Paris) because its townsmen had supported the barons. In 1266, the burgesses tried to regain their liberties by promising to hunt down the king's enemies, a band of the 'disinherited' noblemen, who had occupied a nearby island in the Wash. The plebeian militia were not their match; outflanked by the better-armed and trained noblemen, the plebes failed miserably, and were either slaughtered on the island, or returned to face derision at home.[14]

As noted above, the *Annals of Thomas Wykes* saw bachelors in almost every town in England holding open meetings during this revolt, with violence breaking out between the grandees of towns and other citizens.[15] Yet Wykes' chronicle followed the events of the revolt in only one town – London.[16] Indeed, London seems to have been a principal battlefield of the baronial revolt with the king at Westminster, his son Edward in fields next to Merton, and the troops of de Montfort

---

[9] Noël Denholm-Young, *Richard of Cornwall* (Oxford, 1947), p. 121.

[10] Ibid., p. 116. On Henry's illness in Paris and the devastation to his household advisers, see Powicke, *King Henry III and the Lord Edward*, II, p. 430.

[11] *Annals of Osney*, pp. 139–41.

[12] Powicke, *King Henry III and the Lord Edward*, II, p. 450. In September 1264, the baronial government ordered the mayor and bailiffs of Oxford to suppress illicit assemblies and confederacies of townsmen joined by outsiders and Jews coming into town (probably escaping persecution from London) 'posing a threat not only to your town but to the entire realm' (*CCR 1261–4*, pp. 363–4).

[13] John of Taxster, *Chronicle*, in *The Chronicle of Florence of Worcester, with Two Continuations, Comprising Annals of English History from the Departure of the Romans to the Reign of Edward I*, trans. Thomas Forester (London, 1854), p. 334.

[14] *Matthew Paris's English History*, III, pp. 361–2.

[15] *Annals of Thomas Wykes*, p. 138.   [16] Ibid., pp. 134, 140–3.

encamped south of the city at Southwark.[17] Much more clearly than in 1215, the events of 1263 split the capital between commoners and city elites, who by some sources supported the king, but according to others, sided cautiously with the barons.[18] Either way, the elites wished to keep city gates locked, chains in place to keep both armies from entering, while commoners enthusiastically backed de Montfort and ultimately revolted against their mayor and aldermen to open London to his army. Their actions benefited not only the barons but themselves, with the election of a new populist mayor, Thomas fitzThomas, who held a folkmoot in the open air outside St Paul's, where craft guilds won rights of self-determination for the first time in the city's history.[19]

Contempt for the king and his council flared in the midsummer of 1263, with the king short on funds and unable to obtain loans from London. Royal officers broke into the city treasury kept at the Templars' London headquarters and stole £1,000, which provoked riots against them and other royal councillors residing in London. Commoners broke into their houses, killed their horses, and forced the king's men to flee.[20] Several days later (13 July), when the queen left her residence by barge at the Tower to meet her son at Windsor, London plebes mounted the Thames' bridges to hurl abuse and blasphemy. Calling her a whore and an adulterer, they pelted her and her noble entourage with mud, eggs, and stones: the mayor had to rescue her, and she was forced to return to the Tower.[21] Furthermore, the king was not allowed to enter the city until the mayor gave him safe passage to St Paul's, where he was protected in the bishop's palace. Meanwhile, according to the *Annales Londonienses*, the better-heeled citizens had sided with the king.[22] Until December, de Montfort's troops were kept out of the city, despite his efforts to persuade the city grandees ('majoribus civitatis'). But on 11 December, citizens led by John de Gisors[23] revolted against the mayor and aldermen, broke the city chains, opened the gates, and

---

[17] *Gesta Regum* in *The Historical Works of Gervase of Canterbury*, ed. William Stubbs, 2 vols. RS, 73 (1879–80), II, p. 230.
[18] See, for instance, Reynolds, *An Introduction*, p. 110.
[19] Powicke, *King Henry III and the Lord Edward*, p. 447.
[20] *Annals of Dunstable*, III, pp. 222–3.
[21] *Annales Londonienses*, p. 222. A number of chronicles reported this event: *Annals of Thomas Wykes*, p. 134; *Chronicle of Pierre de Langtoft*, II, p. 140; and *Willelmi Rishanger*, p. 18.
[22] *Annales Londonienses*, pp. 222–3.
[23] According to Williams, *Medieval London*, p. 69, John de Gisors had become the most eminent of the royal merchants by the 1250s. Other leaders of the revolt against the older aldermanic dynasties also came predominantly from London's elites; they were not men of lower crafts, despite a subsequent 'revolutionary change in personnel' in London's officials with later charters and the incorporation of cordwainers, girdlers,

allowed de Montfort's awaiting troops to enter. On hearing of their entry, the king and his son abandoned their positions.[24]

According to Arnald Fitz-Thedmar (an eye-witness and sheriff of London), the leaders of London's sedition, who favoured the barons, were in fact barons themselves – Thomas de Piwelesdone, elected as constable, and Stephen Buckel, as their marshal, along with the king's justiciar at the Tower, Hugh Despenser: 'all the people of the city' armed and assembled under these men's standards. The Londoners lacked their own rebel leaders, even ones from the city elites. The city militia then went from London as far as Isleworth (in Middlesex), where they laid waste to the manor of the King of Almaine (i.e., Richard of Cornwall, the king's brother), burned his mills, and destroyed his fish ponds. According to the royalist Fitz-Thedmar, 'this was the beginning of woes, and the source of that deadly war, through which so many manors were committed to the flames, so many men, rich and poor, were plundered, and so many thousands of persons lost their lives'.[25] The revolt had other consequences, especially for Jews and the city's foreign communities, to be examined later.

To these descriptions, the Patent Rolls add little. The revolt had certainly spread to towns further afield than Oxford. In 1265, the king admitted that 'those of the town of Shrewsbury have borne themselves towards the king otherwise than they should'. 'Among other things', he cited that they had taken the men of Ralph Basset of Drayton, 'keeper of the peace in those parts' and in charge of the town's royal castle.[26] Perhaps reflecting his current weakness, the king commanded the Abbot of Shrewsbury to appeal to the bailiffs and townsmen, bidding them to release the royal officers and grant them safe conduct to see the king.[27]

Northampton was another town that turned against the Crown. In 1268, on condition 'that they behave faithfully henceforward', Henry granted a pardon to 'the mayor and men of the commonalty', after they had detained the town against him 'in the time of the disturbance'. Whether the town was solidly behind the barons or split, as in London, between 'the mayor and good men' and those beneath them cannot be

---

wool packers, and joiners of the saddlers following Walter Hervey's revolt in 1272; ibid., p. 167, chapters 7 and 8.

[24] *Gesta Regum*, II, p. 230.

[25] 'Liber de Antiquis Legibus', p. 65. Williams, *Medieval London*, p. 224.

[26] Basset was constable of the town's castle; less than two months earlier, the king had entrusted him with restoring unity to the region and confiscating the lands and goods of the baronial rebels; *CPR 1258–66*, p. 434, 1265.i.25. In March, he had been the king's officer in charge of delivering the counties of Shropshire and Stafford to the king's side; ibid., p. 411, 1265.iii.7.

[27] Ibid., p. 434, 1265.vi.25.

determined from this document, but the poor do not appear to have raised his 'indignation and rancour'; nor were they later included in the general pardon.[28] On the same day, Henry restored the town's liberties.[29]

The crisis of Edward II

The next crisis of kingship ended Edward II's reign, ushering his son, Edward III, onto the throne, under the guardianship of his mother, Isabella. It was instigated by the queen and her lover, Roger Mortimer, but grew during a long period of tyrannical rule made worse by Edward's privileged and corrupt advisers, principally Hugh Despenser the younger. This time, the conflict focused more narrowly on the capital. However, with the liberation of prisoners, first from the Tower, then from other English gaols, political prisoners and common criminals, including plunderers and murderers ('rapaces et homicides'),[30] allegedly spread strife and spurred civil unrest in towns and cities. Unsurprisingly, these events threatening a king's survival prompted more chronicle accounts than were seen with most examples of urban insurrection.[31] Perhaps more surprisingly, only three chroniclers, two of whom clearly borrowed from one another,[32] felt any sympathy for the hapless Edward, but lamented the assassinations and crimes that followed ('omnes facinorosi').[33] For them the revolt created anarchy; plundering and other crimes were without end: 'ipsi tamen multias rapinas et alias insolentias facere non cessarunt'.[34]

This time, the urban unrest in London did not clearly split the population into opposing factions based on class interests – *populares* versus grandees – with those beneath the ruling elites taking the initiative, supporting the barons, and rebelling against their municipal government. Instead, in 1326 the initiative came from above. The

---

[28] *CPR 1266–72*, p. 225, 1268.v.6.

[29] Ibid. London and its citizens received a pardon for supporting the barons much earlier on 17 September 1263, *CPR 1258–66*, p. 278. Students of Oxford and Cambridge left their universities to start a new (shortly lived) one at Northampton. They joined the barons' cause and as a result, their new university came to an end.

[30] *Vita et mors Edwardi regis Angliae* in *Chronicles of the Reigns of Edward I and Edward II*, pp. 310–11; *Chronicon Galfridi le Baker de Swynebroke*, pp. 23–4.

[31] Ten chronicles in our sample reported the urban events of 1326–7.

[32] *Vita et mors Edwardi regis Angliae*, pp. 310–11 and *Chronicon Galfridi le Baker de Swynebroke*, pp. 23–4.

[33] *Vita et mors Edwardi regis Angliae*, pp. 310–11.

[34] Adam Murimuth, *Continuatio chronicarum, Robertus de Avesbury De gestis mirabilibus regis Edwardi Tertii*, ed. E. M. Thompson (London, 1889), p. 48.

queen and her son sent letters beseeching the mayor and commune of London to come to their aid against the king and his advisers, leaving the London populace ambivalent on what to do.[35] In their initial negotiations, they expressed hostility to the mayor, Hamo de Chigwell, the aldermen, and their sheriffs. Their reservations, however, had to do with procedure, rather than loyalty to the king. Their leaders had offended them by negotiating with rebel barons at Blackfriars and not in the Guildhall with craftsmen in attendance; as a result they were poised to riot through the streets of London. On 15 October, the mayor agreed to meet them and 'in great fear went with them to the Guildhall', where they discussed 'who were the enemies of the queen and the city'.[36] The first to be sought for summary justice was John Marshal, suspected as a spy of Hugh Despenser the younger. Stripped and given confession, he was beheaded in Cheapside. Then the Londoners pursued the king's treasurer, Walter Stapeldon, Bishop of Exeter, first at his home, which they burnt and robbed, and when finding him near the north door of St Paul's, they pulled him from his horse and dragged him through the cemetery to the square in Cheapside, where they 'mercilessly stripped' and beheaded him 'with great ferocity'[37] along with two of his esquires ('armigeris'), leaving 'the nude cadavers exposed in the middle of the square for all to behold'. They sent Stapeldon's head to the queen in Bristol.[38] Hatred of Stapeldon was longstanding among London's commoners and elites alike: as treasurer his fiscal exactions had been resented as excessively harsh.[39] According to an early fifteenth-century chronicle, he was also 'noted for a grete enemye ageyn the liberties of London'.[40]

Londoners then attacked the Tower, assaulting Hugh Despenser's wife and adherents of Henry, third Earl of Lancaster (c. 1280–1345),[41] and liberated all prisoners convicted in connection with the execution in 1312 of Edward's favourite, Piers Gaveston. Londoners now called the political shots, placing the Tower under Edward's younger son, John of Eltham, then 12 years old,[42] and forcing 'the bishops, abbots, priors,

---

[35] *Annales Paulini*, pp. 315–16.
[36] *The Anonimalle Chronicle: 1307–1334, From Brotherton Collection MS 29*, ed. and trans. Wendy R. Childs and John Taylor (Leeds, 1991), pp. 127–9.
[37] *The Chronicle of Lanercost 1272–1346*, trans. Sir Herbert Maxwell (Glasgow, 1913), pp. 251–2.
[38] *Annales Paulini*, pp. 315–16.   [39] Ibid.
[40] Capgrave, *Chronicle of England*, p. 196, who incorrectly dates the revolt to 1324.
[41] Scott L. Waugh, 'Henry of Lancaster, Third Earl of Lancaster', *ODNB*.
[42] *The Chronicle of Lanercost*, pp. 251–2.

earls, barons and other lords of the land to swear to live and die with them in the cause which had now begun'.[43]

Unlike the Barons' War of the 1260s, this dynastic strife that continued after Edward's deposition does not appear to have spread to the lower echelons of burgesses, artisans, workers, and peasants. The Patent Rolls are relatively quiet on the revolt, at least as to how it may have affected lower classes in cities and towns. In 1327, 'bakers, taverners, millers, cooks, poulterers, fishmongers, butchers, brewers, corn-chandlers, and others in the city' 'by day and night' marched through the city of London, armed with swords, clubs, and bucklers, to beat and intimidate citizens. The malefactors may have come largely from the lower echelons of their guilds: the king complained that the misteries of their crafts had been lax in controlling them, and he ordered the mayor to redress the disruptions with corporal punishment.[44] But from the brief description, it is difficult to know whether these artisans and provisioners had any political agenda: were they simply youth gangs out for blood and adventure afforded by the lapse of royal authority? Were there any links between their world of politics and the dynastic crisis swirling above?

From our survey of Patent Rolls, this was the only example at this moment of crisis of heavily armed gangs of guildsmen or their apprentices and journeymen roaming the streets of an English town in pursuit of criminal mischief or political gains. Yet, beyond London, the final crisis of Edward II's reign that led to his deposition and murder spurred on, or at least opened opportunities for, other local riots and incidents that threatened the stability of municipal governments. In 1326, John Lengleyse of Wyrhal [de Englis of Wyram] had been imprisoned for raising troops against the king in the region of Lynn[45] and, according to other documents, had killed the town's mayor.[46] At the same time, a commission was appointed to investigate an uprising in Canterbury, 'touching confederacies and conventicles' that resulted in 'woundings, killings and mutilations of limbs'. But the document does not disclose who the rebels were, or their motives.[47]

The following year, unlawful assemblies of students and violence arose against townsmen in Oxford, and, more seriously, a major political insurrection erupted at Bury. The burgesses laid siege to the monastery and forced the prior and monks to seal a charter of liberties. With neither incident, however, do the Patent Rolls provide evidence that these events were directly tied to warring sides of the royal conflict. Yet again, royal

---

[43] *The Anonimalle Chronicle*, pp. 127–9.   [44] *CPR 1327–30*, p. 185, 1327.xi.8.
[45] *CPR 1324–7*, p. 238, 1326.i.24.   [46] Owen, *The Making of King's Lynn*, p. 40.
[47] *CPR 1324–7*, p. 238, 1326.i.24.

weakness, first with Edward under siege from his queen and her barons, then during the minority of her son (before the prince wrested control from his mother, her lover, and his advisers), opened opportunities for local bitterness and political aims to be pursued. Similarly, protection by one faction in the royal dynasty could allow space for factional ambitions and civil strife to flourish, as at Southampton in 1327, when a faction commanded by the Frost brothers momentarily led a 'genuine popular movement against the ruling faction', attacking the property and ships of several of the town's richest families under cover of protecting the property of the queen mother.[48] With her intervention and the paramour group, charges against the brothers were dropped.

Such opportunities in times of weak kingship and dynastic friction could also swing in the other direction, giving local authorities and royal officers room for exploitation, corruption, and oppression, as appears across towns and counties in Wales in 1327: 'the men of commonalties of Kante Mawr [Cantref Mawr], Cardiganshire, Kanterpenwedyk [Penweddig (Cantref)], Lampeter, Kermerdyn [Carmarthen], and Montgomery' complained 'of oppressions by wardens, sheriffs, constables, chamberlains and other bailiffs and ministers of the late king [Edward II]',[49] now apparently out of control. Finally, and to be discussed later, this crisis set off a wave of burgesses' revolts against ecclesiastical privileges in towns. In addition to the better-known ones at Bury St Edmunds, St Albans, and Abingdon in 1327, townsmen sought charters to extend their rights at Canterbury, Coventry, Plymouth, Dunstable, Barnstaple, and Cirencester.[50]

Further dynastic crises

The baronial revolts in 1263 and 1327 (and perhaps to some extent in 1215–17) galvanized townsmen to join the barons' cause to gain charters of liberties and to overthrow the king. Townsmen were not, however, the prime movers. They were prompted and led by barons, even if London was the principal theatre of violence, at least in two of these revolts against the king. The crisis of Richard II's reign was different in two respects. Firstly, instead of a crisis in a single year or even a single day, as on 15 October 1326, the crisis and discontent with Richard's reign smouldered for almost two decades, from the 1380s to his deposition in 1399 and death early the next year. Secondly, discontent in London ran parallel to the baronial challenges to Richard's throne, first with the

[48] Platt, *Medieval Southampton*, p. 93.   [49] *CPR 1327–30*, p. 72, 1327.ii.15.
[50] David Knowles, *The Religious Orders in England*, 2 vols. (Cambridge, 1950), I, p. 268.

Lords Appellants' rebellion of 1387, which stripped the king of most of his regal powers,[51] then with the attacks and dynastic challenge from his cousin, the Duke of Lancaster's son, Henry of Bolingbroke (Henry IV).[52]

In these dynastic and baronial struggles, however, urban conflict played a less significant role than in the two previous baronial conflicts.[53] The factional conflicts between Northampton and Brembre, complex alliances and strife largely (but not entirely) among victuallers and non-victuallers, were allied to factions within the royal family, first with Richard's uncle, John of Gaunt, and then, fatally for Richard, with John's son, Henry. The fate of London's rival mayors ultimately depended on the dynamics of dynastic power and the mayors' support and protection by leading aristocrats such as Gaunt and the Duke of Gloucester. However, no cause or direction in leadership clearly tied together the two rebellions – urban and dynastic – if indeed there was an urban rebellion at all against Richard. Except for one incident in the countryside and another at the small market town of Bampton in Oxfordshire at the end of Richard's reign (to which none of the chroniclers or the Patent Rolls refer),[54] the only urban theatre of protest

[51] Anthony Goodman, *The Loyal Conspiracy: The Lords Appellant under Richard II* (London, 1971).

[52] See *Chronicles of the Revolution, 1397–1400*.

[53] On the transformation of the role of Londoners in national politics, their reluctance to participate in the martial games of the great magnates, as well as their rebellions against the Crown; see Liddy, *War, Politics, and Finance*, pp. 4–5; C. M. Barron, 'The Later Middle Ages: 1270–1520', in *Historic Towns: Maps and Plans of Towns and Cities in the British Isles, with Historical Commentaries, from Earliest Times to 1800*, ed. M. D. Lobel, 3 vols. (Oxford, 1969–89), III, pp. 44–5. After the Peasants' Revolt, class, and certainly factional strife, intensified in London, but it turned inward, with John of Gaunt and Richard II supporting one faction against the other; see Barron, 'Richard II and London'. Finally, when the merchant elites opposed Lancastrian politics and economic policies on the eve of the Wars of the Roses, they did so by stealth, so much so that it remains difficult for the historian today to map precisely their organizational role; see James L. Bolton, 'The City and the Crown, 1456–61', *London Journal* 12 (1986): 11–24.

[54] See Saul, *Richard II*, pp. 389–90. Prestwich, *Plantagenet England*, p. 470, maintains that Bampton was undoubtedly a village in the early fourteenth century. It does not appear in M. W. Beresford and H. P. R. Finberg, *English Medieval Boroughs: A Hand-List* (Newton Abbot, 1973). With the confusion of government in August 1399, another revolt occurred in Frome, Somerset, recorded by King's Bench, but not by any of our chronicles or Patent Rolls. Townsmen rose against the king's officials and destroyed the Guildhall, 'publicly saying among themselves that they did not wish any longer to be governed or judged there by the laws of England'; cited in Simon Walker, 'Rumour, Sedition and Popular Protest in the Reign of Henry IV' *P&P,* 166 (2000): 49–50. Only two references to Bampton appear in *CPR 1396–9*, both in 1397; neither concerned popular uprising. The Bampton revolt is recorded in several west Oxfordshire court sessions. A case from King's Bench in the same year (*King's Bench*, VII, pp. 94–5) reveals that the rebellion and discontent with Richard ran through villages in Oxfordshire. On Palm Sunday (31 March) 1398, men from several villages assembled

against Richard appears to have been the capital. Unlike the previous two baronial revolts, however, it amounted to little more than the refusal of city rulers to lend the king money. Firstly, in 1387, according to the chronicler Knighton, the king pressured London to raise 'fifty thousand in a short time' (marks or pounds is unclear), to wage war with Scotland. The mayor willingly went forward to the city but 'the greater part of them answered with one voice and mind that they could not and would not go to fight those who were friends of the king and the kingdom'.[55] Exactly who the ones defying the king's wishes were is unclear.

In 1392, the king made further demands for a loan from London. This time street violence erupted, but cannot even be defined as a riot. Certain citizens (the number or magnitude unspecified) assaulted a Lombard, who was willing to lend the sum to the king.[56] During the year, 'crimes against the king' increased in London, with attacks on visitors from the provinces, which Walsingham argued was 'to the detriment of the king'. In the end, the king retaliated, arrested the mayor, the sheriffs, and leading citizens of London, and stripped the city of its liberties. Richard appointed one from his own ranks to govern London, abrogated its laws and ancient charters, and prevented Londoners from electing their mayor.[57] No organized rebellion, not even street action or assemblies of either the previously elected elites or commoners and craftsmen ensued (at least as mentioned by the chroniclers). Instead, on 18 July, the king summoned the former mayor, two ex-sheriffs of London, twenty-four of its last aldermen, and 400 others to Westminster, where they humbly submitted 'their persons and their property to the king'. In return for pardon and restoration of lost liberties, they agreed to pay the Crown £40,000 over the next ten years.[58]

---

at Cockthorpe to assassinate Richard II. One of the leaders, Henry Roper, rode to Burford and other places in Oxfordshire to raise support, was captured, and drawn, hanged, and beheaded; his head was placed on the pillory of Reading, one quarter on the pillory at Colchester, another at Norwich, a third at Northampton, and the fourth at Coventry.

[55] *Knighton's Chronicle 1337–1396*, pp. 406–7.

[56] *The Chronica majora of Thomas Walsingham, 1376–1422*, pp. 286–7.

[57] Ibid. Also see C. M. Barron, 'The Quarrel of Richard II with London 1392–97', *The Reign of Richard II: Essays in Honour of May McKisack*, ed. F. R. H. Du Boulay and C. M. Barron (London, 1971), pp. 173–201. The city was initially fined £100,000, but Richard cancelled it when he restored London's liberties on 19 September 1392; for their refusal to meet Richard's request in 1392, Barron estimates that the city ended by paying around £30,000 from 1392 to 1397 (ibid., p. 200); Barron, 'The Later Middle Ages', pp. 42–3.

[58] *The Westminster Chronicle*, p. 503. Also, Capgrave, *Chronicle of England*, p. 254; and Saul, *Richard II*, pp. 235 and 259.

During the rebellion of 1399, the chroniclers also report little street action in London, or in other towns. Unlike earlier baronial revolts, especially in 1263 and 1326, the deposition of Richard was the work of magnates and their retinues without significant urban support either from organized militias led by mayors, their constables, and aldermen or from popular protest. Only resentment and mumbling now seep from the records. Writing a generation after the events, John Capgrave alleged that during Richard's last year of rule, he borrowed heavily from men of the city without repayment. Further, he threatened any accused of the slightest derogatory word against him with punishment without mercy, no matter the social rank: 'And this mad the puple to hate the Kyng, and caused gret murmour in the puple.'[59] Thomas Walsingham hints that the lower orders ('plebe') may have been hatching secret conspiracies to murder the king, 'because of their hatred' for him; if so, these failed to materialize even to the point of being flushed out by Richard's spies.[60] The French chronicler of *La traïson et mort de Richart* went further, claiming that Henry of Lancaster circulated a 'hundred and fifty pairs of letters' among 'the good towns of the realm'. Allegedly, aldermen of towns then assembled the people and read the letters to them (in London to grandees as well as the poor, 'petiz 't grans') 'falsely railing [them], by different artful fabrications against King Richard and his government'. These stirred the people 'never to mention the king's name' but also, according to the French chronicler, to action: they then murdered royal servants and officers, 'wherever they could be found'.[61] But, according to the more reliable eye-witness account of the French chronicler in verse, Jean Creton, such stirrings surfaced only after Henry had deposed Richard and had 'ceremoniously and triumphantly enter[ed] the city': only then did Londoners come out in force to cheer him on and call for their former king's beheading:

Thus the commons and the rabble of London took their king to Westminster, and the duke made a turn about the city to enter by the chief gate of London, to the end that he might pass through the great street, that they call Cheap-street. He entered the city at the hour of vespers, and came to Saint Paul's. There the people shouted after him through the streets,

[59] Capgrave, *Chronicle of England*, p. 269.   [60] *Annales Ricardi Secundi*, p. 248.

[61] *Chronique de la traïson et mort de Richart deux roy dengleterre*, ed. Benjamin Williams, English Historical Society (London, 1846), pp. 35–40 and 180–2. According to Gransden, *Historical Writing*, II, p. 162, the *Traïson* relied on Creton and has 'little source-value to the historian today'.

'Long live the good Duke of Lancaster', and blessed him in their language with great shew of joy and pleasure.[62]

The mayor and commoners of St Albans also greeted the new king with great fanfare, gathering 'five or six miles' outside their town. 'Clad, each trade by itself, in different garments, drawn up in rows and armed', they assembled to meet Duke Henry 'with a great quantity of instruments and of trumpets, shewing great joy and satisfaction ... shouting, in their language, with a loud and fearful voice, "Long live the good Duke of Lancaster"'.[63]

Henry was not, however, everywhere so eagerly received. Travelling through the Welsh marches and mountains to Coventry in 1400, his English followers met with resistance and their lodgings 'sometimes' set on fire, fanning the flames of a Welsh rebellion against English domination; this rebellion, that of Owain Glyn Dŵr, would continue through the following decade.[64] Moreover, perhaps more in smaller towns than in London, not all had been so happy with Richard's demise and Bolingbroke's rise. Walsingham tells the story within his county of Hertfordshire of a conspiracy to kill Henry on 14 May 1402 (exactly where and by whom is left vague). Rumours spread that Richard was still alive, soon to come out of hiding to reward those who had stayed loyal.[65] The plot was revealed at the Hertfordshire town of Ware, when a priest was captured in possession of a list of those who had supposedly planned or supported the plot. He later confessed that the names of those who he thought might want to kill the king came from his head. Many of the suspects were released, but the priest was drawn and

---

[62] *Translation of a French Metrical History of the Deposition of King Richard the Second* [Creton's metrical history], ed. John Webb, in *Archaeologia: Miscellaneous Tracts Relating to Antiquity*, Society of Antiquarians of London, XX (1824), p. 180.

[63] Ibid., p. 178.

[64] 'The duke set out from Lichfield, and rode on with all his host till he came to Coventry, which is a very good city; but, before he could come there, the Welsh did him much harm and despite, and slew and robbed a great number of his people; sometimes they came to set fire to the lodgings of the English: and, certes, I was right glad of it' (ibid., p. 177). The origins of the conflict go back to a territorial dispute over succession in 1388; harsh fiscal policies, limited possibilities for Welshmen to advance in local government or within the Church, and resentment against the privileges of English settlers brought unity among the Welsh gentry and populace against the Crown. See Llinos Smith, 'Glyn Dŵr', *ODNB* (2008); Davies, *The Age of Conquest*, pp. 443–59; and Davies, *The Revolt of Owain Glyn Dŵr*.

[65] On the legends and rumours of Richard's survival after 1400, see Peter McNiven, 'Rebellion, Sedition, and the Legend of Richard II's Survival in the Reigns of Henry IV and Henry V', *BJRL*, 76 (1994): 93–117; and Walker, 'Rumour, Sedition and Popular Protest', pp. 32–6, supplies examples of those spreading rumours, speaking badly of Henry, and predicting a short reign: a group of Welsh clerks at Oxford gave the new king only two years in 1401.

hanged.[66] Even in London, not all were content with the new king. In 1402, eight Minorite Friars were found guilty and 'indecorously' executed, dragged through the streets, hanged, then decapitated. The brief annalist entry does not explain the friars' reasons for opposing Henry or whether their cause was linked to Londoners' or any secular community's grievances against him.[67]

Furthermore, Patent Rolls show that tensions between Yorkists and Lancastrians sparked wider discontent and political insurrection than was revealed in the chronicles. To be sure, the epicentre was Wales and the Welsh marches with Owain Glyn Dŵr, who from 1400 to 1409 proclaimed himself Prince of Wales. Royal commissions of inquiry chronicle the ebb and flow of that long rebellion from Aberystwyth on the West coast to the Brecon hills in the centre-south, to Glyn, Olghan [Olchon], and Stradewy [Ystrad Tywi] in southern Wales and into England,[68] penetrating southward to Gloucestershire[69] and eastward to Chester. In 1400, the king granted a general pardon to 'all the king's lieges in the county of Chester' – previously Richard's stronghold – for 'all treasons, insurrections, felonies, rebellions and trespasses committed by them from Christmas last to the Purification [2 February, 1400]'. However, a long list of 125 men were exempted from the pardon and remained charged with 'insurrection'. These covered a wide range of professions – five servants, three tailors, two glovers, two goldsmiths, three chaplains, a shipman, a cook, a leche (one who cures or leeches patients for a physician), a skinner, and a flecher (an arrow maker or occasionally a butcher), a coke (cook), a smith, a corviser (cobbler), and three knights (chevalier). Many of these may have been urban commoners, and none was identified as a ploughman, husbandman, bondman, or tiller of the soil.[70] If this revolt was linked to an earlier one in 1393 against the dukes of Lancaster and Gloucester, and the Earl of Derby, it was not made explicit.[71]

---

[66] Walsingham, *The St Albans Chronicle*, II, pp. 316–18.

[67] Ibid., II, pp. 318–19. For the large proportion of clerics involved in conspiracies against Henry IV from 1401 to 1404, especially Franciscans, who were often the ringleaders, see McNiven, 'Rebellion, Sedition', pp. 95–101.

[68] See for instance *CPR 1401–5*, p. 11, 1401.xi.9, p. 22, 1401.xi.23 for North Wales and ibid., pp. 137 and 139, 1402.vii.23 and vii.28 and *CPR 1405–8*, p. 65, 1405.v. for the Brecon hills.

[69] *CPR 1399–1401*, pp. 313 and 357, 1400.v.21 and ix.19.

[70] Ibid., pp. 285–6, 1400.v.22.

[71] For the 1393 revolt, see *Annales Ricardi Secundi*, pp. 159–60; McNiven, 'The Cheshire Rising of 1400', p. 379, especially note 4, and p. 382; Laughton, 'Economy and Society', p. 56; and below, p. 322.

In 1402, the Crown arrested and brought to the Tower of London 'some of the king's subjects' (probably in Cornwall, given that its sheriff and escheator was commissioned to make the arrests). These rebels had attempted 'to subvert the laws and customs and good government of the realm', by telling 'many lies in divers parts of the realm in taverns and other congregations of the people, preaching among other things that the king has not kept his promises made at his advent into the realm and at his Coronation'.[72] A year later, a pardon was offered to twenty-two men, including a knight and six parsons but excluding the mayor and other townsmen of Chester. According to the remission, 'all the people of the town of Chester', including the ecclesiastics, had been present at the battle outside Shrewsbury, had joined the forces of Henry Percy, son of the Earl of Northumberland, and had rebelled against the king.[73] In November, the king offered the mayor and 'commonalty' of Chester a second pardon for their insurrections against him. This time, however, the pardon was in fact a stiff fine either of 800 marks or the expenses to finance the shipping of his soldiers to free the castle of Beaumaris ('Beaumareys') on Angelsey.[74]

At the same time, the rebellion against the king raged in the northeast. Henry ordered all the knights, esquires, and yeomen of Lancashire to go to Northumberland to fight Percy, the rebels, and the king's enemies in Scotland.[75] By 1405 revolt had spread to York, with Archbishop Richard Scrope leading the clergy, lesser burgesses, and greater ones against the king and his taxes. As we shall see, the chronicles devoted far more attention to this revolt; perhaps no other popular rebel of the late Middle Ages has received as much notice as Scrope, Wat Tyler and John Ball included.[76] The king ordered the mayor of York (William Frost, a supporter of Henry IV and who had been in power before the uprising)[77] to confiscate all the property of the archbishop and established a commission to arrest and prosecute those involved in 'all treasons,

---

[72] *CPR 1401–5*, p. 126, 1402.v.11.
[73] Ibid., p. 264, 1403.ix.27. On the 1403 rising, see Peter McNiven, 'The Cheshire Rising of 1400', pp. 393–4, but this has been seen as a revolt of the Palatinate and the gentry in Hotspur's (Henry Percy's) army against Henry IV, and not as an urban revolt.
[74] *CPR 1401–5*, p. 330, 1403.xi.3.   [75] Ibid., p. 292, 1403.vii.27.
[76] See for instance Simon Walker, 'The Yorkshire Risings of 1405: Texts and Contexts', in *Henry IV: The Establishment of the Regime, 1399–1406*, ed. Gwilym Dodd and Douglas Biggs (Woodbridge, 2003), pp. 161–84; *Richard Scrope: Archbishop, Rebel, Martyr*, ed. P. J. P. Goldberg (Donington, 2007); Danna Piroyansky, *Martyrs in the Making: Political Martyrdom in Late Medieval England* (Basingstoke, 2008), pp. 49–73; and other titles consulted below.
[77] See Christian Liddy, 'William Frost, the City of York and Scrope's Rebellion of 1405', pp. 64–85, in *Richard Scrope, Archbishop, Rebel, Martyr*, ed. P. J. P. Goldberg (Donington, 2007), p. 83.

insurrections, rebellions, and felonies within the entire realm'.[78] By 1406, insurrections erupted in Cornwall[79] and at Lynn and its suburbs.[80] In 1408, the king demanded that the chancellor of the University of Oxford, his lieutenants, along with the mayor and bailiffs of the town, interrogate, arrest, and punish students from Ireland, who 'under colour of studying at the university', were acting as spies, revealing 'secrets of the realm' and reporting them back to Ireland either by letter or by returning to Ireland in person.[81] In the same year, insurrection against the king spread to Thetford in Norfolk (though the reasons for it are not stated).[82]

Certainly, not all these revolts were interconnected beyond a common milieu of uncertainties, political intrigues, and treachery opened by various challenges to the throne. Nonetheless, Simon Walker has concluded: 'All over the country during the early years of Henry IV's reign, groups and individuals freely expressed their dissatisfaction with the rule of the new king.'[83] By the end of the Welsh rebellions in 1409, unrest continued to spill eastward, down the Welsh hills into Gloucestershire. At the beginning of that year, the king granted a pardon to a weaver of Cirencester, because of 'the love which he bears towards the king's person' and his recent service at Cirencester 'against the rebels'. He had been indicted for various felonies in pursuit of the king's enemies in Gloucestershire. Perhaps he had fought on both sides, being pardoned also 'for all treasons, insurrections, rebellions, misprisions, robberies, trespasses and felonies committed by him'.[84]

Revolts against weak kings

Baronial challenges did not form the only crucible for urban revolt against the king in late medieval England. But most of them occurred during crises or periods of weakness, much more so than on the

---

[78] *CPR 1405–8*, p. 66, 1405.v.31. The revolt is further described in a pardon of 2 August 1408 to Nicholas Tempest, esquire, who had fought with the archbishop at Shipton Moor outside York and afterwards at Bramham near Tadcaster 'in the company of Henry, late earl of Northumberland'; ibid., p. 463.

[79] Ibid., p. 152, 1406.i.8.   [80] Ibid., p. 152, 1406.ii.7.

[81] Ibid., p. 482, 1408.vii.26. McNiven, 'Rebellion, Sedition', p. 101, shows that Welsh students at Oxford and Cambridge in 1401 and 1402 had returned to Wales to join the rebellion, and in 1402, Oxford's chancellor was instructed to investigate Welsh students, who allegedly 'assemble nightly for the purpose of rebellion'. This inquiry was followed by another headed by Oxford's sheriff to investigate treasons in town committed by Welshmen.

[82] *CPR 1408–13*, p. 65, 1408.xi.26.

[83] Walker, 'Rumour, Sedition and Popular Protest', p. 32.

[84] *CPR 1408–13*, p. 52, 1409.ii.14.

Continent, where another model of revolt was prevalent. In addition to cracks in the ruling order (as with the Revolt of the Ciompi) and periods of uncertainty with ailing kings and the transmission of power to sons in their minority (as with the Jacquerie), aggressive kingship bent on territorial aggrandizement, stripping customary rights of territories and cities, and imposing new forms of taxation also ignited revolt. In fact, several of the most significant and widespread rebellions of the Middle Ages were the consequence of aggressive royal policy, as with Philip le Bel's enterprises in 1297 to 1304, abrogating the virtual autonomy and authority of the Count of Flanders, the imposition of new taxes on commoners in towns and the countryside, as well as imposing new taxes across France without the consent of the three estates in the second decade of the fourteenth century.[85] Similarly, Florence's legal incursions and aggressive fiscal policies against mountain folk along the northern periphery of its territorial state led to waves of successful tax rebellions and defections to Florence's enemies at the beginning of the fifteenth century.[86] By contrast, the actions of strong and aggressive kings such as Edward I and III failed to provoke revolt from below. Popular turmoil during Edward III's reign came instead at two short moments, during the economic and ecological crisis on the eve of the Black Death and in the last fourteen months of his life, when, stricken by illness, he had in fact become a weak king under the spell of certain courtiers and his mistress, Alice Perrers, who formed 'a court covin', embezzled royal resources, and had gained the upper hand.[87] The last months of his life in 1377, along with the transition of power to his 10-year-old grandson Richard, gave rise to mounting civil tensions, created in part by Edward's son, John of Gaunt. His crass alienation of the London population,[88]

[85] The literature on this, as well as the second revolt of Flanders, 1323–7, is extensive: aggressive actions by French kings sparked both; for the second one, the Count of Flanders was allied with the king; for this literature, see Dumolyn and Haemers, 'Patterns of Urban Rebellion'.

[86] Cohn, *Creating the Florentine State*.

[87] Ormrod, *The Reign of Edward III*, p. 117; and Ormrod, *Edward III*, pp. 464–5, 496, 524. This court covin, but especially his mistress, had gained influence over the king as early as the late 1360s with his 'increasing withdrawal into a semi-private existence' (Ormrod, *Edward III*, p. 497). Their corruption provoked reprisals against them, even if these were short-lived, during the trials of the Good Parliament of 1376 (ibid., pp. 496, 534–5). Shortly thereafter, however, their dominance became pronounced during the king's last days of bedridden incapacity. Historians have alleged that Edward was not only ill during his last fourteen months of life but that he also suffered from dementia. Ormrod argues that this has been a presumption of modern historians that finds no evidence in the surviving contemporary sources (ibid., p. 530).

[88] Anthony Goodman, *John of Gaunt: The Exercise of Princely Power in Fourteenth-Century Europe* (Harlow, 1992), pp. 60–2.

corruption of the court, and the circumstances of weak and divided kingship set the stage for the most radical and widespread revolts in England during the Middle Ages, the so-called Peasants' Revolt that reverberated throughout English cities and towns – London, St Albans, Bury St Edmunds, Cambridge, Norwich, Beverley, Scarborough, York, Shrewsbury, Yarmouth, Winchester, Bridgwater, Lynn,[89] and others. All had their own particular antagonisms, class alliances, and cleavages and were not all triggered by the peasant and small-town movements in Kent and Essex of late May and June 1381. Many preceded them that year, as at Shrewsbury, York, Bridgwater, St Albans, and possibly Gloucester and Winchester,[90] or earlier still, originating in 1377.

Historians of the Peasants' Revolt have marked 1377 as a critical year of mounting tensions: the legislation and collection of the first poll tax (which in fact was collected effectively and without great protest)[91] and for rural uprisings, especially in the southwest.[92] Indeed, 1377 may have been a watershed: perhaps for the first time in English social history, peasant protest against their lords now reached beyond single

---

[89] Réville, *Le Soulèvement*, pp. 95–7.

[90] On the conflicts in Shrewsbury and Gloucester, see Holt, 'Gloucester', p. 154. By the middle of July, bailiffs and other prominent townsmen protested against the Crown and were prosecuted. Their grievances are not known, but Holt speculates that they may have revolved around long-standing resentment against the town's royal castle (pp. 154–5); also see Richard C. Holt, 'Thomas of Woodstock and Events at Gloucester in 1381', *BIHR*, 58 (1985): 237–42. Although the major revolt at Winchester occurred in June in tandem with events in Kent, Essex, and London, class tensions and unlawful assemblies had already arisen in 1380; Hinck, 'The Rising of 1381 in Winchester', p. 125.

[91] Only with the third poll tax did the receipts fall off dramatically and did incidents arise such as those in Essex, with John Legge's methods for determining the virginity of young girls and the legend (or fact) of the abuse of Wat Tyler's, John Tyler's, or Jack Straw's daughter on the eve of the revolt; see Lister M. Matheson, 'The Peasants' Revolt through Five Centuries of Rumour and Reporting: Richard Fox, John Stow, and their Successors', *Studies in Philology* 95 (1998): 121–51.

[92] Rosamond Faith, 'The "Great Rumour" of 1377 and Peasant Ideology', in *The English Rising*, pp. 43–73; G. L. Harriss, *Shaping the Nation: England 1360–1461* (Oxford, 2005), pp. 227–29; Elizabeth Hallam, *Domesday Book through Nine Centuries* (London, 1986), pp. 102–4; Miriam Müller, 'The Aims and Organisation of a Peasant Revolt in Early Fourteenth-Century Wiltshire', *Rural History*, 14 (2003), 1–20; Zvi Razi, 'The Struggles between the Abbots of Halesowen and their Tenants in the Thirteenth and Fourteenth Centuries', in *Social Relations and Ideas: Essays in Honour of R. H. Hilton*, ed. Trevor H. Aston, Peter Coss, Christopher Dyer, and Joan Thirsk (Cambridge, 1983), pp. 151–67; Peter Franklin, 'Politics in Manorial Court Rolls: The Tactics, Social Composition, and Aims of a Pre-1381 Peasant Movement', in *Medieval Society and the Manor Court*, ed. Zvi Razi and Richard Smith (Oxford, 1996), pp. 162–98; and Paul V. Hargreaves, 'Seignorial Reaction and Peasant Responses: Worcester Priory and its Peasants after the Black Death', *Midland History*, 24 (1999), 53–78. I thank Miriam Müller for references.

manors or single landlords, to spread across county lines, uniting numerous villages in struggles against multiple lords.[93]

1377 was also a serious year of troubles and perhaps equally a watershed for urban strife in England, at least in the capital. Unfortunately, only one chronicler concentrated on these urban protests – St Albans' Walsingham (although in various recensions, with additions by other authors of his priory).[94] These protests were not only attacks on the Crown and royal policy; they focused on the dignity and ancient liberties of the city against threats by those acting in the king's name during his last days of illness – the king's son, John of Gaunt, Gaunt's brother, Lord Thomas Woodcock, and Lord Henry Percy. The trial of John Wycliffe heightened tensions between Gaunt and Percy on one side, and the city on the other. Wycliffe's defence by Percy against the examination and doctrinal attacks by London's bishop led to heated debate, accusations, and taunts between the bishop and Percy that began with ceremonial protocol – whether Wycliffe had the right to sit, or whether he should stand during his trial. Tensions escalated when John of Gaunt joined the fray. Frustrated by not being able to control matters, he added to the insults against the bishop, 'swearing that he would break not only the bishop's arrogance but that of all the bishops of England', whispering to Percy (at least according to Walsingham's probable invented aside): '"I'd like to grab him by the hair and drag him out of the church, instead of having to put up with such talk"'. Word of these threats incensed Londoners, who 'raised a great clamour, swearing not to allow such an outrage to be inflicted upon their bishop; they would sooner lose their lives than see their bishop so dishonoured in the church and dragged from it with such violence'.[95] Gaunt's insults against their bishop were not the only factor provoking their ire. The duke had already piqued their fury in Parliament the day before [19 February].[96] In the name of the king, Percy, and Thomas of Woodcock, he petitioned to strip

---

[93] See Cohn, 'Revolts of the Late Middle Ages', pp. 276–7. Even the widespread peasant and small-town insurrections in the region of Canterbury in 1318 focused on a single landlord, St Augustine's Abbey of Canterbury.

[94] Walsingham was hardly an unbiased source, especially given his hatred of Gaunt for supporting Wycliffe and insulting the Bishop of London. Ironically, in 1377, in contrast to his venom against the rebels in 1381, he expressed sympathy with the London insurgents, given their loyalty to their bishop and attacks on Gaunt; Walsingham, *Historia Anglicana*, I, pp. 324–5.

[95] Walsingham, *The St Albans Chronicle*, I, pp. 82–4. Before the trial, animosity between Gaunt and the bishop already ran high because of Gaunt's radical anti-clericalism and attempts to tax the clergy in 1377; see Goodman, *John of Gaunt*, p. 60; and Saul, *Richard II*, p. 21.

[96] See Goodman, *John of Gaunt*, p. 60.

Londoners of their rights to elect their mayor, proposed a royal captain to be appointed in his place, and threatened their powers to arrest criminals within the city's jurisdiction; henceforth that authority would pass on to a marshal of England.[97]

The following day, London's grandees summoned a meeting to discuss the treatment of their bishop and threats to their liberties.[98] Roused by a speech by one of these oligarchs, they seized arms, rushed to the marshal's house, broke its doors, and freed the prisoner Sir Peter de la Mare, whom the citizens argued had been unjustly imprisoned, and burnt the wood to which his feet had been bound.[99] Armed bands roamed the city, seeking to punish Lord Percy for his insults and threats. They searched the bedrooms of his palace, 'piercing beds with their lances', investigating even the lavatories, but without success. Afterwards, with 'great haste' they ran to the duke's palace of Savoy, hoping to find Percy and other enemies. According to Walsingham and a continuator of Higden, had the bishop not intervened, the rebels would have done what the London artisans and peasants accomplished four years later, the burning of the Savoy.[100]

The crowd continued with counter-insults against Gaunt and his men, reversing his coat of arms in a main street, on the doors of St Paul's, and at Westminster Hall, signifying that the duke was a traitor. Further, they circulated bills alleging that he was not Edward's son but sired by a Ghent butcher, whose boy had been substituted for a dead royal infant.[101] Others wrote verse slandering the duke, which they posted in

[97] See Ormrod, *The Reign of Edward III*, p. 175; Bird, *The Turbulent London*, p. 25; Pamela Nightingale, 'Capitalists, Crafts and Constitutional Change in Late Fourteenth-Century London', *P&P*, 124 (1989): 21 and 24. The dispute was not resolved during Edward's life, but spilled into Richard's business with a delegation from London headed by John Philpot; see Christian Liddy, 'The Rhetoric of the Royal Chamber in Late Medieval London, York and Coventry', *UH* 29 (2002): 330–1.

[98] Walsingham, *The St Albans Chronicle*, I, pp. 84–93.

[99] Sir Peter, a knight, representative for Herefordshire and steward of the Earl of March, was the 'hero' of the Good Parliament of 1377 and spokesman for the Commons in their negotiations with the Lords; Holmes, *The Good Parliament*, 101–5. He was imprisoned for his courageous protests against the royal court, the only one from the Good Parliament the courtiers succeeded in arresting (ibid., p. 183). On his leadership of the Good Parliament and fate during the closing months of Edward III's reign, see Ormrod, *Edward III*, pp. 553, 567, 585.

[100] 'Continuation of the English Translation', pp. 444–5. According to Walsingham, *The St Albans Chronicle*, I, pp. 90–1, the bishop cautioned them to be mindful 'of that very sacred time – for it was Lent ... lest they defile that sacred time with their civil strife'.

[101] Goodman, *John of Gaunt*, p. 61; *Chronicon Angliae*, pp. 121–6, 126–9, and 131–4. Supposedly, the Bishop of Winchester concocted the rumour and spread it a year earlier, to prevent Gaunt from becoming king; Walsingham, *The St Albans Chronicle*, I, pp. 60–1. It was a story that died hard: a generation later (19 March 1402), a tailor's

different places around the city to damage his name and stir up 'the people's anger'.[102] More violence erupted when one of the duke's knights, Sir Thomas Swinton, a Scot, wishing to curry his favour went on horseback fully armed through the streets in contempt of the citizens, wearing round his neck the duke's badge [*signum ducis*]. He was pulled from his horse, the badge ripped violently from his neck. As a consequence, Walsingham claimed, fashion changed:

for those whom the duke had presented with these badges, whose arrogance the earth could scarcely support, were now thoroughly humiliated: they tore from their necks the chains which they had received from the duke and hid them in their sleeves or gauntlets; these were the badges through which they had believed they could gain riches before heaven and earth. But now the tables had been turned, and those very badges which had previously made them renowned and terrifying, made them men who were despised and mistrusted.[103]

The insults cut to the bone, to which the duke responded with draconian punishments, asking the bishops to excommunicate those who had written and posted the verses. According to Walsingham, these threats split the city: the citizens 'wished to show some regard for the duke, urged the bishops to do what he wanted. They did this to make it clear that they had no hand at all in such actions.' The London magnates and greater citizens went further, wishing to dissociate themselves from the commoners, claiming in a secret meeting before the king that they had not conspired against the duke: the insults happened without their knowledge or assent. The king advised them to have a candle made with the duke's arms inscribed and to carry it in a solemn procession to St Paul's to be burnt perpetually before the image of the Virgin at the city's expense. The candle was made, and a town crier summoned the people. But 'the common people, and in fact all the people among the lower ranks', refused to take part; the city magnates alone participated.

---

wife from a village near Baldock in South Wales allegedly tried to incite resistance against the new king, Henry IV, and to support Owain Glyn Dŵr as the legal prince of Wales and Cornwall. She now spread the story against Henry's father against the son, claiming that Henry was not 'the rightful king' but instead born to a butcher of Ghent; *King's Bench*, VII, pp. 123–4. I thank Paul Strohm for the second reference.

[102] Walsingham, *The St Albans Chronicle*, I, pp. 98–9. On casting of bills and scandalous verse, see Wendy Scase, '"Strange and Wonderful Bills": Bill-Casting and Political Discourse in Late Medieval England', in *New Medieval Literatures*, 2, ed. Rita Copeland, David Lawton, and Wendy Scase (Oxford, 1998), p. 240; and Christian Liddy, 'Bill Casting and Political Communication: A Public Sphere in Late Medieval Towns?', in *La gobernanza de la ciudad europea en la Edad Media*, ed. Jesús Ángel Solórzano Telechea and Beatriz Arízaga Bolumburu (Logroño, 2011), pp. 447–61.

[103] Walsingham, *The St Albans Chronicle*, I, pp. 92–3. Also, Holmes, *The Good Parliament*, p. 190.

The duke, however, was unimpressed: he said the procession instead brought him greater dishonour by displaying his arms in a funerary fashion 'when he was healthy, unscathed and still alive'.[104] Finally, the duke petitioned in Parliament to replace the mayor, sheriffs, and aldermen with newly elected officials and sentence to death those responsible for reversing his arms. Commons agreed only to the change of officials.[105]

As was often the case, chroniclers – the majority of whom were attached, or close, to the court, or from London and its environs, as with the chroniclers of St Albans – focused their attention on the capital. The Patent Rolls, however, show that unrest had spread through the realm during Edward's last year. Disturbances touched a number of counties, towns, and cities that turned on different causes but amounted to another period of heightened unrest in towns, as well as in the countryside. Thanks to the work of Rosamond Faith, Rodney Hilton, and more recently, Miriam Müller, these have come to light in the countryside, but less so in towns. Tensions mounted in both places, even in communities not to explode in 1381. Early in 1377, a split within the University of Oxford over 'certain graces, dispensations and reconciliations' gave rise to 'illicit conventicles, dissensions and discords' in the town: students were terrorized, and the university called the king 'to impose silence'.[106] In June, an 'alliance' of burgesses in Lynn comprised largely of artisans (two tailors, a mercer, a saddler, a glove maker, and a skinner of the twenty-three persons identified by the commission) assaulted their overlord, the Bishop of Norfolk, tried to kill him, butchered twenty of his horses, assaulted his men and servants, and besieged the priory of St Margaret, where the bishop had taken refuge.[107]

The Patent Rolls also reveal further disturbances in the countryside. In September, tenants across Wiltshire and Hampshire confederated and presented their lords with letters patent, 'showing certificates of extracts from Domesday Book', which they claimed released them from services 'due to their lords from time immemorial'. A commission was appointed to arrest the tenants and compel them to find security for good behaviour, 'and if they refuse, to commit them to the nearest gaol'.[108] Other tenants at Christian Malford, Kintbury, and Elendune (possibly Wroughton) had thought of the same, requesting from the

---

[104] Walsingham, *The St Albans Chronicle*, I, pp. 105–7. In addition, the citizens were to erect a marble pillar in the middle of Cheapside with Gaunt's arms on it; Goodman, *John of Gaunt*, p. 61. It is not clear whether it was built, or how John of Gaunt reacted to this plaintive act.

[105] Ibid., *John of Gaunt*, p. 61.   [106] *CPR 1374–77*, pp. 491–2, 1377.ii.26.

[107] Ibid, p. 502, 1377.vi.16. Also, Owen, *The Making of King's Lynn*, p. 36.

[108] *CPR 1377–81*, p. 50, 1377.ix.1.

king's chancery certificates based on extracts from Domesday concerning the lands they toiled, which were owned by Glastonbury Abbey (Wiltshire), Amesbury Abbey (Berkshire), and the Bishop of Winchester.[109] The records do not suggest, however, that they went as far as other tenants in Wiltshire, or those of the county of Southampton, in refusing to work, based on these certificates.

The following year, men of Chichester, led by their mayor, Walter Ouyng, assaulted the under-sheriff of Sussex and his men and prevented the sheriff, his bailiffs, and the king's bailiff from holding the king's court in the city.[110] In July, 'citizens and other inhabitants of the city and suburbs' of Canterbury 'assembled in great numbers and stirred up strife, debates and contentions'. As in Chichester they refused to submit to the king's justice and 'combine[d] by insurrection to resist the king's ministers in the execution of their office, and the said bailiffs'. A royal commission was to hold a hearing to ascertain who the 'malefactors' were and to arrest and imprison them.[111] In the summer two revolts flared in Coventry, which may have been related. The first in July possessed a carnivalesque air. Certain unspecified 'malefactors' assembled 'the commonalty ... and with minstrels went in procession (*modo pomposo*) to the mayor's house'. Against his will, they forced him to accompany them to the fields of Ralph Hunte, where they broke his enclosures, 'threw down the dykes of several fields', carried away his trees, timber, and underwood, and forced others of the town to pay fees at fixed terms 'for maintaining their malice'.[112] A little over three weeks later another commission was charged to investigate further insurrections in town, this time directly against the king, petitioned by the king's clerk and the same Ralph Hunte whose enclosures had been broken a month earlier. No mention, however, was made to the previous event. Instead, as with the revolts a year before at Canterbury and Chichester, the commonalty of Coventry had disrupted 'the king's business in divers courts ... so that they [the king's officers] go in fear of various commoners in the town'. Perhaps this judicial 'business' regarded Ralph Hunte's fields and the damages he had suffered earlier at the hands of the commonalty. If so, the town's guilds may have been the organizational base of both revolts. The commission resolved that 'four of the better sort of every mistery in town give security under a heavy penalty for the good behaviour of all of their mistery, their men and servants', and certified before Michaelmas (29 September).[113]

---

[109] Ibid., p. 15, 1377.viii.5 and 1377.viii.10.   [110] Ibid., p. 252, 1378.v.30.
[111] Ibid, p. 304, 1378.vii.16.   [112] Ibid., p. 303, 1378.vii.20.
[113] Ibid., pp. 305–6, 1378.viii.15.

Less emerges from the records the following year. In Boston, 'certain persons' with ladders scaled the walls of the Friar Preachers, broke their doors and windows, assaulted the prior and the friars in their beds, and, when the town's bells were rung, assaulted the constables, resisted arrest, and carted off the prior's property.[114] As with so many of the incidents examined by 'oyer et terminer' commissions, it is often difficult to know whether the unrest had political connotations over competing rights and liberties, or was simply opportunistic crime, or to know who those 'certain persons' may have been. In 1380, however, unrest with clearer political ends and resistance to the Crown mounted again. In January, Parliament complained that 'commons of the realm have fallen into utter destitution by reason of the multiple payments of tenths, fifteenths, and other subsidies and from other causes'. A commission was appointed to investigate the 'condition of the realm, the conduct of the king's officers and ministers, the state of his revenues, the fees paid to the king's officers and other expenses of the household'.[115] In February the king suffered a further affront when across the counties of York, Lancaster, Westmorland, and Cumberland, certain men, 'religious as well as others', refused to grant alms of a 'thrave of corn yearly from every plough' to the hospital of St Leonard in York, which the kings of England had founded and which continued to be the special patronage of the current king.[116] In the same month, twenty-one men (including a carpenter and a vicar) assaulted the sheriff of Lincoln, when he was holding his court at Caister-on-Sea.[117]

In November, yet another commission heard the complaints of 'the mayor and good men of the town of Shrewsbury'. As we will see, it was one of the few struggles, especially outside the principal cities and towns of England, to witness a clear split between 'the more sufficient men of the town' and 'men of less sufficiency'.[118] Finally, in the same month, a factional dispute erupted in York. It concerned possibly another split between 'sufficient' and lesser citizens, with the latter contesting the election of John de Gysburn, who, according to Parliament, had been duly elected. 'Certain evildoers' assembled, chased Gysburn from town,

---

[114] Ibid., p. 421, 1379.xi.10.

[115] Ibid. p. 459. The Patent Roll dated 2 March 1380 refers to 'the present parliament', which was in January; also see *PROME*, Richard II, January 1380, membranes no. 8, item 15.

[116] *CPR 1377–81*, p. 465, 1380.ii.18.

[117] Ibid., p. 467, 1380.ii.20. See Map 2. Also, further resistance erupted in the countryside: in November, bondmen at the manor of Strixton in Northamptonshire withdrew their services and 'assembled and confederated together by oath' against their landlord; ibid., p. 578, 1380.xi.24.

[118] Ibid., p. 579, 1380.xi.24. Also see Holt, 'Gloucester', p. 154.

and with axes attacked and entered the Guildhall, where they chose Simon de Quixley, supposedly against his will, to be mayor. They then 'compelled many good men of the city by threats to recognise him', drew up their own ordinances 'to the subversion of good government', and commanded the citizenry to assembly and agree to the ordinances 'when the bells on the bridge of York should ring backward (aukeward)'.[119] According to other documents, however, this conflict had been brewing for much longer, and with a more distinctive class dimension. The commoners had chosen Quixley, an export merchant, little different in social and economic background from Gysburn, as leader. However, the rank-and-file, who chased Gysburn from office, were staffed and led by butchers and demanded greater representation for commoners beneath the ranks of the international merchants currently in charge. Government corruption and a new tax, the 'schamel toll' (a penny a week), on butchers had brought these artisans and provisioners into the streets. The causes of these disturbances at York were similar to those that would spark widespread rebellion six months later with the Peasants' Revolt, especially in towns, increased taxes, financial policy, governmental abuse, and the desire to extend citizens' liberties.[120]

In 1381, tensions surfaced in early February in the first of the revolt's two epicentres, Kent, suggesting already some passive resistance to the new taxes. To establish the tax lists for the new subsidy, Kent's sheriff was ordered to record 'the number, names, abode and condition of all laypersons in that county over the age of fifteen, men, women, and servants' and was given power to arrest and imprison 'the disobedient'.[121] The same provisions were then made for other counties of England.[122] In March, the tensions between haves and have-nots in Shrewsbury and the elections of new bailiffs by those without property either was re-examined by a new commission, or new tensions between the two classes arose: the lesser men, now labelled 'those who have no lands or tenements', again elected their own bailiffs against the official elections by 'their betters'.[123]

In summary, the crisis of the transition of power from the once powerful but now ill and ineffective Edward to the boy-king Richard

---

[119] *CPR 1377–81*, p. 580, 1380.xii.5. Christian Liddy, 'Urban Conflict in Late Fourteenth-Century England: The Case of York in 1380–1', *EHR*, 118 (2003): 1–32.

[120] See Liddy, 'Urban Conflict'; and Liddy, *War, Politics and Finance*, pp. 88–91. The latter emphasizes the class and ideological aspects of the revolt and similarities with the Peasants' Revolt. For the revolt as a complex of factional and class discontent over taxes and with Gysburn, see Hilton, *English and French Towns*, pp. 142–3.

[121] *CPR 1377–81*, pp. 627–8, 1381.ii.2; and p. 630, 1381.iii.3.

[122] Ibid., p. 628, 1381.ii.2.   [123] Ibid., pp. 631–2, 1381.iii.26.

under the questionable tutelage of his hated uncle[124] sparked as much resentment and popular insurgency in towns as in the countryside. Except for London, York, Beverley, and Scarborough, and to some extent Winchester, Canterbury, and Bridgwater, the urban anticipation of the so-called Peasants' Revolt has yet to be fully investigated, especially for places such as Chichester, Coventry, and Shrewsbury.[125] Against models of 'preindustrial' revolt, clearly these struggles were not solely 'reactive' or attempts to shore up the status quo. In the cases described above, 'lesser men' took advantage of the spaces suddenly opened to them by weak kingship embattled by a corrupt court to gain or expand their liberties, while villeins across counties sought to win their freedom mostly from ecclesiastical lords through legal and extra-legal means.

Jack Cade's Rebellion

The revolt that ends this study, Jack Cade's in 1450, appears at first glance to have been a repeat performance of events that had taken place in 1381, including English failings and defeats in the Hundred Years War, territorial losses (first Maine, then all of Normandy), dynastic conflicts and struggles among the magnates, uprisings in Kent, pressures of taxation, convergence on London, encampment on Blackheath, the execution of key advisers and royal ministers, the following in large part of 'solid members of village society', this time, however, supported more substantially by the lesser gentry (although they also made a significant appearance among the rebels, and as leaders of 1381, in Cambridgeshire, Suffolk, and Norfolk).[126] What most emphatically distinguished the

---

[124] See Goodman, *John of Gaunt*.

[125] For urban insurrection during the Peasants' Revolt, see Réville, *Le soulèvement*; Liddy, 'Urban Conflict'; R. B. Dobson, 'The Rising in York, Beverley and Scarborough, 1380–1381', in *The English Rising of 1831*, ed. Rodney Hilton and T. H. Aston (Cambridge 1984), pp. 112–42, who speculates that urban struggles probably touched all English towns *c.* 1381; we do not know of them either because of the absence of historical research or because of the disappearance of documents (ibid., pp. 112–13). Even towns as small as Rochester and Guildford had their revolts in 1381 (p. 112). On Canterbury, see A. F. Butcher, 'English Urban Society and the Revolt of 1381', in *The English Rising of 1831*, ed. Rodney Hilton and T. H. Aston (Cambridge, 1984); on Winchester, see Hinck, 'The Rising of 1381 in Winchester'; on Bridgwater, see T. B. Dilks, 'Bridgwater and the Insurrection of 1381', *Proceedings of the Somerset Archaeological and Natural History Society* 73 (1927): 57–69.

[126] Historians disagree on the social composition of Cade's rebels (and even of Cade himself), especially since Griffiths' analysis of the extensive Acts of pardon found in *CPR* (*The Reign of King Henry VI*, pp. 617–23). He argued that large numbers of those pardoned had not been rebels; instead, they included men anxious about the revolt's

rebellion of 1450 from 1381 was the absence of servitude in most of England and therefore the later absence of demands to the king to end serfdom.[127] The Patent Rolls suggest other differences, especially as regards the role of towns. In both rebellions, London may have been the target and climax of revolt, but unlike the period immediately preceding the Peasants' Revolt, the Patent Rolls point to no significant urban protests or riots mounting in the years immediately preceding Cade's revolt. The one possible exception occurred on Irish soil; the town in question, Waterford, was, however, not the crucible of rebellion but instead its butt: rebel violence came from the countryside.[128]

---

outcome, who wished to hedge their bets. Some of these stayed on the sidelines; others even opposed and later prosecuted Cade. Griffiths concluded that the rebels came 'from the lower orders', that they were 'of commoners, ill-organized, poorly armed, and badly disciplined' (pp. 622–3). Later, he appears to contradict himself: in contrast to the Peasants' Revolt (which he sees at least in Kent as 'primarily a rural movement spearheaded by a peasantry in economic and social difficulties' [pp. 629–30]), 'the rebel complaints of 1450 reflect the frustrations and resentments of practically all sections of Kentish society, including the substantial and well-to-do, the townsmen and traders as well as the peasantry and yeomen' (p. 630). Montgomery Bohna, 'Armed Force and Civic Legitimacy in Jack Cade's Revolt, 1450', *EHR*, 118 (2003): 563–82 has challenged Griffiths over the pardon lists and the character of Cade's Rebellion. Instead of being 'ill-organized, poorly armed, and badly disciplined', Bohna maintains they were a well-armed and disciplined peasant militia commanded by officers, many of whom received royal pardons on 7 July 1450. These peasants and yeomen had benefited from the array of arms assembled in May, a month before, to protect England's southern coastline against French piracy and invasion. This may well be the case, but it fails to refute Griffiths' interpretation of the multiple and ambiguous use of pardons by the king. Here, Cade's revolt was no exception. Pardons had been bought by non-participants and sympathizers of the Crown as protection against possible future royal actions, as seen in numerous pardons issued by Richard II in 1377, in 1381–2, and 1398; see Helen Lacey, '"Grace for the Rebels": The Role of the Royal Pardon in the Peasants' Revolt of 1381', *JMH*, 34 (2008): 40, 47–8, and 50–1; and Eiden, 'Joint Action', pp. 8–9 and 19. For the strategies of Richard's pardons in 1397 and 1398 for individuals and groups, see C. M. Barron, 'The Tyranny of Richard II', *BIHR*, 41 (1968): 9–10.

[127] In contradistinction to others, Griffiths, *The Reign of King Henry VI*, p. 630, shows that customary dues on estates such as those of the Archbishop of Canterbury had not disappeared and even prosperous burgesses remained villeins of the abbot at Battle and took advantage of the revolt to refuse their customary payments. In one of Cade's manifestos, a grievance was made against the Statutes of Labourers, recently re-enforced by Parliament in 1445 (p. 638). For Griffiths, the most profound difference between the revolts of 1381 and 1450 was the absence in the latter of an egalitarian or anti-clerical movement. Its manifestos carefully explained that the rebels were petitioners and 'did not blame all lords, all gentlemen, all lawyers, all bishops, all priests, nor "alle that biene aboute the Kynges persone"' (p. 637).

[128] *CPR 1446–52*, p. 132, 1448.iv.8. No doubt, archival research will uncover more, but will it reveal that its prelude was as contentious as the build-up to 1381? From the published municipal records, one can point to the electoral conflicts, with Ralph Holland's pleas in 1442 and Gladman's ritualistic revolt of 1443 (see pp. 32 and 260–1 below).

The last urban riot to occur on English soil before Cade's in our survey was in London almost a decade earlier, despite losses in France, mounting corruption, judicial abuse, and aristocratic violence and criminality over the previous decade.[129] Moreover, this riot hardly appears to have been of great significance; it was confined mostly to a single parish within the city, and may not even have been a popular uprising. The description comes from a royal pardon on 15 February 1442 to an esquire of London. Nearly a year earlier (2 March) he had killed the constable of the parish of St Mary Mounthaut, the constable of St Nicholas Coldabbey, and four others as they were trying to keep the peace at St Nicholas. The pardon provides no details of the unrest the constables were trying to quell or the motives of the 'assembled many evildoers and disturbers of the peace'. The pardoned esquire also had a previous history of criminal violence.[130]

Moreover, Cade's Rebellion did not possess, during or afterwards, the same urban sweep of 1381, from the Welsh marches to York. The mandates and commissions of the Patent Rolls ordering sheriffs and establishing special commissions to investigate, punish, and later pardon rebels ranged across southern England – the counties of Surrey,[131] Northampton,[132] Oxfordshire,[133] Wiltshire,[134] Derby,[135] Gloucestershire,[136] Essex,[137] and especially Kent[138] with a scattering of rebels pardoned from other adjacent counties of Worcester, Huntingdon, and Nottingham.[139] They focused, however, more intensely than in 1381 on southern England without penetrating deeply into the Midlands, or reaching the north, or the far southwest.

In addition, although London was the rebels' focus and the place for presenting their demands, as in 1381,[140] urban revolts per se were now rare, as seen in the royal mandates and commissions. Salisbury,[141] Colchester,[142] and Norwich[143] may have been the exceptions, but for Salisbury and Norwich, the Rolls fail to show direct links to Cade and his

---

[129] See Griffiths, *The Reign of King Henry VI*, especially Chapter 20.
[130] *CPR 1441–6*, p. 75, 1442.ii.15. I. M. W. Harvey, *Jack Cade's Rebellion of 1450* (Oxford, 1991), comes to a similar conclusion: 'Up until 1449 popular unrest in Henry's time had been rare. The only exceptional year was 1431 during Henry VI's minority' (p. 23).
[131] *CPR 1446–52*, p. 381, 1450.iv.11.   [132] Ibid., p. 383, 1450.iv.26.
[133] Ibid., pp. 386–7, 1450.v.23.   [134] Ibid., p. 434, 1451.ix.20.
[135] Ibid., p. 431, 1450.ix.5.   [136] Ibid., p. 433, 1450.ix.28.
[137] Ibid., p. 431, 1450.ix.8.
[138] Ibid., p. 383, 1450.iv.14; p. 431, 1450.ix.8; p. 432, 1450.ix.22; p. 437, 1451.i.13; p. 443, 1451.iii.16.
[139] Ibid., p. 443, 1451.iii.16.
[140] See for instance, ibid., p. 388, 1450.vii.1; and p. 431, 1451.ix.5.
[141] Ibid., p. 433, 1450.xi.18.   [142] Ibid., p. 415, 1451.ii.23.
[143] Ibid., p. 432, 1450.xi.1.

rebellion. At Norwich, the wording of the commission was vague and formulaic: to make enquiries into and to commit to justice all those guilty of 'trespasses, oppressions, extortions, misprisions, offences, maintenances, usurpations, champerties, unlawful leagues, conceal-ments, conspiracies, excesses, injuries, grievances, and misdeeds'.[144] The records do not list those indicted or describe the specific actions rebels may have committed within Norwich's city walls, and leave no hint that their trespasses were connected with Cade. For Salisbury, the charges were equally vague, except in addition to arresting those 'gathering in riots, routs, and congregations in the city', the mayor and bailiffs were commanded to proclaim 'that none fabricate or publish false news'. But the commission fails to specify what that suspected 'false news' might have been.[145]

Outside London, only in nearby Colchester (according to Richard Britnell not a hot-bed of urban rebellion in 1381), did specific charges link urban disturbances to the spread of Cade's Rebellion. The commission registered two revolts, one on 8 July 1450; the other on 17 February, the year after Cade's capture and brutal execution. Following the second revolt, the royal mandate made the connection explicit, calling the revolt a 'war against the king at Colcestre'. On the Tuesday after the Exaltation of the Holy Cross (17 September) the fuller 'John Shaket, with others, armed with swords, staves, bows, arrows, "jakkes" and "palettes",[146] to the number of a hundred ... broke the gaol' and threatened to kill the town's bailiff. Later this leader proclaimed 'that John Cade alias John Mortimer, captain of Kent, was living, and that they would stand with him and die in his treasons'.[147] Other archival sources also point to a plot at Bury St Edmunds on 6 March 1450 to overthrow the king and replace him with the Duke of York. The principal instigators, however, were earls, knights, and esquires without any hints of it being an insurgence of burgesses, if in fact, the plot existed at all.[148] Instead, the larger urban areas rejected Cade, along with other popular movements between 1450 and 1454, which anticipated, or were after-tremors of, Cade's Rebellion. In January, the merchants of Canterbury vigorously repulsed a movement led by Thomas Cheyne to enter the city, and in June, Cade advanced on its western suburbs but was denied entry, and so he headed to London.[149] Eventually, Cade was able

---

[144] Ibid.   [145] Ibid., p. 433, 1450.xi.18.
[146] Palettes were armour to protect the armpit.   [147] Ibid., p. 415, 1451.ii.23.
[148] Harvey, *Jack Cade's Rebellion*, pp. 116–17.
[149] Ibid., pp. 79, 103–4; and Griffiths, *The Reign of King Henry VI*, p. 610. His messages were also met with suspicion in Kentish port towns of Lydd, Rye, and Romney.

to enter London but by force and not with the support of a wide swathe of the city's population, from artisans to probably aldermen, as had happened in 1381: no ground swell within the city now supported a careful coordination of forces with the dual-pronged entry of peasant rebels from Kent and Essex. Cade's rebels remained encamped outside the city in Southwark, where they were defeated by royal troops and by Londoners.[150]

Despite these differences, however, Cade's Rebellion follows a pattern of revolts that can be traced back to baronial troubles of the thirteenth century. Periods of royal weakness with dynastic and other political cracks at the top of aristocratic society occasioned the outbreak of rebellion in towns and the countryside. One exception to the patterns traced above might have been the last decade of Richard II's reign, from his humiliation with the Appellants' successful challenge to his rule and his failure to consult and honour the opinions of the principal earls, dukes, and magnates of his realm. In this decade, plebes, whether in cities or the countryside, mounted few challenges to royal control. As Nigel Saul has shown, however, this decade, despite two short moments of crisis, was not marred by weak kingship. After the Appellants' purge in 1387, Richard changed tack and quickly re-established his grip on London and the realm. Even in the last two years of his rule, with and after his vengeful assault on his old enemies of the 1380s, he strengthened his hold over central government, constructing a new courtier society and rule that anticipated the Tudor revolution in court and county politics during the reign of Henry VII.[151] He built new patronage networks between his court and the provinces as well, thereby weakening the power structures of old magnate families such as the Berkeleys in Gloucestershire.[152] 'By the end of 1397, the government of the counties had been almost wholly assimilated to the structures and political imperatives of the courtier-led regime.'[153] This was Richard's legacy for the formation of a new statecraft of bureaucrats totally committed to the king that would develop again with Tudor kingship.[154] In the last decade of Richard's rule, the Bampton uprising of 1398 in Oxfordshire was the only open challenge to his rule from below.

Unlike on the Continent, popular revolt in England rarely emerged in periods of strong and assertive kingship, as with long stretches of the reigns of Edward I and Edward III, no matter how intrusive their royal policies, threats to urban liberties, tax burdens, purveyances, or other impositions. Nor had the misery of economic and social conditions

---

[150] Harvey, *Jack Cade's Rebellion*, pp. 81, 93–5.   [151] Saul, *Richard II*, pp. 440–2.
[152] Ibid., pp. 382–4 and 442–4.   [153] Ibid., p. 384.   [154] Ibid., p. 441.

during periods of great destitution at the end of the thirteenth century and the 1330s provoked more than rumbling from commoners, even though royal demands for purveyances and taxation reached their peaks. Crises of kingship, as the following chapter will examine, may not have been, however, the only ones to provoke urban revolt.

5   The Black Death and urban protest

Another crisis, not just for England, but across Europe and beyond, was the depression immediately preceding the Black Death of 1348 and the years of serious social, political, and economic dislocation that followed. Our survey of the narrative sources and a sampling of archival ones for Italy, France, and Flanders showed widespread insurrections especially in towns in the years leading up to the plague, but with its arrival, their numbers dropped precipitously and remained at a low ebb until around 1355, when they began to rise again, reaching levels never witnessed before by the final decades of the fourteenth century, when their numbers quadrupled, compared to the late thirteenth and early fourteenth centuries. Did the same patterns characterize the English experience?

From the view of the English chronicles, the patterns were not similar. When revolts were on the rise in the troubled years before the plague on the Continent, nothing of note appears in the English chronicles until after the Black Death and then only three incidents for the next decade, all from Oxford (in 1352, 1354, and 1355), all between burgesses and the university or its students, and none of which specified the motives for the outbreaks, or whether rights were contested. With their greater attention to smaller riots and disturbances beyond the capital, Oxford, and a clutch of monastic centres, the Patent Rolls expose a richer vein of popular unrest during these years of demographic disaster immediately before and after the Black Death. These records reflect some similarities with, but also differences from, the Continent. First, as on the Continent, the years immediately preceding the plague, 1345 to 1348, were not ones of social calm. Although the English sources reveal no machine breaking, strike action, or mass risings of disenfranchised cloth workers as seen in Siena, Florence, and towns of Flanders and northern France, these years for English towns appear as troubled. In 1346, grain prices rose in England to their highest levels since the Great Famine, with labourers' real wages sinking to their lowest point since the 1320s.[1] Despite these ecological circumstances, however, none of the disturbances of the late 1340s turned explicitly on bread prices or describe food riots and famine as occurred occasionally in places such as Florence and Siena in the years leading to the plague's outbreak. Moreover, unlike the prelude to the English Peasants' Revolt or Cade's Rebellion, the mid- and late-1340s were a period of English success in warfare in France and Scotland, with crowning victories at Neville's Cross in 1346, Crécy, the same year, and Calais in 1347.

Nonetheless, the frequency of revolts, particularly against the king and his ministers, began to mount in 1345, probably linked to the great expeditions of 1346 and the need to strengthen northern defences. At Carlisle, some 'led by a most wicked spirit' made agreements with the Scots and schemed to turn the king's town of Carlisle and other castles along the border over to the enemy.[2] Towards the end of summer, a major revolt arose at Carlisle between the royal soldiers of its garrison and the city's 'commonalty', with many casualties on both sides. According to the royal commission, the revolt seriously jeopardized the security of England's borders with Scotland, and if not settled, would encourage 'a hostile invasion of the Scots'. The revolt may have also been connected with deteriorating conditions of food supply: many of the city and castle as well as of the vicinage 'daily' stole victuals and other goods brought there, which they then sold in their own markets. The disruptions may have been, however, more politically inspired. The rebels were involved in 'divers homicides, plunders, felonies, oppressions, extortions and other misdeeds' that led the royal commission to be concerned with the security and provisioning of the city and castle.[3] Further troubles followed in September, this time between the city's 'rich and powerful' and the poor, the latter alleging that the rich, who collected taxes for paving streets and repairing city walls (pavage and murage), were pocketing the proceeds to the city's detriment. The Crown was called to investigate,[4] and the mayor and bailiffs came under suspicion, further exacerbating class tensions. The commission charged that the city's rulers had drawn and hanged men for sedition without the king's warrant, but had allowed Scots and others indicted by Crown courts to remain safe in the city, protected by the mayor and bailiffs.

---

[1] John H. Munro, 'Wage-stickiness, Monetary Changes, and Real Incomes in Late-Medieval England and the Low Countries, 1350–1500: Did Money Matter?' *Research in Economic History*, 21 (2003): 210; and Dobson, *The Peasants' Revolt*, p. 69.

[2] *CPR 1343–5*, p. 492, 1345.ii.2. Two days later, the king's sergeant-at-arms at Carlisle forced confessions from those plotting to overthrow the city; ibid. Also, Summerson, *Medieval Carlisle*, I, p. 274.

[3] *CPR 1343–5*, p. 584, 1345.ix.6.   [4] Ibid., p. 587, 1345.ix.17.

Moreover, the Crown accused the mayor and bailiffs of assembling townsmen along with Scots indicted for sedition to attack the royal castle, its constable, and the Bishop of Carlisle (who possessed rights to the garrison), wounding 'wickedly and atrociously' with arrows, quarrels, and other arms those of the royal garrison. Finally, the city leaders and its commonalty constructed a long street on the castle's dyke, claiming the soil as their own, not the Crown's, along with two parts of the castle in 'contempt of the king and the peril of the loss of the city and castle'.[5]

In 1345 conflict spread to other parts of northern England. The burgesses of Newcastle upon Tyne challenged the water rights of the Friars Minor, breaking the doors and locks to their well and the pipes that brought water to their friary, to divert the water for themselves and against the Crown's support of the friars.[6] Around the same time, men at Liverpool 'feloniously and seditiously' unfurled banners, prevented the king's justices from holding their sessions, and 'wickedly killed, mutilated, plundered' their goods.[7] By the end of the year, troubles against the Crown and its officers flared further south at Worcester. The town's 'commonalty' assaulted the king's recent appointee as the keeper of peace, William de Beauchamp, and beat his men when they tried to arrest those charged with trespass.[8] These problems lasted to the following year: the town's two bailiffs with four other burgesses assembled 'a huge multitude of malefactors of the commonalty', assaulted the royal officer, beat his men, and imprisoned him.[9] Early in 1346, those of Ipswich assaulted a royal tax collector, preventing him from collecting the taxes of the tenth and the fifteenth.[10] Further conflict erupted between burgesses of Oxford and the university over rights to hold the twice yearly court of frankpledge[11] and to supervise the assize of weights and measures.[12] Troubles surfaced again the same month, with 'frequent complaints' that 'disturbers of the peace pretending to be apprentices of the Bench at Westminster' formed illegal confederacies

---

[5] Ibid., p. 588, 1345.ix.16.   [6] Ibid., p. 496, 1345.iii.5.

[7] Ibid., pp. 498–9, 1345.iii.8.

[8] CPR 1345–8, p. 36, 1345.xii.26. On the Beauchamp family in Worcestershire, see Christopher Dyer, Lords and Peasants in a Changing Society: The Estates of the Bishopric of Worcester, 680–1450 (Cambridge, 1980), pp. 48, 50, 56, 76, and 156–7; also see Christine Carpenter, 'Beauchamp, William (V), First Baron Bergavenny', ODNB.

[9] CPR 1345–8, p. 97, 1346.ii.3.

[10] Ibid., p. 98, 1346.ii.10.

[11] Originally, a manorial court before one's peers of the tithing in Anglo-Saxon villages, later extended to towns. These concerned trials of those apprehended through the hue-and-cry.

[12] Ibid., p. 102, 1346.ii.8.

in town to assault and detain students, to ransom them and steal their goods. They were also accused of killing and mutilating others.[13] Late that summer, a third conflict arose at Oxford between burgesses on the one hand and the monastery of St Frideswide and the Crown on the other. The mayor and bailiffs, 'with the assent and abetting of the commonalty' assaulted the monastery's bailiffs and ministers, preventing them from collecting tolls and profits at their annual fair, amounting to £1,000.[14] In November, 'a great multitude of armed men' of the liberty of Holderness disputed the king's fair of Withernsea, gravely assaulting two of the king's bailiffs and three of their deputies charged with collecting the market tolls.[15]

The number of incidents of collective violence against the Crown and the king's ministers continued with the same frequency in 1347, one of the worst years for commoners since the Great Famine.[16] Edward's long siege of Calais, and his need both to requisition ships, and to impose new taxes, heightened tensions further.[17] In May, sheriffs of London and the king's sergeants-at-arms were appointed to arrest Master John de Hynton, parson of the church of Rayleigh in Essex, and Thomas de Hynton, indicted for sedition against the king and the people of London.[18] Unrest spilled into rural areas, but also involved towns, with armed confederacies at Tredington (Worcestershire, now Warwickshire), Kettering (Northamptonshire), and places in Lancashire, 'emboldened by [the king's] absence from England'.[19] Rebels took over churches, stole tithes, assaulted royal sheriffs, expelled royal clerks, took over the king's possessions, attacked town fairs, and extorted fines and ransoms.[20]

As will be explored, townsmen at Bristol, Lynn, Boston, Thetford in Norfolk, and places in Kent, Somerset, and Yorkshire during the summer and autumn, 'assumed to themselves the royal power', boarded ships provisioned for English troops in Gascony and the north of France, confiscated corn from merchants and sold it to their townspeople at

[13] Ibid., p. 98, 1346.ii.16.

[14] Ibid., p. 184, 1346.viii.5. Also, in a similar attack on the annual fair of Wells, men from the county wounded the king's bailiff and collector of corn, and 'many others in various counties' were plotting to kill his ministers, ibid., p. 106, 1346.ii.15.

[15] Ibid., p. 235, 1346.xi.28.   [16] See note 1, above.

[17] Parliament did not sit in 1347, but in its next session, January 1348, Commons petitioned the king, recalling its supplications from 1344, which had also been repeated in the last session of Parliament in 1346. It decried the tax burdens placed on the populace (the fifteenths, ninths and tax on wool) to support war efforts in France; *PROME*, Edward III, January 1348, membranes no. 2, items 16, 20–2, no. 4, items 44 and 57, and no. 5, item 59.

[18] *CPR 1345–8*, p. 319, 1347.v.20.   [19] Ibid., p. 455, 1347.ix.11.

[20] Ibid., pp. 383, 1347.vii.20; 589, 1347.x.10; p. 455; p. 382, 1347.vii.8.

prices they deemed just, and took over municipal governments.[21] These revolts, heretofore unnoticed by historians, were not, however, food riots of the miserable, as seen in Rome, Florence, Siena, and other towns in Italy in the 1320s and 1340s; rather, they concerned liberties and anticipated those of E. P. Thompson's 'moral economy' in eighteenth-century England.[22]

The riots and offences against the Crown continued apace in towns and the countryside[23] into the year of the Black Death and failed to ease appreciably after pestilence reached English shores during the summer. At the beginning of the year, 'a very great multitude, confederate[d] and armed' disrupted the Abbot of Abingdon's annual fair and weekly markets.[24] In February, 'unlawful assemblies of felons and evildoers' at Peterborough attacked and captured 'the king's lieges', forcing fines and ransoms from them, and committed homicides and other crimes 'by day and night'.[25] Whether the violence was the work of criminal gangs or social protest, it shows the Crown's weakness in another urban area. The same month, the king pressured the mayor and bailiffs of Bristol to arrest and punish 'a large confederacy of evildoers', who were preventing his sergeant from exercising his authority in town. Perhaps Bristol's elected officials were colluding: the king accused them of doing nothing to bring the men to justice.[26] In March, those of Bristol were indicted again for boarding ships laden with corn for English troops in Gascony. They attacked merchants and sailors and carried away the victuals.[27] Many of the 'confederates', who had challenged the authority of the royal sergeants in February, may have been the same as those in March. Further attacks on purveying food hit other members of the royal family. In May, the men of Thame in Oxfordshire assaulted and detained 'very many' men sent with carts and horses to purvey provisions for the household of Edward III's oldest son, the Black Prince, then off fighting in France.[28] Similar attacks against him recurred at Fordington in Dorset, Dorchester, and Chalk in Kent.[29]

Unlike on the Continent, the appearance of the Black Death did not appreciably slow the spread of popular insurrection in England. Instead,

---

[21] Ibid., p. 392, 1347.vii.8. On the fiscal crisis of 1347, see G. L. Harriss, *King, Parliament, and Public Finance in Medieval England to 1369* (Oxford, 1975), pp. 325–6.

[22] E. P. Thompson, 'The Moral Economy of the English Crowd in the Eighteenth Century', *P&P,* 50 (1971): 76–137; also see Chapter 6, p. 141; and for seventeenth-century examples, Wood, *Riot, Rebellion and Popular Politics,* pp. 96–106.

[23] For instance, men of the region at Galtres in Yorkshire burnt hedges 'in contempt of the king' and rioted against his enclosures; *CPR 1348–50,* p. 63, 1348.ii.6.

[24] Ibid., p. 62, 1348.i.30.   [25] Ibid., p. 64, 1348.ii.8.   [26] Ibid., p. 59, 1348.ii.8.

[27] Ibid., p. 72, 1348.iii.2.   [28] Ibid., pp. 156, 1348.v.20.   [29] Ibid., pp. 157–8, 1348.v.20.

riots and revolts similar to those of the previous several years continued through the summer and into the following year of pestilence. Men of York, including two spurriers, two skinners, two saddlers, two tailors, a baker, and a smith attacked the king's castle and imprisoned his ministers charged with keeping the peace.[30] Men around Salisbury 'with armed force' attacked the king's clerk, who held the prebend of St Mary's in Salisbury Cathedral, ejected him from his prebend and carried away his tithes.[31] At Sudbury, townsmen assaulted the collector of the tenth and the fifteenth, when he was attempting to collect the town's portion and make distraints of cattle against them. The townsmen rescued the cattle, chased the collector and his men from town as far as Great Waldingfield, and ripped up the king's writ.[32] In the early autumn, further insurrections against tax collectors, refusals to pay the recently granted tenths and fifteenths, and attacks on the king's men making distraints spread through towns and villages in Nottinghamshire, Essex, Suffolk, Norfolk, Northamptonshire, Oxfordshire, Kent, Derbyshire, and parts of Holland in Lincolnshire, registering geographically the most widespread tax resistance to the Crown before the Peasants' Revolt.[33] In November, the sheriff and mayor of Cambridge were appointed to apprehend men from the town and county who had killed John de Wodhull, knight, 'atrociously wounded' the under-sheriff of Cambridge, and assaulted others of the king's bailiffs and ministers, his men-at-arms, and archers while on 'important business' for the Crown. They had plundered 'great sums' of the king's money and had made off with 'very many writs directed to the sheriff'.[34] As usual, the commission did not comment on the rebels' motives.

A struggle for liberties, however, clearly motivated a final case of that year: led by their bailiffs, 'the commonalty' of Worcester assembled 'with unwonted clamour', rebelled against the priory of its cathedral, and challenged the Church's liberties. 'With force of arms and furious onset', they took the body of one of their citizens, who had been killed in the cathedral churchyard, from the liberty of the church to the town to be examined by their coroner and not by the royal coroner of the hundred. The men then went armed to the priory, broke its gates, assaulted the prior's servants, and chased the prior and his monks from the church, 'shooting with bows and arrows and throwing other weapons at them'. After this 'terrible siege', they 'brought up fire' to burn them out.[35] In December, a second commission described this revolt again, listing

---

[30] Ibid., p. 166, 1348.vii.1.   [31] Ibid., p. 175, 1348.viii.28.
[32] Ibid., p. 235, 1348.ix.20.   [33] Ibid., pp. 235–6, 1348.ix.22.
[34] Ibid., p. 243, 1348.xi.2.   [35] Ibid., p. 245, 1348.xi.23.

seventy-nine indicted, including butchers, bowyers, clerks, sergeants, tavernkeepers, chaplains, tailors, spice men, fishmongers, skinners, servants, and a glazier.[36]

By 1349 and over the next several years the number of incidents, as on the Continent, finally began to decline; most of the reports and mandates of popular insurrections concerned the countryside, and none of these can compare with the tax resistance of the previous year that had spread through nine counties. Yet the plague had not killed off popular protest to the extent it had on the Continent: incidents persisted in the capital and in other major English towns. At Southampton, 'a huge multitude of evildoers' assembled and assaulted the king's sergeant-at-arms, who was commissioned with arresting ships to transport troops to serve in Gascony.[37] In the summer, the mayor led the commonalty of Winchester to usurp lands of the monastery of St Peter, owned by the bishop, 'to make markets, fairs and other injurious occupations'.[38] Because of the plague, the enclosed ground was now needed for burial. 'In warlike array and with din of arms'[39] and 'noisy threats of burning the cathedral', burgesses assaulted the cathedral's monks and those burying the plague dead in the cathedral's new graveyard. After digging up the bones and 'casting these into vile places without the graveyard', townsmen occupied the spot and constructed dykes to build new houses.[40] In November, the mayor and commonalty argued in royal courts against the plot being the monastery's ancient graveyard but lost their case, even though the bishop admitted the plot may not have belonged to the cathedral. The mayor was arrested, the town fined £40, and the king 'granted licence for the bishop to enclose the plot according to the metes, bounds, and limits found by the inquisition with

---

[36] Ibid., p. 249, 1348.xii.19.   [37] Ibid., p. 322, 1349.vi.12.

[38] A later *Inspeximus* of the case on 21 November, ibid., p. 424, specified the property's boundaries.

[39] The *Inspeximus* specified that the townsmen were armed with swords, bows, and arrows. While expressions such as *vi et armis* might have been formulaic, specification of the weapons or banners they carried certainly was not. On the *vi et armis* formula and historians' arguments that it exaggerated violence to receive legal attention, see Attreed, 'Urban Identity', p. 581; and Kleineke, 'Why the West was Wild', p. 79. Expanding on the work of S. F. C. Milson, Phillip R. Schofield, 'Trespass Litigation in the Manor Court in the Late Thirteenth and Early Fourteenth Centuries', in *Survival and Discord in Medieval Society: Essays in Honour of Christopher Dyer*, ed. Richard Goddard, John Langdon, and Miriam Müller (Turnhout, 2010), pp. 145–60, especially pp. 147 and 153, instead shows that trespass litigation could be successfully admitted in the courts without the *vi et armis* formula. In fact, certain courts, such as the Sheriffs' Courts, disallowed from adjudicating serious cases of *vi et armis* or *contra pacem domini Regis*, occasionally did so by avoiding these formulas; see Tucker, *Law Courts and Lawyers*, p. 98.

[40] *CPR 1348–50*, p. 384, 1349.vi.20.

a stone wall'.[41] At the end of the year, the mayor, sheriffs, and aldermen of London informed the king's justices of increased 'concourse of aliens and denizens to the city and suburbs', who are 'found wandering by night', breaking the peace. 'Now that the pestilence is stayed', the king insisted that they arrest, imprison, and punish such evildoers.[42]

In 1350, the number of assaults on manors increased, with challenges to royal power. This insurgency, however, now focused on the countryside or small market towns. Unfortunately, few of these insurgents were identified by profession, making it difficult to evaluate who the 'persons', 'evildoers', or 'rebels' were. But if they had been knights or chevaliers, their status would have been specified. Further cases erupted in towns: when the Bishop of Bath and Wells paid his usual visitation and held his court in Yeovil in Somerset, townsmen (including a tailor, a tanner, and a skinner) assaulted and chased him from town, preventing his visitation and his right to exercise justice.[43] At Newark in Nottinghamshire, 'evildoers' confederated and resisted attachments made by the king's constable and assaulted him, imprisoned merchants, and attacked the king's men passing 'in a little ship' down the river Trent with corn and victuals to munition the king's castle of Nottingham. In addition, they assaulted the men and servants of the Bishop of Lincoln.[44] In March, the king was informed that 'very many rebels' had refused to pay their tenths and fifteenths and that under-collectors and others had retained some of the sums levied. The king appointed a commission to arrest and imprison 'all such rebels and defaulters'.[45]

In April, the mayor and bailiffs of York assembled the commonalty against the Abbot of St Mary's to challenge his jurisdiction in the city's suburbs.[46] Troubles arose for the Bishop of Ely and his attempts to exercise justice within his liberty, the Isle of Ely, and to make distraints against its inhabitants. Various residents confederated, rescued one of their citizen's attached property, assaulted the bishop's bailiffs, besieged the king's castle of Wisbech (Cambridgeshire), 'and what is worse' daily threatened the constable of the castle and his ministers and servants 'with loss of life and mutilation of their limbs'. As a result, the officers were unable to remain there 'without a great multitude of armed men'. Because of the threats, the royal servants refused to leave the castle to

[41] Ibid., p. 424.
[42] Ibid., p. 458, 1349.xii.20. Other cases of revolt against taxes and the king's men are seen in Northamptonshire at Cogenhoe, Wappenham, and Weedon; ibid., p. 458, 1349.xii.27.
[43] Ibid., p. 516, 1350.ii.1.   [44] Ibid., p. 521, 1350.ii.15.
[45] Ibid., p. 526, 1350.iii.16.
[46] The following chapter explores these struggles in greater detail.

execute the king's mandates, keep the peace within the liberty, and levy his farms, tolls, and other sources of revenue due to the king.[47] By August, the king's sergeant-at-arms and 'echevin' of the town of Calais had been holding 'unlawful assemblies' with townsmen and 'confederacies'. The king appointed the castle's constable to arrest his sergeant and bring him to the Tower of London, thereby preventing the conspiracy from materializing.[48] In November, men of Whitby rebelled against their abbey, the town's lordship, which 'from time immemorial' had possessed rights to hold its court over the men and tenants of the borough. They assaulted the abbot and his servants, preventing him from holding court and buying provisions to feed himself and his monks.[49]

Serious revolts in towns and challenges to the king and his ministers continued into 1351, but declined in number. Edward III continued to face resistance to collecting his tenths and fifteenths in Somerset. Furthermore, the under-collectors of hundreds, boroughs, and towns – probably from these communities – as well as the king's bailiffs were 'very lukewarm and negligent' in collecting the levies.[50] In March, a chaplain and four others, all from Witham in Essex, were indicted for attacking and chasing 'from the king's service' twenty carpenters brought by the sheriff of Essex to repair the royal castle of Hertford.[51] The next uprising was a rare instance in these documents, when townsmen petitioned or protested against aristocratic violence, disorder, and their usurpation of power. An armed gang led by Sir Gerard Salvayn,[52] 'assumed royal power' by dismissing the king's bailiffs in his town of Hull and assaulting an under-bailiff to free 'malefactors' awaiting justice. The burgesses claimed that the knight and his confederacy of accomplices were scheming to surround the town to kill and do 'evil to' the men, who had been responsible for arresting the malefactors, as well as to their friends, well-wishers, the mayor, bailiffs, and 'good men of the town'. They claimed to be so threatened that they could not leave town, array ships for the king's army, trade, or till their soil.[53]

---

[47] Ibid., p. 583, 1350.vi.1.

[48] Ibid., p. 590, 1350.viii.5. This is significant in light of Geoffrey de Charny's attempts to retake Calais in 1349; see Jonathan Sumption, *The Hundred Years War*, 3 vols. (London, 1990–2009), II: *Trial by Fire*, pp. 60–2.

[49] *CPR 1350–4*, p. 29, 1350.xi.24.

[50] Ibid., p. 80, 1351.ii.28.   [51] Ibid., p. 80, 1351.iii.3.

[52] In the previous year to November, he had been escheator in Yorkshire; ibid., p. 9, 1350.xi.1; and p. 13, 1350.xi.25.

[53] Ibid., p. 102, 1351.vi.6. Historians have argued that this town was free of riots and rebellion throughout the later Middle Ages; Edward Gillet and Kenneth A. Machon, *A History of Hull* (Hull, 1989) mention none, and according to Jenny Kermode,

On 6 July, the Patent Rolls exposed one of the earliest collective acts of resistance to Edward's new Statutes of Labourers approved by Parliament four months before.[54] Justices of oyer et terminer came to Tottenham, north of London, to hear cases of homicide, felonies, and trespasses 'as well as all things contrary to the statute of workmen, artificers and servants'. 'In no small numbers and assuming the royal power', men of the village assaulted the justices, freed the 'evildoers' to be adjudged from the king's prison and drove the justices from their session, preventing them from fulfilling their royal commission.[55] In the following year, five men broke into the townhall of Great Torrington (Devon) and took away the stocks, which justices had placed there to punish violators of the Statutes of Labourers.[56]

The question of royal taxes and post-plague loans split the townsmen of Coventry, leading one group said to be 'certain burgesses', who acted 'in their own name and the name of the commonalty' against the town's mayor and bailiffs and others appointed to levy a forced loan for the king. The rebellious burgesses besieged the townhall, assaulted the elected officials, and appointed their own tax collectors, inflicting 'so many and great injuries' that those assisting with the royal levy dared not to leave the hall and ceased their assessments for the king.[57]

In 1352, disturbances were widespread but confined mostly to the countryside and may have been mostly criminal acts without political objectives. The only urban revolt was the continuing struggle between the Abbey of St Mary's and the burgesses of York led by the city's mayors and bailiffs over liberties and jurisdiction.[58] In the countryside, however, the queen's tenants, ministers, and servants inflicted a wide arc of disturbances against her, breaking her parks and closes, felling her trees, hunting in her free warrens and her free chaces, carrying away her deer, hares, rabbits, pheasants, and partridges, and rescuing cattle that her officers had impounded from her tenants. These charges involved seventy places across twenty-three counties; they concentrated on her

'Obvious Observations on the Formation of Oligarchies in Late Medieval English Towns', in *Towns and Townspeople in the Fifteenth Century: Colloquium on Fifteenth Century History*, ed. John A. F. Thomson (Sutton, 1988), pp. 87–106: 'In Hull no-one profoundly resented their rulers, since no co-ordinated opposition was recorded' (p. 99).

[54] Dobson, *The Peasants' Revolt*, p. 63.
[55] *CPR 1350–4*, p. 158, 1351.vii.6. On land holding and commercialization of land in Tottenham in the late fourteenth and fifteenth centuries, see Douglas Moss and Ian Murray, 'Signs of Change in a Medieval Village Community', *Transactions of the London and Middlesex Archaeological Society*, 27 (1976): 280–7.
[56] Cited in Hilton, 'Resistance to Taxation', p. 176.
[57] *CPR 1350–4*, p. 201, 1351.x.15.   [58] Ibid., pp. 392–3, 1352.xi.26; see Chapter 6.

vast rural estates but also included her holdings within Bristol. In addition, she complained that many of her ministers had allied with others to conceal and withdraw 'rents, escheats, wards, marriages and other profits' pertaining to her lordship, along with 'very many extortions, damages and grievances to her men'.[59] The charges were extended in November to other market towns such as Pontefract and Knaresborough, along with thirty-two further villages.[60]

In summary, the view from the English chronicles reflects in one respect a pattern not so dissimilar from that on the Continent: with the Black Death and the years immediately after, popular revolt had reached a low point. In contrast to the Continent, however, the troubled years of economic depression and famine in many regions seen in these sources did not spark riots in England as they had in the 1340s on the Continent. The more voluminous and detailed reports scattered through the Patent Rolls, however, sketch a different picture. Even if royal commissions, pardons, and other documents in these collections rarely stated rebels' motives, they show that collective acts of violence in towns and the countryside against ecclesiastical lords and the Crown had not disappeared with the Black Death. In addition to resistance to royal taxes and forced loans that Edward needed to continue his wars in France, tensions between the Church and urban governments rose over liberties in towns and ownership of central parcels of land. Did these post-plague disturbances and revolts then increase from the mid-1350s to the supposed 'cluster of revolts' at the end of the 1370s, as they had across many areas of Europe?

Revolts from the mid-1350s to 1377

Through the 1350s to the eve of the Peasants' Revolt, unrest in urban and rural areas of England continued with at least twenty-eight revolts or serious conflicts between one social group and another from market towns to the capital: in Richmond, Huntingdon, Norton, Shrewsbury, Sudbury, Yeovil, Northampton, York, Ipswich, Melcombe, Doncaster, Derby, Aylesbury, Norwich, Peterborough, and Boston; twice in Newcastle upon Tyne and Colchester; and three times in Oxford, London, Bristol, and Exeter in this quarter century alone. These included a wide range of urban disputes – struggles by burgesses for

---

[59] Ibid., p. 331, 1352.ii.18.
[60] Ibid., p. 388, 1352.xi.10. Still more places were added in commissions of 24 February (p. 287) and 26 November (p. 391) that year.

liberties in monastic boroughs as at Abingdon in 1353[61] and Peterborough in 1375,[62] armed struggles over liberties, justice, and jurisdiction between burgesses and its cathedral chapter at Exeter in 1362 and again in 1366,[63] between townsmen and the archdeacon at Ipswich over jurisdiction in the same year,[64] and between burgesses and the parish church at Yeovil in 1363.[65] Conflicts between the university and burgesses led by their mayor at Oxford continued apace, as in the years just before and after the Black Death, in 1353, 1354, 1355, and 1361;[66] struggles over the town's dominant monastery and its monopoly over mills at Richmond in 1354,[67] townsmen resisting arrest, imprisoning their mayor, and forcing him to renounce his office at Bristol in the same year;[68] discords over the elections for mayor at Newcastle upon Tyne in 1364,[69] York in 1365,[70] and London in 1376;[71] struggles between newcomers, who had immigrated to Shrewsbury from its hinterland since the Black Death, and the town's old order on the eve of England's second wave of pestilence in 1361;[72] and a struggle at Aylesbury in 1371, where the town's constable and its tax collectors assessed the commonalty's 'poorer sort' at excessive rates, 'sparing the rich and powerful', who assaulted those who complained and chased them from town, 'so that they dared not return'.[73]

Despite this variety, however, only just over one a year (30) appears in the Patent Rolls over the quarter century, 1353–76, marking a significant decline from what had been the rate around the time of the Black Death, from 1345 to 1352, when fifty-seven urban revolts took place in eight years – or seven per annum. And if 1352 is subtracted, the number rises to eight per annum, or eight times the rate over the next quarter century. The trend of popular insurrection in England once again diverged from the Continent: the two were mirror opposites. For France, Flanders, and especially Italy, the sources show popular insurgency against oligarchies, royal power, taxation, and abuses of justice

---

[61] *CPR 1350–4*, pp. 456–7, 1353.iv.20.   [62] *CPR 1374–7*, p. 1375.xii.10.

[63] *CPR 1361–4*, 1362.vii.12; *CPR 1364–7*, 1366.ii.3.

[64] *CPR 1364–7*, p. 279, 1366.ii.10.   [65] *CPR 1361–4*, 1363.vii.10.

[66] *CPR 1350–4*, p. 517, 1353.x.3; *CPR 1354–8*, 1355.iii.6, 15 and v.20; 1361.iv.12 and vi.1; also see Walsingham, *Historia Anglicana*, p. 278; and Walsingham, *Ypodigma Neustriae*, for the discord of 1354, the only post-plague rift at Oxford that he mentions. Perhaps this was the most violent town–gown confrontation of the 1350s, more so than the more famous riot of St Scholastica's Day in 1355, a year later.

[67] *CPR 1354–8*, p. 128, 1354.x.14.

[68] Ibid., pp. 69–70, 1354.v.18; also see p. 180, 1355.ii.20.

[69] *CPR 1364–7*, 1364.ix.24; and ibid., 1364.x.8.   [70] Ibid., 1365.xii.9.

[71] *CPR 1374–7*, 1376.xi.30.   [72] *CPR 1358–61*, p. 538, 1361.ii.6.

[73] *CPR 1370–4*, p. 178, 1371.x.12.

mounting dramatically after 1355, increasing more than three-fold from around 1355 to the end of the century, and for certain types of revolt, such as those against taxation, the increase was seven-fold.[74]

However, one new source of conflict – the Statutes of Labourers – sparked new class conflict, at least in the countryside. While much work has been done on the effects of this legislation and prosecution of individual cases, fines and evasion,[75] less has been said about collective resistance to the laws, except for the speculation that it was one of the long-term causes of the English Peasants' Revolt thirty years later, implied perhaps in the rebels' battle cry to kill all lawyers, and in Wat Tyler's desire to gain a commission from the king 'to behead all lawyers, escheators and others who had been trained in the law'.[76] Of course, there were other reasons to hate lawyers and judges – corruption in local justice, abuses of power with oyer et terminer commissions, and especially those with special powers granted by the Ordinance of Trailbastons.[77] Another aspect of this unequal, abusive justice is seen in cases illustrated above: the extreme rarity of peasants or other commoners, whether apprentices in London or more substantial groups, winning cases against employers, lords, town oligarchies, or the Church. As Edward Powell has found, 'Tenants' daily experience of the courts was a sour parody of their expectations of equity and justice, promoted by contemporary sermons and royal propaganda.'[78] 'One recurrent theme' of the rebels of 1381, Andrew Prescott has cogently argued, was 'a demand for justice'.[79] Popular cries against lawyers and their venality, in fact, reached further back than the Peasants' Revolt: they had been conventional in the complaint and protest literature from the

---

[74] Cohn, *Lust for Liberty*, pp. 228–9.

[75] B. H. Putnam, *The Enforcement of the Statutes of Labourers During the First Decade After the Black Death 1349–1359*, Studies in History, Economics and Public Law, vol. XXXII (New York, 1908); L. R. Poos, 'The Social Context of Statute of Labourers Enforcement', *Law & History Review*, 27 (1983): 27–52; Chris Given-Wilson, 'Service, Serfdom and English Labour Legislation, 1350–1500', in *The Fifteenth Century, I: Concepts and Patterns of Service in the Later Middle Ages*, ed. A. Curry and E. Matthews (Woodbridge, 2000), pp. 21–37; and Judith Bennett, 'Compulsory Service in Late Medieval England', *P&P* 209 (2010): 7–51.

[76] Walsingham, *Historia Anglicana*, trans. in Dobson, *The English Peasants' Revolt*, p. 375; also the *Anonimalle Chronicle* claimed the same: ibid., pp. 159–60. On the significance of these cries, see Green, 'John Ball's Letters', pp. 184–5; and Crane, 'The Writing Lesson of 1381', pp. 204–5. See especially Harding, 'The Revolt against the Justices', pp. 165–93, on the centrality of justice in the grievances and ideology of the rebels of 1381.

[77] Harding, 'The Revolt against the Justices', p. 169; and J. R. Maddicott, *Law and Lordship: Royal Justices as Retainers in Thirteenth- and Fourteenth-Century England*, *Past & Present* Supplement, 4 (Oxford, 1978), pp. 31, 60–7.

[78] Powell, *Kingship, Law, and Society*, pp. 19 and 44.

[79] Prescott, 'London in the Peasants' Revolt', p. 138.

thirteenth century.[80] By 1381, peasants and artisans had grown sceptical and resentful of the legal channels offered to them. As a consequence, in June 1381, when Richard offered the rebels encamped on St Katherine's Hill the opportunity to put their grievances in writing, they refused, seeing it as 'nothing but a trifle and a mockery' and returned to London, crying round the city that all lawyers, men of the Chancery and Exchequer, 'and everyone who could write a writ or a letter should be beheaded'.[81]

As for the labour laws more specially, Christopher Dyer has found only two rural rebels of 1381 with previous convictions for violating these laws, and one was a landowning employer.[82] Nonetheless, popular anger and resistance against the laws was one of the few instances when a royal innovation and a new and aggressive stance towards commoners, instead of momentary royal weakness or a king's absence from the realm, provoked popular unrest. Even though many other regions (though not everywhere) in Europe passed similar laws after the Black Death, nowhere were they enforced so vigilantly as in England and as a result, only England appears to have sparked so many incidents of this kind of collective resistance.[83] The peak in enforcement and protest against them, however, came a generation before the Great Rising.

As we have seen, only several months after their parliamentary approval, the statutes had provoked workers and tenants in Tottenham to attack royal justices, free those condemned by the new laws, and to prevent these sessions from continuing. Other cases of mass arrest and resistance appear in the Patent Rolls between 1354 and 1357. These did not pertain solely to the countryside or concern rural labourers alone. On 2 July 1354 the king appointed six separate commissions of oyer et terminer 'touching trespasses against the statute of labourers' in the counties of Oxford, Rutland, Derby, Wiltshire, Buckingham, and Southampton; on 25 July the charges applied to Northamptonshire; to

---

[80] Green, 'John Ball's Letters', p. 189; and John Peter, *Complaint and Satire in Early English Literature* (Oxford, 1956), p. 84.

[81] See note 76 above and W. M. Ormrod, 'Introduction: Medieval Petitions in Context', pp. 1–11, in *Medieval Petitions: Grace and Grievance*, ed. W. M. Ormrod, Gwilym Dodd, and Anthony Musson (York, 2009), pp. 9–10.

[82] Dyer, 'The Social and Economic Background', p. 18.

[83] See Samuel K. Cohn, Jr, 'After the Black Death: Labour Legislation and Attitudes towards Labour in Late-medieval Western Europe', *EcHR*, 60 (August 2007): 457–85; and Robert Braid, '"Et non ultra": politiques royales du travail en Europe occidentale au XIVeme siècle', *Bibliothèque de l'Ecole des Chartes*, 161 (2003): 437–91. For the legal and political history of the ordinances and statutes, see Braid, 'Peste, prolétaires, et politiques'. This 'histoire totale' of the laws does not investigate their reception, or the history of protest against them.

Kent on 26 September; 'in the town of Scarborough' on 3 October;
Leicestershire on 20 October; 'within the liberty of the dean and chapter
of the church of St Peter, York' on 8 November;[84] in the county
of Huntingdon on 12 November;[85] again in Northamptonshire on
26 November, in the county of Cornwall on 16 December, and in
Bedfordshire; for the town of Huntingdon on 20 January 1355;[86] for
the liberty of the Abbot of Reading in Berkshire on 12 January, 1356;[87] in
Essex on 14 February 1356 and Suffolk two days later;[88] for Derbyshire
on 10 March; Sussex on 12 March; the town of Boston, the next day;
in the manors within the towns of Cheshunt and Bassingbourn owned
by the Earl of Richmond, and the borough and liberty of Wycombe on
20 March; and finally in Northamptonshire again on the 26th.[89] Specially
appointed royal commissions to investigate and arrest violators of
the new legislation and collective breaches of the peace against the
new laws amounted to thirty-eight cases in these records across
counties, manors, and towns in 1356 alone. Several, moreover, focused
on towns and cities such as the city and suburbs of Lincoln, the
Archbishop of York's liberty of Ripon, the towns of Nottingham,
Newark, Shrewsbury, and the liberty of the hospital of St Leonard
in York.[90] The Patent Rolls also contain pardons to labourers who
violated the ordinance and statute, as with a 'drivar' (a ploughman)[91]
of Longdon in Worcestershire, who took 12d in excess from various
employers for his stipend.[92] They include petitions to gain exemptions
from the statutes, such as on 5 October 1355, when the Carthusian
brethren of Hinton in Somerset beseeched the king, 'for want of
labourers and servants from the time of the last pestilence'.[93] They
contain commissions to investigate corruption by law enforcers of the
new laws, as in Scarborough in 1356, directed against their 'sheriffs,
stewards, bailiffs, ministers and others who by colour of the statute
have delivered labourers and servants taken for the same, on their own
authority, by fines and ransoms to be applied to their own use'.[94]

After 1356, however, commissions to investigate and prosecute the
statutes' violators declined sharply along with pardons and investigations
into collective action provoked by them. Curiously, they do not rebound
with the waves of communal actions against bondage after the Good

---

[84] *CPR 1354–8*, pp. 123–4.   [85] Ibid., p. 160.   [86] Ibid., pp. 123–4.
[87] Ibid., p. 334.   [88] Ibid., p. 389.   [89] Ibid., p. 391.   [90] Ibid., pp. 392–4.
[91] Gustav Fransson, *Middle English Surnames of Occupation 1100–1350*, Lund Studies in
    English, III (Lund, 1935), p. 55.
[92] *CPR 1354–8*, p. 256, 1355.vi.26.   [93] Ibid., p. 282, 1355.x.5.
[94] Ibid., p. 494. 1356.x.30. Also see the same for Sussex on 5 February 1357; ibid.,
    pp. 549–50.

Parliament. A similar pattern is seen with surviving cases of prosecutions of the labour statutes found in other court records; for Essex they peaked in 1352.[95] More globally, Simon Penn and Dyer have found that large numbers of cases were brought to court in the early 1350s, but afterwards they 'dealt with only a few hundred offenders in each county'.[96] By these trajectories, had the Statutes of Labourers been a key for widespread revolt, then the English Peasants' Revolt should have happened about the time of the French Jacquerie (1358), not a generation later.

In conclusion, the rhythm and trajectory of popular revolt in England differed from that of the Continent: we hypothesize that the strength of kingship here overruled the weight of demographic, economic, and ecological factors. As with dynastic crises, so with the Middle Ages' principal disaster: these disruptions in England created space and opportunities for cities, towns, and villages to assert rights and challenge royal authority from petty theft and the assault of royal officers to wide-scale tax revolts. But the king's absence in these years, especially in 1347, may have been more crucial.[97] After the disruption of the Black Death, the deaths of key government officials, and panic in the winter of 1349, Edward III adroitly reasserted control over tax revenues and English politics[98] until the last year of his life, thus altering the general pattern of revolt in England from that then brewing in Italy, France, and Flanders.[99] With his illness and loss of control over his courtiers during the last months of his life, a new chapter in English revolt opened. That

---

[95] Poos, 'The Social Context'.

[96] Simon Penn and Christopher Dyer, 'Wages and Earnings in Late Medieval England: Evidence from the Enforcement of the Labour Laws', *EcHR*, 43 (1990): 359. In part, the decline may have resulted from a deterioration of recordkeeping; see Judith M. Bennett, 'Compulsory Service in Late Medieval England', *P&P*, 209 (2010): 16 (but from other records she finds the same dwindling in the number of cases by the 1360s). Furthermore, most cities had their own separate sessions for these cases, that no longer survive.

[97] A number of documents regarding social violence in *CPR* points to the problem of the king's absence that year, while 'beyond the seas for important business affecting the state and safety of his crown'; see for instance *CPR 1345–8*, pp. 247, 5.ii.1347; 249, 16.ii.1347; 307, 2.iii.1347; 543, 296, 20.x.1347; 8.vi.1347; 312, 20.iv.1347; 314–15, 25.iv.1347; 544, 11.vii.1347. Edward's second son, Lionel, then 9 years old, was left in charge, as 'keeper of England'.

[98] W. M. Ormrod, 'The English Government and the Black Death of 1348–49', in *England in the Fourteenth Century: Proceedings of the 1985 Harlaxton Symposium*, ed. W. M. Ormrod (Woodbridge, 1986), pp. 175–88; and W. M. Ormrod, *Edward III*, Chapter 13: 'The decade after the Black Death marked a period of remarkable reconstruction for the English crown' (p. 383). According to Ormrod, that success depended on 'the firm leadership' of the king.

[99] For the dismal post-plague fate faced by John II in France, see Ormrod, 'The English Government', pp. 187–8.

chapter centred on London but, as research since Réville at the end of the nineteenth century has emphasized, London was not the only city or town to be rocked by social violence and class strife during this, another crisis period of royal transition and weakness.[100] We now turn to the late medieval narrative of collective violence in towns other than London.

---

[100] From chancery and court records, Prescott, 'Judicial Records', argues vigorously that the Peasants' Revolt was even less centred on London than Réville found over a hundred years ago.

6   Urban revolts against the Crown outside London: the case of Bristol

As presented by chroniclers, popular protest in towns against the Crown occurred overwhelmingly in London. Except for the sweep of revolts in cities and towns during the year of the English Peasants' Revolt, conflicts in other urban places, if touched at all by contemporary narrative sources, were seen mostly as minor incidents. It is open to debate whether some of these, like one mocked by Matthew Paris, qualified as 'popular' revolt. The chronicler sniffed that the king's court-iers in this dispute, as was often their way, 'made mountains of mole hills (saepe ex levibus nanciscentes)'. It concerned the monks' refusal at Winchester to obey the king's choice of bishop in 1241. Paris did not know the cause of their disobedience, but sided with his fellow clerics against the courtiers who brought the suit. After the prior's inquisition, the monks found guilty were ejected from the monastery, 'without regard to age, sex, or order, or to the reverence due to the church or the cloister'. '[T]o the dishonour of the whole monastic order', they were 'imprisoned, starved, and subjected to every kind of reproach, insult and indignity'.[1] A second incident, also reported by Paris was more serious. In 1260, Justices in Eyre of the king (the royal circuit court), were sent to Hereford to fulfil their duties, but were not allowed to enter town. The chief men of that part of the country alleged that the justices' coming was contrary to the Statutes of Oxford. They returned without accom-plishing their mission.[2]

A third case – the 1405 revolt at York against Henry IV – was more important, one of the few in the north of England to be reported by chroniclers. Moreover, other than the wave of revolts set off in 1381, it was only the second revolt against the Crown seen in this sample of English chronicles where taxes and their weight on the poor were seen as central to the revolt (not including those in London during Richard II's reign, when forced loans, not taxes, were at issue and concerned the

---

[1] *Matthew Paris's English History*, I, pp. 337–8; and *Chronica majora*, IV, pp. 107–8.
[2] Continuator of Matthew Paris, *Matthew Paris's English History*, III, p. 333.

wealthy of the capital).[3] At least two chronicles reported it: one was an anonymous chronicle found in only two manuscripts; the other, the *St Albans Chronicle*.[4] As with so many of these English revolts (in contrast to Continental ones), the 1405 one at York began at the top of the social hierarchy, this one as a dispute over inheritance, extensive lands, and the heritable rights of the office of Lord Marshal of England. It ended with royal troops entering Yorkshire and beheading the Earl Marshal Lord Mowbray, Sir William Plumpton, and most spectacularly, the Archbishop of York, Richard Scrope, who immediately became a martyred saint of the populace. His legend had political ramifications for kings of England, forming a part of Yorkist propaganda to the Wars of the Roses and beyond.[5]

Mowbray sought the archbishop's support against King Henry's decision to circumvent what Mowbray saw as his rightful inheritance and to grant estates and the office of the marshal to the Earl of Westmorland [Ralph Neville].[6] By 'exhorting and stirring the people' from his pulpit, the archbishop was able to connect these troubles far removed from popular protest in towns as 'evils and misgovernment of the realm'. Masterfully, he convinced the urban populace that such issues of succession and the lands of a single magnate's son were exemplary of the king's current injustice and a cause of York's poverty and decline of trade ('in grete consideracion the grete pouerte off marchaundez in whom wasse wonte to be the substaunce off the riches off all the londe'). As an anonymous chronicle explained, the archbishop was able to interweave the question of Mowbray's inheritance into a popular cause: 'that the heirs of noble men and of lords of the land be restored to their inheritance wholly along with everyman, regardless of his class ("degre") or birth'. Scrope charged the Crown with oppression and corruption, 'the raising of taxes, tallages, and customs under the guise of loans' and attacked the king's council for its greed in taking property ordained for the common good that made the king all the more wealthy. In addition to sermons, Scrope preached his cause by circulating bills 'writton yn Englessh' posted on York's

---

[3] The other was Longbeard's revolt in 1196.

[4] Except where indicated, *An English Chronicle, 1377–1461*, pp. 35–6, has been followed; the other was Walsingham, *The St Albans Chronicle*, II, pp. 440–59.

[5] J. W. McKenna, 'Popular Canonization as Political Propaganda: The Cult of Archbishop Scrope', *Speculum*, 45 (1970): 608–23; Lorraine C. Attreed, *The King's Towns: Identity and Survival in Late Medieval English Boroughs* (New York, 2001), pp. 287–9; Simon Walker, 'Political Saints in Later Medieval England', in *The McFarlane Legacy: Studies in Late Medieval Politics and Society*, ed. R. H. Britnell and A. J. Pollard (Stroud, 1995), pp. 84–5 and 93–4; and Piroyansky, *Martyrs in the Making*, pp. 49–73.

[6] Walsingham, *The St Albans Chronicle*, II, pp. 440–1.

gates[7] and sent to curates in neighbouring towns to preach from their pulpits. At the outset, he used the written word to propagandize his cause, posting in English the list of grievances against the king that he and the Earl Marshal had drawn up together. These appeared in streets, public places, and on the gates of city monasteries; a copy even arrived south at St Albans, which its chronicler translated into Latin.[8]

With his sermons and casting of bills, Scrope raised, organized, and led an army of 'the crowd of people' and 'citizens of York, with many people from elsewhere' along with clergymen – regulars and seculars – knights, esquires, and other commoners from city and countryside to fight the Earl of Westmorland, aided by royal troops.[9] A truce was agreed, but Scrope and Mowbray were betrayed, captured, and beheaded, and Henry marched triumphantly into York. Citizens came barefooted, 'their belts loosened ("ungirt") and with halters round their necks', to kneel before the king, 'beseeching mercy and grace because they had risen with the archbishop'. Henry's mercy was to fine those who had taken part in the revolt.[10] Walsingham reported the miracles that occurred where Scrope, 'a glorious martyr', had been beheaded and at his place of burial:

And at once the common people began a vigorous worship of the ashes of the now defunct archbishop, whom they had previously loved when he was alive. This lasted until they were forbidden to do so by some of the king's men, and so became afraid to make further visits to the archbishop's tomb.[11]

The chronicles, however, mention few other popular revolts in towns outside London, even ones where the populace joined the barons in periodic struggles against the Crown. Other sources, however, especially the Patent Rolls, reveal a wholly different picture. Some of the most audacious and successful revolts took place in towns outside London, but perhaps because of the slim notice chroniclers took of them, modern historians have also given them little attention. We begin with the longest lasting of these.

---

[7] Ibid.

[8] Ibid., pp. 442–51. On the archbishop's casting of bills, see Scase, '"Strange and Wonderful Bills"', p. 240.

[9] Walsingham, *The St Albans Chronicle*, II, pp. 440–1. Because of small numbers of pardons to burgesses and the light penalties meted out to the rebels, Liddy, 'William Frost, the City of York and Scrope's Rebellion', has speculated that clergymen comprised the bulk of this rebellion in York, and where burgesses were concerned, it was mostly factional strife between Frost's supporters and elites opposed to his domination, which reached back to the eve of the Peasants' Revolt, and the struggle between Gysburn and Quixley. On the social composition of Scrope's followers, see Piroyansky, *Martyrs in the Making*, pp. 67–71: it centred on the laity, men and women alike.

[10] Walsingham, *The St Albans Chronicle*, II, pp. 440–1.   [11] Ibid.

The Bristol revolt of 1312–16

The most significant revolt against the Crown occurred in Bristol from 1312 to 1316. In fact, it may be considered to have been the most remarkable and successful revolt in England of the Middle Ages – those in London and ones that accompanied the Peasants' Revolt of 1381 included. Its rise and success depended crucially on a difficult moment within a weak kingship, when Edward II was mostly absent from England, overstretched in his campaigns against the Scots, was about to suffer from humiliating defeat at Bannockburn (1314), and lacked the military strength in England to make good his demands against Bristol's rebels.[12] For four and a half years, Bristol was in effect an independent town, freed from royal taxes, with royal officials and their troops unable to enter to execute justice. Even at the end of these years, with the return of Edward's troops from Scotland and the subjugation of Bristol, the eighty or so town rebels ordered to stand trial, outlawed for disobeying the king's constable, and guilty of armed conflict against royal officials, and of rescinding the liberties of Bristol's fourteen wealthiest men in 1313, never came to justice.[13] Despite the duration and success of this revolt in one of England's most prominent towns, crucial to the realm's economy and trade with Gascony and other foreign ports, only one chronicler reported the events; that chronicle – an anonymous author of a life of Edward II – moreover, survives by a thin thread. The only copy that remains is a transcription of a single manuscript which was lost in a fire in the early eighteenth century.[14]

In addition, this lone chronicle collapses the four and a half years of the Bristol revolt into two or so years, with most of the drama taking place in 1316, that is, at its very end, when it was being repressed. In addition, it presents the revolt principally as an internal affair ('dissensio') springing from questions of economic privileges to the town's port, its market, and 'aliis rebus', which the fourteen most powerful citizens ('quatuordecim de majoribus') controlled. Against this elitist view of the 'commune', other burgesses held that 'these privileges

---

[12] On Bannockburn's significance for English internal politics, see Phillips, *Edward II*, pp. 236–43: it 'undid completely the political and financial stability' Edward had achieved in 1313 and led to a period of internal upheaval, which endured until the 'political settlement in autumn of 1318' (pp. 238 and 243).

[13] The names of seventy-one of these men appear in lists of the Fine, Close, and *CPR*. Fuller, 'The Tallage of 6 Edward II', p. 182.

[14] Wendy R. Childs, 'Introduction', in *Vita Edwardi Secundi: The Life of Edward the Second*, ed. Wendy R. Childs (Oxford, 2005), pp. xvii–xix. On the historiography of the Bristol revolt, see Cohn, 'Revolts of the Late Middle Ages', p. 281.

and liberties' belonged equally to all Bristol's citizens and commoners. The elite fourteen then requested the intervention of royal justice, which decided in their favour and stripped the commoners of their economic and political rights. In the court room, cries of corruption and favouritism rang out, and with fisticuffs and sticks, the commoners rioted, leaving twenty dead. Others out of fear jumped from the top-floor courtroom into the square below, breaking their legs. Eighty of the rebels were sentenced in absentia in the king's court at Gloucester but refused to surrender, chanting that they would 'defend their liberties until they died' and claimed their actions in no way violated the king's authority ('nec in dominum regem nichil deliquimus'). The fourteen fled Bristol, and 'for two years and more' commoners resisted the king. The king summoned the knights and magnates of Gloucestershire to London to plan an assault on Bristol. Eventually, the Earl of Pembroke ordered a siege, which began on 19 July 1316, and the town surrendered a week later.[15] The chronicle then reflected on the revolt's lessons: to resist the king is to forfeit one's own life; 'an island' cannot possibly succeed in rebelling against the king.[16] It concludes that '[t]he Bristolians now know that they have made a bad mistake, that their rebellion achieved nothing'. The chronicler fails, however, to admit that the ringleaders were never punished, or that the town's liberties were fully restored less than six months later. Not only were the citizens granted a general pardon without mass executions preceded by brutal displays of torture, as seen after insurrections at Norwich in 1272 or Bury St Edmunds in 1327 and 1328, but the king did not here demand theatres of supplication and humiliation, as preceded most collective royal pardons, as in York in 1405, when its citizens were forced to strip off, 'prostrat [ing] themselves naked on the ground, almost as if it were another Judgment day'.[17] Instead, several of the Bristol eighty went on to have successful political careers in town and at Parliament.

The Close, Fine, and Parliament, but principally the Patent Rolls recount a longer story of local conflicts between the elite fourteen and the rest of Bristol's citizens and commoners, but these also portray the conflict as one that quickly became centred against the Crown: royal taxation, the arrogance and hatred of the king's constable, Bartholomew de Badlesmere (later hanged and beheaded in 1322),[18] stationed at

---

[15] J. R. S. Phillips, *Aymer de Valence, Earl of Pembroke 1307–1324: Baronial Politics in the Reign of Edward II* (Oxford, 1972), pp. 102–3.

[16] *Vita Edwardi Secundi*, p. 129.   [17] *The Chronicle of Adam Usk*, p. 203.

[18] On his importance in factional politics of Edward II's reign, see Phillips, *Edward II*, pp. 166, 245, 273–4, 385, 397–8, 411, and other places.

Bristol's royal castle, and his attempts to control the town. The anonymous chronicler of Edward II's reign hardly mentions these matters. The
story told by the Patent Rolls and other royal documents differs in other
respects.[19] Commoners' antagonism to the fourteen does not appear to
have been a longstanding class divide. Instead, William Randolf, one of
the most prominent of the fourteen and later a leader of that group (as
suggested by the ordering of names in royal commissions with his at
the top), had been mayor of Bristol earlier and had defended ordinary
burgesses and their liberties against encroachments, oppression, and
violence of magnates with rights over certain neighbourhoods. In
1305, Mayor Randolf issued a complaint to the king that resulted in a
commission of 'oyer et terminer' against Thomas and Maurice de
Berkeley – prominent local lords and often members of royal commissions.[20] Randolf alleged that the Berkeleys had usurped the fee and
lordship of a street and district in Bristol, Redcliffe (Radeclivestrete),
a wealthy industrial suburb of cloth manufacturers that they had
claimed as a part of their manors since the early years of Henry III's
reign[21] and mistreated its burgesses, punishing them for refusing to
appear before the Berkeleys' tribunal on charges of trespass. Because
Randolf defended the burgesses of that street, the Berkeley brothers,
with twenty-seven of their cronies, assaulted him while he was attending

---

[19] Fuller, 'The Tallage of 6 Edward II', pp. 171–278, has assembled many, but not all, of
these documents.

[20] During the civil war between Edward II and his queen in 1326, the Berkeleys sided with
the queen (see Walsingham, *Historia Anglicana*, I, p. 183) and participated in the
rebellion against the Crown and the Dispensers in 1321–2; Edward II was kept
prisoner in the Berkeleys' castle, and some allege that Sir Thomas Berkeley put him
to death; see Christian Liddy, 'Bristol and the Crown, 1326–31: Local and National
Politics in the Early Years of Edward III's Reign', pp. 47–66, in *Fourteenth Century
England*, III, ed. W. M. Ormrod (Woodbridge, 2004), pp. 50–2; and Ormrod, *Edward III*,
pp. 66 and 93–4. On the importance of this family later in the fourteenth century and its loss
of power and patronage at the end of Richard II's reign, see Ralph Hanna III, 'Sir Thomas
Berkeley and his Patronage', *Speculum*, 64 (1989): 849–77; Nigel Saul, *Knights and
Esquires: The Gloucestershire Gentry in the Fourteenth Century* (Oxford, 1981); and Saul,
Richard II, p. 383.

[21] Hilton, 'Towns in English Society', p. 26; and especially, Liddy, 'Bristol and the
Crown'. In the aftermath of the Civil War, the Berkeleys were able to reinstate their
rights to Redcliffe because of their ties with the queen. Although Thomas de
Berkeley was forced to forfeit his rights to the neighbourhood in the 1330s, citizens
of Bristol did not gain complete judicial independence from the Berkeleys until
1373, when the town was incorporated; see D. J. Keene, 'Suburban Growth'
[1976], in *The English Medieval Town: A Reader in English Urban History 1200–1540*,
ed. R. C. Holt and G. Rosser (London, 1990), p. 111. Unlike most suburbs of
medieval English towns, which housed predominantly the poor, these residents'
assessed wealth exceeded by half that of other Bristolians during the reign of John;
ibid., p. 115.

the fair of Dundry at Chew Magna [Chyu], Somerset, in 1305, breaking his shins until 'the marrow ran out'.[22]

The impetus for the shin-breaking originated earlier and may have been a long, ongoing vendetta between Bristol's burgesses and the Berkeleys, whose seigneurial claims over streets and neighbourhoods challenged citizens' liberties. In March 1305, Maurice de Berkeley, 'while in Scotland on the king's service and under royal protection' lodged a complaint and ordered a commission to investigate charges that twenty-four named burgesses, along with others, assembled by ringing the town's common bell, had besieged his manor of Bedminster, broken his gates and doors, and carried away his goods. Their motive was to rescue a resident of Redcliffe (Robert de Cornubia), whom Maurice's bailiffs (exercising their seigneurial rights to the neighbourhood) had arrested and imprisoned for murder. Further, the knights complained of infringements to their judicial and economic liberties. The burgesses had prevented Maurice's men from holding his court at Redcliffe, and as with other 'strangers', had prevented his men from buying and selling corn and other goods within town.[23] Randolf was among these rebels (in fact, probably also mayor). The crowd, as best can be seen from the list of rebels, moreover, was not comprised solely of merchant elites or of Bristol grandees. It included a dyer ('teynturer'), tailor, skinner, shearer ('scer'), 'trekere' (perhaps a porter or carter),[24] and Richard Colpek and John Snowe (or Snogh), who a decade later would become leaders of the burgesses and commoners in their attacks against the king's constable and the wealthy fourteen in defence of communal liberties.[25]

Early the next month, the citizens initiated several commissions of oyer et terminer against the Berkeleys, first for 'usurping the fee and lordship' in Redcliffe; secondly for coming to town with a great multitude of horsemen and foot-soldiers to assault burgesses within their alleged jurisdiction. They claimed that these citizens had refused to appear before their court on charges committed within Redcliffe. The Berkeley men injured the burgesses' horses, dragged citizens from their homes, and threw them into a pit. When the burgesses' wives came to their aid, the Berkeleys beat and 'trampled' them, some to their death. Also, they maimed so badly the king's bailiff that he died soon afterwards. A third commission charged Thomas, Maurice, and their men of besieging Bristol after attending a fair at Tetbury[26] and beating many

---

[22] *CPR 1301–7*, p. 352, 1305.iv.7.   [23] Ibid., 1305.iii.12.
[24] If it were instead 'theker', he was a roofer; Fransson, *Middle English Surnames*, pp. 178–9.
[25] On Colpek, see Fuller, 'The Tallage of 6 Edward II', p. 205.
[26] About 50 km northeast of Bristol.

inside and outside their homes 'whom they knew to be burgesses of the said street and those who refused to declare before them that they were not the king's men of that street'. In addition, the Berkeleys violated the king's justice by taking his felons condemned to hang as thieves and delivering them to be tried in their own court by their juries. Further, the Berkeleys entered shops along the river and set up fittings to ship their merchandise 'as though the lordship of that water belonged to them and not the king'. On the same day, a burgess in a fourth commission accused the Berkeleys and four of their henchmen of assaulting him in his home, dragging him out, and throwing him into a cesspool.[27]

During the next decade, these alliances and divisions changed. Thomas de Berkeley, enemy of Bristol's commoners and elites alike and usurper of royal prerogatives, was regularly appointed to serve and lead royal commissions to examine and adjudicate rebellious crimes in Gloucestershire and elsewhere into the 1340s.[28] A new conflict began in Bristol at the beginning of 1312, this one sparked by the Crown's demands to fight its wars in Scotland. These were to be enforced in Bristol by the new royal constable Badlesmere, appointed by Edward II in 1307 as the constable of the royal castle overlooking town, to requisition troops from the townsmen and collect tallages.[29] In this atmosphere, fourteen of Bristol's wealthiest burgesses, who perhaps represented the town's ancient merchant guild, sought to control the city. They backed the king's new constable, while the mass of townsfolk, who claimed equal rights with the fourteen, were incensed by the levy of new customs to furnish supplies and military engines for the castle to discipline and control townsmen. In other words, from the Patent Rolls, royal intervention and policy was the catalyst that split the town in two, where earlier it had been united in common cause against its feudal overlords. On 13 September, the king stripped the town of its liberties and put them in the hands of Badlesmere, but by November it was clear that 'the Mayor, Bailiffs and worthy men' of the town were not 'intendant and respondent' to the constable; they disobeyed him, 'pretending' to have custody and Barton of their town 'by pretext of a certain mandate' of the king, but which he called 'frivolous and in contempt' of himself and his mandates.[30]

[27] *CPR 1301–7*, p. 352, 1305.iv.7.

[28] See for instance, *CPR 1313–17*, p. 605, 1313.vi.10. On 1 August 1326, the king appointed him to keep the king's peace in the county of Gloucester; on 12 June 1330 (now called 'baron'), he was on a panel with other justices of the King's Bench to hear a complaint of duress that involved force from Hugh Despenser the elder; *CPR 1327–30*, p. 565; and on 25 January 1340, he was appointed to hear and determine trespasses in a popular uprising in Worcester, *CPR 1338–40*, p. 485.

[29] What follows derives mainly from Fuller, 'The Tallage of 6 Edward II'.

[30] *Bristol Charters 1155–1373*, pp. 48–51.

The revolt continued, led by John le Taverner, mayor from 30 September 1312 to 31 May 1313. Burgesses and other commoners[31] refused to supply the castle with weapons. The rift between the Bristol fourteen and the mayor and burgesses became evident. With William Randolf at their lead, the fourteen protested to the king that the current mayor had stripped them of their liberties as citizens and had taken and distrained their merchandise. They charged that the mayor's actions were in retaliation to their alleged siding with the constable, who had oppressed citizens by unjustly imprisoning several in the royal castle and by permitting foreigners to trade in town without the mayor's permission, 'to the prejudice of the liberty of the town and contrary to their oath'.[32]

The king and his commissioners complied, ordering the sheriffs of Gloucestershire, Somerset, and Dorset to force the town to obey Badlesmere and restore the fourteen's rights and property. To punish the mayor and his assembled citizens, the king annulled the liberty of the town. But, unlike almost every other English town during the late Middle Ages, including London, Bristol faced royal power and punishment without humbly submitting and begging for forgiveness. They resisted the constable's efforts to enter town, 'beat and imprisoned his men', and constructed wooden barriers and towers to defend themselves against the royal castle. They even built a new city wall across the town with crenellations for shooting into the royal castle, fundamentally reshaping the town's topography. Further, they successfully prevented the constable and his men from entering to collect taxes and expropriated these funds 'for their own use'.[33] On 16 December 1312, the king ordered a survey to assess the fifteenth on goods and a tenth on rents, but the burgesses prevented the commissioners entering the town to make the assessments.

In May 1313, the mayor, John le Taverner, was arrested and sent to the Tower of London, which incensed the townsmen further and emboldened them in their resistance to pay their tallages. Surprisingly (given the fate of other revolts as we shall see), the king backed down and freed le Taverner on bail. In June, however, Edward insulted townsmen further by putting their old feudal enemy Thomas de Berkeley at the head of an oyer et terminer commission to inquire into the rift between Bristol's fourteen and the rest of the burgesses. This resulted in renewed

---

[31] Certainly, the rebels cannot be identified as the poor or craftsmen alone. Fuller, 'The Tallage of 6 Edward II', p. 205, calculated the combined assessed wealth of four of the prominent rebels – le Taverner, R. Martyn, R. Colpek, and W. de Clif – at £840.
[32] *CPR 1307–13*, p. 524, 1313.i.16.   [33] Fuller, 'The Tallage of 6 Edward II'.

rebellion, with bell ringing, the death of twenty, and the jumping from courtroom windows with which our single chronicler of the rebellion opens his account (though without mentioning the king's misguided, perhaps vengeful, appointment of Lord Berkeley as the lead commissioner). In June, the royal assessors finally were permitted to make their assessments, which were forwarded to London and still survive in the Pipe Rolls. They were not excessive; in fact, the sums were less than was demanded during King John's reign (£289 as compared with £333). Because of continued opposition to the constable, it took three further years, however, before Edward received any tax revenue from Bristol.

In these years, the king made further efforts to bring the rebel government and its leaders to justice and to reinstate the rights, property, and leadership of Randolf and his coterie of rich merchants. Although Edward had stripped Bristol of its liberties, it was to no avail: elections for mayor, bailiffs, and other offices continued as usual into 1316, and the municipal government assumed the right to tax its community as they chose. In 1315, the constable and William Randolf attempted to appease the burgesses and negotiate a settlement, but failed. Warrants were sent again to arrest le Taverner and five other rebels. On several occasions, the king's sheriff of Gloucestershire arrived at Bristol's gates but was turned away, unable to execute his orders. For these arrests, the sheriff assembled 'the whole commonalty' of Bristol in 1316 but failed again; the burgesses answered 'unanimously': none of their men would be arrested. On this try the sheriff then made arrests, but the commonalty forcibly freed the arrested. The sheriff then raised 'a great posse of his county' and returned to invade Bristol. The burgesses locked their gates, and 'the whole community', fortified by Welshmen who had levied war against the king, resisted the invasion. Their preparation and reconstruction of defences had proved for now successful: they drained the castle ditch, destroyed the castle mill, and dug a new twenty-four-foot-wide ditch, and fortified the town with a strong tower, barriers, chains, springalds, and other engines to fight and attack the castle. With 'banners raised', they held their town against the king and the nobility of Gloucestershire.

In June 1316 the king made new attempts to regain his city, sending in the forces of the Earl of Pembroke. Finally, on 9 August 1316, after a siege with heavy stones and a blockade, the 'active rebellion came to an end'. But matters were not settled until December; surprisingly, the penalties were not excessive: the town was fined 2,000 marks and in return on 18 December, its liberties were restored and a general pardon granted to all citizens except for ex-mayor le Taverner, his son, and Robert Martyn. Clearly, the rebels still could bargain, and none of the eighty earlier condemned to death was executed. Even the three excluded from the general pardon were pardoned in 1321, when their escheated lands and forfeited goods were returned to them. Several of the condemned were later chosen as members of Parliament for Bristol.[34] The old alignments and antagonisms soon returned to what they had been before 1312. The local magnate Thomas de Berkeley and his encroachments on town liberties united Bristol again, stimulating urban revolt lasting as late as 1330. The king initiated a commission of oyer et terminer to investigate a complaint by Lord Thomas, who accused Bristol's burgesses of rioting against his rights of the assize of bread and ale, tumbrel, pillory, and 'other liberties' now in another 'suburb' of Bristol, as burgesses had done at Redcliffe a generation earlier. As at the beginning of the century, the rebel leaders were the town's officials, starting with its mayor, but also including bailiffs and town clerks. In 1330, the rebels included several from decades earlier, such as John Fraunceys the younger, now a bailiff, who in January 1313 had been among those imprisoned by Badlesmere. Perhaps more remarkably, William Randolf, no doubt now aged, once the leader of the elite fourteen, and a long-term stalwart of Badlesmere and the king, crossed the barricades a third time, rejoining the commonalty's rebels against their ancient enemies, the feudal lords of Gloucestershire. As in the past, town leaders assembled the commonalty 'by public ringing of the bell', broke Lord Thomas' pillory and tumbrel,[35] assaulted his bailiffs, and 'with armed force' prevented the Berkeleys from holding their court or exercising their office. In addition, they took one of his bailiffs to Bristol's Guildhall, where they compelled him to swear never again to exercise court powers in that suburb.[36]

---

[34] Phillips, *Edward II*, p. 274.

[35] A cart for carrying condemned prisoners, also an instrument of torture.

[36] *CPR 1327–30*, p. 571, 1330.viii.20. McKisack, *The Fourteenth Century*, p. 50, wrongly dates the insurrection to the period of famine, 1315–16, and assumes that it was provoked by these conditions. Further, she mistakenly depicts it as a revolt easily and immediately suppressed by Edward II. Here, the earlier works of the early nineteenth-century antiquarian Samuel Seyer, *Memoirs Historical and Topographical of Bristol*, 2 vols. (Bristol, 1821–3), II, pp. 86–108, and Fuller, 'The Tallage of 6 Edward II', give a more comprehensive and accurate picture of events. A revolt at Sandwich sometime in 1274 was another significant resistance to royal power that finds no reference in chronicles and also occurred in a period of royal transition and weakness, when the young Edward I, recently crowned, had just returned to England after five years on Crusade. The mayor and commonalty of Sandwich resisted the warrener and sergeant of Dover Castle when their knights came to make distraints on cattle belonging to a citizen of Sandwich. With 'a public proclamation in the town', the citizens came out with swords and cudgels, beat the sergeants, and 'robbed them of their nags and their arms'. They then defended their town with chains and by digging trenches, preventing

1347

The tradition of opposing royal power erupted again in Bristol, a generation later, in 1347, during the next period of war, royal crisis, and the absence of a king. 'Malefactors of the town' assumed 'to themselves the royal power' and elected one of their number as captain. They issued proclamations and with armed force boarded ships in the town's port that the king had licensed and stocked with provisions headed for troops in Gascony. The rebels attacked the ships' masters and sailors, plundered the corn and other goods aboard the vessels and committed 'other misdeeds' within the town and the counties of Gloucester and Somerset.[37] Recently, this incident has been taken as the first grain or food riot in English history.[38] Yet from this document there is little evidence that this was a grain revolt of starving masses, even if it occurred at a moment of grain scarcity with sharply rising prices. Instead, it was a political rebuff to the Crown and its heavy-handed requisitioning of ships and grain for the king's war in France.[39]

Bristol was not the only town to resist the king's means of provisioning his troops in 1347. In the same month, another two royal commissions investigated almost identical insurrections in other prominent English ports of the fourteenth century, Boston and Lynn, and supplied further details. At Boston, the insurgents also elected their own leader, Thomas de Hocham, cordwainer, in this case to be 'their captain and mayor'. They boarded ships, which the king had licensed, laden with corn and other victuals. They plundered the ships and imprisoned 'good men' of the town, who would not consent to these raids, as well as others who came from outside to oppose them. 'By fear of death' the insurgents

royal intervention for 'a month or more'. On 8 March 1275, the constable penetrated the town's defences. As a consequence, Sandwich lost its liberties, its townsmen were forced to fill in the trenches and remove the barbicans and other fortifications at their expense, and an unspecified number of the rebels were taken to Dover and imprisoned; *King's Bench*, I, pp. 13–14.

[37] *CPR 1345–8*, p. 392, 1347.vii.12. Law and order appear to have already been breaking down in Bristol by April. Because of increased disturbances by those who 'wander and run about by day and night perpetrating in divers ways damages, evil-doings and excesses', a royal charter granted the mayor, bailiffs, and 'worthy men' increased powers to punish 'evil-doers' and 'make anew one cage for prisoners within the town' as 'used in London'; *Bristol Charters 1155–1373*, pp. 8–11.

[38] Buchanan Sharp, 'The Food Riots of 1347 and the Medieval and Social Conflict', in *Moral Economy and Popular Protest: Crowds, Conflict and Authority*, ed. Adrian Randall and Andrew Charlesworth (Houndmills, 2000), p. 35.

[39] From the end of May, Edward III had been preparing a major offensive against the French. The English preparations reached their peak at the end of July; see Sumption, *The Hundred Years War*, I: *Trail by Battle*, pp. 577–9.

'maintain[ed] their misprisions' and continued their 'quarrels against the king, his royal power and his people'.[40] According to the commission, the insurgents of Boston also assumed royal power and made 'royal proclamations' to all those who had left town because of the dissension and demanded that they return within a certain time, otherwise their houses would be destroyed, 'the timber thereof and all goods of the owners in the town to be burned forthwith'. The commission charged that these rebels had made other proclamations 'daily' (but did not specify them) with similar 'grievous penalties' to be inflicted on townsmen who failed to comply with their ordinances. In neither Bristol nor Boston did these royal reports point to matters of famine, high grain prices, or suspicions of merchant hoarding; instead, both turned on commoners' zeal to elect their own leaders and resist royal authority, to enact their own proclamations and ordinances against the backdrop of England's most extensive efforts to provision its troops for invasion in France at the end of that summer, with 699 requisitioned vessels drawn from eighty-three English ports from Bamburgh to Bristol and with thirty-seven hired vessels from Bayonne, Castile, and the Low Countries.[41]

A third insurrection against the king's ships during the same month, and which according to the commission 'by example' spread to Thetford and other towns in Norfolk, further details these politics of grain and requisitioning foodstuffs imposed by the Crown during the summer of 1347. According to the commission, 'a large confederacy of evil doers' now at Lynn assumed 'to themselves the king's power' and boarded ships in the port 'freighted with his licence with corn of victuals'. This time the document is clearer; it was 'for the sustenance of his lieges in Gascony'. It is also clearer regarding some of these rebels' aims: they discharged the cargoes against the will of the ships' owners, and brought the grain and other provisions to land to sell 'at their own price'. This commission specifies 'other misdeeds' rebels may have also been committing 'daily' at Bristol and Boston. After bringing the confiscated corn to town for sale, Lynn's rebels arrested the corn merchants and by force of arms and 'without process of law' brought them to the town's pillory, where they were tried. They further assumed power in the town, arresting the mayor and 'many of the good men of the town', and with death threats compelled them to abide by the rebels' 'divers quasi-royal proclamations'.[42] In the following month, these armed protests against this gigantic provisioning of troops to fight France had spread to the two

---

[40] *CPR 1345–8*, p. 381, 1347.vii.16.
[41] Sumption, *The Hundred Years War*, I, p. 578.   [42] Ibid., p. 388, 1347.vii.12.

ends of England. Rebels in Yorkshire and Kent, which also included parsons and other clergy, assaulted royal officers and prevented the provisioning of ships for the king's war.[43] Royal politics were here the spark of insurrection.[44] Despite Edward III's remarkable leadership, his fifty-year reign was not entirely immune from revolt by his subjects, as some have alleged.[45]

Whether the Bristol insurgents had any memory of the town's four-and-a-half-year resistance to Edward II, his justices and tax collectors a generation earlier, or used it to rally their forces can only be conjectured. Clearly, at Boston and Lynn, such a tradition and collective memory was not essential to achieve the same goals, although as we shall see, Lynn also had had a major insurrection against the Crown during the same years of Edward II's absence from England while fighting the Scots.[46] The summer of 1347, with Edward III's massive requisitioning of grain and victuals for his troops set off a short but widespread and violent wave of municipal insurrections across England's port towns, which has yet to receive notice from historians. Had the longer period of Edward II's weakness, caused by his overextension in Scotland, permitted a similar wave of insurrection?

[43] Ibid., pp. 398–9, 1347.ix.1.

[44] The records do not reveal how long these revolts succeeded in enforcing rebels' proclamations, their occupation of town governments, or if they were punished. I find no trace of them in *CCR 1346–9*, or *CFR 1347–56*. A search through King's Bench might shed more evidence on them.

[45] See the conclusion of Ormrod, *Edward III*: 'But Edward's successful avoidance of any hint of armed revolt among his subjects for over four decades – an achievement unparalleled in historical memory, and not surpassed again for at least two centuries – is a vivid reminder of the enviable state of stability for which he stood' (p. 603).

[46] It is difficult to know if the king's licensing of this vast number of ships caused further insurrections. In May, further indictments 'of sedition against the king' now investigated the 'people in the city of London', but the two charged had escaped, and the commission did not state their objectives; *CPR 1345–8*, p. 319, 1347.v.20.

7   A wave of insurrection, 1312–18?

The weak kingship of Edward II, his disastrous campaigns in Scotland, culminating in defeat at Bannockburn, coupled with increases in taxation,[1] provided space for insurrection in places other than Bristol. But, as with the Bristol revolt, chroniclers largely ignored them and, as a result, they have been mostly unnoticed by later historians. One exception is a revolt recorded by *William Thorne's Chronicle* of those on the manors and market towns owing rents and services to St Augustine's Abbey, Canterbury at the mouth of the Thames estuary. In 1318, these rural and market town tenants withheld rents, assembled unlawfully, taxed themselves to wage battle against the abbey, assaulted the abbot's bailiff, and prevented the abbot from holding his view of frankpledge and other courts at Minster. When the abbot imposed 'distraints', the tenants organized six hundred men and gathered further support from townsmen of the Cinque Ports. 'With bows, arrows, swords and sticks', they besieged the abbey's manor houses on several occasions. Their attacks continued for over five weeks, during which they held meetings, swore oaths in writing, made assessments and raised funds ('divers tallages amongst themselves') amounting to £26. 'By such conspiracies and collections' and 'by tumult and excessive shouting', they prevented the abbot from holding his court at Minster. Ultimately, the abbot had to appeal for royal intervention. The tenants were found guilty and forced to pay the enormous sum of £200 for damages to the abbot.[2] In 1318, Edward II appointed the same lord, Bartholomew de Badlesmere, constable of Bristol from 1313 to 1316, as his chief officer, now at England's other end, despite his inability to quell England's longest urban revolt of any period in its history, including the early modern

---

[1] The heaviest taxation of Edward II's reign came after the defeat at Bannockburn, in 1315–16, but the impositions of these years hardly reached the levels of the mid-1290s or the 1330s. For periods of high taxation, see Maddicott, *The English Peasantry*, pp. 6–7.

[2] *William Thorne's Chronicle of Saint Augustine's Abbey Canterbury*, ed. and trans. A. H. Davis (Oxford, 1934), pp. 432–4.

and modern periods.[3] Badlesmere again sided with the elites, in this case, the abbot against his tenants, both rural and urban.[4]

The estates of St Augustine's Abbey were not the only other places to experience rebellion during the second decade of the fourteenth century; moreover, the major arena of these conflicts, c. 1312 to 1318, was towns. Although these years coincided in part with the famines of 1315 to 1317, no evidence points to dearth as the trigger of protest. None pictures impoverished commoners, or records the cries of starving widows and the wretched, with their shouts of 'Misericordia', as happened at Siena's Piazza del Campo in 1329.[5] Instead, zeal among citizens to maintain or extend town liberties against the Crown and other lords drove these revolts. Neither their leadership nor the rank-and-file were impoverished; rather, they were of the upper echelons and were mayors, bailiffs, and other elected officials.

Yet chronicles and Patent Rolls were certainly not blind to problems posed by this, Europe's worst famine in medieval and modern history, and reported it with interest and passion. A chronicler mentioned that 'the clamour of the people (ad clamorem populi excitatus)' in London in 1316 moved the king to regulate the grain market in the capital, but did not lead to riot.[6] 'The unusual scarcity of corn and other victuals in the realm and the famine oppressing the people thereof' did precipitate crime, even internationally. Against the king's protection, and safe conduct granted to merchants from Spain, Sicily, and Genoa, then provisioning England with emergency grain, 'certain persons' carried off a Genoese

[3] Badlesmere was Kentish and had represented the county in Parliament (1307) before being posted to Bristol; see Maddicott, 'Badlesmere, Sir Bartholomew, c. 1275–1322', rev. ODNB.

[4] Two royal commissions provide further details of the revolt. In January 1318, fifty-seven men were charged with gathering 'a great mob', surrounding the abbot's dwelling at Salmaston (near Margate), and attempting to burn down the abbot's manor (an attack not mentioned in the chronicle); CPR 1317–21, p. 98, 1318.i.4. A second oyer and terminer commission, this one headed by Badlesmere, added that the rebels assaulted the abbot's men appointed to the custody of his manors of Salmaston and Minster 'in the open market there', causing the abbot to lose his market profits; ibid., p. 172, 1318.iii.4. Conflicts with the abbey's villages and market towns of Thanet reached back as far as 1176, when 'tenants insisted that they were not obliged to attend the abbot's court in Canterbury once every three weeks'; Gilbert Slater, 'Social and Economic History', in VCH: Kent, ed. William Page (London, 1932), III, pp. 348–9.

[5] Cohn, Lust for Liberty, p. 71. However, on much of the Continent, this famine rarely provoked revolt; ibid., p. 70. William Jordan, The Great Famine: Northern Europe in the Early Fourteenth Century (Princeton, 1996), claims that 'grain riots did characterize urban life of the famine years' (p. 165); yet he produces only one grain riot during the famine, at Magdeburg (Germany) in 1316.

[6] Johannes de Troklowe et Henricus de Blaneforde, Chronicas et annales, regnantibus Henrico III, Edwardo I, Edwardo II, Ricardo II et Henrico IV, ed. Henry T. Riley, RS, 3 (1866), pp. 95–6.

vessel, a 'great ship, called a *Dromond*', docked at Sandwich, that had transported wheat and other cereals. The 'malefactors' were not, however, starving women, children, or other *miserabiles*; rather they were foreign agents later found to have been employed by the French Crown.[7]

Taxation, rights to govern, possession of a town's castle, justice, and the preservation or extension of liberties were the issues that prompted townsmen and others to revolt in these years. In at least two of these cases, Patent Roll descriptions begin not with grain prices or scarcity, but by stating that they occurred 'while the king was absent beyond the seas'[8] along with other of his chief officials during their 'absence in Scotland'.[9] Royal absence, not grain prices, was the essential backdrop to the disorders. Although the chronicles report only two incidents, 1312–18, that challenged local lords backed by the king or against the king himself – Bristol and Thanet (both by a chronicle a piece) – the Patent Rolls provide a rich array of riots and revolts, the geographical extension of which appears as broad as that of the English Peasants' Revolt in 1381.

On 8 September 1312, a royal commission investigated a revolt in Winchester led by twenty-seven 'confederates', 'disturbers of the city'. As with the Bristol revolt, royal mandates provoked a city's division and the eruption of conflict. Here, however, the alignments and support of the Crown differed from Bristol's. At Winchester, the elected officials supported the Crown, and the rebels prevented the mayor, his ministers, and justices from exercising their offices, which included 'executing the king's mandates'. Against the mayor's and king's prohibitions, the rebels held meetings, refused to be brought to justice, 'deprived certain citizens of the city of their liberty', and perhaps most seriously, as suggested by its position in the document, 'of their own authority . . . admitted strangers to that liberty' and imposed tallages on 'some of the citizens . . . not only to the prejudice of the mayor and king's minister, but also in derogation and contempt of the king's mandates . . . to the impoverishment of the city of Winchester'.[10] As with the terse and formulaic administrative language of most of these records, it is difficult to know the rebels' social position, motives, or demands. With the granting of citizenship to outsiders and exacting their own taxes, had they established a parallel government to challenge that of the mayor and elites backed by the Crown?

[7] *CPR 1313–17*, pp. 501–2, 1316.v.23; on the identity of the raiders, see *Foedera, conventions, literae, et cujuscunque generic acta public, inter reges Angliae . . .*, ed. Thomas Rymer, 10 vols. (London, 1704–35), III, p. 894. I thank Dr Bryan Dick for the reference.

[8] See for instance *CPR 1313–17*, 1317.v.24, pp. 57–8.

[9] See for instance ibid., p. 105, 1314.iv.27.   [10] *CPR 1307–13*, p. 534, 1312.ix.8.

In the same year, on a lesser scale (in terms of the size of the town and the incident), five men, with a daughter of one the rebels and 'others', assaulted a royal clerk and his servants who were on the king's business at the market towns of Cheshunt and Ware in Hertfordshire. They imprisoned the officials and carried away their goods.[11] Another commission of 1312 investigated the 'riotous behaviour' of six named rebels, including a tailor and unnamed 'others of their confederates', who broke the peace and committed 'divers outrages upon the citizens of Carlisle and other men of Cumberland'.[12]

The following year, cases of collective violence against magistrates in cities and towns and acts of disobedience against the Crown mounted in importance. On 24 July, a commission of oyer et terminer (which included Bartholomew de Badlesmere) drew up one of the longest lists of rebels and most detailed accounts in the Patent Rolls of collective violence found over its near two hundred and fifty years of published documents.[13] Robert de Montalt [de Monte Alto], 'lord of the port of the town of Bishops Lenn',[14] in a complaint to the king indicted individually 223 men and a woman, who comprised only part of a 'great crowd of rioters' of townspeople at Lynn.[15] Served by inspectors ('perceners') and bailiffs, Robert possessed the rights, as a farm from the king, over Lynn's tollbooth, where the port's fees were collected, and to a tribunal that enforced the port's regulations and laws and the sea surrounding it.[16] As he 'peacefully approached the town', the prior of Lynn, John de Brompholm, first named and probably the leader, 'armed in a warlike manner with banners displayed', assaulted Lord Robert,

---

[11] Ibid., p. 544, 1312.xii.1.   [12] Ibid., p. 541, 1312.xi.8.

[13] The pardons after Cade's Rebellion list more; these, however, were many separate entries stretching over several months, not a single commission.

[14] In an acquittal of Robert on 8 February 1310 for scutage during Edward I's wars in Wales, his brother Roger was identified as a tenant-in-chief of the late king and a minor in the king's wardship; CCR, 1307–1313, p. 194. In March 1311, Robert went to Scotland in the king's service; ibid., p. 311. With his wife, he possessed the manor of Aylesbury, which was presumed to belong to the king's demesne, and on 7 April 1313, the sheriff of Buckingham ordered him to collect royal tallages from his tenants; ibid., p. 519. A licence in CPR of 23 November 1316 shows that Robert and his wife Emma were linked by inheritance to the highest members of Edward II's court. They held in dower property that after the death of Emma would ascend to Robert de Baldock, archdeacon of Middlesex, a favourite of Edward II and Despenser, and then to Hugh Despenser the younger, Hugh the elder, and to Edward's son Hugh the younger and his heirs; CPR 1313–17, p. 402.

[15] CPR 1313–17, pp. 57–8, 1313.vii.24.

[16] According to the Close Rolls of 22 November 1308, Margaret, the queen mother of Edward II, sold the tollbooth of Lynn with its pleas and perquisites (which had belonged to the deceased Robert de Tateshale) to the king's clerk William de Carleton for £546 13s 4d; CCR, 1307–1313, p. 84.

besieged the inn where he stayed, carried away his goods, and beat and imprisoned him and his men, until they were delivered by writs from the king. For 'a long time' they lost their services (and presumably their fees from the port). Although Robert may have approached the town peacefully on that day of the rebels' assembly, clearly a longer history preceded the strife. 'Through fear of death', the rebels forced Lord Robert 'to release all manner of actions which he had against the mayor and commonalty of the town'. Unfortunately, the commission does not specify what these actions concerned. However, it goes beyond most Patent Rolls by stating more clearly what had been at stake and even sketching the broad ideological outlines behind the rebels' assemblies and 'warlike' actions.

The demands of the Lynn rebels may have even reached beyond those of the Bristolians, who always insisted that they were not disobeying the king, or making incursions against his authority, but sought only to restore the status quo, which amounted to their previously ensured town liberties. The townsmen of Lynn made no attempt to gloss over their radicalism. They compelled the royal agent, Lord Robert, to turn over the profits of the port as well as his office to the commonalty of Lynn for twenty-one years, along with other agreements that the commission did not specify. Not only did the rebels force him to write and secure these liberties to the town with his seal; they brought him to the marketplace, 'compelled him to stand aloft on a stall before a great multitude of men assembled there', and upon the Host, brought by their chaplain, swear he would not contravene any of the agreements stated in his sealed document. He was further forced to bind himself by a £2,000 surety to be paid to the mayor and the commonalty if he violated any of the agreements. In addition, the 'rioters' removed his bailiff and appointed their own to collect the port's fees. The revolt was clearly an attempt to extend the economic and political rights of the town, to seize the liberty and revenues of what had been a royal toll farmed out to a nobleman. Unlike resistance to the Crown at Bristol or Winchester, this one did not last as long or split the town into warring factions. Only thirty of the 223 are listed by occupation, and one by a title, that of the town's leader and prior, John de Brompholm. But those identified by profession show a wide cross-section of crafts and victuallers: five taverners, four goldsmiths, four tailors, three furriers, two barbers, eight soap makers ('soperes'),[17] a cooper, a shipman, and a fisherman.[18]

[17] See Fransson, *Middle English Surnames*, p. 71.
[18] On occupations in Lynn and under-representation of those in the cloth industry, see Owen, *The Making of King's Lynn*, pp. 57–9.

As was generally the case, the Patent Rolls reveal little of the success or failure of the revolt. The municipal archives of Lynn, however, show that the results were mixed: the rebels forced Robert de Montalt to lease his share of the tollbooth to them, but they paid for it, as they were eventually saddled with a fine of £4,000, which took years to pay off.[19] Instead of creating division, however, this revolt appears to have healed a rift in Lynn's urban society. Nine years before, 'the poor' of Lynn had petitioned the king against 'the rich', who they accused of embezzlement in the form of levying tallages and a fine for the king, collecting more than the sum specified, and extorting 'grievous distraints from the commonalty', converted to 'their own uses'.[20]

Towards the end of 1313, two further urban revolts arose against the Crown that concerned economic and political liberties. In October, burgesses of the port of Ravenserodd, once at the mouth of the Humber estuary (Yorkshire),[21] 'conspired' and passed ordinances against the king 'and his state'. These sought to curtail the powers of royal bailiffs and other officers within the town and gave new powers to local merchants. With the new laws, burgesses assumed charge over regulating who among foreign merchants could enter their town and sell merchandise, giving the burgesses rights to seize for the town contraband merchandise that previously would have gone to the king. Further, they withheld the king's customs charged on goods as their own and imposed penalties on those who violated the ordinances 'to the prejudice of the king and the manifest impoverishment of foreign merchants and others resorting to the town'.[22]

The next day, another royal inquiry exposed a conspiracy at Nottingham. The rebels 'made confederacies among themselves, by drafting an oath' pledging to support one another if any were indicted for the mayor's murder, and with this agreement they murdered the mayor and assaulted six royal guards at Nottingham Castle. After one of the 'confederacy' had been apprehended, they made good their promise: ringing the town's bells, they raised a posse to rescue the felon imprisoned in the royal castle. The document makes no mention of the outcome, who the rebels were, or their motives for deposing the mayor and king's men. Was it similar to what was happening in Bristol at the same time, an outrage against the impositions of a royal castle and royal

---

[19] Ibid., p. 38.   [20] *CPR 1301–7*, p. 61, 1304.vii.5.

[21] Built on sandbanks in the estuary, it was a major port in the thirteenth century before being swept into the sea at the end of the fourteenth; see Prestwich, *Plantagenet England*, pp. 471–2.

[22] *CPR 1313–17*, p. 63, 1313.x.23.

taxation, or as at Winchester, Lynn, and Ravenserodd, were they fighting to extend their economic rights and privileges? Whatever the case, as it had at Winchester, it split the town, with the elected officials siding with the king against an unspecified group of citizens or disenfranchised residents opposed to both municipal and royal authority.[23]

For the next year, the Patent Rolls do not present urban revolts as significant as ones the previous year with clear economic or political objectives against royal mandates. Nevertheless, two further outbreaks of organized collective violence threatened the king and hindered his men from executing justice and other royal duties. On 10 March, William Tuchet[24] and unnamed others comprised 'an armed multitude' of rebels, who threatened and terrorized judges and jurors from holding their court sessions ('assise of novel disseisin') at Northampton concerning properties in five nearby villages. The king set another day for the justices to meet in town but the same persons 'and many others' with armed force prevented the court from being held again.[25] Whatever their motives, it shows effective collective, even mass, armed resistance to the king and his assizes in an urban place, while he was overextended, fighting his wars in Scotland.

A similar breakdown in royal authority appears that year in Oxford. 'Before leaving for Scotland', Edward had demanded that his peace be preserved in Oxford between students and townsmen, but brawls and pitched armed conflict between the two continued. He then ordered the sheriff of Oxford to make it known in the university that anyone inciting conflict would be arrested (under pain of forfeiture). Nonetheless, despite the proclamation, town–gown disputes remained rife, with 'homicides and other offences ... committed in contempt of his mandates'. On 28 June, the king tried again to alleviate the unrest, commanding the sheriff to arrest without delay any found guilty of violence, whether clerks or others. Its success was not recorded.[26]

Revolts also erupted in London. A royal commission found that 'rioters' had held unlawful assemblies in the city and suburbs and had risen against their mayor, John de Gisors,[27] and magistrates of the king,

---

[23] Ibid., pp. 62–3.

[24] William Tuchet was a local knight, who served in Edward II's Scottish campaigns in 1311 and 1319 but sided with the Earl of Lancaster against the king in 1322. The family claimed to have come to England with William the Conqueror.

[25] *CPR, 1313-17*, p. 141.   [26] Ibid., p. 153.

[27] This was John de Gisors the Third, grandson of the founder of this London dynasty, and a populist mayor of London in 1246, who supported Simon de Montfort in 1263. John the Third's father was also an alderman and mayor of London. In 1321, John III was found guilty of predating the grant of freedom to a committed felon in order to release him on bail, which provided Edward II with the pretext to arrest him and suspend the

pelting them with mud and stones. The insurgents ran through the streets 'uttering a great and horrible noise' that 'excited the people against the king and his ministers', breaking into and plundering houses. Unfortunately, none of the confederates was listed or described beyond the word 'rioters', and their aims and grievances are difficult to ferret out, but the document points to one motive – to prevent 'the king's laws and assizes to be observed'.[28] With this case, the chroniclers provide more flesh and insight into the nature and causes of the revolt. A perceived miscarriage of justice among artisans had sparked discontent. In the summer before, London's courts had punished a baker by torture, drawing him upon the hurdle, while another (presumably guilty of the same crime) went free.[29] The following day 'the people' insulted the mayor, calling him a rogue; many were 'imprisoned and impoverished' by the mayor's 'malice and scheming'. The rift and antagonism between Gisors and commoners, moreover, continued after the oyer et terminer inquiry of 1314. In 1317, the French chronicler of London reported succinctly but blandly, 'there was great discord between the commons and him [Gisors]'. The commoners drew up their demands in a new charter presented to the mayor, 'a thing . . . much against [his] will'.[30] During the summer, unrest against Edward also broke out in the countryside and possibly in towns in Stafford and Shropshire. The king's assessors and collectors of the twentieth, recently granted by Parliament, reported that under the pretext of the king failing to observe 'the great charter of liberties of England, the charter of the forests, and the ordinances made by the prelates, earls and barons', their duties had been impeded.[31]

In 1315, violence erupted against Edward I's widow, Margaret (1279?–1318), at her urban holdings in Oxford, Worcester, Gloucester, and Hereford, which she held in dower from the king. Her sergeant locked the doors and windows of the houses and stalls she owned in these towns and sealed them because of unpaid rents and services. 'Certain persons' then forcibly broke the seals and opened the doors

---

mayoralty of London. The family was prominent in the wine trade and harmed by royal support of Gascon importers, which drew the Gisors into conflict with Edward; see Elspeth Veale, 'Gisors, John (I) de', *ODNB*.

[28] *CPR 1313–17*, pp. 410–11.

[29] *French Chronicle of London 1259–1343*, in *Chronicles of the Mayors and Sheriffs of London 1188–1274*, ed. Henry T. Riley (London, 1863), pp. 251–2.

[30] Ibid., p. 252. This could have been a misdated reference to the revolt and demands of 1319 that fundamentally restructured London's constitution, limiting terms of office and broadening the franchise, giving craftsmen greater possibilities of citizenship; Williams, *Medieval London*, p. 283.

[31] *CPR 1313–17*, p. 568.

and houses. To what extent these acts were coordinated across the four towns is difficult to know. By the queen's complaint, her urban tenants further 'prevented [her] from levying the rents and services due to her',[32] suggesting a consciously organized rent strike aided by violence.

The breakdown in royal control is seen not only from the perspective of riots in towns and the countryside in these years; corruption, abuses of justice, and lack of control over royal magistrates further expose Edward's weakness. It provoked rare instances when commoners were able to petition the king successfully into appointing special commissions to examine abuses by his own officials. On 10 March the 'people' of Norfolk and Suffolk were granted a special commission to investigate the complaint of 'conspiracies and confederacies and the maladministration of justice in those counties'.[33] Three months later, the commonalty of the king's Welsh town of Builth lodged a complaint.[34] First, the king's men and bailiffs stationed at the town's castle enacted an elaborate ruse against the townsmen, feigning to besiege their own castle, shooting arrows at it, then pinning the blame on the burgesses. With trumped-up charges, they imprisoned 'very many' townsmen in the castle and wounded and mistreated others, thereby preventing the townsmen from defending themselves in court 'according to the liberty of the town'. Furthermore, the royal officials used these opportunities to steal 'victuals and other things' from burgesses' homes. They killed their swine and violated their liberties to possess hand mills, forcing them to grind their corn at these bailiffs' mills and pay 'a heavy toll' fixed at the officers' will, as though they were seigneurial lords. Any burgess who resisted was imprisoned, as well as any who approached the king to complain. The burgesses further accused the officers of committing other acts 'to the destruction of the liberty of the town' and their 'impoverishment'.[35]

The last year of the Bristol revolt and resistance to the Crown in 1316 saw further attacks against the Crown across England. On 1 January, a commission once more investigated the king's problems with collecting royal taxes, the twentieth and fifteenth, now in Yorkshire. The revolt began with the king's bailiffs themselves. Along with locally elected bailiffs, the king's men disobeyed royal mandates and resisted royal taxes. These bailiffs even led those who had refused to pay or could not pay 'in contempt of the king' to break the royal pounds where their property had been impounded.[36] Again in Yorkshire, a commission investigated a plot hatched by twenty-three men 'and others' (including

---

[32] Ibid., p. 573, 1315.viii.2.   [33] Ibid., p. 564.   [34] Town in Powys, central Wales.
[35] CPR 1313–17, p. 325, 1315.v.27.   [36] Ibid., p. 424.

two chaplains) from Scarborough to kill the town's royal bailiff. It suggests a motive. The bailiff had tried to bring the rebels to justice for trespasses against him, breaking 'his houses and walls', dragging him by his hair, and abducting Katharine, a minor in his custody.[37] But from the Patent Rolls alone, it is difficult to know why these men made their attack in the first place. From other unpublished records of the oyer et terminer commissions and trials, however, the incident appears as the culmination of struggles within Scarborough among groups of the rich, poor, and middling burgesses that had been stirring over the first thirteen years of Edward II's reign.[38]

In the same year, collective disobedience to the Crown sprouted in the southeast. Discord between the men of Yarmouth and the barons of the Cinque Ports opened afresh after agreements enforced during the reign of Edward I, and after Edward II had commanded representatives to appear regularly before him and his council, threatening that any deed jeopardizing the peace between them would be punished severely. Yet, 'having no consideration for his prohibition or the ordinances', the men of Great Yarmouth, under the guise of trading with foreign ports, put to sea 'a great fleet of armed ships' to attack the Cinque Ports and other merchants at Portsmouth, near the Isle of Wight, and elsewhere around Southampton. The commission was to gather the names of those who manned the armed ships – the 'lords, masters, mariners and others in the said ships, and of all aiding and abetting them', and to punish all found guilty.[39] Finally, across to Wales, a rebellion against the king led by Llewelyn Bren in parts of Glamorgan and South Wales was quelled towards the end of March.[40] The inquiry shows, however, that the rebellion had not been confined to these Welsh regions alone; rather 'many men', English as well as Welsh, in those lands and neighbouring regions, had supported the rebellion.[41]

The return of troops from Scotland and suppression of the Bristol revolt in 1316 mark a decline of popular revolt against the Crown until the years of baronial reactions led by Queen Isabella and Roger de Mortimer.[42] In 1317, only two revolts appear that in any way involved

---

[37] Ibid., pp. 586–7, 1316.viii.21; 593, 1316.x.3; 493–4, 1316.iii.6.
[38] See Kaeuper, 'Law and Order', p. 780.   [39] CPR 1313–17, p. 583, 1316.vii.8.
[40] Llewelyn surrendered unconditionally to the Earl of Hereford on 18 March 1316 and was hanged at Cardiff Castle a year later.
[41] CPR 1313–17, p. 492, 1316.iii.26.
[42] The baronial revolt of 1321–2 appears to have had no significant ripples among burgesses as seen in chronicles or CPR. According to Valente, The Theory and Practice of Revolt, p. 147, this revolt was strikingly different from the 1260s: in 1321–2, townsmen comprised only 1 per cent of identified rebels.

the Crown. One of these, moreover, infringed only indirectly on the king, and the second, which resulted from the absence of a king's agent supporting Edward's war with Scotland, was not an urban rebellion, or at least did not occur in a prominent town, even by late medieval English standards. The first was largely a local jurisdictional conflict between the Abbey of St Mary's in York and the burgesses of the city, who possessed the rights over the York suburb, the borough of Bootham.[43] Against the town's claims, the abbot argued that the Earl of Richmond had granted it to the abbey and had been confirmed by the king and his progenitors. On 4 May, the abbot lodged a complaint against York's mayor, its clerk, five previous city bailiffs and four present ones, two previous chamberlains, and eight other burgesses, including a furrier, girdeler, armourer, and tailor, that they assembled 'a multitude of malefactors', who marched to Bootham, where they arrested 'certain men and tenants of the abbot'. York's citizens charged those of Bootham of illegally baking bread and brewing ale contrary to the city's rights of assize over the borough. They took the men to York, put some in city pillories and imprisoned others. Further, they assessed and imposed various taxes ('tallages') on the abbot, his men, and tenants, as if the borough were the City of York, which the abbot asserted it was not. Nonetheless, the burgesses made distraints for the unpaid taxes and 'committed other excesses upon the abbot'.[44] The conflict was essentially one between the city hierarchy and the Abbey of St Mary's, but in which the king had an interest, as the abbey's defender.[45]

The same month, an attack on the king and one of his ministers impinged much more directly on matters of royal control in the Forest of Dean. While the king's custodian of the castle of St Briavels and of the Forest had been transferred and was then on duty as the custodian of the Scottish border town of Berwick-upon-Tweed, two brothers of St Briavels gathered 'a crowd', held 'unlawful conventicles', resisted the deputy custodian of the castle, and prevented other royal ministers from performing their duties, such as the seizing of property ('distraints and attachments') for unpaid taxes and debts, holding the court of the hundred, and levying taxes, rents, and other debts due to the custodian's farm over the castle and forest. Furthermore, they assaulted the custodian's deputy and servants.[46]

---

[43] To the northeast of York's city walls and of St Mary's, outside the walls. In 1275 it was declared as a free borough belonging to St Mary's; Beresford and Finberg, *English Medieval Boroughs*, p. 186.

[44] *CPR 1313–17*, pp. 692–3, 1317.v.4.

[45] In 1333, for instance, the king appointed the Abbot of St Mary's temporally as the crown's treasurer; Ormrod, *Edward III*, p. 154.

[46] *CPR 1313–17*, 1317.v.24 p. 697; the forest was administered from St Briavels.

Further attacks or revolts against the king or his ministers in localities followed in 1318, which continued to reflect the pressures and aftershocks of the war with Scotland. On 15 April, a writ of aid was directed to the king's sheriffs, bailiffs, and other ministers at Berwick-upon-Tweed,[47] resulting from the political and military instability of this recently acquired frontier town on the Scottish border. After guarantees from the town's mayor, bailiffs, and commonalty, the king granted them custody over the town.[48] Yet 'owing to their default', the Scots entered the town and occupied it. The king appointed John de Weston to arrest and seize all the goods of the burgesses and commonalty of Berwick, as well as those belonging to them outside the town.[49] A second attack on the Crown was probably less significant. As the king's tax collectors of the scutage for the armies in Scotland approached York, thirteen named men and 'others' assaulted them, thereby delaying the collection.[50] On the same day, ninety-one men, including some of the thirteen, broke into the houses of an attendant of the tax collectors, pried open his chests, and stole his cattle, money, and other goods.[51]

On 6 August 1318, the elected bailiffs of Norwich led a revolt of burgesses against a certain John de Cove. Seventy-four men were named. By their occupations, they appear to represent the upper echelons of the city – six drapers, three spice merchants, two goldsmiths, and a 'coltiller' (knife maker or dealer). They rang the city bells and closed its gates. Cove's men took refuge in the royal castle, and the rebels besieged it for more than three days and stole their horses.[52] The royal inquiry leaves opaque the motives and outcome of this organized town rebellion against an individual under royal protection.

The significance of these protests, revolts, and large-scale rebellions, as with Bristol's four-and-a-half-year resistance to the Crown and Lynn's ousting of the king's tollbooth collector, and demands that the commonalty possess economic and political liberties, must be considered quantitatively. Overall, by our assessment, 263 incidents of popular attacks against the king or his officials, or of the Crown intervening in the affairs of towns to restore 'the king's peace', are recorded in the 170 years of the published Patent Rolls – fewer than two a year. By contrast, in the period

---

[47] It had been taken from the English in 1296.

[48] In a royal mandate of 18 December 1317, 700 marks collected from a recently conceded tax on the clergy in the province of York (the tenth) were granted to the mayor, bailiffs, and commonalty of Berwick-upon-Tweed, because they had 'covenanted under certain conditions to hold their town for the king against the Scots'; *CPR 1317–21*, p. 65.

[49] *CPR 1317–21*, pp. 132–3, 1318.iv.15.   [50] Ibid., p. 305, 1318.xii.12.

[51] Ibid., pp. 305–6.   [52] Ibid., p. 277, 1318.viii.6

from 1313 to 1318, when Edward II was preparing war in Scotland, overstretched by massive troop deployment and then faced with humiliating defeat, at least thirty-five attacks against him or his bailiffs, tax collectors, justices, and other ministers in localities appear – over five per annum – and between 1313 and 1316, the years of the Bristol revolt, they rise to over eight per annum.

In addition, these years witnessed urban conflict and rebellion of various other sorts, such as that of commoners against oligarchies, or the struggles of city and town magistrates and the commonalty for economic and political liberties against abbeys, priories, and other ecclesiastical institutions – which will be examined in the following chapters. The king's weakness and absence during these troubled years opened opportunities for burgesses to combat economic monopolies and the juridical and political domination by the Church as well as by urban oligarchies and, if only momentarily, to widen their town liberties. While the brunt of these protests and revolts was not aimed directly against the Crown, they concerned royal power and authority. In 1314, for instance, the Abbot of St Albans sought royal intervention on six occasions in February and May to prosecute burgesses and other tenants of the abbey. Each case concerned the abbey's monopoly rights 'as lord of the town' over the grinding of grain at the abbot's mills. Certain tenants had constructed hand mills in their homes, and when the abbot's bailiff sought to enter and remove the upper stone of the mill called 'the distraint', the burgesses resisted.[53] This was not the first time townsmen resisted the abbey's monopoly over hand mills. Instead, it had surfaced in the records in 1274[54] – at another moment of royal weakness, the transition to Edward I's reign after he had returned from five years on crusades. But then no further incidents occur until 1314, and afterwards none until an urban revolt of 1327, at yet another moment of royal weakness and civil war. This time, it instituted radical reforms and established the town temporally as a borough with its own charters that remained partially intact until yet another crisis in royal control, that of 1381.[55]

It would be an exaggeration to maintain, as Norman Trenholme once did, that a 'violent revolutionary element' ensued from the end of the twelfth century until the dissolution of the monasteries, and that monastic towns were in 'a constant state of political unrest'.[56] As we shall see, clashes between burgesses and their monastic lords came to a head in

---

[53] *CPR 1313–17*, pp. 137 and 148, 1314.ii.1 and 1314.v.2.
[54] Freeman, *St Albans*, pp. 96–8.   [55] Ibid., pp. 98–9.
[56] Trenholme, *The English Monastic Boroughs*, p. 1.

only a few towns.[57] But even in places such as St Albans and Bury
St Edmunds, with long and often violent histories of strife between
burgesses intent on gaining town liberties and recalcitrant monastic
lords bent on upholding the status quo, struggles rose only at several
junctions across the long period of the later Middle Ages, c. 1200 to
1450. These were moments when burgesses could make their voices
heard and overturn, if only temporarily, privileges and monopolies of
monastic and other ecclesiastical lords, and these correspond closely
with moments of royal crisis. One of these was the years c. 1312 to 1318.

Furthermore, this period of royal weakness spurred on other forms
of economic revolt that focused on town liberties, as in 1315, when a
merchant bought cloth at markets in St Ives and transported them for
sale to Cambridge. The commonalty of Cambridge knew in advance of
the merchant's business and confronted his servants carrying the cloth
on the road to Cambridge at Girton.[58] There the mayor of Cambridge,
with the town's four bailiffs, and seventy-two others named in the
commission, assaulted the servants and followed them into Cambridge,
where others of the commonalty, already assembled, imprisoned the
merchant's servants and confiscated the cloth.[59] The mayor and townsmen had in effect assumed royal power.

Economics were also certainly at stake (though poorly specified) in a
petition sent to the king and his council in November 1318, concerning
the stannary men, or tin workers, of Devonshire. It is one of the few
documents found in the Patent Rolls or chronicles to describe a revolt
that stemmed from a specific occupational group, and the revolt of this
particular group in Devonshire would surface again in the latter part
of the fourteenth century, at another point of deep political crisis for
the Crown.[60] In 1318, the stannary men were accused of trespassing,
assaulting men of the county outside the boundaries of the stannary, and
resisting arrest 'daily'. They beat the king's bailiffs, imprisoned them in
their own prison, and demanded ransoms. Further, the petition alludes

---

[57] For the absence of revolt in Westminster, see Rosser, *Medieval Westminster*; for Reading,
C. F. Slade, 'Reading', in *Historic Towns: Maps and Plans of Towns and Cities in the British
Isles, with Historical Commentaries, from Earliest Times to 1800*, ed. M. D. Lobel, 3 vols.
(Oxford, 1969–89), I; and Trenholme, *The English Monastic Boroughs*, p. 41; for
Banbury, P. D. A. Harvey, 'Banbury', in *Historic Towns: Maps and Plans of Towns and
Cities in the British Isles, with Historical Commentaries, from Earliest Times to 1800*, ed.
M. D. Lobel, 3 vols. (Oxford, 1969–89), I.

[58] About four miles north of Cambridge.   [59] *CPR 1313-17*, p. 330, 1315.vii.3.

[60] See their 'felonies, trespasses, conspiracies ... against the king' in 1365, 1376, and
1380; *CPR 1364-7*, p. 148, 1365.v.13; *CPR 1374-7*, p. 328, 1376.vii.6; and *CPR 1377-81*,
pp. 569–70, 1380.vii.3. See John Hatcher, *English Tin Production and Trade Before 1550*
(Oxford, 1973).

to economic motives. They were charged with 'many acts of extortion', digging for tin outside the limits of the stannary, and seizing royal bailiffs sent to collect debts and 'the tenth of the refined mineral' due to the lord of the soil.[61]

Although this upsurge in urban revolt, 1312–18, coincided in part with the climatic crisis that led to Europe's most severe food shortages and famine of the Middle Ages,[62] the political strife began before its onset and soaring bread prices, and coincided more closely with a period of increased warfare, royal absence, and royal weakness. Furthermore, none of these revolts gives any sign that the impoverished were the ones to rise up; none of the rebels' complaints or demands referred to skyrocketing of corn prices or scarcity of other victuals. Instead, these conflicts, as with the larger ones at Bristol or Lynn, were positioned at the opposite end of the urban social spectrum, led by mayors and bailiffs and staffed by substantial artisans and shopkeepers, even merchants, and often local parsons. The long Bristol rebellion might be viewed at least in part as a factional dispute between two parties within the ruling urban elites; yet ultimately it focused on the retention, if not extension, of urban liberties against the juridical and fiscal impositions of the Crown. Moreover, contrary to the impressions given by chroniclers, who generally remained close to the concerns of their local institutions or instead focused on the national, and even the international, politics of the Crown, the Patent Rolls show that urban challenges to the Crown from 1312 to 1318 did not derive exclusively from the capital. Instead, overwhelmingly, they arose in provincial cities and towns – Bristol, Lynn, and Winchester, and once-proud ports such as Boston and Ravenserodd. With Edward's kiss of peace and temporary reconciliation with his cousin, Thomas of Lancaster, and the Treaty of Leake in 1318, his political fate changed from weakness to strength, at least until 1324, or perhaps as late as 1326, when Isabella went to France. Moreover, after the fall of Thomas, his execution, and the destruction of most of Edward's magnate opponents in 1322, the Crown enjoyed an unusual period of financial stability, even wealth.[63] As far as our sources reflect, a corresponding period of stability and quiescence in towns ensued from 1318 to the London revolt against the king's men in October 1326.

---

[61] *CPR 1317–21*, p. 240, 1318.xi.28.

[62] In 1318, grain prices declined to their lowest level since 1288; another harvest failure occurred in 1321; by the autumn of 1318, however, the worst was over; Phillips, *Edward II*, p. 330.

[63] Ibid., chapters 7–9.

8 Tax revolts

For many years, historians have connected the Black Death and the precipitous fall in population of the second half of the fourteenth century with increased popular unrest and insurrection. The case has perhaps been made best for England and its Peasants' Revolt of 1381. Here, scholars have pointed to the rise of labour legislation as a long-term determinant of revolt. In the face of economic dislocation, spiralling prices, particularly of foodstuffs, and the dramatic change in the supply and demand for labour, Edward III and his advisers tried, not only to keep wages stable, but pegged to 1346 – a deflationary year of economic crisis.[1] Had these wage levels been followed to the letter, numerous peasants, workers, and artisans would have starved to death. As we have seen, social protest against these laws peaked early on, as measured by surviving numbers of prosecutions against violators and evidence of collective social unrest in the Patent Rolls. Possibly the indignity of the statutes were remembered in 1381 and contributed to the peasant resentment of lawyers, but no evidence from the rebels' demands or chronicles pinpoints the Statutes of Labourers as central to their discontent.[2]

---

[1] B. H. Putnam, *Proceedings before the Justices of the Peace in the Fourteenth and Fifteenth Centuries, Edward III to Richard III* (London, 1938), p. cxxiii, cited by E. B. and Natalie Fryde, 'Peasant Rebellion and Peasant Discontents', in *The Agrarian History of England and Wales*, ed. Joan Thirsk, *Volume III, 1348–1500*, ed. Edward Miller (Cambridge, 1991), p. 760, made the case emphatically: 'It is no accident that "the area of the greatest intensity of the revolt [1381] coincides with the area for which there is definite evidence of the greatest efforts at enforcement of the labour laws"'. Also see E. B. Fryde, 'Introduction to New Edition', in Oman, *The Great Revolt*, p. xxviii; and Hanawalt, 'Peasant Resistance', p. 37. Christopher Dyer, 'The Causes of the Revolt in Rural Essex', in *Essex and the Great Revolt: Lectures Celebrating the Six Hundredth Anniversary*, ed. W. H. Liddell and R. G. E. Wood, Essex Record Office Publication no. 84 (Essex, 1982), pp. 31–4, points to the Statutes of Labourers as a principal cause, but places resentment to the laws in the wider context of seigneurial reactions to depopulation after the Black Death. On 1346, see Poos, 'The Social Context', p. 28.

[2] Hilton, 'Popular Movements in England', p. 233, maintains that the Mile End programme makes a clear reference to the labour legislation; however, he makes no reference to it and the three principal chronicle descriptions of it (the *Anonimalle*, Knighton, and Walsingham) leave little hint of it (Dobson, *The Peasants' Revolt*,

A better link between the Black Death and the English Peasants' Revolt is demand for new and increased taxation[3] to fund military campaigns and states' desires for territorial aggrandizement, as can be seen across Europe with the Hundred Years War, John of Gaunt's adventures in Spain and Portugal, or in Italy, the snowballing of a myriad of city-states towards five or six territorial states from the Black Death to the fifteenth century, fuelled by warfare. This curious post-plague leap in military expense and ambition by states seemingly spurred on by the monumental mass death of the Black Death has yet to be fully explained by historians.[4] These new military expenditures and increased destruction to population were made all the more difficult in that states had to rely on drastically reduced tax bases, cut by as much as a half or more in many regions across Europe. Community taxes based on pre-Black Death estimates of population and wealth could no longer function, and governments depended increasingly on indirect taxes largely tied to commodities of consumption[5] or in England on new poll or head taxes.[6] Both were regressive, whereby the poor paid almost as much as the rich, despite instructions with the last English poll tax of 1380 that 'the sufficient . . . shall aid the lesser'.[7]

---

pp. 159–61, 182–3, and 190–2, respectively). Later, Hilton, 'Resistance to Taxation', suggests that the rebels' demand against the Statute was only implicit in Wat Tyler's call that 'noone should serve any man except voluntarily and by *convenant taille*' (p. 176).

[3] Among others to emphasize taxation as the principal cause of the Peasants' Revolt, see Dobson, 'Remembering the Peasants' Revolt', p. 18; and Dyer, 'The Causes of the Revolt', p. 35.

[4] On this question, see Samuel K. Cohn, Jr, 'The Black Death: The Consequences', in *Renaissance and Reformation On-line Bibliographies*, ed. Margaret L. King (Oxford, 2010). For the breakdown in peace negotiations between France and England in the later fourteenth century, see J. J. N. Palmer, *England, France and Christendom 1377–99* (London, 1972).

[5] For the Low Countries, see Dumolyn and Papin, 'Y avait-il "révoltes fiscales"', pp. 8–9 (based on earlier work of Blockmans); for Italy, among other places, see Charles-Marie de la Roncière, 'Indirect Taxes or "Gabelles" at Florence in the Fourteenth Century: The Evolution of Tariffs and Problems of Collection', in *Florentine Studies*, ed. Nicolai Rubinstein (London, 1968), pp. 140–92.

[6] Other than custom taxes on wool export, the English Crown was late in developing sales (or excise) taxes, unlike in France and Italian city-states. Parliament considered them in 1380, but they were not implemented until the early modern period; see W. M. Ormrod, 'Poverty and Privilege: The Fiscal Burden in England (13th–15th Centuries)', in *La Fiscalità nell'economia europea secc. XIII–XVIII*, pp. 637–56, ed. S. Cavaciocchi, Atti delle "Settimane di Studi", 39, 2 vols. (Florence, 2008), II, p. 652.

[7] Cited in Christopher Dyer, 'Taxation and Communities in Late Medieval England', in *Progress and Problems in Medieval England: Essays in Honour of Edward Miller*, ed. R. H. Britnell and John Hatcher (Cambridge, 1995), pp. 168–90; see p. 174, for the third poll tax of 1380–1. For peasants' and artisans' awareness of regressive taxation, see Hilton, *English and French Towns*, p. 135, and for concrete examples of it, Cohn, *Lust for Liberty*, p. 100; Cohn, *Popular Protest*, document nn. 157 and 169.

In England, these inequalities were further compounded: to reverse the sinking fortunes of the English at war in France, the new taxes for the first time charged 'thousands of small-holders, craftsmen, and wage earners', along with teenage children, who had previously been exempted from direct taxation.[8] In Italy, France, and Flanders, tax revolts increased more sharply than any other form of revolt after the Black Death to the end of the century.[9] The fiscal demands to finance wars, first by the dying Charles V, then by his young son, stirred waves of revolts between 1378 and 1382, centred in towns, first in the south – Montpellier, Clermont de Lodève, Le Puy, Alès, Béziers, Narbonne, Nîmes, and Toulouse – then the north – the Maillotins of Paris, the Harelle of Rouen, and in smaller towns such as Saint-Quentin and Laon in Picardy.[10] As Graeme Small has argued, 'Highpoints of dissidence clearly match periods of heavy demands from the crown, notably the revolts of the 1350s, the later 1370s to early 1380s, and the 1430s.'[11] Yet it was not increases in taxes alone that so embittered populations; it was also, even more so, changes in taxation – their fundamental unfairness and inequalities.[12] Although the English Peasants' Revolt had many causes that can be separated into the long, medium, and short terms – the weakness of the Crown from the mid-1370s, the defeats in France, threats to the Kentish coast, the arrogance of the Duke of Lancaster and his alienation of the merchant class and commonalty of London[13] – the spark was the imposition of the third poll tax and trebling of rates in the winter of 1380. The first rumblings in Kent and Essex coincided with efforts to collect this regressive tax in early June 1381 or, as seen in the Patent Rolls, even earlier, in February that year.[14]

Despite these 1381 connections, tax revolts were not paramount in the history of English uprisings as they were in Italy, France, and Flanders, where they constituted over a fifth of popular insurrections and increased seven-fold after the Black Death to comprise 40 per cent

---

[8] Dyer, 'The Causes of the Revolt', p. 35; also Dyer, 'Taxation and Communities', p. 174.

[9] See Cohn, *Lust for Liberty*, pp. 228–9.

[10] Cohn, *Popular Protest*, pp. 261–337; Cohn, *Lust for Liberty*, pp. 81–3.

[11] Small, *Later Medieval France*, p. 198.

[12] On fiscal revolts never being exclusively matters of taxes but often more about justice and rights, see Cohn, *Popular Protest*, document no. 157; and, more recently, Dumolyn and Papin, 'Y avait-il "révoltes fiscales"'.

[13] For succinct presentations of causes, see E. B. Fryde, *The Great Revolt of 1381*, Pamphlet of the Historical Association (London, 1981); Rodney Hilton, *Bond Men Made Free: Medieval Peasant Movements and the English Rising of 1381* (London, 1973); Dyer, 'The Social and Economic Background', especially p. 42; Dyer, 'The Causes of the Revolt', pp. 21–36; and an earlier account, Oman, *The Great Revolt*; for the sequence of events, Saul, *Richard II*, pp. 56–82.

[14] See p. 106, above.

of all revolts. Yet protests in England against taxes, and movements spurred on by both these inequalities and corruption by tax collectors, appear from the earliest times in our study. Taxes and aids to the Crown were at the crux of one of the best known of English popular rebellions of the Middle Ages, that of William fitzOsbert, called Longbeard, in 1196. According to the chronicler Roger of Howden (who took a more sympathetic view than other commentators), new impositions 'to no small amount' were imposed on the realm because of the king's captivity and 'other accidents', and the rich, 'sparing their own purses, wanted the poor to pay everything'.[15] 'Inflamed by zeal for justice and equity (*zelo justitiae et aequitatis accensus*), Longbeard became the champion of the poor', holding that all should pay according to his means.[16] Known for his wit, eloquence, 'and moderately skilled in literature',[17] he fought the cause of the poor against the rich in public assemblies, first as a city magistrate, then by convening meetings of the poor, preaching on street corners, and organizing 'a conspiracy'. According to William of Newburgh's far-fetched estimate, Longbeard drew a following of 52,000 (probably more than London's total population at the time), and caches of iron tools were hidden to burst open the well-secured homes of London patricians.[18] These were discovered, the conspiracy quashed. Longbeard with his mistress took sanctuary in London's church of St Mary Arches, where by orders of the Archbishop of Canterbury, Hubert Walter, chief justiciar, he was smoked out, the church reduced to flames, its tower burnt to the ground.[19] Longbeard was taken to the Tower, tied by his feet to the tail of a horse and dragged through London to his place of execution, his skin ripped apart by cobblestones along the

---

[15] *The Annals of Roger de Hoveden, Comprising the History of England and of Other Countries of Europe from AD 732 to AD 1201*, trans. Henry T. Riley (London, 1853), pp. 388–9. But even according to William of Newburgh (*The History of William of Newburgh*, trans. Joseph Stevenson, [London, 1856; Lampeter, 1996], pp. 652–6), the rich had imposed the entire tax burden on the poor (p. 652). On these accounts, see John Gillingham, 'The Historian as Judge: William of Newburgh and Hubert Walter', *EHR*, 119 (2004): 175–87. Howden's sympathy for fitzOsbert may have been connected to their past as crusaders.

[16] *The Annals of Roger de Hoveden*, p. 388; and *Memoriale fratris Walteri de Coventria: The Historical Collections of Walter Coventry*, ed. William Stubbs, 2 vols. (London, 1872–3), II, pp. 97–8: 'volens quod unusquisque, tam dives quam pauper, secundum mobilia et facultates suas daret ad universa civitatis negotia' (p. 97).

[17] *The History of William of Newburgh*, p. 652.   [18] Ibid., pp. 652–6.

[19] On the consequences of the archbishop's actions, charges of sacrilege, complaints from his own clergy, his eventual resignation in 1198, the propaganda battle to justify his actions, and papal criticisms against English prelates assuming high secular offices, see Gillingham, 'The Historian as Judge'; and C. R. Cheney, *Hubert Walter* (London, 1967), pp. 94, 97–100. According to Howden, Innocent III implored Richard I not to permit the archbishop 'or any other bishop or priest to [accept] secular office' (ibid., p. 100).

way ('demolitis carnibus ad silices obiter positos'). Bound in chains, he was hanged with eight of his accomplices.[20]

Immediately after his execution, he became a martyr of the poor. To the consternation of the rich and powerful, his supporters gathered nightly at his place of 'flagellation': the chains that had bound him, the gibbets of his hanging, and the ground beneath it became his relics, so much so that, to William of Newburgh's disdain, the 'idiot rabble' scrapped away at the supposed sacred ground by the handfuls, 'as if consecrated by the blood of the executed man', leaving a large ditch beneath his site of execution. With crowds growing nightly, the king sent out his chief justice to disperse them and guard the place from any returning. He punished a ringleader priest, who fanned the enthusiasm for fitzOsbert's relics and 'invented' his miracles.[21]

Until 1381, no other revolt sparked by taxes or that revolved around them in English medieval history received as much attention in chronicles. Especially as compared with the Continent, chronicle reports of tax revolts were remarkably rare. Of 231 riots and revolts from our sample of chronicles, only fourteen tax revolts appear (6 per cent), and only a further four concerned church tithes, or other ecclesiastical tallages. Moreover, not all of these had taxes as their primary cause or objective. 'The Great Tumult' of London in October 1271 was in fact a disputed election between 'the Aldermen and more discreet citizens' on the one hand and the 'mob of the city' on the other, which 'violently and unjustly impeded' the election of the aldermen's candidate, putting Walter Hervey 'in the seat of the mayoralty'. His great support from 'the vast multitude of a countless populace', according to a chronicler, in fact one of the present aldermen of London, came from Hervey's election promise: as mayor he assured the populace that they would be 'exempt from all tallages, exactions and tolls, and would keep the City

---

[20] *The Chronicle of Gervase de Canterbury*, in *The Historical Works of Gervase of Canterbury*, 2 vols., RS, 73 (1879-80), I, pp. 534–5; at least nine chronicles describe fitzOsbert's horrific execution. This revolt and its leadership appear similar to that of Henri de Dinant, seventy years later at Liège: both were well-known for their oratory; both led revolts against unfair taxes; both were class traitors. On Henri de Dinant, see Godefroid Kurth, *La Cité de Liège au moyen âge*, 3 vols. (Brussels, 1909–10), I, pp. 179–215; Godefroid Kurth, 'Henri de Dinant et la démocratie liégeoise', *Academie Royale des Sciences des Lettres et de Beaux-arts de Belgique: Bulletins de la Classe des Lettres* (1908): 384–410.

[21] *The Chronicle of Gervase de Canterbury*, p. 535. *The History of William of Newburgh* devotes an entire chapter to Longbeard's martyrdom. On Longbeard's revolt, see Williams, *Medieval London*, pp. 4–5; Christopher Brooke, *London 800–1216: The Shaping of a City* (London, 1975), pp. 48–9; Edward Miller and John Hatcher, *Medieval England: Towns, Commerce and Crafts 1086–1348* (London, 1995), p. 284; Hilton, *English and French Towns*, p. 136.

acquitted of all its debts, both as towards the queen as towards all other persons'. In fact, the king had recently tried 'to extort' from citizens a great sum of money. Taxes, no doubt, were in the background of the revolt but per se were not the immediate cause.[22] Similarly, the revolt at the end of our analysis, Cade's, touched on fiscal inequality. As the *English Chronicle, 1377–1461* put it: 'the commyn profette was sore hurte and decresed so that the commyn people, with sore taxes and sore talages and other oppressions done be lordes'. In addition, the rebels had been embittered by, and protested against, unauthorized purveyances of grain over the past five years or more, listed as one of the rebels' grievances in one of its surviving manifestos.[23] However, these did not play a pivotal role as had the poll tax on the eve of the Peasants' Revolt of 1381.[24] Instead, the catalyst was the perception of misgovernance – the 'gouvernance' of Henry VI and 'rule by untrue counsell'.[25] Rather than new fiscal schemes or other means by the Crown to aggrandize or centralize power at the expense of subjects, Cade's Rebellion was a case par excellence of a revolt against a weak government, its failures at war, the loss of Maine, then Normandy, and the growing belief, especially along the southern littoral, that the government was no longer capable of ensuring the nation's security.[26] Certainly, other revolts counted above as tax revolts, such as the one led by Scrope in 1405, had causes and objectives other than fiscal policy. Like Cade's, royal misgovernance was at the forefront of this revolt, with taxation simply a symptom of that misrule. Perhaps as remarkable, only one major revolt described in the chronicles that touched on taxes was not centred on London – Scrope's of 1405 – and only two major ones clearly spread beyond the capital – the English Peasants' Revolt and Cade's Rebellion.

More remarkable still, given trends on the Continent and the historio-graphy of popular revolt in England, is the chronology of the English tax revolts found in chronicles. Of the fourteen, six occurred before the Black Death and another seven before 1381. Neither plague, with its shifts in demography, nor the Peasants' Revolt sparked new levels of collective action against the Crown's needs for more money, despite imposing greater demands per capita on the peasantry and commoners

---

[22] 'Liber de Antiquis Legibus', pp. 153–8. Among the aldermen who appealed to the king against the trumped-up election, Fitz-Thedmar was hardly a disinterested source; yet he showed no sympathy for the king's new impositions on London.

[23] See Griffiths, *The Reign of King Henry VI*, p. 638.

[24] Harvey, *Jack Cade's Rebellion*, p. 8.

[25] *An English Chronicle, 1377–1461*, pp. 67–70.

[26] On these military failures and raids on coastal towns and villages in Kent, see ibid., p. 110.

in cities. Nor did the post-plague environment, physical or psychological, unleash a new self-confidence as it had on the Continent to
oppose new taxes, loans, and other 'oppressions', which became more
burdensome and less equitable during the second half of the fourteenth
and early fifteenth centuries. This is all the more surprising given the
tendency in English towns, especially after the Black Death, to extend
taxes to as many wage earners as possible, shifting the tax burden from
the wealthy to the less affluent.[27]

Nonetheless, as the numbers reveal, tax revolts were also rare before
the Black Death. After the fitzOsbert revolt of 1196, troubles over royal
finance and taxation did not arouse the 'middle and lower orders' of
London again until 1258.[28] And this time their actions appear to have
been limited to courts and complaints to the king. According to the
chronicles, those appointed to collect the funds to rebuild city walls had
'fraudulently' pocketed most of the proceeds 'to the injury of the lower
order of citizens'. Here was a rare moment when a chronicler, Matthew
Paris, sympathized with the lower sort, claiming that officials had done
the same 'in all the collections and talliages they had made'. The officials
were found guilty, but with intervention by the king's chief clerk,
John Mansel,[29] their lives were spared.[30] If this were a tax revolt, it
appears to have been a peaceful one, as with the next one against taxes
by London's lower orders, a 'murmuratio' in 1269 that also failed to
blunt the Crown's resolve.[31]

After Walter Hervey's 'Great Tumult' of London in 1271, with its
appeals to lower the tax burden on the populace, the next tax revolt
appears in 1319, but received only a brief and cryptic notice from a
single chronicle: on St Edmund's day [20 November], a serious dispute

---

[27] Dyer, 'Taxation and Communities', pp. 188–9. The lay subsidies in 1334, whereby
communities distributed and collected the tax burden among themselves once target
amounts had been set centrally, may have alleviated tensions; however, such systems of
taxation also characterized tax structure and collection on the Continent, as with
cadastre in France and estimi in Italy; yet there tax revolts mounted after the Black
Death and not solely against indirect taxes.

[28] Williams, Medieval London, p. 7, reports a revolt against tallage in 1255, which does not
appear in our survey of chronicles.

[29] Mansel was one of Henry III's closest advisers and royal clerks, who in 1258
was charged with rescinding the city's liberties; see Jeremy Catto, 'Fitzthedmar,
Arnold (1201–1274/5)', ODNB; and Robert C. Stacey, 'Mansel, John (d. 1265),
Administrator and Royal Councillor', ibid. For his importance to Henry III's reign,
see Powicke, King Henry III and the Lord Edward, I, pp. 227; II, pp. 420, 430.

[30] Paris, Chronica majora, V, p. 663.

[31] Annals of Thomas Wykes, p. 228. Moreover, one of the causes behind the London
citizens' alliance with the barons in 1263 was taxation; see Williams, Medieval London,
p. 92.

erupted in the London Guildhall between the commonalty and 'some others', over a tax increase by stealth. The commonalty sent messengers to the king, presumably to make a royal complaint with a special commission and inquiry to follow, but the chronicler makes no further mention of it or of whether the Londoners' pleas had any effect.[32] In 1340, a fifth tax protest erupted in London but this, too, hinged on more than taxes. The king sent his justices to every county of the realm to investigate collections of the tenth, fifteenth, and other taxes, such as wool customs. London, however, took these inquiries as violations of their liberties and refused to answer the justices' questions. Certain commoners staged 'a great revolt' in front of the Tower of London, where the king had installed his justices until after Easter. The revolt 'gravely offended' the king; he sought to ferret out the ringleaders but failed. Eventually, he got over his anger; the justices left the Tower and held no further inquiries in the city that year.[33] It is one of the few successes of a popular revolt seen in these sources. The same appears to have been the outcome of a sixth tax revolt, again limited to London, that occurred on the eve of the Peasants' Revolt. Yet, despite the chronicler calling this revolt anticipatory to 1381, 'a big one over taxes between the leading men and commoners (*Suboritur grandis tumultuatito inter proceres and commuens pro taxis levatis*)', it received only scant attention from him. With the ringing of the bells, the 'rebelling plebs' forced the elected leaders from the city, but attacked only certain houses, those they believed had been the counsellors of the new tax.[34]

After the Peasants' Revolt, only five more protests against taxation appear. Moreover, none was a major revolt and the first not actually a tax revolt: Richard's demands for a loan of £1,000 in 1392 failed to split the city into warring factions or between class interests, as they had in the past. Nor did the protest appear to spill into the streets; instead, it was limited to the elites.[35] The only reported violence by Londoners was against a Lombard, who had offered the king the money. The king retaliated against them, calling together the leading nobles of the kingdom.[36] The Londoners enjoyed no victory: on 25 June, Richard II convicted the mayor, sheriffs, aldermen, and leading citizens; the mayor

---

[32] *Annales Paulini*, p. 287. This was the year when London craftsmen won their 'Great Charter'.

[33] *Chronicon Galfridi le Baker de Swynebroke*, p. 73; the same incident is described by Murimuth, *Continuatio chronicarum*, pp. 118–19, but dated 1341.

[34] Thomas Otterbourne and Johannes Whethamstede, *Duo rerum Anglicarum scriptores veteres. Ab origine gentis Britannicæ usque ad Edvardum IV* (Oxford, 1732), p. 153.

[35] Walsingham, *Historia Anglicana*, II, pp. 207–8.

[36] Walsingham, *Chronica maiora*, pp. 286–7; and *The Westminster Chronicle*, p. 497.

and sheriffs were imprisoned, the city's liberties rescinded.[37] From a vague chronicle description, the next protest against royal taxes or finances again is difficult to define as a tax or popular revolt. It involved more than London's citizens, and the protests were not limited to taxation. At the end of Richard's reign (1399), resentment and anger against him mounted, especially in the capital against his forced loans of 'grete summes'. But again these concerned the rich, not the poor or middling sort. Writing a generation after the events, Capgrave claimed that the king's unfair practices spilled over to 'every person, of what degree he was'. But by Capgrave's report, these practices concerned speech, not taxes: if they said as much as a single word 'in derogacion of the Kyng', no mercy was shown. 'And this mad the puple to hate the Kyng, and caused gret murmour in the puple.'[38]

In the second year of Henry IV's reign (1401) Adam Usk reports three riots prompted by taxes, made all the more insulting by Henry's false promise not to tax while campaigning against his cousin. These, however, appear to have been small, localized conflicts, limited to individual attacks on tax collectors. On 1 May at Norton St Philip, a rural centre for wool and cloth trade near Bath, drapers and other merchants killed one of the king's tax collectors of tolls or sales tax on cloth in the middle of the marketplace. The royal justices were unable to arrest the perpetrators because they were defended by local townsmen; the king had to intervene.[39] Around the same time, people of Dartmouth in Devon[40] attacked a tax collector, and at Bristol, the wives 'undertook this task on behalf of their husbands', attacking tax collectors, 'exchanging blows . . . in a similar skirmish'.[41] After these questionable 'tax revolts', the chronicles describe no further riots of any sort that even mention fiscality

[37] This case and its dire consequences for the city have received wide attention from historians; see Goodman, *John of Gaunt*, p. 151; Charles Petit-Dutaillis, 'Introduction historique' in *Le soulèvement des travailleurs d'Angleterre en 1381* (Paris, 1898), p. cxxxiii; Barron, 'The Quarrel of Richard II'; C. M. Barron, 'London 1300–1540', in *CUHB*, p. 409; Nightingale, *A Medieval Mercantile Community*.

[38] Capgrave, *Chronicle of England*, p. 269.

[39] *The Chronicle of Adam Usk*, p. 130–1. The Norton St Philip 'insurrection' is also reported in *CPR 1399–1401*, pp. 516–17, 1401.iv.29. It further specifies that the tax collector, Thomas Neuton, was mortally wounded in a hundred places, while collecting the aulnage on cloths (taxes paid on cloth produced for sale) for Somerset, but may not have been the victim of Norton St Philip's protest. On the aulnager, see E. M. Carus-Wilson, 'The Aulnage Accounts: A Criticism', in *Medieval Merchant Venturers: Collected Studies* (London, 1954), pp. 279–91.

[40] Dartmouth provided more ships for the Hundred Years War than any other port in England; see Maryanne Kowaleski, *Local Markets and Regional Trade in Medieval Exeter* (Cambridge, 1995), pp. 29–30.

[41] *The Chronicle of Adam Usk*, p. 130.

until Cade's Rebellion in 1450. As far as the chronicle evidence goes, the self-confidence of peasants, artisans, and the middling sort during the Peasants' Revolt failed to set a trend towards increased protest against increasingly inequitable taxation. If 1381 were a watershed, then the water was flowing in the opposite direction.

Of course, neither royal nor municipal taxes were the only ones imposed on commoners; the Church had its tithes and tallages. Chroniclers, however, scarcely notice any protest against these. In 1222, one of the few examples of what was possibly a popular revolt emerges from a Scottish chronicler: the Bishop of Caithness, also 'sometime abbot' of Melrose, claimed tithes [teinds] and other ecclesiastical rights from his subjects. On Sunday 11 September, three hundred assembled, attacked the bishop, 'beat, bound, wounded and stripped him',[42] and, according to Walter Bower and the Melrose chronicle, then stoned him.[43] After that, they tossed him into his kitchen, set it on fire, and scorched him to death. He was later found buried under the stones used to stone him. Despite the local earl not heeding the call of the bishop's servants, the rebels' actions did not long remain unpunished. Hearing the news while in Jedburgh, King Alexander changed his plans, raised an army, and subjected those responsible to 'various tortures', beginning by cutting off their limbs.[44]

In 1229, a conflict between the Abbey of Dunstable and its burgesses forced the king to intervene and redact new ordinances between the two, of which Church taxes and customary payments were among the liberties contested – 'deforciantes, de servitiis, et consuetudinibus, sectis, tallagiis, et aliis rebus'.[45] In 1240, rectors of parish churches in Berkshire refused to hand over their tithes to the pope to support his war against the emperor, but no evidence suggests that these actions were provoked by popular protest against tithes.[46] Finally, after Londoners' refusal to grant Richard his £1,000 request in 1392, Walsingham burst

[42] John of Fordum, *Chronicle of the Scottish Nation*, trans. F. J. H. Skene, ed. W. F. Skene (Edinburgh, 1872), pp. 284–5.

[43] Walter Bower, *Scotichronicon*, 8 vols., ed. D. E. R. Watt (Aberdeen, 1990–4), V, pp. 113–15; and *Early Sources of Scottish History AD 500 to 1286*, ed. and trans. Alan Orr Anderson, 2 vols. (Edinburgh, 1922), II, pp. 449–50.

[44] Bower, *Scotichronicon*, p. 115. The incident was also reported in the *Annals of Dunstable*. According to Barbara E. Crawford, 'The Earldom of Caithness and the Kingdom of Scotland, 1150–1266', in *Essays on the Nobility of Medieval Scotland*, ed. K. J. Stringer (Edinburgh, 1985), pp. 28–30, it resulted from 'tensions between the local northern tradition and the new ecclesiastical authority in Caithness'. The new exactions concerned teinds on butter and hay; the rebels were farmers, and Caithness was not alone in its refusal to pay. At least passive resistance spread throughout the Hebrides. I thank Dauvit Broun for this reference.

[45] *Annals of Dunstable*, pp. 118–24.   [46] Paris, *Chronica majora*, IV, pp. 38–43.

into a tirade against the capital's citizens; they 'surpassed all other nations for pride, arrogance and greed ... had little belief in God ... supported the Lollards, slandered monks ... impoverished the common people', and 'refused to pay tithes'.[47] Walsingham, however, gives no evidence of any revolt by Londoners against the Church or their collection of tithes. After the Black Death, chronicles produce not a single fiscal protest against the Church.

Tax revolts in the Patent Rolls

The Patent Rolls reveal more cases of tax disputes and protests, both peaceful and by force of arms, against corruption in cities and the impositions of the Crown. Several of these have already been described. They sketch a wider geography of protest than with chronicles, where London overwhelmingly appears at the centre. Yet Patent Rolls corroborate the patterns sketched by chronicles, and few can be seen as essentially tax revolts. In 1336 a collector of the king's custom at Southampton arrested goods for debts of a recently deceased burgess. A draper, a chaplain, his widow, and others retaliated, knocked down the doors and windows where the arrested goods were kept, entered and broke the locks of the coffers, chests, and bailiff's seals, taking away £200 and other goods.[48] Was this a tax revolt?[49] Breaking of pounds and assaults of tax collectors, however, could extend beyond the possible business of criminal gangs or organization by family or friends to avoid taxes. In 1316, the king's bailiffs in Yorkshire, along with those in the city, 'resisted' other royal officials collecting the king's twentieth and fifteenth and organized commoners to break the king's pounds and rescue their property.[50] Had the officials' actions originated from tax payers themselves? Again, was this a tax revolt?

Occasionally, the Patent Rolls describe protests that were without doubt community tax protests. In 1304 'the poor men' of Lynn complained to the king, charging that the rich who levied the taxes on the community for the king collected more than their due and 'extort[ed]

---

[47] Walsingham, *Chronica maiora*, pp. 286–7; Walsingham, *Historia Anglicana*, II, p. 208.
[48] *CPR 1334–8*, p. 298, 1336.vii.3.
[49] Similar cases are found in the countryside: in 1336 armed 'confederates' at Hardwick by Panton murdered the collector of the tenth and fifteenth in Lincolnshire and made off with the king's taxes (ibid., p. 362); tenants at Cogenhoe and Weedon, Northamptonshire, rescued the goods taken as distraints against unpaid royal taxes and debts; *CPR 1348–50*, p. 458, 1349.xii.27; several men in Cumberland attacked the collector of royal tolls and customs appointed by the mayor and bailiffs of Carlisle; *CPR 1364–7*, p. 137, 1365.ii.8.
[50] See p. 152 above.

grievous distraints' from the commonalty, which they converted to their own uses.[51] In addition to the four and a half years of opposition to the Crown, when Bristol prevented the king's ministers from collecting their tallages and customs, the town's burgesses again defied the king, refusing to send him one hundred armed men at Stanhope in County Durham in 1329 for his war in Scotland. Instead, they claimed they held the farm of the town from Queen Isabella and therefore were entitled to levy a tallage for their own use. They also levied 'illegal customs' (according to the king's inquiry) on wine and other goods brought to the town for sale.[52] Clearly, these fiscal protests were as much concerned with communal liberties as with taxes. In 1345, a group led by their parson attacked the two royal collectors of the tenth and fifteenth and their ministers in Gloucestershire.[53] As we have seen, the collection of taxes for pavage and murage in the same year split Carlisle between rich and poor, the poor accusing the rich of peculation. In 1346, the commoners of Ipswich assaulted the royal tax collector of the tenth and fifteenth, while in 1351 the burgesses of Coventry in 'the name of the commonalty' assaulted the mayor and bailiffs of the town and others who assessed and collected a forced loan for the king.[54]

The chronological trends uncovered in chronicles, as with the more voluminous and geographically expansive records of the Patent Rolls, show that changes of community tax rates established by the subsidy of 1334, despite increased corruption and fiscal inequalities, especially in towns, failed to fan increased tax rebellion. Nor did the Black Death spark a new trend. The next urban tax dispute in the Patent Rolls did not arise until 1365. Two individuals were named in the commission and 'others' attacked a tax collector appointed by the mayor and bailiffs of Carlisle to collect royal tolls and customs. But this may have been no more than a gang out for profit; moreover, it happened at Plumpton, a village in the forest of Ingelwode, not in town.[55] The next incident, in 1371, more clearly concerned collective action by townsmen and, in this case, the poor: the constable and under-taxers of Aylesbury were accused of exploiting the poor and chasing them from town when

---

[51] *CPR 1301–7*, p. 280, 1304.vii.5. Also, Owen, *The Making of King's Lynn*, p. 40. Five years later, these men obtained pardons from the king.
[52] *CPR 1327–30*, p. 424, 1329.ii.21.   [53] *CPR 1343–5*, p. 514–15, 1345.vi.8.
[54] *CPR 1350–4*, p. 201, 1351.x.15.
[55] *CPR 1364–7*, p. 137, 1365.ii.8. In addition, it does not appear in Beresford and Finberg, *English Medieval Boroughs*, whose cut-off date is 1509. Cases such as those at Suffolk in 1350 and at Somerset in 1351 that mandated the arrest of 'rebels' who 'rebelliously' resisted paying the tenth and the fifteenth may have included towns but mentioned none and therefore were not counted; *CPR 1348–50*, p. 526, 1350.iii.16; and *CPR 1350–4*, p. 80, 1351.ii.28.

they complained, but this, too, was not necessarily a tax revolt: their actions, no matter how brave, appear not to have gone beyond the legal channels of the king's courts.[56] Early in 1380, a harbinger of things to come the following year was sounded by a complaint in Parliament that led the Crown to appoint a larger number of commissioners than usual, composed of a wide array of dignitaries – the Archbishop of York, bishops of Winchester, Hereford, Rochester, the earls of Arundel, Warwick, Stafford, three bannerets, three knights, two citizens of London (John Philipot, who had been mayor, and William de Walleworth or Walworth, shortly to become London's illustrious mayor at the time of the Peasants' Revolt), and a citizen of York. It reported bluntly 'the complaint of the king's subjects', 'that the commons of the realm have fallen into utter destitution by reason of the multiplied payments of tenths, fifteenths, and other subsidies'. Further, the commission admitted that the sources of their perilous discontent reflected the 'condition of the realm', and resulted from 'the conduct of the king's officers and ministers, the state of his revenues, the fees paid to the king's officers ... annuities granted, the expenses of the household, etc'.[57] A year later, on the very eve of the Peasants' Revolt, the Speaker, Sir Richard Waldegrave, voiced similar warnings in Parliament again.[58] Although prompted by 'murmurs' from the populace over excessive taxes, extravagant expenditures, and possible corruption, these investigations did not yet, however, point to collective action from below.

Finally, as with the chronicles, the Patent Rolls fail to show any upsurge in tax revolts following the Peasants' Revolt and into the fifteenth century. Instead, with the Great Revolt over, these forms of protest had almost ceased altogether. Beyond the 1405 dispute led by York's archbishop and Cade's Rebellion at the end of this study, only two possible tax disputes surface in Patent Rolls. The first, immediately after the Peasants' Revolt, did not, however, concern royal taxes; nor was it clearly a tax revolt. A commission was called to investigate those who had prevented the Bishop of Carlisle's officer from collecting the clerical subsidy within his diocese at Penrith.[59] The second, at Chesterfield in

---

[56] *CPR 1370–4*, p. 178, 1371.x.12.

[57] *CPR 1377–81*, p. 459, 1380.iii.2. The composition of this reforming commission resembled closely one to reform the king's household after Archbishop Courtenay had been dismissed as Lord Chancellor and general pardons and a policy of reconciliation had replaced mass executions and repression; see Saul, *Richard II*, p. 81.

[58] Among other places see John Gillingham, 'Crisis or Continuity? The Structure of Royal Authority in England 1369–1422', in *Das spätmittelalterliche Königtum im europäischen Vergleich*, ed. Reinhard Schneider (Sigmaringen, 1987), p. 60.

[59] *CPR 1381–5*, p. 356, 1383.xi.12.

1408, involved the collection of customs but was hardly a major revolt. Four named men with others threatened a royal bailiff and the bailiff of the Earl of Kent's widow, hindering them collecting the town's tolls and profits from its fair, weekly markets, farms, rents, and other services owed to the earl's widow. In addition, the protest appears to have turned as much on liberties and resistance to seigneurial impositions as on taxes.[60]

These protests, large and small, against new or old taxes were remarkably rare and limited in scale.[61] Not including disruptions and thefts of monastic tolls most often perpetrated by those from the countryside, not townsmen, or efforts to break pounds to recover property distrained because of tax arrears, usually of individuals and not communities, only thirty-seven investigations into collective attacks on tax collectors, refusals to pay taxes (whether royal, municipal, or ecclesiastical), or any other disputes that concerned taxes appear in our survey of 651 incidents of popular protest in cities and towns in the Patent Rolls, less than 6 per cent of the cases, less, that is, than found in chronicles.

King's Bench

Cases from the published records of King's Bench corroborate these findings. Resistance to royal taxation was rare and on a small scale. In 1276, a clerk, sergeant, and five other men were charged with obstructing the king's assessors of the fifteenth from making their assessments of goods and chattels in the market town of Wisbech in the Fens. They then 'assaulted, beat, and wounded' the sheriff ordered to arrest them.[62] In 1302 there may have been resistance to paying the papal tenth in aid of the Holy Land, and the collection of the tax ended. The action, however, came not from popular revolt but from a royal council held at York.[63] Complaints must have reached the king's commissioners about their

---

[60] *CPR 1408–13*, p. 63, 1408.x.8.

[61] Rodney Hilton, 'Resistance to Taxation and to Other State Impositions in Medieval England', in *Genèse de l'état moderne: prélèvement et redistribution. Actes du colloque de Fontevraud, 1984*, ed. J.-Ph.Genet and M. Le Mené (Paris, 1987), pp. 176–7, concludes with some surprise that social classes 'not involved in negotiations with king, crown or state did not indeed frequently offer violent resistance against tax collection' and attributes the absence to 'the embryo state – the monarchy embedded in its feudal-military environment'. Why then did tax revolts flourish on the Continent, where monarchies and other states were less developed than the English Crown? Curiously, two years later, Hilton, 'Révoltes rurales et révoltes urbaines', concluded that 'fiscality in France as in England appears to have been the origins of most conflicts [in towns]' (p. 27).

[62] *King's Bench*, I, p. 27.   [63] Ibid., III, pp. 114–15.

assessors and collectors of the fifteenth in townships in the East Riding in the late 1330s, and in 1340 an assessor was found guilty of percolation and of assessing communities 'at his own discretion', and not according to their wealth. But despite his corruption and unfairness, the records give no signs that collective violence ensued.[64] The only tax protest found on a larger scale in these records comes later. Yet to what extent it may have been popular in character is difficult to gauge. Given the description of the rebels' weapons and armour, noblemen comprised at least part of its rank-and-file. If it were a popular revolt, however, it was not by townsmen; instead, it was one of the few examples seen in our sources where those of the surrounding countryside turned against a town. On Michaelmas (29 September) 1392, six men from the villages of Thorne, Hatfield, Sykehouse, and Tudworth in Yorkshire[65] led 300 from the demesne of Hatfield with force and arms, shields, breastplates, palettes, swords, bows, arrows, axes, and staves. They granted 'to themselves royal authority', and invaded Doncaster. In the middle of town before its high cross in the market square, they read out a public proclamation:

We command on behalf of the king of England and the duke of Lancaster, the duke of York and the lords of this town that there be no man of this town . . . as to take any custom, pannage or toll from the tenants of the duke of Lancaster or the duke of York on pain of losing his life.

They then returned to Thorne, where eleven men formed a 'covin' of 200, assaulted the bailiff and intimidated him from collecting taxes and tolls.[66]

Indicative of these findings is the negative evidence supplied by F. M. Powicke's comprehensive *King Henry III and the Lord Edward*.[67] Despite detailed attention to Henry III's tax increases and demands for new ones, his exhaustive narrative reports not a single tax revolt arising from either the countryside or towns during the combined ninety-one years of Henry III's (1216–72) and his son's (Edward I, 1272–1307) reigns. More recently, J. R. Maddicott has shown that the two decades of the heaviest fiscal demands placed on the English populace before the Black Death were the 1290s (especially 1294 to 1298)[68] and the 1330s.

---

[64] Ibid., V, pp. 123–4.   [65] Places northeast of Doncaster.
[66] *King's Bench*, VII, no. 42, p. 86.
[67] See in particular the periods of new and high taxation in the 1220s, from 1245 to 1252, and in Edward's reign – in the 1270s and especially following his expulsion of the Jews in 1279; Powicke, *King Henry III and the Lord Edward*, I, pp. 33–6, 154, 304, 363–4; and II, 726 and 737.
[68] On Edward I's dismal finances in his last decade as king, collapse of the Lucchese Riccardi bank in 1299, the absence of Italian finance for five years, and the legacy of

Yet these decades do not record peak levels of urban revolt of any sort; they were relatively calm, at least as far as popular revolt goes.[69] For the troubled years of the 1330s, with bad harvests, famine, frequent direct taxes, increased purveyances, and indirect taxes, tax payers may have 'grumbled, protested against specific cases of corruption, but in the end paid up' as Christopher Dyer has commented, and as the exchequer records show.[70] During the long reign of Edward III (1327–77), despite increased taxation with increasing shares imposed on towns, urban tax revolts were rare. As W. M. Ormrod has concluded, except for a petition (not a revolt) of 1348, when several towns pleaded to have their quotas of the tenth lowered, their 'silence is almost unbroken' during Edward's reign.[71] This is all the more remarkable given the tax reforms of 1334 that put the responsibility of distributing tax burdens on the rural and urban communities themselves. The new freedom led urban elites, but not those in the countryside, to evade taxation, shifting its fiscal burdens to the less affluent.[72] Yet, in stark contrast to trends on the Continent from the mid-1350s into the following century, neither the plague nor the Peasants' Revolt initiated a new phase of anti-fiscal activity in English towns. As with English popular revolts in general, tax revolts in England were not 'reactive' to new and aggressive royal initiatives.

royal debt for Edward II, see Richard W. Kaeuper, 'Royal Finance and the Crisis of 1297', in *Order and Innovation in the Middle Ages: Essays in Honor of Joseph R. Strayer*, ed. William C. Jordan, Bruce McNab, and Teofilo F. Ruiz (Princeton, 1976), pp. 103–10. On the general political crisis of these years, see Michael Prestwich, *War, Politics and Finance under Edward I* (London, 1972), Chapter 12.

[69] Maddicott, *The English Peasantry*, p. 7. In 1290, a complaint was made in Parliament that 'the potentes' of Gloucester 'were levying immoderate tallages on the other inhabitants', but no revolt ensued; see N. M. Herbert, 'Medieval Gloucester 1066–1547', pp. 13–72, in *VCH: Gloucester. Vol. IV: The City of Gloucester*, ed. N. M. Herbert (Oxford, 1988), p. 32; and M. D. Lobel and J. Tann, 'Gloucester', in *Historic Towns: Maps and Plans of Towns and Cities in the British Isles, with Historical Commentaries, from Earliest Times to 1800*, ed. M. D. Lobel, 3 vols. (Oxford, 1969–89), I, p. 6. Ormrod, *Edward III*, pp. 241–2, argues that Parliament in 1341 conceded 'the single heaviest tax raised in England in the entire period between the beginning of the thirteenth century and the end of the fifteenth century'; yet this crisis led to no revolt (pp. 244–6).

[70] Dyer, 'Taxation and Communities', p. 172: 'In contemporary France taxes met with some violent opposition and were not gathered with the same efficiency.'

[71] Ormrod, *The Reign of Edward III*, p. 180. On the multiplicity of taxes and their mounting burden on the poor after 1334 until the third poll tax of 1380, see Hilton, 'Resistance to Taxation', especially p. 170.

[72] Ormrod, 'Poverty and Privilege', pp. 641–2; and Dyer, 'Taxation and Communities', pp. 168–90. Recently, Christian Liddy, '"Bee War of Gyle in Borugh": Taxation and Political Discourse in Late Medieval English Towns', in *The Languages of the Political Society*, ed. Andrea Gamberini, Jean-Philippe Genet, and Andrea Zorzi (Rome, 2011), pp. 473–9, has challenged this view, arguing that taxation became tied to citizenship and that in cities such as Norwich, taxes were progressively distributed according to neighbourhood in the fifteenth century, even if the elites continued to fiddle the system.

Manipulation of coinage

The same is seen with the absence of popular protest against another royal provocation that sparked several of the most reported popular revolts in towns by contemporary chronicles on the Continent, particularly for Paris. These implemented tax rises and, simultaneously, the lowering of urban labourers' wages by stealth, achieved through currency debasement or chipping the coins paid to labourers, as with Philip the Fair's devaluations in 1306, 1311, and 1313. All three spurred the *menu peuple* into action.[73] In 1306, the 'small people' first went against the provost of the Parisian merchants, the city's wealthiest bourgeois, and then against the king. They prevented him from leaving the Templars' palace and threw the meat delivered to him in the mud. In 1356, royal devaluation mobilized the merchants and artisans of Paris to rise up against the dauphin, leading two years later to Étienne Marcel's revolt against the Crown. Furthermore, royal policies of devaluation were among the causes to spark popular revolt and a reign of terror with the Parisian butchers' revolt in 1413, and other popular uprisings in Paris in 1421, 1422, and 1425. Major revolts erupted against currency manipulations also at Tournai in 1423.[74] The Florentine *popolo minuto* during the Revolt of the Ciompi (1378) protested against governmental manipulation of currency, seeing it as the mechanism that lowered wages, and again in 1380, apprentices and other workers forced the government of the Minor Guilds to debase the gold florin, thereby increasing the value of their money of common exchange to enhance their standard of living.[75]

Late medieval English kings may not have gone to the extremes of the Valois kings in coin clipping and devaluation; nonetheless, to improve royal finances, strong kings such as Edward I and Edward III introduced new currencies and revalued old coins, as in 1279 after the persecution of the Jews for allegedly clipping coins. Edward I again devalued monies used by commoners in the last years of the thirteenth century and their use of foreign coins called 'pollards and crockards'. From 1343 to 1351, with the minting of England's first gold coin in 1344, Edward III debased the common currency further, culminating in a pound of silver being worth 300 pennies, inflated from the old standard of 243.[76] Despite cutting deeply into commoners' living standards, the policies

---

[73] For monetary manipulation as a general cause of revolts in the Low Countries, see Dumolyn and Papin, 'Y avait-il "révoltes fiscales"', p. 5.
[74] Lantschner, 'The Logic of Political Conflict', p. 163.
[75] Cohn, *Lust for Liberty*, pp. 66–7.
[76] Michael Prestwich, *Edward I*, 2nd edn, Yale English Monarchs Series (New Haven, 1997), p. 247; Michael Prestwich, *The Three Edwards: War and State in England,*

failed to provoke a single incident of popular protest seen in Patent Rolls or chronicles. In contrast to the Continent, only Parliament and barons chastised kings for them, and they alone negotiated compromises with the Crown.[77] As seen with other patterns of revolt, commoners in English towns did not rise up against such aggressive royal initiatives as happened in France, when kings were strong. Instead, English towns-people had to wait for opportunities when dynasties were divided with kings weak or absent, waging wars in France or Scotland; as Patent Rolls often put it, when the populace became 'emboldened by his [the king's] passing to parts beyond the seas'.[78]

1272–1377, 2nd edn (London, 2003), pp. 150, 199, 210–12; Prestwich, *Plantagenet England*, pp. 127, 177, and 287–8; and Ormrod, *Edward III*, pp. 258 and 371–2.

[77] See, for instance, the baronial ordinances imposed on Edward II in 1311 (Prestwich, *Plantagenet England*, pp. 35–6). Also, municipal governments might manipulate coinage illegally, as opponents of York's mayor John de Gysburn claimed he had done between 1369 and 1375, transmuting English pennies into false Scottish coins; see Prescott, 'Judicial Records', p. 227. The claims may have heightened factional antimonies but did not lead to popular revolt.

[78] See for instance *CPR 1313–17*, p. 57, 1313.vii.24; *CPR 1343–5*, p. 69, 1343.ii.4; *CPR 1345–8*, p. 179, 1346.vii.6; ibid., p. 235, 1346.xi.25; ibid., p. 315, 1346.iv.25; ibid., p. 382, 1346.vi.16; ibid., p. 459, 1346.x.2; and *CPR 1348–50*, p. 524, 1350.iv.20; *CPR 1416–22*, p. 421, 1422.ii.5. According to G. L. Harriss, 'Political Society and the Growth of Government in Late Medieval England', *P&P*, 138 (1993): 28–57: 'agrarian society was cushioned against intolerable taxation by the productive tax on wool exports which underpinned the crown's war finance. Thus taxation ... was very rarely met by refusal or revolt' (p. 42). The descriptions of extortionate purveyances combined with burdensome war taxes and excessive taxes and loans on Jews, then foreigners, call into question this explanation, especially in periods of military over-extension in France and Scotland from the 1250s to the Black Death; see Maddicott, *The English Peasantry*; Robin R. Mundill, *England's Jewish Solution: Experiment and Expulsion, 1262–1290* (Cambridge, 1998); Powicke, *King Henry III and the Lord Edward*; and other sources. Ormrod, *The Reign of Edward III*, pp. 180–9, argues that while direct taxes were never so burdensome on towns, indirect subsidies, forced loans, and customs were, and towns assumed an increasing burden of these costs as Edward III's reign continued. In *Edward III*, he further argues that 'England was certainly no tax paradise' (p. 114), especially at moments such as the late 1330s (pp. 210–11) and with the third poll tax passed in Parliament in November 1380 (p. 586).

9   Revolts: poor against rich

We have already seen several revolts that divided urban populations, not only into factions, but by social status, wealth, and access to power. These turned on disputes over the distribution of taxes, and on claims by the poor of peculation and extortion by the rich, as at Lynn in 1304, Carlisle in 1345, Aylesbury in 1371, London in 1380, and most famously, in Longbeard's revolt of 1196.[1] Mayoral elections also sparked tensions within towns between rich and poor as with Walter Hervey's championing the poor in his London electoral bid in 1271, or in cases such as Scarborough in 1307 for reasons not clearly delineated by the sources.[2] These examples may give the impression that such struggles were common in English towns, as common perhaps as the rise of the *popolo* and their struggles against old regimes of magnates in Italian city-states in the thirteenth and fourteenth centuries, the *popolo minuto* in struggles for guild recognition and citizenship, or the rise of the *menu peuple* in France and Flanders. Indeed, A. R. Bridbury has claimed, 'whenever urban complaint can be heard [in England], it is the complaint of the lesser people, who say they are being exploited, that we hear'.[3] He refers, however, to less than a handful of examples and

---

[1] Court records also reveal tensions and complaints of the poor or lesser burgesses against unfair tax distributions imposed by elites as in Gloucester, 1290 (p. 174, note 69), and after the king's departure in 1326, when the 'middle people' of Norwich complained to the king that their bailiffs and the rich levied new taxes without consent and threatened to raise taxes 'from one day to another at their will'; *The Records of the City of Norwich*, I, pp. 61–2. Colby, 'The Growth of Oligarchy', pp. 644–5, claims that protests between rich and poor over taxes became frequent with Edward I's reign but cites few cases of it (at Gloucester, Oxford, and Stamford); moreover, these were legal proceedings.

[2] The *CPR* do not clarify or even mention the strife among various social rungs of burgesses; the documents that mention inter-class strife do not point to taxes or elections as the causes. According to Colby, 'The Growth of Oligarchy', p. 646, the struggle between middle-class and poor burgesses against the *divites* began as a law suit in the exchequer court. Kaeuper, 'Law and Order', p. 780, adds little more, despite the fact that the conflict continued to flare until Edward III's reign.

[3] Bridbury, 'English Provincial Towns', p. 17.

provides no statistics. By contrast, petitions, royal commissions, and chronicles rarely mention such splits by class or between rich and poor.[4]

Chroniclers describe only twenty such splits among the 231 incidents of urban riot and revolt (less than 9 per cent of them), and not all of these mobilized street action. As described above, Londoners 'of the middle and lower orders' in 1258 accused those appointed to collect the tallages to rebuild city walls of lining their pockets. The complaint, however, did not lead to social revolt.[5] In 1273, class tensions again flared in London, with Hervey once more playing a leading role. Gregory de Rokesle, an alderman representing the current mayor, and 'other discreet citizens' contested charters Hervey redacted when he had been mayor as without force of law, since the aldermen and discreet citizens of the city had not approved them. After 'a wordy and most abusive dispute' in the Guildhall, Hervey took his cause 'to the people of the trades' to whom the charters had been granted and assembled 'a great multitude' in the church of Saint Peter in Cheapside. He then marched through 'the streets and lanes of the city, preaching and enticing the populace' to join him against the mayor and wealthy, promising 'to maintain them in their integrity'. His street-corner campaigning did not lead to popular insurrection, however. The barons and the king's council got wind of the threats, and the king sent writs to the mayor and sheriffs.[6] It is not clear, however, that the elites had succeeded entirely in heading off insurrection from below. According to a brief notice in the *Annales Londonienses*, a conflict erupted that year between aldermen and commonalty over the mayoral election, and the city had to be placed under the custody of William of Cornhill and his son.[7]

In 1317, dissension between the mayor, John de Gisors, and the commonalty over the city's charter brewed, but no evidence suggests that the split was along class lines.[8] Similarly, in 1328, another disputed mayoral election rocked London, when Hamo de Chigwell was deposed and John of Grantham put in his place, but again the chronicles give no evidence that the divisions cut across class with the

---

[4] Such clashes between rich and poor also appear rarely in Parliament rolls. The Michelmas roll of 1281 presents grievances of a now-lost petition against the mayor of Carlisle for overtaxing the city's poor, probably prompted by inequities in collection of murage. The mayor may have feared a popular uprising and in 1279 built a palisade outside his house, but there is no evidence of violence in 1281, only a petition. Moreover, Summerson, *Medieval Carlisle*, I, pp. 170–7, concludes that the tensions of 1281 were exceptional in Carlisle's social history. When the next complaints of fiscal misappropriation arose, the sheriff, 'not the humbler citizens', complained (p. 177).
[5] See above, p. 165.   [6] 'Liber de Antiquis Legibus', pp. 169–70.
[7] *Annales Londonienses*, pp. 82–3.   [8] *French Chronicle of London*, p. 252.

lesser sorts opposing the rich.[9] Instead, it seems this was a power play between elite factions on a national scale, connected to the deposition of Edward II and the fall of Hugh Despenser's men.[10] In 1364, another conflict divided the mayor from the commonalty, but the single chronicler of these events left undefined the issues, as well as the social character of the division within the commonalty.[11] Two years later, however, a council of discreet men ('sub manucaptione probus civium') deposed another London mayor, replacing him with one of their own and of the king's choice. This time, the election created a class cleavage. The 'populares' assembled, defied the king's will, and threw out the newly elected mayor, proclaiming they would have no one other than the previously elected mayor, Adam de Bury. To avert further disaster, the body of elder statesmen ('sanior consilio') convened and elected two hundred 'trustworthy citizens', twenty from each ward, along with the aldermen, to prevent the rabble ('vulgi') from coming to power. Furthermore, the elites sought to punish the commoners gravely. In February, the elites were able to install a mayor, 'worthy of the position'.[12] As we have seen, the insults of John of Gaunt and Lord Percy, first to the Bishop of London, then to the citizens of London, provoked a united front against Gaunt in 1377. But after efforts to murder Percy, burn down Gaunt's palace, and reverse his coats of arms, city leaders agreed in secret to placate the duke, which isolated and insulted commoners, who refused to do their bidding. Yet, despite the class bitterness, few actions beyond posting of libellous verse followed, and no insurrection.[13]

In the years leading to the Peasants' Revolt, further strife divided London's 'proceres' and 'plebs' in 1380 over taxation. Yet, during the Peasants' Revolt itself, it is not clear that the city was split sharply. Certainly, the Peasants' Revolt created deep fissures within the political and social life of the city across several axes – attested to by the rebels' brutal massacre of Flemish artisans and prostitutes in Southwark, as well as by conflicts within the aldermen class, with violence and later legal opposition between those such as alderman John Horn, who was

---

[9] *Annales Paulini*, p. 342.

[10] According to Nightingale, *A Medieval Mercantile Community*, p. 146: 'The process by which Despenser's men consolidated their power began with the election of Hamo de Chigwell as mayor in October 1319.'

[11] *Chronica Johannis de Reading*, p. 161.

[12] Ibid., pp. 169–70. Acts in *LB, G*, p. 168, do not allude to these disturbances, but on 5 August the aldermen investigated 'a disturbance raised by men of divers misteries on the Feast of St Peter ad Vincula [1 Aug]'.

[13] Walsingham, *The St Albans Chronicle*, I, pp. 105–11; and above, pp. 101–22.

possibly sympathetic to the rebels,[14] and the mayor, William Walworth, and other wealthy merchants, such as Nicholas Brembre.[15] In the aftermath of the Peasants' Revolt, the scars left in the upper classes by the pre-revolt conflict resurfaced, fuelling factional dispute between leading aldermen and elected mayors. The factions supported by different classes now entered their most contentious phase in the history of medieval London, at least since the days of Walter Hervey, lasting from 1382, if not earlier,[16] to the end of the century. Again, these conflicts centred on mayoral elections, in this case, between John of Northampton and Nicholas Brembre and their supporters. To what extent this cleavage reflected deeper class interests has been debated.[17] Certainly, contemporary chroniclers saw the lower and middling groups of guildsmen as taking an active part and, as we have seen, John of Northampton appealed to a broad base against the high cost of provisioning enjoyed by fishmongers and grocers. In one revolt, the 'cordewaner' or cobbler, John Constantyn, stirred up the crowds and paid for it with his head, placed above Newgate after his execution. According to the *Westminster Chronicle*: 'excited as some will have it, by a spirit sent from the Devil, [Constantyn] careered through the streets of London urging the populace to rise against the mayor, whom he declared to be bent on smashing all those who supported John of Northampton'.[18] Ultimately, the testimony of middling guildsmen against Brembre in the Appellants' vengeful trial of Richard II's inner circle during the Merciless Parliament of 1386 ended Brembre's life by the same fate.[19]

In 1388, in a surprisingly rare incident for these documents, especially in comparison to France and Italy, magnates and their troops from outside threatened London's security and led to another split within London: the nobles demanded entry into the city but the mayor refused them. Eventually, the mayor bowed to the magnates' wishes, not only because of their might but because of opposition from the 'undisciplined

---

[14] See Bernard Wilkinson, 'The Peasants' Revolt of 1381', *Speculum*, 15 (1940): 29 and 32; and Rexroth, *Deviance and Power*, pp. 137–8.

[15] On these factional divides, see Bolton, 'London and the Peasants' Revolt', *London Journal*, 7 (1981): 123–4; Dyer, 'The Social and Economic Background', pp. 39–40; and Prescott, 'London in the Peasants' Revolt', pp. 130–3 and 136–7. On the edited inquisitions and false charges against the aldermen, John Horn, Adam Karlile, Walter Sibil, William Tonge, and John Fresh, see Dobson, *The Peasants' Revolt*, pp. 212–26.

[16] According to Walsingham, the conflict began with Northampton's 'persecution' of the fishmongers that lowered fish prices in 1382; Walsingham, *Historia Anglicana*, II, p. 66.

[17] See discussion in Chapter 1.

[18] *The Westminster Chronicle*, p. 65; also see *LB, H*, pp. 229 and 235; and Walsingham, *Chronica maiora*, p. 214, who sees Northampton as the revolt's organizer; also *The Westminster Chronicle 1381–1394*, pp. 63–4.

[19] Saul, *Richard II*, pp. 184 and 193.

mob', which had accompanied the lords and applied pressure from within. 'The commons of the city and the poor', who Walsingham asserted were 'always keener on trouble than peace', were ready to admit the lords and, according to Walsingham, 'to ransack the houses of the rich for valuables'. The mayor, Nicholas Exton, however, averted rioting by allowing the troops to enter and by distributing wine, beer, bread, and cheese to all.[20] A final conflict between commons at least of the guild community and London's elites broke out in 1440, stirred by another mayoral election: 'strife erupted in the Guildhall with the changing of the mayor provoked by the craft of the tailors'.[21]

Outside London, chroniclers presented urban conflicts as united fronts against an adversary, either the Church or the king, usually in defence of liberties or in efforts to gain rights and independence. These ranged from large and violent conflicts, as in Norwich in 1272, to various struggles of townsfolk in monastic boroughs such as St Albans fighting to preserve their hidden household hand mills. A case in point is York's remarkable revolt of 1405 with the archbishop galvanizing support against the Crown across the social spectrum: 'Knights, esquires and communes from city and countryside thronged in great numbers around the archbishop[22] ... havynge in grete consideracion the grete pouerte off marchaundez in whom wasse wonte to be the substaunce off the riches off all the londe; and also the raysynges off taxes, tallages, and customez undir colour of borrowynge'.[23] Not a single chronicler described class confrontation between rich and poor, 'the sufficient' and less so outside London. As presented by the *Vita Edwardi Secundi*, the 1315 insurrection in Bristol comes closest to class conflict within the ranks of urban classes, which according to the chronicler erupted because of control by the city's fourteen wealthiest men over Bristol's port. The commonalty of Bristol resented it as a breach of their liberties, proclaiming 'that all the burgesses were of one rank and therefore equal'.[24] But, as we have seen, those who opposed the fourteen were not the poor.

Urban class conflict in the Patent Rolls

Patent Rolls present a different picture. London was not the only place split by class conflict within the ranks of burgesses or between burgesses

---

[20] Walsingham, *Chronica maiora*, p. 259.
[21] *Chronicle of the Grey Friars of London*, p. 17. On this election and the conflicts that ensued, see Barron, 'Ralph Holland'.
[22] Walsingham, *Chronica maiora*, p. 336.   [23] *An English Chronicle, 1377–1461*, pp. 35–6.
[24] *Vita Edwardi Secundi*, pp. 122–3.

and disenfranchised residents; such conflicts in fact figured in provincial towns and cities more prominently than in the capital, with petitions by the poor to the king or action in the streets against the corruption, extortion, and oppression by elites, who controlled tax assessment, as in Lynn in 1304, Carlisle, 1345, and Aylesbury, 1371. Other disputes also divided urban communities, as were created by Edward III's purveyances for his war efforts in 1347 with Bristol, Boston, Lynn, Thetford, and other places in Gloucestershire, Kent, Somerset, and Yorkshire, when rebels elected their own captains, drew up proclamations, boarded ships requisitioned by the king, sold the victuals according to their sense of fair price, and took over municipal governments.[25]

In fact, the wide range of possibilities for individuals and communities to file complaints with the king and his councils witnessed in Patent Rolls may have provided greater scope for lower classes to express their grievances within urban communities than in other regions of Europe during the later Middle Ages, and thus allow the historian of England a closer view of such splits within the social fabric of towns than is available from Continental sources such as town minutes[26] or the *provvisioni* of central and northern Italian city-states.[27] While petitions found in the Continental sources contain supplications to the state for tax exemptions and special considerations because of military or ecological disasters and occasionally disruptions between guildsmen, they rarely created an arena that enabled lower social groups to complain against those above them on matters of taxation, rigged elections, or the malfeasance, corruption, and oppression of royal officials. At times, such as in 1330, the king actively solicited petitions against oppressions committed by magnates or by corrupt ministers against commoners.[28] On the Continent, given the strength of cities such as Florence, certainly no such legal avenues would have openly invited the *popolo minuto* to voice such concerns. We hear of class clashes instead in criminal acts or pardons followed by fines, capital punishments, or the occasional acquittal.

By contrast, Patent Rolls registered such complaints between different layers of society, as with the charges of 'the people of the counties of

---

[25] See above, pp. 141–3.

[26] For a recent study of town minutes, see Graeme Small, 'Municipal Registers of Deliberations in the Fourteenth and Fifteenth Centuries: Cross-Channel Observations', in *Les idées passent-elles la Manche?*, ed. Jean-Philippe Genet and F-J. Ruggiu (Paris, 2007), pp. 37–66.

[27] For petitions from villages and towns of Florence's territorial state, see Cohn, *Creating the Florentine State*, part 3.

[28] Ormrod, *Edward III*, p. 107.

Norfolk and Suffolk' in 1315 against 'the maladministration of justice in those counties';[29] or for England as a whole as in 1380.[30] Through these channels, such complaints could be voiced even against aristocratic landlords, as in 1398, when tenants challenged their lord, Maurice de Berkeley, who without licence from the king had enclosed land and made a park near Stoke in the lordships of Winterbourne and Frampton, Gloucestershire. They argued that they possessed common rights of pasture on these lands 'from time immemorial'.[31] Although 'lesser sorts' almost inevitably lost their cases, at least their complaints were heard, written down, and investigated.[32]

The same is seen within urban communities. Elected officials of municipalities, commoners, burgesses out of power, and 'the poor', could lodge complaints that established royal commissions to investigate grievances against social superiors, as well as ones by the upper echelons against their inferiors. To be sure, making such complaints cost money and may have required patronage behind the scenes not revealed in the documents, and many of the descriptions remain too vague to determine whether strife cut across class. For example, a royal mandate in 1272 'to the bailiffs, burgesses and the whole commonalty of Yarmouth' ordered the suppression of 'contentions and discords' that 'easily arise' from those 'who wander night and day' and arouse 'sinister suspicion'.[33] The mandate fails to clarify who the town wanderers were: rebels out of power with a cause, loitering vagrants, or criminal gangs threatening rich and poor alike? Other cases suggest class cleavages but may have been factional conflict, as with the king's intervention at Winchester in 1274. Because of discords within the city, he appointed a royal clerk as mayor to re-establish order before a new election could be held. The interim mayor was given powers to select bailiffs from 'the better men of the city who have taken no part in the contentions'.[34]

Other cases with multiple documents can be integrated to gain clearer pictures. In 1414, the king appointed two commissions to enquire into and resolve tensions between 'two parties' of the burgesses within the town of Lynn. Sometime before May he called representatives of the 'said parties' before his council to 'get true information from either party' and reach a compromise. In December, another commission dealt with the discord, giving a clearer sense of the controversy. Thirty-nine men were listed who had opposed the election of the present mayor and tried to resist his rule. Despite all the parties concerned being 'burgesses'

[29] *CPR 1313–17*, p. 314, 1315.iii.10.   [30] See above, p. 105.
[31] *CPR 1396–9*, p. 1398.iv.28.   [32] See Scase, *Literature and Complaint in England*.
[33] *CPR 1266–72*, p. 677, 1272.ix.10.   [34] *CPR 1272–81*, p. 60, 1274.x.14.

and the opponents labelled 'parties', this factional dispute over an election now appears to have had a class dimension. The occupations of those who contested the election clustered at the lower end of the urban spectrum even for a middle-sized English town such as Lynn: four tailors, a cobbler ('souter'), a smith, a barber, and a braiser. Moreover, the king supported the mayor (who was, in fact, his own appointment, against the town's elected candidate) and threatened the commonalty with a £1,000 pound fine for any disobedience.[35] In a case from Bath in 1422, a commission gave the mayor and bailiffs special powers to arrest and force all the city's inhabitants then forming 'congregations and conventicles in taverns and other suspected places' with 'making rancour, dissension, and discord'.[36] The intentions and meeting places may

---

[35] *CPR 1413–16*, p. 345, 1414.v.10, and p. 411, 1414.xii.3. The brief chronicle of events by Lynn's town clerk, William Asshebourne, gives further details, especially regarding the king's intervention and the strife it engendered between burgesses and the Crown, not mentioned in *CPR*.

[36] *CPR 1416–22*, p. 447, 1422.vii.11. For taverns and alehouses as places of seditious meetings, planning, and preaching, see below for Bury's rebellion in 1327–8; the telling of 'many lies' in taverns in Cornwall, 1402, about Henry IV's broken promises; the organization of the 1381 revolt in Cambridge in a tavern at Bridge Street, witnessed by John Shirle's indictment on 18 July 1381 (Dobson, 'Remembering the Peasants' Revolt', pp. 3–4); Ian Forrest, *The Detection of Heresy in Late Medieval England* (Oxford, 2005), p. 188, for Oldcastle's in 1414; Hilton, 'Révoltes rurales et révoltes urbaines', p. 31, for 'covins' of journeymen in late medieval London. Also, the *CPMR*, III, pp. 88–9, 1368.vi.20, describes artisans and journeymen holding their illegal meetings in taverns. For meetings of rebels and political discontents in alehouses of late fifteenth- and early sixteenth-century York and Bruges, see Christian Liddy and Jelle Haemers, 'Popular Politics in the Late Medieval City: York and Bruges', *EHR* (forthcoming), pp. 24 and 26. In addition, as texts throughout this book describe, of those rebels identified by occupation, tavernkeepers were one of the most prevalent groups of English rebels, even more so than craftsmen in the cloth industry. The fourteenth-century moralistic and satirical literature also condemned taverns and alehouses, not only for gluttony, foul language, sloth, promiscuity, theft, and the like, but for being where 'manifold frauds, plots, and conspiracies' were hatched; places of 'debate', 'illicit oaths' and 'tumult' (see for instance John Bromyard's *Summa Predicantium*); G. R. Owst, *Literature and Pulpit in Medieval England: A Neglected Chapter in the History of English Letters & of the English People*, (Oxford, 1961), pp. 432 and 439. As places of sociability and possibly 'subversive talk' in which women played a prominent role, see Rodney Hilton, 'Women Traders in Medieval England', in *Class Conflict and the Crisis of Feudalism: Essays in Medieval Social History* (London, 1983), pp. 214–15. For the social distinction between taverns and alehouses, see Rexroth, *Deviance and Power*, pp. 164–5: in the former, guildsmen, including aldermen, would gather, while the latter were the haunts of the poor. Also, see Peter Clark, *The English Alehouse: A Social History 1200–1830* (London, 1983), p. 5, who distinguishes a social hierarchy of three types of victualling houses in declining order of social status – the inn, tavern, and alehouse – but cautions that there were 'no hard and fast' distinctions among the three; also see p. 29: the words 'alehouse' and 'tavern' could be used interchangeably in the late Middle Ages. In our documents, alehouses are never mentioned.

suggest a class divide between city rulers and those the king wished to arrest. However, without further details of aims, occupations, or labels such as the poor, the lesser sort, etc., it is uncertain whether the conventicles were of a criminal underclass, a political faction, or artisans or others seeking liberties.

Still other tantalizing Patent Rolls supply too little information for us to know whether a 'disruption' was a revolt, even when the occupations of the groups in questions are known, as with a royal mandate to the mayor and sheriffs of London in 1320 to arrest and punish bakers, taverners, millers, cooks, and others of the city guilty of 'disorderly and riotous conduct'.[37] Was this a drunken revelry, guild entertainment turned bad, or a revolt involving political demands that posed a serious threat to London's rulers? Similarly, in Cirencester in 1414, the king granted pardons to 104 men 'for all treasons, insurrections, felonies, trespasses, inobediences, rebellions, negligences, misprisions, main-tenances, contempts, councils, abetments, conventicles, confederacies, extortions, oppressions, offences, impeachments and other evil deeds'. Given the occupations' heavy concentration in the cloth industry – six weavers, three tailors, two glovers – plus an ironmonger, this may have been a rare occurrence of an industrial or craft revolt in the cloth industry, either against the king or municipal elites. But by this document alone, despite its long but vague list of insurgent crimes, the historian cannot know whether the insurgents' actions had a craft or a decidedly class dimension.[38] Only by its date and context with other sources might we suspect that these 'insurrections etc.' may have been linked with Oldcastle's cause of political and religious dissent backed by the sort now galvanized by Lollardy[39] or by the new king's pre-emptive strike to wipe-out any possible dissent.[40] If connected to Oldcastle's cause, then conditions of work probably were not central; artisans instead were merely the ones most attracted to his cause.

A case in point comes earlier, when more than one document from the Patent Rolls draws a clearer picture of the social relations between competing factions or classes in an urban setting. In 1303, twenty

---

[37] *CPR 1317–21*, p. 478, 1320.ii.23.   [38] *CPR 1413–16*, pp. 168–9, 1414.ii.15.

[39] On Oldcastle's rebellion and Lollardy, see J. H. Wylie, *The Reign of Henry the Fifth*, 3 vols. (Cambridge, 1914–29), I, pp. 40, 63, 250–4, 519; III, pp. 85–96; K. B. McFarlane, *John Wycliffe and the Beginnings of English Nonconformity* (London, 1952), pp. 173–5; John A. F. Thomson, *The Later Lollards 1414–1520* (Oxford, 1965); Margaret Aston, 'Lollardy and Sedition 1381–1431', *P&P*, 17 (1960): 1–44, revised in Margaret Aston, *Lollards and Reformers: Images and Literacy in Late Medieval Religion* (London, 1984), pp. 1–48; and pp. 297–301, below.

[40] Paul Strohm, *England's Empty Throne: Usurpation and the Language of Legitimation, 1399–1422* (New Haven, 1998), pp. 65–86.

men, a woman (Isabella Borrey), and others 'conspired together by bonds and oaths', besieged the town of Shrewsbury, assaulted the three bailiffs elected by the commonalty, took over the bailiffs' peacekeeping functions and other matters pertaining to their office, took away their wands, and replaced these officers with their own unelected bailiffs. Further, they intimidated the men of the commonalty from trading in the town or outside it.[41] This may have been an outside invasion but none was identified from other places even by the common toponymical 'atte'. Economic motives may have been a cause – competition between members of the ruling elite of traders, or oppression by them. Was the conflict factional or one of class?

Although none was identified by an occupation except for the local parson, the first-named, Isabella, only five days before, had filed a complaint against seventy-five men, including four tailors, three pamenters (another type of tailor), a 'galey', shearer ('scherer'), barber, and a carpenter, plus 'others'. This document gives us a better idea of the conflict that followed. Isabella was not an outsider to Shrewsbury, impoverished, or from the labouring classes. Her complaint charged that the group she wished to indict, probably the back-bone of the burgesses, later to be stripped of their elected officials, had invaded her dwelling-place at Shrewsbury, broken her gates and houses therein, and beaten and maimed her servants.[42] What may appear initially as a revolt of an underclass led by a fire-brand woman against elected elites, now clearly emerges as the opposite: the out-of-power wealthy revolting against legitimately elected officials, whose professions suggest a municipal government centred on a middling artisan class. From the second document, Isabella now surfaces as leader of Shrewsbury's *coup d'état* five days later, a coup from above. Her elite status is further highlighted by other archival documents. Twenty years later, the king would grant her special protection and privileges, and she became identified as 'the king's hostess (*hospes Regis*)', by which she received a guarantee that 'nothing is to be taken of her corn at [her manor of] Campden or elsewhere, and no bailiff or other minister of the king shall be lodged within her dwelling place at Shrewsbury'.[43] Moreover, her wealth went beyond manors: she acted regularly as a banker, making extensive loans for as much as £100 to merchants, mercers, and knights throughout Shrewsbury's hinterland.[44]

---

[41] *CPR 1301–7*, p. 271, 1303.xi.30.   [42] Ibid., p. 270, 1303.xi.25.

[43] *CPR 1321–4*, p. 53, 1322.i.25.

[44] She appears eighty-three times in debtor–creditor relations (TNA, C 241, Chancery: Certificates of Statute Merchant and Statute Staple) and as creditor in all but six, with loans from 40s. to £100.

Thus, the wresting of power from elected officials was indeed class conflict, but tilted in the opposite direction from what we may initially have supposed from the reading of a single commission. Unfortunately, the great majority of cases present single documents alone, with a mandate, commission, or pardon only to go by.

Nonetheless, other documents in the Patent Rolls reveal more about class tensions in urban places: strife between those called by a variety of terms and phrases – the 'greater' and 'lesser sort', the 'rich' and 'poor', the 'young' and the established order, 'certain men of less sufficiency' and 'their betters', 'more worthy citizens' and those who apparently were less so. As seen earlier, the young men of Scarborough in the 1280s allied with outsiders to create a second power structure within town that defied municipal elites, the Church, and king. They appropriated rents from the town's mills and farm, imposed their own taxes, violated Church liberties, and resisted the justice of legitimately elected officials.[45] In 1301, 'poor men of Cirencester' lodged a royal complaint against their urban lords, the Abbot of Cirencester, two of his fellow monks, and seven laymen who, the poor charged, had extorted from them 'great sums of money by undue distraints'. The poor claimed that these Church elites had entered their homes, assaulted and imprisoned some, and consumed or taken away their goods and animals.[46] In 1323, the poor of the commonalty of Dover complained that 'the rich men' of town, against the customs of the port, and 'to the detriment of the common advantage and infringement of the usages of the town', appropriated ships equipped and financed by the town's twenty-one wards for their own profit, which led to 'dissensions between the poor men and the said rich men with loss of life on both sides' with 'worse to be feared'.[47]

Occasionally, urban divisions arose between certain occupational groups in conflict with municipal authorities, lords, or the king. As seen earlier, the mistery of the cobblers of Bristol petitioned the king against their mayor in 1363, because he changed guild customs preventing cobblers to buy fresh hinds or tan them in town, which caused shoe prices and other leather goods to soar. In turn, these impositions caused 'great clamour and strife among the people'.[48] In 1384, a fraternity or guild comprised of 'labourers and workmen' in Coventry, called the Nativity of Jesus Christ, which the king had authorized to acquire lands and rents to hire a chaplain, used 'the guise of the gild' to league together to oppose the city's mayor and bailiffs as well as the king's ministers

---

[45] *CPR 1281–92*, p. 50, 1282.x.20; and see p. 73, above.
[46] *CPR 1301–7*, p. 49, 1301.ii.18.   [47] *CPR 1321–4*, pp. 375–6, 1323.ix.26.
[48] *CPR 1361–4*, pp. 297–8, 1363.ii.1.

'to the subversion of the good government of the city'.[49] In 1362, sailors and mariners residing in thirteen 'towns' in Essex – Colchester, Aylesford, Brightlingsea, St Osyth, East and West Mersea, Fingringhoe, Peldon, Peet [near Peldon], Wigborough, Salcott, Tollesbury, and Goldhanger – took an oath and petitioned the king. They charged that Lionel of Bradenham, a justice of the Statute of Labourers from at least 1355,[50] had usurped their common fishing rights in three bodies of sea water issuing from the Colne, which they and their ancestors had enjoyed without hindrance 'time out of mind'. Lionel claimed the waters belonged to his lordship, and that the men to whom he leased the waters had fixed large piles, obstructing the entrances to the waters. Further, he abused his position as justice of labourers, fining the sailors who signed the petition and confiscating their boats on these waters. For their release he demanded ransoms or used the boats for his own purposes. In addition, he abused his position by keeping for his own profit the half penny from fines charged on violations of the Statutes of Labourers, which should have gone to the commonalties for payments of the fifteenth.[51] W. R. Powell has shown that this was a longstanding controversy between the unscrupulous Bradenham, out for profit, and the burgesses of Colchester, intent on maintaining their liberties.[52]

After the Black Death, in stark contrast to the Continent, only a handful of cases explicitly show divisions within towns even vaguely along class lines; several of these, moreover, were resolved by arbitration or in royal courts. In 1378, commoners of Norwich felt aggrieved by what they judged as an unfair distribution of a new tax for coastal defence by the city's 'Prudhommes' with the burden shifted onto the poor. Commoners took their case to the Crown and (uncharacteristically) won: the king's ministers determined that only those who possessed property worth £10 or more should be assessed,[53] and as a result, the protest did not escalate into armed confrontation.[54]

In 1380, 'certain men of less sufficiency' in Shrewsbury 'banded together by covin' and in effect took over the reins of the municipal government. On St Giles day the latter customarily elected the town's two bailiffs. The poorer sort banded together 'by covin' with the counsel

[49] *CPR 1381–5*, p. 497, 1384.vii.11.
[50] *CPR 1354–8*, p. 294, 1355.viii.28, and p. 296. On his career, see W. R. Powell, 'Lionel de Bradenham and his Siege of Colchester in 1350', *Essex Archaeology and History: Transactions of the Essex Archaeological Society*, 22 (1991): 67–75; and the incident of 1362, pp. 70–3. The fishery dispute went back to 1350 or earlier.
[51] *CPR 1361–4*, p. 283, 1362.vii.3.   [52] Powell, 'Lionel de Bradenham'.
[53] McRee, 'Peacemaking', p. 846.
[54] This case appears neither in the chronicles nor *CPR*.

of eleven named men, including a draper, a saddler, a souter (cobbler), and a shearman, hijacked the elections and chose their own bailiffs. They took money from the town treasury, allegedly 'to squander', rose up against 'their betters', assaulted and imprisoned one of them, and refused to obey the king's writ for his release, so that the sons of the one imprisoned 'died of grief'.[55] Four months later, probably many of the same, now described as 'with no lands', tried again to prevent 'the customary election of bailiffs'. The king appointed a commission to arrest and imprison them.[56] In 1393, another election of mayor and bailiffs split a town along class lines. In this case, the dean and chapter of the cathedral of Lincoln allied with the commonalty against 'the more worthy citizens'. Apparently it was a touchy matter; even the king was reluctant to intervene. First, he handed it over to his chancellor, the Archbishop of York, but he refused to decide, claiming 'urgent affairs of state' prevented him from doing so. It then passed to a royal commission, but they too refused to assume the burden because of 'perils likely to arise' without a 'special mandate' from the king.[57] As we have seen, commoners of Norwich protested against the city elites in 1414 for abrogating the commoners' electoral prerogatives since 1404. But as with their complaints of 1378, the protest did not escalate into collective protest in the streets; this time, the expense of a suit brought to royal courts was averted, settled by a mutually elected arbiter, Sir Thomas Erpingham.[58]

Finally, in 1437, the king sent a mandate to the mayor and sheriffs of Norwich to cry throughout the city that those 'stirring up strife between the greater and lesser men' and who formed unlawful assemblies would be punished 'under pain of loss of life and limb'.[59] The mandate gives no reason why the 'lesser men' had gathered, or what their grievances might have been. A single surviving document in the national archives, however, reveals that this incident was the final straw after four years of negotiations and arbitration, first through Norwich's bishop, then the Earl of Suffolk, against attempts by ex-mayor William Wetherby to extend his term of office in violation of Norwich statutes and corporate codes of behaviour. The archival source and the string of negotiations over the previous four years suggest that the 1437 melee did not, however, divide Norwich sharply between a broad base of commoners

---

[55] *CPR 1377–81*, p. 579, 1380.xi.24; and see p. 105, above.
[56] *CPR 1377–81*, pp. 631–2, 1381.iii.26.
[57] *CPR 1391–6*, p. 240, 1393.iii.5; Hill, *Medieval Lincoln*, does not comment on this dispute.
[58] See p. 57 above.   [59] *CPR 1436–41*, p. 146, 1437.xi.29.

and elites, as suggested in the oyer et terminer investigation, or as had been the case with the earlier electoral dispute of 1414, when 'Prudhommes' had ruled against any participation in elections to higher posts by 'persons of the smallest reputation in the city'. Rather, the 1437 conflict was more clearly factional with Wetherby and his cronies on one side, and commoners allied with aggrieved elites on the other.[60]

Many of the disputes dividing urban communities erupted on the eve of elections for mayors and bailiffs.[61] In addition to those described above, the Patent Rolls reveal others: Winchester in 1274,[62] Newcastle upon Tyne in 1341,[63] and two more times in 1364,[64] York in 1365[65] and in 1380,[66] London in 1376,[67] Lynn in 1414,[68] and Liskaerd [Cornwall] in 1439.[69] For the most part, it is difficult to determine whether they were factional or drawn between oligarchic citizens and those with few, if any rights. For some, as with a Newcastle upon Tyne discord of 1341, when tensions were rising between Scotland and England, the language of the petition suggests a factional division: 'one confederacy' elected a mayor 'and another confederacy' elected another. King's Bench, however, further unravels the character of this revolt: several men were accused of having 'wrongfully set themselves apart as a body' against the mayor and bailiffs. The two principal ringleaders, Richard of Acton and his wife Maud, roused a 'great proportion of the lesser people of the town' – 'ignorant and unknowledgeable men' – to assemble at

---

[60] See McRee, 'Peacemaking', pp. 853–64. He does not mention the *CPR* source. Wetherby resurfaces again during the Gladman Insurrection, with backing of the priory, the Duke of Suffolk, and privy council: once again he succeeds in ruling the city; see Chris Humphrey, *The Politics of Carnival: Festive Misrule in Medieval England* (Manchester, 2001), p. 72.

[61] However, it would be going too far to agree with Reynolds, *An Introduction*: 'Riots and disorders when they occurred nearly all happened at mayoral elections' (p. 186). In the chronicles, only 10 of 231 cases concerned or happened at times of elections – less than 5 per cent. In *CPR*, they were rarer still: 12 of 651 cases, or under 2 per cent.

[62] *CPR 1272–81*, p. 60, 1274.x.14.   [63] *CPR 1340–3*, pp. 320–1, 1341.x.16.

[64] *CPR 1364–7*, pp. 18–19, 1364.ix.24; and ibid., p. 44, 1364.x.8.

[65] Ibid., p. 44, 1365.xii.9.   [66] *CPR 1377–81*, p. 580, 1380.xii.5.

[67] *CPR 1374–7*, p. 387, 1376.xi.2.

[68] *CPR 1413–16*, p. 411, 1414.xii.3. 'Muniments of the Borough of King's Lynn', housed in Lynn's municipal archives, also describes it (Owen, *The Making of King's Lynn*, pp. 395–401). The dispute arose because Henry V intervened in mayoral elections to prevent the victor, John Bilney, from becoming mayor. With his supporters, Bilney broke into the Guildhall and forced the previous mayor to swear him in as mayor. It was a revolt as much, if not more, in defiance of the king as against another faction or social class within the city. When elections approached again in 1416, the king was clearly anxious about renewed violence and ordered artisans to remain at their shops and stalls, forbidding them to congregate in conventicles for 'rioting and insurrection'; ibid., doc. no. 498, pp. 401–4.

[69] *CPR 1436–41*, p. 371, 1439.xii.10.

St Nicholas' church, and by their confederacy, illegally elected Richard as mayor.[70] The principals were pardoned, but only after paying high fines of either £100 or £200. In York, the electoral struggle of 1380 between Gysburn and Quixley shows elements of factional dispute and class conflict, as do those between Northampton and Brembre in London in the 1380s, or the capital's electoral disputes in the early 1440s. Still others remain completely opaque as in 1439, when 'divers congregations, riots, routs and other unlawful assemblies have lately occurred at Liskaerd in connection with the election of a mayor'.

But despite the great variety of divisions created over elections, or which arose because of abuses and other grievances, open class revolt between rich and poor or of similar designations remain extremely rare in late medieval English urban society, especially in comparison with the late medieval histories of popular revolt in Italy, France, and Flanders.[71] The Patent Rolls uncover only twenty-six cases manifesting explicit social or class divisions within towns of the 651 complaints and incidents seen as riots or revolts in urban places, and some of these may have hinged more on factional than class strife. By contrast, revolts of the 'popolo', 'bourgeois', or middling sorts against knights, magnates, and privileged citizens on the Continent constituted the largest number of revolts, 311 of 1,112 – or over a quarter of them. Added to these, revolts by the disenfranchised *menu peuple* or *popolo minuto*, who took up arms to become citizens or to struggle against their rulers' abuses, came next in line, with 112 revolts.

Equivalent terms, often with concrete juridical meaning, such as *popolo*, *menu peuple*, and *popolo minuto*, do not even appear in the late medieval English sources. As we have seen, both chronicles and royal commissions present a wide, varied, but vague nomenclature for those at the bottom of urban society – 'the poor', 'the lesser sort', 'the less worthy', 'men of less sufficiency'. Moreover, these were not reported with any consistency from one document to the next, even in the same cities; nor were they tied to specific professions or legal restrictions determining which groups could possess citizenship, as chronicles,

---

[70] *King's Bench*, V, pp. 47–8.
[71] Systematic searches through King's Bench and local court records would produce further incidents as in Oxford, 1253, when the 'lesser commune' (*minor communia*), also called the 'lesser burgesses', and the poor petitioned the king against their treatment by the 'greater burgesses', concerning various crimes but principally over excessive and fraudulent taxation; see *Snappe's Formulary and Other Records*, ed. H. E. Salter, Oxford Historical Society, 80 (Oxford, 1924), pp. 270–80; and cited in Powicke, *King Henry III and Lord Edward*, II, p. 446. The actions of these minor burgesses, however, were limited to a meeting in Oxford's church of St Giles, where they affixed their seal to the grievances.

statutes, and other legal documents in France and Italy often specified with juridical precision. New research into civic records of English towns, no doubt, will shed further light on these class distinctions.[72] For now, we hypothesize that one reason for this comparative lack of clarity in English towns may have resulted from the high percentage of those with burgess rights in many English towns, especially smaller ones, as with Shrewsbury, which included many as citizens – weavers, tailors, shearmen, and others in the cloth industry – who would have been excluded from such rights in many Continental towns.[73] Moreover, in places such as St Albans, wealthy merchants, along with the poor, were equally labelled 'villeins'. The proportion of urban revolts which turned on class division was certainly one of the most crucial differences distinguishing popular protest in England from the Continent: while for England they comprised 4 per cent of urban revolts and riots in Patent Rolls (26 of 651), for Italy, France, and Flanders, they made up 40 per cent of them (423 of 1,112).

Burgess struggles against the secular nobility

Another dimension of class conflict which was curiously infrequent in English towns was struggles between burgesses and secular magnates, whether knights from the countryside, or magnates of the realm with residences in towns and cities.[74] The absence is all the more surprising given the historiography, that English towns must be seen in the larger

[72] Watts, 'Public or Plebs', p. 245, discusses briefly the class distinctions between commons and others of lesser rank or outside the commons, such as 'lesser burgesses'. He does not show, however, that they were distinguished with the juridical or occupational clarity that can be seen in towns and cities on the Continent.

[73] Also see Dale, 'Social and Economic History', p. 34, who asserts that in Leicester, 'as in other towns membership of the Guild Merchant was theoretically open to all manner of traders and craftsmen, with the exception of women'. By contrast, many artisans, even highly skilled ones, especially in the cloth industry, were excluded from the guild community and citizenship in places such as Siena and Florence for most of the late Middle Ages, and in cities and towns of Flanders until 1305. In larger cities such as London and Norwich, large numbers of inhabitants were not members of guilds or part of the citizenry; for London, Hilton, 'Popular Movements in England', p. 237, has argued that the class structure of late medieval London may not have differed so greatly from Florence's: less than a quarter of London's inhabitants were citizens; for Norwich, see Liddy, '"Bee war of gyle in borugh"', p. 478, who is less precise but argues that only citizens were members of guilds, at least by the fifteenth century, and that they were privileged politically and economically.

[74] According to Hilton, 'Towns in English Society', p. 26, unlike in Italy and southern France, secular nobles did not have permanent residences in late medieval towns; nonetheless, magnates were involved in urban economies as rentiers and in the running of weekly markets and seasonal fairs; see Dyer, *Making a Living in the Middle Ages*, p. 147.

context of agrarian lordship, that private lords possessed 'many more than two-thirds of market towns' and, through their stewards, exercised considerable control at the meetings of the portmoot. Their presence in towns was significant, with fortresses within or on the outskirts of towns possessed by magnates, such as Gaunt's at Lincoln and Knaresborough. Feudal lords still imposed levies on certain artisans and on the owner-ship of urban property, even if that presence was on the decline after the Domesday Book (1086).[75] As we will see, a major struggle throughout our period was between townsmen and ecclesiastical lords in monastic boroughs, as well as outside them. Yet surprisingly, seldom did strife erupt between townsmen and their secular lords, as seen in the late medieval documentation.

By contrast, such struggles filled Italian medieval history. They char-acterized the earliest forms of class strife, when *pedites* challenged the rule of *milites* in towns in the eleventh century.[76] The struggle between the *popolo* and magnates, both rural and urban, was the central force of Italian city-state constitutional developments, to the end of the four-teenth century, if not longer. Such movements also spread through cities in France and Flanders, with bourgeois challenges to seigneurial rights at Marseilles in 1257, Limoges in 1274, Valenciennes in 1291, and the Revolts of Flanders, 1297–1304 and 1323–8, when, in addition to attacking the French, a broad coalition of peasants, artisans, and shop-keepers rose against their lords in cities and the countryside.[77] Struggles between commoners in Bruges and the nobility of their 'franc', or hinterland, over privileges in the city and for hegemony in neighbouring towns were longstanding through the fifteenth century.[78] Furthermore, 'jacquerie' to slaughter noblemen and ladies were not limited to the Jacquerie of 1358 or to rural areas, but also flared at Gaeta in 1353, Toulouse and its region in 1364, Viterbo in 1367, and Naples in 1374. Even during the Peasants' Revolt, urban rebels (as opposed to rural ones) targeted few properties, palaces, or rural estates belonging to secular lords, especially compared with the Jacquerie of 1358 or the Ciompi in 1378. The property townspeople burnt in 1381 – the Savoy, estates at Highbury, the hospital of Clerkenwell, the College of Corpus Christi at Cambridge – were targeted principally because of their con-nection with key figures of the royal government, first and foremost the king's uncle, John of Gaunt, then the royal treasurer and master of

---

[75] Hilton, 'Towns in English Society', p. 25.
[76] Cohn, *Lust for Liberty*, pp. 9–10.
[77] Among other places, ibid., pp. 53–7, 78–9, and 107.
[78] Liddy and Haemers, 'Popular Politics', p. 23.

the hospital of Clerkenwell, Robert Hales, and not as secular lords per se, independent of the Crown and the royal courts.[79]

Finally, military campaigns organized by guilds or governments of burghers against noble strongholds in the countryside were common on the Continent from the end of the eleventh to the fifteenth century, as with the battles between Piacenza's *pedites* against their lords in 1090, Parma on numerous occasions through the late thirteenth and early fourteenth centuries,[80] the government of Cola di Rienzo before and after the Black Death,[81] Florence with its wars to 'exterminate' the Guidi, and other noble clans on its mountainous fringes across the late Middle Ages,[82] Siena with raids and military campaigns against noble strongholds in its *contado*, Sint-Truiden against the stronghold possessed by the noble family of Hers after their youth had murdered an artisan in 1384, and more.[83] Such struggles were rare in the English late medieval sources, especially when the targeted magnates were not among the king's immediate family. During the Barons' War of the 1260s, the constable and marshal of London, appointed by the citizens, summoned 'all the people of the city' with the sound of 'the great bell of St Paul's' to follow the leaders' standards into the countryside, where they 'laid waste and ravaged with fire' Richard of Cornwall's manor of Isleworth, destroyed his fisheries, and burnt his mills. They destroyed his mansion at Westminster and those of other magnates sympathetic to the king, and properties of his clerks, barons of the Exchequer, and justices of the Bench. The London militia encircled London, ravaging the lands of Henrician magnate supporters such as William de Valence, Philip Basset, Peter of Savoy at Cheshunt, Walter de Merton at Merton and his manor at Finsbury, and James de Audley's land at Tottenham.[84] According to the alderman chronicler of London, 'so many manors were

---

[79] On 24 June 1381, the king appointed high-ranking magnates to examine insurgents' destruction of property during the past twenty days of revolt. Eight commissions indicted rebels, listing numerous properties destroyed on manors in Cambridge, Hertford, Essex, Bedfordshire, Norfolk, and Suffolk, but only one shows townsmen equalling scores against a secular lord – John of Gaunt and his possessions in the city and suburbs of London (*CPR 1381–5*, p. 76). An exception may have been raids of Cambridge burgesses joined by country rebels against manors in the surrounding countryside. The two leaders, John Hanchach and Geoffrey Cobbe, were, however, substantial county landowners; see Dobson, *The Peasants' Revolt*, doc. n. 37. For rural rebels, the picture was different, but even here Dyer, 'The Social and Economic Background', pp. 10–14, has concluded: 'Serious personal violence against lords seems to have been unusual' (p. 14).

[80] Cohn, *Lust for Liberty*, p. 10.   [81] Ibid., p. 5.

[82] See Cohn, *Creating the Florentine State*.

[83] For these and more examples, see Cohn, *Lust for Liberty*.

[84] Denholm-Young, *Richard of Cornwall*, p. 126; and Williams, *Medieval London*, p. 224.

committed to the flames, so many men, rich and poor, were plundered, and so many thousands of persons lost their lives'.[85] This is the closest any group in English history (not counting the Crown) came to staging a 'Jacquerie' against the secular nobility.

Yet, these raids were not independent actions of Londoners to extend communal rights against magnates. Instead, they were raids led by Hugh Despenser, the baronial justiciar in Simon de Montfort's war against Henry III. Moreover, the properties targeted were mostly those of the king's immediate family and supporters. Essentially, these were attacks against the Crown. A less dramatic but better case comes from Colchester in the 1340s, when burgesses invaded Lexden Park against the fitzWalters, to assert their rights of pasturing, hunting, and fishing.[86] 'John fitzWalter and his retinue laid siege to the town and ambushed merchants until townsmen bought him off'.[87] It was a case, however, not recorded by chronicles or Patent Rolls. Another example, well recorded by these sources, was the 1405 attack on the forces of the Earl of Westmorland, when the Archbishop of York led citizens into battle.[88] However, the origins of this dispute did not concern the interests and liberties of the city; as we have seen, this was first and foremost a dispute among the highest magnates of the realm over aristocratic inheritance.[89] We have also examined the threats and demands of the nobility to enter London in 1388, when the mayor first refused them entry but then felt forced to allow them in. Placated by wine and hospitality, the threat, however, never exploded into the armed conflict that had been feared. Like the others, this friction did not, moreover, concern burgess privileges against a rural or urban aristocracy.[90]

Our best case concerns the conflicts between the mayors and burgesses of Bristol against their seigneurial lords, the Berkeleys, which stretched across the first half of the fourteenth century. It was an extraordinary case but, as far as our survey goes, a singular one. Their struggle for rights and power, moreover, was not that of an entire city, as with the magnate–*popolo* wars in Italy or in southern France, but was against the Berkeleys' feudal rights to courts and other privileges in Bristol neighbourhoods, first with Redcliffe, and later another city suburb. Here, the Berkeleys held their own courts and collected tolls and fees as though these urban neighbourhoods were seigneurial manors. As previously seen, citizens resisted these lords' infringements,

[85] 'Liber de Antiquis Legibus', p. 65.   [86] Powell, 'Lionel de Bradenham', pp. 68–9.
[87] Britnell, *Growth and Decline in Colchester*, p. 31.   [88] See pp. 131–2, above.
[89] Walsingham, *Chronica maiora*, p. 336; and *An English Chronicle, 1377–1461*, pp. 35–6.
[90] Walsingham, *Chronica maiora*, p. 259.

arrogance, and violence, their rides into town and their assaults on burgesses and their wives, which included breaking of shins, draggings from homes, and tossings in pits and cesspools. For three decades or more, the burgesses organized marches into the countryside against the lords, broke into their manors, disrupted their courts, and destroyed the instruments of their oppression, the pillory and tumbrel.[91]

The Bristol case was unusual in a second way. The few other examples of strife between secular lords and burgesses came from small or medium-sized market towns, not from commercial centres, where the king's will would have more likely prevailed over the juridical or economic interests of contending secular lords. Led by the parson of the church of St George in Sudbury, eleven men and a woman, along with other burgesses of this Suffolk market town – a seigneurial borough controlled by the king's son, Lionel, Duke of Clarence – confederated together in 1363 to disrupt and prevent his deputies holding sessions of his leet court,[92] their weekly markets, and annual fair. They assaulted the duke's steward, sergeant, and other court officers and imprisoned the sergeant, took over his market and fair, and appraised the merchandise brought there 'at less than it was worth, and had their will of it', thus 'usurping royal power'.[93]

In 1365, a knight and others including a draper and a slater led armed burgesses of Doncaster to prevent their lord, Lady Margaret, widow of Peter Mauley [de Malo], the fifth, from holding her court and collecting tolls and other profits. Further, they entered her manors at Doncaster and eleven other villages, hunted her warrens and fished her fisheries, toppled her carts laden with crops, hay, and wood, assaulted her servants, and threatened her tenants so that 'they have withdrawn from her lordship and dare not dwell there'.[94] Two years later, five named men of Doncaster, including a chaplain, inflicted further threats to Lady Margaret's lordship. In armed confederacy, they rescued one of the town's bakers from the town's pillory, who had been prosecuted in her

---

[91] See above, pp. 135–7, 140.

[92] A criminal tribunal that was larger than the view of frankpledge.

[93] *CPR 1361–4*, p. 358, 1363.ii.14.

[94] *CPR 1364–7*, p. 146, 1365.v.12. The first named of this group and the likely leader, Sir John fitzWilliam from nearby Sprotborough, does not appear to have been an outlaw or criminal in further documents between 1364 and 1367; in three other cases he appears once for trespass against an outlaw (ibid., p. 45, 1364.xi.28) and twice as a Crown appointee to commissions (ibid., pp. 280–1, 1366.ii.10; and p. 365, 1366.x.26). On a commission of oyer et terminer, he sat in judgement on a complaint lodged by a Peter Mauley, not the fifth, the deceased husband of Lady Margaret, but perhaps her son, or another in-law. The case concerned breaking parks and warrens on seven of his manors. None of the other named defendants appears during these years of *CPR*.

court – the assize of bread. Afterwards, they prevented her steward from holding further court sessions and her ministers from collecting tolls and profits from her market and fairs. Finally, they dug her soil and hunted and fished in her free warrens and fisheries in Doncaster and in eight other manors, and laid ambushes for her servants: 'so threatened and injured' were her men and tenants that they 'withdrew from her lordship'.[95]

On the eve of the Peasants' Revolt, John of Gaunt suffered uprisings and troubles, not only in London, but on his rural estates and market towns. His courts were disrupted; tenants and others illegally dug in his mines; his servants were assaulted; and residents refused to honour his rights to turn stray animals over to him.[96] In 1380, men of Bridgwater challenged the rights of another baron prominent within the royal circle, William la Zouche [the third],[97] who was lord of two parts of the town. They attacked his rights to hold the view of frankpledge. Unusually, the attack was not led by the burgesses' elected officials; instead, the master of the town's hospital of St John Baptist, three of its brothers, a knight and his son, a chamberlain, and one named William Webbe (who may or may not have been a weaver) led the assault. In addition to preventing the lord's steward holding court, the men took its profits, stole a cow, and broke his close at a nearby village, where they hunted, depastured his corn, and assaulted his servants.[98]

After the Peasants' Revolt, despite freeing his bondmen, at least in Kent, Gaunt continued to face rebellion on his estates, and in particular in two towns where he possessed lordship. In his capacity as Earl of Lincoln, he had custody and ward over the town's castle, with privileges of holding and profiting from 'fairs, markets, royalties, liberties, and free customs' in the city, including the view of frankpledge with its profits from the chattels of waifs, fugitives, and felons convicted there. In 1390, four previous mayors of Lincoln, the present mayor, a previous bailiff and the present one, two former servants of the mayor and bailiffs, and seven other men, including a saddler and a butcher, entered the castle bailey with other 'evildoers', broke stalls and stakes and prevented merchants from selling there. Where the market once stood, they erected houses and buildings within the castle dykes, charged rents, established their own assize of bread and ale, and violated the duke's jurisdiction by

[95] *CPR 1367–70*, pp. 60–1, 1367.xi.10.
[96] *CPR 1377–81*, p. 468, 1380.ii.13; and ibid., p. 511, 1380.v.1.
[97] See Eric Acheson, 'Zouche [de la Zouche] Family, (per c. 1254–1415), Magnates', *ODNB*.
[98] *CPR 1377–81*, p. 570, 1380.vii.3. Also, Dilks, 'Bridgwater'. Curiously, he does not mention Webbe. Perhaps by 1381 he was no longer around.

levying fees and attaching persons, amounting to losses of £1,000.[99] On the same day, the duke lodged another complaint against the burgesses of Knaresborough, where he also was lord, 'touching treasons, felonies, murders, homicides, robberies, insurrections and other offences in John, duke of Lancaster's lordship and liberty of Knaresburgh and in the forest and chace thereof'.[100]

Finally, in 1401, tenants of Abergavenny rebelled against their lord, William Beauchamp,[101] to free three men from the gallows and in so doing shot arrows and killed the knight, Sir William Lucy, sheriff of Hereford, charged with carrying out the execution. As far as Usk's brief report reveals, this action of a few armed men did not challenge the rights of the lord.[102] On the other hand, according to two commissions, more may have been at stake. The rebels were accused of assemblies in various places through South Wales within the lordship of Abergavenny ('Bergevenaby'), where they committed homicides and were moving into the Marches 'to do worse'. They besieged the castle of Abergavenny, leaving Lord Beaumont and his wife Joan locked up there until at least 18 May, six days after the initial attack and the freeing of the three sentenced to be executed. The local knight John Chaundos and the sheriff of Gloucester were commissioned to raise a posse of all 'fencible men of the county' to go 'without delay' to free the lord and his wife and bring the besiegers to justice.[103] From these descriptions, the rebels may have been men more from the county than the town, and the incastellated enclave of Abergavenny can only be considered on the cusp of being a town at the beginning of the fifteenth century.

The Patent Rolls are filled with thousands of mandates and special commissions to inquire into complaints brought by owners of manors, and by knights, earls, and members of the royal family, against long lists of men and sometimes women, who broke closes and parks, hunted and fished properties, depastured fields, broke chests, and stole or destroyed muniments. Yet our survey reveals only two significant struggles between burgesses and secular lords (other than against the king himself) over the two and a half centuries of these records. One of the two, moreover,

---

[99] *CPR 1389–92*, p. 270, 1390.iii.10.   [100] Ibid., pp. 269–70, 1390.iii.10.

[101] William Beauchamp was granted justice of South Wales for life; *CPR 1399–1401*, 1399.x.30, p. 33. After the incident, on 27 August 1401, Henry revoked the office, because Beauchamp had not exercised it for a year 'and the men of the country have not been governed'; ibid., p. 538.

[102] *The Chronicle of Adam Usk*, pp. 130–3.

[103] *CPR 1399–1401*, pp. 518 and 520, 16 and 18.v.1401. For Lady Joan's later involvement in private warfare, mass murder, and criminality in the 1430s, see Griffiths, *The Reign of Henry VI*, p. 142.

touched a secular lord who was not only of the royal household but was perhaps at that time England's most powerful individual. The struggles at Bristol against the Berkeleys during the first thirty years of the fourteenth century and the 1390 attack at Lincoln were the only confrontations in major towns when burgesses engaged in arm conflict against their secular lords over political and economic liberties.[104] Not even the Peasants' Revolt sparked burgesses to demand their rights, courts, and markets from secular lords (as opposed to ecclesiastical ones). At the beginning of the twentieth century, Charles Oman generalized: 'The history of the majority of English towns in the fourteenth century, just like that of Italian or German towns during that same period, is in a great measure composed of the struggles of the *inferiors* against the *potentiores*.'[105] Instead, our survey shows the opposite: the history of popular revolt in English towns did not reflect the same social dynamics as seen on the Continent; class cleavages within towns, whether between the poor and 'better sort' of elected officials and their ilk or between the commonalty and magnates of the realm or large landowners in surrounding regions were rare.[106] The picture changes dramatically, however, when burgesses confronted ecclesiastical lords; here chronicles and Patent Rolls forcibly corroborate the difference.

---

[104] There were of course minor clashes between burgesses and magnates that did not spill into recorded violence, such as in 1315, when 'certain magnates and lords' in the hinterland of Southampton, violated burgesses' liberties by evading tolls; *CPR 1313–17*, pp. 308–9, 1315.ii.26; and Platt, *Medieval Southampton*, p. 87.

[105] Oman, *The Great Revolt*, p. 14. Green, *Town Life*, pp. 190–1 and 207, drew a similar picture based on several examples: 'the broad chasm … breaks the whole industrial society itself into two factors – merchant traders versus artificers and small retail dealers. Incessant riots declared the discontent of the commons.'

[106] Other sources reveal tensions between burgesses and nobility in seigneurial boroughs, such as at High Wycombe in 1227 or 1228, when burgesses complained that their lord, Alan Basset, had acted contrary to liberties they held from the king. The lord then granted them rents, markets, and fairs, and other things belonging to a free borough, but in return demanded rent and the service of one knight due to the king. Further, Basset maintained 'the right to take tallage in the borough whenever the king tallaged his demesnes'; C. Jamison, 'Social and Economic History', in *VCH: Buckingham*, ed. William Page (London, 1908), II, p. 38. The complaint and its settlement did not go beyond court action.

Part III

Church and city

10   Revolts in monastic boroughs

Struggles between townsmen and the Crown may have been the most important of urban conflicts in the later Middle Ages. They are the best known in the political histories of England and for constitutional developments, such as the alliances of barons with townsmen against the king in 1263–6 or in 1326–7, the urban conflicts of the Peasants' Revolt of 1381, Richard II's troubles, and the factional alliances and struggles that ensued in London, such as those between Northampton and Brembre and their coteries from 1382 to the end of the century. But as far as chronicle reporting of urban protest goes, struggles between towns and the Crown were not the most frequent. In number, struggles between burgesses and ecclesiastical bodies – competition over privileges and liberties and for political, economic, and juridical control involving archbishops, bishops, priories, canons, hospitals, and monasteries – were greater. If conflict between burgesses and universities (another ecclesiastical body) is added, then over a quarter of all the urban conflicts in our sample of chronicles were ones in which burgesses contested ecclesiastical bodies (59 of 231 incidents), and this not counting the English Peasants' Revolt of 1381, which also entailed attacks on churches, hospitals, and a college at Cambridge. If conflicts within these ecclesiastical bodies are added, the proportion climbs to over 40 per cent. In fact, the one revolt to receive the most attention from the chronicles was neither against the Crown nor located in London, the most reported-upon urban place during the Middle Ages; rather, it was the Norwich burgess–Church struggle of 1272.[1]

This preponderance of conflicts involving ecclesiastical bodies and townsmen did not result simply because the great majority of late medieval English chroniclers were monks. In the various Acts of the Patent Rolls initiated for the king's business and peace and redacted by his clerks, commissioners, and lawyers, the number of conflicts between

---

[1] At least fifteen chronicles reported this revolt in our sample.

burgesses and the Church was almost as great: a third of them involved ecclesiastical bodies (213 of 651 Acts).

This predominance, and especially those against monastic lords, is yet another aspect that differentiated England from the Continent. To be sure, conflicts between townsmen and local bishops occurred in Italy. In 1319, for instance, a bishop with papal backing excommunicated the town of Recanati, because of its support of their lord, Federico of Montefeltro, whom the pope and bishop accused of idolatry and heresy. The townsmen responded by staging a mock funeral of the bishop, carrying a straw effigy of him, which they burnt ceremoniously with chants in a great funerary pyre.[2] Moreover, municipal archives in France show that conflict between towns and bishops had not ended with the central Middle Ages,[3] but they had become infrequent, and ones between townsmen and local monasteries had become extremely rare, if they continued at all. Even in towns such as Langres, where the bishop and the Duke of Burgundy never wished their townsmen to form a commune, the bishop by 1356 was forced to accept it, and no violence ensued.[4]

These conflicts, moreover, often differed from English ones: not only were the Continental ones less frequent (8 per cent, or 89 of 1,112 revolts); by the thirteenth century, almost invariably, they formed part of larger and long-running conflicts between the pope and regional, even international powers. For instance, the one in Recanati concerned the larger universe of papal versus imperial politics within the pope's back-yard, the Papal States. In the colourful revolt of the *Harelle* at Rouen on 25 February 1382, the city bourgeois attacked the privileges of the

---

[2] Cohn, *Lust for Liberty*, pp. 101–2. Also similar attacks took place at Osimo and Perugia in the early fourteenth century.

[3] I thank Graeme Small for this observation.

[4] For examples of conflicts between small towns and villages and the Archbishop of Bremen, with revolts spreading into East Frisians and the Stedingers from 1204 to the 1230s, against tithes and other taxes, the archbishop's use of excommunication, and the pope calling an international crusade to crush the uprisings, see Bas J. P. van Bavel, 'Rural Revolts and Structural Change in the Low Countries, Thirteenth–Early Fourteenth Centuries', in *Survival and Discord in Medieval Society: Essays in Honour of Christopher Dyer*, ed. Richard Goddard, John Langdon, and Miriam Müller (Turnhout, 2010), pp. 251–2 and 262; and other examples, pp. 252–3 and 262. The rebels were also accused of worshipping evil spirits and paganism. For France, see Bernard Chevalier, *Les bonnes villes de France: Du XIVe au XVIe siècle* (Paris, 1982), who describes no violent conflicts between townsmen and their bishops or monasteries; for the case of Langres, see p. 201. For attacks by commoners against individual bishops or archbishops, as at Sens in 1315 and Florence in 1390, see Cohn, *Lust for Liberty*, pp. 74 and 79. The period of conflict between bishops and citizens over episcopal rights and hegemony of urban territories in northern and central Italy reached its peak by the end of the thirteenth century, if not earlier; see Scott, *The City-State in Europe*, Chapter 3, p. 9.

ancient monastery of Saint-Ouën, forcing the monks to destroy their old charters and swear to new ones devised by the rebels.[5] It occurred within the larger framework of simultaneous revolts against Charles VI and his new subsidies that spanned towns of northern France and reached those of Flanders.[6] These conflicts differed in a third respect. In the myriad struggles in England between burghers and their ecclesiastical lords, questions over religious doctrine with accusations of heresy almost never figured. The issues instead were economic and political – hard-headed matters of rights of elections, courts, land, monopolies, and profits from markets. In Italy, France, and Flanders, only the long history of political and economic rights in the Episcopacy of Liège resembled those of various English towns, but also here the struggle differed. At Liège, the conflict was between the bishop and his canons allied with an entrenched patriciate, on the one hand, against guildsmen, artisans, some merchants, and other townspeople, on the other.[7]

Conflict in monastic boroughs over liberties between clerics and townsmen is one of the few areas of class struggle where English historians have gone beyond the study of individual towns or individual periods such as de Montfort's baronial or the Peasants' Revolt of 1381. In 1927, Norman Trenholme analysed English monastic boroughs from their earliest foundation charters of Henry I in the early twelfth century to the dissolution of the monasteries in 1536.[8] In addition to chronicling the most important of these – in Dunstable, Abingdon, St Albans, and Bury St Edmunds – his analysis of the causes, ideology, and patterns of these revolts stands the test of time. He saw 'a close connection between national and local politics'[9] of the monastic boroughs. As we have seen with urban revolts against the Crown, Trenholme found three principal waves of monastic revolts: one accompanied the baronial revolt against Henry III in the 1260s; a second followed the queen's revolt against Edward II in 1326, and the third coincided with the Peasants' Revolt of 1381. Yet, at the same time, he saw these revolts as more or less constant, even on an upward spiral, prompted by growing monastic recalcitrance and their failure 'to recognize the growing corporate spirit of the townsmen'. Secondly, he argued that monastic power and privileges in these boroughs survived largely intact because of England's 'highly centralized government', with the Crown careful to suppress local disaffection 'and to support the vested interests of the great abbeys and priories, most of which were royal foundations'.[10]

---

[5] Cohn, *Popular Protest*, pp. 306–7.   [6] Ibid., pp. 191 and 225.
[7] Ibid., pp. 235–42; and Lantschner, 'The Logic of Political Conflict', especially Chapter 4.
[8] Trenholme, *The English Monastic Boroughs.*   [9] Ibid., p. 31.   [10] Ibid., p. 1.

Finally, Trenholme contrasted the history of late medieval popular revolt in towns with communal movements of Italy, France, and Germany, concluding that outside monastic boroughs, the 'violent revolutionary element' seen on the Continent, 'scarcely appears in the political development of English towns': the ordinary accounts of English municipal history give witness to 'comparatively few references to internal troubles or communal insurrections'. Trenholme's study, however, was written a generation before Gwyn Williams' on medieval London, and towns that were not monastic boroughs did not enter Trenholme's research. As we have seen, several of the most remarkable communal uprisings spread through towns and cities such as Bristol, Lynn, Norwich, Shrewsbury, Winchester, Lincoln, Bath, Ipswich, and Scarborough that were not monastic boroughs. Moreover, conflicts between townspeople and church authorities, which were not within monastic boroughs – ones against local bishops, canons, and abbots (who did not possess lordship over towns) could be as stormy, if not more so, as at Norwich with its priory. The monastic borough was hardly unique, even exceptional, in witnessing popular insurrection, as Trenholme assumed, and not all monastic boroughs experienced the same troubled relations and outbreaks of popular violence. It was absent from the monastic boroughs of Reading, Leominster, and Westminster[11] and rare for others such as Cirencester, Coventry, Peterborough, and Whitby. Instead of the rule, St Albans, Bury St Edmunds, and Abingdon were the exceptions.

The chronicles

The best known of the revolts between townsmen and Church were those within monastic boroughs, especially at St Albans and Bury St Edmunds during the English Peasants' Revolt. These rekindled protests that reached back at least to the late thirteenth century and focused on liberties, namely burgesses' claims to be bound to the king alone and not as monasteries' villeins. In Bury, the rebels of 1381 forced the monks to search through their archives for a supposed charter granting them the liberties confirmed by the monastery's founder, King Cnut.[12] At St Albans, the revolt was less violent; not a single monk lost his life, but similarly, in the case of St Albans, the insurgents demanded ancient charters going back into the mists of history, and supposedly granted by the Saxon King Offa. In both towns, rebel success was short-lived:

---

[11]   Rosser, *Medieval Westminster*; and Slade, 'Reading'.
[12]   See Walsingham in Dobson, *The Peasants' Revolt*, pp. 243–8 and 269–77.

their new charters and agreements were rescinded almost immediately; the ringleaders were executed; and in the case of Bury, the townsmen were fined heavily and excluded from the general amnesty granted across the realm by Richard in December. Rebels at Dunstable also forced a charter on their abbot granting burgess liberties, even though the Peasants' Revolt hardly touched Bedfordshire. Its mayor, Thomas Hobbes, was at St Albans during the unrest, but then returned to Dunstable, and organized a rebellion against the priory.[13] Yet against the historiographical grain that the Peasants' Revolt supposedly provoked a new wave of revolt through England into the early modern period, the pattern seen from the chroniclers charts the opposite: the monastic revolts of 1381 were a last-ditch stand, marking the end, rather than the beginning, of a new invigorated phase of popular self-confidence and urban insurrection for liberties.

The earliest of these monastic revolts found in our sample of chronicles goes back to 1227, when a dispute broke out in Dunstable over notions of trespass ('super misericordiis delictorum'), leading townspeople to demand a charter from the abbey. Its clauses focused entirely on the abbey's juridical rights over the town, ending the prior's authority to conduct inquisitions against townsmen, arrest them within the town ('burgam'), seize their chattels anywhere in England, and bring them before King's Bench, thus liberating them from all monastic tribunals.[14] The following year, another dispute arose between the prior and ten burgesses over offerings made at weddings and funerals, for which the ten were excommunicated. The townsmen ('populus'), however, in defiance of the abbey, continued to communicate with the ten, accompanying them to their parish church with the rest. As a result, monks, as well as the parish priest, ceased to celebrate mass from the beginning of August to the feast of St Denis (9 October).[15]

A year later, Henry III came to Dunstable. Hosted by the prior, he declared himself the monastery's patron and sought to bring peace between the monks and burgesses. The better sort of the people ('majores populi') admitted to wrongdoings and submitted to the king's peace, thus reinstating the monastery's tribunals and juridical rights over them. But as soon as the king left, the townsmen rejected the agreements. The prior appealed to the king and the Earl of Bedford to intervene, accusing the burgesses of violently resisting their services, customs, taxes ('tallagiis'), and refusing to pursue suits in the abbot's

---

[13] C. Gore Chambers, 'Political History', in *VCH: Bedford*, ed. William Page (London, 1908), II, p. 35.
[14] *Annals of Dunstable*, III, p. 73.   [15] Ibid., p. 110.

courts ('sectis'). With royal pressure, the prior again forced the townsmen to recognize the abbot's assize of bread and ale and frankpledge:
any burgess wishing to pursue a case against another at Dunstable could
do so only at the abbot's tribunal. The townspeople, 'men as well as
women' rose up again, resisting the abbot's juridical authority and taxes.
Outside forces – the Earl of Bedford's bailiff and the Bishop of Lincoln,
who used his powers of excommunication – quelled the fury; by the
monastery's annals, 'this pestilential storm' transformed quickly into 'a
gentle breeze'. The monastery's privileges were reconfirmed in the royal
courts, a copy preserved at the monastery.[16]

In 1243, the year of the Winchester burgesses' revolt against their
newly elected bishop and of baronial troubles for the Crown, a dispute
also erupted at St Albans over the juridical decisions of its monastic
court over a boy found guilty and hanged. Similarly, at Reading its abbot
executed several found guilty of murdering servants of the abbey.[17]
According to the monastic chronicle *Annales de Tewksbury*, both incidents seriously upset the king, but the chronicler gives no indication of
why they did or whether he intervened. That year, yet another conflict
flared between the Church and townspeople but this one not in a
monastic borough. At Cambridge, 'a violent revolt exploded between
the clergy and burgesses; several were ruthlessly murdered, and the
weight of war fell on clerics'.[18] The coincidence of incidents probably
hinged on the disruption of the realm, the first of Henry's troubles with
his barons since Richard Marshal's revolt in 1233.

Another baronial war against the king that led to civil war and, in this
case, to the deposition and death of Edward II, opened space for two of
the most violent and successful revolts of monastic boroughs – those of
St Albans and Bury St Edmunds – even if their successes were short-
lived.[19] By some accounts, St Albans was the first, and may have been
inspired by agents from London, who encouraged St Albans' burgesses
to erect a block with an axe in the town square, threatening any who
refused to join them with decapitation. Then they forced the prior to
concede a charter of liberties, granting them their own common seal, a
guild merchant, and power to elect their alderman independently of the
abbot. By the charter, townspeople could collect their own taxes, possess
custody over minors and orphans, and appoint the town's gate-keepers.

---

[16] Ibid., pp. 119–24.   [17] *Annales de Tewksbury*, p. 134.   [18] Ibid.
[19] See Freeman, *St Albans*, p. 98; Michele Still, *The Abbot and the Rule: Religious Life at
St Albans, 1290–1349* (Aldershot, 2002), pp. 115, 70; Rosamond Faith, 'The Class
Struggle in Fourteenth Century England', in *People's History and Socialist Theory*,
ed. R. Samuel (London, 1981), p. 54; Rigby and Ewan, 'Government, Power, and
Authority', p. 297.

St Albans' parish priests and friars, who also despised the monastery's monopolies and rule, joined them, led rebel processions, and sent ambassadors to Rome to negotiate on their behalf with the pope.[20]

At Bury, the revolt of 1327 went further and lasted longer. An extraordinary monastic register – in effect, a chronicle of this revolt alone (*Depraedatio Abbatiae Sancti Edmundi*) – gives a more detailed narrative of a popular uprising than for any other revolt of medieval England, except the Peasants' Revolt. This account, though hardly without bias, describes the outbreak of grievances and violence between townsmen and the monastery well before Easter (the date given by the *Annales Paulini*)[21] and gives direct testimony of provocation and communication among rebels: 'malefactors' from the capital came to Bury just after Epiphany (6 January) and gathered with residents (called 'villeins' by the register) in a local tavern to plan 'the plunder and destruction' of the monastery.[22] After lunch the following day, the 'able-bodied' called a mass meeting in the town's Guildhall to foment plans and drew up demands to present to the abbot and convent. The register did not specify what these entailed, but others did. According to the *Annales Paulini*, they contested the 'liberties and customs enjoyed by the abbey and monks', which the burgesses insisted be 'snatched away'. In their place, new charters were to be redacted 'carefully and industriously' and to be preserved by the monks.[23] Another chronicle transcribed a copy of the new and revolutionary demands.[24]

The Bury register continues with the monastery's view of events. On 14 January 3,000 townsmen[25] attacked and broke into the monastery, imprisoned ten monks in their Guildhall, robbed the treasury, stole their papal charters, removed the monastery's gate guards, replaced them with townsmen, elected John de Berton as their alderman, prohibited the convent from ringing its bells, and imposed their own on the town. Several days later (as at St Albans) they set up a block with an axe in the marketplace, and 'by threats, gifts, and lies' won others to their side.

---

[20] Trenholme, *The English Monastic Boroughs*, pp. 38–9; and *British Borough Charters 1307–1600*, ed. Martin Weinbaum (Cambridge, 1943), p. 3.

[21] *Annales Paulini*, pp. 333–4.

[22] According to M. D. Lobel, 'A Detailed Account of the 1327 Rising at Bury St Edmunds and the Subsequent Trial', *Proceedings of the Suffolk Institute of Archaeology*, 21 (1933): 216, the tavern meeting was on Tuesday 13 January.

[23] Annales Paulini, pp. 333–4.   [24] *Cronica Buriensis*, pp. 46–7.

[25] Lobel, 'A Detailed Account', p. 216, reckons this was a gross exaggeration since the town counted only 2,445 in 1377, but she does not mention that the population may have shrunk by 50 per cent or more after the Black Death or that the 1377 record underestimates the population.

When the revolt erupted, the abbot had been attending Parliament and heard the news only by 29 January. He returned and faced the rebels, who forced him to sign a new charter of rights to townsmen.[26] The abbot escaped and returned to Parliament, which enraged the townsmen into renewed plundering. With their promises, 'many thousand more', freemen and villeins, joined the rebels' cause.[27] On 19 May 'more than ten-thousand men' laid siege to the monastery. Burgesses were not the only rebels. Two clerics from the churches of Saint Mary's and St James', dressed in tunics, armed and carrying military banners, led the commoners; they entered the monastery, dismantled the doors, which they hauled back to town, occupied the convent's tower, and fortified it in a military manner.[28] In the meantime, all the monastery's tithes and offerings had been withheld. The king took the abbey and town into his hands. But with his departure for Scotland in the autumn, townsmen seized the chance to rebel a third time.[29] On 18 October through continual ringing of the bells of the tollhouse and St James', they summoned 'all the greater and lesser' inhabitants of the town, including twenty-eight priests and rectors. Here, a document other than the abbey's gives insight into causes of the burgesses' renewed offensive. An undated letter from Bury's aldermen and burgesses to London seeking advice and support outlines the reasons for their third revolt of 1327. They charged that the monks on the Feast of St Luke (18 October) imprisoned many of their women and children while they were attending church services in the monastery's close. When the burgesses demanded their release, the monks assaulted them. 'Thereupon the commons rose up and burnt a great part of the abbey, though the church was saved by the townsmen and monks.'[30] In the week that followed (18–25 October) the burgesses took their battle to the countryside, plundering and burning twenty-two of the

---

[26] Lobel maintains that he returned on the 28th; ibid., p. 217.

[27] According to Lobel, the abbot was allowed to return to Parliament to get the new charter confirmed; ibid., p. 218.

[28] The tower may have been the great Norman gate still in existence. The *Annales Paulini*, p. 334, dates this second major onslaught to 13 May, when burgesses held large meetings, supposedly without any notable organization ('sed nullo modo valentes concordari'). They burnt its houses, stole 'many precious objects' from its treasury, pulled the monks out, beat them, and locked them in prison. The account does not mention the leadership of clerics from St Mary's and St James'.

[29] Knowles, *The Religious Orders*, I, pp. 226–7. On 16 October, Sir John Howard was made guardian, with power to arrest the rebels who had harmed the abbey; Lobel, 'A Detailed Account', p. 222.

[30] *CPMR*, I, p. 35. Prestwich, *Plantagenet England*, p. 478, assumes that this account refers to the original revolt of the burgesses in January.

abbey's manors. An inventory of the destroyed properties, manor by manor, survives in the monastic register.[31]

According to the *Annales Paulini*, the king established a royal inquiry into the revolt on 28 October. But unlike royal commissions in normal times, this one seems to have languished. According to the *Depraedatio*, the abbot could not follow up the inquiry that would obtain an order calling Norfolk's sheriff or royal troops to Bury until mid-December. However, when they finally arrived, they liberated the monks, who had been imprisoned in St Mary's, and hanged several burgesses, 'their excommunicated bodies' put in wooden boxes and thrown from town 'in the manner of dead dogs'. On 16 December, the sheriff loaded thirty carts of prisoners and shipped them to Norwich to be tried, and the king sent four justices from London to try the town and mete out punishments: nineteen were sent to the scaffolds, and the town was fined the colossal sum of 140 thousand [pounds] for damages and expenses.[32] Neither the conflict nor the sentences, however, ended here. In the new year, three of the ring-leaders, thirty-two rectors and clerics, thirteen women, and another 153 men were sentenced for various crimes during the past year of revolts. Yet with the aid of Friars Minor, two leaders escaped, gathered supporters, and resisted arrest. In October they laid siege to one of the abbot's manors and abducted him,[33] first to London, where he was hidden with the assistance of an ex-mayor of London (Hamo de Chigwell). The rebels moved the disguised abbot from house to house, then to Dover and across the sea to Diest in Brabant, where he was incarcerated until April 1329. When he was liberated, his captors were arrested and hanged. Moreover, in Bury, other rebel prisoners broke out of gaol, many escaping to Cambridge and other places. The following year, the pope excommunicated all who had taken part in the plundering and burning of the abbey, the destruction of its manors, and the abbot's abduction. But young Edward III, fresh on the throne, did not achieve a final settlement between abbey and town until 6 April 1331, when he felt compelled to travel to Bury to bring about a reconciliation, that is, almost four-and-a-half years after the first tavern meeting to extend the burgesses'

---

[31] *Depraedatio Abbatiae Sancti Edmundi*, in *Memorials of St Edmund's Abbey*, ed. Thomas Arnold, RS, 96 (1892), pp. 340–7.

[32] By Lobel's calculation ('A Detailed Account', pp. 227 and 230), fines from three suits came to £133,000, which on 6 April 1331 was reduced to £122,333 6s. 8d. There is no evidence that the townsmen ever paid off the full amount (p. 231).

[33] According to Lobel, 'A Detailed Account', p. 228, two women of Bury St Edmunds were prominent among these insurgents.

rights at Bury.[34] Moreover, after-tremors of the revolt continued, with townsmen rioting on 15 October.[35]

The weakness of the Crown following Edward II's deposition and the new king's absence to wage war in Scotland opened space for further revolts against monastic control of towns. On 27 April 1327, townsmen of the monastic borough of Abingdon, aided by students from Oxford (for undisclosed reasons) invaded the abbey. 'With force of arms', the burgesses threw the monks out and carried away their goods.[36] The chronicler did not specify the burgesses' motives. A royal commission dated 24 May, however, supplies further details. Although it does not mention the assistance from the Oxford students, it suggests the attacks were more serious than those described by the chronicler with 'large numbers of malefactors in the counties of Oxford and Berks, confederating together'. They attacked the town and abbey, 'burnt houses, assaulted and beat the monks ... killing some and detaining others in prison until they paid fines ... carried away chalices, vestments and ornaments of the church'.[37]

The revolt at Abingdon, whose motives are left vague by its single chronicle, is given considerable more detail in five further royal inquiries at the beginning of 1328. In addition to detailing the revolt's targets and destruction, they list 137 rebels and describe attacks that were not limited solely to destruction of buildings, beatings, and theft of sacred ornaments. A commission of 6 January listed seventy-three rebels: none was listed as a student but five were from Oxford. Thirteen others identified by occupation reflect the occupational structure of a small market town: five bakers, a town clerk, a notary, a butcher, a skinner, a cobbler ('suour'),[38] a furrier, a needle worker ('nieleward'), and a taverner. In addition, two women were named as rebels. They comprised only part of 'a multitude of other persons', who 'in warlike manner',

---

[34] Lobel, 'A Detailed Account', p. 230. Richard Yates, *An Illustration of the Monastic History and Antiquities of the Town and Abbey of St Edmund's Bury* (London, 1805), pp. 128–36, claimed that the final decision did not come until 1332, on the Thursday after the feast of the Holy Trinity. The abbot was able to pack the jury with his own men, including his former steward as a justice; see Prestwich, *Plantagenet England*, pp. 478–9.

[35] Lobel, 'A Detailed Account', p. 231.

[36] *Annales Paulini*, p. 332. According to *British Borough Charters*, p. 3, the charter granted to Abingdon's burgesses in 1327 was 'short-lived'. According to Trenholme, *The English Monastic Boroughs*, p. 42, the mayor of Oxford accompanied burgesses and scholars to Abingdon. Also, Knowles, *The Religious Orders*, I, pp. 267–8.

[37] *CPR 1327–30*, 1327.v.24. Another commission, dated 5 October 1327, investigating the rebels' attack adds no further details. According to Cooper and Crossley, 'Medieval Oxford', p. 17, the revolt was 'partly fomented by the queen and her supporters'. It was led by Philip de Eu and included the mayor, bailiffs, and other prominent burgesses.

[38] Fransson, *Middle English Surnames*, p. 131.

besieged the abbey, burnt its gates and houses within the abbey and at Berton and Northcote, and broke abbey walls and stalls. Once inside, they carried away its timber, books, chalices, vestments, church ornaments, and other goods. The 'other goods' lend insight into the rebels' aims: they contained 'divers chapters, writings obligatory, agreements, and other muniments' that pertained to the townsmen.

The commission gives further clues that the revolt, as with the others in 1327, centred on liberties. The rebels took Robert de Halton, the prior, 'then sick within the abbey', to Bagley Wood in Radley, where they threatened to behead him if he did not do their bidding, then brought him back to the abbey, broke open a coffer conserving the abbey's common seal and forced him to seal three obligatory charters. The first held the abbot and convent to their promises, securing them with a bond of £1,000. The other two 'released' townspeople from 'quit-claim of all trespasses from the beginning of the world till the date of sealing'. Still other charters granted 'the men of Abyndon' the liberty to elect annually a provost and bailiffs for the custody of the town and 'have power to make profit of [xxxx – unreadable] the wastes opposite their houses towards the king's highway in the town'.[39]

The conflict between burgesses and abbey did not finish with these acts of violence and demands for liberty. Another commission on 5 January investigated the collective action of twenty-nine men and two women, including two bakers, two butchers, and 'others'. They disrupted the abbot's weekly market and yearly fair, and prevented his bailiffs from collecting rent from stalls and other profits, as well as from holding his court that had been granted to the monastery by the king. The rebels took over the monastic tribunals and assaulted the abbot's bailiff.[40] The abbot issued two further complaints, both on 2 March 1328, one regarding the rebels' successful disruption of the abbot's markets, fairs, and courts; the other about the siege of the monastery. They add further names: the first lists two spice dealers, two tanners, a cobbler, a nappare,[41] and the 'prior's esquire'.[42] The second, containing 133 names, includes a woman, nineteen from Oxford (although none identified as students), a town clerk, two notaries, again, the prior's esquire, two spice dealers, three fishermen, six bakers, two barbers, a tanner, two butchers, three chandlers, four cobblers, two furriers, two tailors, two goldsmiths, a mulleward (keeper of a mill), a manciple (steward of a monastery or college), a taverner, and a draper. With the draper, a town clerk, two notaries, two goldsmiths, and the prior's

---

[39] CPR 1327–30, pp. 221–2, 1328.i.6.   [40] Ibid, p. 223, 1328.i.5.
[41] One who raises the nap on cloth.   [42] CPR 1327–30, p. 287, 1328.iii.2.

esquire, the rebels represent Abingdon's elites and the barbers, tanners, and cobblers, the middling sort, if not the lower echelons of this market borough. As with other burgess struggles against monastic rule, this one presents a united front across social lines and status, without evidence of any from the laity supporting the abbey. Finally, a royal mandate sent to the sheriff of Bedford to take and imprison men of Dunstable who were lying in wait for the prior suggests that yet another insurrection against monastic lordship flared in 1327.[43]

After this wave of revolts, urban uprisings against monastic rule in towns all but disappear from the chronicles until 1377, the moment of another crisis of dynastic transition, the last months of Edward III's life, his isolation, the corruption of his courtiers led by his mistress, and the opening years of Richard II's reign at 10 years old.[44] In that year, St Albans imposed a new demand that angered its burgesses. Similar to the ritual demands of the bishop at Lynn that sparked a revolt in the same year, the St Albans protest differed from economic and political demands of the past. With the death of Edward III, the abbey formed a confraternity to honour its patron, Alban. Without the townsmen's consent, the abbot ordered them to process, carrying the martyr's image and twelve torches, at their expense. The 'common people' rebelled, as Walsingham sneered, 'showing that they were not the brothers of St Alban but of the synagogue of Satan'. Annoyed by the new ordinance, their anger escalated into rejecting the abbot's lordship entirely: they destroyed the cloisters, 'threatened the destruction of the monastery', and perpetuated 'their radical ideas' against monastic rule in neighbouring towns.[45] No further reports of burgesses' violence in monastic boroughs appear until 1381, when the breakdown in royal power gave vent to major insurrections again at St Albans and Bury St Edmunds, and Dunstable, where burgesses presented the abbot with a charter of liberties. The same, moreover, would have happened at Peterborough had Henry Despenser, Bishop of Norfolk, not arrived with his troops in the nick of time and suppressed the burgesses, as Knighton approved, 'some being put to death, some committed to prison and fetters, none being spared'. The Leicester monk judged that those who had fled to the church for sanctuary 'did not deserve the church's protection': townspeople were 'struck down by lances and swords at the altar'.[46]

[43] Trenholme, *The English Monastic Boroughs*, p. 44.
[44] During this interval, the only revolt to challenge monastic control from our sample was not from a monastic borough but by small-town tenants on the estates of St Augustine, Canterbury; see pp. 144–5, above.
[45] Walsingham, *The St Albans Chronicle*, I, p. 123.
[46] Knowles, *The Religious Orders*, I, pp. 268–9; and *Knighton's Chronicle 1337–1396*, pp. 224–5.

In the first half of the fifteenth century, antagonisms between abbots and their subject urban communities may have continued to rumble on, but at a low pitch. At St Albans, where two monastic chroniclers survive with their attention pinned to local events, little is revealed, nothing compared to the rebellion of the late medieval past. In 1424, when the abbot was absent, the urban 'tenants' (whom the chroniclers continued to call 'villanorum et terrae tenentium villae') accused the monastery of breaching their liberties. Burgess attacks, however, no longer included the earlier armed raids, threats on abbots' lives, killing of servants and monks, destruction of churches and manors, burning of charters and the enforced sealing of new ones. Now, the most monastic chroniclers could charge was that their urban villeins had attacked the monks with 'swords of words and whips of bombast (cum linguarum gladiis et ampullarum fustibus)'. Once the abbot returned, matters rapidly returned to normal: townsmen retired and begged for forgiveness.[47]

Neither the Black Death nor the Peasants' Revolt spawned a new era of popular rebellion as far as burgess revolts in monastic boroughs go. Instead, these were concentrated in the thirteenth and early fourteenth centuries and coincided closely with periods of royal absence, weakness, and civil war between the barons and king. This is all the more curious given the history of heresy in England: Lollardy comes to prominence only after 1381. Possible instances of Lollardy accompanying burgess struggles for rights against the Church might be spotted, but they surface only obliquely and at best in municipal records, not in chronicles or Patent Rolls. During the early 1420s, craftsmen in the cloth industry, tanners, butchers, and others who worked with animals in Coventry protested against the decisions of the mayor and city elites to enclose common pasture that previously had been open on Lammas Day for citizens to graze their animals. The priory of St Mary was the overlord of these lands. Maureen Jurkowski has speculated that anti-clericalism mounted over resentment to these enclosures and lost rights, fuelling the appeal of the Lollard preacher John Grace, when he came to preach in Coventry in 1424. His followers were largely artisans in the cloth industry.[48] But here it was residual economic conditions that may have fanned Grace's following, not the other way around, and even if Jurkowski's connections between Lollardy and burgess rights at Coventry are correct, the alliances had

---

[47] *Annales ... Amundesham*, I, pp. 187–94.

[48] Maureen Jurkowski, 'Lollardy in Coventry and the Revolt of 1431', in *The Fifteenth Century, VI: Identity and Insecurity in the Late Middle Ages*, ed. Linda Clark (Woodbridge, 2006), pp. 156–61.

changed: burgesses no longer presented a united front; now the mayor and city elites were allied with the Church.

The story from Patent Rolls: Bury St Edmunds

The royal commissions reveal further incidents of strife between burgesses and abbots who controlled towns; several were major revolts for political and economic liberties. Of monastic boroughs, Bury appears to have had the most violent and contentious history during the later Middle Ages and was best covered by the chronicle sources; nevertheless, Patent Rolls, along with the monastery's rich archive, provide more information, reveal further riots and revolts, and provide new wrinkles to the 1327–8 revolt so passionately told by the monastic chronicles. These disputes reach back to the last decade of the twelfth century, to the time of Abbot Samson, when with payment of an annual farm to the abbey, the burgesses received a merchant guild and recognition of burghal rights.[49] The next serious challenge to the abbey's privileges came with the baronial revolt in the 1260s, which swept through a number of towns and monastic boroughs, such as St Albans. For Bury, however, it appears only obliquely from a single chronicle and is dated to 1266, the second revolt of the youth guild of burgesses: 'There was also at that time a quarrel between the abbot ... and the burgesses.'[50] Curiously, the *Chronica Buriensis 1212–1301* does not mention it. A commission of oyer et terminer, however, reveals more, shedding light on the townsmen's objectives, and showing that at least initially they succeeded. Against the abbot, they established 'their own authority' and held their own law courts against monopolies authorized by the kings of England to the abbey.[51] Based on other archival records, H. W. C. Davis argued that this was the first instance when Bury's townspeople made a serious attempt to form their own commune with a constitution. These sources suggest that the core of the rebels, a force of three hundred men, were 'the bachelors' of the Gilda iuventum: influenced by the example of London, they rebelled soon afterwards against the greater burgesses of Bury and the monastery.[52]

---

[49] Lobel, *The Borough of Bury St Edmund's*, p. 121.
[50] John of Taxster, *Chronicle*, p. 340; also Lobel, *The Borough of Bury St Edmund's*, p. 127.
[51] *CPR 1258–66*, p. 375, 1264.x.29.
[52] H. W. C. Davis, 'The Commune of Bury St Edmunds, 1264', *EHR*, 24 (1909): 313–17. Also, Yates, *An Illustration*, pp. 124–5; and more definitively, Lobel, *The Borough of Bury St Edmund's*, pp. 126–32. Yates (*An Illustration*, p. 128) reports struggles between the abbey and townsmen in 1292, 1302, and 1305, for 'infringing the rights of the monastery'; withholding fines, tolls, and other customs; resisting officers employed in enacting distraints against townsmen; and in the last incident, 'throwing stones upon,

Entries in the Patent Rolls report further quarrels at Bury. In 1304, sixty-two burgesses of Bury, 'with others', conspired 'by oaths of confederacy' and 'unlawful conventicles'.[53] According to the abbot, they usurped his liberties as 'lord of the town', which included the right to appoint bailiffs, hold his court, execute distraints, and 'other things pertaining to bailiffs'. The rebels collected fines and profits from the assize of bread and ale, took custody over lands, tenements, and rents descended by hereditary right to wards and orphans, took control over the town's gates, ruled on mercantile forstallings, and collected tolls, murage, and pavage on goods entering the town.[54]

As we have seen, several chronicles describe in great detail (even if exclusively from the abbey's point of view) the burgesses' next attempt to cast off monastic rule and monopolies in 1326–7. The intervening sixty years, however, had not been entirely peaceful; tensions between burgesses and abbey had continued to grow, with sparks along the way. In the late 1280s and 1290s 'Abbot John was dogged by trouble with the town' over their demands to control town gates, for free election of aldermen, rights to levy their own taxes, and jurisdiction over distraints against foreign merchants in town.[55] By 1290, townsmen's complaints escalated to direct action. From meeting in the Guildhall, they marched out to a dam, newly constructed by the abbey in a marsh northeast of town that diverted townsmen's water and caused flooding, and they tore it down. The abbot appealed to the king, and justices were appointed.[56] In 1297, two influential townsmen, one a future alderman, who had led the opposition in the early 1290s, obtained duplicates of charters from the reigns of Henry I and John, which had granted burgesses among other rights, freedom from the abbey's tolls. Without the abbot's knowledge, the men read out the charters publicly at the tollhouse. Although the charters and their grants were not questioned, the abbot appealed to Edward I, who summoned the two ringleaders before him and confiscated the duplicate charters. Early in 1298, the most important

---

and damaging the roof of the church', stoning the workmen repairing the roof, beating servants of the abbey, and interrupting the bailiff of the convent in discharging his office.

[53] Thirteen were identified by profession: a laner (wool trader), a smermonger (lard dealer), an ironmonger, a clerk, a spicer, a goldsmith, a coinur (minter), a schereman (shearer), a turnur (carpenter), a wafrur (maker of sacramental wafers?), a reder (thatcher), a roper, and a mawer.

[54] *CPR 1301–7*, pp. 283–4, 1304.viii.29.

[55] Antonia Gransden, 'John de Northwold, Abbot of Bury St Edmunds (1279–1301) and his Defence of its Liberties', in *Thirteenth Century England, III: Proceedings of the Newcastle upon Tyne Conference, 1989*, ed. S. D. Lloyd and P. R. Coss (Woodbridge, 1991), p. 108.

[56] Ibid., pp. 108–9; and Lobel, *The Borough of Bury St Edmund's*, pp. 132–3. The commission documents do not survive in *CPR*.

burgesses were ordered to appear before the abbot and were bound to deposit 320 marks for surety against further actions that violated or threatened the abbey's liberties.[57] In 1304, the abbot filed a complaint to the king against sixty-two named men and women accused of unlawful conspiracy by exacting fees from merchants coming to the abbot's market days, and of obstructing the abbot's courts.[58]

In addition, three documents from the Patent Rolls add further details to the chronicle reports of the revolts of 1327. After May, the rebels also attacked the king's men and his custody over the town, while he was away fighting the Scots in the borders. After repeated injunctions, the townsmen assembled companies of armed men again, beat the abbey's servants, and prevented the dean and other ministers from exercising their spiritual office, further blocked the abbot and convent from holding their courts, exercising justice in town, and collecting farms, rents, tolls, and other customs. They broke the abbey's conduit, cut the abbey's water supplies, felled more of the abbot's trees, mowed his grass, took away sluices, flooding his fish ponds and killing his fish, destroyed abbey houses, threatened to burn the church, and 'besieged the monks with a great multitude of armed men'. As seen in the *Depraedatio*, their attacks ventured into the countryside, where they invaded the abbot's manors in thirteen villages. According to the commission, however, the burgesses' actions were not just destructive: they took it on 'themselves, by their own authority' to hold courts, 'levied amercements for their own use', and 'assessed themselves to maintain these assemblies and wrongs'. To remedy matters, the earl was commanded to arrest and imprison the rebels by raising the 'posse comitatus' in Norfolk and Suffolk.[59]

A third document of 1327, a royal complaint initiated by the abbot, listed 172 townspeople, who 'with a great multitude of other persons' besieged and broke the gates of the abbey, assaulted the abbot's servants, broke his chests and stole 'gold and silver chalices, books, vestments and ornaments of the church, vessels, gold and silver spoons, cups and other household utensils, goods, and money worth £500', along with various charters. The rebels apprehended the abbot and twelve monks, imprisoned them, and forced them to seal an obligatory

---

[57] Gransden, 'John de Northwold', pp. 108–9. These complaints do not appear in *CPR* but in manuscript collections of the British Library, Cambridge University, and *The Pinchbeck Register: Relating to the Abbey of Bury St Edmund's*, ed. Francis Hervey (London, 1925).

[58] Lobel, *The Borough of Bury St Edmund's*, p. 137. Again, the document does not survive in *CPR*.

[59] *CPR 1327–30*, p. 106, 1327.v.26; on 26 July, the king repeated the mandate; ibid., p. 156; for the above, ibid., pp. 213–14, 1327.x.24.

note, stating that the abbot and convent owed six townsmen £10,000, and a letter of release and quit-claim of all actions and suits of debts and trespasses, which the convent might make against the six.[60]

Of the 172, one was a woman and fifty-two were identified by occupation, comprising a large number of clerics – eighteen chaplains, three parsons and two clerks (who may have been lay or clerics). As Trenholme has maintained for St Albans,[61] so too, for Bury: the secular clergy were also deeply aggrieved by the monastic lords' zealous hold onto privileges. The other occupations suggest that this crowd was not composed of the poor, unskilled labourers, or even predominantly skilled artisans; instead, they were of the middling, even the upper, sort. Within the cloth industry, only one tailor and four dyers ('listere') (one of whom was the woman) were named, in contrast to five drapers and two mercers (who often were cloth merchants). Among the others were six bakers, another kind of baker ('pestour'), two butchers, two upholders, an ironmonger ('romongour'), and a ploughwright.

Despite the greater detail provided by Patent Rolls and other archival sources, the chronological trend of revolts at Bury traced by the chronicles remains much the same, if not more concentrated, in the late thirteenth and early fourteenth centuries. With the exception of the burgesses' revolt during the Peasants' Revolt, only one further attack appears to the end of our survey,[62] and this one does not suggest earlier well-organized assaults that succeeded, even if only temporarily, in cancelling monastic privileges and granting burgesses their own courts, rights of election, and control over taxation. On 1 September 1384, the king appointed bailiffs and aldermen for the town, with instructions to arrest and pay a hefty indemnity for all those persons 'of mean estate of Bury' who unlawfully assembled 'night and day' to injure the abbot and convent of Bury, 'against whom they have a grudge'.[63] The grudge is not specified, but does not point to any rights. Moreover, matters had changed in another way from earlier revolts, when Bury's secular elites allied with clerics and others in their mutual quest for liberties. Now the better sort had been given some plums – a little authority, with positions of aldermen. Perhaps consciously, the Crown had adopted a new strategy to divide secular society and isolate the meaner sort. Well before

---

[60] In addition, the complaint repeated many points summarized in the chronicles; ibid., pp. 217–18, 1327.xi.2.

[61] Trenholme, *The English Monastic Boroughs*, pp. 38–9.

[62] In 1379, other documents reveal a disputed election of a new abbot, when townsmen supported the candidate more sympathetic to their rights; Lobel, *The Borough of Bury St Edmund's*, p. 151.

[63] *CPR 1381–5*, p. 501, 1384.ix.1.

the early modern period, a gap between rich and poor among a population legally still defined as 'villeins' had widened, if not economically, then politically, that dampened possibilities for widespread, united popular protest.[64]

Two further entries appear in Patent Rolls concerning rebels of Bury; however, these refer back to the Peasants' Revolt. On 5 February 1385, the king granted remission to twenty-three, who had not been pardoned earlier by the fifth and sixth Parliaments of Richard's reign, for their actions in 1381. The mandate also demanded that the residue of the 2,000-marks fine levied against townsmen for their insurrection be paid no later than Easter week, under penalty of a further £1,000, and stated that 'several men of the town' were refusing to pay. The king instructed that these ones be compelled to pay by imprisonment or other means.[65] As late as 1388, royal pardons to rebels of 1381 lingered on, with one granted to Geoffrey Denham of Bury, 'squier', servant of the prior, 'a principal insurgent in Suffolk' in 1381, who had not been included in earlier pardons. He was now to contribute with the rest of Bury's townsmen to the fine agreed upon to the king.[66] The ability to pay for pardons may have been another means of dividing lay society and blunting future united fronts. But whatever the effect of the exemplary punishments, heavy fines, and pardons following the Peasants' Revolt, instead of spawning a new era of popular insurrection, 1381 was for Bury decisively its end. The townsmen had been cowed. Major disturbances on a national level in 1450 and 1485 no longer prompted them to seek lost liberties or strive for new ones.[67] By the sixteenth century, their civic aspirations had sunk so low they failed to seize the opportunity of acquiring rights of self-government, even with the monasteries dissolved.[68]

St Albans

Entries in the Patent Rolls reveal further disturbances between townsmen of St Albans and their monastic lords, but nothing comparable to the struggle for liberties already seen in the chronicles for 1265, 1274,

---

[64] On the widening gap between rich and poor and growing cultural and political division between labourers and yeomen in early modern England as a reason for decline in popular insurrection, see Wood, *The 1549 Rebellions*, Chapter 5. Hanawalt, 'Peasant Resistance', p. 43, sees this gap widening principally because of economic changes in the countryside during the fifteenth century. Harriss, *King, Parliament, and Public Finance*, pp. 332–3, sees the isolation of the peasantry from the patriarchal support of their landlords widening earlier still, immediately after the Black Death.

[65] *CPR 1381–5*, p. 586, 1385.ii.5.   [66] *CPR 1385–9*, p. 383, 1388.i.24.

[67] Lobel, *The Borough of Bury St Edmund's*, p. 163.   [68] Ibid., p. 167.

1327, or 1381. In 1313, the abbot named two men who erected their own hand mills to grind corn in contravention of monopolies over mills enjoyed by the abbey, and who, when the abbot's bailiff went to take chattels for the illegal mills, resisted and refused to be tried, 'to his great loss and the manifest lessening of his demesne [lordship] in the town'.[69] The same day, the abbot complained further about one of the perpetrators, Benedict Spichfat, along with twenty-two men and two women (including a 'whyte', one who whitewashes or bleaches, a 'suur' or cobbler, a 'cous' or tailor, and a tanner), who forcibly entered the abbot's close in St Albans, felled trees, carried away timber, and assaulted his servant.[70] The following year, the abbot brought three similar charges against his urban tenants, that they had constructed hand mills in their homes, violating the abbot's and the bishop's liberty over the town, and had resisted the bailiff when he tried to seize the mills' upper stones.[71]

Other than the urban revolt of 1381 against the monastery, the only other riots, or even criminal violations, that were remotely related to St Albans, came from its rural tenants or those outside St Albans' immediate precinct.[72] In 1410, the prior of the small Benedictine priory of Wymondham in Norfolk,[73] a cell of St Albans, complained to the king that three men, with other parishioners, broke the priory's tower and hung three bells there 'to govern' their coming and going to church. Wishing not to be disturbed in their divine service, the monks prohibited the parishioners from possessing their own bells. To preserve their rights, the parishioners broke the 'strong walls of the priory', threw the prior from his parlour, locked him in the chancel for three days, and threatened and assaulted his servants. As usual, the royal commissioners sided with the Church, ordered the 'rebels' to remove their bells, repair the walls, and 'amend other trespasses', and threatened that future trespasses would be met with arrest and imprisonment.[74] Even more

---

[69] *CPR 1313–17*, pp. 65–6, 1313.xi.2.   [70] Ibid., p. 66.

[71] Struggles for the rights to mills appear to have been particularly fraught at St Albans. In other towns where such conflicts arose, as with Shrewsbury during the thirteenth century, compromises were made between the dominant abbey and the town. The two even made agreements to finance new mills together; see H. Owen and J. B. Blakeway, *A History of Shrewsbury*, 2 vols. (London, 1825), I, pp. 129–30.

[72] In 1417, bondmen at Barnet 'leagued together to refuse their due customs and services'; *CPR 1416–22*, p. 143, 1417.ix.17. Also, Dyer, *Making a Living in the Middle Ages*, p. 291.

[73] About 16 km. southwest of Norwich; the abbey was founded in 1107.

[74] *CPR 1408–13*, pp. 181–2, 1410.ii.8 Curiously, Walsingham does not mention the incident. From 1393 to 1396 he resided there and wrote a short version of his *Cronica majora*; see Gransden, *Historical Writing*, II, p. 125. Earlier, Wymondham's prior had

starkly than at Bury St Edmunds, burgess attempts at St Albans to wrest privileges from their monastic lords and establish themselves as free burgesses clustered before the Black Death and died with 1381.

Abingdon

Chronicles and the Patent Rolls agree: conflicts between abbey and burgesses at Abingdon also clustered before the Black Death. In addition to the struggles of 1327, which are richly documented by chronicles and commissions, at least two significant attacks against the abbot and his privileges antedated this revolt. In 1295, twenty-one men, including a spice merchant, butcher, and porter with 'a great multitude of men' disrupted the abbot's yearly fair held at his chapel of St Edmund, chased away those coming to the fair, assaulted the abbot's three bailiffs, broke their wands, and moved the fair outside town.[75] In 1315, townsmen again challenged the monastery's economic privileges. Twenty-three named men 'confederated', drew others to their cause, assaulted the abbot's bailiff, prevented him from holding the leet, broke the assize of bread and ale, caused those coming to the abbot's yearly fair to return home, and prevented the abbot from collecting his rents ('stallage') on market days. Townsmen set up their own stalls and 'applied those profits to their own uses'.[76] In January 1348 (before the plague reached England), a great multitude of townsmen, confederated and armed, again disrupted the abbot's fair and challenged his economic privileges, turning away those wishing to attend.[77]

Strife between townsmen and abbey continued after the Black Death. These, however, were legal battles mainly against excessive tolls and taxes levied on them in 1368, 1372, and 1376. They no longer disputed the abbot's right to tax them. By the latter half of the fourteenth century, townsmen and their lawyers had learnt that to succeed at all in royal courts, they could not challenge the abbey's ancient liberties.[78] Finally, even the Peasants' Revolt failed here to spark a last hooray of townsmen to win liberties. Berkshire was not a principal county of unrest in 1381. With the repressive round-up of insurgents across large swathes of

complained that its townsmen had besieged his monks and threatened to burn the priory down; *CPR 1374–7*, p. 318, 1376.iii.20.

[75] *CPR 1292–1301*, p. 211, 1295.xii.8.   [76] *CPR 1313–17*, p. 405, 1315.vii.12.

[77] *CPR 1348–50*, p. 62, 1348.i.30. On 20 April 1353, the abbot complained again of 'a great multitude' of armed men, who laid ambushes against those coming to the abbot's weekly markets and annual fair. The commission fails to specify whether the men were from the town, or if they were fighting to win liberties against the abbey's prerogatives; *CPR 1350–4*, pp. 456–7.

[78] Gabrielle Lambrick, 'The Impeachment of the Abbot of Abingdon in 1368', *EHR*, 82 (1967): 250–76.

England immediately after the Peasants' Revolt, royal commissioners were instructed to arrest and seize the goods of only seven from Abingdon.[79] These rebels, however, had joined insurgents elsewhere; neither chronicles nor Patent Rolls describe any uprisings that year at Abingdon.[80]

At Abingdon, the death knell of armed challenges to monastic authority came earlier, ending on the eve of the Black Death. Post-plague and post-1381 challenges to abbey authority continued only from rural tenants, and these, too, were limited. In 1393, bondmen at Winkfield 'rebelliously' withdrew their services and in assemblies 'confederate[d] by oath to resist the abbot and his ministers'.[81] But it was to the royal courts that the tenants then turned, arguing from Domesday Book that they were the Crown's, not the abbey's, bondmen. The suit continued until 1398, but the bondmen lost and were convicted 'of unlawful assemblies and riots against the king's peace', to be punished 'with the full power of the counties'.[82] As usual, court battles proved no more, and perhaps even less, successful than open rebellion.

Other monastic boroughs

Monastic boroughs were not consistently the hotbeds of popular insurrection, as Trenholme argued, largely from the records of St Albans, Bury St Edmunds, and Abingdon. Instead, these were the exceptions. In Coventry, for instance, where power and authority were divided between the earl and its priory, only one major revolt against the prior appears, and it was during the aftermath of the baronial revolt against Henry in 1268.[83]

---

[79] CPR 1381–5, p. 72, 1381.vi.28; and E. C. Lodge, 'Social and Economic History', in VCH: Berkshire, ed. P. H. Ditchfield and William Page (London, 1907), II, p. 190. For numerous commissions from 28 June to 10 August 'to punish the late insurgents' in various counties and towns – Berkshire, Cambridge, Cambridgeshire, St Albans, Essex, Kent, the Cinque Ports, Surrey, Sussex, Huntingdon, Scarborough 'and neighbouring places', Lincolnshire, Southampton and Wiltshire, Norfolk, Suffolk, Middlesex, and Somerset – see CPR 1381–5, pp. 71–4.

[80] For rebels from Hertfordshire travelling to join revolts in 1381, see M. E. Simkins, 'Political History', in VCH: Hertfordshire, ed. William Page (London, 1908), II, pp. 12–13.

[81] CPR 1391–6, p. 294, 1393.v.14; and SCBKC, pp. ciii–iv and 82–5.

[82] Ibid., p. civ.

[83] Coss, 'Coventry before Incorporation'. The only other revolt of burgesses seen here from the Patent Rolls did not concern the abbey or its privileges. Instead, it was a revolt by 'the commonalty of the town' against a new regressive tax initiated by the king, to be assessed in 1351. Commoners assaulted the king's tax assessors, who levied the same sum on all men of the town with goods valued at £10 or more, 'sparing none'. This split the town between commoners and their mayor and bailiffs, whom the king had instructed to assist his ministers. The commoners besieged them in the Guildhall, inflicting 'so many and great' injuries that they dared not to leave the hall 'for a long time' or levy the king's tax; CPR 1350–4, p. 201, 1351.x.15.

Peterborough was another monastic borough for which the records reveal little conflict, other than threats made by burgesses in 1381. Only one armed conflict of townsmen against their monastic lords appears in the Patent Rolls, and none in the chronicles. At the end of 1375, the abbot charged nine townsmen (none identified by profession) and others of making alliances, violating the abbot's privileges to hold his courts of frankpledge and the assize of bread and ale, and hindering his steward from collecting dues. They broke into the abbot's house, where they threatened him, his monks, and servants, who were afterwards afraid to leave the abbey to pray for the king's safety, or celebrate mass outside the abbey.[84] Finally, armed conflict between townsmen and their monastic lords has yet to be uncovered in several major monastic boroughs, and others leave few traces of it.[85] One reason for this may have been lessons learnt from burgess attacks at Bury and St Albans: invariably the Crown intervened and burgesses lost, to be saddled with harsh penalties that ranged from stiff fines taking decades to pay off, to mass execution. As David Knowles concluded long ago: 'Abroad the king or emperor often supported the town against a dangerous vassal; in England the king always supported the monastery.'[86]

[84] *CPR 1374–7*, p. 229, 1375.xii.10. During the Peasants' Revolt, Peterborough's rural tenants rebelled against the abbey; Petit-Dutaillis, 'Introduction historique', cvii.
[85] For Whitby's one revolt against its monastic lord, see p. 121.
[86] Knowles, *The Religious Orders*, I, p. 269.

11 Church struggles in towns other than monastic boroughs

On 11 August 1272, the citizens of Norwich,[1] armed to the nines, along with women of the city, laid siege to the cathedral and its monastic cloister.[2] Not able to knock down the massive doors, they set them ablaze and burnt precious ornaments, books, paintings, and statues, along with the great almshouse ('ad magnam domum elemosinariam'), the bell-tower of Saint Gregory, and its bells. The townsmen shot missiles into the choir and destroyed dormitories, the refectory, a wing of the hospital, the infirmary and its chapel, and 'almost every building of the curia', except the chapel of the Blessed Mary, which 'miraculously' was saved.[3] Many of the servants, clerics as well as lay, and seven monks died in the blaze; others were imprisoned.[4] After entering, the citizens carried away 'every sacred vase, the books, the gold and silver, vestments, and anything else yet to be consumed in the flames. Still not content, their malice continued for three days with further conflagration, murder, and plunder.'[5] The anonymous *Opus chronicum* compared the citizens' assault to the ferocity of rhinoceroses ('mores rhinocerotis'), 'such that the fear of God had been swept aside'.[6] Other documents, however, expose the biased exaggeration of the ecclesiastical chroniclers. The incident began during a sporting competition among citizens

---

[1] According to *The Chronicle of Bury St Edmunds*, pp. 50–2, the rebels numbered 32,000, a figure that probably then exceeded Norwich's population. Along with others, this chronicle adds that men and women composed the crowd.

[2] Much of what follows comes from one of the longest reports on the Norwich revolt, Cotton, *Historia Anglicana*, pp. 146–9.

[3] The continuator of Matthew Paris, in *Matthew Paris's English History*, pp. 380–1, made the same point; another, in Murimuth, *Continuatio chronicarum*, p. 28, said it was the chapel of Walter; *The Chronicle of the Abbey of Bury St Edmunds*, p. 50, maintained that three or four buildings survived the flames, although they were 'hardly worth mentioning'.

[4] According to *The Chronicle of Bury St Edmunds*, p. 50; according to Rye, 'The Riot', p. 23, only thirteen died on both sides.

[5] Cotton, *Historia Anglicana*, pp. 146–9. Others followed in a similar vein with additional remarks and listed further objects destroyed by the citizens.

[6] *Opus chronicum*, p. 28.

(not mentioned by the chroniclers), when spectating servants of the priory scrambled for the broken truncheons and spears. The monks drew the first blood, shooting a Norwich merchant, and later rebuffed citizens' efforts for peaceful arbitration.[7]

After describing the atrocities, the chroniclers focused on the national reactions that followed, beginning with royal letters sent to 'all the ports of England and every maritime position' ordering the arrest of any rebel who tried to escape.[8] Norwich's bishop convened a meeting at Ely to excommunicate all citizens who had rebelled. The following day (1 September) Henry III convened the bishops and knights of the realm at Bury to advise on how to proceed against 'the malefactors', and on 14 September,[9] he went personally to Norwich to take vengeance on the citizens ('ad vindicandum facinus praedictum'). Fearing the king's entry, many fled. Henry took custody over the city and for thirteen days deliberated on who to punish. Finally, the condemned were drawn by horses to the place of execution, hanged, and their bodies burnt.[10] Despite this brutality, the Bury St Edmunds chronicler lamented that Henry had inflicted 'only partial justice': only thirty-four men and one woman 'from the great multitude paid the penalty for the rest'. In addition, the burgesses were fined £3,000 and held responsible for rebuilding large parts of the cathedral and monastic complex. Damages to Ethelbert Gate into the cathedral close remain witness to the citizens' war with their priory. The penalties did not end in 1272, or with the king. The following year, the monks travelled to Rome and acquired a papal letter further condemning the citizens. More than any other conflict between burgesses and a local church, this one assumed not only national but international proportions.[11]

Yet, despite their attention, chroniclers reveal little about the citizens' motives beyond 'the spirit of the devil'. They focused instead on the horrors of destruction and the punishments that followed. One of the shortest of these accounts is among the few to give any inkling of why the burgesses had become so enraged; surprisingly, it was a monastic chronicle. The *Annals of Osney* first reported that the altercations between monks and citizens had not sprung suddenly or spontaneously, as though prompted solely by the devil. Instead, their 'monstrous rage'

---

[7] Rye, 'The Riot', pp. 21 and 28–9.   [8] Cotton, *Historia Anglicana*, p. 146.

[9] 11 September, according to *The Chronicle of Bury St Edmunds*.

[10] According to *The Chronicle of Bury St Edmunds*, some were dragged, others hanged, and others burnt, and some suffered all three. *Annales monasterii de Wintonia (AD 519–1277)*, in *Annales monastici*, II, p. 111, said the same, but added that some were imprisoned. Other chronicles claimed the condemned were also quartered.

[11] Cotton, *Historia Anglicana*, pp. 150–1.

had many causes and had existed for some time. These concerned taxes and rights or privileges ('super quibusdam tallagiis et libertatibus').[12]

Certainly, few of the controversies between citizens and Church reached such levels of warfare, violence, and penal retribution, but behind most were similar ideological motives – questions of taxes, fees, courts, markets, tolls, and their profits. For others, the causes were often less apparent. At Winchester, for instance, violence erupted between the burgesses and its principal monastery, as well as between the burgesses and the cathedral and its canons, on several occasions. In 1243, a dispute arose from the king's 'election' of a new bishop, which led the mayor and the most powerful citizens of Winchester ('magnates civitatis') to refuse the bishop entry, when he arrived barefooted at the city's gates to celebrate mass on Christmas Eve. The bishop retaliated, placing an interdict on the city, and the king became indignant. Supporting a rival candidate, he established in effect a blockade on the diocese, prohibiting 'food or anything else' from entering the city.[13] This revolt by citizens may, however, be interpreted also, or even more so, as a revolt against the king. By one account, the monks and clerics of the priory, defending their liberties against Henry's interference in episcopal elections, united with the citizens and became 'entangled' by the same interdict.[14] That unity two decades later, however, disappeared. Those of Winchester (Wyntonienses) rose up ('insurrexerunt') against the prior and monastery of St Swithin in a fashion that may have proven as destructive as the much better-known struggle at Norwich in 1272. Winchester's burgesses destroyed the monastic buildings and moveable property, leaving seven monks dead – the same as at Norwich. But, unlike the well-documented events of Norwich, this revolt was only noticed by one surviving chronicle, and it failed to specify any reasons for the 'iniquitous' violence that ensued.[15]

In 1274, the principal monastery of Winchester was caught again in armed conflict, this time between the bishop and a former prior of St Swithin, who returned to Winchester with a 'multitude of armed

---

[12] *Annals of Osney* in *Annales monastici*, ed. Henry Richards Luard, 5 vols., RS, 36 (1864–9), IV, p. 249.

[13] *Annales Londonienses*, p. 30; *Annals of Dunstable*, pp. 162–3; also, Paris, *Historia Anglorum*, II, pp. 473–4.

[14] *Annales Londonienses*, p. 30: 'totam civitatem cum ecclesia cathedrali et omnibus aliis interdicto supposuit, et omnes monachos sequaces et fautores priores intrusi per potestatem regiam defuncti anathematis vinculo innodavit'. Prestwich, *Edward I*, p. 21; and Clive H. Knowles, 'Savoy, Boniface of (1206/7–1270)', *ODNB* (2007).

[15] *Annales monasterii de Wintonia*, p. 101.

men' to regain the cathedral priory. Fortified by the Dominicans and other allies ('fidelibus'), the bishop resisted the prior's take-over, then assembled all the priests of the city and excommunicated the former prior and monks, who had supported the prior. These actions were insufficient to restore peace; several days later, the king sent his royal judges (including Nicholas Stapeldon, to be beheaded by rebels in 1326) to hold a judicial inquisition: many were captured and imprisoned; others fled the city.[16] The citizens' role in this internecine Church battle remains unclear.

Revolts against the Church also occurred in towns which were neither monastic boroughs nor cathedral cities, as in Inverkeithing, Fife, in 1282, when burgesses murdered their parish priest, 'resenting the indignity inflicted upon them'.[17] Unfortunately, the chronicler does not explain what the priest's offences had been. Another case comes from the royal borough of Lynn in 1377. Its bishop – that of Norwich – visited to impress on the mayor and townsmen that he was the town's lord. Here, unlike many of the controversies, which turned on concrete economic demands such as breaking monopoly rights over mills, electing one's own officials, or freeing townsmen from the indignities of ecclesiastical servitude, this incident concerned ritual and honour.[18] The bishop challenged town protocol, whereby the mayor possessed the right to carry a staff whenever he walked down the town's streets, while the bishop could carry 'only a wand with a black horn attached to each end'. The new bishop demanded that the aldermen grant him the same ceremonial honours. They begged him to withdraw the demand, fearing it would anger commoners (whom the bishop called rascals). The bishop persisted, baited the aldermen as cowards, and had one of his men carry the staff in front of him. As the aldermen predicted (perhaps even prompted), the commoners took this breach of ritual as a violation of their town liberties and rebelled: they closed the town's gates, bent their bows and shot arrows, wounding the bishop, his horse, and one of his men, and then fled into the darkness.[19] Such wrangles over protocol in processions died hard at Lynn. In 1449, another dispute between townspeople and bishop flared, this time over townsmen's rights to carry a ceremonial sword before their mayor. Eventually, a compromise was negotiated: the

---

[16] Ibid., p. 465.   [17] *The Chronicle of Lanercost*, pp. 29–30.
[18] Owen, *The Making of King's Lynn*, p. 36; the bishop was the famous warrior and later failed crusader, Henry Despenser. Owen maintains that the participants were artisans.
[19] Walsingham, *The St Albans Chronicle*, I, p. 113.

townsmen won the right, but at the expense of paying the bishop £140 per annum as a lease for the township.[20]

These examples present a rich array of conflict between townsmen and Church concerning a wide variety of issues, from fights over the rituals and rights of leadership to struggles over economic and political liberties. They were hardly confined to monastic boroughs. Yet, as in monastic boroughs, they clustered in the second half of the thirteenth and early fourteenth centuries and erupted especially with two late medieval crises of the Crown – the baronial revolt sparked by Simon de Montfort in the 1260s and that of Queen Isabella and her lover which ended Edward II's rule in 1327. The chronicles fail to show either the Black Death or the Peasants' Revolt sparking a new wave of urban self-confidence that emboldened townsmen to challenge ecclesiastical privilege in towns that were not monastic boroughs. Do the Patent Rolls corroborate these patterns?

The story from the Patent Rolls

Firstly, accounts of conflicts between townsmen and the Church in non-monastic towns are much more numerous in the Patent Rolls than in chronicles, and in both sources, struggles against the Church are more numerous outside monastic boroughs. The conflicts in non-monastic towns remain numerous even if we count only those that explicitly reveal struggles for rights, or resentment against impositions of ecclesiastical tolls, stallage, monopolies over mills, etc., within towns. In addition, the Patent Rolls present a myriad of attacks against ecclesiastical holdings, including the breaking of closes, pasturing of animals, stealing of goods, and destroying of charters that may have also been ideologically charged. Furthermore, the geographic distribution of these struggles was far more extensive in the Patent Rolls than in the chronicles. Conflicts appeared not only in the capital and cathedral cities, but also in smaller towns, such as Richmond in Yorkshire. We will briefly survey some of these struggles between townsmen and monastic institutions, friaries, and hospitals, in towns that were located in boroughs not controlled by an abbey.

Monastic strife: Norwich

Compared to revolts against the king and his ministers, or against monastic lordship in monastic boroughs, conflicts between townsmen

---

[20] Owen, *The Making of King's Lynn*, p. 36 (from the Muniments of the Borough of King's Lynn and not found in our samples of chronicles or *CPR*).

and other Church bodies surface later in the Patent Rolls. None appears during the Barons' War against Henry III, no doubt because the Crown had yet to form regular inquiries of oyer et terminer. The first major revolt against a priory in these records was the 1272 assault on Norwich priory. The royal condemnation of the revolt was as passionately anti-burgess as any voiced in the monastic chronicles. The royal commissions labelled the Norwich townsmen 'sons of blasphemy', called their acts, 'sacrileges', their purpose, 'subversion of ecclesiastical liberty', and their revolt, 'an offence to the name of God', which caused the king 'dishonour', 'anguish, and grief all the more vehement because such detestable crimes have never been heard of hitherto'.[21]

Yet neither the international notoriety of this rebellion nor its unusually severe repression put an end to Norwich's pursuit of liberties from the Church. Less than four years later, fifty men 'and many others of the commonalty' invaded the priory again,[22] and in 1303 another conflict flared between the two. Here, the commission makes clear what was at stake: jurisdiction and liberties over governance within the city and suburbs against the claims of the Church. The prior complained that the city's coroner and bailiffs, along 'with the whole commonalty' had invaded and exercised their justice and privileges in two central wards, Tombland and Ratunrowe, which the prior claimed did not belong to the 'liberty of the town' but to the king's hundred of Blofield. The prior and his predecessors held their annual fair here and therefore city bailiffs were not to carry their wands during the fair or exercise authority there. Yet city bailiffs and their coroner extended their power in the district, made summons, attachments, and distraints on property, and examined corpses. The dispute was triggered when the county coroner came to examine a body found dead at the priory's fair. Led by their officials, the commonalty of Norwich assaulted the county coroner and his bailiff, 'snatched the coroner's rolls from his hands, and tore and trampled them', preventing him from executing his office and merchants from trading at the fair. According to the prior, the town's rebels also 'extorted' customs from merchants, who had come from outside the city, preventing the prior from levying and collecting his toll and other customs.[23] After further examinations in 1304 and 1305, however,

---

[21] *CPR 1266–72*, p. 675, 1272.ix.5. Rye, 'The Riot', p. 29, claims the king and secular courts were more even-handed in their attitudes towards the rebels, and that they even viewed them favourably. The language of the Patent Rolls does not support these claims.

[22] *CPR 1272–81*, p. 179, 1276.vii.13. The rebels carried away 200 marks of property; the commission does not specify their aims.

[23] *CPR 1301–7*, p. 190, 1303.v.7. On 10 July, the county coroner made the same complaint against the mayor, bailiffs, and commonalty of Norwich; ibid., p. 193; commissions

matters between the priory and citizens cooled: only one further controversy between the two appears to the end of our analysis, and this one – Gladman's procession and Shrove Tuesday celebration – may not have seriously challenged the bishop and priory's privileges.[24] Instead, trust and partnership between burgesses and Church appears to have grown in the fifteenth century. With a disputed mayoral election of 1433, the citizens turned first to their bishop, William Alnick, to mediate and resolve these civic differences, and in 1448, they instituted the religious guild of St George as a permanent body to negotiate future conflicts of a civic character.[25]

York

On 26 May 1275, the earliest traces appear in the Patent Rolls of a long conflict between the mayor, citizens, and bailiffs of York on the one hand, and the Abbot of St Mary's on the other; however, Parliamentary inquiries into the dispute had already been sounded.[26] In 1317, the dispute between the two became clearer: as described above, it involved territorial rights in York's western suburb of Bootham, where St Mary's was located and which the abbot held as a monastic borough. The mayor, clerk, six previous bailiffs, four present ones, and three chamberlains of the city assembled 'a multitude of malefactors', invaded the suburb, attacked the monastery, and, against the monastery's liberties, taxed the suburban residents and abbot's tenants for baking and brewing, contrary to the abbey's assize. Further, they took certain men from Bootham to York, put them in stocks, imprisoned others, and assessed those of the suburb for various tallages as though they were citizens of York.[27]

were set up to examine the case on behalf of the prior on 6 February 1304 (p. 273) and 8 April 1305 (p. 357). The second commission maintained that Tombland and Ratunrowe were held by the Crown, a grant of King William, but upon which the mayor and bailiffs exercised liberties as if they belonged to the town. In claiming that Norwich was 'Europe's most religious city', Norman Tanner, 'Religious Practice', in *Medieval Norwich*, ed. Carole Rawcliffe and Richard Wilson (London, 2004), pp. 152–3, quickly brushed aside the disastrous revolt of 1272 and mentioned the 'Gladman Insurrection' of 1443, in which 'nobody was killed', as only the second eruption of violence between burgesses and the Church. For another picture of city–priory relations, especially from 1443 to the Reformation, see Attreed, 'Urban Identity', pp. 584–5, with failed attempts at arbitration over rights in Norwich's suburbs, complaints of daily attacks on the prior, the intervention of Henry VII in 1492, because of the inability by prior and city to make peace, assaults on a city sheriff by priory monks in 1506, and finally, Wolsey's personal intervention in 1524.

[24] For Gladman's 'insurrection', see pp. 260–1 below.
[25] McRee, 'Peacemaking', pp. 856 and 865.   [26] *CPR 1272–81*, pp. 692–3, 1275.v.4.
[27] *CPR 1313–17*, pp. 692–3, 1317.v.4.

Seventeen years later, questions of juridical status arose again, each side airing its views, and alleging crimes and usurpations of rights by the other over the intervening years.[28] In 1350, the issue of Bootham flared for a fourth time: the abbot complained that the mayor, bailiffs, and citizens of York had attacked the monastery and threatened to torch it, kill the abbot, and 'crucify' his men. 'Occupied about his passage beyond the seas', the king placed control over Bootham in the hands of two ministers.[29] But they failed to solve the jurisdictional squabbles. In 1352, the abbot complained again, now outlining the history of the dispute that reached back to Edward I, when York's mayor and bailiffs had argued their case before Parliament, ruling in the abbey's favour, and finding that the residents should not be tallaged with the citizens of York or pay tolls to the city. The abbot charged that the mayor, bailiffs, and five other citizens had once again assembled 'a great company of evildoers' and that 'disturbers of the peace' entered the borough several times, usurped the abbot's rights of justice, took distraints, made attachments in the borough, taxed those in the borough, placed tolls there, and extorted money from the abbot's men and tenants, causing some to leave the suburb.[30] Afterwards, the abbot made further accusations of armed attacks, but these pertained to his manors in the countryside and, as best can be seen, did not involve organized groups of citizens.[31] Shortly following the Black Death, the near-century-long dispute involving armed combat and litigation over Bootham was resolved, or at least had faded from the royal commissioners' view.[32]

The Bootham affair had not, however, entirely ended struggles between burgesses and the Church. In 1358, the mayor and commonalty were embroiled with another religious institution, the free chapel of St George, over possessions and rights to a plot called La Holme within the city, between the king's castle and the river Ouse. According to the chaplain's complaint, 'time out of mind' the land had been the warden's possession and had been enclosed. Yet from as early as 1318,

---

[28] *CPR 1334–8*, p. 15, 1334.ix.24.   [29] *CPR 1348–50*, p. 497, 1350.iv.20.

[30] *CPR 1350–4*, pp. 292–3, 1352.xi.26.

[31] See for instance, *CPR 1361–4*, 1363.v.1 and *CPR 1370–4*, 1373.x.28.

[32] According to R. B. Dobson, 'The Risings in York, Beverley and Scarborough', in *The English Rising of 1381*, ed. Rodney Hilton and T. H. Aston (Cambridge, 1984), p. 118, the townsmen had definitively won their juridical battle over St Mary's at that date. According to Griffiths, *The Reign of King Henry VI*, p. 568, citizens in 1443 'clashed head on with abbot of St Mary's'. He cites *CPR 1441–6*, p. 578 (a page in the index). The only reference in this volume to the abbey is on 12 March 1444 (pp. 282–3), when it was granted a licence to enclose two plots in Bootham: no conflict, implicit or explicit, emerges here with citizens. On the Bootham conflict, also see Liddy, *War, Politics and Finance*, p. 201.

'many' of York's 'commonalty' had occupied it, to build ships and to shoot arrows, wrestle, and play there on feast days. The king ordered the sheriff to summon the mayor, bailiffs, and the citizens who occupied the plot to justify their actions, and then ruled in the wardens' favour.[33] Nine months later, however, not all the citizens had accepted the judgement: 'certain evil doers' on various occasions broke into the chapel grounds, dug its soil, and carried it away, along with lead, timber, stone, and glass from the chapel's roof, windows, and doors. But the mayor now no longer supported those breaking and entering the close: the king's order of 1358 had ended city claims.[34]

In the summer of 1359, another case of rights and liberties between city and Church was disputed, this time between the sheriff, mayor, bailiffs, and citizens on the one hand, and York's Friars Minor on the other. According to the friars' guardian, the secular officials had abused their authority by arresting felons who sought sanctuary in the friars' hospice and church. 'Nefariously', they entered the order's enclosures and 'sacrilegiously' pummelled and dragged the fugitives away 'in contempt of the friars and their ecclesiastical liberty'. Further, they broke their houses and walls, and treaded down their gardens, 'violating their liberty and celebration of mass'. As a consequence, the king took 'the friars and all things within [their] fences' into his protection, prohibiting citizens and their officials 'under heavy forfeitures' from entering to pursue fugitives.[35] This was the last conflict over rights in these published documents between York's citizens and any religious order or church.[36]

Oxford

Historians have claimed that Oxford was 'the most riotous population' of any English town in the Middle Ages.[37] These conflicts concentrated on town–gown rivalries, but as we have seen, they could unite burgesses and students in conflicts that turned against other ecclesiastical organizations, as with the assault of Osney in 1238.[38] After this *cause célèbre*,

[33] *CPR 1358–61*, pp. 154–5, 1358.x.18.   [34] Ibid., p. 281.

[35] Ibid., p. 255, 1359.vii.28.

[36] Ibid., p. 281, 1359.vii.18. Conflict between St Mary's and the city erupted in 1500, after the abbot enclosed land in Bootham and erected a tower against the city's liberties; see Attreed, 'Urban Identity', pp. 588–9.

[37] Trenholme, *The English Monastic Boroughs*, p. 42; also see Charles Hammer, Jr, 'Patterns of Homicide in a Medieval University Town, Fourteenth-Century Oxford', *P&P* 78 (1978): 3–23.

[38] *CPR 1232–47*, p. 297, 1238.vii.23.

matters appear to have settled between the two: the next conflict between them does not arise in the Patent Rolls until 1418, when two cases surface. Firstly, the abbot charged the mayor, its two bailiffs, and twenty-four other named men of invading the priory's properties in North and South Osney. The titles and occupations show a wide swathe of Oxford's population – three gentlemen, five fishermen, two brewers, two chapmen (merchant or dealer), a butcher, a brass founder ('brasyer'), a goldsmith, a draper, a town clerk, a sergeant, a cobbler ('coryur'), a dyer, a cook, a skinner, a repairer or dealer of used goods ('upholder'), a labourer, 'and other evildoers'. By the abbot's complaint, they had carried away nine of the prior's horses, fished his ponds, and assaulted, wounded, imprisoned, ill-treated, and threatened his men, tenants, and servants on three of his manors in the outskirts of Oxford. The same day, one of the Oxford bailiffs counter-charged: the abbot, two of his canons, three yeomen from North Osney, and a barber from Oxford had assaulted him at Oxford.[39] It is difficult to know what lay behind the spat. Ten days later, however, another case suggests a connection. The abbot, with his henchmen, had assaulted one of the town's tax collectors while he was hearing mass at St Mary Magdalene's in Oxford. They dragged the collector, 'with bleeding wounds' from church, imprisoned him in town, and threatened to kill him and his servants if they sued. The reason for the assault was now clear: earlier, the collector had made a distraint against the abbot of 45 shillings for unpaid taxes.[40] Evidently, the abbot saw himself as being above the law.

The mayor and burgesses of Oxford had a more sustained battle over rights with another priory within town precincts, the Augustinian house of St Frideswide: this one stretched over forty-six years.[41] In 1336, the abbot complained that ten named men and others 'besieged' his priory, carried away goods including two cart loads of corn, and impounded fifty of his swine, which they kept without feeding them, so that thirty died. Further, they captured the abbot and nine of his canons, imprisoned them, and threatened to burn them alive. This was not just a savage attack for economic gain (as it might at first appear); it concerned rights and authority. The mayor and burgesses also forced the abbot and

---

[39] *CPR 1416–22*, p. 207, 1418.xii.1.

[40] Ibid., p. 208, 1418.xii.11. From the Oxford archives, Cooper and Crossley, 'Medieval Oxford', p. 20, give further details of the conflict: that the town's tax collectors distrained the abbot for a tenth of his moiety of Castle mills, which sparked fighting between townsmen and the abbot's men. The abbot charged that the mayor, bailiffs, and two aldermen led the townsmen against him, broke his weirs, fished his fishery, and assaulted and imprisoned his servants.

[41] After the dissolution of the monasteries, it became Christ Church.

canons to swear an oath to observe the town Statutes of Oxford.[42] In 1344, Oxford and St Frideswide confronted one another again over liberties. The abbot claimed the right to hold a fair on the abbey's saint day and for five days afterwards. But Oxford's mayor, bailiffs, 'and others of the commonalty' prevented the abbot from collecting the profits, assaulted his bailiffs and ministers, and took over the tolls, which were worth £1,000.[43] The same complaints were repeated in 1345 and 1346.[44] The next controversy involving St Frideswide's appears to have been an internal affair – a contested election over its new prior in 1378. This time, the mayor of Oxford and his bailiffs, along with the chancellor of the university and the king's sergeant-at-arms, served on the commission to settle the controversy. Several canons with certain laymen held that one of the canons was the legitimate prior and not the one elected. The canons and laymen held the priory 'like a castle with a power of armed men and archers' against the newly elected prior and his men. Allegedly, the rebel canons 'wasted' the priory's goods and carried away its treasures and jewels. The commissioners, including the mayor and his men, with the help of a posse, were empowered to remove the pretender and his men, arrest and imprison any disobedient canons, and punish others 'according to their deserts'.[45]

Finally, in 1382, another royal commission investigated 'certain undetermined disputes' between the prior, city, and chancellor of the university, concerning 'their respective rights and franchises'.[46] Afterwards, no more is heard of these disputes, or any further ones involving citizens with any other priory, abbey, or religious order. Neither the Black Death nor the Peasants' Revolt was a fillip to increased rebellion; instead, insurrections clustered in the first half of the fourteenth century.

Canterbury

Despite the survival of three chronicles from Canterbury in our sample – *The Chronicle of Gervase de Canterbury*, *The Chronicle of Anonymous of Canterbury 1346–1365*, and especially *William Thorne's Chronicle of Saint Augustine's Abbey Canterbury*, which is so attentive to popular uprisings in the hinterland of Kent – it is striking how peaceful relations appear between burgesses and Church in this cathedral city, despite its strong,

---

[42] *CPR 1334–8*, p. 359, 1336.viii.28.
[43] *CPR 1343–5*, p. 423, 1344.xii.8. The same charges were repeated on 5 August 1346; *CPR 1345–8*, p. 184.
[44] *CPR 1343–5*, p. 576, 1345.vii.18; and *CPR 1345–8*, p. 184, 1346.xii.8.
[45] *CPR 1377–81*, p. 302, 1378.vii.27.   [46] *CPR 1381–5*, p. 1382.xi.18, p. 202.

and, as we have seen, assertive monastic institutions. The Abbey of St Augustine of Canterbury aggressively protected its liberties, resorting to armed force and extensive litigation in the royal courts against its tenants on large manors such as Chislet and Minster, and in market towns. As early as 1266, the priory charged townsmen of Stonar (Stonore) and Sandwich of being 'forgetful of their own salvation' by burning two water mills belonging to the abbot.[47] In 1318, these townsmen joined a widespread revolt across towns and rural manors in northeastern Kent along the southern portion of the Thames estuary against the priory. In 1368, another conflict led by a certain Thomas Crabber arose when men of Stonor and Sandwich, along with others, including the 'barons and men' of the Cinque Ports, stole by force of arms chattels that the abbot had impounded 'for certain customs and services due to him'.[48] It is not clear, however, that the capture of the property resulted from a rent strike or that the actions were provoked by ideological stirrings against the abbot's seigneurial claims over these townsmen. By contrast, conflict between the abbey and the citizens within Canterbury's city limits hardly appears. The single struggle between the two, moreover, concerned the countryside. In 1257, they quarrelled over jurisdiction to fields in Barton Manor, where the priory possessed a farm. Led by their mayor, the citizens attacked an abbey mill at St Radegund's 'to the sound of the Boroughmoot Horn'.[49]

The early 1340s brought another wave of conflict, in which Patent Rolls make clearer burgesses' motives. These concentrated on the priory of Christ Church and challenged the archbishop. In August 1343, three commissions of oyer et terminer describe the confederacy and armed attacks against the priory's possessions in the city and suburbs. As with many of these revolts, they were organized from above by elected officials, in this case, the city's bailiffs, and appear to have represented a united front that did not cross class lines or exacerbate factional fissures. 'Unduly usurping the royal power', the bailiffs summoned 'all persons' of the liberty of Canterbury between the ages of sixteen and sixty (presumably men and women) to assemble and 'hear certain matters

---

[47] *William Thorne's Chronicle*, p. 249.   [48] Ibid., pp. 494–5.
[49] William Urry, *Canterbury under the Angevin Kings*, University of London Historical Studies, XIX (London, 1967), p. 168, from a patent letter preserved in the Corporation Archive of Canterbury. Butcher, 'English Urban Society', p. 102, maintains that citizens also struggled for liberties against either the cathedral priory or the Abbey of St Augustine in 1327, but does not make clear which institution was involved or the rebels' targets; nor is the source cited. Also, Urry, *Canterbury*, p. 168, and Knowles, *The Religious Orders*, I, p. 268, mention a revolt in this year, but without citing the source. In our survey of the chronicles and *CPR*, no revolt at Canterbury appears for 1327.

to be laid before them and lend their assent, council and aid to what would be treated of there'. It was, in effect, a town meeting, in the commission's words, to 'enter into divers unlawful confederacies prejudicial to the king and his royal power, binding themselves by oath to maintain the same and threatening some men and fellow-citizens who refused to join'.[50] They then planned an attack against the priory in the city's suburbs – perhaps the ones described in greater detail in another commission issued five days before, with 'the assent of the commonalty of Canterbury' and led by their bailiffs, in which twenty-one men were listed (but only two, a spicer and a chandler, by profession). They broke the priory's closes, destroyed its buildings, took forty horses, twenty oxen, and twenty cows, and attacked its men and servants.[51] At the end of the year, and early in 1344, commissions show that this movement may have reached beyond city walls and into the countryside, with coordinated raids of citizens, small townsmen, and villagers. 'Aided and abetted' by the bailiffs and others of the city, a 'great number of evildoers' from Canterbury allied with others in the county to prevent appointees to juries and assizes investigating and adjudicating 'assaults, murders, mutilations, robberies, and other outrages in divers parts of the county'.[52] Perhaps these related to the assaults on the priory of the previous year. No further collective actions by burgesses which challenged Church rights appear in Patent Rolls or chronicles in this arch-cathedral city until the Peasants' Revolt, and then none thereafter in our samples.[53]

Burgess struggles with religious orders in other urban places

Nowhere else, not even in London, do major riots and conflicts between burgesses and monasteries or other religious orders arise. For London, the closest was the wrestling match between city youth and servants of the Abbot of Westminster in 1223, which has been discussed above. Although this incident erupted into serious violence, with the mayor

---

[50] *CPR 1343–5*, p. 167, 1343.viii.16.   [51] Ibid., p. 166, 1343.viii.11.

[52] Ibid., p. 284, 1344.ii.7. A second commission the same day charged others listed from Canterbury with breaching the peace in Kent, again 'with the aid and assent' of the city's bailiffs; ibid., p. 278.

[53] *William Thorne's Chronicle*, pp. 563–4, hints that a social or economic conflict between Canterbury's burgesses and the Abbey of St Augustine occurred around 1358. The chronicler recorded an 'Agreement between the abbot and the citizens of Canterbury on the mills'. However, no commission or chronicle reports any conflict preceding the agreement.

leading his troops against the abbot, it was a struggle about pride, not over rights, fairs, assizes, tolls, taxes, or questions over jurisdiction of plots of land. Nor do any other conflicts arise over rights between London's mayors, bailiffs, and citizens, and its plethora of monastic institutions, hospitals, and religious orders. Even during the Peasants' Revolt, these institutions appear to have been mostly spared. The attack on the hospital of St John at Clerkenwell had nothing to do with rights or alleged usurpations of power; rather it was targeted because Robert Hales, the royal treasurer, was its master.[54] The Patent Rolls reveal other ecclesiastical institutions on the outer environs of London which were targeted in 1381. Sometime before 25 June, 'evildoers' 'assembled and made insurrection' on the Abbey of Waltham Holy Cross, attempting to destroy the abbey and its charters. A royal grant to the abbot identifies four, but none by occupation, or specified as a Londoner.[55] In August, another uprising on London's outskirts, again in Essex, this one against the Abbey of Stratford, shows clearly that the insurgency went beyond plotting, but again gives no evidence of any Londoner playing a part. Instead, the rebels were the abbey's tenants, who strove to break their bonds of dependency and burn the abbey's charters. The only clear evidence of Londoners influencing a revolt against an ecclesiastical body came earlier, when they travelled to St Albans and Bury St Edmunds, mingled in taverns with local burgesses, and supposedly helped plan these towns' rebellions. Their motives were not directed solely against the Church, and certainly not against their own in London, but against Edward II and the misrule of his advisers.[56]

Struggles between burgesses and monasteries in other towns appear at best episodic, not matters that dragged on with periodic eruptions for fifty years or more, as in York. The one exception may have been a conflict between Winchester burgesses and the Anglo-Saxon Abbey of Hyde just beyond the city gates. It concerned, however, rights outside the city, in fact, outside the county, first at a manor near Southampton, then at another in the same county. In 1282, the Abbot of Hyde complained that the mayor and bailiff, 'with a great multitude' from Winchester, entered the abbey's enclosures in the hundred of Micheldever, seized the attachments for certain trespasses, and arrested its men and ministers. The commission does not explain why they travelled the distance to attack these rural possessions or arrest its men or what, if any, rights were challenged.[57] The motives for a second conflict

---

[54] Petit-Dutaillis, 'Introduction historique', lxxxvi–lxxxvii; Dobson, *The Peasants' Revolt*, pp. 156 and 158.
[55] *CPR, 1381–5*, p. 27, 1381.vi.25.   [56] *Depraedatio*, pp. 329–30.
[57] *CPR, 1281–92*, pp. 47–8, 1282.vii.24.

between the two are even less clear. In 1314, sixty-nine armed men 'and others', covering a wide array of professions – drapers, fishmongers, bakers, cobblers, taverners, a dyer, a rope maker, a copyist or bookbinder, a cooper, and a poultry dealer – attacked the abbey's manor of la Breton, assaulted its men, carried away goods, and broke sluices, causing flooding to a hundred acres of meadowland.[58] Finally, just before the Black Death (1 July 1348), the abbey clearly faced a conflict over rights, with villagers, however, and not with townsmen. The abbey had bought Sanderstead in Surrey in 1292 and now refused to pay its share of the tax farm on the tenth and fifteenth of wool; instead they shifted the burden onto the villagers.[59]

From the Patent Rolls, no other cities or towns had sustained conflicts with priories, hospitals, friaries, or their parish priests, who may have exercised rights over towns. Only isolated incidents occurred. In 1337, thirty-eight men and a woman of the town of Daventry (Northampton-shire) 'by force' prevented the prior and his servants exercising their right 'time out of mind' of grinding all the malt for brewing within the town.[60] In 1341, the men of Newcastle upon Tyne prevented the Friar Preachers from enclosing property in their town with new fences and gates.[61] Three years later, the mayor, its four bailiffs, and thirteen named burgesses, including two chaplains and a cobbler, led its commoners to contest by force the friars' water rights. The guardian claimed the friary possessed a conduit of water from a well in the town to their manse and rights from the king to enclose and keep it locked 'long before the town was walled'. Against his claims, the mayor and his men broke the well door and the conduit's pipes along the high street and in other places, diverting water from the friars' manse.[62] In 1345, the men of Bodmin (county seat of Cornwall), led by their mayor, bailiff, nineteen men, and a woman, formed a 'confederacy among themselves' to hinder the Abbey of Bodmin from holding its view of frankpledge.[63] In the same year, a dispute between the men of the town of Godmanchester[64] and the prior and convent of the church of St Mary, Huntingdon, arose over rights to mills and control of waterways. The prior charged that certain of the

---

[58] *CPR, 1313–17*, pp. 145–6, 1314.v.6.   [59] *CPR, 1348–50*, p. 162, 1348.vii.1.
[60] *CPR, 1334–8*, p. 440, 1337.iii.8.   [61] *CPR, 1340–3*, p. 352, 1341.xii.6.
[62] *CPR, 1343–5*, p. 412, 1344.x.15.
[63] Ibid., p. 572, 1345.vii.6. In 1379, nineteen men, including three carpenters, two sutors, a fisherman, and a milward, broke into two of the prior's manors in Cornwall, destroyed a weir, felled trees, and fished his ponds. The commission does not indicate if the men were from towns or whether their motives went beyond theft.
[64] Now a suburb of Huntingdon, presently in Cambridgeshire.

town's 'evildoers' had prevented the abbey from repairing their gullies and mete (granted to them in a charter of Henry II), so that water no longer supplied their mills. As usual, the king's commission resolved the case by punishing the townsmen.[65]

In the year of the Black Death, the priory of Worcester Cathedral (St Mary's), initiated two royal commissions against their townsmen. The controversy appears to have begun over town challenges to Church liberties and jurisdiction not within its precincts, but in the hundred of Oswaldslow. Led by Worcester's two bailiffs, the commonalty assembled 'with unwonted clamour', marched to the cathedral churchyard and 'with force and arms' took away the body of a fellow citizen, usurping the rights of the county coroner. Further, eleven men of the commonalty (including a butcher and a bowyer) went – whether at the same time or afterwards is unclear – armed to the church, broke the priory's gates, and assaulted its men and servants, shooting arrows and throwing other weapons at them. After 'a terrible siege', they tried to burn the monks from their priory. The men then invaded the priory's manors outside the city, fished their ponds, and hunted their rabbits.[66] Less than a month later, another commission indicted seventy-nine of the commonalty, including the town clerk, two sergeants, three butchers, a bowyer, a spice dealer, a taverner, a chaplain, a glazier, a baker, a skinner, a fisherman, a tailor, a water boy, and a lord, for the 'terrible' assault of St Mary's.[67] But, despite its violence, no further struggles over liberties and jurisdiction appear at Worcester in the remaining Patent Rolls.

The next struggle between a town and its priory again concerned mills and rights over water. This one originated from a complaint of the prior of St Margaret in the castle town of Marlborough (Marleberghof) in 1359 and involved a complex alliance of interests not only between the town and the priory, but with a tangle of rights claimed by knights, the queen, and king (separately) over mills at a royal castle and sluices to divert water from the mill to the borough and priory.[68] In 1363, thirty-one named rebels of Yeovil, Somerset, including a skinner, a tanner, a cobbler (souter), and a tailor, took oaths and plotted to prevent their parish priest ('lord of that town') from exercising his view of frankpledge, opening his weekly market, and other liberties. The townsmen assaulted the parson and his men and took over their judicial and economic rights.[69]

---

[65] Ibid., p. 577, 1345.vii.26.   [66] CPR, 1348–50, p. 245, 1348.xi.23.

[67] Ibid., p. 249, 1348.xii.19. This list included ten of the eleven named in November.

[68] CPR, 1358–61, p. 292, 1359.x.18. The controversy seems to have been resolved in the courts.

[69] CPR, 1361–4, p. 443, 1363.vii.10.

Although attacks on abbeys, priories, hospitals, and friaries certainly continued through the post-plague period, it was not until 1399 that any urban uprising outside a monastic borough explicitly championed extending town liberties against the ancient privileges of any ecclesiastical institution. Led by its mayor, the commons of Bristol 'riotously assembled' and destroyed the mills of the town's convent of St Augustine and placed planks to divert its water course. The mayor and commons alleged that the abbot and servants who ran the mill had violated the citizens' rights of way and use of their ferry. As a result, the mayor and commons arrested and imprisoned the convent's canons and servants.[70]

For the first half of the fifteenth century, attacks by urban commonalties against monastic privileges remain as rare. The one dispute between an urban commonalty and convent that concerned rights was mild by comparison with the full-scale revolts and violence of the late thirteenth and early fourteenth centuries. In 1420, a dispute between the mayor and commonalty of Bath and the prior and convent of the cathedral church (now Bath Abbey) arose over the ringing of bells, but this was not entirely a trifling matter: the king was called to intervene while he was in Rouen. 'Time out of mind', the men of Bath were not allowed to ring their bells before the prior and convent had rung theirs in the morning, or after their sounding of the nightly curfew. But lately, the mayor and commonalty had violated the custom. The prior complained that his priests could 'hardly celebrate canonical hours and other divine obsequies ... without great bodily harm', but the citizens continued to ring theirs first, even after the king had sent letters from France ordering the mayor to abide by ancient custom.[71] Besides the use of bells to organize secular time, they were symbolic of urban autonomy and order as seen at Wymondham.

Monastic boroughs were not the principal crucible of struggle between the Church and burgesses as has been assumed. As seen in mandates and other acts of the Patent Rolls, riots and revolts between burgesses and ecclesiastical bodies outside monastic boroughs actually

---

[70] *CPR, 1396–9*, p. 585, 1399.v.8. In February the same year, a royal commission investigated 'malefactors' in Bristol accused of assembling 'in large numbers and in warlike array', who broke the close, houses, and chests of the prior or keeper of St John's hospital, Bristol, and carried away 'divers bags containing charters and writings'. Was the theft of documents meant to erase the hospital's rights in the city? Ibid., p. 510, 1399.ii.8.

[71] *CPR, 1416–22*, p. 205, 1420.viii.30. A later case, 5 January 1439, may have involved rights. The abbot of a monastery at Lilleshall, Shropshire, complained that Shrewsbury's two bailiffs and commonalty occupied and enclosed monastic land with hedges and dykes, and threatened his tenants within town so that they 'dared' not pay their rents and services; *CPR 1436–41*, p. 268.

occurred almost five times as often as ones within them (175 incidents compared to 38). Even conflicts between monasteries and burgesses over rights in towns that were not monastic boroughs were more numerous than in towns that were (61 compared to 38). However, few were as long-lasting or as violent as those seen within the monastic boroughs of St Albans or Bury St Edmunds that endured from the early thirteenth century to the Peasants' Revolt. Only in Oxford does a major revolt against a monastery appear in the documents we have surveyed before the Barons' Revolt of the 1260s, and that one, against the priory of Osney, just outside the town, was led by scholars of the university, and does not appear to have contested town liberties. As with conflicts in monastic boroughs, those outside them show a wide variety of issues, including battles over: water rights and mills; the grinding of malt for brewing; jurisdiction over suburbs and precincts within city limits; exemptions from taxation; the election of mayors and aldermen; views of frankpledge and the assize of bread and ale; and the right to serve distraints, hold leet courts, ring bells, or collect profits and tolls from weekly markets and annual fairs. Moreover, they cover a wide swathe of England, from the eastern tip of the Thames estuary, to Bodmin in Cornwall, Yeovil in Somerset, Shrewsbury in the Welsh marches, and Newcastle upon Tyne in Northumberland.

As with townsmen's revolts in monastic boroughs, here even more decisively, the chronology of urban struggles for rights against the Church fails to show the Black Death or the Peasants' Revolt as a significant divide in the growth of urban self-confidence. Instead, few conflicts followed the Peasants' Revolt, and by 1400 they had virtually disappeared. No rising zeal for liberties progressed inexorably from the late Middle Ages to the Reformation, as has been hypothesized, when these ecclesiastical institutions finally lost their hold over urban places by fiat from above. With the failures of the Peasants' Revolt, but in most places a generation or more before, townsmen had already lost their struggles with the Church, because of the Crown's swift and effective intervention in support of a wide range of ecclesiastical bodies. Conflict now became restricted mostly to court battles, in which burgesses pursued lesser goals, which no longer questioned the principle of ecclesiastical privilege.[72]

---

[72] In addition to cases cited above, conflicts between burgesses and ecclesiastical institutions continued in the courts in places such as Newcastle against the Bishop of Durham, the monastery of Durham, the hospital of St John of Jerusalem, and the monastery of Tynemouth over rights to fairs, seizing fish and ships, avoiding payment of tithes, and questions of jurisdiction. One court battle between townsmen and bishop over a tower the burgesses constructed on a bridge crossing the Tyne continued in royal

Over the course of the later Middle Ages, conflicts in urban places with monastic neighbours, priories, parsons, or hospitals, whether in monastic boroughs or not, were far more prevalent and violent in England and concentrated on economic, political, and ideological principles of self-rule and economic freedom more than any such revolts seen in late medieval Italy, France, or Flanders. With the possible exception of Liège, the character of these Continental revolts, moreover, was different: rarely did Continental rebels attack priories of monks, canons, or the old Benedictine orders; instead (although still rarely) the mendicant orders were the usual butt of their anger. And here, the challenges were not over jurisdiction in suburbs, plots of land within cities, struggles over waterways, mills, fairs, tolls, taxes, courts, and the like; rather, they concerned the friars' role as papal inquisitors and the urban laity's defence against the Church on doctrinal grounds[73] – another issue that fails to emerge in our survey of England's late medieval city–Church conflicts.

Struggles in the countryside

It is important to compare, if only briefly, patterns of protest between city and countryside. Contrary to what might be expected, the struggles of bondmen in the English countryside do not follow the same chronology as conflicts in towns but show one overriding similarity: ecclesiastical lords, rather than secular ones, were the object of their revolt. Although failure to pay rent, or rent strikes, can be found in the manorial rolls for places such as Park on the estates of St Albans in 1246, 1265, 1270s, 1309, and every year from 1318 to 1327, or refusal to bring grain to the abbey's mill as early as 1237,[74] widespread resistance against lords of any sort, anywhere in England, came later and crystallized only in the years leading up to the Peasants' Revolt, at least as seen in the Patent Rolls. For the period before 1377, historians using principally manorial rolls have highlighted examples of protest that fit better with James C. Scott's notion of 'weapons of the weak' than with collective

---

courts from 1383 to 1416, before being decided in the bishop's favour. These court battles do not appear, however, to have escalated into armed combat and are not found in the chronicles or *CPR*; see *History of Newcastle and Gateshead*, ed. Richard Welford, 3 vols. (London, 1884–7), I, pp. 9, 33, 38, 141–2, 238, 246, and 257–8; and Christian Liddy, *The Bishopric of Durham in the Late Middle Ages: Lordship, Community and the Cult of St Cuthbert* (Rochester, 2008), pp. 175–86.

[73] See Cohn, *Lust for Liberty*, pp. 132–3, and Guy Geltner, 'Mendicants as Victims: Scale, Scope, and the Idiom of Violence', *JMH* 36 (2010): 126–41.

[74] Faith, 'The Class Struggle', p. 51.

rebellion.[75] These include small bands assaulting lords, and acts of resistance limited mostly to individuals and families, such as neglecting to repair buildings after the Black Death, refusing to perform labour services, or doing them badly, burning the lord's mill and refusing to reroof it, neglecting to attend the lord's courts, or electing simpletons or the blind as rent collectors or reeves. Collective action was marshalled within the law: peasants raised funds to bring suits before the king's courts, arguing that their tenancies were free 'according to the customs of the ancient demesne'.[76] As we have seen, matters changed in 1377, when protest spread beyond individual manors, with peasants collectively refusing to work their lords' fields in at least forty villages in Wiltshire, Surrey, Sussex, and Devon.[77] More remains to be found for this pivotal date. Miriam Müller has uncovered further organization of, and assertiveness by, English villeins at Badbury in that year, when the villeins went beyond their pleas for ancient demesne status, which had been lodged in 1348, to enlist peasants across other manors in Wiltshire in struggles against bondage.[78]

Evidence from the Patent Rolls corroborates this picture. No cases of bondmen withholding or refusing services to manorial lords antedate the Black Death, and only one concerns men rescuing a bondman. In 1338, the prior of the Abbey of Tynemouth, near Newcastle upon Tyne, and his men were taking one of their bondmen to justice and his beasts to be impounded, when men from Newcastle freed the man and broke the pound.[79] The commission gives no reason why these men freed him; as far as the document reveals, they were not fellow bondmen; nor did they have any obligations to the monastery. Instead, the first hints of an organized revolt of bondmen against a manorial lord came only in

---

[75] James C. Scott, *Weapons of the Weak: Everyday Forms of Peasant Resistance* (London and New Haven, 1985).

[76] See pp. 55–7 and nn. 86–7 above; see examples of peasant passive resistance in Frederick Bradshaw, 'Social and Economic History', in *VCH: Durham*, ed. William Page (London, 1907), II, pp. 218–22, who argues that these cases increase dramatically after the Black Death. For the land of the Bishop of Durham, see R. H. Britnell, 'Feudal Reaction after the Black Death in the Palatinate of Durham', *P&P*, 128 (1990), pp. 40–6, who shows the effects of passive resistance to the Bishop of Durham's harsh estate policies after the Black Death. The measures taken, which included flight from the bishop's lands, tumults in court, refusal to obey laws, disobedience to reeves, village refusal to send jurors to the Halmotes, collective complaints against high rents, and bargaining for better terms of tenure, had, by 1380, succeeded in ending labour services.

[77] Faith, 'The "Great Rumour"'; Harriss, *Shaping the Nation*, pp. 227–9; and Hallam, *Domesday Book*, pp. 102–4.

[78] Müller, 'Aims and Organisation of a Peasant Revolt', pp. 15–16.

[79] *CPR 1338–40*, p. 67, 1338.ii.20.

1349, either during or immediately after the plague. On 24 February, the Countess of Pembroke charged that certain unspecified 'evil doers' had ambushed her men, who were being taken to justice in Cambridgeshire, because of 'disobedience and rebellion'.[80] Later that year, men identified as servants attacked the steward of the prior of Ely, prevented him from putting a rebellious bondman in stocks, and 'with armed force' pressured the steward to issue and seal a letter declaring the bondman's deliverance.[81] In 1352, a commission investigated several men who attacked the manors of the Bishop of Worcester at Henbury in Saltmarsh, when the bishop was the king's chancellor and under his special protection. In addition to attacking the bishop's servants and stealing his goods, they persuaded the bishop's bondmen and other tenants, 'by conspiracy', to refuse to work the bishop's land. The bishop had to pay 'a great sum before he could compel them by law ('justiciare') to do the said services'.[82]

Seven years later, in a curious reversal of roles, an abbot and his fellow monks and servants broke the closes of a manor at Shipden in Norfolk, assaulting the men and servants of the manor and destroying the stocks that held three of the lord's bondmen who had refused to serve him.[83] In 1360, the Abbot of Meaux contested the identity and status of three men, who twenty years earlier had escaped to the town of Waghen[84] with their chattels and children and claimed to be the king's bondmen. The abbot claimed that the fugitives were his bondmen – as had been their ancestors – not the king's, and that they should return to his manor of Dimlington.[85] No further cases of bondmen refusing service or being freed from stocks appear in the Patent Rolls until 1378 (most likely reflecting incidences of the previous year and its widespread array of peasant uprisings). These cases suggest larger and more organized forms of protest than those following the Black Death. Now the commissions describe 'divers assemblies', 'mutual confederations', with alleged outside instigation and leadership. Most significantly, many more disobedient bondmen now comprised these confederacies. On 8 April, a commission investigated the bond tenants of the Bishop of Winchester at his manor of Farnham, 'who have long rebelliously

[80] CPR 1348–50, p. 313.   [81] Ibid, pp. 453 and 454.
[82] CPR 1350–54, p. 275, 1352.ii.7. Dyer, Lords and Peasants, p. 275, finds from the bishop's manorial accounts that this revolt had little success. Saul, Richard II, p. 61, cites incidents of widespread withdrawal of services in the 1350s, and again in the 1380s, on manors of the Archbishop of Canterbury at Otford and Wingham in Kent.
[83] CPR 1358–61, p. 284, 1359.vii.28.   [84] In Holderness, Yorkshire.
[85] Dimlington in Holderness, Yorkshire. CPR 1358–61, p. 481, 1360.vii.12. This case was still being adjudicated ten months later; CPR 1361–4, p. 67, 1361.iv.23.

withdrawn the customary service due to him ... and in divers assemblies have mutually confederated and bound themselves by oath to resist him and his ministers'.[86]

These protests cut beyond the boundaries of single manors. Similar assemblies, oaths, and long-term resistance were said 'to have been done' on three manors of the Abbot of Chertsey, at Chobham, Thorpe, and Egham in Surrey.[87] A month later, the case against the abbot's tenants was repeated with further details. They had 'long refused the customs and services' due the abbot, 'at the instigation of certain counsellors, maintainers and abettors', and in addition to confederating in various assemblies bound by oath to resist the abbot, they congregated 'daily ... to do further mischief'.[88] On that day (20 May), and on 2 June and 23 June, 'the like' was reported on four estates of the Abbess of Shaftesbury in Wiltshire (now Dorset), and Bradford, Liddington, Donhead, and Downton, and on a further four of her estates in Dorset (Hinton, Fontmel, Cheselbourne, and Iwerne). Thus the disobedience and revolt that had risen on forty Wiltshire manors in 1377 now appears to have been even more extensive, including still further villages, and crossing county boundaries into Dorset. The bondmen on two manors of the prior of Bath and the Barton of Bath at Exton in Somerset similarly organized assemblies and withdrew services, as did those on the manor of Richard de Molyns and his wife at Aston Bampton, Oxfordshire.[89] In 1380, bondmen of Thomas Preyers at Strixton, Northamptonshire, refused to work or pay customs, and by oath confederated with others to resist him.[90]

Unlike protest in English towns, as far as the chronicles and the Patent Rolls reveal,[91] revolt in the countryside did not fade with the Peasants' Revolt. Less than four months after the men of Kent had begun their march on London, rebels rose up there again, at Boughton Malherbe on 30 September.[92] It is one of the few documents of protest in the Patent Rolls, in which a leader is explicitly identified (rather than just appearing

---

[86] *CPR 1377–81*, p. 204, 1378.iv.8.   [87] Ibid.
[88] Ibid., p. 251, 1378.v.18.   [89] Ibid., p. 251.   [90] Ibid., p. 578, 1380.xi.24.
[91] King's Bench continues to describe small uprisings in towns: see for instance, in November 1381, when the clerk John Tubb led burgess attacks in Huntingdon against its prior, culminating in a special commission of oyer et terminer in December; JUST 1/357. But these appear to have been fewer and less significant than those before 1381. I thank Andrew Prescott for this reference.
[92] Even earlier, on 17 June 1381, almost a week after peasant rebels from the south had marched to London, tenants formed an association and by sworn oath joined together to destroy wood belonging to the prior of Canterbury at Mersthan in Surrey, claiming it was common land and threatening to kill any who opposed them; see Prescott, 'Judicial Records', p. 337.

as the first named) and that expresses rebel ideology, especially in the countryside. By 'procurance'[93] of the yeoman Thomas Hardyng,[94] the rebels sought 'to extort' rights earlier demanded: they 'rose in insurrection to compel the king to grant them the liberties and pardons demanded of the king in the late insurrection at Milende [Mile End]'. Further, a curious twist of fate is revealed in two pardons, separated by two months, granted to the same John Cote of Lose in the parish of Maidstone, Kent, a mason, who had organized 'covins' in Kent but had turned 'approver' (state's witness) against his fellow rebels.[95] The rebels had heard from pilgrims 'from northern parts', journeying to Canterbury, that John of Gaunt had freed his bondmen on his estates. If the rumour were true, the rebels wished to 'conspire together to make him king of England'. In February, they investigated the rumour by sending messengers to the duke. Whether they communicated directly with him or not, by the time the second pardon was issued, in April, the rebels in Kent had become convinced that the pilgrims' report was true.[96] According to Cote's confession[97] they made Gaunt 'their Lord, and King of England', and 'with the said Duke, for life and death' now were allied against Richard.[98]

A year later, rebels in Norfolk conspired to kill the Bishop of Norwich and force those attending St Faith's fair to join them to occupy the Abbey of St Benet Holme.[99] In 1386, bondmen of the knight James de Audele [Audley] at his manor of Fordesham, Shropshire,[100] 'rebelliously' withdrew their services and by oath conspired against him.[101] In 1393, bondmen of the Abbot of Abingdon on his manors of

---

[93] Description of this revolt derives from two pardons to John Cote, one on 14 February 1383, the other on 14 April; *CPR 1381–5*, pp. 237 and 264–5.

[94] On 31 August 1381, a Thomas Hardyng of Manytre had been a mainstay of royal power, commissioned, along with the king's sergeant-at-arms and the sheriff of Essex, to bring nine men before the king's council; *CPR 1381–5*, p. 77, 1381.viii.31. The two Thomases, however, may not have been the same man.

[95] On approvers' appeals, and this case in particular, see Prescott, 'Judicial Records', pp. 233–5.

[96] Cote had been the king's approver on 13 July 1382, when he appealed on behalf of a Kent rebel, who was pardoned, and gave evidence leading to the capture of fellow rebels; *CPR 1381–5*, p. 158. Despite Gaunt's possible change of sentiment after the Peasants' Revolt, he still aroused anger and insurrection among his tenants and others within his vast tracts of towns and countryside. As we have seen, in 1390, 'treasons, felonies, murders' etc. spread across 'his lordship' of Knaresborough; *CPR 1389–92*, pp. 269–70, 1390.iii.10.

[97] *Coram Rege Roll*, Michaelmas Term, 5 Ric. II [1381], published in W. E. Flaherty, 'Sequel to the Great Rebellion in Kent of 1381', *Archaeologia Cantiana*, 4 (1861): 83–6.

[98] Ibid., p. 85.   [99] Prescott, 'Judicial Records', pp. 78–9.

[100] TNA online identifies it as 'Ford ?'; SC6/HenVII/1051.

[101] *CPR 1385–9*, p. 314, 1386.v.29.

Hurst, Winkfield, and Whistley [Wysseley] in Berkshire did the same.[102]
A detailed 'exemplification' of 1396 requested by the prior of the
Hospital of St John of Jerusalem (Knights Hospitaller) enumerated the
customs that provoked the bondmen of the prior of Balsall, Warwickshire, to withhold their services and payments. It reflected on an earlier
case, when sixteen bond tenants assembled two years earlier to resist
paying the prior's duties, following the death of one of his tenants.
Afterwards they 'threw themselves upon the king's grace, praying to be
admitted to make a fine therefor', but 'in accordance with statute' lost
their plea, were imprisoned, and then fined by the prior individually at
varying amounts.[103] No evidence suggests that this possible appeal to
the prior of the hospital did them any more good than their earlier
supplication at the feet of the king. For peasant rebels, as with townsmen, legal action appears almost inevitably to have ended badly.

Cases of peasant revolt and resistance continued into the first half of
the fifteenth century, though the pace slowed. In 1413, one of two cases
of bondmen residing in a town and resisting their lord appears; this one
at Cirencester opposed the abbot of the town.[104] In 1423, bondmen of
the Abbot of Waltham Holy Cross on four of his manors in Essex
(Waltham, Nazeing, Epping, and Loughton) rebelliously gathered 'at
the procurement of certain of their councillors', refused to perform their
services, and by oath resisted the abbot and his ministers.[105] A further
inquiry a month later may have been related: an esquire, who previously
had been a sheriff of Henry V, named twenty-four men, including nine
husbandmen, two skinners, a draper, a carpenter, a weaver, a school-
master, a tanner, a carter, a fletcher, and a bondman from several
villages in Essex, along with 'other malefactors', who 'arrayed in manner
of war', laid in wait for him at Waltham Holy Cross. They threatened
him with death and mutilation, and 'abused him' so that he could not
execute a royal writ as sheriff of Essex.[106] Finally, in 1427, the bondmen
of the prior of Bridlington, Yorkshire also with advice from 'their maintainers and abettors' confederated by oath and refused him customs and
services at Burton Fleming.[107] Whether all of these protesters were rural
tenants or a mixture of rural and urban rebels, as seen in enclosure riots
of the sixteenth and seventeenth centuries,[108] is difficult to know; none
was identified.

---

[102] *CPR 1391–6*, p. 294, 1393.v.11. The following year, another commission had to be
appointed to investigate and prosecute these 'rebellious bond-tenants'; ibid., p. 444,
1394.v.29.

[103] *CPR 1396–9*, pp. 112–13, 1396.xii.27.   [104] *CPR 1413–16*, p. 38, 1413.vi.12.

[105] *CPR 1422–9*, p. 174, 1423.xi.24.   [106] Ibid., pp. 216–17, 1423.xii.21.

[107] Ibid., p. 402, 1427.ii.14.   [108] Manning, *Village Revolts*, pp. 43 and 104.

Later cases of bondmen assembling by oath to resist their lords fail to appear in the published records of the Patent Rolls. No doubt, the change reflects the success of rural resistance against servitude since the Peasants' Revolt, the decline of serfdom, and the diminished power of lords on their manors, as Rodney Hilton, Christopher Dyer, and others[109] have convincingly argued. From manorial rolls and other royal judicial records such as King's Bench, and escheators' records, more cases of bondmen resistance and support by villagers and towns post-1381 certainly could be amassed. Resistance simmered under the surface, with increasing trespasses on lords' demesnes, refusals to perform service in manorial offices, and the withholding of rents. Occasionally, these flared into regional revolts, as in Norfolk during the autumn of 1382.[110] Such post-1381 instances of resistance recently supplied by Herbert Eiden, however, come exclusively from the countryside.

The Patent Rolls suggest two conclusions: (1) the chronology of protest in rural areas differed from those of towns against Crown, Church, and in rare instances, the secular nobility; (2) incidents of bondmen resistance concentrated overwhelmingly on the estates of monastic orders, not of bishops, or of secular lords.[111] Of the seventeen cases of 'rebellious' activity of bondmen, one occurred on an estate of a bishop, one on land possessed by the king, and in one, the lord's name was unspecified. The other fourteen arose on the estates of abbeys or in one case, on that of a hospital. If the number of rebellious manors is instead counted, the preponderance of Benedictine priors as the embattled and recalcitrant lords becomes more pronounced. All cases of multiple manors revolting were against monastic lords (in one case that of an abbess): by this count, twenty-seven of the thirty manors listed in these protests were possessed by Benedictines. The contrast with the

---

[109] Christopher Dyer, 'The Political Life of the Fifteenth-Century English Village', in *The Fifteenth Century, IV, Political Culture in Late Medieval Britain*, ed. Linda Clark and Christine Carpenter (Woodbridge, 2004), especially pp. 144–7; and Hilton, *Bond Men Made Free*, p. 231; against the claims of Dobson, *The Peasants' Revolt*: 'In general the results of the great revolt seem to have been negative where they were not negligible' (p. 27). Post-plague changes in the economic strategies of lords also accounted for the decline in demesnal farming.

[110] Eiden, 'Joint Action', pp. 29–30; and Eiden, 'Norfolk, 1382'.

[111] The same pattern appears also with attacks during 1381, especially if the manors of Gaunt are not considered; Eiden, 'Joint Action', p. 22: most of the manors that had their documents burnt belonged to religious institutions; for numerous riots on the estates of Westminster Abbey and burning of its monastic rolls in 1381, see Barbara Harvey, *Westminster Abbey and its Estates in the Middle Ages* (Oxford, 1977), pp. 269 and 305. She also shows the monks' remarkable insensitivity to market forces, and as a result their reluctance to change tenancies and their estate management well into the sixteenth century; see especially, pp. 304–5, 311, 321, and 331.

French Jacquerie of 1358 could not be starker: its targets were secular, not monastic. In England, monasteries appear to have been as recalcitrant in preserving their ancient privileges and rights of servitude in the countryside as in towns, but for the former they were less successful, as the post-1381 history of servitude in England well attests. The Black Death had not killed off the hope and resistance of rural dependants, as it had for urban rebels. This divergence in the histories of political and economic rights in the city and the countryside has yet to be investigated. No doubt, the differences depended in part on a divergence in opportunities presented in the wake of plague.

12   Urban conflict against bishops and universities

Chronicles reflect on few conflicts between bishops and burgesses, even if monastic priories attached to cathedrals at places such as Norwich are included as struggles between burgesses and episcopal authority.[1] Most of these have already been considered in other contexts. They amount to less than a handful and in the case of Winchester's disputed election of a new bishop in 1243, the revolt was more one against the king, who had made the appointment. The most colourful of these conflicts was one between the Archbishop of York and Durham, over which he possessed ecclesiastical authority. For years, the priors of St Cuthbert at Durham had taken displeasure over the archbishop's visitation of their monastery, and periodically, they challenged the archbishop's rights to examine them. These were mostly internecine ecclesiastical battles. However, in 1283, the struggle percolated beyond clerics. The people of Durham (Dunelmenses) refused the archbishop entry to their city to conduct his visitation. Part of the reason may have hinged on the collection of papal taxes ('Romana extra [ecclesia] de censibus exactionibus et procuracionibus'). Nonetheless, according to the bishop's register, a body of young men from the borough rushed into the church, chased him from the pulpit, out of the building, down the stairs to a school, and to the waterside. In the pursuit, they clipped an ear off his palfrey. According to the chronicle of the monastery of Guisborough, the monks battled against the archbishop with sticks and swords, but it was the town's women who came out and chased him away, throwing rocks at him, causing his horse to stumble. His clerks found him another and whisked him off to the city's hospital.[2]

In London, protests, if not revolts, can be detected between the mayor, John of Northampton, and the bishop on the eve of the trial of

---

[1] As Knowles, *The Religious Orders*, I, observed: unlike on the Continent, '[I]n England the monasteries were more important boroughs than were the bishops, and the struggle came later than abroad' (p. 265).
[2] *The Chronicle of Walter of Guisborough*, pp. 349–51.

Wycliffe in 1377. When commoners united behind their bishop against Gaunt's and Percy's support of Wycliffe, all Londoners may not have so patriotically backed their bishop. Walsingham reports the rise of a Wycliffian morality among them that had already been used against the jurisdiction and authority of the bishop. According to the St Albans' scribe, the citizens supported their 'arrogant' mayor and punished women, presumably more severely than the Church thought correct, for acts of fornication and adultery: the women were incarcerated in a prison called 'The Tun', their locks shorn 'like Theor's'. They were brought out 'for public inspection and, preceded by trumpeters and pipers, were marched around for all the people of London to see'.[3]

An incident of 1393 may be a clearer case of outrage and riot by urban commoners against a bishop over secular authority in London. A servant of the Bishop of Salisbury ('yomon off the Bishoppe'), while the bishop was resident in the capital, robbed and assaulted a baker. The 'people' came out and tried to arrest him, but he fled to the bishop's place. To protect the thief, the Bishop of London closed the gates on the constables of London, thereby provoking a larger crowd to gather, who threatened to burn the palace down. The mayor and sheriffs of London arrived 'sesed the malice off the communes, and made euery man goo hom and kepe the peasse'. Yet, despite their successful intervention, the bishop lodged a complaint, first with the treasurer of England, then with the chancellor, Lord Arundel, and finally the king, who deposed the mayor and sheriffs.[4] This incident, however, may have had less to do with Londoners' own bishop than with the Bishop of Salisbury. As we have seen, sixteen years earlier, Londoners had rallied round their own bishop against the insults of Gaunt and Percy.[5]

---

[3] Walsingham, *The St Albans Chronicle*, I, pp. 612–15; and Walsingham, *Historia Anglicana*, II, p. 65. Instead of draconian moral enforcement, Walsingham's gripe may have instead hinged on the infringement of the mayoral courts on ecclesiastical jurisdiction; see Bird, *The Turbulent London*, pp. 63–5. On the Tun and its changing function as a temporary gaol for moral offences, see *Memorials of London*, p. 40; and Rexroth, *Deviance and Power*, pp. 63, 112, 149, 176–7, 292, and 313. For Northampton's use of musical accompaniment for new ceremonies of punishment in 1382, and his use of biblical language and populist morality to appeal to the sturdy working classes of London, see ibid., pp. 143–56 and 314. In addition to persecuting prostitutes, Northampton launched an attack on false beggars and against the laxity of the clergy. He thereby differentiated himself from the previous mayor of his rival party, William Walworth, who had established a bathhouse and brothel in one of his houses in Southwark (ibid., p. 150). Northampton also passed decrees lowering prices of bread and ale, fees for saying masses, and performing christenings and weddings that assisted artisans and labourers (ibid., p. 150).

[4] *An English Chronicle, 1377–1461*, p. 16.

[5] Bird, *The Turbulent London*, speculates that Londoners had achieved so many rights vis-à-vis their bishop by the fourteenth century, that there was no need for further struggle

Similarly, in York, their archbishop, instead of provoking resentment among the populace, led them in revolt and, with his execution, became their martyred saint.

By contrast, the Patent Rolls reveal more tension, resentment, and open revolt by burgesses against their bishops and canons, even if they were less frequent than protests against abbots. Protests against Episcopal lords appear later than those against monasteries, clustering in the early and mid-fourteenth century. By the 1380s, however, as with urban revolts against ecclesiastical institutions in general, those against bishops declined sharply. Several of these, moreover, were minor incidents, as with our earliest case. In 1275 'certain persons of the commonalty' of York threatened the archbishop's servants, followed and beat them when, 'as courteously as possible', they supposedly were protecting certain boys, who had been confirmed at the church of the Friar Preachers, from the crush of the crowd.[6] The commission fails to explain why the commoners' animosity towards the archbishop and his servants arose.

In 1287, the appointment of a new constable of the castle of Dover makes a brief mention of 'discord' between citizens of Canterbury and England's other archbishop over market stalls and plots in the market-place that were empty and not rented. The document, however, does not specify whether the discord erupted into violence or went to the courts.[7] The next protest does not appear until the early fourteenth century. Although it began at Canterbury, the unidentified men probably came from a market town in Kent. The incident was a rare description of popular protest in these, as well as other, documents that hinged on ritual humiliation: 'Notwithstanding the king's ordinance for the preservation of the peace during his absence in Scotland', certain persons at night attacked the archbishop's palace in Canterbury, 'broke the gates, assaulted his servants and ministers, carried away his goods'. Their principal mission, however, appears not to have been directed at the archbishop as such, but to capture and humiliate his dean of Osprenge, appointed at Sellinge [Sellingges] in Kent,[8] whose duty was 'to make certain citations and do other things that were incumbent upon him by reason of his spiritual office'. The men threw him 'into filthy mud, and with his face turned to his horse's tail, holding the tail in his hand instead

with the clergy, and 'one reason for their early success' was because bishops had frequently been royal officials, 'who thought less of the claims of [their] See than of the finances of the central government' (p. 117).
[6] *CPR 1272–81*, p. 173, 1275.xi.23.   [7] *CPR 1281–92*, p. 289, 1287.xii.4.
[8] Sellinge was probably no more than a small market village.

of the bridle', compelled him to ride *chiarivari* (in the humiliating position of facing backwards) through the middle of the town. They continued the ritual, cutting off his horse's tail, lips, and ears, and throwing him again into the mud, and led him through town with songs and dances.[9]

Further popular protests against episcopal power continue through the first half of the fourteenth century: according to the Patent Rolls, it marked the hallmark of popular protest against bishops in late medieval England. These riots and revolts, moreover, were more clearly focused on the pursuit of liberties. In 1326, seventy men[10] were accused of assembling a 'great multitude' by ringing the town bell of Ely. They attacked the bishop's bailiff and other servants, broke into the bishop's dwelling, where his court was in session, and prevented them from holding the view of frankpledge. In 1338, eighty-eight men, including two tavernkeepers, two bakers, two chaplains, two tailors, a bowyer, a skinner, a porter, and a servant, attacked a servant of the Bishop of Coventry and Lichfield, then collecting the tolls at the bishop's Wednesday market.[11]

In 1342, men of Chichester took letters from servants of their bishop commanding him, along with his chapter, priests, and regular clergy within his diocese, to pray for the king while he was overseas. On a separate occasion, many of the same men assaulted the bishop and his servants, arresting him, then expelling him from the city, and refusing him re-entry. The case was repeated three months later, this time listing ninety-two rebels. The second adds that the townsmen had also imprisoned the bishop's servants, preventing the bishop from performing his 'business'. Neither case, however, explains why the townsmen had risen up and ripped apart royal letters.[12] The longer list of rebels of the second commission suggests that the conflict was not just between townsmen and bishop, but was divided also internally within the cathedral. The list begins with four canons, followed by four parsons, two chaplains, and twelve vicars of various parishes within the city. Nonetheless, the laity predominated with a wide spectrum of artisans and shopkeepers – two tavernkeepers, a baker, a saddler, a goldsmith, a cobbler, a tapermaker (candlemaker), and a brewer. They made

---

[9] *CPR 1301–7*, p. 198, 1303.xi.6. Another commission investigated the case on 6 October 1305; ibid., pp. 403–4.

[10] *CPR 1324–7*, pp. 350–1, 1326.viii.15; only six were identified by occupation – two clerks, a chaplain, a baker, a butcher, and a cook ('keu').

[11] *CPR 1338–40*, pp. 64–5, 1338.ii.12.

[12] *CPR 1340–3*, p. 587, 1342.xi.15; and Edward III, 6, p. 69, 1343.ii.4.

an 'alliance and confederacy', suggesting one that allied clerics and burgesses against the bishop and his policies.[13]

In 1343, men of Wells revolted against episcopal rule, especially against the bishop's rights to the view of frankpledge, his hundred court, and his fairs, with their tolls and profits on stalls.[14] The following year 'by force and arms', they prevented him from executing certain writs within his jurisdiction and assaulted his bailiff.[15] In the same year, Salisbury's burgesses also interrupted and prevented their bishop from exercising justice within his city. Thirty-three men 'with others'[16] assaulted the bailiff and other ministers of the bishop, while he held his court in the city's Guildhall. The townsmen locked the courtroom and imprisoned the bishop's bailiff and ministers as well as the suitors to the court. They took the court rolls and memoranda and prevented him from holding his tribunal, at a loss of profits 'for a great time'.[17] Finally, men of the market town Croydon, on the feast of John the Baptist in that year, assaulted and prevented the bailiffs and ministers of the Archbishop of Canterbury from collecting tolls at his yearly fair there.[18] This period of Edward III's absence, waging of war in France, and

[13] According to Dyer, 'Bromsgrove', p. 46, 1342 was 'a troubled year in a number of English towns'; he mentions, however, only two conflicts, and they were at the small end of the urban spectrum: in priory courts at Shipston and Bromsgrove, tenants were charged with violations against their lord, the cathedral priory of Worcester. Neither can be characterized as a large-scale revolt against episcopal privileges, as seen above at Chichester. At Bromsgrove, it is unclear whether the actions went beyond the courts.

[14] *CPR 1343–5*, p. 99, 1343.vii.18. Twenty-nine men were indicted, including a salter (seller of salt), a somenour (summoner, a petty officer, who warns persons to appear in court), a dyer, a skinner, and a barber. David Gary Shaw, *The Creation of a Community: The City of Wells in the Middle Ages* (Oxford, 1993), pp. 114–24, places the protest in a wider context. On 17 July 1341, Edward III granted the burgesses a charter that included rights to elect their own mayor and bailiff, and other privileges. Less than fifteen months later, probably because of the bishop's protests to the Crown, the king revoked the charter, and the burgesses revolted against the bishop. According to Shaw, the indicted burgesses represented a cross-section of the urban population. He argues that they must not have been guilty of using force of arms, because the Crown did not inflict corporal penalties and the fine of £3,000 was low. However, such an amount for a city Wells' size (less than 2,500) would have been a severe punishment. According to Shaw, 'Social Networks and the Foundations of Oligarchy in Medieval Towns', *UH*, 32 (2005): 206, the burgesses comprised about half Wells' population. Not counting women and children, about 300 people would have been responsible for paying £10 per head or possibly more – no small fee for a small townsman before the Black Death. To argue that the penalties imposed on Wells were lenient, Shaw compares them only with one revolt, Bury's in 1327–8, one of the longest and bloodiest in medieval English history, which ended with multiple executions and a vast fine. In addition, Wells' only medieval mayor was excommunicated. Curiously, Shaw does not use the record above, citing 'force of arms' reported in *CPR*.

[15] *CPR 1343–5*, p. 421, 1344.xi.10.

[16] Only one was identified by an occupation, a draper.

[17] *CPR 1343–5*, p. 420, 1344.xii.3.   [18] Ibid., p. 386, 1344.vi.26.

heightened taxation, set the political parameters for the most significant cluster of attacks by burgesses on bishops in their towns and on their manors.

A second cluster came during, or just after, the Black Death, in 1349 and 1350. The 'deadly pestilence' and its mounting bodies directly provoked the first of these: an armed conflict between Winchester's burgesses and their bishop over property rights and their uses, the bishop's desire to use a plot adjacent to the cathedral for the plague's overflow versus the town's alleged 'usurpation' of it for their markets, festivals, housing, and other matters of the living.[19] The case continued to be adjudicated until 21 November, when the king judged in favour of the cathedral and fined the city.[20] In 1350, Edward again sided with a bishop against a mayor and commonalty, this time at Lynn over the view of frankpledge, which the mayor and commonalty had in fact earlier purchased from the previous bishop for £40 a year. Yet, '[F]or the removal of any ambiguity ... for the security of the bishop and his successors', Edward now granted the court to the bishops 'for ever' and 'revoked entirely' the previous grant, though he acknowledged that it had been made to the mayor and burgesses.[21] Three-and-a-half months later, the same bishop sought further royal support while in the king's service at Calais. Men at Haddiscoe[22] attacked his commissary general appointed in his absence, tore his rolls and memoranda to shreds, and threatened to kill his ministers if they acted against them.[23] Further riots against bishops, their ministers, their privileges, courts, and distraints took place in 1350 at Yeovil (against the Bishop of Bath and Wells) and Newark-on-Trent (against the Bishop of Lincoln).[24]

The Black Death, however, failed to spur burgesses into a new period of struggle to extend their liberties against the impositions of their episcopal lords.[25] The next conflict between burgesses and a bishop or cathedral chapter does not appear for sixteen years, and this one was vague, referring only to 'discords and dissensions' that had been stirred up by malefactors between the mayor and town of Exeter on one side,

---

[19] *CPR 1348–50*, p. 384.

[20] Ibid., pp. 424–5. On bishops' tight control over their monopolies of funerals and burials, even with the mass burials that ensued during the plague, see Ian Forrest, 'The Politics of Burial in Late Medieval Hereford', *EHR*, 125 (2010): 1110–38.

[21] *CPR 1348–50*, p. 551, 1350.v.16. Also see Owen, *The Making of King's Lynn*, p. 36.

[22] A village southwest of Great Yarmouth.   [23] *CPR 1348–50*, p. 592, 1350.ix.1.

[24] Ibid., p. 516, 1350.ii.1; and p. 521, 1350.ii.15.

[25] Certain types of conflict not involving armed conflict and not seen in chronicles or *CPR* may have increased after the Black Death, such as those uniting parish priests and their congregations against jealously guarded rights of bishops over monopolies of funerals and burials within cathedrals; see Forrest, 'The Politics of Burial'.

and the dean, canons, vicars, chaplains, clerks, and ministers of the cathedral of St Peter, Exeter, on the other. As a consequence, the latter 'dare not go from their college to the church to perform divine service'. To remedy matters, the king took the dean and chapter into his special protection for two years.[26] The mayor and commonalty did not, however, take the decision lightly. Three days later, a commission based on information from the dean and chapter accused a newly elected mayor of rallying his citizens against them. Locking their doors, they came armed 'in array of war' before the royal justices authorized to investigate the charges against the previous mayor and town's bailiffs for trespass against the cathedral. The burgesses so threatened the dean, chapter, and jurors 'that they dared not prosecute the taking of the inquisition or proceed to examine the truth'.[27] Three years later, resentment against episcopal judicial prerogatives spread to another town within the diocese of Exeter. The men of 'the suburb and town' of Brampton had 'newly formed' themselves into congregations of men-at-arms, confronted the episcopal authorities of the dean and chapter 'to correct defaults and notorious crimes', and prevented them exercising justice, thus violating 'the ecclesiastical liberty' and 'the king's peace'. The king authorized the sheriff of Devon and bailiffs of Exeter to arrest any citizen who bore arms.[28]

The period from the late 1370s to the Peasants' Revolt, so rich in civil and political unrest in the countryside, failed to spawn a new wave of challenges by burgesses to episcopal privileges and authority. In Edward III's tumultuous last year and loss of power, only one incident appears: artisans and other burgesses of Lynn tried to kill their bishop by laying an ambush for him; they chased him into the priory of St Margaret's, refused to allow him to leave for some time, killed twenty of his horses, and assaulted his men and servants. The commission unfortunately gives no explanation for their organized outrage.[29] Nor did the Peasants' Revolt prompt a new willingness among burgesses to challenge bishops' prerogatives; attempts by burgesses to gain such liberties had at that point declined even more steeply than their challenges to priories and monasteries.

---

[26] *CPR 1364–7*, pp. 278–9, 1366.ii.3.   [27] Ibid., p. 278, 1366.ii.6.

[28] *CPR 1367–70*, p. 352, 1369.xii.1.

[29] Twenty-three men were named, nine by occupation: two tailors, two glovers, two saddlers, a bower, a skinner, and a mercer; *CPR 1374–7*, p. 502, 1377.vi.16. Also, see the chronicle description, p. 103 above; and Owen, *The Making of King's Lynn*, p. 35, which lists several other controversies between Lynn's burgesses and their bishop in *CPR* and other sources. These clustered in the thirteenth century – 1227, 1234, and 1236 – and not all of them resulted in riots or violence.

The few incidents to appear, moreover, occurred in places far removed from the hot spots of the Peasants' Revolt. In 1383, townsmen of Penrith staged what appears to have been a tax revolt against the Bishop of Carlisle, preventing his appointee from collecting a clerical subsidy.[30] In 1390, a territorial dispute between the dean and chapter of the cathedral of Lincoln and the city's burgesses erupted. The mayor and city's two bailiffs, along with twenty-one others, including a saddler, a butcher, and a dyer ('littester'), broke the cathedral's close, and 'conspired' to take lands around the cathedral into the city's jurisdiction. They also opposed the economic and juridical privileges of the Church, confiscating money the bishop had levied on merchants for fines in his court, called 'le Galilee'. The rebels instead compelled merchants to appear before their tribunal at the Guildhall and levied fines on the chapter's dean, to the episcopate's loss of £1,000.[31]

The first half of the fifteenth century witnessed still fewer struggles between burgesses and bishops.[32] Until the end of the published Patent Rolls in 1452, only three further bouts between towns and bishops or their canons emerge. In 1410, men of the market town Taunton, in Somerset, challenged the liberties of their 'lord of the town', the Bishop of Winchester. They assaulted those of his servants appointed to levy tolls at his fair and at a court called 'the piepowder'. Further, four hundred townsmen banded together in what was clearly an illegal guild or confraternity, and 'made a livery of four hundred caps and more of one suit to live and die against him and his ministers'.[33] In 1434, the dean and chapter of the cathedral of St Peter, Exeter, charged that the mayor and 'other malefactors, arrayed in manner of war', took away

---

[30] *CPR 1381–5*, p. 356, 1383.xi.12.   [31] *CPR 1389–92*, pp. 270–1, 1390.v.11.

[32] Between 1401 and 1404, disputes between Lynn's burgesses and their bishop (Henry, Bishop of Norwich) flared over attempts to force the bishop to repair his pier in town. Although the burgesses at one point failed to appear in court because of alleged threats of violence, these disputes were confined to courts and find no mention in chronicles or *CPR*; see Owen, *The Making of King's Lynn*, pp. 36 and 381–2; and *Anglo-Norman Letters and Petitions from All Soul's MS 182*, ed. M. D. Legge, Anglo-Norman Text Society, 3 (1941), pp. 45–7, 92, and 112.

[33] *CPR 1408–13*, p. 179, 1410.ii.2. For a similar case of a town showing its unity by donning the same livery, see Scarborough in the summer of 1381, when townsmen, across social classes and guilds, took 'a solemn oath of mutual self-support and a common livery ... a white hood with a red liripipe or tail'; Dobson, 'The Risings in York, Beverley and Scarborough', p. 136. Livery and maintenance with illegal fraternities, oaths of allegiance, and revolt may have increased in the last decade of the fourteenth and early fifteenth century; see Andrew Prescott, 'The Yorkshire Partisans and the Literature of Popular Discontent', in *Medieval Literature in English*, ed. Elaine Treharne and Greg Walker (Oxford, 2010), pp. 325–44, on the band of Collingham and riots at Beverley, Benningholme, and Hull from 1386 to 1392.

cattle 'lawfully taken' from two of the bishop's tenants in town for unpaid customs and services and assaulted the bishop's steward while holding a session of the bishop's view of frankpledge.[34] Finally, in 1436, the dean and chapter of the cathedral of Lichfield accused eleven men (all but two identified by occupation) – two yeomen, a smith, a clerk, a parchment maker, a tailor, a skinner, and a cobbler ['corveser'] – who broke the gates of the chapter house and with slings 'and other engines' shot a 'great many stones over the walls'. By 'day and night' they attempted to enter the chapter house to slay the bishop's men and laid in wait for nine ministers of the cathedral and other servants 'so that they dared not stir abroad for a great while'. The commission fails to reveal the reasons for the townsmen's anger.[35] However, as with the two other cases of burgess–bishop conflict during the first half of the fifteenth century, townsmen no longer appear to have challenged bishops' broad liberties or asserted their own.[36]

To these fifteenth-century attacks, three further incidents might be added from the chronicles – one that occurred in London, and two that took place in Salisbury. None of them, however, explicitly questioned Church privileges or religion. The first sprang from a conflict of national dimensions in 1425, between Humphrey, Duke of Gloucester, the king's uncle and protector of the realm, and Henry Beaufort, Bishop of Winchester, and royal chancellor. The city of London felt oppressed by Beaufort, not as a bishop, but instead as a chancellor, especially because of his harsh policies towards citizens and his protection of alien merchants at their expense. Earlier that year, the people demonstrated against him at Wine Crane's wharf, with slanderous bills circulated against Flemings nailed to his door.[37] Now, they moved to murder him in his inn at Southwark; to throw him into the Thames to teach him 'to swim with wings'.[38] The gates of London Bridge, however, were well patrolled, and the Londoners were unable to cross. Nonetheless,

---

[34] *CPR 1429–36*, 1434.v.20.   [35] *CPR 1436–41*, p. 84, 1436.xi.18.

[36] Municipal records and bishop registers show further strife in Carlisle, where the bishop was responsible for city defences and controlled its citadel. But also here, cases of riot and violence were rare. In 1345, tensions over purveyances and duties to share the city's defence against Scottish incursions led to widespread violence between Bishop Kirby and citizens. Decked out in military armour, he directed rampages against citizens with bows, arrows, and other weapons, wounding and killing many. Nine years later, he excommunicated thirteen citizens who obstructed his officers from buying victuals, probably to purvey his castle. Finally, in 1389, the citizens quarrelled with the cathedral canons, though without apparent violence; Summerson, *Medieval Carlisle*, pp. 275–7 and 352–4. None of these, however, challenged episcopal rights.

[37] Griffiths, *The Reign of King Henry VI*, p. 74.   [38] Ibid., p. 75.

according to an anonymous English chronicler, the bitterness and hatred against the bishop persisted for a 'longe tyme after'.[39]

The second incident, from the same chronicler, was a brutal attack on the Bishop of Salisbury by the 'people' of Wiltshire, while he performed mass at a church in Edington at the end of June 1450. They dragged him from the altar with his 'orbe and stole around his neck', took him up a hill near the church and 'slogh hym horribly, thair fadur and thair bisshoppe'.[40] Again, the chronicler leaves no hints as to the rebels' motives, whether townsmen were involved, or if the incident were connected to the political discontent that stirred Cade's rebellion. Documents from King's Bench, however, give a fuller picture. The bishop, William Aiscough, a close companion of the king, had married Henry to Margaret of Anjou in 1445, and was long resented in Wiltshire, where he was seen as one of the traitors within Henry's close circle of temporal and spiritual advisers. On the same day that his tenants at Edington hacked the bishop to death, those of Salisbury attacked the dean and chapter of the cathedral, and, several days later, Aiscough's urban palace, ransacking the episcopal archives.[41]

Finally, the colourful and ritualistically rich 'Gladman's Insurrection' in Norwich in 1443 remains open to debate as to its causes and meaning. It was a conflict that cut across a number of divides within late medieval Norwich society – factional rivalries with class dimensions, involving present and previous mayors, landed magnates of the county, and the old battle lines between artisans and burgesses against the privileges and impositions of the bishop, the cathedral priory, and the Abbey of St Benet's Hulme.[42] It began as a riot of artisans on 23 January against decisions by a county court upholding St Benet's jurisdictional claims to water rights on the river Wensum, but escalated to a larger insurrection of Shrove Tuesday, allegedly against the bishop, the priory, and the abbey. It took the form of a procession led by John Gladman, described as a merchant but possibly a

---

[39] *An English Chronicle, 1377–1461*, pp. 58–9. On the controversy between the Duke of Gloucester and Beaufort and the reasons for London's popular affection for the duke, see Lucy Rhymer, 'Humphrey, Duke of Gloucester and the City of London', in *The Fifteenth Century, VIII: Rule, Redemption, and Representations in Late Medieval England and France*, ed. Linda Clark (Woodbridge, 2008), pp. 47–58.

[40] Ibid., p. 67.

[41] See Griffiths, *The Reign of King Henry VI*, pp. 644–5, based largely on the 1975 London thesis of J. N. Hare, 'Lords and Tenants in Wiltshire, c. 1380–c. 1520', which uses records of King's Bench.

[42] This abbey was also a chief target of the Norfolk insurgents of 1381. According to A. W. Reid, 'The Rising of 1381 in South West and Central Norfolk', in *Studies Towards a History of the Rising of 1381 in Norfolk* (Norwich, 1984), p. 26, it was not an anti-clerical revolt, but one against the monastery's manorial privileges and impositions.

smith, dressed as a king at the head of a group of twenty-four craftsmen and followed by a further hundred on foot or horseback. By the city's version, this was simply an artisan celebration of Shrove Tuesday – the ritualistic turning of the world upside down for a day.[43] By the county court version, supporting the ecclesiastical interests in the city, the incident was not so innocent: the mayor and commonalty attacked the priory, stole its charters, and forced the priory to abandon its jurisdiction.[44] Historians have often doubted the city version because the procession occurred in January, five weeks before Shrove Tuesday (5 March), and the punishments meted out to citizens – destruction of their mills, loss of liberties, and imprisonment of the mayor – suggest more than play and theatre.[45] Moreover, these events reached King's Bench, reporting burgesses' destruction of the prior's stocks, 'symbols of the punitive means by which the cathedral party usurped the jurisdictional rights of the city', and the Crown intervened, seized Norwich's liberties for four years, and sentenced the city and individuals with stiff fines.[46] Nonetheless, it is curious that the Patent Rolls leave little trace of these events,[47] and as Philippa Maddern comments, 'accounts of these events outside the law courts are extremely scanty'[48] as with its only reference in a local chronicle: sometime after Christmas [1442] a *magna insurrexio* happened in the city of Norwich with the citizens rising up against the Monastery of Christ [the priory] and as a consequence the citizens lost their franchise.[49]

---

[43] On these rituals in late medieval and early modern England, see Charles Pythian-Adams, *The Desolation of a City: Coventry and the Urban Crisis of the Late Middle Ages* (Cambridge, 1979).

[44] The description of this insurrection comes from court documents, *Records of the City of Norwich*, II, pp. 230 and 312 and has been described at length by Philippa Maddern, *Violence and Social Order: East Anglia 1422–1442* (Oxford, 1992), pp. 175–205; Hilton, *English and French Towns*, pp. 123–5; Humphrey, *The Politics of Carnival*, pp. 63–82; and McRee, 'Peacemaking', p. 865.

[45] On the historiography, see Humphrey, *The Politics of Carnival*, p. 76.

[46] Attreed, 'Urban Identity', p. 584.

[47] On 8 February 1444, *CPR 1441–6*, pp. 232–3, a mandate refers to letters patent dated 25 May of the previous year that describes a controversy between the priory and bishop on the one hand and the mayor and commonalty on the other, regarding juridical rights to streets and places in the city and countryside. The mandate resolved that the places belonged to the county, not the town. Nothing, however, is mentioned about Gladman or any violence to the bishop or priory. A commission of 11 February 1443 charged the mayors, sheriffs, and aldermen of Norwich with misgovernance and may be referring to the supposed riot of 23 January, but does not accuse the mayor or anyone else of violence, much less revolt against the county court, bishop, or priory.

[48] Maddern, *Violence and Social Order*, p. 175.

[49] *John Benet's Chronicle for the Years 1400 to 1462*, ed. G. L. Harriss and M. A. Harriss, *Camden Miscellany*, XXIV, CS, 4th series, 9 (1972), p. 189: 'Et post Natale facta est magna insurrexio in civitate Norwyc. Nam cives insurrexerunt contra Monasterium Christi in eadem civitate propter quam amiserunt suam frawnchesiam.'

As with protest against abbots, open revolts against bishops and their chapters declined sharply by the mid-fourteenth century. Although hatred towards individual bishops and clerics may not have disappeared,[50] it is surprising how steep the decline in violent opposition to bishops had become, especially given the late fourteenth century's concomitant rise of Lollardy, its cries against clerical wealth, special privileges, hierarchy, usurpation of power, corruption, and the Church's jealous hold over doctrine – all of which became principles stimulating Lollard piety, resentment, and rebellion.

Struggles between burgesses and universities

Numerous revolts and conflicts, even war, arose between burgesses and clerics within England's two principal university towns. Several appear from chronicle descriptions as little more than town–gown fights turning on rowdy student misbehaviour or townies preying on easily targeted scholars – matters of criminality and youth culture, rather than urban revolt. In 1223, for example, a rare case of conflict between 'scholares' and townsmen flared outside the two major university towns: a fight ('rixa') between burgesses and students at Dunstable left many wounded and a burgess killed. What it concerned is left to our imagination.[51] Such conflicts could have more serious consequences, as with a battle at Oxford in 1228 that left dead bodies scattered through alleyways and squares. The 'people' were forced to pay 50 marks to be distributed between rich and poor students.[52] In addition to fines, the 'cives' often suffered from interdicts and sentences of excommunication, as at Oxford in 1228, 1352, and 1354, the last lasting until 1357.[53] These dissensions could also have disastrous consequences for universities. Prompted by the hanging of two, or possibly three, Oxford students for the murder of a woman, and fearing the king's 'tyranny', almost all the students left Oxford in 1209, some going to Reading, others to Paris, and others to Cambridge, which marked the beginnings of the latter as a university.[54]

---

[50] For instance, the struggles between Exeter's citizens and its cathedral over rights and immunities continued from at least the thirteenth century to the Reformation, with the cathedral winning the upper hand by 1448; these conflicts, however, were fought and negotiated in royal courts; see Attreed, 'Arbitration'; and Attreed, 'Urban Identity', p. 577.

[51] *Annals of Dunstable*, pp. 78–9.   [52] Ibid., pp. 109–10.

[53] Ibid., pp. 109–10 and 476; *Malvern Continuation of Higden in Ranulphi Higden monachi Cestrensis*, VIII, p. 356, which is the continuation from 1348 to 1377 by John of Malvern at Worcester; Otterbourne and Whethamstede, *Ab origine*, p. 299; Walsingham, *Ypodigma Neustriae*, pp. 295 and 301.

[54] *Memoriale fratris Walteri de Coventria*, II, p. 201; Paris, *Historia Anglorum*, II, p. 120; and Paris, *Chronica majora*, II, pp. 525–6. In addition, see Cooper and Crossley, 'Medieval

In 1240, Oxford students again fled after a dispute with burgesses, this time to Cambridge, where they were able to negotiate 'some liberties' and a charter from the king.[55] The flow of students was not exclusively eastward: in 1249, quarrels and fist-fights between burgesses and scholars at Cambridge, again for unexplained reasons, led to robberies and house breaking, with numbers wounded and murdered. These were significant enough to 'reach the king's ear' by Easter and sparked a student mass exodus to Oxford.[56]

Violent conflict between townsmen and scholars appears, however, to have predominated in Oxford. In 1352, the 'populi' there rose up against students; books were burnt and much of the university destroyed. An ecclesiastical interdict was imposed on the citizens until they signed a peace with the university, promising to treat students well.[57] The pact had little effect. Two years later, citizens and students fell out again, with 'many students' killed. Again, the citizens were placed under interdict and again had to pay homage to the students.[58] In 1355, another war between citizens and scholars flared, perhaps Oxford's most serious, or at least its best-remembered one, the St Scholastica's Day riot.[59] It began as a bar-room brawl at Swindlestock tavern, Carfax, between a student and the tavernkeeper, in which a wine sack was split across the tavernkeeper's head (by other accounts wine was thrown in his face). After nearly two days, a religious procession ended the fighting that left many laymen wounded and twenty dead, with a similar death toll for students. After a brief armistice, conflict erupted, again killing more. The bodies of young students were thrown into town latrines, their books ripped to shreds, their property stolen. As a result, numerous students left and others refrained from enrolling at the university. The king intervened, carried off four of Oxford's most powerful citizens to the Tower of London, fined the citizens £250, stripped the mayor of his privileges, and seized the assize of wine and beer from them

---

Oxford', p. 12: documents in the university archives reveal that the king fined the town in 1214 for these conflicts and forced the mayor, bailiffs, and fifty leading burgesses to take a public oath promising no further violence against the university; also see Hastings Rashdall, *The Universities of Europe in the Middle Ages*, 2nd edn, F. M. Powicke and A. B. Emden, 3 vols. (Oxford, 1936), III, pp. 33–4; and Jonathan Davies, *Culture and Power: Tuscany and its Universities 1537–1609* (Leiden, 2009), p. 160.

[55] Paris, *Chronica majora*, IV, pp. 7–8. The students left again after a disputed election over their chancellor in 1287; Capgrave, *Chronicle of England*, p. 168.

[56] Paris, *Chronica majora*, V, pp. 67–8; and also C. H. Cooper, *Annals of Cambridge*, 5 vols. (Cambridge, 1842–52), I, p. 45.

[57] *Malvern Continuation*, VIII, p. 356; see Gransden, *Historical Writing*, II, p. 56.

[58] *Annals of Bermondsey*, p. 476.

[59] See Rashdall, *The Universities of Europe*, III, pp. 96–102; Alan B. Cobban, *The Medieval English Universities: Oxford and Cambridge to c. 1500* (Aldershot, 1988), p. 263; and Alan B. Cobban, *English University Life in the Middle Ages* (London, 1999), pp. 193–4.

and handed it to the chancellor of the university.[60] Little hint is given as to why the antagonisms grew.

Other quarrels arose between students and citizens whose causes and objectives remain obscure in the sources, but which called for the king, nobles, or bishops to intervene. On occasion, peace came only 'after a long time', as with strife at Oxford in 1236.[61] Sometimes, these were internecine struggles that may have hinged on wider national conflicts and called for baronial intervention, as at Oxford in 1258, where a violent split occurred between the various nations of the university – Scots, Welsh, northerners, and southerners – or at Oxford in 1388, and again in 1389, when Welsh students allied with southerners against northerners.[62] In 1388, the conflict had to be resolved by an Act of Parliament, which removed the university's chancellor. But disturbances continued; 'for the Welsh students ... were never quiet'. More deaths resulted and Thomas of Woodstock, Duke of Gloucester, was called in with troops. Many of the Welsh were expelled and 'as they left', the northerners stood by the gates to humiliate them further, forcing them to exchange kisses.[63]

Student alliances and conflict could cut in other directions, as seen in the last student tumult from our sample of chronicles, a 'commotio' of 1431, fought between scholars and monks of the Black Order at Oxford.[64] Internecine brawls between students could snowball into wider conflicts that exploded into war between the university and town, such as one dated variously by different chroniclers, to 1295 or 1296, and correctly, by the *Annales of Worcester*, to 1298. Two 'boys of different nations (diversae nationis)' came to blows, escalating into a fight with 'everyone, clerics and lay' coming from their homes to join the fray. Burgesses robbed the houses of clerics, and a church rector was killed. News reached the king's court; royal justices were sent in; burgesses were fined £200 (200 marks by other accounts), and the Bishop of Lincoln threatened any who broke the peace with

---

[60] Robert of Avesbury, *De gestis mirabilibus regis Edwardi Tertii*, ed. E. M. Thompson, RS, 93 (London, 1889), pp. 421–3. Also, Ormrod, *The Reign of Edward III*, p. 177; and Cooper and Crossley, 'Medieval Oxford', p. 18: six clerks were killed and twenty-one seriously wounded; there are no figures for the townsmen's casualties. The burgesses may have won the war, but they lost the peace (p. 18).

[61] Paris, *Chronica majora*, III, pp. 371–2.

[62] *Knighton's Chronicle 1337–1396*, pp. 431 and 529; and *CPR 1385–9*, p. 331, 1389.xi.27.

[63] *Knighton's Chronicle 1337–1396*, p. 529. Adam Usk, who was indicted as 'the chief instigator and leader of the Welshmen', reports the struggle. He was acquitted only after 'great difficulty', from which he learnt 'the power of the king' and 'to fear' him; *The Chronicle of Adam Usk*, pp. 14–17.

[64] *Annales ... Amundesham*, I, p. 57.

excommunication.[65] No doubt the Anglo–Scottish war, begun in 1296, contributed to the heightened tensions between the 'nations'.[66]

In 1362, again at Oxford, the chancellor prosecuted a student – a Carmelite friar – for 'rebellion and disobedience', and ordered him punished, but the friar and his supporters resisted, making 'daily' citations and appeals in the royal courts against the chancellor.[67] In 1380, the provost of an Oxford college, 'Le Quenehall' (Queen's college), charged the previous provost of the college and other masters with embezzlement and theft of charters, books, and jewels from the college.[68]

Despite these manifold divisions, our sources do not point to rifts between students and masters. In fact, the two appear united, as with a labour dispute in 1334 at Oxford between these scholars and their attendants and servants.[69] At other times, scholars came out united with their servants, as in 1345, when the chancellor of Oxford was unable to punish 'such a multitude of scholars and servants', who assembled to prevent royal justices from discharging their office. The chancellor had to call for reinforcements from the Crown.[70] Finally, students and burgesses could unite, as at Osney in 1238, as well as the year before, during a crisis in high politics, when Oxford students joined Abingdon townsmen to attack the abbey, and presumably its privileges.[71]

As in the chronicles, the lion share of cases at both universities in the Patent Rolls concerned violence either between students or between students and townsmen, in which rights were not mentioned. For instance, clearly the town of Oxford and the university were divided politically and ideologically during the Barons' War. These divisions continued to 1264, but the Patent Rolls reveal no demands made by either burgesses or the university, despite major dissension between 'scholares & burgenses'.[72] Before setting off for his wars in Scotland, Edward II in 1314 sought to restore peace between the two at Oxford,

---

[65] *Opus chronicum*, p. 59, dates the incident to 1295; Walsingham, *Historia Anglicana*, II, pp. 62–3, to 1296.

[66] None of the chronicles or the *CPR*, however, refers to the war as a condition of these hostilities.

[67] *CPR 1361–4*, p. 282, 1362.vi.18.   [68] *CPR 1377–81*, p. 470, 1380.ii.7.

[69] *CPR 1334–8*, p. 66, 1334.ix.20.   [70] *CPR 1343–5*, p. 501, 1345.iii.14.

[71] *Annales Paulini*, p. 332.

[72] *CPR 1258–66*, p. 328, 1264.vi.27; *CCR, 1261–4*, pp. 363–4; and *Medieval Archives of the University of Oxford*, ed. H. E. Salter, 2 vols., Oxford Historical Society, LXX and LXXIII (Oxford, 1920–1), I, doc. nn. 16–17, pp. 24–6. The university at Northampton, newly created by scholars from Cambridge and Oxford in 1260, also resisted Henry. As a result, the king revoked its licence; Cobban, *English University Life*, p. 194.

threatening heavier penalties against violators of the peace. He was informed that 'there are constant disputes between the scholars and others, whereby homicides and other offences have been committed in contempt of his mandates',[73] lending some credence to the remarkably high murder rates compiled by Charles Hammer, Jr for fourteenth-century Oxford, which dwarf any from twentieth-century cities in the West.[74] But could these deadly bar-room brawls that spilled into Oxford's streets have arisen from more fundamental ideological questions over rights and privileges? The laconic commissions rarely afford clues: in 1400, for example, the chancellor of the University of Oxford was appointed to investigate 'evildoers who assemble unlawfully' to assault and mistreat members of the university, to the 'loss' and 'hindrance of clerks studying there'. The report specifies no motive for the assemblies, not even if the 'unlawful' ones were those of the town's laity.[75] On other occasions, it is difficult even to know who the perpetrators of violence against scholars were: other students or the laity. In 1261, twenty-eight men were pardoned from previous assaults on certain northern students at Cambridge, but only two were identified by title or profession; both were 'masters'.[76] This may have been connected to an inquiry the previous year concerning complaints by a master and 'his fellows, scholars of Cambridge', that certain malefactors, 'clerics as well as lay' of the town had broken into their lodgings, beaten them, and plundered their goods.[77]

Chroniclers occasionally point to causes beyond the loss of tempers or rites of youth culture, when issues such as liberty came to the fore. In 1263, during the baronial disturbances against Henry, burgesses attacked the university's royal privileges and imprisoned students. The conflict between clerics and burgesses, called 'war' by a chronicler,[78] lasted from 21 September to 24 June – far longer, and probably with more casualties, than the now more famous St Scholastica uprising of 1355.[79] The burgesses led their charges with military banners, one of

---

[73] *CPR 1313–17*, p. 153, 1314.vi.28.
[74] Hammer, 'Patterns of Homicide'; and criticisms of it, Maddern, 'Order and Disorder', pp. 188–212.
[75] *CPR 1399–1401*, p. 313, 1400.v.20. A further royal proclamation of 1353, which described 'assemblies or unlawful conventicles … and the carrying of arms' and prohibited the university's chancellor from hearing pleas from these 'evildoers', suggests the disputes between university and town continued; *CPR 1350–4*, p. 517, 1353.x.3.
[76] *CPR 1258–66*, p. 146, 1261.–.–.   [77] Ibid., pp. 180–1, 1260.xi.24.
[78] *Annales de Tewksbury*, p. 449; also see *Annales monasterii de Wintonia*, p. 101.
[79] *Annals of Osney*, pp. 139–41. Its fame derives from Rashdall's description of it (*The Universities of Europe*, III, pp. 96–102).

which the students succeeded in ripping to shreds.[80] Another case involving rights at Oxford did not concern the burgesses but instead was a controversy between the university and a bishop. In 1257, nine masters of Oxford went to St Albans to lodge a complaint with the king against the Bishop of Lincoln on charges that he had infringed 'on the liberties of the scholars contrary to the old and approved statutes of the university'.[81] Perhaps the best known of the medieval struggles between an English university and burgesses, however, was not at Oxford but Cambridge, whose history of town–gown strife was much less contentious or frequent than Oxford's: it spread from the Peasants' Revolt, when the mayor and burgesses of Cambridge challenged the rights and privileges of the university and destroyed its ancient charters.[82]

In the Patent Rolls, disturbances between universities and burgesses explicitly touching town liberties, jurisdictions of tribunals, and other forms of rule are rarer still. The closest comes from Oxford in 1346, when burgesses revolted against the university's right of frankpledge.[83] In 1298, 'controversies and discords between the chancellor and scholars of the university' on the one hand, and the mayor, burgesses, and commonalty of the town on the other, suggest that questions of rights or jurisdiction were at stake, but the commission has left them opaque.[84] At any rate, the revolt itself (as with the later, more famous, one of St Scholastica's Day, 1355) brought contested juridical relations and privileges between university and town to the forefront. After having been attacked by students and had their mace taken,[85] the bailiffs asked the chancellor for permission to arrest the 'evil-doers' but were refused, and threatened with excommunication. The conflict then escalated, with 1,500 clerks by one account, and 3,000 by another, in organized assault on laymen 'with bows and arrows, swords and bucklers, slings and stones'. According to the university, the townsmen rallied against the scholars with 'bells, horns, and a common battle cry'. By both accounts, the riots were organized and premeditated.[86] Even the famous

---

[80] *Annales monasterii de Wintonia*, pp. 100–1.   [81] Paris, *Chronica majora*, V, p. 618.

[82] Oman, *The Great Revolt*, pp. 50 and 123; Reynolds, *An Introduction*, p. 183; Helen Cam, 'Medieval History', in *VCH: Cambridge and the Isle of Ely*, ed. J. P. C. Roach (London, 1959), III, pp. 8–12; J. P. C. Roach, 'The University of Cambridge: The Middle Ages', pp. 150–66, in *VCH: Cambridge and the Isle of Ely*, ed. J. P. C. Roach, (London, 1959) III, p. 152.

[83] See p. 115 above.   [84] *CPR 1292–1301*, p. 378, 1298.iv.26.

[85] The mace was the principal symbol of a town's constitutional powers granted by the king; Attreed, 'Urban Identity', p. 577.

[86] *Medieval Archives*, I, doc. nn. 32–41, pp. 43–81. In the university archives more documents survive on this revolt (including a version of events from townsmen) than on any others, even the the riot of St Scholastica's Day in 1355.

St Scholastica war of 1355, presented by chroniclers as the spontaneous violence of a bar-room brawl gone mad, takes a different husk in the Patent Rolls: burgesses rang their 'common bell' and with banners unfurled marched to the dwellings of masters and scholars, imprisoned some, mutilated others, and burnt their gates and doors. Their objective was 'to break up the university'.[87]

Two cases from Cambridge, however, were more explicit about rights than any at Oxford. The first, in 1322, named 155 in one commission and 267 in another the same year. In both, men alone appear as rebels, representing a wide variety of provisioning trades and crafts. Leadership came from the town's elected officials – the mayor, its four bailiffs, and a town clerk. 'Acting in the name and with the authority of the commonalty', townsmen attacked the inns of masters and students, climbed their walls, broke doors, 'imprisoned some, mutilated others', and killed a parson. They took away books and other goods, 'so that no person dare go to the University of the said town for study'.[88] But this was no mad jacquerie. The second commission adds that the townsmen trampled in the mud a writ concerning the university's privileges, first when it was presented to townsmen and again when it was attached to the tollbooth.[89]

The Patent Rolls also record Cambridge's second, more famous, uprising against the university during the Peasants' Revolt. In comparison with the commission reports of 1322, these provide less insight into burgess aims and actions. Several documents in the late summer of 1381 – mostly commissions to arrest insurgents for entering and destroying manors, carrying away horses, cattle, jewels, and other goods in a long list of counties including Cambridge – fail to specify any of the rebels' aims other than implicit ones of economic gain from thievery, fleecing the university, its chancellor, masters, and scholars.[90] Royal complaints lodged by John of Gaunt and the houses of Corpus Christi and St Mary, under the duke's patronage, were only slightly more informative. The commission listed eleven men 'and others' who broke into these houses, took timber, doors, windows, books, and jewels, and

---

[87] *CPR 1354–8*, p. 215, 1355.iii.20; also see ibid., p. 234, 1355.iii.6; *CPR 1358–61*, p. 294, 1360.v.16; and *Medieval Archives*, I, doc. nn. 98–9, 101–2, 107–9, pp. 149–52, 157–60, 168–72.

[88] *CPR 1321–4*, pp. 151–3 and 169–71, 1322.v.18.

[89] Ibid., pp. 177–8, 1322.v.18. Also, Roach, 'The University of Cambridge', p. 152; and Cobban, *The Medieval English Universities*, pp. 264 and 319 (based on Cooper, *Annals of Cambridge*, I, pp. 79–80). In addition to townsmen, the mayor and the town's four bailiffs were charged.

[90] *CPR 1381–5*, p. 271, 1381.viii.10.

broke open the common chest and other cabinets to rip up or carry off various charters. Before the assault, the burgesses proclaimed that they would come to the college 'to destroy and spoil it' and threatened to kill the masters, scholars, and their servants.[91] Was the burgesses' rage against that college provoked only because Gaunt was its patron?[92] Other documents suggest that the town's objectives were broader and revolved around questions of rights and privileges. They burnt the university chest and archives of St Mary's Church, attacked the house of a university bedel,[93] and broke into the university treasury, burning their royal charters, papal bulls, and other muniments. They forced the chancellor and scholars to deliver sealed letters to the mayor and burgesses that bounded the university by large sums of money not to take criminal or civil action against the rebels for any reason. At the November session of Parliament in 1381, the townsmen still possessed these written bonds against the university and only by 11 December were they ordered to release them.[94]

As with other forms of revolt or riot in English towns, those involving students and the university predominated in the thirteenth and early fourteenth centuries. Of twenty-six student disturbances, or ones by burgesses against the university, found in our sample of chroniclers, a third (seventeen) occurred before 1300 and only two flared in the fifteenth century. Again, neither the Black Death nor the Peasants' Revolt sparked a new wave of disputes, a new zeal by burgesses to assert their liberties against university privileges. More astonishing (and yet to be observed by English historians) was Cambridge's weak presence in these disturbances, where only four (possibly five) of the twenty-six riots and insurrections recorded by chroniclers occurred.

Entries in the Patent Rolls suggest a chronological pattern that is slightly at variance with the chronicles'. Although the heyday of student unrest preceded the Peasants' Revolt, the Black Death seems to have set off more large-scale collective violence than at any other time. Of twenty-nine cases of student conflict (not including repeat cases, or

[91] Ibid., 1382.v.24.
[92] According to Cobban, *The Medieval English Universities*, p. 265, it was because Corpus Christi was the third largest landowner in the town; he fails to mention that Gaunt was its patron.
[93] Ibid., p. 265. *PROME*, Richard II, iii, 108, item 54.
[94] Ibid., Richard II, iii, 106, item 45. Also, Cooper, *Annals of Cambridge*, I, p. 121. From Cooper's search through college and other archival sources, few riots appear that were not recorded in chronicles or *CPR*. The most important was a brawl between northern and southern scholars in 1261, in which townsmen joined, and students, along with Oxford exiles, left to found a new university; sixteen townsmen were executed; Cooper, *Annals of Cambridge*, p. 48.

various pardons to rebels referring to single incidents), seven occurred in the thirteenth century, seven in the fourteenth before the Black Death, nine before the Peasants' Revolt, and one during it. Afterwards, however, they decline precipitously: only two occurred before the end of the century and three during the first half of the next century. Moreover, two of the post-Peasants' Revolt commissions did not exactly describe revolts or disturbances but were based on Crown suspicions about whether Irish students had entered England as spies, under the guise of being students, to gather state secrets. In both cases (1387 and 1408), moreover, the Crown admitted getting it wrong, having arrested 'trusty' Irish students.[95] Rather than acting as a stimulus for further insurrection between students and burgesses or against university privileges, the Peasants' Revolt had the opposite effect: when the alleged cases of spying are subtracted, a mere three incidents appear in the last seventy years of our analysis. Secondly, although revolts and disturbances by students, or against them and the university at Cambridge, were not as rare in Patent Rolls as in chronicles, such acts, nonetheless, predominated at Oxford, with twenty-four of the twenty-nine cases, or 83 per cent of them, occurring there.[96]

---

[95] *CPR 1405–8*, p. 482, 1408.vii.26. Another commission in 1402 reported that Welshmen 'assemble nightly in divers unlawful congregations for the purpose of rebellion'. They were not, however, specified as students; *CPR 1399–1401*, p. 132, 1402.vii.18.

[96] Other sources, using court records, city and university archives, point to further riots and rebellions, such as a dispute between Cambridge's mayor, John Bilneye, and the university in 1420. It seems to have been, however, a private affair: he refused to convert one of his houses into a student hostel. Scholars attacked the house and threatened his life; the university appealed to the king and Bilneye was excommunicated; see Cobban, *The Medieval English Universities*, p. 272; and Cooper, *Annals of Cambridge*, I, pp. 164–6. G. G. Coulton, *Social Life in Britain from the Conquest to the Reformation* (Cambridge, 1919), p. 66, describes another incident at Cambridge in 1418 involving Bilneye, this time in his role as mayor: 'armed in warlike manner', the scholars laid in wait to kill him and his officers; failing in their plot, they nailed a libellous scroll to his gate to insult him and other citizens. (Also, cited in Scase, '"Strange and Wonderful Bills"', pp. 232–3.) From archival materials, several further cases of riot appear for Cambridge. Two were internal conflicts: a brawl between the university and the Dominicans and Franciscans in 1303 (*Annals of Cambridge*, I, p. 70); and a violent clash between northern and Irish students in November 1267 (*Medieval Archives*, I, doc. n. 19, pp. 26–8). From the Oxford University archives: in May 1287 (ibid., n. 30, pp. 41–2) townsmen were charged with 'various transgressions and injuries' and violating university privileges, and on 21 April 1329 (ibid., n. 71, pp. 113–14), a royal commission (that does not survive in TNA) investigated 'frequent quarrels' in public and private, night and day, between scholars and townsmen, resulting in 'beatings, woundings, mutilations, killings ... and fires [that] disturbed and terrorized the university and the people'. Adding these riots to the ones tallied from the chronicles and *CPR* does not alter significantly the previous patterns: one occurred in Dunstable, thirty-eight in Oxford, and ten in Cambridge (where only 21 per cent of the incidents took place); twenty

On the evidence of the chronicles and the Patent Rolls, conflicts within universities and between universities and townsmen appear to have differed in several ways from town–gown violence in France and Italy during the later Middle Ages. Firstly, they were more common in England, especially at Oxford.[97] Secondly, unlike those on the Continent, which often brought students into conflict with their masters, the English ones do not show any such internal hierarchical cleavages; instead, the two were united in violence.[98] Thirdly, the English sources show few peaceful strikes by students, with threats to leave for other cities or to set up rival universities, as the Bolognese students did in 1321 and in 1325, forcing their Alma Mater to agree to their conditions. Fourthly, abuses of justice and unfair trials by town authorities of individual students, as in Paris in 1230, or in Bologna in 1321,[99] rarely sparked student strikes or violence in England. Finally, the question of university liberties and their privileges over towns, granted in royal charters, was a powerful irritant to burgesses, and fuelled town–gown rivalries, occasionally provoking violence and open warfare in England. This was explicit in only three revolts in England, but implicit in others. On the Continent, I know of no revolts during the Middle Ages staged by burgesses against resident universities to gain new rights over assizes, or other aspects of town governance. With priories, monasteries, colleges of canons, parish priests, bishops, and universities, the Church's secular power in towns, backed by the Crown, was a principal irritant to burgesses and the major source of collective protest in late

---

occurred in the thirteenth century, eight in the fourteenth, before the Black Death, eight between the Black Death and the Peasants' Revolt, another four (including 1381) to the end of the century, and seven from 1401 to 1450.

[97] From our sources, this trend goes against the generalizations of Alan B. Cobban, 'Medieval Student Power', *P&P* 53 (1971): 28–66; and Cobban, *The Medieval English Universities*: 'the scholars of Oxford and Cambridge maintained a more effective level of co-operation with their citizen hosts than was achieved in some of the Continental universities, especially those of a strong cosmopolitan character, where relations with the citizens tended to be excessively turbulent' (p. 274). Furthermore, he sees the history of town–gown conflict in the two English universities as essentially the same.

[98] This may have resulted from the structure of Italian, and to a lesser extent French, universities, in which students had greater power than at universities in England and other northern countries, at least until the fourteenth century; see Cobban, 'Medieval Student Power', pp. 60–1. Cobban, however, argues that because English students tended to be younger, economically more dependent, and less powerful than their southern European counterparts, they were less inclined to violence. Paul F. Grendler, *The Universities of the Italian Renaissance* (Baltimore, 2002), pp. 500–5, repeats his conclusions. Oxford's turbulent town–gown relations fail to square with this picture.

[99] Cohn, *Lust for Liberty*, pp. 5 and 92–3.

medieval English towns. Of course, struggles for political rights and economic privileges were not the only reason for collective violence in urban settings. We now turn to movements of hatred that brought crowds into the streets of late medieval England. Against longstanding assumptions, these were not always, or even principally, the work of the poor or the oppressed.

13   Urban risings of hatred: Jews, foreigners, and heretics

Although persecutions against Jews ended abruptly in England with Edward I's expulsion of them in 1290, our survey shows more violent incidents against Jews in England in the century before than appear in the sources we examined for Italy, France, and Flanders combined. Perhaps German-speaking areas would supply comparable numbers to England's. In France, the persecutions of Jews by the Crown and others were often linked with the English ones: one influenced the other, especially in English possessions such as Gascony, but also in other regions of France during the thirteenth century.[1] In France, as well as in other parts of Europe, however, the English often took the lead, as with the invention of blood libel, ritual crucifixion, the stigmatization of entire Jewish populations as coin-clippers and criminals, and traditions of local, then national, expulsion set in France by the English example of Gascony.[2] As yet, however, no quantitative comparisons have been made. In Italy and Flanders, few examples of riots or massacres against Jews emerge from the chronicles in the thirteenth century, despite this century's reputation in the historiography as being at the pinnacle of a 'persecuting society'.[3] The most prominent incident was

---

[1] For the Anglo-French link of the second half of the thirteenth century, see Mundill, *England's Jewish Solution*, pp. 276–85. Also see Robin R. Mundill, 'Out of the Shadow and into the Light – the Impact and Implications of Recent Scholarship on the Jews of Medieval England 1066–1290', *History Compass* 9 (2011): 572–601; and Anthony Julius, *Trials of the Diaspora: A History of Anti-Semitism in England* (Oxford, 2010), Chapter 3, for an overview of the period.

[2] On the importance of the 1286 expulsion from Gascony as a model influencing Jewish expulsions in Anjou, Saintonge, and Poitou in 1290, see Mundill, *England's Jewish Solution*, p. 283. On the spread of accusations of ritual murder to Blois in 1171, see Colin Richmond, 'Englishness and Medieval Anglo-Jewry', in *The Jewish Heritage in British History*, ed. T. Kushner (London, 1992), pp. 54–5. Jews had been earlier expelled from Britanny in 1239–40, and temporarily in parts of France by Philip Augustus in 1182, and under Louis IX in 1248–9; Steven T. Katz, *The Holocaust in Historical Context, I. The Holocaust and Mass Death before the Modern Age* (New York, 1994), pp. 375–7.

[3] See Friedrick Heer, *The Medieval World: Europe, 1100–1350*, trans. Janet Sondheimer (London, 1962); R. I. Moore, *The Formation of a Persecuting Society: Power and Deviance*

the Shepherds' Crusade in 1251, when Jews and clerics were massacred in various places in France. Other than this wave of religious hatred, little else comes to fore. The later crusades during the early thirteenth century – the Fourth, from 1202–4, and Fifth, from 1213–21 – did not stimulate the levels of anti-Semitic violence experienced during the First, Second, and Third crusades, and even these earlier ones (before our analysis) did not spread to Flanders and Italy as they had down the Rhineland and into German-speaking regions and with the Third, across towns and cities in England.

Other than the Shepherds' Crusade of 1251 (which did not affect Italy), the only anti-Semitic riot found in our earlier survey of chronicles of the thirteenth-century Italy was in a remote mountain village, Nerito, on the slopes of the Gran Sasso, when 'citizens' in 1289 killed Jews in the region, probably an attack against their seigneurial lords of the Benedictine monastery of Santa Maria, who protected the Jews as their vassals.[4] In France, more incidents of anti-Jewish riots arise in the fourteenth century, first with the Second Crusade shepherds in 1320–1, then, more significantly, with the burning of Jews during the Black Death and its immediate aftermath. Demographically, this was the most important anti-Semitic massacre of the Middle Ages, spreading through parts of Spain and eastern and southern France, down the Rhineland, across great swathes of German-speaking Europe, and into the Low Countries. Little, if any, of this violence, however, had its origins in popular movements.[5] Finally, though with much less ferocity and few Jewish deaths, anti-Semitic incidents accompanied popular uprisings and tax revolts against Charles VI in 1380 in Paris and in 1382 in Paris, Rouen, and other cities of northern France.[6]

---

in *Western Europe, 950–1250* (New York, 1987); and Gaven I. Langmuir, 'At the Frontiers of Faith', in *Religious Violence between Christians and Jews: Medieval Roots, Modern Perspectives*, ed. Anna Sapir Abulafia (Basingstoke, 2002), p. 148. Late twelfth-century riots against Jews appear in northern France, with the circulation of myths of the ritual murders of Christian boys for Passover blood; see, for example, R. B. Dobson, *The Jews of Medieval York and the Massacre of March 1190* (York, 1974), p. 19. But England led these anti-Semitic mythologies, and various forms of anti-Jewish persecution were more frequent and violent in England; see Richard C. Stacey, 'Anti-Semitism and the Medieval English State', in *The Medieval State: Essays Presented to James Campbell*, ed. J. R. Maddicott and D. M. Palliser (London, 2000), pp. 163–78; Richmond, 'Englishness'; and Geraldine Heng, 'Jews, Saracens, "Black Men", Tartars: England in a World of Racial Difference', in *A Companion to Medieval English Literature, c. 1350–1500*, ed. Peter Brown (London, 2007), pp. 249–55.

[4] Cohn, *Lust for Liberty*, p. 102.
[5] See Samuel K. Cohn, Jr, 'The Black Death and the Burning of Jews', *P&P* 196 (2007): 3–36.
[6] Among other places, see ibid.

Persecution against Jews in England appears more frequent and vicious than is seen elsewhere, with the possible exception of the Rhineland. Chronicles describe the majority of these incidents and are thus well known to late medieval English history. Two of the most infamous waves of anti-Semitic violence antedate our analysis – the massacre of Jews at Norwich for the reputed ritual of blood libel, the first of its kind since the early first century; and the killing of Jews in 1189–90 at London, Lynn, Bury St Edmunds, Lincoln, Northampton, Stamford, Colchester, Thetford, Ospringe, and especially York, which was sparked by zeal for the Third Crusade.[7] To what extent these were popular movements is unclear: the massacres at York culminated in a bonfire of records of Jewish loans that benefited the propertied classes, and at York and Lincoln in 1190, citizens and country landlords were the perpetrators.[8] William of Newburgh talks of 'strange youth' who came to Lynn and attacked Jews, loaded their ships with plunder, and quickly departed. Their status is not specified, but they appear to have been young knights and others wealthy enough to possess ships and join the crusades. At York, he alleges, those who 'thirsted for' Jewish blood and plunder were 'with great poverty ... oppressed by tax–gathers to satisfy the usurers' (e.g. the Jews). Yet these were hardly peasants or workers; they had had 'their own estates' and 'those who urged them on' (according to Newburgh) were 'persons of higher rank, who owed large sums to those impious usurers'. However, later he claims 'the nobility of the city and the more respectable citizens' cautiously refrained from entering the fray; instead 'the whole class of workmen', 'the young men of the city' and 'a great mob of country people', assisted by military men, 'performed a service to God' by killing the Jews, while at the same time seeking 'their own private advantage'.[9]

Persecution and popular violence against Jews appears to have intensified in England during the thirteenth century. In 1210, the chronicler of Dunstable reported that 'throughout all of England' Jews were despoiled of their landed property, possessions, and credits ('cartis et debitis'). 'All the rich ones were imprisoned and many others killed.' The impetus of this pogrom, however, came from the king, with demands for 66,000 marks from the English Jewish community, 10,000 of which were taken from a single Jew after his teeth, according to Roger of Wendover,

---

[7] Dobson, *The Jews of Medieval York*; and Mundill, *England's Jewish Solution*, p. 17.
[8] Miller and Hatcher, *Medieval England: Towns, Commerce and Crafts, 1086–1348* (London, 1995), p. 388. Also, Richmond, 'Englishness', especially p. 57, argues that the perpetrators were the Crown and English elites.
[9] *The History of William of Newburgh*, pp. 564, 566, and 568.

had been extracted. The chronicles do not specify if any of the subsequent violence to the Jews came from a popular movement.[10] In 1234, Jews of Norwich were imprisoned on charges of circumcising a little Christian boy. Similar accusations were brought again at Norwich in 1239, 1240, and 1245. In 1240, four Jews were tied to the tails of horses, drawn and hanged.[11] On 25 March 1244, 'clerics' of the University of Oxford (probably including students) attacked the town's Jews and broke into their homes, stealing 'an immense quantity of their possessions'. Forty-five of the clerics were imprisoned for their deeds but soon were acquitted at the insistence of Bishop Robert of Lincoln, who argued that their actions had not disturbed the king's peace and thus were not acts of felony.[12]

Because of its wide dissemination in ballades, chronicles, and Geoffrey Chaucer's 'The Prioress's Tale', the next anti-Semitic massacre is the best known of the century (if not of English medieval history) – the supposed kidnapping, flogging, and crucifixion of a beautiful ('elegantissimum forma') 8-year-old boy in Lincoln (1255). His mother went after the Jews and called for the king's intervention. Eighteen of Lincoln's wealthiest Jews were drawn and hanged, and another sixty-eight (ninety-one by other accounts) were brought to the Tower of London, where they were given similar, or more brutal, sentences. One was quartered, his four parts displayed on London's four gates.[13] To preserve the memory of these punishments, the story was ordered to be retold in all churches of the city.[14] According to Richard C. Stacey, the Lincoln incident was a turning-point of English anti-Semitism: for the first time, the Crown threw its full weight behind the new myth of ritual crucifixion.[15] To what extent this prosecution and persecution of Jews depended on mob

---

[10] *Annals of Osney*, pp. 91–2; *Annals of Dunstable*, p. 32; and Paris, *Historia Anglorum*, II, p. 121, dates the capture of Jews throughout England, 'men and women', to 1210 and attributes it to the king's desire to extort money from them. *Annales monasterii de Wintonia*, p. 81, is less informative: 'Judaei totius Angliae multis miseriis affecti sunt'.

[11] Paris, *Historia Anglorum*, II, p. 375. In addition to the charge against Jews in Norwich circumcising a Christian boy in 1239, for which four Norwich Jews were hanged, the same year saw a major destruction and extermination of Jews on 22 June; ibid., III, p. 543, and IV, pp. 30–1; *The Chronicle of Bury St Edmunds*, pp. 10–11; and *Continuatio chronici Florentii Wigorniensis*, II, p. 177. For 1245, see *Calendar of the Plea Rolls of the Exchequer of the Jews Preserved in the Public Record Office*, ed. J. M. Rigg, Hilary Jenkinson, and H. G. Richardson, 4 vols. (London and Edinburgh, 1905–1972), I, p. 111.

[12] *Annals of Thomas Wykes*, p. 91.

[13] According to Stacey, 'Anti-Semitism', p. 174, nineteen were executed and nearly a hundred imprisoned.

[14] See Cotton, *Historia Anglicana*, pp. 132–3; Paris, *Historia majora*, V, pp. 516–19; and Hill, *Medieval Lincoln*, pp. 224–32.

[15] Stacey, 'Anti-Semitism', p. 174.

violence is unclear. A decade later, Jews accused of conspiring to burn down London with Greek fire were captured in Northampton and burnt to death.[16]

The next wave of violence against Jews was more significant, coming from barons and in places probably from the populace as well.[17] Sparked by Simon de Montfort's revolt against Henry III, these opened the gates to various forms of popular violence. The first broke out in London, when a Jew allegedly wounded a Christian with a knife, drawing 'a countless multitude of people' into the streets in pursuit of the Jew, and at nightfall led to the looting of Jewish homes. This time, the governing elites put an end to the violence: many more Jewish homes would have been broken into 'had not the mayor and sheriffs repaired to the spot and driven away those offenders by force of arms'.[18] At least seven chronicles describe a massacre of 9 and 10 April, 'the week before Palm Sunday' in London, 1263(4).[19] The chronicler Arnald Fitz-Thedmar claimed it 'destroyed' Jewry in London: all their property was carted off, their bodies 'stripped naked, despoiled and afterwards murdered by night in sections'. He estimated that 500 were murdered and the few to survive did so thanks to intervention by the Justiciars and mayor. They also saved the Jews' 'Chest of Chirographs', that had been placed in safekeeping at the Tower of London before the slaughter began.[20] The *Annals of Thomas Wykes* provides the longest account, describing in detail the brutality of killings 'without regard for sex or age, murdering women with infants nursing at their breasts', but baronial politics are not mentioned. The motivation by this account was simply greed; the opportunity to profit by pillaging the Jews' wealth.[21]

---

[16] *Eulogium*, p. 120.

[17] For instance, *Continuatio chronici Florentii Wigorniensis*, II, p. 192, says that barons with Londoners plundered and murdered the Jews, but does not specify who the 'Londoners' were.

[18] 'Liber de Antiquis Legibus', p. 54.

[19] *French Chronicle of London*, p. 234; 'Liber de Antiquis Legibus', p. 66; *Annales Cambriae (AD. 444–1288)*, ed. J. Williams ab Ithel (London, 1860), p. 49; *Annales monasterii de Wintonia*, p. 101; *Annals of Osney/Thomas Wykes*, p. 450; *Annals of Thomas Wykes*, pp. 141–3; and *Continuatio chronici Florentii Wigorniensis*, II, p. 192. The *Annales monasterii de Wintonia*, p. 101, dates what probably was this slaughter to 1262 and claims 700 Jews were killed, their synagogue desecrated ('datae dedecori'). Modern historians have settled on the lower estimate of 500; see Mundill, *England's Jewish Solution*, p. 41.

[20] On Jewish chirographs, *archae*, and their protection by the Crown, see H. G. Richardson, *The English Jewry under Angevin Kings* (London, 1960), pp. 16–22; and Robin R. Mundill, *The King's Jews: Money, Massacre and Exodus in Medieval England* (London, 2010).

[21] *Annals of Thomas Wykes*, pp. 141–3. Also see the mandate to the mayor and sheriffs of London to prosecute any molesting 'the Jews or their households', who had taken refuge in the Tower. The king had taken them 'under his special protection' and granted them

Were the perpetrators, the mass of artisans and workers? The chronicle identifies only one of its 'auctores', a John fitzJohn, who with his own hands killed one of the most renowned of London's citizens ('famosissum civitatis') the Jew Kok, son of Abraham.[22]

Moreover, the baronial conflict unleashed further pogroms with anti-Semitic riots in Canterbury, Northampton,[23] Winchester,[24] Worcester, Bury St Edmunds, Lincoln,[25] and Cambridge, lasting as late as August 1266.[26] Earlier, Simon de Montfort had expelled the Jews from his town of Leicester and had annulled all debts owed to them.[27] In many of these places, the remnant of de Montfort's barons orchestrated the atrocities, with the pillaged treasures carted off to 'the Disinherited's' headquarters at Ely. Finally, a continuator of Florence of Worcester reported that Jews at Northampton crucified a boy on 14 September 1279 and 'under this pretext, numerous Jews of London were torn to pieces by dragging and hanged'.[28]

To these incidents – at least seven of them afflicting Jews in sixteen or more towns in less than seventy years – others can be added from the Patent Rolls. The soil for renewed anti-Semitic violence was already fertile on the eve of de Montfort's baronial revolt. At the end of 1259, the Crown was still making appointments of enquiry and mandates to sheriffs to pursue Jewish outlaws charged with the murder of Hugh of Lincoln.[29]

---

safe passage to return to their homes; *CPR 1258–66*, p. 322, 1264.vi.11. In 1266, the king appointed thirty-five Londoners with the special mandate of protecting the city's Jews and prosecuting any who molested them; ibid., p. 577, 1266.-.-.

[22] *Annals of Thomas Wykes*, p. 142.

[23] On 2 June 1264, the king mandated twenty-four Northampton burgesses 'to protect the Jews who lately on account of the disturbance of the realm and especially on account of the battle at Northampton, fled to the castle of Northampton and have not since dared to leave it'. *CPR 1258–66*, pp. 320–1, 1264.vi.2.

[24] Locke, 'Political History', pp. 310–11.

[25] The king appointed twenty-one citizens of Lincoln to ensure the Jews' well-being; *CPR 1258–66*, pp. 421–2, 1265.v.6. A year later, he granted 'their pledges named in the chirographs made between them and their debtors' to two Jews 'and other Jews of the city' for 'losses and grievances at the hands of his enemies in the conflict at Lincoln'; ibid., p. 617, 1266.vii.14.

[26] *Annales Londonienses*, p. 71, dates the slaughter and pillaging as August 1265; Cam, 'Medieval History', p. 5, as August, 1266. Also see the mandate to protect the town's Jews; *CPR 1258–66*, 1266.-.-. For references to the other towns, see Reynolds, *An Introduction*, p. 138.

[27] Maddicott, *Simon de Montfort*. Also, see Fergus Oakes, 'How and Why were the Towns of England Involved in the Barons' War of 1264–67' M.Litt. thesis, University of Glasgow (September 2010).

[28] John of Eversden (?), *Chronicle*, in *The Chronicle of Florence of Worcester, with Two Continuations Comprising Annals of English History from the Departure of the Romans to the Reign of Edward I* trans. Thomas Forester (London, 1854), p. 361.

[29] *CPR 1258–66*, p. 109, 1259.xii.20; *The Great Chronicle of London*, p. 12; Paris, *Chronica majora*, V, pp. 516–19. For an analysis and ramifications of these allegations and blood

In November 1261, burgesses of Derby anticipated trends of the next generation – expulsion from Gascony in 1287, then England's 'Final Solution' of 1290.[30] For a fee ('fine'), the Crown granted the town 'the liberty', to expel its Jews: 'no Jew or Jewess by the king and his heirs or others shall henceforth remain or dwell in the said town'.[31] A month later, Canterbury's 'clerks as well as lay' attacked the houses of the city's Jews at night with axes, set them alight, and beat the Jews as they tried to escape. The presence of clerics suggests that this was not a riot exclusively of the rabble, a conjecture supported by a second charge of the royal enquiry: the bailiffs of Canterbury and others from Kent turned a blind eye to the disturbances and failed to raise the hue and cry or keep the king's peace.[32]

After the sweep of baronial rebellion through numerous towns and cities of England, Henry III appointed burgesses and others in several towns to protect Jews against further violence, restore their property, honour their debts, and ensure them safe passage to their homes from royal castles and other places where they had taken refuge. Yet in 1264, the Jews of Northampton were still held in the town's castle, where they had fled after the battle of Northampton. With Henry's defeat of the barons, Jews were granted safe passage to their homes, along with protection and security, with twenty-four appointed burgesses to guard them.[33] Between 1264 and 1266, the king made similar mandates and appointments to protect Jews, or honour previous loans registered and kept in chests of chirographs that had been stolen or destroyed during the Barons' Revolt in London,[34] Canterbury,[35] Wilton (Wiltshire),[36] Cambridge,[37] Lincoln[38] and Bristol.[39] Clearly, these provisions and guarantees were not inevitably successful: by 1266, the king heard a complaint from Jews of York that 'certain persons' had broken his special protection, jeopardizing 'their bodies and goods, whereby they fear grave peril'. He appointed the mayor of York and sixteen other citizens to protect the city's Jews.[40] From a royal enquiry of 1269 into

---

libel, see Gavin Langmuir, 'The Knight's Tale of Young Hugh of Lincoln', *Speculum*, 47 (1972): 459–82.

[30] Earlier expulsions had been made in England, beginning with Abbot Samson's expulsion of Jews from Bury in 1190, and de Montfort's from Leicester in 1231; see Richmond, 'Englishness', p. 50; Maddicott, *Simon de Montfort*, pp. 14–17; and Mundill, *England's Jewish Solution*, p. 265. Also, Jews of Cambridge were expelled in the mid-1270s; *Continuatio Chronici Florentii Wigorniensis*, II, pp. 215–16; for other local expulsions, see Julius, *Trials of the Diaspora*, p. 139.

[31] *CPR 1258–66*, 1261.v.21, p. 153.   [32] Ibid., p. 229, 1261.xii.28.

[33] Ibid., p. 320, 1264.vi.2.   [34] Ibid., p. 322, 1264.vi.11; and ibid., p. 577, 1266.iv.3.

[35] Ibid., p. 470, 1265.x.25.

[36] Ibid., p. 521, 1265.xii.14. Also, Powicke, *King Henry III and Lord Edward*, II, p. 516.

[37] *CPR 1258–66*, p. 577, 1266.iv.3   [38] Ibid., 617, 1266.vii.18.

[39] *CPR 1266–72*, p. 13, 1266.xii.4.   [40] Ibid., p. 679, 1266.x.8.

the 'depredations and trespasses committed by certain citizens of Winchester and others' against a Jewish couple in the city, it is difficult to estimate the extent of violence against Jews in Winchester that year:[41] did the violence pertain solely to the couple, or was it indicative of general anti-Semitic violence, that couple being the only ones wealthy enough to have a royal commission appointed? In September and December, a mandate and an appointment to enquire by a jury in Southampton concerning the 'depredations and trespasses' against the couple expose the chief culprit as the cathedral prior of Winchester, St Swithun's, who owed the husband £100 and refused to honour it. The jury ruled in favour of the Jewish moneylender as far as the loan was concerned, but acquitted the prior of charges of violent assault.[42]

Other documents provide further examples of anti-Semitism merged with popular revolt and violence. In 1235, when the king passed through Norwich, 'the greater part of the men and women', along with the city's priests and clerks, assembled to accuse his sheriff and bailiffs of false arrests and wrongful seizure of cattle. They also took the opportunity to complain against the Jews: there were simply too many of them, 'to the city's detriment'; they beseeched the king to limit their number. Moreover, the alleged false arrests were in fact connected to the citizens' anti-Semitism: they concerned burning of Jewish homes and further maltreatment and beatings of Jews on two occasions, to which the royal sergeants rang the communal bell and tried to defend the Jews, but instead 'a great crowd of citizens' called on for assistance 'evily beat' the sergeants.[43] In the spring of 1274, seventeen of Southampton, armed 'with swords, axes, bows, arrows' and 'with the assent and consent of all the community of the town' rang the town's common bell, raised the hue and cry, and assaulted a Jewish money-lender, authorized to collect his outstanding debts by the king. They threw him from his horse, stripped him of his tabard and supertunic, robbed him of six marks, wounded him in the arm, and maltreated him, 'to his damage, £200'.[44] Edward I sided with the Jew, seized the town, deprived the burgesses of their liberties for two years, fined them £20, and increased their annual tax farm by forty marks.[45]

An older historiography has maintained that Henry III's heavy tallages on the Jews, combined with the massacres by barons, had reduced

---

[41] *CPR 1266–72*, p. 223, 1269.ix.4.   [42] Ibid., p. 400, 1269.ix.3; and 1269.xii.28.

[43] *Select Cases of Procedure without Writ under Henry III*, ed. H. G. Richardson and G. O. Sayles, Selden Society, 60 (London, 1941), pp. 21–3.

[44] *Calendar of the Plea Rolls of the Exchequer of the Jews*, II, pp. 130–1.

[45] Platt, *Medieval Southampton*, p. 59.

England's Jewish communities to utter ruin.[46] With further inflictions
by the Crown in the reign of Edward I – first with the 'Statutum de
Judaismo' of 1275, which forbade Jews to lend on usury, then the
prosecutions and mass executions of Jews for allegedly clipping coins
in 1278–9[47] – the Jewish community no longer was of financial utility to
the Crown. By the time of their expulsion, they had become a frail,
wrecked community: expulsion was inevitable. More recently, historians
have shown that the Jews had never been as vital to Crown finances
as once supposed; nor had they become so utterly destroyed after
the Barons' revolt. Instead, they responded positively to Edward I's
anti-usury 'experiment' of 1275, redirecting assets from pawning and
banking to successful mercantile activities. Tallies from tallages and their
bonds continued to show a vigorous financial community to the moment
of their expulsion.[48] The Patent Rolls do not supply any new economic
data on Jewish finances, but they do show that Jews could solicit royal
commissions to examine their complaints and could win lawsuits even
against powerful adversaries such as city priories, more so, in fact, than
is seen with peasants, artisans, or even merchants, in their collective
pursuit of liberties through the royal law courts, where almost inevitably,
the king sided with churchmen against even upper-class urban prosecu-
tors and defendants.

In addition, cases such as the Jews' early expulsion from Derby, initiated by burgesses in 1261, and the 1274 massacres in Southampton, lend
support to the view, based on anti-Semitism in Europe, that their persecution came from below: indigenous populations of artisans, workers, and
peasants were envious and embittered by Jewish wealth and usurious
loans, while secular authorities, especially the king, defended the Jews.[49]

The bulk of the English evidence described above (and more so, from
the Continent) challenges these longstanding generalizations of hate
percolating from below. Threats of excommunication by the Bishop of
Hereford afford glimpses of Christian–Jewish relations that point to an
intermingling, even friendship, between Christian commoners and Jews
that alarmed authorities, especially those at the top of the ecclesiastical
hierarchy. On 6 September, 1286, the bishop wrote to the dean of the
cathedral, urging him to take stringent actions against citizens and
others in the city and county who had ignored his earlier warnings

---

[46] For this literature, see Mundill, *England's Jewish Solution*, chapters 6–8.
[47] Walsingham, *Ypodigma Neustriae*, p. 172; *Continuatio chronici Florentii Wigorniensis*, II,
pp. 221; and other chronicles report it. On the mythology and prosecutions of coin
clipping, see Stacey, 'Anti-Semitism', p. 175: 600 Jews were imprisoned; 269 hanged.
[48] Mundill, *England's Jewish Solution*, especially chapters 6 and 8.
[49] On this general theme in medieval Jewish history, see Cohn, 'The Black Death'.

against befriending and entertaining Jews in their homes, 'eating, drinking, playing, joking, and even acting in plays together (seu quod-cumque ystrionatus officium exercendo)': such acts 'brought shame on Christianity'.[50] Two months later, the bishop circulated through his parishes a bull of Pope Honorius IV, issued on 18 November, that instructed the Archbishop of Canterbury 'to check the familiar inter-course between Christians and Jews, which has encouraged the perverse infidelity of the latter, occasioning grave scandals to the faithful'. The bull described further 'indecorous' exchanges between Christians and Jews: Jews hired Christian servants on Sundays and feast days, admitted other Christians into their homes and brought up ('educandos') Christian children and infants, where they 'cohabitated' with Jewish families. It pointed particularly to shameless conviviality between Christian and Jewish women, their eating and drinking together, with frequent visits to one another's homes. On the eve of the Jews' expulsion, this bull was circulated throughout England, suggesting that Hereford's interfaith tolerance and friendship may not have been exceptional. The Church hierarchy at its highest levels, starting with the pope, had led the charge against Jews.[51] Such trust and conviviality may well have reached further back in English–Jewish history. Even stories such as the purported blood-libel and crucifixion of Hugh of Lincoln show elements of integration. By Matthew Paris' account, Hugh had been playing with Jewish boys his own age; without suspicion or abrogation, he visited one of these boys' homes.[52] Before the alleged murder, neither Hugh's mother nor the Christian community found their play or friendship in

---

[50] *Registrum Ricardi de Swinfield, episcopi Herefordensis, 1283–17*, ed. W. W. Capes, Canterbury and York Series, 6 (London, 1909), pp. 121–2. The extent to which such warm relations may have characterized Hereford (much less the whole of England) is difficult to assess. A Jewish wedding in 1286 to which Christians had been invited appears to have provoked the Bishop of Hereford's first warning; see Mundill, *England's Jewish Solution*, pp. 262–3. The Bishop was indignant that 'so many Christian acquaintances of the Jewish couple had accepted their invitation'; R. B. Dobson, 'The Role of Jewish Women in Medieval England', pp. 127–48, in *The Jewish Communities of Medieval England: the Collected Essays of R. B. Dobson*, ed. Helen Birkett (York, 2010), pp. 135–6, supplies further evidence of trust between Jewish and Christian families during the last three decades of Jews in medieval England, evinced, for instance, by Jews under threat leaving their valuables on deposit with Christian friends.
[51] Ibid., pp. 139–40, 1286.xi.19. Also see Mundill, *England's Jewish Solution*, p. 272; for a transcription of the papal bull, a short commentary and bibliography on it, see Shlomo Simonsohn, *The Apostolic See and the Jews. Documents: 492–1404*. Pontifical Institute of Mediaeval Studies (Toronto, 1988), document n. 255, pp. 262–64. Also, Solomon Grayzel, *The Church and the Jews in the XIIIth Century*, vol. 2, 1254–1314, ed. K. R. Stow (New York, 1989), pp. 157–62.
[52] Paris, *Historia majora*, V, pp. 516–19.

any way unusual or offensive. It took, after all, three days after the boy had been seen playing with his Jewish friends and had gone missing before either the mother or others bothered to raise an alarm.[53]

Hatred of foreigners

Jews were not the only outsiders to be persecuted by elites, popular movements, or the clergy in late medieval England. In 1231 and 1232, an organized group of conspirators wrote threatening letters to English bishops demanding that foreigners possessing English benefices be driven from the country; the unnamed writers claimed to have had the support of noblemen and commoners alike. By December 1231, their movement turned to action. First, armed masked men attacked a group of foreign clergy as they left a Church council at St Albans. In the following year, the attacks became more widespread. The perpetrators confiscated, stole, destroyed, or distributed to the poor the goods, grain, and livestock of foreign clergymen, mostly Italians, pillaging one foreigner's estate for two weeks until it became worthless. They attacked even well-protected papal messengers, killing one, badly beating another, and ripping to pieces and trampling in the mud their papal bulls. The movement, whose members were never revealed, were probably mainly lower clergymen; however, it touched the upper echelons of civil and clerical society. The Bishop of London and Hubert of Burgh, royal justiciar, were accused and sent to Rome for papal pardon, and the nobleman Sir Robert Twenge, called William Wither, was a principal leader. Furthermore, Henry III was ambivalent in bringing charges against the perpetrators. His leniency may have resulted from the general popular anger against papal interference since John's submission to the pope in 1213 and the mounting numbers of Italian clergy, who had been granted English benefices by the papal curia. According to the chroniclers, who passionately opposed the foreign prelates, these foreigners siphoned off native resources while failing to preach and render their

---

[53] On a general European-wide perspective that elites within Church and state were the prime movers of anti-Semitism in the Middle Ages to the mid-thirteenth, see Moore, *The Formation of a Persecuting Society*; for the period following the Black Death, see Cohn, 'The Black Death'. For further stories of Christian and Jewish children peacefully playing together without suspicion and condemnation before horrors ensued, see Miri Rubin, *Gentile Tales: The Narrative Assault on Late Medieval Jews* (New Haven, 1999), especially pp. 7–39. For a 'kindlier world' of close relations between Christians and Jews in England at the end of the twelfth century, see Richardson, *The English Jewry under Angevin Kings*, pp. 46–9, but he argues that the atmosphere changed in the thirteenth.

customary clerical services to English parish communities.[54] Despite these protests and conspiracies, papal interference and imposition of Italian prelates, priors, and abbots on English ecclesiastical institutions continued through the later Middle Ages and beyond.[55]

The Barons' Revolt of the 1260s not only ignited rioting against Jews; Simon de Montfort presented Henry III with political demands 'which exploited popular antipathy towards aliens, particularly the hated Cahorsins'.[56] London's mayors and justiciars had anticipated that violence would afflict foreign merchants of the city: the money belonging to 'the men of Italy and Quercy' that had been deposited in priories and abbeys for safe custody was carried off to London.[57] In this atmosphere of suspicion and hatred of the outsider, London's citizens, keeping watch and ward, rode nightly throughout the city, hunting aliens.[58] In February 1260, a gang of youths chased Italian clerics and murdered them in broad daylight.[59] According to Gwyn Williams, these years were marred by further 'irrational outbreaks of passion and xenophobia'.[60] At Oxford, according to the continuator of Matthew Paris, the barons swore to cleanse the kingdom of foreigners to restore the good laws.[61]

This undercurrent of alien hatred did not end with Henry's restoration of power in the late 1260s. The early decades of the fourteenth century saw Londoners in 'running guerrilla' warfare against foreigners, particularly against Gascons, to the extent that it became a constant theme in London politics.[62] In the summer of 1301, a riot broke out between English servants and those of the Florentine companies of the

---

[54] For this movement see Hugh MacKenzie, 'The Anti-Foreign Movement in England, 1231–2', in *Anniversary Essays in Medieval History by Students of Charles Homer Haskins*, ed. C. H. Taylor and J. L. La Monte (Boston, 1929), pp. 183–203, who relies on the chroniclers Roger of Wendover; Matthew of Westminster, *Flores historiarum*; and the *Chronicle of Dunstable*. In 1245–6, another organized attempt to rid the country of foreign clerics arose that spilled into violence, resulting in a papal nuncio being chased from the country. In addition to these acts of violence against foreign prelates, chroniclers often expressed anger against them, papal taxes, and papal threats to native Church liberties. They were incensed by royal favouritism to alien merchants and craftsmen, as expressed by the *Osney Chronicler* in the 1260s; see Gransden, *Historical Writing*, I. p. 426, and 431.

[55] See, for instance, protests by Commons in January 1348 against papal interference with free elections of the Church and imposition of 'aliens and unsuitable people' on abbeys and priories 'to the destruction and ruin of the religious of England'; *PROME*, Edward III, membrane no. 4, item 50. A later item in this session, recalling an earlier objection of Parliament in 1344, went further: 'no alien should have a benefice in the realm of England by the provision of the court of Rome'; ibid., no. 5, item 63.

[56] Nightingale, *A Medieval Mercantile Community*, p. 78.

[57] '*Liber de Antiquis Legibus*', p. 66.   [58] Ibid., p. 58.

[59] Williams, *Medieval London*, p. 224.   [60] Ibid., pp. 214–15.

[61] Valente, *The Theory and Practice of Revolt*, p. 85.   [62] Ibid. pp. 264–5 and 269.

Frescobaldi and Spini.[63] During the next baronial *coup d'état* led by the queen and her lover in 1326–7, journeymen rose up not only against their masters but also sought out aliens and brought the leader of London's Gascon community to a 'No-Man's Land', where they beheaded him.[64] With the loss of its franchise over monopolies of trade (1351), competition with foreign merchants intensified in London, and with it assaults on Lombards, particularly by those of the mercers' guild. Through the 1370s, the mayor and aldermen treated foreign merchants with prejudice, refusing or delaying justice to them, and revived enquiries against usurers.[65] In 1355, the king ordered a proclamation in London forbidding further molestation of Flemish artisans. Four years later, the proclamation had to be repeated twice.[66] 'With force and arms' in 1359, London mercers attacked the Lombards dwelling in the Old Jewry.[67] In 1379, the Genoese merchant Janus Imperial was assassinated, an act arranged by London merchants in resentment over new royal ordinances that threatened their monopolies, giving Southampton an opportunity to become England's principal port for Italian commerce.[68] The jury absolved a young grocer, John Algor, who confessed to having been inspired to kill the Genoese by talk of London's impending ruin, heard at the homes of wool merchants and from servants of some of London's wealthiest merchants, such as Nicholas Brembre, William Walworth, Richard of Preston, and John Philipot.[69] As Paul Strohm has argued, the threat of foreign exporters of wool united the merchant class across divisions soon to spark London's longest lasting factional rivalry, that between Brembre and Northampton. The trial scripts show that more than threats to London's wool trade was at stake. The cover-up and exoneration of many others involved in the assassination rested on hatred of foreigners and xenophobia.[70]

[63] *CEMCR*, pp. 115–17.   [64] Ibid., p. 296.

[65] Nightingale, 'Capitalists, Crafts', p. 11–13.

[66] Martha Carlin, *Medieval Southwark* (London, 1996), pp. 157–8.   [67] *ML*, pp. 302–3.

[68] Nightingale, *A Medieval Mercantile Community*, pp. 259–61; Platt, *Medieval Southampton*, p. 91; Walsingham, *Ypodigma Neustriae*, p. 330; Walsingham, *Historia Anglicana*, I, pp. 407–8 and 449; and *King's Bench*, VII, pp. 40–1. In 1380, John de Kyrkeby was dragged and hanged for the killing. 'Continuation of the English translation', p. 451, refers to a slaying by Londoners of a Genoese wine and spice merchant around that time (the entry is not dated): by this chronicler's account, Londoners murdered this Genoese merchant for undercutting their prices. French employment of Genoese crossbowmen during the Hundred Years War may have also fanned prejudice against the Genoese.

[69] Nightingale, 'Capitalists, Crafts', p. 24; Benjamin Z. Kedar, *Merchants in Crisis: Genoese and Venetian Men of Affairs and the Fourteenth-Century Depression* (New Haven, 1976), pp. 31–7; and *King's Bench*, VII, pp. 40–1.

[70] Paul Strohm, 'Trade, Treason, and the Murder of Janus Imperial', *JBS*, 35 (1996): 16, 19–21.

Soon afterwards, according to the chronicle of Otterbourne and Whethamstede, the anger led to a London crowd killing any they could find from Genoese galleys.[71] And another possible foreigner, Richard Lyons, who had advanced loans to King Richard in 1379, was beheaded by London rebels along with the Flemings in 1381.[72]

Fights between residents of English ports and foreign merchants and sailors who landed there may have been endemic. On occasion, they burst into significant diplomatic rows, as in 1324, when five Venetian galleys docked at Southampton. A battle ensued between the Venetian merchants and sailors on the one hand, and the men of Southampton and the Isle of Wight on the other, leaving several dead. As a consequence, the Venetians demanded special pardons and guarantees that they would not be tried or imprisoned for these deeds in Parliament and from the king on 2 February.[73] In part, this anti-alien sentiment and violence could be seen as attacks against the king, and resentment against the special privileges he had granted foreign trading communities, in order to tap sums for the crown quickly.[74] As we have seen, against city interests and solidarity, foreign bankers might break ranks with indigenous citizens to rescue Crown finances, as in 1392. The Lombard who answered Richard II's call paid dearly for his generosity.[75]

In February 1425, serious anti-alien outbursts erupted in London and anonymous bills hostile to Flemish residents circulated through the city, alarming the chancellor, Bishop Beaufort, to protect the foreign community with armed force, which in turn contributed to the city's growing hostility to him.[76] In the same year, following claims of unjust foreign profiteering, Parliament passed a law requiring aliens to be hosted with Englishmen while trading within the realm.[77] In 1427, Londoners attacked its Lombard community again, but this time their violence appears limited to property, not bodies. They accused Lombards

---

[71] Otterbourne and Whethamstede, *Ab origine*, p. 153. Also, Walsingham, *Historia Anglicana*, I, pp. 407–8; and Walsingham, *Ypodigma Neustriae*, p. 330.

[72] Bird, *The Turbulent London*, pp. 28–9. Given Lyons' past as part of the 'court covin' during the 1370s, guilty of corruption and embezzlement of royal funds, there were certainly various motives for his murder. On Lyons' activities in the 1370s and condemnation by the Good Parliament, see Fryde, 'Introduction to New Edition' in Oman, *The Great Revolt of 1381*, p. xxvii; and Ormrod, *Edward III*, pp. 496 and 543.

[73] *Foedera*, IV, p. 39.

[74] For instance, at the end of the thirteenth century, royal generosity towards the old aldermanic elites of London dried up; the greater posts passed to Gascons and Italians; see Williams, *Medieval London*, p. 251.

[75] See p. 92, above.

[76] Griffiths, *The Reign of King Henry VI*, p. 74. Also described in *Gregory's Chronicle*, cited in Gransden, *Historical Writing*, II, p. 238.

[77] Ibid.

of adulterating the sweet wines they sold to inns, to poison Londoners. With the mayor at their head, Londoners dragged casks of wine from the Lombard taverns and broke them to bits, 'the unwholesome liquor, like torrents of rain-water, ran down through the midst of the City'.[78] Finally, general anti-alien hostility, and belief that foreigners enjoyed inordinate wealth, led Parliament in 1439–40 to impose an alien head tax of 1s4d for three years, extended to a further two.[79] In 1449, Parliament imposed a new subsidy on all aliens, whether permanently or temporarily resident in England, which 'shifted perceptibly the burden of taxation from the king's subjects to the foreigner'.[80] Even before these special alien taxes, foreign merchants from the mid-fourteenth to the fifteenth century shouldered increasingly heavier tax burdens placed on wool exports. According to John Munro, the wool subsidy imposed on foreign merchants had increased so much that by the 1430s it accounted for 65 to 70 per cent of aliens' pre-finishing production costs, which led to sharp declines in imports of English wool by Flemish and Italian cloth manufacturers during the fifteenth century.[81] As regards financial discrimination and degradation, foreigners were fast becoming the Jews of England. Indeed, already in 1376, Parliamentary commons blamed the downturn in trade and outflow of English bullion on denizen Lombard communities, which they cursed as 'Jews and Saracens and secret spies'.[82]

Such attacks, however, did not fall exclusively on merchant elites. The most infamous and bloodiest attack against foreigners erupted during the Peasants' Revolt in London, Southwark, and Essex when '140 or 160' Flemish textile workers were butchered 'in various places, thirty-five in one batch' in London alone.[83] According to Jean Froissart, under their captains John Ball, Jack Straw, and Wat Tyler, after the siege of the Savoy and the attack on Gaunt's hospital of St Johns, the crowd 'went from street to street and slew all the Flemings that

---

[78] Riley 'Introduction' and *Chronicon . . . Monasterio S. Albani*, I, pp. xxxi and 18–19.
[79] Griffiths, *The Reign of King Henry VI*, pp. 555 and 558.   [80] Ibid., p. 380.
[81] See John H. Munro, 'The Rise, Expansion, and Decline of the Italian Wool-Based Textile Industries, ca. 1100–1730: a Study in International Competition, Transaction Costs, and Comparative Advantage', *Studies in Medieval and Renaissance History*, 3rd series, 9 (forthcoming), p. 28.
[82] Ormrod, *Edward III*, pp. 540–1. Commons in the same session of Parliament cried out against alien clerics, their absentee benefices, and disservice to English parishioners 'to the great impoverishment and destruction of holy Church and of this land'. They were worse 'than all the Jews and Saracens in the world'; *Prome*, Edward III, April, 1376, membrane 338, item 97. Perhaps, it is only a coincidence that during the later Middle Ages, the Lombards resided in the area called 'the Old Jewry'.
[83] Oman, *The Great Revolt*, p. 69; Fryde, *The Great Revolt*, p. 23; and Carlin, *Medieval Southwark*, p. 158. The report comes from *The Anonimalle Chronicle*, which maintained that these workers were concentrated in the Vintry ward by the Thames.

they could find in church or in any other place'.[84] More grizzly still was the report of the Westminster chronicle: the rebels spent the entire day roaming through Cheapside and 'beheaded without judgement or trial all the Flemings they found; so that mounds of corpses were to be seen in the streets and various spots were littered with the headless bodies of the slain'.[85]

Mayoral minutes of London confirm the chroniclers' horrors, reporting 'a very great massacre of Flemings': 'in one heap there were lying about forty headless bodies of persons, who had been dragged forth from the churches and from their homes'.[86] King's Bench indicted still others of massacring Flemings: Robert Gardiner of Holborn, was accused of gathering 'a great crowd of rebels' at Clerkenwell on 13 June, killing seven Flemings, and was pardoned on 2 February 1382.[87] At Manningtree, near Colchester, by order of the leader, John Hardyng, the rebels decapitated a Fleming on 13 June,[88] and on 30 March 1385, Adam Michel of Colchester was pardoned for having been among the rebels who executed Flemings from 1 May to 1 November 1381, the number killed, unspecified.[89] Further rebel executions of Flemings occurred at Yarmouth and at Maldon in Essex,[90] and before entering London, the Kent rebels sacked a brothel of Flemish prostitutes in Southwark.[91] Other rebels attacked Flemings outside the city, as had John de Spayne of Lynn, 'a chief captain in the great insurrection', pardoned in 1382 for murdering, with others, a Fleming during the revolt.[92] In Lynn's rising on 17 June 1381, artisans went after 'traitors': their first victim was a Fleming, and the next day they incited villagers of Snettisham to join them to search for, and kill, Flemings.[93] Len Scales argues that these aspects of the English Peasants' Revolt, embarrassing to historians today, were the most memorable ones for contemporaries

---

[84] Dobson, *The Peasants' Revolt*, p. 188.
[85] *The Westminster Chronicle*, pp. 6–9. As compensation, friends of the murdered Flemings (according to the chronicle) were given permission to execute the murderers, and 'the wives of victims were given the authority to behead their husbands' murderers' (pp. 16–17).
[86] Dobson, *The Peasants' Revolt*, p. 210.
[87] See *The Anonimalle*'s description of their crossing; Dobson, *The Peasants' Revolt*, p. 156. [87] Réville, *Le soulèvement*, p. 203; ibid., pp. 96–7, 125, 162, 217–18.
[88] Ibid., p. 216. For the murder of the Flemish weaver at Manningtree, see Dyer, 'The Causes of the Revolt', p. 28.
[89] Réville, *Le soulèvement*, pp. 217–18.   [90] Prescott, 'Judicial Records', pp. 117–18.
[91] Carlin, *Medieval Southwark*, p. 158; also *Anonimalle Chronicle* (Dobson, *The Peasants' Revolt*, p. 162).
[92] *CPR 1381–5*, p. 272, 1382.v.21. On John de Spayne's case before King's Bench in 1383, see Prescott, 'Judicial Records', p. 358.
[93] Réville, *Le soulèvement*, pp. 96–7, 125, 162, 217–18.

such as Geoffrey Chaucer, whose only reference to the revolt was Jack Straw's supposed rallying to kill Flemings.[94] But were such ethnic slaughters of artisans by artisans typical of late medieval rebellion across Europe, as Scales goes on to suggest?

Flemings were also killed during different phases of the Florentine Tumulto dei Ciompi, but unlike the English Peasants' Revolt, there were only five such incidents. These, moreover, were wholly different and can hardly be seen as murders by the mob. Instead, the new governments, first of the Medici reformers in June 1378, then, later that summer, the new revolutionary government of Ciompi, tried the Flemings by due process, found them guilty, and executed them: four for robbery; one for murder. In addition, I know of no other late medieval revolts, when foreign artisans (as opposed to foreign soldiers or clerics) became key targets for large numbers of murders, as happened in London and other English towns and villages in 1381.[95] Despite rebel cries to 'kill all the lawyers', and resentment against landlords and the king's advisers as the authors of excessive taxation and English losses in France, Flemish artisans bore the brunt of English rebel violence with their lives; no other group – lawyers, landlords, or royal officers – comes close to their 1381 death tolls.[96]

Nor did hatred of foreigners by those beneath city elites, especially in London, end with the Peasants' Revolt: they continued through the first half of the fifteenth century and beyond the chronological confines of this study. Ralph Flenley has maintained that the first half of the fifteenth century 'saw a steady increase' in feelings against aliens in England

---

[94] Len Scales, 'Bread, Cheese and Genocide: Imaging the Destruction of Peoples in Medieval Western Europe', *History* 92 (2007): 284–300, p. 285.

[95] Jan Dumolyn concurs: he knows of no examples of Fleming artisans attacking fellow artisans because they were foreigners, or even attacks against foreign merchants resident in the Low Countries, such as Italian bankers, who were so often the targets of hate and violence, individual and collective, in London. For the multicultural and multilingual world of the late medieval Low Countries and its tendencies for inclusion and exclusion, see Marc Boone, 'Langue, pouvoirs et dialogue. Aspects linguistiques de la communication entre les ducs de Bourgogne et leurs sujets flamands (1385–1505)', *Revue du Nord* 91 (2009): 9–33.

[96] In spite of rebels' cries against lawyers and questmongers and attacks on the apprentices' law chambers at the Temple, where they burnt charters and destroyed houses of jurors and questmongers, none reports the seizure or killing of any lawyers in these two major attacks on the legal profession. The number of lawyers killed appears limited, despite the torment and beheading of a few prominent ones, such as John Cavendish, Chief Justice of the king's Bench, and the 'questmonger' Roger Leget or Legat; see Saul, *Richard II*, pp. 64–5; and Prescott, 'London in the Peasants' Revolt', pp. 133–4, for Legat and his friend, the lawyer John Doget of Butterwick, also a sheriff of Middlesex; Harding, 'The Revolt against the Justices', pp. 172 and 179.

(although he provides no quantitative evidence for it).[97] According to Ralph Griffiths, anti-alien feeling swept across parts of England after the Treaty of Arras (1435) with the alliance between the French and Charles the Bold, Duke of Burgundy, and reached its climax with the loss of Normandy in 1449–50.[98] In 1436, 573 aliens (mostly Flemings) of London, Southwark, and suburban parishes of Middlesex, sought protection, presumably from artisan mobs.[99] Hatred was not then limited to the Flemings; according to Griffiths, deadly prejudice against Italians, especially the Genoese, was rife in London.[100] In 1450, riots against aliens spread to Southampton, when men from Romsey invaded the town 'riotously' threatening the Lombards.[101] As with the Peasants' Revolt, Cade's fanned anti-alien sentiment, even if it did not result in the same Flemish slaughter as sixty-nine years earlier. Before marching into London, Cade sent a letter demanding that Lombards and other aliens supply the rebels with weapons, horses, and one thousand marks. If they failed to do so, he threatened to kill them ('the heads of as many as we can get of them'). According to Flenley, this bullying increased Cade's popularity within the capital.[102] Riots against Flemings, and especially London's Italian merchant community, flared again in 1456 and 1457, with houses burnt and looted, resulting in the mass evacuation of the Italian merchant community to Winchester.[103] Beyond our period, an artisan conspiracy of Londoners threatened to cross the Thames to Southwark in 1468, to cut off the thumbs and hands of Flemish craftsmen, so that they should never again practise their trades again. The following year, Charles the Bold, concerned with the fate of Flemish workers in London, sent letters to London's mayor and people, urging them to keep the peace; if they turned against their resident Flemings, he would seek revenge.[104]

Finally, similar suspicion and hatred could be cast against 'foreigners' from other places under Crown control within the British Isles. With the influx of Irish refugees in 1381–2, the Crown ordered them expelled

---

[97] Ralph Flenley, 'London and Foreign Merchants in the Reign of Henry VI', *EHR*, 25 (1910): 644–55.
[98] Griffiths, *The Reign of King Henry VI*, pp. 167–71.
[99] Bolton, 'Introduction', pp. 3 and 30.
[100] Griffiths, *The Reign of King Henry VI*, p. 554.
[101] Platt, *Medieval Southampton*, p. 137.
[102] Flenley, 'London and Foreign Merchants', p. 647.
[103] Ibid., pp. 650–3. On these riots, corrections to Flenley's earlier narrative, the participants from servants of London mercers to the probable involvement of the city's wealthiest merchants, and the reasons for attacks on Italian merchants, see Bolton, 'The City and the Crown'.
[104] Bolton, 'Introduction', pp. 3 and 39.

from Wales and England if they did not buy licences to remain.[105] Sentiments against both the Welsh and Irish ran high at Oxford and Cambridge, where students were accused of spying during tense moments of Richard II's reign, in 1388, and in Henry IV's, in 1408. We have also seen the bitter rivalries between students of the three British 'nations' at these universities and that even child's play with war games could get out of hand, when the vying make-believe troops were posed as Scots and English. Further, suspicions, accusations, and violence arose between resident populations and Scottish, Irish, and Welsh students at Oxford and Cambridge in 1429. Firstly, at Cambridge, the Irish were accused of burning down schools and extorting funds from locals by new methods of intimidation – the sending of threatening letters. These resulted in petitions to Parliament banning all Irish, Scottish, and Welsh students from Oxford, Cambridge, or elsewhere in England, who could not maintain themselves with lands and tenements or benefice of Holy Church. Further, Irish scholars were required to give surety for their good behaviour and had to present letters to the chancellors at Oxford and Cambridge. At Oxford, their malice led them to be labelled 'Wylde Irisshmen'.[106] The Welsh and Scots, although not charged with the extortions, nonetheless were tarred by the same brush.[107] Prejudice against the Welsh in English towns intensified during the decade of Owain Glyn Dŵr's revolt, particularly in the border town of Chester. The Crown issued draconian measures that went beyond questions of military security: all Welshmen and women, as well as any of Welsh extraction or with sympathies towards the Welsh, were ordered to leave the city by nightfall; those who remained were threatened with execution.[108] And in 1422 and 1430, Parliamentary decrees ordered Irish residents of Chester to return to their homeland.[109]

---

[105] Peter Fleming and Kieran Costello, 'Identity and Belonging: Irish and Welsh in Fifteenth-Century Bristol', in *The Fifteenth Century VII: Conflicts, Consequences and the Crown in the Late Middle Ages*, ed. Linda Clark (Woodbridge, 2007), p. 178.

[106] Riley, 'Introduction', pp. xlv–xlvi and *Chronicon . . . Monasterio S. Albani*, p. 46. Earlier, in 1422, Irish disorderliness led to their mass expulsion and stringent controls on those without a profession; see Griffiths, *The Reign of King Henry VI*, p. 168.

[107] For further discriminatory laws against those of Irish, Welsh, Italian, Dutch, and German origin, from Owain Glyn Dŵr's revolt to the 1430s, expulsion of the Irish, laws against the Welsh purchasing property in Welsh boroughs and in England, and special poll taxes levied on aliens in the 1430s and 1440s, see Griffiths, *The Reign of King Henry VI*, pp. 167–71.

[108] Jane Laughton, 'The Control of Discord in Fifteenth-Century Chester', in *Survival and Discord in Medieval Society: Essays in Honour of Christopher Dyer*, ed. Richard Goddard, John Langdon, and Miriam Müller (Turnhout, 2010), pp. 225–6.

[109] Laughton, *Life in a Late Medieval City*, p. 105.

Antipathy towards the Irish and Welsh was not, however, everywhere the same. Unlike in Chester, neither Owain Glyn Dŵr's rebellion, nor the influx of Welsh people into Bristol, precipitated prejudicial laws or violence against them. They appear to have integrated well with the artisan population; some even served as aldermen. Perhaps, the assistance given by the Welsh militia to Bristol's citizens a century earlier during their revolt against the Crown had been remembered. Bristol's late fourteenth- and fifteenth-century experience of Irish residents was, however, different. They were considered 'aliens', forced to pay the new 1440 subsidy on 'aliens', even though, like the Welsh, they were born within 'the king's allegiance'. When the Crown, in 1455, finally clarified that Irishmen were not legally aliens, the mayor and commons of Bristol sought to pass laws to redefine them as such.[110]

To be sure, foreigners incited a wide range of popular revolt on the Continent during the late Middle Ages, including the rage against the French during the Sicilian Vespers of 1282, the Revolt of Flanders from 1297 to 1304, and in particular, the Brugse Metten of 1302, when artisans sliced up French soldiers into 'pieces like little tunny fish', the assault against the Breton mercenaries butchered at Cesena in 1377, and more.[111] None of these Continental revolts, however, erupted from economic resentment against foreign competition or the struggle over labour against equals, or especially against those socially beneath them; instead, the oppression, arrogance, and humiliation of foreign territorial occupation accompanied by robbery, acts of violence and abuse of a resident population's wives, daughters, and servants sparked these revolts. By contrast, at least after the Norman Conquest, no English town suffered such humiliation at the hands of foreign mercenaries, and no such revolts resulted. Here again, the late medieval English experience differed from the Continent's.

Heresy and Lollardy

Conflict between burgesses and the Church – whether the monastery, hospital, bishop, or university – predominated in England to a far greater extent than on the Continent, especially relative to social conflict with

---

[110] Fleming, 'Identity and Belonging', pp. 178–84. John A. F. Thomson, 'Scots in England in the Fifteenth Century', *The Scottish Historical Review*, 79 (2000): 3–4, 12, 16, also argues that active hostility towards Scots differed regionally in England: they were treated with less suspicion in smaller communities than in larger ones and generally better in cities in the south than the north, until their arrival in larger numbers at court, following the union of the Crown.

[111] See Cohn, *Lust for Liberty*, pp. 103–5.

secular lords and magnates within towns and cities, or between different social tiers or groups within urban society.[112] When chroniclers or commission reports, mandates, and pardons expressed the motives for violence between burgesses and the Church, they concerned political and economic rights, not doctrine. In contrast to the Continent, none of these conflicts was laced with accusations of heresy, as with those struggles for political hegemony in the Marche and Umbria in the 1320s, or throughout much of northern Italy from the mid-1370s to 1378, when both sides questioned the orthodoxy of the other. Despite numerous struggles between burgesses and ecclesiastical institutions in towns, the English sources show nothing similar to the social, political, and religious movements of the thirteenth and early fourteenth centuries on the Continent. These included the Albigensians; Fra Dolcino's radical communities in the hills of Novara in 1305–7; similar movements in towns of Provence; the Poveri Lombardi; Waldensians; the 'Great Alleluia' movement across wide swathes of northern and central Italy from 1319 to 1322; radical Ghibellines in Umbria and the Marche from 1319 to 1322; and flagellant and peace movements, some local, others regional, one of which stretched across the Alps and another of which swept Continental Europe.

Before Wycliffe, collective accusations of heresy in England were rare.[113] Even cases of individual heretics are difficult to spot in chronicles before the Peasants' Revolt,[114] although the English chronicles give notice of the large heretical movements then spreading across

---

[112] For a concise analysis of what Lollardy meant in the fifteenth century, its various ideas, and intersections with earlier popular beliefs such as millenarianism, witchcraft, and magic, its anti-clerical, anti-authoritarian, and, on occasion, anti-sacramentalism combined with scriptural fundamentalism and common-sense rationalism, its attack on transubstantiation and images, see Thomson, *The Later Lollards*, pp. 239–50; for a more detailed account of their beliefs and practices, see Anne Hudson, *The Premature Reformation: Wycliffite Texts and Lollard History* (Oxford, 1988).

[113] According to Aston, 'Lollardy and Sedition': 'Before 1381, though the English governing classes had encountered heretics as well as rebels against society, they had never had to deal with either on a large or concerted scale' (p. 1). Neither she nor others have compared chronological trends of popular rebellion and heretical movements in England with those on the Continent. The only mass persecution of heretics before the Lollards was the expulsion of thirty Populicani from Oxford in 1163; see Moore, *The Formation of a Persecuting Society*, pp. 63, 156–8; according to *The Chronicle of Walter of Guisborough*, pp. 58–9, these 'men and women' were German speakers and their punishment – expulsion – was mild, compared to the mass butchering of Albigensians, Fra Dolcino and his followers, and other heretics at the same time on the Continent.

[114] Paris, *Chronica majora*, IV, pp. 32–4, reports the seizure of a Carthusian at Cambridge accused of heresy for allegedly claiming that the pope was not head of the Church. Paris also reports the much broader prosecution of heretics at Milan, who were burnt at the stake; ibid., III, p. 63.

France and other parts of Europe in the thirteenth and early fourteenth centuries. The continuator of Florence of Worcester, Walsingham, and Matthew Paris all mention the first of the Shepherds' Crusades of 1251; by Paris' account, it had a following in England but failed to take on the violent and heretical tones developed across the Channel; nor did it stir the anti-Semitic pogroms seen in France and Spain. This is all the more surprising given the exceptionally rich top-soil for Jewish hatred in England.[115] The second Children's Crusade of 1320 also had a footing on English shores, but again failed to develop into the violent anti-clerical, heretical movement that ensnared the Continent with mass murder, first and foremost of lepers, then Jews and clergymen. The chronicler Adam Murimuth maintained that as on the Continent, 'many shepherds, women, and others of England gathered ... wishing to acquire the Holy Land and kill the enemies of Christ', but he reports no such incidents arising from this movement in England. Instead, it was in 'parts of the region of Toulouse and Aquitaine' where the killing of Jews and the violence against authorities took place.[116] Similarly, the later flagellant movement during the Black Death arrived in London at the end of September 1349 – with 120 or more from Zeeland, Holland, and Flanders.[117] Again, the Continental mass religious ecstasy, with its overtones of anti-clerical and anti-Semitic consequences, found little appeal for the English.

Not until 1377, with Thomas Walsingham's description of Wycliffe's trial in London, do traces of home-grown English heresy in our sample of chronicles finally come to the fore. But, here, as seen earlier, Wycliffe's ideas were not yet part of any popular movement. In fact, the opposite is true: Lord Percy and Gaunt were Wycliffe's supporters, while 'citizens of London' and commoners rallied behind the orthodoxy of their bishop, Wycliffe's prosecutor.

With rebellion, did Londoners and peasants suddenly turn about-face in 1381? In the years leading up to the insurrections of 1381 had 'Wycliffe and his followers ... extended their preaching throughout the country to the pollution of the people' as Walsingham later alleged?[118] Had Wycliffe's 'Pestilential doctrines' 'provoked the people to rebellion'; had John Ball been his disciple two years before the revolt? Had a 'secret fraternity' travelled 'around the whole of England', preaching Wycliffe's

---

[115] Paris, *Chronica majora*, V, pp. 251–2; Walsingham, *Historia Anglicana*, I, p. 278; *Continuatio chronici Florentii Wigorniensis*, II, p. 183.

[116] Murimuth, *Continuatio Chronicarum*, pp. 31–2. Also, Walsingham, *Historia Anglicana*, I, pp. 157–8.

[117] Avesbury, *De gestis mirabilibus regis Edwardi Tertii*, pp. 407–8.

[118] Walsingham translated in Dobson, *The Peasants' Revolt*, p. 367.

beliefs, as the *Fasciculi Zizaniorum* purported?[119] Historians deny
Wycliffe's influence on the revolutionary preachers of 1381 and that Ball
confessed before his execution to have been Wycliffe's disciple, or to
have preached 'the heresy of the altar'.[120] Margaret Aston has pointed
to the Feast of Corpus Christi as the central day of the Peasants' Revolt
when pincer movements from Essex and Kent converged on Blackheath.
However, she ends by admitting that 'no evidence' implicates any rebels
of being moved by Wycliffe's arguments or of preaching against the
sacramental teachings on the Eucharist. Instead, the association with
Corpus Christi day fed the minds of those who later denounced the
rebels for their rupture of civil unity on the very day in the Christian
calendar that celebrated that unity.[121] Certainly, Wycliffe himself did not
identify with the rebels; like Luther later, he condemned them, and
sympathized with those who suffered at their hands.[122]

The chronicler Henry Knighton appears nearer the mark: Ball
was Wycliffe's precursor and possibly 'prepared the way for Wycliffe's
opinions'.[123] The ideological importance of preachers during the
Peasants' Revolt cannot be dismissed. Notions such as those presented
in the peasants' demands at Smithfield that the religious hierarchy
should be levelled so that there would be only one bishop of England
and beneath him no shades of difference within the ranks of the clergy,
that mendicants should be compelled to return to pristine doctrines of
poverty, that all monks would be disbanded, except for two houses of
religion, and that 'the goods of the Holy Church should not remain in
the hands of the religious, not of parsons and vicars, and other churchmen'[124] would certainly have been judged as heresy on the Continent.[125]

[119] Ibid., pp. 376–8.
[120] Ibid., pp. 376–8, for the account of the *Fasciculi Zizaniorum*; and p. 378 for Dobson's
doubts. Also, Aston, 'Lollardy and Sedition', pp. 4 and 5, which questions this
chronicle's claims of Ball's apprenticeship and connections between Wycliffe's
teaching and the revolt of 1381. However, Hilton, 'Popular Movements', p. 164, has
suggested that even if Ball had not been Wycliffe's disciple, the effect was much the
same. Also see Rodney Hilton, 'Inherent and Derived Ideology in the English Rising of
1381,' in *Campagnes médiévales: l'homme et son espace, études offertes à Robert Fossier*, ed.
Elisabeth Mornet, Histoire ancienne et médiévale, 31 (Paris, 1995), p. 403.
[121] Margaret Aston, 'Corpus Christi' and Corpus Regni: Heresy and the Peasants' Revolt,'
P&P, 143 (1994): 46–7.
[122] Among other places, Aston, 'Lollardy and Sedition', p. 3.
[123] Knighton, translated in Dobson, *The Peasants' Revolt*, p. 376.
[124] '*The Anonimalle Chronicle*' in ibid., pp. 163–4. Also Hilton, *Bondmen Made Free*, p. 228.
[125] For the condemnation of radical Franciscans, spiritualists, and Fraticelli in the late
thirteenth and early fourteenth centuries, see among other places, Malcolm Lambert,
Medieval Heresy: Popular Movements from Bogomil to Hus, 3rd edn (Oxford, 2002),
Chapter 11; and Charles T. Davis, 'Ubertino da Casole and his Conception of
"Altissima Paupertas"', *Studi Medievali*, 3rd series, 22 (1981): 2–56.

Moreover, even if John Ball may loom larger in chronicles (as in Walsingham's damning account) than the role he actually played,[126] he nonetheless had been excommunicated eight or nine times,[127] and was imprisoned on the eve of the revolt, freed just in time to preach and lead the insurgents.[128] As Rodney Hilton has suggested, instead of being influenced by Wycliffe or Lollardy, the militant preachers of the Peasants' Revolt had anticipated the radical ideology of the Lollards.[129]

Furthermore, Parliament, at least by the spring of 1383, saw a relationship between insurgence and troublesome preachers and gave statutory authority to sheriffs with a bishop's approval to arrest and imprison would-be John Balls in the future.[130] Perhaps G. R. Owst was not exaggerating when he concluded that 'the preaching not merely of friars but of other orthodox churchmen of the day was ultimately responsible for the outbreak of the Peasants' Revolt'.[131] Yet in the numerous commissions that run from 5 July 1381 through 1382, with knights and high magnates of the realm such as Hugh la Zouche, Robert Bealknap, William Walworth (mayor of London), Thomas, Earl of Buckingham (the king's uncle), Robert Knolles, Robert Tresilian, and others, appointed 'to keep the peace in the country and put down risings of rebels', not a single one mentions heresy as one of the many crimes charged against them, or in the individual and general pardons that followed.[132] Before 1381, none of the urban revolts described by chronicles or Patent Rolls shows any such ideological and religious sentiment or programmes, even in the most bitter and violent of Church-city struggles. Afterwards, as commissions show, pressure by Church and state against heresy mounted; increasingly the Crown tarred

---

[126] See Andrew Prescott, 'Ball, John (d. 1381)', *ODNB* (2004). Aston, 'Corpus Christi' p. 17–24, positions him as the most prominent clerical leader of the Peasants' Revolt.

[127] Aston, 'Corpus Christi', p. 21.

[128] Walsingham, translated in Dobson, *The Peasants' Revolt*, p. 373–4; according to Knighton, ibid., pp. 135–6, he was freed from the archbishop's prison on 13 May.

[129] Hilton, 'Popular Movements in England', pp. 239–40; and Rodney Hilton, 'Social Concepts in the English Rising of 1381', in *Class Conflict and the Crisis of Feudalism: Essays in Medieval Social History* (London, 1983): 'Wycliffe, then, was not only too late but too traditional in his social teaching to have inspired the rebels of 1381. If the bringing of theory to the movement can be attributed to any one man, that man must be John Ball, though he may have been one of a number of pre-Wycliffe poor preachers' (p. 223).

[130] Aston, 'Lollardy and Sedition', p. 4.

[131] Owst, *Literature and Pulpit*, p. 304; 'Sacred orators of the Church, as hostile to class war, to earthly revenge and social revolution as any Luther, were here themselves unconsciously formulating a revolutionary charter of grievances' (p. 295).

[132] According to J. A. Tuck, 'Nobles, Commons and the Great Revolt of 1381', in *The English Rising*, p. 211, the churchmen saw a connection between the unrest of 1381 and movements against Church authority.

insurgents (legitimately or not) as heretics in long lists of their 'treasons, insurrections, felonies, trespasses', etc.

Henry Knighton seems again nearer the mark than Walsingham: he argues that it was after the Peasants' Revolt that heresy became a reason to suppress political and social movements in England. Evidence of it, in fact, is charted by Walsingham. In 1382, he saw Wycliffe's doctrines motivating some in the entourage of the new populist mayor of Northampton, his supposed 'usurpation of episcopal rights' and use of secular courts instead of the bishop's to punish with especial severity moral and sexual crimes.[133] These supposed followers of Wycliffe, more-over, reproached prelates of London, harassing them for their neglect, greed, 'zealousness for money', and unwillingness to use the full penal-ties of the law on those guilty of fornication, giving 'impunity to live in their sins with their [the clergy's] approval'. As a consequence of these sins, the heretics preached that 'the whole city would suffer ruin when God took vengeance upon them', inflicting plague or war, unless they purged the city of its defilement.[134] Walsingham coupled these with the same popular groups that cheered on Northampton's new legislation against the fishmongers that lowered prices of fish and other victuals in the city.[135] To what extent these early Lollards may have comprised a popular movement is difficult to determine: no evidence from Patent Rolls, at least in the 1380s, supports his views, certainly nothing occurred that was akin to the Hussite's moral crusades in Prague of the next century.[136] However, in 1382, the great magnates of the Crown began to abandon Wycliffe and his doctrines: Gaunt did so in that year; the king followed suit a few years later.

In 1392, Walsingham again turned against Wycliffe's supposed sup-porters in London for their 'arrogance' in defying Richard II's request for £1,000 and for their beating a Lombard almost to death for offering it. Yet Walsingham connected these supporters, whom he now called Lollards, not with artisan rebels, but with the city's noble citizens, known for their arrogance and greed, who 'had little belief in God and the traditions of their ancestors. They slandered monks, refused to pay tithes, and impoverished the common people'.[137] This undergrowth of religious and political sentiment, however, grew not so much with the nobility, or among those who first protected Wycliffe, such as Percy and Gaunt, but among artisans of market towns and the capital, culminating in John Oldcastle's conspiracy against the Crown at the beginning of

---

[133] See p. 252, above.   [134] Walsingham, *The St Albans Chronicle*, I, p. 612–15.
[135] Walsingham, *Historia Anglicana*, II, p. 66.   [136] See Saul, *Richard II*, p. 300.
[137] Walsingham, *Chronica maiora*, pp. 286–7.

Henry V's reign in 1414. Again, Walsingham railed against the heretics. At night, sometime after Christmas, Oldcastle, 'by extravagant promises of the Lollards' and by 'hiring them at his own expense', enticed crowds to flock together at St Giles' fields outside London, their goal 'to destroy first the monastic houses of Westminster, St Albans and St Paul's and all the friars of London', followed by 'the wholesale destruction of king, nobles, prelates, property-owning monks, mendicant friars, and citizens'. The king's troops uncovered the plot; the rebels lost heart; many were arrested, but Oldcastle escaped. Not even the king's offer of a thousand-mark reward could entice any to reveal Oldcastle's hiding place. Walsingham concluded, 'almost the whole country had embraced the Lollard madness'.[138]

During the summer (1414), so-called Lollards rose up again 'vomiting blasphemies against the king, making grand claims, and scattering their threats over written documents that they fastened to the doors of the churches, and in many other places'. Again, their goals combined politics and religious doctrine: they strove to overthrow the king and subvert the 'orthodox faith'. Again, as in revolts of cities against the Crown from the thirteenth century, the rebels waited till the king 'had started on his journey overseas' 'to spat out' their insults, 'urging each other on'. At this moment, according to the St Albans' chronicler, they began to murmur: 'Now that the prince of priests has departed and our enemy has gone away, a favourable time has smiled upon us in which ... to avenge our injuries with impunity'.[139] Finally, the later chronicler John Capgrave reported a third attempt by Oldcastle to topple Henry in 1417, while he was celebrating Christmas at Kenilworth: in every inn of St Albans, Reading, and Northampton, bills of 'gret malice ageyn God and the Kyng' had been cast.[140] In 1431, another Lollard conspiracy was uncovered. Again bills preaching against clerical possessions were scattered, this time in Abingdon, London, Coventry, Oxford, and other towns.[141]

Finally, at midsummer 1440, the priest and vicar in Essex, Richard Wyche (Weyde), was burnt for heresy in front of Colchester's town hall,

---

[138] Ibid., pp. 394–5; and in a much abridged version, Otterbourne and Whethamstede, *Ab origine*, p. 274.

[139] Walsingham, *Chronica maiora*, p. 405; Walsingham, *Historia Anglicana*, II, pp. 291–7 and 306. According to Capgrave, *Chronicle of England*, p. 310, after the crowds had been dispersed, they found Oldcastle's armour, money, and a costly painted banner with the Host and Chalice, and others depicting Christ's sufferings, 'to make simil folk to suppose that he was a trew zelator of the Feith' (p. 310).

[140] Capgrave, *Chronicle of England*, p. 317; also, Walsingham, *Historia Anglicana*, II, p. 317.

[141] *Annales ... Amundesham*, p. 284.

causing uproar among townsmen, with some commoners calling him a saint and others, a heretic. At night, men and women went to the spot of his execution to offer money and wax images. They knelt praying to him 'as they wolde haue don to a seynte', kissing the ground, scooping up his ashes as his relics. This went on for eight days, until London's mayor and aldermen sent armed men to put an end to 'that false ydolatrie' of the 'symple and lewde people': many were arrested and imprisoned.[142]

The Patent Rolls specify fewer cases of heresy, which involved any sense of a popular movement; all of these, moreover, occurred in the fifteenth century; the earliest focused on Oldcastle's conspiracy. Two commissions were put in force immediately after the botched (or, more likely, government-orchestrated)[143] conspiracy of 10 and 11 January to collect information and pursue the arrest of 'the king's subjects commonly called Lollards'. The first concentrated on rounding up the insurgents of London's city and suburbs and the county of Middlesex; the second, on the punishments to be meted out to those who 'traitorously planned' the king's death 'and other things to the destruction of the Catholic faith and the estate of the lords and magnates of the realm'.[144] The second commission revealed more, showing that the king supposedly suspected a revolt far more vast than a city uprising in London. His instructions for capturing and punishing those of Lollard opinions were sent to sheriffs in twenty counties – Hertford, Bedford, Buckingham, Northampton, Rutland, Gloucester, Salop, Nottingham, Derby, Devon, Southampton, Somerset, Dorset, Worcester, Warwick, Leicester, Oxford, Berkshire, Kent, and the town of Bristol.

The most extensive document within the Patent Rolls on Oldcastle's conspiracy, however, was a pardon granted to two London fullers. In it, the royal clerks summarized their views of the general aims of Lollardy. Those 'vulgarly called Lollards', had 'longheld divers heretical opinions against the Catholic faith and other manifest errors repugnant to the

---

[142] *An English Chronicle, 1377–1461*, p. 61. Also, *The Great Chronicle of London*, pp. 174–5, which maintains that 'many ulernyd, as specially women' came to his place of execution, where they erected a cross on 'an huge hepe of stonys', made offerings and said that he worked miracles. He was accused also of fostering a popular cult for financial profit; see McKenna, 'Canonization as Political Propaganda', p. 609. For his career and cult, see Thomson, *The Later Lollards*, pp. 15 and 148–50. Wyche had been a supporter of Oldcastle in the early fifteenth century, wrote a letter to Jan Hus in 1410, and may have supplied books to Bohemians around that date, but appears not to have participated in Oldcastle's rebellion. See Powell, *Kingship, Law, and Society*, p. 146; Anne Hudson, 'Which Wyche? The Framing of the Lollard Heretic and/or Saint', in *Texts and the Repression of Medieval Heresy*, ed. Caterina Bruschi and Peter Biller (York, 2003), pp. 221–37; Hudson, *The Premature Reformation*, p. 160.

[143] See Strohm, *England's Empty Throne*, pp. 65–86.

[144] *CPR 1413–16*, p. 175, 1414.i.10 and p. 177, 1414.i.11.

Catholic law'. Since they were unable to practise their views 'so long as the royal power and estate and office of the prelatial dignity persevered within the realm in prosperity and tranquillity', they schemed to destroy the royal estate, the office of prelates and the religious orders, 'to kill the king and his brothers and prelates and other magnates, to provoke religious men to mundane occupations, to spoil cathedrals and other churches and religious houses of relics and other ecclesiastical goods and level them to the ground'. To achieve their plans, they sought to appoint John Oldcastle 'regent of the realm'. The commission claimed that 20,000 armed rebels from various parts of England had planned to assemble on the Wednesday after Epiphany in the parish of St Giles (10 January), just beyond the Old Temple, outside the city walls, 'to kill the king and his brothers Thomas, Duke of Clarence, John de Lancastre and Humphrey de Lancastre and do other evils'.[145] On the following Thursday, Oldcastle was sentenced to be drawn through the middle of the city to St Giles to be hanged on the new gallows.[146] The conspiracy may have stretched through cities, small towns, and the countryside, but given the 'pitifully small' numbers of pardons issued – 47 accused of Lollardy and rebellion, 115 of rebellion alone, and 52 of Lollardy alone[147] – the planned gathering appears to have been far smaller than the royal commission claimed. Furthermore, given the timing of events – that the supposed mass gathering at St Giles, the formation and sitting of a royal commission to try the traitors, and the commissioners' celebratory breakfast all took place on the same day (10 January), Paul Strohm has convincingly argued that the Crown orchestrated it, as a propaganda stunt to shore up the new king's authority and to enforce obedience and conformity.[148] In the following months, several others received pardons for participation in the revolt. As Aston concluded from other lists, the accused heretics represented a wide range of occupations, but centred on crafts. In the royal commissions of the accused in 1414, only one was an esquire; one, a mercer; and one, a clerk; but only one was from the countryside – a 'plowman'. On the other hand, there were two parchment makers, two carpenters, two weavers, an ironmonger,

---

[145] Walsingham's estimate was even larger – '50,000 servants and apprentices, together with some of their masters from among the citizenry', cited in Strohm, *England's Empty Throne*, p. 76.

[146] Ibid., p. 162, 1414.i.23.   [147] Powell, *Kingship, Law and Society*, p. 155.

[148] Strohm, *England's Empty Throne*, pp. 65–86; also see Marx, 'Introduction', in *An English Chronicle, 1377–1461*, pp. lxxi-iii, in support of Strohm; and Clive Burgess, 'A Hotbed of Heresy? Fifteenth-Century Bristol and Lollardy Reconsidered', pp. 43–62, in *The Fifteenth Century, III: Authority and Subversion*, ed. Linda Clark (Woodbridge, 2003), p. 49. Henry V was crowned in 1413.

a cobbler, and a student ('scoler').[149] Given the expenses of lodging
and winning royal pardons, these, moreover, may have represented
Oldcastle's better-heeled followers.

After his failure, further Lollard revolts and conspiracies appear in
the Patent Rolls. The term Lollardy was added to blanket condemnations investigating 'rebellious misdeeds', such as one in London and
its suburbs of 1450, 'touching all treasons, insurrections, felonies,
trespasses, lollardries, conspiracies, confederacies'. No mention of
Cade or his rebellion is here specified,[150] and historians such as
Aston have concluded that Lollards decided against participation in
this rebellion.[151] Yet contemporaries may have suspected a connection
between the two, as is suggested by the wording of an inquisition from
Essex on 12 February 1451, 'touching all heretics and Lollards'.[152]
Similarly, in 1438, another commission 'touched on' 'insurrections,
rebellions, felonies, lollardries, robberies etc. throughout the county of
Kent'.[153] The document, however, fails to clarify the particulars,
precise locations, or names, of alleged rebels, but other documents
expose it to have been another revolt associated with Lollardy, this
one led by the knight Sir Nicholas Conway at Tenterden, Kent; five
men were executed for heresy.[154] After 1414, unlike before, during, or
immediately after the Peasants' Revolt, heretic hunting had now
become a normal response to popular protest by the Crown and secular
powers.[155]

---

[149] Ibid., p. 237, 1414.ix.19; p. 250, 1414.xi.6; p. 271, 1414.xii.6, 15 and 18; and p. 299,
1414.vii.3. For the trials of Oldcastle and two of his chief leaders, Walter Blake
of Bristol, chaplain, and Sir Roger Acton of Shrewsbury, see *King's Bench*, VII,
pp. 217–20.

[150] *CPR 1446–52*, p. 388, 1450.vii.1.

[151] Aston, 'Lollardy and Sedition', p. 38: 'If the Lollards avoided involvement in the rising
of 1450 this does not prove that they had given up all hope of another rebellion of their
own'.

[152] *CPR 1446–52*, p. 440.

[153] *CPR 1436–41*, p. 1438.vi.1. The same charges arose again for those in Kent on
20 December 1445, spelling out further, 'lollardries and heresies, and errors
contrary to the Catholic faith', and other offences in Kent; *CPR 1441–6*, p. 422,
and another on 4 July 1451, *CPR 1446–52*, p. 477. The martyred priest Sir Richard
Wyche had livings in Kent in the 1420s and 1430s, and in 1428, the Archbishop of
Canterbury sought to arrest Lollard suspects in Kent; Aston, 'Lollardy and Sedition',
p. 23. In addition, as Thomson, *The Later Lollards*, p. 180, has commented, the anti-
clericalism of Cade's rebellion suggests that 'some heretical motivation' may have been
possible.

[154] *CPR 1436–41*, p. 398, 1438.vi.1; and Thomson, *The Later Lollards*, p. 178.

[155] Aston, 'Lollardy and Sedition', p. 34–5. Also, according to Thomson, *The Later
Lollards*: 'After 1414 persecution was intensified, and the officials of the secular
government played a more active part in it, not only acting as executioners but also
taking an active part in hunting down offenders' (p. 5).

Perhaps Lollardy, after Oldcastle, had simply become a term of abuse.[156] On the other hand, the Patent Rolls used it sparingly. They even refrained from branding two well-known Lollard insurrections as 'Lollardy'. Their descriptions, however, clearly linked heretical and unauthorized preaching with the supposed destruction of the Catholic faith and conspiracies to overthrow the king. The second England-wide conspiracy of Lollards led by William Perkins, alias John or Jack Sharp, finds only one reference in the Patent Rolls, and it is not an inquisition or commission to suppress the conspiracy but a grant by the House of Lords of 6,000 marks a year to Humphrey, Duke of Gloucester, as long as he was lieutenant of England, or 5,000 marks after the king's return. He was rewarded for his capture and execution 'of that horrible heretic and iniquitous traitor who called himself John Sharp'. But the term 'Lollardy' was not used.[157]

The Crown suppressed another wave of 'seditious' revolt at the end of 1424, but again did not call it Lollardy, commissioning the king's sergeant-at-arms to arrest John Grace, 'a false prophet, who with no licence to preach[158] had 'rouse[d] terrible seditions among the people to the damage of the peace and the likely overthrow of the Catholic faith'. According to the mandate, John preached in various places, but especially at Coventry, with 'riots and unlawful assemblies'. Riots also 'increased' in Staffordshire, Warwickshire, and Shropshire, and the king

---

[156] See Burgess, 'A Hotbed of Heresy?' and Clive Burgess, 'A Repertory for Reinforcement: Configuring Civic Catholicism in Fifteenth-Century Bristol' in *The Fifteenth Century, V: Of Mice and Men: Image, Belief, and Regulation in Late Medieval England*, ed. Linda Clark (Woodbridge, 2005), pp. 85–109 for his charges that the historiography has overestimated the spread and threat of fifteenth-century Lollardy and heresy, which actually hardly constituted a network. Others have taken the Lollard threat more seriously. According to Chris Given-Wilson, 'The Problem of Labour in the Context of English Government, c. 1350–1450', in *The Problem of Labour in Fourteenth-Century England*, ed. James Bothwell, P. J. P. Goldberg, and W. M. Ormrod (York, 2000), pp. 85-100, had Henry V not begun to act as the supreme governor of the Church of England, the country might have gone the way of Bohemia – 'an outcome which clearly seemed far less implausible to contemporaries than it has to some historians' (p. 90). Also, Hudson, *The Premature Reformation*, pp. 116–19, 153–4, 508–17, has argued that Lollard following from 1381 to 1413 was much more serious than Burgess suggests.

[157] *CPR 1429–36*, pp.184–5, 1431.xi.28. On the other hand, chroniclers describe Sharp's rising at Abingdon and his execution, but here, too, the *Great Chronicle of London*, pp. 155–6, does not call it 'Lollardy'. On Sharp's pseudonym and desire to gain support from social rebels who would associate him with Jack Straw, see Thomson, *The Later Lollards*, p. 59. On the Duke of Gloucester's role in suppressing the movement in 1431 and sentencing the leaders, and on how his reputation was enhanced as a result, see Griffiths, *The Reign of King Henry VI*, p. 140, and Jurkowski, 'Lollardy in Coventry', p. 158.

[158] In fact, Grace was an anchorite friar who had obtained a preacher's licence.

censured sheriffs for 'neglecting to take measures to arrest the said John' and ordered them 'to stop such riots and assemblies'.[159]

By the beginning of the fifteenth century, legal writing and statutes against heresy mounted,[160] and jottings by chroniclers, such as those of an unknown St Albans' monk, and those of John Amundesham, become punctuated with references to Lollardy and heresy, to ordinances enacted by Parliaments and by their own monastery against them; and to notices of executions of individual heretics, as well as of leaders of heretical and seditious movements. In 1426, the Abbot of St Albans held a synod to pass ordinances against those inimical to the Church, false preachers, and persons possessing books in the vernacular, who were summoned before him;[161] in 1428, Lollards were burnt at Norwich;[162] in 1429, heresy was uncovered at Lincoln;[163] in 1430, a Lollard was burnt on Tower Hill;[164] another at Maldon in Essex; and a Lollard priest at Chelmsford, 'who held the sacraments in contempt'. In 1431, the Bishop of Ely and Abbot of St Albans met at Hertford to combat Lollards, and in the same year, Jack Sharp cast his bills in various towns and was executed with seven other leaders at Oxford.[165]

Lollardy was not the only heresy or 'evil practice' to emerge during the first half of the fifteenth century which secular and religious authorities suddenly felt needed to be stamped out. In 1405, the Bishop of Lincoln headed a commission to examine and imprison 'all fortune-tellers, magicians, enchanters, necromancers, diviners, soothsayers, and wizards within his diocese'.[166] Four years later, the king instructed the Bishop of Bath and Wells to make proclamations within his diocese and the town of Bristol, condemning 'certain satellites of Satan' who preach 'divers new and unheard of doctrines and false opinions and wickednesses and manifestly contrary to the Catholic faith'. They were reputed to 'hold schools in occult' that attracted many of the king's subjects. The bishop was empowered to arrest and imprison all who disobeyed the proclamation.[167] On 1 August 1426, a commission formed to hunt and prosecute a knight, a yeoman, 'and other malefactors of their covin', 'unmindful of the salvation of their souls, and not

---

[159] *CPR 1422–9*, p. 1424.xii.14. Also, Griffiths, *The Reign of King Henry VI*, p. 131. On Grace's preaching at Coventry, see Jurkowski, 'Lollardy in Coventry', p. 157.
[160] See Forrest, *The Detection of Heresy*, pp. 105–6.
[161] *Annales ... Amundesham*, I, pp. 222–4 and 225.
[162] *Chronicon ... Monasterio S. Albani*, p. 29.
[163] Ibid., p. 35.   [164] Ibid., pp. 46, 50, 51, 61.   [165] Ibid. pp. 63, 64.
[166] *CPR 1405–8*, p. 112, 1406.i.2. For the possible connection between magic and heresy in the minds of Church authorities in the early fifteenth century, see Thomson, *The Later Lollards*, pp. 30–1.
[167] *CPR 1408–13*, p. 109, 1409.vi.7.

having God before their eyes'. They were accused of practising 'sooth-saying, necromancy and the art of magic, to weaken and annihilate, subtly consume and altogether destroy by the said arts'. Another commission appointed the same day was charged to root out similar black arts in Dorset and another in Cornwall.[168] Before 1405, Patent Rolls reveal no fears of black arts, magic, or witches in any of its commissions and mandates from their inception in the early thirteenth century.[169]

These black offences and conspiracies also begin to enter the chronicles. At St Albans, for instance, an unknown chronicler describes a covin of women who, around Christmas 1430, came from across England to London to kill the king. The language of the chronicle suggests witchcraft: they were called 'quedam maleficae'; their mission was to be achieved by certain machinations ('quae machinatae'). Unfortunately, the chronicler does not allude to the women's motives or how they communicated across England and then banded together in London.[170] Furthermore, other documents such as the Parliamentary rolls reveal an increase in the Crown's fear of magical activity – 'prophecy, divination, necromancy' – from 1397 through the fifteenth century. At the end of our period, the Crown branded Jack Cade not only as a political conspirator, but tarred him 'as a dabbler in sorcery and consorter with the devil'.[171] According to Simon Walker, by the fifteenth century, 'associations of involvement in sorcery and divination became the currency of domestic politics'.[172] Perhaps most famous of these accusations for political propaganda was the Duke of Bedford's offensive, based on

---

[168] *CPR 1422–9*, p. 363, 1426.viii.1.

[169] Thomson, *The Later Lollards*, p. 241, suggests that popular beliefs, Lollard ideas, and witchcraft may have been intertwined by the mid-fifteenth century. Yet politically motivated charges of necromancy against individuals can be found earlier, as in 1325 against a master John, who allegedly was bribed to use his arts to kill the king, the Earl of Winchester, Sir Hugh le Despenser, and others [KB 27/259, m. 24]; cited by Helen Lacey in 'Perceptions of Royal Governance and Westminster in Fourteenth-Century England', at the International Medieval Congress, 11 July 2011. Already, in 1323, Despenser felt threatened by black arts and wrote to the pope for advice; see Natalie Fryde, *The Tyranny and Fall of Edward II* (Cambridge, 1979), p. 162. I thank Dr Lacey for this reference. Another high-profile case comes in 1376, during the Good Parliament, with antagonism against Alice Perrers. Knights of the Parliament captured her physician, the Dominican friar Palange Wyk, accused of practising black arts on her behalf; Carole Rawcliffe, 'The Profits of Practice: the Wealth and Status of Medical Men in Later Medieval England', *Social History of Medicine*, I (1988): 73; and J. R. Maddicott, 'Parliament and the Constituencies, 1272–1377', in *The English Parliament in the Middle Ages*, ed. R. G. Davies and J. H. Denton (Manchester, 1981), pp. 79–80.

[170] *Chronicon ... Monasterio S. Albani*, pp. 56–7.   [171] Walker, 'Political Saints', p. 88.

[172] Ibid., pp. 88–9. As far as we see, little has been done on this fascinating new development in English politics.

accusations that Joan of Arc was a heretic and witch, before, during, and after her trial and burning in May 1431.[173] A decade later, now within England, enemies of Humphrey, Duke of Gloucester, used charges of necromancy, black arts, and witchcraft to prosecute his second wife, Eleanor, and two of her religious associates, a canon of St Stephen's, Westminster, and an Oxford priest, first to blacken further her reputation, then to end the Duke's influence in national politics and, ultimately, his life.[174]

A case from 1356 brought before King's Bench against a vicar of the parish of Aldbury, Hertfordshire, near Tring, and a religious hermit highlight this change in sentiment and use of heresy to blacken popular movements and the Crown's enemies by the early fifteenth century. The two preached publicly against the Statutes of Labourers, proclaiming that labourers, artisans, and servants should feel free to take as much as they pleased from their labour, that 'the statute and ordinance were falsely and wickedly made'. They used their pulpits and open-air preaching to excommunicate any who dared support or execute these laws to indict, punish, or prevent labourers from 'obtaining wages, even abnormal wages'. They used their religious authority to cross the secular divide, proclaiming that 'the aforesaid ordinances and statutes are abolished'. The two carried big sticks to waylay the king's justices assigned to enforce the laws, and threatened them 'with death and mutilation, arson, and other hideous and unspeakable evils'. According to the indictment, their preaching had comforted and emboldened workers and artisans throughout Hertfordshire, 'nurturing their wrongdoing'. As a consequence, these labourers 'until now and still are more rebellious and bolder in their outrages and trespasses in disobeying court processes and judgements'. Of the accusations against the two on the bottom rungs of the religious hierarchy, the court never used the word 'heresy'.[175] Certainly, after Oldcastle, much milder and vaguer offences against royal power and authority would have been tarred as such, even by those without religious positions, who made no references to doctrine, or use of the pulpit, to support the poor and rebuke the state.

By the fifteenth century, the Crown had become more zealous in suppressing not only 'false religious doctrine', but all forms of speech

---

[173] Griffiths, *The Reign of King Henry VI*, p. 219.
[174] Bennett, *Six Medieval Men and Women*, pp. 15–16; and Walker, 'Political Saints', p. 89.
[175] *King's Bench*, VI, pp. 110–11. Also, Prescott, 'Judicial Records', pp. 306–8. Tring and Aldbury had been hot-beds of insurrection in 1381; Réville, *Le soulèvement*, pp. 33, 35, 37, 39, 161.

that threatened its status. With a new vigour, it enforced earlier legislation of Richard II, mandating mayors and bailiffs in cities and sheriffs in
the counties to arrest any who 'fabricate or publish false news'.[176] Yet
during Richard's reign, the use of these statutes of Westminster never
appears in the Patent Rolls to investigate or prosecute any accused of
spreading such libellous reports.[177] In the surveillance of speech and the
prosecution of libellous or critical words voiced against those in power,
London appears to have led the way. The first of these, at least as seen in
any of the published court records, Letter-books, or memoranda of the
mayors and aldermen, surfaces a year and a half after the Peasants'
Revolt, during the mayoralty of Northampton. In December 1382, the
court imprisoned John Filiol, a fishmonger, 'for opprobrious words
against the mayor'. He was freed only after his friends paid £100 to
ensure 'his good behaviour towards the officers of the city'.[178] Four
months later, the court summoned William Spaldying, a tailor, to the
Guildhall, where he was accused of 'speaking evil and shameful words'
against one from the mistery of tawyers, that such talk could have caused
discord.[179] And two months after that, another was imprisoned for
disseminating false news of Despenser's crusade in Flanders.[180] The
avalanche of mayoral court cases, imprisonment, and fines against those
accused of speaking ill of government and particularly against its mayor
came, however, with Brembre's mayoralty, in fact immediately after
his contested election and the execution of the cordwainer, John
Constantyn: on 18 May 1384, the court charged William Mayhew,
grocer, for speaking out against the mayor, accusing Brembre of
governing the city badly, and for having 'falsely and iniquitously'
condemned Constantyn to death. In the editor's 'selected cases' alone,
sixty-seven more cases against those who rumoured, cried out, or
opposed Brembre's government with 'false words' were brought before

---

[176] *CPR 1446–52*, p. 433, 1451.ix.18.
[177] In fact, no examples of this article against libellous speech in the Statutes of
Westminster against groups or individuals appear in *CPR* until 1450. Instead,
citations to these statutes are complaints against violations of fishing regulations to
preserve stocks of lampreys, samlets, and mature salmon from off-season fishing, illegal
nets, and 'other engines' used on English rivers. One insurrection before Richard's law
points to 'loose tongues' on 12 November 1354, when 'conventicles, confederacies,
and conspiracies in London . . . excite[d] the people' against the king, his ministers, and
'the good men of the city', with insurgents 'loosing their tongues opprobiously against
the king'; *CPR 1350–4*, p. 164. On these statutes and others against seditious speech in
the fifteenth century, see John Watts, 'The Pressure of the Public on Later Medieval
Politics', in *The Fifteenth Century, IV: Political Culture in Late Medieval Britain*, ed.
Linda Clark and Christine Carpenter (Woodbridge, 2004), pp. 170–1 and 177–8.
[178] *CPMR*, IV, p. 36, 1382.xii.6.   [179] Ibid., p. 40, 1383.iii.19.
[180] Ibid., p. 36, 1383.v.31.

the mayor's chambers: these constituted the overwhelming proportion of Brembre's mayoral business in these records. Several, moreover, involved multiple condemnations, as with eleven goldsmiths accused of calling his government 'perverse and evil'. For speech alone, they were imprisoned but 'by favour of the mayor' were delivered on bail under penalty of £100.[181] As far as heresy and speech go, England's trajectory again differed from the Continent's, where such measures of a 'persecuting society' evolved much earlier, during the late twelfth and thirteenth centuries. In England, they blossomed after the Peasants' Revolt of 1381, but intensified only during the fifteenth century.

In conclusion, the chronology of heretical revolt and its persecution, as charted by chronicles and Patent Rolls, differs from the Continent. For late medieval Italy, France, and Flanders, the major revolts, social movements, and suppression of heretics peaked in the thirteenth and early fourteenth centuries, then disappeared altogether after the flagellant movements of 1349, until the 1420s, when supposed small groups of Hussites formed in towns of northern France and Flanders. These later heretical movements and their persecution pale by comparison with the pan-regional religiously inspired revolts of the thirteenth and early fourteenth century on the Continent, or those which were to erupt in German-speaking provinces and Hungary by the beginning of the sixteenth century.[182] In England, the chronological pattern was precisely the opposite. No heretical revolts or religious social movements of consequence appear on English soil before the Peasants' Revolt. Then, as they disappear in Italy, France, and Flanders, they spring forth as Lollardy in England, along with accusations and persecution against magical incantations, witchcraft, and a new zeal by the Crown and municipal authority to suppress seditious speech and the written word (bill casting) by urban commoners. This chronological pattern is all the more surprising given English history's anti-Jewish persecution from the late twelfth century to its 'final solution', along with heightened English xenophobia against Flemings, Lombards, the Welsh, Scots, and Irish seen in chronicles and royal commissions, courts, and mandates. In England, persecution of the other – Jews, women, witches, heretics, and foreigners – did not neatly run in tandem with the increasing power

---

[181] Ibid., IV, pp. 60, 61, 62, 65, 66–7. These included charges against artisans, for instance, the cordwainer John Remes, the barber William Frere, the cutler Edmund Wodhull, John Coraunt, and eleven other goldsmiths, who assembled their mistery to protest the elections, along with others of the 'middle sort belonging to divers misteries', including 'divers tailors'.

[182] See *Lust for Liberty*, p. 234 and Tom Scott, *Town, Country, and Regions in Reformation Germany*. Studies in Medieval and Reformation Traditions (Leiden, 2005), pp. 125–48.

of a 'persecuting state', as has been argued was the reason for these groups' suppression in Europe of the High Middle Ages.[183] English persecution of its Jews was as vicious as anywhere in thirteenth-century Europe, spearheading the way with new myths for mass hatred and expulsion. Yet its persecution of heretics was delayed, all but absent from its shores, until the end of the fourteenth century. The reasons for this English disjunction in hate await new research and thought.

[183] Most importantly, see Moore, *The Formation of a Persecuting Society*; Carlo Ginzburg, *Ecstasies: Deciphering the Witches' Sabbath*, trans. Raymond Rosenthal (London, 1991); and Jeffrey Richards, *Sex, Dissidence and Damnation: Minority Groups in the Middle Ages* (London, 1991).

14   Conclusion

It has been assumed that little happened in the way of revolts and popular movements in medieval English towns. Instead, the theatre of medieval English class conflict has been perceived as the countryside, where revolts occurred more frequently and possessed a more sophisticated and radical ideology. Popular protest in the countryside has been studied more widely over various disciplines, and more thoroughly in England than for any other area of medieval Europe. By contrast, the few studies of revolts in English urban areas to appear have been confined mostly to individual towns. Few of these have peered, even momentarily, beyond local confines to establish patterns, or to compare the English case with histories across the Channel. When historians have episodically placed their findings in broader comparative frameworks, as with Gwyn Williams' classic work on medieval London, it has been to draw parallels and not to see the differences. In particular, Williams saw London's revolts of the mid- and late-thirteenth century, such as those led by the mayors Thomas fitzThomas and Walter Hervey, as part of a larger Continental movement that swept across towns in Italy and Flanders, where artisans contested the control of cities by patricians and entered government for the first time.[1] After Williams, Hilton's *Bondmen Made Free* did much the same for peasant revolt across Europe, placing the Peasants' Revolt of 1381 within the wider contexts of European development. Despite describing a rich panoply of revolts – all with their own particularities – this seminal work saw English revolts as part of broad movements that hinged on similar ecological, social, and economic developments. From a politically diametrically opposed perspective, Mollat and Wolff's *Ongles bleus* a few years earlier had also placed English revolts (at least the Peasants' Revolt of 1381) into a single European perspective. In their view, a supposed European cluster of popular revolts sprang forth between 1378 and 1381, provoked by the

---

[1] Williams, *Medieval London*, pp. 168.

long-term consequences of the Black Death[2] with the English Peasants' Revolt and its long-term causes emblematic of that post-Black Death European development. Finally, the last chapter of Hilton's final book, *English and French Towns in Feudal Society*, is the most sustained comparison of popular revolt between England and any part of the Continent (even if only France). Throughout, it stresses the similarities: revolts in English towns fit seamlessly with those on the Continent – more so than what he discovered earlier, with peasant revolts.[3]

Rather than similarities, the present book has discovered differences between late medieval popular revolt in English towns and the Continent. Despite a background of similar ecological and economic developments, the histories of popular reaction to these overarching conditions were not cut of a single cloth, formed more or less by European-wide economic, social, and epidemic realities. The growth of towns and craft industries in the twelfth and thirteenth centuries, economic and demographic stagnation by the end of the thirteenth century, or demographic collapse and the resetting of environmental, economic, social, political, and psychological factors in the second half of the fourteenth and early fifteenth centuries did not produce uniform political or social responses from labouring classes across Europe.

Instead, politics and institutional political differences – kingship and the precocious development of centralized and unified power in England[4] – made the big difference. Firstly, descriptions of artisans and disenfranchised workers in trades such as textiles in combat against their employers, city oligarchies, or the Crown, do not appear in the chronicles or Patent Rolls for England as they do in narrative and administrative sources for Continental Europe. Moreover, even in the capital, where municipal court records and Letter-books of the mayor and aldermen survive in great numbers regarding artisan groups such as tailors, tawyers, and tanners, few examples of labour strife between workers and bosses or lesser and greater guilds appear. For the

---

[2] Michel Mollat and Philippe Wolff, *Ongles bleus Jacques et Ciompi: les révoltuions populaires en Europe aux XIVe et XVe siècles* (Paris, 1970). Later, Hilton, 'Popular Movements in England', contrasted revolts in towns between England and the Continent, especially with Florence. For questioning such a European-wide cluster, see Cohn, *Lust for Liberty*, pp. 205 and 218–27.

[3] Also, see his 'Unjust Taxation and Popular Resistance', *New Left Review*, 180 (1990): 178–84, which stresses the similarities in urban revolts across the later Middle Ages between France and England.

[4] For the contrast in state development – royal administration, justice, and taxation – between England and France during the thirteenth and fourteenth centuries, see Richard W. Kaeuper, *War, Justice, and Public Order: England and France in the Later Middle Ages* (Oxford, 1988), especially pp. 381–92. Also, Dyer, *An Age of Transition?*, p. 111.

Continent, by contrast, these occurred not only in textile-producing cities such as Bruges, Ypres, Ghent, and Florence but in numerous smaller towns across France, Italy, and the Low Countries, and even in places with few textile workers, such as Liège.

Secondly, the amalgam of disputes in English towns differed from that on the Continent. Although the papacy could make deep inroads into English politics, as F. M. Powicke showed for Henry III's reign, papal exactions or decisions and threats by papal legates rarely provoked popular revolts. To be sure, papal politics were a major source of urban organized violence mainly in Italian city-states, but as with the clash of rival popes Urban VI and Clement VII, in the 1370s and 1380s, these politics could stir popular emotions as far north as Liège and in England. Another source of popular violence and protest – resentment to billeting of foreign troops and the abuses they inflicted on urban societies – provoked some of the most horrific and widespread revolts on the Continent during the Middle Ages. They hardly appear in late medieval England, for towns or the countryside, even with troops stationed for long periods near the Scottish borders.

Thirdly, protests by children, peace marches or efforts to goad a city into war, as seen in Naples, Florence, Parma, Paris, and other Continental towns, are absent from the English sources. Except for the revolts of 'bachelors' during the baronial revolts of the 1260s (of which we know so little) and a few others, as with Scarborough in 1282, revolts of youth against ruling oligarchies also appear rarely in late medieval England.

Fourthly, and perhaps most surprising is the relative rarity of tax revolts in England; surprising, because of the importance of the English Peasants' Revolt, the most studied revolt of the Middle Ages, which in large part was a tax revolt, sparked by the third poll tax of 1380 and its collection the year after. Yet, despite vigorous efforts by the Crown to tax populations including the clergy by various subsidies – ninths, tens, fifteenths, pavage, murage, purveyances, various wool customs, and more – to enhance the Crown's courtly splendour and wage wars, few tax protests flared in English cities or the countryside, even when tax exactions reached their peaks in the late 1250s, the last decade of the thirteenth century, and the 1330s. In contrast to a vertiginous climb in tax revolts on the Continent, the opposite occurred in England – when its governments faced increased military expenditures financed by greatly reduced populations after the Black Death, fiscal revolts in post-plague England almost disappeared. Finally, internal struggles within English towns, between social groups defined vaguely as 'rich' and 'poor', those of 'sufficiency' or not, and by other class characteristics, pale by comparison with struggles between the juridically defined and occupationally specific classes of the *popolo* and magnates, *menu peuple* and bourgeois, or *popolo minuto* and *popolani grassi* in Continental towns, which there comprised 40 per cent of revolts.

What then filled the gap with English urban protest? Firstly, the chroniclers and the Patent Rolls show a greater proportion of popular revolts in towns against the Crown and royal officers. However, when the city-states of Italy, which rarely dealt with kings or princes, except for the Holy Roman emperor, are removed, the preponderance of these protests remains higher in England than in France, the kingdom of Sicily and Naples, and the Low Countries during the later Middle Ages, but only marginally so. More crucial was the high number of English revolts against the Church, struggles for liberties by burgesses over jurisdiction in urban neighbourhoods, rights to hold courts, fairs and markets, to patrol and guard town gates, and above all else to elect their own mayors, aldermen, coroners, and other officials. Best known to historians, these protests erupted in monastic boroughs. But monastic boroughs were not the only, or even the primary, arenas for these contests. Collectively, more protests, and ones which were just as violent, raged between burgesses and bishops, priories, canons, or universities in towns that were not monastic boroughs. Moreover, not all, or even most, monastic boroughs were scenes of such strife: Reading and Westminster, for instance, appear completely free of them.

Finally, the chronological patterns of revolt in England differed fundamentally from those on the Continent. After the Black Death (or at least after 1355), the frequency of insurrection soared by as much as three times until the early fifteenth century in Italy, France, and Flanders, and seven-fold as regards tax revolts. By contrast, the majority of popular violence and protest in English towns, whether against the Crown, the Church, or universities, or between the lesser and greater 'sorts', preceded the Black Death, clustering in the late thirteenth and early fourteenth centuries. Although the changed social and demographic dynamics of the second half of the fourteenth century were much the same for England as for Western Europe, these underlying conditions did not provoke the same trajectories of popular revolt, especially as far as towns are concerned.[5] Nor did the Peasants' Revolt spawn a new wave of self-confidence, a zeal to struggle for personal freedoms and collective liberties, in towns. Incidents of

---

[5] As we have seen, the post-plague trajectory of collective violence in the countryside differed from that in towns.

popular revolt fell more sharply after this famous revolt than after the Black Death.[6] The one exception in this chronological trend in popular movements was heresy, which spouted in England only after the Peasants' Revolt. On the Continent, by contrast, the trend swung in the opposite direction: after the flagellant movement, 1348–50, Western Continental Europe was free of mass religious and heretical movements until the third decade of the fifteenth century, when small groups began banding together in northern France and Flanders, supposedly under the influence of the Hussites.

This book has hypothesized that differences in popular protest between England and Continental Western Europe resulted from the early development of the English state, with its structure of courts and law enforcement, including royal sheriffs, Justices of the Peace, escheators, King's Bench, London's and other municipal courts, special and general commissions of oyer et terminer and inquiry, and the Crown's ability to call on magnates of the realm, as well as local gentry, lesser landowners, and especially after the Black Death, Justices of the Peace, to intervene swiftly into the affairs of local communities.[7] Already, by the reign of Henry I, the English monarchy was ahead of the game: 'by contemporary standards', it was 'immensely strong'.[8] That impressive growth of centralized royal power continued apace through the late Middle Ages, despite temporary setbacks with weak kings and baronial strife. In John Gillingham's assessment: 'by medieval standards England [*c.* 1400] was a much-governed state. Royal authority in England was reinforced by an increasingly elaborate administrative network, both at the centre and in the provinces'.[9] As Christian Liddy has shown, royal control of the provinces, and especially provincial cities, depended increasingly on the integration of local elites into national politics, through finance, Parliament, and ultimately as sheriffs and Justices of the Peace in new urban corporations that achieved county status from 1373 on.[10] By these means, the English Crown could effectively arbitrate and manage the

---

[6] In addition, keyword searches for various terms for revolt or social movements of artisans or peasants in French, English, and Latin in *PROME* did not mark the English Peasants' Revolt as a watershed opening a new epoch of rural or urban disorder in England; see Cohn, 'Revolts of the Late Middle Ages', pp. 279–80.

[7] On differences between the French and English Crown and the extent of centralized control in England compared to other regions of Europe, see Frame, *The Political Development*, pp. 71–2, 99, 171–3, 221–2.

[8] Ibid., p. 99.

[9] Gillingham, 'Crisis or Continuity?', p. 76. On the precociousness of the English Crown, also see Genet, *La genèse de l'état moderne*.

[10] Liddy, *War, Politics and Finance*, p. 228 and elsewhere.

politics of urban places, rewarding its supporters and repressing those who opposed its dictates and notions of hierarchy far more greatly than in other kingdoms or city-states in late medieval Europe. As a result, the frequency and relative effectiveness of popular uprisings in English towns followed closely the fate of its monarchs: their absence while abroad fighting wars, dynastic crises and transition, and baronial civil strife opened avenues for insurrection, not only against the Crown, but against other local authorities and especially the Church, whose rights kings almost inevitably protected against the interests of burgesses. On the other hand, strong monarchs such as Edward I and Edward III (before his final fourteen months of illness and incapacity) with few exceptions could raise taxes to new levels, impose new exactions, and collect crippling purveyances with only faint murmuring and without incurring significant armed threats from cities and towns, whether organized by mayors, bailiffs, or aldermen, or from below by 'the lesser commune' of burgesses and the poor.

At first glance, a glaring exception to this rule might appear to have been England's most famous revolt, the great one of 1381: not only were new burdensome taxes levied; they struck portions of the English population for the first time. However, as is well rehearsed in the historiography, this period of new taxes, 1377 to 1381, was hardly one of royal strength; rather, effective challenges from Parliament, losses in war to the French, loss of security along English coastal waters, the loss of control of an ill and aged king, and the transition of power to the boy-king Richard, with his hated uncle essentially at the helm, opened deep fissures in royal authority and power. Further, although rarely mentioned among its causes,[11] 'the Great Revolt' occurred when 'the only immediately available armed forces were away, north of York, dealing with the Scots'. As had been the case so often in the past, the king's absence from England had been a precondition of insurrection in towns such as Bristol, Lynn, Bury St Edmunds, St Albans, Oxford, Lincoln, and others.[12] The old refrain seen in the Patent Rolls might have been repeated in the summer of 1381: rebels had been 'emboldened by the king's passing to parts beyond the seas' (even if John of Gaunt was not then actually king).[13]

[11] For instance Eiden's detailed list of causes ('Joint Action against "Bad" Lordship', p. 7), mentions neither royal weakness nor the presence of royal troops in the Scottish borders.

[12] H. E. P. Grieve, 'The Rebellion and the County Town' in *Essex and the Great Revolt of 1381: Lectures Celebrating the Six Hundredth Anniversary*, ed. W. H. Liddell and R. G. E. Wood, Essex Record Office Publication no. 84 (Essex, 1982), p. 46.

[13] See pp. 116, 126, 128, 141, 143, 146, 154, 156, 176, 212, 253, 255, above; according to Rexroth, *Deviance and Power*, when Edward III prepared to leave England for France in

Finally, the further decline in the frequency of popular insurrection after the Black Death may be attributed to the development of the crown's powers of surveillance and repressive forces, especially as regards subaltern classes.[14] These involved royal peace commissions, the rise of Justices of the Peace, grants to them to deal summarily with riot, the increased activity of King's Bench, and new laws from the Statute of Treason in 1352 to the Statute of Riots in 1414, which brought the full powers of the state against heresy, treasonous speech, and rebellion, in an era before standing armies and a permanent police force.[15] As a result of these laws and new administrative and judicial structures, popular rebellion declined sharply from its heyday in the early fourteenth century. By the fifteenth century, even long absences of kings, as when Henry V left for northern France to conduct his military campaigns, or during periods of minority and divided loyalties at court, as with much of Henry VI's reign, no longer so easily unleashed opportunities for insurrection.[16]

As argued in *Lust for Liberty*, the model of popular insurrection in 'pre-industrial' or 'pre-modern' times contrived by sociologists, political scientists, and modern historians, and generalized across vague stretches of time from antiquity to the French Revolution, Industrial Revolution,

---

1338, Londoners immediately felt imperilled by the threat of general unrest, an end to the 'king's peace with robbery, plundering and the negation of any civic order' (p. 43).

[14] Even before the Black Death, not every royal crisis automatically or inevitably led to rioting or popular revolt. As we have seen, commoners were absent from the baronial revolt against Edward II in 1322; and Edward III's difficulties in the opening phases of the Hundred Years War, culminating in the crisis of 1341, failed to spark rebellion, baronial or popular. On the latter, see Ormrod, *Edward III*, pp. 239–46.

[15] See Powell, *Kingship, Law, and Society*, especially chapters 2 and 7.

[16] Ibid., pp. 246ff, and 271–2, discusses the limited resources of control in maintaining social order, especially in outlying counties such as Devon, but this discussion focuses on factional conflicts of magnates and gentry. Here, King's Bench and other courts had to rely on conciliation rather than punitive action. Even with disorder at this level of society, Powell maintains that 'a national framework of royal justice and law enforcement had been established' by the early fifteenth century. Because of this growth of royal jurisdiction, levels of social disorder appear paradoxically higher in the fifteenth century (p. 20). On the growing strength of the Crown, its repressive laws, surveillance, and 'unparalleled legislative intervention in the lives of ordinary people' in the late fourteenth and early fifteenth centuries, also see Given-Wilson, 'The Problem of Labour'; R. C. Palmer, *English Law in the Age of the Black Death, 1348–1381: A Transformation of Governance and Law* (Chapel Hill, NC, 1993), and criticisms of their arguments by Prescott, 'Labourers' Lives: some Crown Prosecutions of Artisans, 1420–30', Fifteenth-Century Conference, Royal Holloway College, University of London, 2–4 September 2004.

and by some to as late as the mid-nineteenth century, fails to fit the experience of late medieval popular rebellion on the Continent.[17] Firstly, instead of being the norm, revolts rarely occurred in times of high bread prices and famine. It was the opposite; post-plague revolts coincided with falling bread prices and rising expectations. Women did not comprise the 'crowds' of pre-modern revolts; instead they were conspicuously absent from them, as is seen across a wide range of narrative, judicial, and administrative sources. Peasants, workers, and artisans in late medieval Continental revolts rarely relied on those out-side their ranks – aristocrats, mayors, and clergymen – to lead their protests. Instead, chronicles and judicial sources show a wide array of peasant and artisan leaders – Jan Breydek, the butcher; Jan Heem, the fuller; the better-off peasants Clais Zannekin, Zeger Janzone, and Jacob Peyt, the weaver, 'Peter the king' (Pieter de Coninck), Michele di Lando, a wool comber; Piero Capurro, a sailor or gallery man; the leaders of the Ronco conspiracy who planned Ciompi tactics, who were mostly disenfranchised wool workers; Colart Sade, the big iron man of Longueil-Sainte-Marie, a peasant; Mahieu de Leurel, Étienne du Wès, Jean Flageolet, and Guillaume Cale, of the Jacquerie of 1358; Simon Cabouche, the butcher, and many others of similar backgrounds. 'Pre-modern' insurrections were not inevitably 'reactive', stirred by the state, its new policies of aggrandizement, taxation, and centralization. Instead, revolts such as the Jacquerie and the Ciompi were often oppor-tunistic, directed by their own initiatives, erupting not when states were strong, in pursuit of new aggressive policies, but when weak, divided by factional cracks at the top of society. Late medieval revolts on the Continent fail to match James C. Scott's generalizations.[18] They were neither infrequent nor suicidal, ending inevitably in brutal suppression. Instead, regularly their leaders could cut favourable deals with their

---

[17] For these models of pre-industrial revolt and their variations, see works by George Rudé, Charles Tilly, David Sabean, Patricia Crone, James C. Scott, Sidney Tarrow, Yves-Marie Bercé, Guy Fourquin, and others. For changes in these models as far as the work of Tarrow and Tilly goes, see most recently Michael Hanagan, 'Charles Tilly and Violent France', *French Historical Studies*, 33 (2010): 283–96 and Marcel van der Linden, 'Charles Tilly's Historical Sociology', *International Review of Social History* 54 (2009): 237–74, especially 255–9. The conceptual changes, however, had little to do with the popular protest, collective violence, or 'repertoires of contention' in the Middle Ages; instead, they focused on differences between the eighteenth and twentieth century. Until 1800, 'contentious performances' – Tilly's new term for social protest – remained 'parochial, particular, and bifurcated', as opposed to 'cosmopolitan, autonomous, and modular' from the nineteenth century on. Charles Tilly, *Contentious Performances* (Cambridge, 2008).

[18] Scott, *Weapons of the Weak*, p. xv. Also, Fourquin, *The Anatomy of Popular Rebellion*, p. 25.

social betters and more than occasionally won outright their demands. Finally, the ideology of pre-modern popular revolts was not reactionary in the literal sense, harking back to vague or imaginary lost rights of a mythical golden age that could only be regained *Deus ex machine* through intervention by 'the good king', emperor, or pope. Instead, late medieval rebels on the Continent rarely held their supreme authorities in such esteem and sought means to confront, embarrass, and insult them and their symbols of power when they could.[19]

How well do these pre-modern models characterize popular protest in English towns? In one aspect, English cases fit them even less well than those on the Continent: rarely were English revolts 'reactive' to innovations or pressures coming from on high. In few, if any, did a strong king provoke significant popular revolts through aggressive aggrandizement of power, as resulted with with Philip the Fair's (Philip IV, Philippe le Bel) fiscal and political measures in Flanders that led to the first of two of the most widespread revolts of the late Middle Ages.[20] Instead, the actions of strong kings in England – monetary debasement, new purveyances and taxes for increased warfare, new juridical and administrative structures – provoked at most only vague murmurs from the populace. An exception may have been the yet-to-be studied wave of ship seizures in English ports in 1347, with rebels' momentary take-over of municipal governments in reaction to Edward III's purveyances to supply his troops in Gascony. This resistance, however, was brief, and not a single chronicler mentioned it. Nor did it arise in the next session of Commons, despite numerous

---

[19] See examples in Cohn, *Popular Protest*: the Parisian rising of 1307, when the *menu peuple* held the king hostage and threw meat delivered to him into the mud to show their disrespect (doc. no. 14); the mock humiliation of kingship during Rouen's Harelle of 1382, when rebels dressed a fat burgher as king for a day (doc. nn. 144–5); the chants of the Neapolitan populace in 1347 against their queen: 'Death to the traitors and to the Queen, the whore', Cohn, *Lust for Liberty*, p. 80; and others.

[20] The same is seen in numerous rural revolts in northwestern Germany and the Low countries in the thirteenth and early fourteenth century, 'ignited by fiscal matters and grievances over the centralization of public administration'; see van Bavel, 'Rural Revolts', pp. 254 and 263–7. Also see Peter Hoppenbrouwers, 'Rebels with a Cause: The Peasant Movements of Northern Holland in the Latter Middle Ages', in *Showing Status: Representations of Social Positions in the Late Middle Ages*, ed. Wim Blockmans and Antheun Janse (Tourhout, 1999), pp. 445–82, who analyses seven peasant revolts in northern Holland between 1274 and 1426, all provoked by 'the rude intrusions upon local autonomy via appointed officials' (p. 482) and the count's efforts to centralize power (p. 267). For this model of strong kings and development of the state being the creative force behind popular revolt in the later Middle Ages, see Mollat and Wolff, *The Popular Revolutions of the Late Middle Ages*, and Boone, *A la recherché d'une modernité civique*, p. 59.

petitions against royal taxes, purveyances, and the heavy-handed seizure of ships requisitioned by the king.[21]

In other respects, however, the English case begins to conform to a supposed 'pre-modern' model, at least more closely than with the Continent. Firstly, while women on the Continent were conspicuously absent from popular revolts, in English ones they appear regularly, even if in small numbers, and not solely as followers. Joanna Ferrour may have been a leader during the Peasants' Revolt; she was among an inner core of 'principal' rebels not included in the first general pardons. Along with her husband, she was first active in village risings in Kent, later on 13 June with the burning of the Savoy Palace, and the following day at the Tower of London, with the summary executions of the archbishop, royal treasurer, and king's physician.[22]

Nor was she alone among women as a named participant or leader of a late medieval English revolt. Thomas Brembole, his wife, and daughter were also charged with burning the Savoy and the hospital at Clerkenwell;[23] a certain Katharine Gamen blocked the escape of the Chief Justice of King's Bench, Sir John Cavendish, leading to his capture and ghoulish execution.[24] An old woman, Margaret Starre, who was at the marketplace public burning of university charters in Cambridge, 'gathered the ashes of the burning documents, scattered them to the winds, and exclaimed, "Away with the craft of the clerks, away with it!"'[25] At Petham hundred in Kent, seven were indicted for rebellion in 1381: three were women. From Andrew Prescott's uncovering of thousands of indicted rebels, such a proportion was hardly typical.[26] Yet, in stark contrast to the Continent, at least women appeared.

---

[21] *PROME*, Edward III, January 1348, membranes no. 2, items 16, 20–2, no. 4, items 44 and 57, and no. 5, item 59.

[22] See Sylvia Federico, 'The Imaginary Society: Women in 1381', *JBS*, 40 (2001):159–83; and KB 145/3/5/1 and 27/482 rex, m.39d. She was, however, not found guilty. I thank Andrew Prescott for his transcriptions. Réville, *Le Soulèvement*, Appendix II, documents nn. 199 and 200, had already described her activities.

[23] Petit-Dutaillis, 'Introduction historique', lxxxvi-ii.

[24] Oman, *The Great Revolt*, p. 107; Trenholme, *The English Monastic Boroughs*, p. 56; Powell, *Kingship, Law, and Society*, pp. 41–2; and Prescott, *'The Yorkshire Partisans'*, p. 337. Margaret Wright of Lakenheath was also involved in Cavendish's capture; see Dyer, 'The Social and Economic Background', p. 16. Cavendish was paraded with his head stuck on a pole, his ear first to the mouth of the executed prior of Bury on another pole, then lip to lip, to mock their corrupt friendship.

[25] Cooper, *Annals of Cambridge*, I, p. 121; and Oman, *The Great Revolt*, p. 126.

[26] JUST 1/400 m 23; also translated in Flaherty, 'The Great Rebellion in Kent of 1381 Illustrated from the Public Records', *Archaeologia Cantiana*, 3 (1860), pp. 94–5. The twenty-four pieces from the bundle of court records, now housed in TNA, 'Presentationes de Malefactoribus qui surrexerunt contra Dominum Regem, 4 et 5 Ric. II', names 189 indicted rebels from early June to August. Of these, only the three

In fact, women's participation in popular uprisings in late medieval English towns in general appears more significant than it was in 1381. From the earliest revolts of monastic boroughs – those at Dunstable in 1227 and 1228 – women were named within the crowds rebelling against an abbey's juridical authority and taxes. In 1235, 'the greater part of the men and women' of Norwich assembled to complain to the king of false arrests, wrongful seizure of cattle, and violations against their privileges as burgesses. For its more violent actions in 1272, chronicles describe the citizens 'armed to the nines', with townswomen storming the cathedral and monastic cloister. Of the thousands said to have participated, Henry ultimately decided to execute only its most zealous rebels or leaders; they included thirty-four men and a woman. In the 1283 conflict between the Archbishop of York and the priory of St Cuthbert at Durham, women hurled the rocks and chased the archbishop from town. In the 1313 revolt against the tollbooth and its farm at Lynn, another woman is singled out and named among the 'great crowd of rioters'. In the same year, a complaint from the Abbot of St Albans listed twenty-three men and two women who broke the abbey's monopoly rights on hand mills, refused to be brought to trial, and retaliated against the abbot by entering his close in town, felling trees, carrying away timber, and assaulting his servant. In burgess revolts for liberties and new charters against abbots sparked by the baronial strife of 1327, women were named among the rebels subject to special scrutiny, and at Bury, fourteen were singled out for especially severe punishment. In 1337, a commission named a woman insurgent in Daventry, who 'by force' prevented the prior from exercising the abbey's right 'time out of mind' of grinding all the malt for brewing within town. In Newcastle upon Tyne in 1341, Richard of Acton and his wife Maud gathered the 'lesser people' of the town to oppose the current regime of the mayor and bailiffs. In 1363, a rare revolt in a lay seigneurial borough, that of Sudbury, was led by a local parson, eleven men and a woman, who imprisoned its sergeant and other officials. After the rigged election of Nicholas Brembre in October 1384, Joan, wife of a goldsmith, organized and incited a riot to free Brembre's imprisoned rival, Northampton.[27]

Still other descriptions claim that the 'whole commonalty' of towns revolted against the king, abbeys, and other lords in struggles for liberties, implying that women, as well as men, were among the rebels, as with those at Bristol, who were assembled by their sheriff

women from the Hundred of Petham appear. I thank Andrew Prescott for these references.
[27] Bird, *The Turbulent London*, p. 89, a case found in the *CPMR*, III, p. 67.

in 1316 to resist the arrest of any citizen; those in Norwich in
1303, who invaded two wards within the city, exercised their own
justice, and claimed certain privileges; or those in Canterbury, in
1343, 'instigated by its bailiffs' against the priory of Christ Church,
and so on. Finally, women appear in bold collective political action that
did not result in violence but could have, as in an all-women's march
into Parliament during its session of 1427, led by a woman from
London's stocks market ('Stokkes'). They delivered letters to the Duke
of Gloucester, the archbishops, and lords in attendance, rebuking the
duke for failing to free his wife, Jacqueline of Bavaria,[28] from captivity
and for his open adultery, 'to the ruin of the realm'.[29] In 1430, another
all-women's group banded together; this one to kill the king. Finally,
in anticipation of enclosure riots of the seventeenth century, 'wives,
acting the part of their husbands' led a Bristol tax revolt in 1401.[30]
Nothing comparable is seen on the Continent until well into the early
modern period.

Another contrast between English and Continental revolts regards
their success and repression. Here, the English ones appear in another
world from the Continent. The success rate for the latter, as seen from
chronicles, approached 70 per cent. For England, by contrast, such
success stories are hard to find, even limited ones for short periods.
Most exceptional was Bristol's revolt between 1312 and 1316, when
burgesses resisted royal incursions, and yet in less than six months
following defeat, its liberties were restored. Its eighty rebel leaders never
faced justice and several resurfaced later as mayors, bailiffs, and even
members of Parliament. The revolt of Lynn and capture of its tollbooth
won economic rights to its port, but were gained only with payment of
hefty fines. With both, partial success depended on the internal and
international circumstances of the second decade of the fourteenth
century – on Edward II's weak kingship, his overextension militarily
and financially to fight the Scots. London commoners experienced
further successes, but again, these were momentary, as with the extension of the guild-based government in the 1270s and elections of mayors
favourably disposed to artisan liberties. Finally, the sources fail to report
any repression of the 1347 wave of riots in the port towns that stretched
as far north as Yorkshire, south to Kent, and west to Bristol during

[28] On her assistance to peasant rebels in northern Holland in 1426 and her loss to Duke
Philip of Burgundy, see Hoppenbrouwers, 'Rebels with a Cause', pp. 454–5.

[29] Riley, 'Introduction' and *Chronicon ... monasterio S. Albani*, pp. xxxiii–xxxiv and 20.

[30] Walker, 'Rumour, Sedition and Popular Protest', pp. 56–7, according to the King's
Bench indictments, the rank and file was overwhelmingly women.

another crisis, this one of economic downturn and harvest failures, but triggered by the king's need to provision ships to fight in France.

On the other hand, burgess insurrections that challenged the privileges of monasteries, priories, bishops, canons, and parish priests and their jurisdictions within towns invariably failed. Ecclesiastical lords appealed to the king, his courts, and special commissions, resulting in swift reprisals, stiff fines, and often capital punishment by drawing, quartering, or even death by fire. Here, Guy Fourquin's dictum – revolts led 'only to repression and not to revolution' – comes closer to the mark than is seen with late medieval Continental revolts (for which Fourquin's generalization was mainly intended). Most successful of the burgess revolts for liberties against the Church was at Bury in 1327–8, where it took a year and a half before the Crown could fully restore the abbey's rights, and longer before its last rebels were brutally executed. The delay again depended on a royal crisis, a *coup d'état* that this time led to the king's murder. Once Edward III had restored royal power, penalties for Bury came swiftly and without mercy.

Leadership also distinguished English popular revolts: elected mayors and bailiffs, predominantly from towns' upper echelons, led a united front of citizens and commoners into pitched battle against the king or Church, and occasionally against seigneurs, such as the Berkeleys at Bristol. Even with London's reform movements and efforts by craftsmen to gain rights to assembly, maintain their own religious confraternities, and combat abuses of power and unfair taxes against the privileges of a narrow oligarchy, their leaders were born outside the ranks of the oppressed, as with William fitzOsbert, Thomas fitzThomas, Walter Hervey, John of Northampton, Ralph Holland, and William Cottesbroke. They had held the city's highest offices and were as wealthy, if not more so, than the oligarchs they opposed.[31] At times, their leadership came from higher levels still, as with the nobles who led Londoners to destroy the estates of members of the royal family during de Montfort's revolt against Henry.

The same is seen outside the capital. The leaders of 1312 who first opposed the fourteen oligarchs of Bristol and then royal power were among Bristol's wealthiest tax payers. In addition to clergymen, several leaders of the rebels of 1381 in Norfolk, such as Sir Roger Bacon and Sir Thomas Cornerd, were members of the gentry.[32] A principal rebel

---

[31] Viewing London's rebellious past, Williams, *Medieval London*, p. 228, concluded that popular rebel leaders were mostly of aldermanic rank or belonged to misteries of the patriciate such as those of drapers, goldsmiths, vintners and pepperers.

[32] Hanawalt, 'Peasant Resistance', p. 41; on Bacon and his attacks of Yarmouth, Suffolk, Flegg and south Norfolk, see Barbara Cornford, 'Events of 1381 in Flegg', pp. 39–48, in

leader in Suffolk, Thomas Sampson, owned estates in three Suffolk villages as well as in Norfolk, along with luxury goods, as was revealed in the post-rebellion confiscation of his property.[33] With the first major village revolt of 1381, that at Fobbing, Essex, on 30 May, the villagers' spokesman had been their tax collector,[34] and the bailiff of East Hanningfield, John Geffrey, led the last resistance of the Essex men at the end of June.[35] In Scarborough, two of the three principal instigators were among the town's wealthiest.[36] Three prominent men of the gentry with close ties to the royal family led the Cheshire Rising of 1393, which included archers and 'a considerable number of the rebels who came from the lowest classes'. Its principal leader, Sir Thomas Talbot, owned estates in Yorkshire, Lancashire, Cheshire, and Kent.[37] The most striking example comes from York and its revolt of 1405, when one of the most powerful aristocrats of England, the Archbishop of York, led from the pulpit against unfair and excessive taxation and royal misgovernance and corruption. The leader of the 1414 Lollard conspiracy to topple royal power and assault the rights of the Church to possess property was the aristocrat Sir John Oldcastle, a knight of the realm, previously justice of the peace, sheriff, and member of Parliament representing the knights of Hertfordshire, who had married into one of the principal aristocratic families of Kent.[38] Finally, little is known about the real Jack Cade, but he certainly did not boast working-class or artisan origins;[39] in fact, he assumed the aristocratic family name of Mortimer and took great pains with dress and demeanour to prove he was of nobility, even if 'a new type of lord', wearing a straw hat along with aristocratic armament.[40]

Studies Towards a History of the Rising of 1381 in Norfolk, ed. Barbara Cornford (Norwich, 1984), pp. 39–41; and Prescott, 'Judicial Records', p. 167.

[33] Prescott, 'Judicial Records', p. 343.   [34] Grieve, 'The Rebellion', pp. 41–2.

[35] Eiden, 'Joint Action', p. 14.

[36] Dobson, 'The Risings in York, Beverley and Scarborough', p. 137.

[37] Bellamy, 'The Northern Rebellions', *BJRL*, 47 2 (1965), pp. 261 and 265; and Saul, *Richard II*, p. 219. On the possible connection between the uprising and peace negotiations with France, which threatened these military men's livelihoods, see Laughton, *Life in a Late Medieval City*, pp. 26–7. On Talbot's later involvement with Lollardy, see Thomson, *The Later Lollards*, p. 173; and Powell, *Kingship, Law, and Society*, p. 164.

[38] For his biography, see W. T. Waugh, 'Sir John Oldcastle', *EHR*, 20 (1905): 434–56; and John A. F. Thomson, 'Oldcastle, John, Baron Cobham (d. 1417)', *ODNB* (2004).

[39] Griffiths, *The Reign of King Henry VI*, pp. 617–19, argues that Cade came from the lower ranks of society, but in his negotiations with the archbishops admits he was well-spoken and, if the author of any of the surviving manifestos, was an articulate and skilled rhetorician. According to Simkins, 'Political History', p. 290, he was also 'a man of education' with the capacity to organize an army and draw up proclamations.

[40] Kaufman, *The Historical Literature*, pp. 16, 92, 124, 127, 130. Also, following Cade's victory over the Staffords, he donned 'Sir Humphrey's expensive accoutrements – his

Furthermore, if Montgomery Bohna's arguments regarding the pardon lists of Cade's rebels are accepted, then high-ranking military constables were on the next rung of leaders of the 1450 rebellion.[41]

To be sure, there were exceptions. On the eve of the Peasants' Revolt of 1381, the 'men of less sufficiency' or 'poorer sort' rebelled against 'the mayor and good men of the town of Shrewsbury'. But even these rebels took counsel from men such as the draper Roger Wolrych, who were not of their ranks. In 1384 the 'cordewaner' John Constantyn stirred up London crowds against the oligarchy of Brembre in support of the former populist mayor, Northampton. To what extent Northampton was the behind-the-scenes leader remains, however, unclear. In addition, artisans such as the dyer William Haylyn, who was sent to prison for protesting against the city of London's new charter of 1443 that concentrated judicial power in the hands of London's elite and stripped artisans of their previous electoral rights, may have been artisan heroes, but the sources do not portray them as leaders.[42]

The best example before the English Peasants' Revolt of 1381 of popular leaders from the ranks of those they led may have been the brief wave of popular rebellion that swept through English ports in 1347. Throughout, the Patent Rolls describe a similar organization and actions, suggesting possible networks of communication and leadership beyond individually isolated towns and cities. 'Malefactors' of the towns assumed 'to themselves the royal power and elected one of their number as captain before attacking the ships', plundering corn, and imprisoning the 'good men' of their towns. Only in one port, however – Boston – was that captain named: Thomas de Hocham, cordewaner, who briefly became their 'mayor'.

The English Peasants' Revolt provides the largest repertoire of popular leaders, the only names of non-elite leaders now well-known to students – Wat Tyler, probably a tiler, Geoffrey Lister, a dyer, John Ball and John Wrawe, parish priests, and Jack Straw, for whom nothing is known except from one chronicler, who claimed he came from the Kentish gentry.[43] However, according to Hilton, '[T]he peasant element in the local leadership and membership of rebel bands appears rather

---

brigandise of velvet decorated with gilded nails, his salet, and his spurs; Griffiths, *The Reign of King Henry VI*, p. 612.

[41] Bohna, 'Armed Force', pp. 575 and 581. Also, Helen Lyle, *The Rebellion of Jack Cade* (London, 1950), p. 19, maintains that the constables supporting Cade sent writs in thirty-three hundreds, calling on their military levies, and in seven villages every man of military age answered the summons.

[42] Barron, 'The Political Culture', pp. 129–30.

[43] Hilton, *Bond Men Made Free*, pp. 177–8; supposedly of the Culpeper family.

less prominent when we look at the indictments and the escheators' records of confiscations after the defeat of the rising'.[44] Moreover, outside Kent and Essex, the leaders of the movement were substantial landowners on the cusp between 'well-to-do yeomen' and gentry as with Cambridgeshire's rebel leaders, the wealthy landowner Geoffrey Cobbe,[45] and John Hanchach, whose estates comprised one-fifth of the manorial property in Barham and six other villages.[46]

In the cities and towns of York, St Albans, Cambridge, Bury St Edmunds, Scarborough, Winchester, and Gloucester, the leaders of 1381 were not artisans, workers, or the indiscriminate poor; rather these 'rebels' struggled for power as heads of factions within government, were wealthy merchants, as with the supposedly reluctant new mayor of York, Simon de Quixley, substantial property owners, as with St Albans' heroic William Grindecobbe, or were these towns' traditional mayors and aldermen, leading burgesses to gain town liberties against recalcitrant abbots. At Scarborough, the principal rebel leader was the draper William Marche, who could afford to clad five hundred of his followers in a common uniform of a white hood with a red tail.[47] The rising in Essex and Kent set off a less well-studied revolt in Winchester of craftsmen; its leaders, however, came from the town's ruling elite.[48] In Beverley, the revolt of butchers, fullers, tilers, tailors, and other lesser craftsmen may have been supported by Alexander Neville, Archbishop of York.[49] In Gloucester, ringleaders such as Thomas Biseley and Thomas Compton came from the pinnacle of city society, having served multiple terms in the highest city offices.[50]

For London, less is known of their leaders, who sprang to action even before peasant and small-town rebels had crossed London Bridge, and who probably had been responsible for opening it to them. Factional politics after the revolt led to false accusations against certain aldermen, prominent among London's merchants: Willian Tonge, vintner, Walter Sibil, fishmonger (who controlled the ward of the Bridge with the authority to open London Bridge), John Horn, fishmonger, Adam

---

[44] Ibid., p. 178.   [45] See Oman, *The Great Revolt*, p. 123.
[46] Ibid., pp. 180–1. The mayor was another ringleader at Cambridge and the county. However, the rebels 'brandished axes and swords' and threatened to behead him if he did not lead them; Cam, 'Medieval History', p. 11.
[47] Oman, *The Great Revolt*, p. 142. A commission, however, headed by Gaunt pinned the making of the livery on the artisans, so 'that each should maintain what the other had done herein' (*CPR, 1381–5*, 1381.viii.19, p. 77).
[48] Locke, 'Political History', p. 315; and Hinck, 'The Rising of 1381 in Winchester'.
[49] Kermode, *Medieval Merchants*, pp. 57–8.
[50] Holt, 'Thomas of Woodstock and Events at Gloucester in 1381', *BIHR*, 58 (1985): 239.

Karlille, grocer, and John Fressh, mercer. Yet the indictments against these victuallers came with heightened factional politics in post-rebellion London, with the election of the anti-victualler mayor Northampton and his party's revenge against fishmongers and wholesale grocers.[51] Despite doubts over the post-1381 accusations, the question remains: how did the rebels cross London Bridge seemingly without opposition?[52]

From the Plea and Memoranda Rolls and Parliamentary records, on the other hand, Ruth Bird has emphasized that the London rebels 'were drawn from the lowest classes'. Yet neither her meticulous work nor that of later historians has uncovered prominent names from these classes. London's butchers Adam atte Welle and Roger Harry (who incited Essex men to enter the City) are the furthest down the social ladder she was able to descend in identifying popular leaders.[53] London's antagonism to John of Gaunt, on the other hand, especially among the merchant elites since the Good Parliament provoked in large part by Gaunt's threats to the city's liberties certainly gave those Bird classifies as the 'capitalist class' reasons to join and probably lead and incite the rebels to attack the Crown.[54]

Perhaps the most striking difference between the leaders of the English Peasants' Revolt and late medieval movements on the Continent, however, was the prominence of clergymen. In addition to John Ball, John Wrawe, and the vicar Geoffrey Parfray, Hilton has found at least twenty priests as its major leaders; they included itinerant ones as with Ball, and established parsons, as with the ringleader, Nicholas Frompton, at Bridgwater.[55] 1381 was no exception. As we have seen, names of insurgent clerics fill the mandates, pardons, and commission inquiries of the Patent Rolls that describe popular rebels and their

---

[51] Bird, *The Turbulent London*, p. 53–62; Dobson, *The Peasants' Revolt*, pp. 212–26; and more recently, Marion Turner, *Chaucerian Conflict: Languages of Antagonism in Late Fourteenth-Century London* (Oxford, 2007), pp. 31–9. Wilkinson, 'The Peasants' Revolt', first questioned the validity of the jurors' inquisitions of 1382. According to Rexroth, *Deviance and Power*, Horn 'had demonstrably colluded with the rebels' (p. 137).

[52] See the *Anonimalle Chronicle's* description of their crossing, in Dobson, *The Peasants' Revolt*, p. 156; and Prescott, 'Judicial Records', p. 19. From the chronicles, Wilkinson, 'The Peasants' Revolt', believed the bridge was lowered by force of Southwark and London commoners, without any identifiable leadership. On Horn and the jurors' charges, see ibid. Nonetheless, Wilkinson concluded that Londoners' hatred of Gaunt, including that of 'important aldermen' (p. 32), had galvanized sympathy towards the rebels, but such sympathy says nothing about leadership. Even the jurors' indictments, which sought to frame Horn, Tonge, Sibil, and other aldermen of the summer of 1381 in the worse possible light, did not describe them as leaders of the London, or peasant, rebels.

[53] Bird, *The Turbulent London*, p. 55.   [54] See above, Chapter 4, note 97.

[55] Dilks, 'Bridgwater', pp. 62–3 and 67.

actions. From local parish priests, friars, and apostate preachers, they reached the apex of late medieval England's religious hierarchy. From various towns, friars allied with townsmen in de Montfort's revolt against Henry; in 1327–8, they were among Bury's rebels and later assisted in freeing rebels imprisoned by the abbot. In 1402, they were prominent in the conspiracies against Henry IV; at St Albans they joined forces with the town's parish priests and burgesses against the Benedictine Abbey's economic and political monopolies.

Parish priests were also among the leaders of revolts at the very outset of our investigations: following Longbeard's execution, one led a subversive movement to transform Longbeard's place of execution into a shrine to further fan his fame as the people's martyred saint, and was executed for it. In the assault of May 1327 on the Abbey of Bury St Edmunds, two parish priests, decked out in military tunics, carrying pennants in warlike fashion, led burgesses to tear down the monastery's doors and occupy its tower. In October raids that year, twenty-eight rectors and priests joined burgesses in further attacks against the monastery and then in a week-long plunder of the abbey's rural estates. In 1345, a parson led a tax revolt in Bristol against the collection of the tenth and fifteenth. In 1363, a parson of Sudbury organized a confederacy of burgesses against the courts and other privileges held by the town's seigneurial lord, Edward III's son Lionel, Duke of Clarence. In 1380, the master of the hospital of St John Baptist and three of its brothers in Bridgwater led burgesses against their lord, William la Zouche. At the end of the fourteenth century, an outsider, a wealthy clerical pluralist and canon of Salisbury, the rector Richard Wych, 'helped to ignite the smouldering grievances' in the small town of Shipston-on-Stour, convincing the town's tenants that they were burgesses.[56] Unlicensed preachers such as John Grace led revolts against the Crown in 1424. Hertfordshire appears to have had a tradition of rebel parish priests. In the 1350s, the vicar of Aldbury church and a hermit preached against the Ordinances and Statutes of Labourers. In 1381, a vicar of Ware led a wide cross-section of the town in the Great Rebellion,[57] and in 1402, yet another parish priest of Ware was accused of organizing the town's conspiracy against Henry IV. Finally, contemporaries were astonished at the large numbers of clergymen who joined the burgesses of York and their archbishop in 1405 against the Crown's excessive taxation and attacks on liberties. Different from 1381, these

[56] Dyer, 'Small-town Conflict', pp. 199–202.
[57] Prescott, 'London in the Peasants' Revolt', p. 129; and Prescott, 'Essex Rebel Bands in London', p. 63.

clerical rebels ranged across the Church hierarchy and included secular and regular clerics.[58] By contrast, less than 1 per cent of participants of 1,112 revolts on the Continent were members of the clergy, regular or secular; and clerical leaders can be counted on one hand. Fra Bussolari of Pavia was the most notable exception, and he cited lessons from Roman history rather than the Bible to rouse his townsmen.[59]

Finally, in contrast to the Continent, late medieval English history portrays popular rebels with apparent respect and awe for the king while pouring blame on his corrupt advisers.[60] The rebels of the longest and most successful revolt found in our survey – that against the Crown in Bristol from 1312 to 1316 – took pains to claim that their revolt was not against Edward or royal power. Instead, the *bête noir* of their discontent was their hated royal constable, Bartholomew de Badlesmere. More famous was the rebels' esteem and trust for young Richard during the Peasants' Revolt: the English commoners presented themselves as his self-appointed soldiers, defending him against his evil advisers, from the Duke of Lancaster to petty questmongers and legal scribes.[61] Peasants and small townsmen marched to Blackheath, St Albans, Bridgwater, and elsewhere under the king's banner of St George,[62] while they summarily executed the king's principal advisers at the Tower, burnt the Savoy and manors of Robert Hales and John of Gaunt, destroyed chests and

[58] See Walker, 'The Yorkshire Risings of 1405', p. 175. In comparison with the Continent, the English clergy – secular and regular – was better armed and more disposed to enter armed battle whether in military defence of the realm, factional conflict, or popular insurrection. The kings of England contributed to the clergy's combat readiness with royal writs from Edward III (1369) to Henry V (1418), ordering bishops to command abbots, priors, and other clergy 'to be armed and arrayed', ready to march against enemy invasion from across the Channel or the northern border. According to Bruce McNab, 'Obligations of the Church in English Society: Military Arrays of the Clergy, 1369–1418', in *Order and Innovation in the Middle Ages: Essays in Honor of Joseph R. Strayer*, ed. William C. Jordan, Bruce McNab, and Teofilo F. Ruiz (Princeton, 1976), pp. 313–14, bishops followed these orders with little or no protest, despite canonical prohibitions against bearing arms and shedding blood.

[59] Cohn, *Lust for Liberty*, pp. 114–15.

[60] David Grummitt, 'Deconstructing Cade's Rebellion: Discourse and Politics in the Mid Fifteenth Century', pp. 107–23, in *The Fifteenth Century: VI: Identity and Insurgency in the Late Middle Ages*, ed. Linda Clark (Woodbridge, 2006), p. 122, argues that Cade's rebels 'petitioned against corrupt courtiers and evil counsellors because that is what the discursive conventions of the time identified as the principal reasons for misgovernment'. But, even if this were 'discourse' alone and somehow not related to rebels' beliefs and practices, then it must be recognized that this 'discursive convention' was not common 'for the time' outside England.

[61] Fryde, *The Great Revolt*, p. 18; and Dyer, *Making a Living in the Middle Ages*, p. 288.

[62] David Crook, 'Derbyshire and the English Rising of 1381', *BIHR*, 60 (1987): 9–23, p. 16; Dilks, 'Bridgwater', pp. 64–5; Prescott, '"Meynteyn him als his brother"', p. 11; and Réville, *Le soulèvement*, p. 39 (at Tring).

charters of the lawyers' abode of the Temple, and desired 'to kill all lawyers, questmongers, or any who could write a writ'.[63] The worst disrespect any could show the boy-king himself (and this from the prejudicial account of the St Albans' chronicle) was Wat Tyler, guzzling water and then ale from a jug on a hot summer's day in front of the king.[64] With England's second most celebrated revolt of the Middle Ages, Cade's in 1450, again the rebels sharply separated the king from his evil advisers, as reflected in the bills they circulated: 'The king is informed daily and nightly that evil is good and good is evil; by false means and lies his counsellors make him hate his true friends and love the false traitors'.[65] The surviving manifestos 'above all, affirmed the rebels' loyalty to him, placing their faith in him and the restoration of customary legal process'.[66] They branded themselves the king's 'true liege men and best friends'.[67]

Such sentiments infused popular tales such as those of *Gamelyn* and *Adam Bell* and Robin Hood ballads: 'I love no man in all the worlde/ So well as I do my kyne'.[68] Even magnates in their revolts against the king made similar distinctions. To justify their deposition of Edward II, they accused the king's favourite, Hugh Despenser the younger, of tyranny, not the king; Edward was seen as the victim of Despenser's 'machinations'.[69] Similarly,

---

[63] This was not only the cry of rebels in London as reported by Walsingham and other chronicles, but in other regions such as Norfolk; see Prescott, '"Meynteyn him als his brother"', p. 16.

[64] According to Froissart and Walsingham, peasant rebels entered the Tower and rampaged through the king's and queen mother's private chambers. By Froissart's account they broke her bed, causing her to swoon; according to Walsingham, they asked her to kiss them. The *Anonimalle Chronicle* and *LB, H* cast doubts on these stories: the queen mother was not then at the Tower but accompanying the king at Mile End; see W. M. Ormrod, 'In Bed with Joan of Kent: The King's Mother and the Peasants' Revolt', pp. 277–92, in *Medieval Women: Texts and Contexts in Late Medieval Britain: Essays for Felicity Riddy*, ed. Jocelyn Wogan-Browne, et al. (Turnhout, 2000), especially 277–8; and Strohm, '"A Revelle!"', p. 48. Even if Froissart or Walsingham are to be believed, significantly the rebels did not execute her as they did the Crown's bureaucrats, and in contrast to rebel attempts at Naples against their queen in 1347.

[65] Scase, '"Strange and Wonderful Bills"', p. 234. Also, Mavis Mate, 'The Economic and Social Roots of Medieval Popular Rebellion: Sussex in 1450–1451', *EcHR*, 45 (1992), pp. 663–4: Cade's manifestos followed traditional lines of loyalty of the king and the necessity of removing his evil advisers. With Wilkyns' revolt two years later, rebels of the southeast abandoned the distinction and targeted the king; see Harvey, *Jack Cade's Rebellion*, p. 165.

[66] Griffiths, *The Reign of King Henry VI*, p. 637. Cade's rebels did not see themselves as 'risers' but as those 'coming to the rescue of their king'; see Watts, 'The Pressure of the Public', pp. 160 and 168–9; and Powell, *Kingship, Law, and Society*, p. 40.

[67] Cited in Powell, *Kingship, Law, and Society*, p. 40.   [68] Ibid., p. 39.

[69] Phillips, *Edward II*, pp. 509–10. London plebes hurling mud and abuse on the queen as she tried to escape by barge during the barons' war against Henry III might be considered an exception; yet the queen, not the king, was the butt of these insults.

despite bitterness over Henry IV's usurpation of the throne, followed by excessive taxation that broke his initial promises, the target of York's rebels in 1405, according to their bills nailed to church doors, was not Henry but his 'avaricious and greedy counsellors . . . gorging themselves on the wealth ordained for the common good'.[70]

These differences between England and the Continent, we hypothesize, derive from the strength of the English Crown. When not abroad fighting wars or embroiled in baronial revolts or civil wars at home, kings intervened quickly and decisively into the affairs of towns and cities across the realm. More than on the Continent, revolts coincided with cracks widening within the ruling order. Ecological and demographic factors could also have an impact, as was seen in the economically depressed years preceding the Black Death, but even here, royal politics were at the forefront: more than bad harvests or high bread prices, the king's requisitioning of victuals and ships for war, coupled with his absence from England, led to townsmen's attacks and momentary take-over of town governments. More profoundly, the Black Death failed to cut the crucial divide in the pace and character of popular revolt as it had on the Continent. There, the change in supply and demand for labour gave rise to a new spirit, a 'lust for liberty', to use the chronicler of Saint-Denys' words in the 1380s. In English towns, the Black Death spurred on no such following, even given the exception of the urban risings of 1381.

In terms of the centralization of royal power and the gap between rulers and ruled, late medieval England began to resemble European monarchies of the early modern period more than they did the fragmented powers of late medieval city-states or monarchies on the Continent. This development of the English Crown no doubt benefited from the geo-politics of an island nation. As the chronicler of the life of Edward II put it after the defeat of Bristol's rebellion in 1316: 'For an islander to rebel against an island king is as if a chained man were to try his strength with the warden of his prison.'[71] Even here, the chronicler was thinking more of magnate revolts against the king – 'the tragic fate of the besieged at Bedford' and those who had held the castle at Kenilworth – than of protests by artisans or peasants, who, unlike their social superiors, possessed neither ships to escape nor ready support from across the Channel, the Irish Sea, or the borders of Wales and Scotland. Later, royal and oligarchic powers in Continental Europe would catch up with the English. The division between rulers and ruled

---

[70] Walker, 'The Yorkshire Risings of 1405', p. 172.
[71] *Vita Edwardi Secundi*, p. 129; cited in Phillips, *Edward II*, p. 410.

would there too widen, and as a consequence, the character of popular revolt would change: women would become more prominent within protesting crowds and emerge as leaders, as with la Branlaire in a tax revolt at Montpellier in 1645;[72] leadership would come increasingly from outside the ranks of artisans and peasants, to rely on what Yves-Marie Bercé calls their traditional leaders – the clergy, mayors, and lords[73] – and chances of popular rebels succeeding would diminish. Late medieval England was the harbinger of these changes.

Comparison of popular insurrection in English and Continental towns fails to demarcate an unvariegated *longue durée* of the 'pre-modern', all of one piece as presently imagined by modern historians, political scientists, and sociologists. Fundamental structural differences could vary from one region of Europe to the next, with rhythms of change strongly dependent on power relations between haves and have-nots, rulers and ruled, stemming from institutional developments at the top of society. These facts and relationships in turn would depend on the successes and failures of popular revolt itself.

---

[72] N. Z. Davis, 'Women on Top', in *Society and Culture in Early Modern France* (Stanford, CA, 1975), p. 146. For early modern English examples, see Keith Wrightson, *English Society 1580–1680* (London, 1982), p. 178; Manning, *Village Revolts*, pp. 96, 99, and 115–16; Walter, *Crowds and Popular Politics*, p. 49; and Wood, 'Collective Violence, Social Drama and Rituals of Rebellion in Late Medieval and Early Modern England', in *Cultures of Violence: Interpersonal Violence in Historical Perspective*, ed. Stuart Carroll (Houndmills, 2007), p. 103.

[73] Yves-Marie Bercé, *Revolt and Revolution in Early Modern Europe: An Essay on the History of Political Violence*, trans. Joseph Bergin (Manchester, 1987 [1980]), p. 64.

Bibliography

Primary sources: chronicles

Annales of Burton (AD 1004–1263) in *Annales monastici*, ed. Henry Richards Luard, 5 vols., RS, 36 (1864–9), V, pp. 1004–263.

Annales Cambriae. AD 444–1288, ed. J. Williams ab Ithel (London, 1860).

Annales Londonienses in *Chronicles of the Reigns of Edward I and Edward II, Edited from Manuscripts*, ed. William Stubbs, 2 vols., RS, 76 (1882–3), I, pp. 1–252.

Annales de Margan in *Annales monastici*, ed. Henry Richards Luard, 5 vols. RS, 36 (1864–9), I, pp. 3–42.

Annales monasterii S. Albani, a Johanne Amundesham (AD 1421–1440), ed. Henry T. Riley, 2 vols., RS, 28/5 (1870–1).

Annales monasterii de Waverleia (AD 1–1291) in *Annales monastici*, ed. Henry Richards Luard, 5 vols., RS, 36 (1864–9), II, pp. 129–413.

Annales monasterii de Wintonia in *Annales monastici*, ed. Henry Richards Luard, 5 vols., RS, 36 (1864–9), II, pp. 3–128.

Annales monastici, ed. Henry Richards Luard, 5 vols. RS, 36 (1864–9).

Annales Paulini in *Chronicles of the Reigns of Edward I and Edward II, Edited from Manuscripts*, ed. William Stubbs, 2 vols., RS, 76 (1882–3), I, pp. 253–370.

Annales Ricardi Secundi et Henrici Quarti (1392–1406). RS, 28 (1866), III, pp. 153–420.

Annales de Tewksbury (1066–1263) in *Annales monastici*, ed. Henry Richards Luard, 5 vols., RS, 36 (1864–9), I, pp. 43–180.

Annals of Bermondsey in *Annales monastici*, ed. Henry Richards Luard, 5 vols., RS, 36 (1864–9), III, pp. 421–88.

Annals of Dunstable, partially translated in William Robieson, *The Growth of Parliament and the War with Scotland, 1216–1307* (London, 1914), pp. 9–78.

Annals of Dunstable in *Annales monastici*, ed. Henry Richards Luard, 5 vols., RS, 36 (1864–9), III, pp. 3–408.

Annals of Osney in *Annales monastici*, ed. Henry Richards Luard, 5 vols., RS, 36 (1864–9), IV, pp. 3–5.

The Annals of Roger de Hoveden, Comprising the History of England and of other Countries of Europe from AD 732 to AD 1201, trans. Henry T. Riley (London, Bohn, 1853).

Annals of Thomas Wykes in *Annales monastici*, ed. Henry Richards Luard, 5 vols., RS, 36 (1864–9), IV, pp. 6–354.

The Anonimalle Chronicle: 1307–1334, From Brotherton Collection MS 29, ed. and trans. Wendy R. Childs and John Taylor (Leeds, 1991).

The Anonimalle Chronicle, 1333 to 1381, ed. V. H. Galbraith (Manchester, 1970).

Avesbury, Robert of. *De gestis mirabilibus regis Edwardi Tertii*, ed. E. M. Thompson, RS, 93 (London, 1889).

Barber, John. *The Bruce*, ed. A. A. M. Duncan (Edinburgh, 1997).

Bower, Walter. *Scotichronicon*, 8 vols., ed. D. E. R. Watt (Aberdeen, 1990–4).

Capgrave, John. *Chronicle of England*, ed. F. C. Hingeston, RS, 1 (1858).

Cotton, Bartholomew de. *Historia Anglicana (AD 449–1298)*, ed. Henry Richards Luard, RS, 16 (1859).

Chronica Johannis de Oxenedes (to 1293), ed. H. Ellis (London, 1859).

Chronica Johannis de Reading, et Anonymi Cantuariensis, 1346–1367, ed. James Tait, Publications of the University of Manchester, Historical Series, 20 (Manchester, 1914).

Chronicle of the Abbey of Bury St Edmunds. Jocelin of Brakelond, trans. Diana Greenway and Jane Sayers (Oxford, 1989).

The Chronicle of Bury St Edmunds 1212–1301, ed. Antonia Gransden (London, 1964).

Chronicle of Dieulacres Abbey, 1381–1403, ed. M. V. Clarke and V. H. Galbraith in 'The Deposition of Richard II', *BJRL*, 7 (1930): 125–81.

The Chronicle of Gervase de Canterbury in *The Historical Works of Gervase of Canterbury*, 2 vols., RS, 73 (1879–80).

Chronicle of the Grey Friars of London, CS, old series, 53, ed. J. G. Nichols (London, 1852).

The Chronicle of Lanercost 1272–1346, trans. Sir Herbert Maxwell (Glasgow, 1913).

A Chronicle of London, from 1089 to 1483, Written in the Fifteenth Century, ed. N. H. Nicolas and E. Tyrell (London, 1827).

The Chronicle of Melrose: from the Cottonian Manuscript, Faustina B. IX in the British Museum, ed. A. O. Anderson and M. O. Anderson (London, 1936).

The Chronicle of Walter of Guisborough, ed. H. Rothwell, CS, 3rd series, 89 (1957).

The Chronicle of William de Rishanger, of the Barons' Wars: The Miracles of Simon de Montfort, Edited from Manuscripts in the Cottonian Library, ed. James Orchard Halliwell, CS (1840).

The Chronicles of Enguerrand de Monstrelet, ed. Thomas Johnes (London, 1810).

Chronicles of London, ed. C. L. Kingsford (Oxford, 1905).

Chronicles of the Reigns of Edward I and Edward II, Edited from Manuscripts, ed. William Stubbs, 2 vols., RS, 76 (1882–3).

Chronicles of the Revolution, 1397–1400: The Reign of Richard II, trans. and ed. Chris Given-Wilson (Manchester, 1993).

Chronicon Angliae Petriburgense, ed. J. A. Giles (London, 1845).

Chronicon anonymi Cantuariensis: The Chronicle of Anonymous of Canterbury 1346–1365, ed. and trans. Charity Scott-Stokes and Chris Given-Wilson (Oxford, 2008).

Chronicon brevius ad incarnatione usque ad annum Domini M.CCC.LXIV in *Eulogium (historiarum sive temporis): Chronicon ab Orbe condito usque ad annum Domini M.CCC.LXVI*, ed. Frank Scott Haydon, 3 vols., RS, 9 (1863), III, pp. 245–332.

Chronicon Galfridi le Baker de Swynebroke, ed. E. M. Thompson (Oxford, 1889).

Chronicon rerum gestarum in Monasterio S. Albani (1422–1431) a quodam auctore ignoto compilatum, ed. Henry T. Riley, 2 vols., RS, 28/5 (1870–1).

Chronique de Jean le Bel, ed. Jules Viard and Eugène Déprez, SHF, 317, 2 vols. (Paris, 1904).

Chronique de la traïson et mort de Richart deux roy dengleterre, ed. Benjamin Williams, English Historical Society (London, 1846).

Chroniques de London, ed. G. J. Aungier, CS, 28 (1844).

Commendatio lamentabilis, etc. Monachi cujusdam Malmesberiensis vita Edwardi II in *Chronicles of the Reigns of Edward I and Edward II, Edited from Manuscripts*, ed. William Stubbs, 2 vols., RS, 76 (1882–3), II, pp. 3–24.

Continuatio chronici Florentii Wigorniensis in *Florentii Wigorniensis monachi chronicon ex chronicis*, ed. Benjamin Thorpe, 2 vols. (London, 1848–9).

Continuatio chronici Willelmi de Novoburgo in *Chronicles of the Reigns of Stephen*, ed. R. Howlett, II (1885).

'Continuation of the English translation ... *MS Harl 2,261*' in *Ranulphi Higden monachi Cestrensis*, ed. J. R. Lumby, 9 vols., RS, 41 (1865–6), VIII, Appendix 3, p. 440.

Cronica Buriensis, AD 1020–1346, ed. Thomas Arnold, 3 vols., RS, 96 (1896), III.

Depraedatio Abbatiae Sancti Edmundi in *Memorials of St Edmund's Abbey*, ed. Thomas Arnold. RS, 96 (1892), pp. 327–54.

Diceto, Ralph de. *Radulphi de Diceto decani Lundoniensis Opera Historica. The Historical Work of Master Ralph de Diceto, Dean of London*. ed. William Stubbs, 2 vols., RS, 68 (1876).

Dieulacres Chronicle in *Chronicles of the Revolution 1397–1400: The Reign of Richard II*, trans. and ed. Chris Given-Wilson, Manchester Medieval Sources Series (Manchester, 1993).

'Eighth Book of the *Polychronicon* from Caxton' in *Ranulphi Higden monachi Cestrensis*, ed. J. R. Lumby, 9 vols., RS, 41 (1865–86), VIII, pp. 522–87.

An English Chronicle, 1377–1461, Edited from Aberystwyth, National Library of Wales MS 21068 and Oxford, Bodleian Library MS Lyell 34, ed. William Marx (Woodbridge, Suffolk, 2003).

Eulogium (historiarum sive temporis): Chronicon ab Orbe condito usque ad annum Domini M.CCC.LXVI, ed. Frank Scott Haydon, 3 vols., RS, 9 (1863), III, pp. 1–242.

Fordum, John of. *Chronicle of the Scottish Nation*, trans. F. J. H. Skene, ed. W. F. Skene (Edinburgh, 1872).

'A Fourteenth-Century Chronicle from the Grey Friars at Lynn', ed. Antonia Gransden, *EHR*, 72, no. 283 (1957): 270–8.

French Chronicle of London AD 1259–AD 1343 in *Chronicles of the Mayors and Sheriffs of London 1188–1274*, ed. Henry T. Riley (London, 1863).

Froissart, Jean. *Œuvres de Froissart: chroniques*, ed. M. le baron Kervyn de Lettenhove, 25 vols. (Brussels, 1867–77).

Gesta Edwardi de Carnarven in *Chronicles of the Reigns of Edward I and Edward II, Edited from Manuscripts*, ed. William Stubbs, 2 vols., RS, 76 (1882–3), II, pp. 25–92.

Gesta Regum in *The Historical works of Gervase of Canterbury*, 2 vols., RS, 73 (1879–80), II.

Gray, Sir Thomas. *Scalacronica 1272–1363*, ed. Andy King (Woodbridge, 2005).

The Great Chronicle of London, ed. A. H. Thomas and I. D. Thornley (London, 1938).

L'Histoire de Guillaume le Marechal, ed. P. Meyer, 3 vols., SHF (1891–1901).

Historia sive narracio de modo et forma mirabilis parliamenti per Thomas Favent clericum indicate, ed. M. McKisack, Camden Miscellany, XIV (1926).

The History of William of Newburgh, trans. Joseph Stevenson (Lampeter, 1996).

Incerti scriptoris narratio de rebus in bello sancto gestis 1217–1218, primum edidit ex unico codice, qui in bibliotheca Aulae-Graianae servatur, ed. Joannes Allen Giles (London, 1846).

John Benet's Chronicle for the Years 1400 to 1462, ed. G. L. Harriss and M. A. Harriss. Camden Miscellany, XXIV, CS, 4th series, 9 (1972).

John of Eversden (?). *Chronicle* in *The Chronicle of Florence of Worcester, with Two Continuations Comprising Annals of English History from the Departure of the Romans to the Reign of Edward I*, trans. Thomas Forester (London, 1854).

John of Taxster, *Chronicle* in *The Chronicle of Florence of Worcester, with Two Continuations* . . . trans. Thomas Forester (London, 1854).

The Kirkstall Abbey Chronicles, ed. John Taylor, Thoresby Society, XLII (Leeds, 1952).

Knighton's Chronicle 1337–1396, ed. and trans. G. H. Martin (Oxford, 1995).

Langtoft, Peter de. *Chronicle of Pierre de Langtoft, in French Verse from the Earliest Period to the Death of Edward I*, ed. T. Wright, 2 vols., RS, 47 (1866–8).

'*Liber de Antiquis Legibus*', attributed to Arnald Fitz-Thedmar in *Chronicles of the Mayors and Sheriffs of London 1188–1274: The French Chronicle of London AD 1259–AD 1343*, ed. Henry T. Riley (London, 1863).

Malvern Continuation of Higden in *Ranulphi Higden monachi Cestrensis*, ed. J. R. Lumby, 9 vols., RS, 41 (1865–86), VIII, pp. 352–428.

Mémoires de Pierre de Fenin, comprenant le récit des événements qui se sont passés en France et en Bourgogne sous les règnes de Charles VI et Charles VII (1407–1427), ed. Mlle DuPont, SHF (Paris, 1837).

Memoriale fratris Walteri de Coventria: The Historical Collections of Walter Coventry, ed. William Stubbs, 2 vols., RS, 58 (1872–3).

The Metrical Chronicle of Robert of Gloucester, ed. William Aldis Wright (London, 1887).

Monachi cujusdam Malmesberiensis Vita Edwardi II in *Chronicles of the Reigns of Edward I and Edward II, Edited from Manuscripts*, ed. William Stubbs, 2 vols., RS, 76 (1882–3), II, pp. 155–291.

Munimenta Civitatis Oxonie, ed. H. E. Salter, Oxford Historical Society, 71 (Oxford, 1920).

Murimuth, Adam. *Continuatio chronicarum, Robertus de Avesbury De gestis mirabililbus regis Edwardi Tertii*, ed. E. M. Thompson, RS, 93 (London, 1889).

Oeuvres de Rigord et de Guillaume le Breton, historiens de Philippe-Auguste, ed. H. François Delaborde, 2 vols., SHF (1882–5).

Opus Chronicorum in *Chronicum monasterii S. Albani*, ed. Henry T. Riley, 3 vols., RS, 28 (1866), III, pp. 3–59.

Otterbourne, Thomas and Whethamstede, Johannes. *Duo rerum Anglicarum Scriptores veteres. Ab origine gentis Britannicæ usque ad Edvardum IV* (Oxford, 1732).

Paris, Matthew, *Chronica majora: Matthew Paris's English History: From the Year 1235 to 1273*, trans. J. A. Giles (London, 1852–4).

Chronica majora in *Matthaei Parisiensis monachi Sancti Albani, chronica majora*, ed. Henry Richards Luard, 7 vols., RS, 57 (1874), III.

Historia Anglorum, sive, ut vulgo dicitur, historia minor, ed. Frederic Madden, 3 vols., RS, 44 (1866–9).

The Political Songs of England from the Reign of John to that of Edward II, ed. Thomas Wright, CS, 6 (London, 1839).

Quibus praefigitur Chronicon rerum gestarum in Mon. S. Albani (A.D. 1422–1431), a quodam auctore ignoto compilatum, ed. Henry T. Riley, 2 vols., RS, 28 (1870–1).

Ralph de Diceto. *Radulphi de Diceto decani Lundoniensis opera historica. The Historical Work of Master Ralph de Diceto, Dean of London*, ed. William Stubbs, 2 vols., RS, 68 (1876).

Translation of a French Metrical History of the Deposition of King Richard the Second [Creton's metrical history], ed. John Webb, in *Archaeologia: Miscellaneous Tracts Relating to Antiquity*, 110 vols., Society of Antiquarians of London, XX (1824).

Troklowe, Johannes de and Henricus de Blaneforde. *Chronica et annales, regnantibus Henrico III, Edwardo I, Edwardo II, Ricardo II et Henrico IV*, ed. Henry T. Riley, RS, 3 (1866).

Usk, Adam. *The Chronicle of Adam Usk*, ed. and trans. Chris Given-Wilson (Oxford, 1997).

Vita Edwardi Secundi, ed. Noël Denholm-Young (London, 1957).

Vita Edwardi Secundi. The Life of Edward the Second, ed. Wendy R. Childs (Oxford, 2005).

Vita et mors Edwardi Regis Angliae in *Chronicles of the Reigns of Edward I and Edward II, Edited from Manuscripts*, ed. William Stubbs, 2 vols., RS, 76 (1882–3), II, pp. 297–323.

Vita Sancti Hugonis. The Life of St Hugh of Avalon: Bishop of Lincoln, 1186–1200, ed. R. M. Loomis (New York, 1985).

Walsingham, Thomas. *Annales Ricardi Secundi et Henrici Quarti*, ed. H. T. Riley, 3 vols., RS, 28 (1866), III.

The Chronica maiora of Thomas Walsingham, 1376–1422, ed. James Clark and trans. David Preest (Woodbridge, Suffolk, 2005).

Chronica monasterii S. Albani, historia anglicana, ed. Henry T. Riley, 2 vols., RS, 28 (1863–4).

Neustriae: chronica monasterii S. Albani, Ypodigma Neustriae, ed. Henry T. Riley, 7 vols., RS, 28 (1876), VII.

The St Albans Chronicle: The Chronica maiora of Thomas Walsingham, ed. John Taylor and Wendy R. Childs, trans. Leslie Watkiss, 2 vols. (Oxford, 2003–11).

Wendover, Roger of. *The Flowers of History*, ed. Henry G. Hewlett, 3 vols., RS, 84 (1885–9).

The Westminster Chronicle 1381–1394, ed. L. C. Hector and Barbara F. Harvey (Oxford, 1982).

Willelmi Rishanger, monachi S. Albani, chronica, ed. Henry T. Riley, RS, 28.2 (1865).
William Thorne's Chronicle of Saint Augustine's Abbey Canterbury, ed. and trans. A. H. Davis (Oxford, 1934).

Other primary sources

Anglo-Norman Letters and Petitions from All Soul's MS 182, ed. M. D. Legge, Anglo-Norman Text Society, 3 (1941).
Bristol Charters 1155–1373, ed. M. Dermont Harding (Bristol, 1930).
British Borough Charters 1307–1600, ed. Martin Weinbaum (Cambridge, 1943).
Calendar of the Close Rolls Preserved in the Public Record Office (1227–1509), 63 vols. (London, 1900–63).
Calendar of Coroners Rolls of the City of London, AD 1300–1378 (London, 1913).
Calendar of Early Mayor's Court Rolls Preserved among the Archives of the Corporation of the City of London at the Guildhall A.D. 1298–1307, ed. A. H. Thomas (Cambridge, 1924).
Calendar of the Fine Rolls Preserved in the Public Record Office, 1272–1509, 22 vols. (London, 1911–62).
Calendar of Letter Books Preserved among the Archives of the Corporation of the City of London at the Guildhall: Letter-Book A–K, 9 vols., ed. Reginald R. Sharpe (London, 1899–1912).
Calendar of Patent Rolls Preserved in the Public Record Office, 1216–1452, 49 vols. (London, 1901–9).
Calendar of Plea and Memoranda Rolls Preserved among the Archives of the Corporation of the City of London at the Guildhall, 1323–1482, ed. A. H. Thomas, 6 vols. (Cambridge, 1926–61).
Calendar of the Plea Rolls of the Exchequer of the Jews Preserved in the Public Record Office, ed. J. M. Rigg, Hilary Jenkinson, and H. G. Richardson, 4 vols. (London and Edinburgh, 1905–72), I.
Cohn, Jr, Samuel K., ed. and trans. *Popular Protest in Late Medieval Europe: Italy, France, and Flanders*, Medieval Sources Series (Manchester, 2004).
Dobson, R. B. *The Peasants' Revolt of 1381*, 2nd edn (London, 1983).
Early Sources of Scottish History AD 500 to 1286, ed. and trans. Alan Orr Anderson, 2 vols. (Edinburgh, 1922).
Flaherty, William. 'The Great Rebellion in Kent of 1381 Illustrated from the Public Records', *Archaeologia Cantiana*, 3 (1860): 65–96.
Foedera, conventions, literae, et cujuscunque generic acta public, inter reges Angliae . . ., ed. Thomas Rymer, 10 vols. (London, 1704–35).
History of Newcastle and Gateshead, ed. Richard Welford, 3 vols. (London, 1884–7).
Medieval Archives of the University of Oxford, ed. H. E. Salter, 2 vols., Oxford Historical Society, LXX and LXXIII (Oxford, 1920–1).
Memorials of London and London Life in the XIIIth, XIVth, and XVth Centuries Being a Series of Extracts, Local, Social, and Political from the Early Archives of the City of London AD 1276–1419, ed. Henry T. Riley (London, 1868).
Owen, Dorothy M. *The Making of King's Lynn: A Documentary Study*, Records of Social and Economic History, new series IX (London, 1984).

The Parliament Rolls of Medieval England, 1275–1504, ed. C. Given-Wilson, The National Archives, The History of Parliament Trust (Leicester, 2005).

The Pinchbeck Register: Relating to the Abbey of Bury St Edmund's, ed. Francis Hervey (London, 1925).

'Poem on the Evil Times of Edward II' in *The Political Songs of England from the Reign of John to that of Edward II*, ed. Thomas Wright, CS 6 (1839).

Records of the Borough of Leicester, ed. Mary Bateson, 2 vols. (London, 1899–1901).

Records of the Borough of Nottingham, ed. W. H. Stevenson, James Raine, W. T. Baker, E. L. Guilford, Duncan Gray, and V. W. Walker, 9 vols. (London, 1882–1956).

The Records of the City of Norwich, ed. William Hudson and John Cottingham Tingey, 2 vols. (Norwich, 1906), I.

Regestrum Johannis de Trillek, episcopi Herefordensis, AD 1344–1361, ed. Joseph H. Parry, Canterbury and York Society, 8 (London, 1914).

Registrum Ade de Orleton, episcopi Herefordensis, 1317–27, ed. A. T. Bannister, Canterbury and York Society, 5 (London, 1908).

Registrum Ricardi de Swinfield, episcopi Herefordensis, 1283–17, ed. W. W. Capes, Canterbury and York Society, 6 (London, 1909).

Select Cases before the King's Council 1243–1482, ed. I. S. Leadam and J. F. Baldwin, Selden Society, 35 (Cambridge, MA, 1918).

Select Cases from the Coroners' Rolls 1265–1413, ed. Charles Gross, Selden Society, 9 (London, 1896).

Select Cases of Procedure without Writ under Henry III, ed. H. G. Richardson and G. O. Sayles, Selden Society, 60 (London, 1941).

Simonsohn, Shlomo. *The Apostolic See and the Jews. Documents: 492–1404*, Pontifical Institute of Mediaeval Studies (Toronto, 1988).

Snappe's Formulary and Other Records, ed. H. E. Salter, Oxford Historical Society, 80 (Oxford, 1924).

Statutes of the Realm, 11 vols. (London, 1810–28).

York Civic Ordinances, 1301, ed. Michael Prestwich, Borthwick Papers, no. 49 (York, 1976).

Secondary sources

Acheson, Eric. 'Zouche [de la Zouche] family (c. 1254–1415), magnates', *ODNB*.

Allmand, C. T. *Lancastrian Normandy, 1415–1450: The History of Medieval Occupation* (Oxford, 1993).

Aston, Margaret. 'Corpus Christi and Corpus Regni: Heresy and the Peasants' Revolt', *P&P*, 143 (1994): 3–47.

    Lollards and Reformers: Images and Literacy in Late Medieval Religion (London, 1984).

    'Lollardy and Sedition 1381–1431', *P&P*, 17 (1960): 1–44.

Attreed, Lorraine C. 'Arbitration and the Growth of Urban Liberties in Late Medieval England', *JBS*, 31 (1992): 205–35.

    The King's Towns: Identity and Survival in Late Medieval English Boroughs (New York, 2001).

'Urban Identity in Medieval English Towns', *JIDH*, 32 (2002): 571–92.

Barron, C. M. 'The Later Middle Ages: 1270–1520' in *Historic Towns: Maps and Plans of Towns and Cities in the British Isles, with Historical Commentaries, from Earliest Times to 1800*, ed. M. D. Lobel, 3 vols. (Oxford, 1969–89), III, pp. 42–56.

'London 1300–1540', Secondary sources in *CUHB*, pp. 395–440.

'The Political Culture of Medieval London' in *The Fifteenth Century, IV: Political Culture in Late Medieval Britain*, ed. Linda Clark and Christine Carpenter (Woodbridge, 2004), pp. 111–33.

'The Quarrel of Richard II with London 1392–97' in *The Reign of Richard II: Essays in Honour of May McKisack*, ed. F. R. H. Du Boulay and C. M. Barron (London, 1971), pp. 173–201.

'Ralph Holland and the London Radicals, 1438–1444' in *The English Medieval Town: A Reader in English Urban History 1200–1540*, ed. R. C. Holt and G. Rosser (London, 1990), pp. 160–83.

'Richard II and London' in *Richard II: The Art of Kingship*, ed. Anthony Goodman and James L. Gillespie (Oxford, 1999), pp. 129–54.

'Searching for the "Small People" of Medieval London', *The Local Historian*, 38 (2008): 83–94.

'The Tyranny of Richard II,' *BIHR*, 41 (1968): 1–18.

Barrow, G. W. S. *Robert Bruce and the Community of the Realm of Scotland* (Edinburgh, 1976).

Baswell, Christopher. 'Aeneas in 1381' in *New Medieval Literatures*, ed. Rita Copeland, David Lawton, and Wendy Scase (Oxford, 2003), V, pp. 7–58.

Beik William. *Urban Protest in Seventeenth-Century France* (Cambridge, 1997).

Bellamy, J. G. 'The Northern Rebellions', *BJRL*, 47 (1965): 254–74.

Beloch, Karl Julius. *Bevölkerungsgeschichte Italiens*, 3 vols. (Berlin, 1937–61).

Bennett, H. S. *Six Medieval Men and Women* (Cambridge, 1955).

Bennett, Judith M. 'Compulsory Service in Late Medieval England', *P&P*, 209 (2010): 7–51.

Bercé, Yves-Marie. *Revolt and Revolution in Early Modern Europe : An Essay on the History of Political Violence*, trans. Joseph Bergin (Manchester, 1987 [1980]).

Beresford, M. W. and H. P. R. Finberg. *English Medieval Boroughs: A Hand-List* (Newton Abbot, 1973).

Bird, Ruth. *The Turbulent London of Richard II* (London, 1949).

Bloch, Marc. *Feudal Society*, trans. L. A. Manyon, 2 vols. (Chicago, 1961 [Paris, 1939–49]).

French Rural History: An Essay on its Basic Characteristics, trans. Janet Sondheimer (London, 1966 [Antwerp, 1931]).

Bohna, Montgomery. 'Armed Force and Civic Legitimacy in Jack Cade's Revolt, 1450', *EHR*, 118 (2003): 563–82.

Bois, Guy. *Crise du féodalisme: économie rurale et démographie en Normandie orientale du début du 14e siècle au milieu du 16e siècle* (Paris, 1976).

Bolton, James L. 'The City and the Crown, 1456–61', *London Journal*, 12 (1986): 11–24.

'Introduction' in *The Alien Communities of London in the Fifteenth Century: The Subsidy Rolls of 1400 & 1483-4* (Stamford, 1998).

'London and the Peasants' Revolt', *London Journal*, 7 (1981): 123–4.

Boone, Marc. *A la recherché d'une modernité civique: la société urbaine des anciens Pays-Bas au bas Moyen Age* (Brussels, 2010).

'Langue, pouvoirs et dialogue. Aspects linguistiques de la communication entre les ducs de Bourgogne et leurs sujets flamands (1385–1505)', *Revue du Nord*, 91 (2009): 9–33.

'Urban Space and Political Conflict in Late Medieval Flanders', *JIDH*, 32 (2002): 621–40.

Boone, Marc and Maarten Prak. 'Rulers, Patricians and Burghers: The Great and the Little Traditions of Urban Revolt in the Low Countries' in *A Miracle Mirrored: The Dutch Republic in European Perspective*, ed. Karel Davids and Jan Lucassen (Cambridge, 1995), pp. 99–134.

Bradshaw, Frederick. 'Social and Economic History' in *VCH: Durham*, ed. William Page (London, 1907), II, pp. 175–260.

Braid, Robert, '"Et non ultra": politiques royales du travail en Europe occidentale au XIVeme siècle', *Bibliothèque de l'Ecole des Chartes*, 161 (2003): 437–91.

'Peste, prolétaires et politiques: la législation du travail et les politiques économiques en Angleterre aux XIIIeme et XIVeme siècles. Concepts, réalites et contexte européen', Ph.D. thesis, Université de Paris 7 (Paris, 2008).

Brentnall, Margaret. *The Cinque Ports and Romney Marsh* (London, 1972).

Bridbury, A. R. 'English Provincial Towns', *EcHR*, 34 (1981): 1–23.

Britnell, R. H. 'Feudal Reaction after the Black Death in the Palatinate of Durham', *P&P*, 128 (1990): 28–47.

Growth and Decline in Colchester, 1300–1525 (Cambridge, 1986).

'Town Life' in *A Social History of England 1200–1500*, ed. Rosemary Horrox and W. M. Ormrod (Cambridge, 2006), pp. 134–78.

'The Towns of England and Northern Italy in the Early Fourteenth Century', *EcHR*, 44 (1991): 21–35.

Brooke, Christopher. *London 800–1216: The Shaping of a City* (London, 1975).

Brooks, F. W. 'The Cinque Ports', *The Mariner's Mirror*, 15 (1929): 142–91.

Brooks, Nicholas. 'The Organization and Achievements of the Peasants of Kent and Essex in 1381' in *Studies in Medieval History Presented to R. H. C. Davis*, ed. Henry Mayr-Harting and R. I. Moore (London, 1985), pp. 247–70.

Brown, A. L. *The Governance of Late Medieval England 1272–1461* (London, 1989).

Burgess, Clive. 'A Hotbed of Heresy? Fifteenth-Century Bristol and Lollardy Reconsidered' in *The Fifteenth Century, III: Authority and Subversion*, ed. Linda Clark (Woodbridge, 2003), pp. 43–62.

'A Repertory for Reinforcement: Configuring Civic Catholicism in Fifteenth-Century Bristol' in *The Fifteenth Century, V: Of Mice and Men: Image, Belief, and Regulation in Late Medieval England*, ed. Linda Clark (Woodbridge, 2005), pp. 85–109.

Bush, Michael. 'The Risings of the Commons in England, 1381–1549' in *Orders and Hierarchies in Late Medieval and Renaissance Europe*, ed. Jeffrey Denton (Manchester, 1999), pp. 109–25.

Butcher, A. F. 'English Urban Society and the Revolt of 1381' in *The English Rising of 1381*, ed. Rodney Hilton and T. H. Aston (Cambridge, 1984), pp. 84–111.

Cam, Helen. 'Medieval History' in *VCH: Cambridge and the Isle of Ely*, III, ed. J. P. C. Roach (London, 1959), pp. 8–12.

Carlin, Martha. *Medieval Southwark* (London, 1996).

Carpenter, Christine. 'Beauchamp, William (V), First Baron Bergavenny', *ODNB*.

Carpenter, David. 'English Peasants in Politics 1258–1267', *P&P*, 136 (1992): 3–42.

'"In Testimonium Factorum Brevium": The Beginnings of the English Chancery Rolls' in *Records, Administration and Aristocratic Society in the Anglo-Norman Realm: Papers Commemorating the 800th Anniversary of King John's Loss of Normandy*, ed. Nicholas Vincent (Woodbridge, 2009), pp. 1–28.

The Reign of Henry III (London, 1996).

'Simon de Montfort: The First Leader of a Political Movement in English History', *History: The Journal of the Historical Association*, 76 (1991): 3–23.

Carus-Wilson, E. M. 'The Aulnage Accounts: A Criticism' in *Medieval Merchant Venturers: Collected Studies* (London, 1954), pp. 279–91.

'The First Half-century of the Borough of Stratford-upon-Avon', *EcHR*, 18 (1965): 49–70.

Catto, Jeremy. 'Fitzthedmar, Arnold (1201–1274/5)', *ODNB* (2004).

Chambers, C. Gore. 'Political History' in *VCH: Bedford*, ed. William Page (London, 1908), II, pp. 17–72.

Cheney, C. R. *Hubert Walter* (London, 1967).

Pope Innocent III and England, Päpste und Papsttum, 9 (Stuttgart, 1976).

Chevalier, Bernard. *Les bonnes villes de France: du XIVe au XVIe siècle* (Paris, 1982).

Childs, Wendy R. 'Introduction' in *Vita Edwardi Secundi, The Life of Edward the Second*, ed. Wendy R. Childs (Oxford, 2005), pp. xv–lx.

Clark, Peter. *The English Alehouse: A Social History 1200–1830* (London, 1983).

Cobban, Alan B. *English University Life in the Middle Ages* (London, 1999).

The Medieval English Universities: Oxford and Cambridge to c. 1500 (Aldershot, 1988).

'Medieval Student Power', *P&P*, 53 (1971): 28–66.

Cohn, Jr, Samuel K. 'After the Black Death: Labour Legislation and Attitudes Towards Labour in Late-Medieval Western Europe', *EcHR*, 60 (2007): 457–85.

'The Black Death and the Burning of Jews', *P&P*, 169 (2007): 3–36.

'The Black Death: The Consequences' in *Renaissance and Reformation On-line Bibliographies*, ed. Margaret L. King (Oxford, 2010).

Creating the Florentine State: Peasants and Rebellion, 1348–1434 (Cambridge, 1999).

'Epidemiology of the Black Death and Successive Waves of Plague' in *Pestilential Complexities: Understanding Medieval Plague*, ed. Vivian Nutton, *Medical History*, Supplement no. 27 (London, 2008), pp. 74–100.

Lust for Liberty: The Politics of Social Revolt in Medieval Europe, 1200–1425 (Cambridge, MA, 2006).

'Revolts of the Late Middle Ages and the Peculiarities of the English' in *Survival and Discord in Medieval Society: Essays in Honour of Christopher Dyer*, ed. Richard Goddard, John Langdon, and Miriam Müller (Turnhout, 2010), pp. 269–85.

Women in the Streets: Essays on Sex and Power in Renaissance Italy (Baltimore, 1996).

Colby, Charles W. 'The Growth of Oligarchy in English Towns', *EHR*, 5 (1890): 633–53.

Comba, Rinaldo. 'Rivolte e ribellioni fra tre e quattrocento' in *La storia: I grandi problemi*, ed. Nicola Tranfaglia and Massimo Firpo (Turin, 1988), II, Part 2, pp. 673–91.

Cooper, C. H. *Annals of Cambridge*, 5 vols. (Cambridge, 1842–52).

Cooper, Janet and Crossley, Alan. 'Medieval Oxford' in *VCH: Oxford, Vol. IV: The City of Oxford*, ed. Alan Crossley (Oxford, 1979), pp. 3–74.

Cornford, Barbara. 'Events of 1381 in Flegg' in *Studies Towards a History of the Rising of 1381 in Norfolk*, ed. Barbara Cornford (Norwich, 1984), pp. 39–48.

Cornford, Margaret E. 'Religious Houses of Durham' in *VCH: Durham*, ed. William Page (London, 1907), II, pp. 78–131.

Coss, Peter R. 'Coventry before Incorporation: A Re-interpretation', *Midland History*, 2 (1974): 135–51.

Coulton, G. G. *Social Life in Britain from the Conquest to the Reformation* (Cambridge, 1919).

Crane, Susan. 'The Writing Lesson of 1381' in *Chaucer's England: Literature in Historical Context*, ed. Barbara Hanawalt (Minneapolis, 1992), pp. 201–21.

Crawford, Barbara E. 'The Earldom of Caithness and the Kingdom of Scotland, 1150–1266' in *Essays on the Nobility of Medieval Scotland*, ed. K. J. Stringer (Edinburgh, 1985), pp. 25–43.

Crook, David. 'Derbyshire and the English Rising of 1381', *BIHR*, 60 (1987): 9–23.

Dale, Marian K. 'Social and Economic History, 1066–1509' in *VCH: Leicester, Vol. IV: The City of Leicester*, ed. R. A. McKinley (London, 1958), pp. 31–54.

Davies, Jonathan. *Culture and Power: Tuscany and its Universities 1537–1609* (Leiden, 2009).

Davies, Rees. *The Age of Conquest: Wales 1063–1415* (Oxford, 1987).

The Revolt of Owain Glyn Dŵr (Oxford, 1995).

Davis, Charles T. 'Ubertino da Casole and his Conception of "Altissima Paupertas"', *Studi Medievali*, 3rd series, 22 (1981): 2–56.

Davis, H. W. C. 'The Commune of Bury St Edmunds, 1264', *EHR*, 24 (1909): 313–15.

Davis, N. Z. 'Women on Top' in *Society and Culture in Early Modern France* (Stanford, CA, 1975), pp. 124–51.

Denholm-Young, Noël. *Richard of Cornwall* (Oxford, 1947).

Dijk, Conrad Van. 'Simon Sudbury and Helenus in John Gower's *Vox Clamantis*', *Medium Aevum*, 77 (2008): 313–18.

Dilks, T. B. 'Bridgwater and the Insurrection of 1381', *Proceedings of the Somerset Archaeological and Natural History Society*, 73 (1927): 57–69.

Dobson, R. B. *The Jews of Medieval York and the Massacre of March 1190* (York, 1974).

'Remembering the Peasants' Revolt 1381–1981' in *Essex and the Great Revolt of 1381: Lectures Celebrating the Six Hundredth Anniversary*, ed. W. H. Liddell and R. G. E. Wood, Essex Record Office Publication no. 84 (1982), pp. 1–20.

'The Risings in York, Beverley and Scarborough, 1380–1381' in *The English Rising of 1381*, ed. Rodney Hilton and T. H. Aston (Cambridge, 1984), pp. 112–42.

'The Role of Jewish Women in Medieval England' in *The Jewish Communities of Medieval England: The Collected Essays of R. B. Dobson*, ed. Helen Birkett (York, 2010), pp. 127–48.

'Urban Decline in Late Medieval England' [1977] in *The English Medieval Town: A Reader in English Urban History 1200–1540*, ed. R. C. Holt and G. Rosser (London, 1990), pp. 265–86.

Dumolyn, Jan. '"Criers and Shouters": The Discourse on Radical Urban Rebels in Late Medieval Flanders', *Journal of Social History* 42 (2008): 111–35.

'Privileges and Novelties: The Political Discourse of the Flemish Cities and Rural Districts in their Negotiations with the Dukes of Burgundy (1384–1506)', *UH*, 35 (2008): 5–23.

Dumolyn, Jan and Haemers, Jelle. '"A Bad Chicken was Brooding": Subversive Speech in Late Medieval Flanders', *P&P*, 214 (2012): 45–86.

'Patterns of Urban Rebellion in Medieval Flanders', *JMH*, 31 (2005): 369–93.

Dumolyn, Jan, and Kristof Papin, 'Y avait-il "révoltes fiscales" dans les villes médiévales des Pays-Bas méridionaux? L'exemple de Saint-Omer en 1467', *Revue du Nord* (forthcoming).

Dyer, Christopher, *An Age of Transition? Economy and Society in England in the Later Middle Ages: The Ford Lectures Delivered in the University of Oxford in Hilary Term 2001* (Oxford, 2005).

'Bromsgrove: A Small Town in Worcestershire in the Middle Ages', Worcestershire Historical Society, Occasional Publications, no. 9 (2000).

'The Causes of the Revolt in Rural Essex' in *Essex and the Great Revolt of 1381: Lectures Celebrating the Six Hundredth Anniversary*, ed. W. H. Liddell and R. G. E. Wood, Essex Record Office Publication no. 84 (Essex, 1982), pp. 21–36.

'Did the Peasants Really Starve in Medieval England?' in Martha Carlin and Joel T. Rosenthal, *Food and Eating in Medieval Europe* (London, 1998), pp. 53–71.

Everyday Life in Medieval England (London, 2001).

'The Hidden Trade of the Middle Ages: Evidence from the West Midlands of England', *Journal of Historical Geography*, 18 (1992): 141–57.

Lords and Peasants in a Changing Society: The Estates of the Bishopric of Worcester, 680–1450 (Cambridge, 1980).

Making a Living in the Middle Ages: The People of Britain 850–1520 (New Haven, 2002).

'The Political Life of the Fifteenth-Century English Village' in *The Fifteenth Century, IV: Political Culture in Late Medieval Britain*, ed. Linda Clark and Christine Carpenter (Woodbridge, 2004), pp. 135–57.

'Small-town Conflict in the Later Middle Ages: Events at Shipston-on-Stour, *UH*, 19 (1992): 183–210.

'The Social and Economic Background to the Rural Revolt of 1381' in *The English Rising of 1381*, ed. Rodney Hilton and T. H. Aston (Cambridge, 1984), pp. 9–42.

Standards of Living in the Later Middle Ages: Social Change in England c. 1200–1520 (Cambridge, 1989).

'Taxation and Communities in Late Medieval England' in *Progress and Problems in Medieval England: Essays in Honour of Edward Miller*, ed. R. H. Britnell and John Hatcher (Cambridge, 1995), pp. 168–90.

Ebeling, Dietrich and Franz Irsigler. *Landesgeschichte als multidisziplinäre Wissenschaft: Festgabe für Franz Irsigler zum 60. Geburtstag* (Trier, 2001).

Eiden, Herbert. *'In der Knechtschaft werdet ihr verharren': Ursachen in Verlauf des englischen Bauernaufstandes von 1381* (Trier, 1995).

'Joint Action against "Bad" Lordship: The Peasants' Revolt in Essex and Norfolk', *History*, 83 (1998): 5–30.

'Norfolk, 1382: A Sequel to the Peasants' Revolt', *EHR*, 114 (1999): 370–7.

'Der Richter, der seinen Kopfverlor: Leben und Sterben des Sir John Cavendish (1381), Chief Justice of the King's Bench' in *Landesgeschichte als multidisziplinäre Wissenschaft: Festgabe für Franz Irsigler zum 60. Geburtstag*, ed. Dietrich Ebeling and Franz Irsigler (Trier, 2001), pp. 197–222.

Erskine, Audrey M. 'Political and Administrative History, 1066–1509' in *VCH: Leicester, Vol. IV: The City of Leicester*, ed. R. A. McKinley (London, 1958), pp. 1–30.

Faith, Rosamond. 'The Class Struggle in Fourteenth Century England' in *People's History and Socialist Theory*, ed. R. Samuel (London, 1981), pp. 50–60.

'The "Great Rumour" of 1377 and Peasant Ideology' in *The English Rising of 1381*, ed. Rodney Hilton and T. H. Aston (Cambridge, 1984), pp. 43–73.

Farmer, Sharon. *Surviving Poverty in Medieval Paris: Gender, Ideology and the Daily Lives of the Poor* (Ithaca, 2002).

Federico, Sylvia. 'The Imaginary Society: Women in 1381', *JBS*, 40 (2001): 159–83.

Flaherty, W. E. 'Sequel to the Great Rebellion in Kent of 1381', *Archaeologia Cantiana*, 4 (1861): 67–86.

Fleming, Peter and Kieran Costello. *Discovering Cabot's Bristol: Life in the Medieval and Tudor Town* (Bristol, 1998).

'Identity and Belonging: Irish and Welsh in Fifteenth-Century Bristol' in *The Fifteenth Century, VII: Conflicts, Consequences and the Crown in the Late Middle Ages*, ed. Linda Clark (Woodbridge, 2007), pp. 175–93.

Flenley, Ralph. 'London and Foreign Merchants in the Reign of Henry VI', *EHR*, 25 (1910): 644–55.

Forrest, Ian. *The Detection of Heresy in Late Medieval England* (Oxford, 2005).

'The Politics of Burial in Late Medieval Hereford', *EHR*, 125 (2010): 1110–38.

Fourquin, Guy. *Anatomy of Popular Rebellion in the Middle Ages*, trans. A. Chesters (Amsterdam, 1978).

Frame, Robin. *The Political Development of the British Isles 1100–1400* (Oxford, 1990).

Franklin, Peter. 'Politics in Manorial Court Rolls: The Tactics, Social Composition, and Aims of a Pre-1381 Peasant Movement' in *Medieval Society and the Manor Court*, ed. Zvi Razi and Richard Smith (Oxford, 1996), pp. 162–98.

Fransson, Gustav. *Middle English Surnames of Occupation 1100–1350*, Lund Studies in English, III (Lund, 1935).

Freeman, Mark. *St Albans: A History* (Lancaster, 2008).

Fryde, E. B. *The Great Revolt of 1381*, pamphlet of the Historical Association (London, 1981).

'Introduction to New Edition' in Charles Oman, *The Great Revolt of 1381* (Oxford, 1969), pp. xi–xxxii.

Fryde, E. B. and Natalie Fryde. 'Peasant Rebellion and Peasant Discontents' in *The Agrarian History of England and Wales*, ed. Joan Thirsk, *Volume III, 1348–1500*, ed. Edward Miller (Cambridge, 1991), pp. 744–819.

Fryde, Natalie. *The Tyranny and Fall of Edward II* (Cambridge, 1979).

Fuller, E. A. 'The Tallage of 6 Edward II (Dec. 16, 1312) and the Bristol Rebellion', *Transactions of the Bristol and Gloucestershire Archaeological Society* 19 (1894–5): 171–278.

Geltner, Guy. 'Mendicants as Victims: Scale, Scope, and the Idiom of Violence', *JMH*, 36 (2010): 126–41.

Genet, Jean-Philippe. *La genèse de l'état moderne: culture et société politique en Angleterre* (Paris, 2003).

Gillet, Edward and Machon, Kenneth A. *A History of Hull* (Hull, 1989).

Gillingham, John. 'Crisis or Continuity? The Structure of Royal Authority in England 1369–1422' in *Das spätmittelalterliche Königtum im europäischen Vergleich*, ed. Reinhard Schneider (Sigmaringen, 1987), pp. 59–80.

'The Historian as Judge: William of Newburgh and Hubert Walter', *EHR*, 119 (2004): 175–87.

Ginzburg, Carlo. *Ecstasies: Deciphering the Witches' Sabbath*, trans. Raymond Rosenthal (London, 1991).

Given, James. *Society and Homicide in Thirteenth-Century England* (Stanford, 1977).

Given-Wilson, Chris. *Chronicles: The Writing of History in Medieval England* (London, 2004).

'The Problem of Labour in the Context of English Government, c. 1350–1450' in *The Problem of Labour in Fourteenth-Century England*, ed. James Bothwell, P. J. P. Goldberg, and W. M. Ormrod (York, 2000), pp. 85–100.

'Service, Serfdom and English Labour Legislation, 1350–1500' in *The Fifteenth Century, I: Concepts and Patterns of Service in the Later Middle Ages*, ed. A. Curry and E. Matthews (Woodbridge, 2000), pp. 21–37.

Goldberg, P. J. P., ed. *Richard Scrope: Archbishop, Rebel, Martyr* (Donington, 2007).

Goodman, Anthony. *John of Gaunt: The Exercise of Princely Power in Fourteenth-Century Europe* (Harlow, 1992).

The Loyal Conspiracy: The Lords Appellant under Richard II (London, 1971).

Gransden, Antonia. *Historical Writing in England*, 2 vols. (London, 1974–82).

'John de Northwold, Abbot of Bury St Edmunds (1279–1301) and his Defence of its Liberties' in *Thirteenth Century England, III: Proceedings of the Newcastle upon Tyne Conference, 1989*, ed. S. D. Lloyd and P. R. Coss (Woodbridge, 1991), pp. 91–112.

Grayzel, Solomon. *The Church and the Jews in the XIIIth Century*, 2 vols., ed. K. R. Stow (New York, 1989).

Green, Mrs J. R. [Alice Stopford]. *Town Life in the Fifteenth Century*, 2 vols. (London, 1894).

Green, Richard F. 'John Ball's Letters: Literary History and Historical Literature' in Barbara Hanawalt, *Chaucer's England: Literature in Historical Context* (Minneapolis, 1992), pp. 176–200.

Grendler, Paul F. *The Universities of the Italian Renaissance* (Baltimore, 2002).

Grieve, H. E. P. 'The Rebellion and the County Town' in *Essex and the Great Revolt of 1381: Lectures Celebrating the Six Hundredth Anniversary*, ed. W. H. Liddell and R. G. E. Wood, Essex Record Office Publication no. 84 (Essex, 1982), pp. 37–53.

Griffiths, Paul. *Youth and Authority: Formative Experiences in England 1560–1640* (Oxford, 1996).

Griffiths, Ralph A. 'Local Rivalries and National Politics: The Percies, the Nevilles, and the Duke of Exeter, 1452–1455', *Speculum*, 43 (1968): 589–632.

The Reign of King Henry VI: The Exercise of Royal Authority, 1422–1461 (London, 1981).

Gross, Charles. *The Gild Merchant: A Contribution to British Municipal History*, 2 vols. (Oxford, 1890).

Grummitt, David. 'Deconstructing Cade's Rebellion: Discourse and Politics in the Mid Fifteenth Century in *The Fifteenth Century: VI: Identity and Insecurity in the Late Middle Ages*, ed. Linda Clark (Woodbridge, 2006), pp. 107–23.

Haemers, Jelle. 'A Moody Community? Emotion and Ritual in Late Medieval Urban Revolts' in *Emotions in the Heart of the City (14th–16th Century)*, ed. Elodie Lecuppre-Desjardin and Anne-Laure Van Bruaene, Studies in European Urban History, 5 (Turnhout, 2005), pp. 63–81.

Hallam, Elizabeth. *Domesday Book through Nine Centuries* (London, 1986).

Hammer, Jr, Charles. 'Patterns of Homicide in a Medieval University Town, Fourteenth-Century Oxford', *P&P*, 78 (1978): 3–23.

Hanagan, Michael. 'Charles Tilly and Violent France', *French Historical Studies*, 33 (2010): 283–96.

Hanawalt, Barbara. *Medieval Crime and Social Control* (Minneapolis, 1999).

'Peasant Resistance to Royal and Seignorial Impositions' in *Social Unrest in the Late Middle Ages: Papers of the Fifteenth Annual Conference of the Center for Medieval and Early Renaissance Studies*, ed. Francis X. Newman (Binghamton, New York, 1986), pp. 23–47.

Hanna, Ralph III. 'Sir Thomas Berkeley and his Patronage', *Speculum*, 64 (1989): 849–77.

Harding, Alan. *England in the Thirteenth Century* (Cambridge, 1993).

'Plaints and Bills in the History of English Law, Mainly the Period 1250–1330' in *Legal History Studies 1972: Papers Presented to the Legal History Conference, Aberystwyth, 18–21 July 1972*, ed. Dafydd Jenkins (Cardiff, 1975), pp. 65–87.

'The Revolt against the Justices' in *The English Rising of 1381*, ed. Rodney Hilton and T. H. Aston (Cambridge, 1984), pp. 165–93.

Hare, J. N. 'Lord and Tenant in Wiltshire, c. 1380–c. 1520, with Particular Reference to Regional and Seigneurial Variations', unpublished Ph.D. thesis, University of London (1976).

Hargreaves, Paul V. 'Seignorial Reaction and Peasant Responses: Worcester Priory and its Peasants after the Black Death', *Midland History*, 24 (1999): 3–78.

Harriss, G. L. 'Humphrey [Humfrey or Humphrey of Lancaster], Duke of Gloucester', *ODNB* (2004).

King, Parliament, and Public Finance in Medieval England to 1369 (Oxford, 1975).

'Political Society and the Growth of Government in Late Medieval England', *P&P*, 138 (1993): 28–57.

Shaping the Nation: England 1360–1461 (Oxford, 2005).

Harvey, Barbara. *Westminster Abbey and its Estates in the Middle Ages* (Oxford, 1977).

Harvey, I. M. W. *Jack Cade's Rebellion of 1450* (Oxford, 1991).

Harvey, P. D. A. 'Banbury' in *Historic Towns: Maps and Plans of Towns and Cities in the British Isles, with Historical Commentaries, from Earliest Times to 1800*, ed. M. D. Lobel, 3 vols. (Oxford, 1969–89), I.

Hatcher, John. *English Tin Production and Trade Before 1550* (Oxford, 1973).

'The Great Slump of the Mid-Fifteenth Century' in *Progress and Problems in Medieval England: Essays in Honour of Edward Miller*, ed. R. H. Britnell and John Hatcher (Cambridge, 1996), pp. 237–72.

Heer, Friedrick. *The Medieval World: Europe, 1100–1350*, trans. Janet Sondheimer (London, 1962).

Heng, Geraldine. 'Jews, Saracens, "Black Men", Tartars: England in a World of Racial Difference' in *A Companion to Medieval English Literature, c. 1350–1500*, ed. Peter Brown (London, 2007), pp. 247–69.

Herbert, N. M. 'Medieval Gloucester 1066–1547' in *VCH: Gloucester: Vol IV: The City of Gloucester*, ed. N. M. Herbert (Oxford, 1988), pp. 13–72.

Herlihy, David. *Opera Muliebria: Women and Work in Medieval Europe* (New York, 1990).

Herlihy, David and Christiane Klapisch-Zuber. *Les Toscans et leurs familles: une étude du catasto florentin de 1427* (Paris, 1978).

Hill, J. W. F. *Medieval Lincoln* (Cambridge, 1948).

Hilton, Rodney. *Bond Men Made Free: Medieval Peasant Movements and the English Rising of 1381* (London, 1973).

Class Conflict and the Crisis of Feudalism: Essays in Medieval Social History (London, 1983).

English and French Towns in Feudal Society: A Comparative Study (Cambridge, 1992).

'Inherent and Derived Ideology in the English Rising of 1381' in *Campagnes médiévales: l'homme et son espace, études offertes à Robert Fossier*, ed. Elisabeth Mornet, Histoire ancienne et médiévale, 31 (Paris, 1995), pp. 399–405.

'Popular Movements in England at the End of the Fourteenth Century' in *Il Tumulto dei Ciompi: Un momento di storia fiorentina ed europea* (Florence, 1981), pp. 223–40.

'Resistance to Taxation and to other State Impositions in Medieval England' in *Genèse de l'état moderne: prélèvement et redistribution. Actes du colloque de Fontevraud, 1984*, ed. J.-Ph. Genet and M. Le Mené (Paris, 1987), pp. 169–77.

'Révoltes rurales et révoltes urbaines au Moyen Age' in *Révolte et société: actes du IVe colloque d'histoire au present, Paris, mai 1988*, ed. Fabienne Gambrelle and Michel Trebitsch, 2 vols. (Paris, 1989), I, pp. 25–33.

'Small Town Society in England before the Black Death' in *The English Medieval Town: A Reader in English Urban History 1200–1540*, ed. R. C. Holt and G. Rosser (London, 1990), pp. 71–96.

'Social Concepts in the English Rising of 1381' in Rodney Hilton, *Class Conflict and the Crisis of Feudalism: Essays in Medieval Social History* (London, 1983), pp. 216–26.

'Towns in English Society' in *The English Medieval Town: A Reader in English Urban History 1200–1540* (London, 1990), ed. R. C. Holt and G. Rosser, pp. 19–28.

'Towns in Societies – Medieval England', *Urban History Yearbook* (1982): 7–13.

'Unjust Taxation and Popular Resistance', *New Left Review*, 180 (1990): 178–84.

'Women Traders in Medieval England' in *Class Conflict and the Crisis of Feudalism: Essays in Medieval Social History* (London, 1983), pp. 205–15.

Hinck, Helmut. 'The Rising of 1381 in Winchester', *EHR* 125 (2010): 112–30.

Hindle, Steve. *State and Social Change in Early Modern England, c. 1550–1640* (London, 2000).

Holmes, George. *The Good Parliament* (Oxford, 1975).

Holt, Richard C. 'Gloucester in the Century after the Black Death', *Transactions of the Bristol and Gloucestershire Archaeological Society*, 103 (1985): 149–61.

'Thomas of Woodstock and Events at Gloucester in 1381', *BIHR*, 58 (1985): 237–42.

Holt, Richard C. and G. Rosser. 'Introduction: The English Town in the Middle Ages' in *The English Medieval Town: A Reader in English Urban History 1200–1540*, ed. R. C. Holt and G. Rosser (London, 1990).

Hoppenbrouwers, Peter. 'Rebels with a Cause: The Peasant Movements of Northern Holland in the Later Middle Ages' in *Showing Status: Representations of Social Positions in the Late Middle Ages*, ed. Wim Blockmans and Antheun Janse (Tourhout, 1999), pp. 445–82.

Hudson, Anne. *The Premature Reformation: Wycliffite Texts and Lollard History* (Oxford, 1988).

'Which Wyche? The Framing of the Lollard Heretic and/or Saint' in *Texts and the Repression of Medieval Heresy*, ed. Caterina Bruschi and Peter Biller (York, 2003), pp. 221–37.

Humphrey, Chris. *The Politics of Carnival: Festive Misrule in Medieval England* (Manchester, 2001).

Jacob, E. F. *Studies in the Period of Baronial Reform and Rebellion, 1258–1267* (Oxford, 1925).

Jamison, C. 'Social and Economic History' in *VCH: Buckingham*, ed. William Page (London, 1908), II, pp. 37–93.

Jones, Michael K. 'War on the Frontier: The Lancastrian Land Settlement in Eastern Normandy, 1435–50', *Nottingham Medieval Studies*, 33 (1989): 104–21.

Jordan, William C. *The Great Famine: Northern Europe in the Early Fourteenth Century* (Princeton, 1996).

Julius, Anthony. *Trials of the Diaspora: A History of Anti-Semitism in England* (Oxford, 2010).

Jurkowski, Maureen. 'Lollardy in Coventry and the Revolt of 1431' in *The Fifteenth Century, VI: Identity and Insecurity in the Late Middle Ages*, ed. Linda Clark (Woodbridge, 2006), pp. 145–63.

Justice, Steven. *Writing and Rebellion: England in 1381* (Berkeley, 1994).

Kaeuper, Richard W. 'Law and Order in Fourteenth-Century England: The Evidence of Special Commissions of Oyer and Terminer', *Speculum*, 54 (1979): 734–84.

'Royal Finance and the Crisis of 1297' in *Order and Innovation in the Middle Ages: Essays in Honor of Joseph R. Strayer*, ed. William C. Jordan, Bruce McNab, and Teofilo F. Ruiz (Princeton, 1976), pp. 103–10.

War, Justice, and Public Order: England and France in the Later Middle Ages (Oxford, 1988).

Katz, Steven T. *The Holocaust in Historical Context, I. The Holocaust and Mass Death before the Modern Age* (New York, 1994).

Kaufman, Alexander L. *The Historical Literature of the Jack Cade Rebellion* (Farnham, 2009).

Kedar, Benjamin Z. *Merchants in Crisis: Genoese and Venetian Men of Affairs and the Fourteenth-Century Depression* (New Haven, 1976).

Keene, D. J. 'Suburban Growth' in *The English Medieval Town: A Reader in English Urban History 1200–1540*, ed. R. C. Holt and G. Rosser (London, 1990), pp. 97–119.

Kermode, Jenny. *Medieval Merchants: York, Beverley and Hull in the Later Middle Ages* (Cambridge, 1998).

'Obvious Observations on the Formation of Oligarchies in Late Medieval English Towns' in *Towns and Townspeople in the Fifteenth Century: Colloquium on Fifteenth Century History*, ed. John A. F. Thomson (Sutton, 1988), pp. 87–106.

Kleineke, Hannes. 'Why the West was Wild: Law and Disorder in Fifteenth-Century Cornwall and Devon' in *The Fifteenth Century, III: Authority and Subversion*, ed. Linda Clark (Woodbridge, 2003), pp. 75–93.

Knapp, Fritz Peter and Niesner, Manuela (eds.), *Historisches und fiktioales Erzählen in Mittelalter* (Berlin, 2002).

Knowles, Clive H. 'Savoy, Boniface of (1206/7–1270)', *ODNB* (2007).

Knowles, David. *The Religious Orders in England*, 2 vols. (Cambridge, 1950).

Kowaleski, Maryanne. 'The Commercial Dominance of a Medieval Provincial Oligarchy: Exeter in the Late Fourteenth Century' in *The English Medieval Town: A Reader in English Urban History 1200–1540*, ed. R. C. Holt and G. Rosser (London, 1990), pp. 184–215.

Local Markets and Regional Trade in Medieval Exeter (Cambridge, 1995).

Kriehn, George. *The English Rising in 1450* (Strasbourg, 1892).

Kurth, Godefroid. *La cité de Liège au moyen âge*. 3 vols. (Brussels, 1909–10).

'Henri de Dinant et la démocratie liégeoise', in *Academie Royale des Sciences des lettres et de beaux-arts de Belgique: bulletins de la classe des lettres* (1908): 384–410.

Labarge, Margaret Wade. *Gascony, England's First Colony 1204–1453* (London, 1980).

Lacey, Helen. '"Grace for the Rebels": The Role of the Royal Pardon in the Peasants' Revolt of 1381', *JMH*, 34 (2008): 36–63.

'Perceptions of Royal Governance and Westminster in Fourteenth-Century England' at the International Medieval Congress (11 July 2011).

Lambert, Malcolm. *Medieval Heresy: Popular Movements from Bogomil to Hus*, 3rd edn (Oxford, 2002).

Lambrick, Gabrielle. 'The Impeachment of the Abbot of Abingdon in 1368', *EHR* 82 (1967): 250–76.

Lander, J. R. *Conflict and Stability in Fifteenth-Century England*, 3rd edn (London, 1977).

Langmuir, Gavin. 'At the Frontiers of Faith' in *Religious Violence between Christians and Jews: Medieval Roots, Modern Perspectives*, ed. Anna Sapir Abulafia (Basingstoke, 2002), pp. 138–56.

'The Knight's Tale of Young Hugh of Lincoln', *Speculum*, 47 (1972): 459–82.

Lantschner, Patrick. 'The Logic of Political Conflict in the Late Middle Ages: A Comparative Study of Urban Political Conflicts in Italy and the Southern Low Countries, c. 1370–1440', D.Phil. thesis, University of Oxford (2012).

la Roncière, Charles-Marie de. 'Indirect Taxes or "Gabelles" at Florence in the Fourteenth Century: The Evolution of Tariffs and Problems of Collection' in *Florentine Studies*, ed. Nicolai Rubinstein (London, 1968), pp. 140–92.

Laughton, Jane. 'The Control of Discord in Fifteenth-Century Chester' in *Survival and Discord in Medieval Society: Essays in Honour of Christopher Dyer*, ed. Richard Goddard, John Langdon, and Miriam Müller (Turnhout, 2010), pp. 213–29.

'Economy and Society, 1350–1500' in *VCH: Chester*, ed. C. P. Lewis and A. T. Thacker (London, 2003), V, part 1, pp. 34–90.

Life in a Late Medieval City: Chester, 1275–1520 (Oxford, 2008).

Liddy, Christian. '"Bee War of Gyle in Borugh": Taxation and Political Discourse in Late Medieval English Towns' in *The Languages of the Political Society*, ed. Andrea Gamberini, Jean-Philippe Genet, and Andrea Zorzi (Rome, 2011), pp. 461–85.

'Bill Casting and Political Communication: A Public Sphere in Late Medieval Towns?' in *La gobernanza de la ciudad europea en la Edad Media*, ed. Jesús

Ángel Solórzano Telechea and Beatriz Arízaga Bolumburu (Logroño, 2011), pp. 447–61.

The Bishopric of Durham in the Late Middle Ages: Lordship, Community, and the Cult of St Cuthbert (Rochester, 2008).

'Bristol and the Crown, 1326–31: Local and National Politics in the Early Years of Edward III's Reign' in *Fourteenth Century England*, III, ed. W. M. Ormrod (Woodbridge, 2004), pp. 47–66.

'The Rhetoric of the Royal Chamber in Late Medieval London, York and Coventry', *UH* 29 (2002): 323–49.

'Urban Conflict in Late Fourteenth-Century England: The Case of York in 1380–1', *EHR*, 118 (2003): 1–32.

War, Politics, and Finance in Late Medieval English Towns: Bristol, York and the Crown 1350–1400 (Woodbridge, 2005).

'William Frost, the City of York and Scrope's Rebellion of 1405' in *Richard Scrope: Archbishop, Rebel, Martyr*, ed. P. J. P. Goldberg (Donington, 2007), pp. 64–85.

Liddy, Christian and Jelle Haemers. 'Popular Politics in the Late Medieval City: York and Bruges', *EHR* (forthcoming).

Lobel, M. D. *The Borough of Bury St Edmund's: A Study in the Government and Development of a Monastic Town* (Oxford, 1935).

'A Detailed Account of the 1327 Rising at Bury St Edmunds and the Subsequent Trial', *Proceedings of the Suffolk Institute of Archaeology*, 21 (1933): 215–31.

Lobel, M. D. and J. Tann. 'Gloucester' in *Historic Towns: Maps and Plans of Towns and Cities in the British Isles, with Historical Commentaries, from Earliest Times to 1800*, ed. M. D. Lobel, 3 vols. (Oxford, 1969–89), I, pp. 1–14.

Locke, A. Audrey. 'Political History' in *VCH: Hampshire and the Isle of Wight*, ed. William Page (London, 1912), XII, pp. 293–358.

Lodge, E. C. 'Social and Economic History' in *VCH: Berkshire*, ed. P. H. Ditchfield and William Page (London, 1907), II, pp. 165–213.

Lyle, Helen. *The Rebellion of Jack Cade* (London, 1950).

McFarlane, K. B. *John Wycliffe and the Beginnings of English Nonconformity* (London, 1952).

McIntosh, Majorie K. 'Local Responses to the Poor in Late Medieval and Tudor England', *Continuity and Change*, 3 (1988): 209–45.

McKenna, J. W. 'Popular Canonization as Political Propaganda: The Cult of Archbishop Scrope', *Speculum*, 45 (1970): 608–23.

MacKenzie, Hugh. 'The Anti-Foreign Movement in England, 1231–2' in *Anniversary Essays in Medieval History by Students of Charles Homer Haskins*, ed. C. H. Taylor and J. L. La Monte (Boston, 1929), pp. 183–203.

McKisack, May. *The Fourteenth Century 1307–1399* (Oxford, 1959).

'London and the Succession to the Crown during the Middle Ages' in *Studies in Medieval History Presented to Fredrick Maurice Powicke*, ed. Richard W. Hunt, William A. Pantin, and Richard W. Southern (Oxford, 1948), pp. 76–89.

McNab, Bruce. 'Obligations of the Church in English Society: Military Arrays of the Clergy, 1369–1418' in *Order and Innovation in the Middle Ages: Essays in*

Honor of Joseph R. Strayer, ed. William C. Jordan, Bruce McNab, and Teofilo F. Ruiz (Princeton, 1976), pp. 293–314.

McNiven, Peter. 'The Cheshire Rising of 1400', *BJRL*, 52 (1969–70): 375–96.

'Rebellion, Sedition, and the Legend of Richard II's Survival in the Reigns of Henry IV and Henry V', *BJRL*, 76 (1994): 93–117.

McRee, Benjamin R. 'Peacemaking and its Limits in Late Medieval Norwich', *EHR*, 109 (1994): 831–66.

Maddern, Philippa. 'Order and Disorder' in *Medieval Norwich*, ed. Carole Rawcliffe and Richard Wilson (London, 2004), pp. 188–212.

Violence and Social Order: East Anglia 1422–1442 (Oxford, 1992).

Maddicott, J. R. 'Badlesmere, Sir Bartholomew, c.1275–1322', rev. *ODNB*.

The English Peasantry and the Demands of the Crown 1294–1341, *P&P* Supplement, 1 (Oxford, 1975).

Law and Lordship: Royal Justices as Retainers in Thirteenth- and Fourteenth-Century England, *P&P* Supplement, 4 (Oxford, 1978).

'Parliament and the Constituencies, 1272–1377' in *The English Parliament in the Middle Ages*, ed. R. G. Davies and J. H. Denton (Manchester, 1981), pp. 61–87.

Simon de Montfort (Cambridge, 1994).

Manning, Roger B. *Village Revolts: Social Protest and Popular Disturbances in England, 1509–1640* (Oxford, 1988).

Mate, Mavis. 'The Economic and Social Roots of Medieval Popular Rebellion: Sussex in 1450–1451', *EcHR*, 45 (1992): 661–76.

Matheson, Lister M. 'The Peasants' Revolt through Five Centuries of Rumour and Reporting: Richard Fox, John Stow, and their Successors', *Studies in Philology*, 95 (1998): 121–51.

Miller, Edward and John Hatcher. *Medieval England: Towns, Commerce and Crafts 1086–1348* (London, 1995).

Mollat, Michel and Wolff, Philippe. *Ongles bleus, Jacques et Ciompi: les révolutions populaires en Europe aux XIVe et XVe siècles* (Paris, 1970).

The Popular Revolutions of the Late Middle Ages, trans. A. L. Lytton-Sells (London, 1973).

Moore, R. I. *The Formation of a Persecuting Society: Power and Deviance in Western Europe, 950–1250* (New York, 1987).

Moss, Douglas and Ian Murray. 'Signs of Change in a Medieval Village Community', *Transactions of the London and Middlesex Archaeological Society*, 27 (1976): 280–7.

Müller, Miriam. 'The Aims and Organisation of a Peasant Revolt in Early Fourteenth-Century Wiltshire', *Rural History*, 14 (2003): 1–20.

Mundill, Robin R. *England's Jewish Solution: Experiment and Expulsion, 1262–1290* (Cambridge, 1998).

The King's Jews: Money, Massacre and Exodus in Medieval England (London, 2010).

'Out of the Shadow and into the Light – the Impact and Implications of Recent Scholarship on the Jews of Medieval England 1066–1290', *History Compass*, 9 (2011): 572–601.

Munro, John H. 'The Rise, Expansion, and Decline of the Italian Wool-Based Textile Industries, ca. 1100–1730: A Study in International Competition, Transaction Costs, and Comparative Advantage', *Studies in Medieval and Renaissance History*, 3rd series, 9 (forthcoming).

'Wage-stickiness, Monetary Changes, and Real Incomes in Late-Medieval England and the Low Countries, 1350–1500: Did Money Matter?', *Research in Economic History*, 21 (2003): 185–297.

Musson, Anthony and W. M. Ormrod. *The Evolution of English Justice: Law, Politics and Society in the Fourteenth Century* (Basingstoke, 1999).

Nicholas, David. *The Later Medieval City, 1300–1500* (Harlow, 1997).

Medieval Flanders (London, 1992).

The Metamorphosis of a Medieval City: Ghent in the Age of the Arteveldes, 1302–1390 (Leiden, 1987).

The van Arteveldes of Ghent: The Varieties of Vendetta and the Hero in History (Ithaca, 1988).

Nightingale, Pamela. 'Capitalists, Crafts and Constitutional Change in Late Fourteenth-Century London', *P&P*, 124 (1989): 3–35.

A Medieval Mercantile Community: The Grocers' Company and the Politics and Trade of London, 1000–1485 (New Haven, 1995).

Oakes, Fergus. 'How and Why were the Towns of England Involved in the Barons' War of 1264–67?', M.Litt. thesis, University of Glasgow (2010).

Oman, Charles. *The Great Revolt of 1381*, new edition with introduction by E. B. Fryde (Oxford, 1969).

Ormrod, W. M. *Edward III*, Yale English Monarchs Series (New Haven, 2012).

'The English Government and the Black Death of 1348–49' in *England in the Fourteenth Century: Proceedings of the 1985 Harlaxton Symposium*, ed. W. M. Ormrod (Woodbridge, 1986), pp. 175–88.

'In Bed with Joan of Kent: The King's Mother and the Peasants' Revolt' in *Medieval Women: Texts and Contexts in Late Medieval Britain: Essays for Felicity Riddy*, ed. Jocelyn Wogan-Browne (Turnhout, 2000), pp. 277–92.

'Introduction: Medieval Petitions in Context' in *Medieval Petitions: Grace and Grievance*, ed. W. M. Ormord, Gwilym Dodd, and Anthony Musson (York, 2009), pp. 1–11.

'Murmur, Clamour and Noise: Voicing Complaint and Remedy in Petitions to the English Crown, c. 1300–c.1460' in *Medieval Petitions: Grace and Grievance*, ed. W. M. Ormord, Gwilym Dodd, and Anthony Musson (York, 2009), pp. 135–55.

'Poverty and Privilege: The Fiscal Burden in England (13th–15th Centuries)' in *La Fiscalità nell'economia europea secc. XIII–XVIII*, ed. S. Cavaciocchi, Atti delle 'Settimane di Studi', 39, 2 vols. (Florence, 2008), II, pp. 637–56.

The Reign of Edward III: Crown and Political Society in England 1327–1377 (New Haven, 1990).

Owen, H. and J. B. Blakeway. *A History of Shrewsbury*, 2 vols. (London, 1825).

Owst, G. R. *Literature and Pulpit in Medieval England: A Neglected Chapter in the History of English Letters & of the English People*, 2nd edn (Oxford, 1961).

Palmer, J. J. N. *England, France and Christendom 1377–99* (London, 1972).

Palliser, D. M. 'Introduction' in *CUHB*, pp. 3–15.

'Towns and the English State: 1066–1500' in *The Medieval State: Essay Presented to James Campbell*, ed. J. R. Maddicott and D. M. L. Palliser (London, 2000), pp. 127–46.

Palmer, R. C. *English Law in the Age of the Black Death, 1348–1381: A Transformation of Governance and Law* (Chapel Hill, NC, 1993).

Penn, Simon and Christopher Dyer. 'Wages and Earnings in Late Medieval England: Evidence from the Enforcement of the Labour Laws', *EcHR*, 43 (1990): 356–76.

Peter, John. *Complaint and Satire in Early English Literature* (Oxford, 1956).

Petit-Dutaillis, Charles. 'Introduction historique' in *Le soulèvement des travailleurs d'Angleterre en 1381* (Paris, 1898), pp. xix–cxxxvi.

Phillips, J. R. S. *Aymer de Valence, Earl of Pembroke 1307–1324: Baronial Politics in the Reign of Edward II* (Oxford, 1972).

Phillips, Seymour. *Edward II*, Yale English Monarchs Series (New Haven, 2010).

Piroyansky, Danna. *Martyrs in the Making: Political Martyrdom in Late Medieval England* (Basingstoke, 2008).

Platt, Colin. *The English Medieval Town London* (London, 1976).

Medieval Southampton: The Port and Trading Community, AD 1000–1600 (London, 1973).

Poos, L. R. 'The Social Context of Statute of Labourers Enforcement', *Law & History Review*, 27 (1983): 27–52.

Powell, Edward. *Kingship, Law, and Society: Criminal Justice in the Reign of Henry V* (Oxford, 1989).

Powell, W. R. 'Lionel de Bradenham and his Siege of Colchester in 1350', *Essex Archaeology and History: Transactions of the Essex Archaeological Society*, 22 (1991): 7–75.

Powicke, F. M. *King Henry III and the Lord Edward: The Community of the Realm in the Thirteenth Century*, 2 vols. (Oxford, 1947).

The Thirteenth Century 1216–1307 (Oxford, 1953).

Prescott, Andrew. 'Ball, John (d. 1381)', *ODNB* (2004).

'Essex Rebel Bands in London' in *Essex and the Great Revolt of 1381: Lectures Celebrating the Six Hundredth Anniversary*, ed. W. H. Liddell and R. G. E. Wood, Essex Record Office Publication no. 84 (Essex, 1982), pp. 55–66.

'Judicial Records of the Rising of 1381', Ph.D. thesis, Bedford College, University of London (1984).

'Labourers' Lives: Some Crown Prosecutions of Artisans, 1420–30', *Fifteenth-Century Conference*, Royal Holloway College, University of London (2–4 September 2004).

'London in the Peasants' Revolt: A Picture Gallery', *London Journal*, 7 (1981): 125–43.

'"Meynteyn him als his brother": Rebellion, Power and Knowledge in Late Medieval Britain' (forthcoming).

'The Yorkshire Partisans and the Literature of Popular Discontent' in *Medieval Literature in English*, ed. Elaine Treharne and Greg Walker (Oxford, 2010), pp. 321–52.

Prestwich, Michael. *Edward I*, 2nd edn, Yale English Monarchs Series (New Haven, 1997).

Plantagenet England 1225–1360. The New Oxford History of England (Oxford, 2005).

The Three Edwards: War and State in England, 1272–1377, 2nd edn (London, 2003).

War, Politics and Finance under Edward I (London, 1972).

Putnam, B. H. *The Enforcement of the Statutes of Labourers during the First Decade after the Black Death 1349–1359*, Studies in History, Economics and Public Law (New York, 1908), XXXII.

Proceedings Before the Justices of the Peace in the Fourteenth and Fifteenth Centuries, Edward III to Richard III (London, 1938).

Pythian-Adams, Charles. *The Desolation of a City: Coventry and the Urban Crisis of the Late Middle Ages* (Cambridge, 1979).

Rashdall, Hastings. *The Universities of Europe in the Middle Ages*, 2nd edn, ed. F. M. Powicke and A. B. Emden, 3 vols. (Oxford, 1936).

Rawcliffe, Carole. 'The Profits of Practice: The Wealth and Status of Medical Men in Later Medieval England', *Social History of Medicine*, I (1988): 61–78.

Razi, Zvi. *Life, Marriage, and Death in a Medieval Parish: Economy and Demography in Halesowen 1270–1400* (Cambridge, 1980).

'The Struggles between the Abbots of Halesowen and their Tenants in the Thirteenth and Fourteenth Centuries' in *Social Relations and Ideas: Essays in Honour of R. H. Hilton*, ed. T. H. Aston, Peter R. Coss, Christopher Dyer, and Joan Thirsk (Cambridge, 1983), pp. 151–67.

Reid, A. W. *Resistance, Representation, and Community*, ed. Peter Blickle (Oxford, 1997).

Reid, A. W. 'The Rising of 1381 in South West and Central Norfolk' in *Studies towards a History of the Rising of 1381 in Norfolk* (Norwich, 1984), pp. 11–31.

Réville, André and Charles Petit-Dutaillis. *Le soulèvement des travailleurs d'Angleterre en 1381* (Paris, 1898).

Rexroth, Frank. *Deviance and Power in Late Medieval London*, trans. Pamela Selwyn (Cambridge, 2007).

Reynolds, Susan. *An Introduction to the History of English Medieval Towns* (Oxford, 1977).

Rhymer, Lucy. 'Humphrey, Duke of Gloucester and the City of London' in *The Fifteenth Century, VIII: Rule, Redemption, and Representation in Late Medieval England and France*, ed. Linda Clark (Woodbridge, 2008), pp. 47–58.

Richards, Jeffrey. *Sex, Dissidence and Damnation: Minority Groups in the Middle Ages* (London, 1991).

Richardson, H. G. *The English Jewry under Angevin Kings* (London, 1960).

Richmond, Colin. 'Englishness and Medieval Anglo-Jewry' in *The Jewish Heritage in British History*, ed. T. Kushner (London, 1992), pp. 42–59.

Rigby, S. H. 'Urban "Oligarchy" in Late Medieval England' in *Towns and Townspeople in the Fifteenth Century*, ed. John A. F. Thomson (Gloucester, 1988), pp. 62–86.

and Elizabeth Ewan, 'Government, Power, and Authority 1300–1540', *CUHB*, pp. 291–312.

Roach, J. P. C. 'The University of Cambridge: The Middle Ages' in *VCH: Cambridge and the Isle of Ely*, ed. J. P. C. Roach (London, 1959), III, pp. 150–333.

Rodger, N. A. M. *The Safeguard of the Sea: A Naval History of Britain, I, 660–1649*, 2 vols. (London, 1997).

Rosser, Gervase. *Medieval Westminster 1200–1540* (Oxford, 1989).

'Crafts, Guilds and the Negotiation of Work in the Medieval Town', *P&P*, 154 (1997): 3–31.

Rubin, Miri. *Gentile Tales: The Narrative Assault on Late Medieval Jews* (New Haven, 1999).

Rye, W. 'The Riot between the Monks and Citizens of Norwich in 1272', *Norfolk Antiquarian Miscellany*, first series, 2 (1880): 17–42.

Saul, Nigel. *Knights and Esquires: The Gloucestershire Gentry in the Fourteenth Century* (Oxford, 1981).

Richard II, Yale English Monarchs Series (New Haven, 1997).

Scales, Len. 'Bread, Cheese and Genocide: Imaging the Destruction of Peoples in Medieval Western Europe', *History*, 92 (2007): 284–300.

Scase, Wendy. *Literature and Complaint in England, 1272–1553* (Oxford, 2007).

'"Strange and Wonderful Bills": Bill-Casting and Political Discourse in Late Medieval England' in *New Medieval Literatures*, 2, ed. Rita Copeland, David Lawton, and Wendy Scase (Oxford, 1998), pp. 225–47.

Schofield, Phillip R. 'Trespass Litigation in the Manor Court in the Late Thirteenth and Early Fourteenth Centuries' in *Survival and Discord in Medieval Society: Essays in Honour of Christopher Dyer*, ed. Richard Goddard, John Langdon, and Miriam Müller (Turnhout, 2010), pp. 145–60.

Schulze, Winfried. 'Peasant Resistance in Sixteenth- and Seventeenth-Century Germany in a European Context' in *Religion, Politics and Social Protest: Three Studies on Early Modern Germany*, ed. Kaspar van Greyerz (London, 1984), pp. 61–98.

Scott, James S. *Weapons of the Weak: Everyday Forms of Peasant Resistance* (London and New Haven, 1985).

Scott, Tom. *The City-State in Europe, 1000–1600: Hinterland – Territory – Region* (Oxford, 2012).

Freiburg and the Breisgau: Town-Country Relations in the Age of Reformation and Peasants' War (Oxford, 1986).

Town, Country, and Regions in Reformation Germany. Studies in Medieval and Reformation Traditions (Leiden, 2005).

Seyer, Samuel. *Memoirs Historical and Topographical of Bristol*, 2 vols. (Bristol, 1821–3).

Sharp, Buchanan. 'The Food Riots of 1347 and the Medieval and Social Conflict' in *Moral Economy and Popular Protest: Crowds, Conflict and Authority*, ed. Adrian Randall and Andrew Charlesworth (Houndmills, 2000), pp. 33–54.

Shaw, David Gary. *The Creation of a Community: The City of Wells in the Middle Ages* (Oxford, 1993).

'Social Networks and the Foundations of Oligarchy in Medieval Towns', *UH*, 32 (2005): 200–22.

Simkins, M. E. 'Political History' in *VCH: Hertfordshire*, ed. William Page (London, 1908), II, pp. 1–46.

Simonetta, Stefano. 'Wyclif e la rivolta di 1381' in *John Wyclif: logica, politica, teologia, atti del convegno internazionale, Milano, 12–13 febbraio 1999*, ed.

M. Fumugalli Beonio Brocchierri and Stefano Simonetta (Florence, 2003), pp. 143–79.

Slade, C. F. 'Reading' in *Historic Towns: Maps and Plans of Towns and Cities in the British Isles, with Historical Commentaries, from Earliest Times to 1800*, ed. M. D. Lobel, 3 vols. (Oxford, 1969–89), I, pp. 1–9.

Slater, Gilbert. 'Social and Economic History' in *VCH: Kent*, ed. William Page (London, 1932), III, pp. 348–9.

Small, Graeme. *Later Medieval France* (Basingstoke, 2009).

'Municipal Registers of Deliberation in the Fourteenth and Fifteenth Centuries: Cross Channel Observations' in *Les idées passent-elles la Manche?* ed. Jean-Philippe Genet and F-J. Ruggiu (Paris, 2007), pp. 37–66.

Smith, Llinos. 'Glyn Dŵr', *ODNB* (2008).

Stacey, Richard C. 'Anti-Semitism and the Medieval English State' in *The Medieval State: Essays Presented to James Campbell*, ed. J. R. Maddicott and D. M. Palliser (London, 2000), pp. 163–78.

Stacey, Robert C. 'Mansel, John (d. 1265), Administrator and Royal Councillor', *ODNB*.

Stemmler, Theo. 'Der Bauernaufstand von 1381 in der zeitgenössischen Literatur Englands' in *Historisches und fiktioales Erzählen in Mittelalter*, ed. Fritz Peter Knapp and Manuela Niesner (Berlin, 2002), pp. 45–62.

Still, Michele. *The Abbot and the Rule: Religious Life at St Albans, 1290–1349* (Aldershot, 2002).

Strickland, Matthew and Hardy, Robert. *The Great Warbow: From Hastings to the Mary Rose* (Stroud, 2005).

Strohm, Paul. *England's Empty Throne: Usurpation and the Language of Legitimation, 1399–1422* (New Haven, 1998).

'A Peasants' Revolt?' in *Misconceptions about the Middle Ages*, ed. Stephen J. Harris and Bryon L. Grigsby (New York, 2007), pp. 197–203.

'"A Revelle!": Chronicle Evidence and the Rebel Voice' in *Hochon's Arrow: The Social Imagination of Fourteenth-Century Texts* (Princeton, 1992), pp. 33–56.

'Trade, Treason, and the Murder of Janus Imperial', *JBS*, 35 (1996): 1–23.

Summerson, Henry. *Medieval Carlisle: The City and the Borders from the Late Eleventh to the Mid-Sixteenth Century*, 2 vols. (Stroud, 1993).

Sumption, Jonathan. *The Hundred Years War*, 3 vols. (London, 1990–2009).

Swanson, Heather. 'The Illusion of Economic Structure: Craft Guilds in Late Medieval English Towns', *P&P*, 121 (1988): 29–48.

Tait, James. *The Medieval English Borough: Studies on its Origins and Constitutional History* (Manchester, 1936).

Tanner, Norman. 'Religious Practice' in *Medieval Norwich*, ed. Carole Rawcliffe and Richard Wilson (London, 2004), pp. 137–56.

TeBrake, William H. *A Plague of Insurrection: Popular Politics and Peasant Revolt in Flanders, 1323–1328* (Philadelphia, 1993).

Thompson, E. P. 'The Moral Economy of the English Crowd in the Eighteenth Century', *P&P*, 50 (1971): 76–137.

Thomson, John A. F. *The Later Lollards 1414–1520* (Oxford, 1965).

'Oldcastle, John, Baron Cobham (d. 1417)', *ODNB* (2004).

'Scots in England in the Fifteenth Century', *The Scottish Historical Review,* 79 (2000): 1–16.

Tillotson, John H. 'Peasant Unrest in England of Richard II', *Historical Studies,* 16 (1974): 1–16.

Tilly, Charles. *Contentious Performances* (Cambridge, 2008).

Trenholme, Norman Maclaren. *The English Monastic Boroughs: A Study in Medieval History.* The University of Missouri Studies 3 (1927).

Tuck, J. A. 'Nobles, Commons and the Great Revolt of 1381' in *The English Rising of 1381,* ed. Rodney Hilton and T. H. Aston (Cambridge, 1984), pp. 194–212.

Tucker, Penelope. *Law Courts and Lawyers in the City of London, 1300–1550* (Cambridge, 2007).

Turner, Marion. *Chaucerian Conflict: Languages of Antagonism in Late Fourteenth-Century London* (Oxford, 2007).

Urry, William. *Canterbury under the Angevin Kings,* University of London Historical Studies, XIX (London, 1967).

Vale, Malcolm. *The Angevin Legacy and the Hundred Years War 1250–1340* (Oxford, 1990).

Valente, Claire. *The Theory and Practice of Revolt in Medieval England* (Aldershot, 2003).

van Bavel, Bas J. P. 'Rural Revolts and Structural Change in the Low Countries, Thirteenth–Early Fourteenth Centuries' in *Survival Discord in Medieval Society: Essays in Honour of Christopher Dyer,* ed. Richard Goddard, John Langdon, and Miriam Müller (Turnhout, 2010), pp. 249–68.

van der Linden, Marcel. 'Charles Tilly's Historical Sociology', *International Review of Social History,* 54 (2009): 237–74.

Veale, Elspeth. 'Gisors, John (I) de', *ODNB.*

Walker, Simon. 'Political Saints in Later Medieval England' in *The McFarlane Legacy: Studies in Late Medieval Politics and Society,* ed. R. H. Britnell and A. J. Pollard (Stroud, 1995), pp. 77–106.

'Rumour, Sedition and Popular Protest in the Reign of Henry IV', *P&P,* 166 (2000): 31–65.

'The Yorkshire Risings of 1405: Texts and Contexts' in *Henry IV: The Establishment of the Regime, 1399–1406,* ed. Gwilym Dodd and Douglas Biggs (Woodbridge, 2003), pp. 161–84.

Walter, John. *Crowds and Popular Politics in Early Modern England* (Manchester, 2006).

Watts, John. 'The Pressure of the Public on Later Medieval Politics' in *The Fifteenth Century, IV: Identity and Insurgency in the Late Middle Ages,* ed. Linda Clark (Woodbridge, 2006), pp. 159–80.

'Public or Plebs: The Changing Meaning of "The Commons", 1381–1549' in *Power and Identity in the Middle Ages: Essays in Memory of Rees Davies,* ed. Huw Pryce and John Watts (Oxford, 2007), pp. 242–60.

Waugh, Scott L. 'Henry of Lancaster, Third Earl of Lancaster', *ODNB.*

Waugh, W. T. 'Sir John Oldcastle', *EHR,* 20 (1905): 434–56.

Weinbaum, Martin. *The Incorporation of Boroughs* (Manchester, 1937).

Wilkinson, Bernard. 'The Peasants' Revolt of 1381', *Speculum,* 15 (1940): 12–35.

Williams, Gwyn A. *Medieval London: From Commune to Capital* (London, 1963).

Wood, Andy. *The 1549 Rebellions and the Making of Early Modern England.* (Cambridge, 2008).

'Collective Violence, Social Drama and Rituals of Rebellion in Late Medieval and Early Modern England' in *Cultures of Violence: Interpersonal Violence in Historical Perspective*, ed. Stuart Carroll (Houndmills, 2007), pp. 99–116.

Riot, Rebellion and Popular Politics in Early Modern England (Houndmills, 2002).

Wrightson, Keith. *English Society 1580–1680* (London, 1982).

Wylie, J. H. *The Reign of Henry the Fifth*, 3 vols. (Cambridge, 1914–29).

Yates, Richard. *An Illustration of the Monastic History and Antiquities of the Town and Abbey of St Edmund's Bury* (London, 1805).

Index

* Except for John, English kings are listed
  by name and number alone; other kings are designated also by nation.

9 781107 529359